S0-ACC-053

DB2 UNIVERSAL DATABASE
APPLICATION PROGRAMMING INTERFACE
(API)
DEVELOPER'S GUIDE

McGraw-Hill Enterprise Computing Series

DB2 Universal Database Developer's Guide for Call Level Interface by Sanders
ISBN 0-07-134572-8

Enterprise Java Developer's Guide by Narayanan/Liu
ISBN 0-07-134673-2

Web Warehousing and Knowledge Management by Mattison
ISBN 0-07-0041103-4

ODBC 3.5 Developer's Guide by Sanders
ISBN 0-07-058087-1

Data Warehousing, Data Mining & OLAP by Berson/Smith
ISBN 0-07-006272-2

Data Stores, Data Warehousing and the Zachman Framework by Inman
ISBN 0-07-031429-2

DB2 Universal Database Application Programming Interface (API) Developer's Guide

Roger E. Sanders

McGraw-Hill
New York • San Francisco • Washington, D.C. • Auckland
Bogotá • Caracas • Lisbon • London • Madrid • Mexico City
Milan • Montreal • New Delhi • San Juan • Singapore
Sydney • Tokyo • Toronto

McGraw-Hill

A Division of The McGraw·Hill Companies

Copyright ©2000 by The McGraw-Hill Companies, Inc. All Rights Reserved. Printed in the United States of America. Except as permitted under the United States Copyright Act of 1976, no part of this publication may be reproduced or distributed in any form or by any means, or stored in a database or retrieval system, without the prior written permission of the publisher.

1 2 3 4 5 6 7 8 9 0   AGM/AGM   9 0 4 3 2 1 0 9
P/N: 0-07-135390-9
Part of ISBN: 0-07-135392-5

The sponsoring editor for this book was Simon Yates, and the production supervisor was Clare Stanley. It was set in Century Schoolbook by D&G Limited, LLC.

Printed and bound by Quebecor/Martinsburg.

Throughout this book, trademarked names are used. Rather than put a trademark symbol after every occurrence of a trademarked name, we used the names in an editorial fashion only, and to the benefit of the trademark owner, with no intention of infringement of the trademark. Where such designations appear in this book, they have been printed with initial caps.

Information contained in this work has been obtained by The McGraw-Hill Companies, Inc. ("McGraw-Hill") from sources believed to be reliable. However, neither McGraw-Hill nor its authors guarantees the accuracy or completeness of any information published herein and neither McGraw-Hill nor its authors shall be responsible for any errors, omissions, or damages arising out of use of this information. This work is published with the understanding that McGraw-Hill and its authors are supplying information but are not attempting to render engineering or other professional services. If such services are required, the assistance of an appropriate professional should be sought.

 This book is printed on recycled, acid-free paper containing a minimum of 50% recycled de-inked fiber.

DEDICATION

To my son, Tyler Marek Sanders.

ACKNOWLEDGMENTS

A project of this magnitude requires both a great deal of time and the support of many different people. I would like to express my gratitude to the following people for their contributions:

- Paul Rivot—IBM
  Worldwide Brand Manager, Database Servers
  Paul provided me with DB2 Universal Database, Version 5.2 software, coordinated the delivery of the DB2 Universal Database documentation, and provided me with a key contact at the DB2 development lab in Toronto, Canada.

- Sheila Richardson—IBM Toronto Lab
  IBM Consulting Editor
  Sheila was my key contact at IBM Toronto. She was instrumental in providing me with DB2 Universal Database documentation and in getting me technical help when I needed it.

- Rick Swaggerman—IBM Toronto Lab
  DB2 Language Architect
  Rick provided me with information about upcoming SQL changes in DB2 Universal Database, Version 6.0.

- Robert Begg—IBM Toronto Lab
  Software Developer
  Robert provided me with information about upcoming CLI changes in DB2 Universal Database, Version 6.0, and he provided technical support about CLI cursor support and the `SQLSetPos()` function.

- Matthew Huras—IBM Toronto Lab
  Senior Technical Staff Member
  Matthew provided me with information about upcoming API changes in DB2 Universal Database, Version 6.0.

- Roger Zheng—IBM Toronto Lab
  Advisory Software Developer
  Roger tested the in-doubt transaction API examples for me and provided additional information about in-doubt transaction processing.

- Hershel Harris—IBM
  Director, Database Technology
  Mr. Harris was one of the behind-the-scenes authorizers that made it possible to include an evaluation copy of DB2 Universal Database in this book.

I would also like to thank my editor, Simon Yates; my project manager, Alan Harris, who worked with the production staff; and the staff at McGraw-Hill for their help and support.

Most of all, I would like to thank my wife, Beth, for all of her help and encouragement, and for once again overlooking the things that did not get done while I worked on this book.

CONTENTS

Contents

Contents

Contents

FOREWORD

Relational database technology was invented in IBM research more than 20 years ago. In 1983, IBM shipped the first version of DB2 for MVS. In 1997, IBM delivered its flagship relational technology on the AS/400 and OS/2. As we enter the 21st century, IBM has continued to extend its award winning database technology with additional function and support for additional platforms. Today, DB2 Universal Database is the most modern database on the planet, supporting the world's most popular system platforms (IBM OS/390, IBM OS/400, IBM RS/6000, IBM OS/2, Sun Solaris, HP-UX, Microsoft Windows NT, SCO OpenServer, and Linux).

DB2 Universal Database, which first shipped in 1997, has evolved to meet the rapid-fire changes within corporations around the world. Traditional companies are transforming their core business processes around the Internet. New e-companies are being formed, and a new generation of Web-based applications are being written. You might ask, "What is an e-business anyway?" e-business is buying and selling on the Internet. e-business is being open 24-hours-a-day, seven-days-a-week, without having to be there at the company. e-business is about reaching new customers, and e-business means working together in different ways. Some have said that e-business changes everything—or does it?

e-business demands highly scalable, available, secure, and reliable systems. e-business demands industrial strength database technology—the kind that DB2 has delivered to more than 40 million users over the last 15 years. IBM's DB2 Universal Database team has been hard at work delivering enhancements to DB2 Universal Database to make it the foundation for e-business. Today, users can access DB2 Universal Database from the Web. Application developers can write DB2 applications and stored procedures using Java or JDBC. Database administrators can administer DB2 databases from Web browsers, and DB2 is the most highly scalable, available, robust database in the world.

e-business poses a number of new requirements on the database, as well—access from any type of device. New, pervasive devices will be used to access DB2 databases. e-businesses will have a growing need to leverage information and knowledge, which will drive business intelligence and knowledge-based applications which require support for multi-terabyte databases to grow to petabytes. These applications will require advanced analytical functions to be supported in the database engine. They will also require access to rich content—documents, images, text, video, and spatial data. DB2 Universal Database has been extended to deliver this rich content today.

The next millennium will bring with it enormous change. The next millennium also will bring with it incredible opportunity for information technology professionals and those who support database systems. The new economy will be based on information exchange, and database professionals will be the stewards of this critical corporate asset. I encourage you to take advantage of the opportunity that Roger Sanders is providing to learn more about DB2 Universal Database. I also encourage you to obtain a certification in DB2 Universal Database. Your time will be well spent. DB2 Universal Database is the foundation for e-business for thousands of companies today, and we have only begun.

Janet Perna
General Manager, Data Management Solutions
IBM Corporation

INTRODUCTION

DB2 Universal Database is a robust database management system that is designed to be used for a variety of purposes in a variety of operating system environments.

DB2 Universal Database is not a new product; it has existed in some form or another since 1989. The earliest version was called Database Manager, and that version was bundled with OS/2 in a product called OS/2 Extended Edition. This product was IBM's first attempt to put its popular Database 2 product (which had been available for MVS operating systems on IBM mainframes since 1983) on a PC. Through the years, IBM's PC version of DB2 has matured to the point where the program is now one of the most powerful database products available for a wide variety of platforms.

DB2 Universal Database provides a rich set of programming interfaces (Structured Query Language, a Call-Level Interface, and numerous Application Programming Interface function calls) that can be used to develop several different kinds of applications. This book, one of a series of books that describe each of these programming interfaces in detail, is designed to provide you with a conceptual overview of DB2 Universal Database—as well as a comprehensive reference that covers DB2 Universal Database's Application Programming Interface.

Why I Wrote This Book

Although DB2 Universal Database has been available since 1989, only a handful of books have been written about the product. And, as the DB2 product evolved, many of the books that were written were not revised to reflect the differences in the product. Eventually, they went out of print. By 1993, when the DB2/2 GA product was released (with DB2/6000 following shortly after), no book existed that focused on DB2 application development. Robert Orfali and Dan Harkey's *Client / Server Programming with OS / 2 2.1* contained four chapters covering the Extended Services 1.0 database manager and later DB2/2. However, because this book addressed client/server programming rather than DB2 application programming, its information about DB2 was limited. This situation meant that IBM's product manuals and online help were the only resources available to application developers writing applications for DB2/2.

In the summer of 1992, while developing a specialized DB2 application (then called the Extended Services 1.0 Database Manager) that used many of DB2's *Application Programming Interface* (API) calls, I discovered how lacking (particularly in the area of examples) some of the IBM manuals for this product really were. Because there were no other reference books available, I had to spend a considerable amount of trial-and-error programming to complete my DB2 application. I immediately saw the need for a good DB2 programming reference guide.

This inspiration ultimately led to the writing of my first book, *The Developer's Handbook to DB2 for Common Servers*.

Since that book was written, DB2 has undergone two more revisions, and several new features have been added to an already rich application development toolset. As I began revising my original book, I discovered that it would be impossible to put a thorough reference for this toolset in a single book. My editor, Simon Yates, decided to do the next best thing: to put this information in a series of books, where each book addressed a specific aspect of DB2 Universal Database's rich development toolset.

Who Is This Book For?

This book is for anyone who is interested in creating DB2 Universal Database applications using DB2's Administrative *Application Programming Interfaces* (APIs). The book is written primarily for database application programmers and analysts who are familiar with DB2 and are designing and/or coding software applications that perform one or more DB2 administrative tasks. Experienced C/C++ programmers with little experience developing DB2 database applications will benefit most from the material covered in this book. Experienced DB2 API application developers who are familiar with earlier versions of the DB2 product will also benefit from this book, because the book describes in detail new features that are only available in the latest release of DB2 Universal Database. In either case, this book is meant to be a single resource that provides you with almost everything you need to know in order to design and develop DB2 database applications using DB2 APIs.

To get the most out of this book, you should have a working knowledge of the C++ programming language. An understanding of relational database concepts and *Structured Query Language* (SQL) will also be helpful, although not crucial.

How This Book Is Organized

This book is divided into three major parts. Part 1 discusses basic relational database concepts. Before you can successfully develop a DB2 API application, you must first have a good understanding of DB2's underlying database architecture and data consistency mechanisms. Two chapters in this section are designed to provide you with that understanding: Chapter 1 and Chapter 2.

Chapter 1 explains relational database concepts and describes the components of a DB2 Universal Database. This chapter also describes the internal file structures used by DB2 for data and database object storage. Chapter 2 discusses the mechanisms that DB2 provides for maintaining data integrity. These mechanisms include transactions, isolation levels, row- and table-level locking, and transaction logging. Together, these two chapters lay the groundwork for the rest of this book.

Part 2 discusses DB2 application development fundamentals. Once you have a good understanding of DB2's underlying database architecture and consistency mechanisms, you also need to understand general database application development as it applies to DB2. The two chapters in this section, Chapters 3 and 4, describe the different types of applications that can be developed for DB2 and provide you with an understanding of the methods used to develop applications using DB2 APIs.

Chapter 3 discusses the application development process as it applies to DB2. This chapter describes basic DB2 application design and identifies the main elements of a DB2 application. The chapter also explains how the database application development and testing environment are established before the application development process begins.

Chapter 4 explains how to write *Application Programming Interface* (API) applications and identifies the main components of a API application. This chapter also describes the steps you must take to convert API application source-code files into executable programs.

Part 3 contains information about each DB2 API function that can be used in an application. This section is designed to be a detailed API function reference. The ten chapters in this section group the API functions according to their functionality.

Chapter 5 examines the basic set of DB2 APIs that are used to prepare and bind embedded SQL applications, along with the APIs that are typically used in all DB2 API applications. This chapter also contains a detailed reference section that covers each program preparation and general application development API function provided by DB2. Each API function described in this chapter is accompanied by a Visual C++ example that illustrates how to code the API in an application program.

Chapter 6 shows how an application can start, stop, and to a certain extent, control the DB2 Database Manager background server processes. This chapter also contains a detailed reference section that covers each API function that can be used to interact with the DB2 Database Manager. Each API function described in this chapter is accompanied by a Visual C++ example that illustrates how to code the API in an application program.

Chapter 7 describes how DB2 uses configuration files to manage system resources. This chapter also contains a detailed reference section that covers each API function that can be used to view, modify, or reset DB2 Database Manager and DB2 database configuration files. Each API function described in this chapter is accompanied by a Visual C++ example that illustrates how to code the API in an application program.

Chapter 8 examines the sub-directories that DB2 uses to keep track of databases, remote workstations (nodes), and DRDA servers. This chapter also contains a detailed reference section that covers each API function that can be used to scan and retrieve entries stored in the database, node, and DCS sub-directories. Each API function described in this chapter is accompanied by a Visual C++ example that illustrates how to code the API in an application program.

Chapter 9 shows how DB2 database tables can be stored in different table spaces, and how data stored in tables can be reorganized so faster access plans can be generated. This chapter also contains a detailed reference section that covers each API function that can be used to manage tables and table spaces. Each API function described in this chapter is accompanied by a Visual C++ example that illustrates how to code the API in an application program.

Chapter 10 examines the mechanisms that DB2 provides for migrating, backing up, restarting, and restoring databases. This chapter also contains a detailed reference section that covers each API function that can be used to migrate, backup, restart, restore, and perform a roll-forward recovery on a DB2 database. Each API function described in this chapter is accompanied by a Visual C++ example that illustrates how to code the API in an application program.

Chapter 11 shows how data stored in a database table can be exported to an external file, and how data stored in external files can be imported or bulk-loaded into database tables. This chapter also contains a detailed reference section that covers each API function that can be used to move data between a database and one or more external files. Each API function described in this chapter is accompanied by a Visual C++ example that illustrates how to code the API in an application program.

Chapter 12 looks at database partitioning and node (workstation) management in an multi-partitioned database environment. This chapter also contains a detailed reference section that covers each API function that can be used to manage database nodes and obtain partitioning information. Each API function described in this chapter is accompanied by a Visual C++ example that illustrates how to code the API in an application program.

Chapter 13 examines the database activity monitor and two-phase commit processing. This chapter also contains a detailed reference section that covers each API function that can be used to monitor database activity and manually process indoubt transactions that were created when a critical error occurred during two-phase commit processing. Each API function described in this chapter is accompanied by a Visual C++ example that illustrates how to code the API in an application program.

Chapter 14 describes the mechanisms used by DB2 to work with threads in multithreaded applications. This chapter also contains a detailed reference section that covers each API function that can be used to manage thread contexts. Each API function described in this chapter is accompanied by a Visual C++ example that illustrates how to code the CLI API in an application program.

NOTE: *The concepts covered in Chapters 1–3 are repeated in each book in this series. If you have another book in this series and are already familiar with this information, you may want to skip these three chapters.*

About the Examples

The example programs provided are an essential part of this book; therefore, it is imperative that they are accurate. To make the use of each DB2 API function call clear, I included only the required overhead in each example and provided limited error-checking. I have also tried to design the example programs so they verify that the API function call being demonstrated actually executed as expected. For instance, an example program illustrating database configuration file modification might retrieve and display a value before and after the modification, to verify that the API function used to modify the data worked correctly.

I compiled and tested almost all of the examples in this book with Visual C++ 6.0, running against the SAMPLE database that is provided with DB2 Universal Database, Version 5.2. Appendix C shows the steps I used to create the test environment and the steps I used to reproduce and test all of the examples provided in this book.

Feedback and Source Code on the CD

I have tried to make sure that all the information and examples provided in this book are accurate; however, I am not perfect. If you happen to find a problem with some of the information in this book or with one of the example programs, please send me the correction so I can make the appropriate changes in future printings. In addition, I welcome any comments you might have about this book. The best way to communicate with me is via e-mail at `r-bsanders@mindspring.com`.

As mentioned earlier, all the example programs provided in this book have been tested for accuracy. Thus, if you type them in exactly as they appear in the book, they should compile and execute successfully. To help you avoid all that typing, electronic copies of these programs have been provided on the CD accompanying this book.

Limits of Liability and Warranty Disclaimer

Both the publisher and I have used our best efforts in preparing the material in this book. These efforts include obtaining technical information from IBM, as well as developing and testing the example programs to determine their effectiveness and accuracy. We make no warranty of any kind, expressed or implied, with regard to the documentation and example programs provided in this book. We shall not be liable in any event for incidental or consequential damages in connection with or arising out of the furnishing, performance, or use of either this documentation or these example programs.

PART 1

Basic Database Concepts

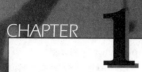

CHAPTER 1

DB2 Database Architecture

Before you begin developing DB2 database applications, you need to understand the underlying architecture of DB2 *Universal Database* (UDB), Version 5.2. This chapter is designed to introduce you to the architecture used by DB2 UDB. This chapter begins with a description of the relational database model and its data-handling operations. This is followed by an introduction to the data objects and support objects that make up a DB2 database. Finally, the directory, subdirectory, and file-naming conventions used by DB2 for storing these data and system objects are discussed. Let's begin by defining a relational database management system.

The Relational Database

DB2 UDB, Version 5.2, is a 32-bit relational database management system. A *relational database management system* is a database management system that is designed around a set of powerful mathematical concepts known as *relational algebra*. The first relational database model was introduced in the early 1970s by Mr. E. F. Codd at the IBM San Jose Research Center. This model is based on the following operations that are identified in relational algebra:

SELECTION—This operation selects one or more records from a table based on a specified condition.

PROJECTION—This operation returns a column or columns from a table based on some condition.

JOIN—This operation enables you to paste two or more tables together. Each table must have a common column before a JOIN operation can work.

UNION—This operation combines two like tables to produce a set of all records found in both tables. Each table must have compatible columns before a UNION operation can work. In other words, each field in the first table must match each field in the second table. Essentially, a UNION of two tables is the same as the mathematical addition of two tables.

DIFFERENCE—This operation tells you which records are unique to one table when two tables are compared. Again, each table must have identical columns before a DIFFERENCE operation can work. Essentially, a DIFFERENCE of two tables is the same as the mathematical subtraction of two tables.

INTERSECTION—This operation tells you which records are common to two or more tables when they are compared. This operation involves performing the UNION and DIFFERENCE operations twice.

PRODUCT—This operation combines two dissimilar tables to produce a set of all records found in both tables. Essentially, a PRODUCT of two tables is the same as the mathematical multiplication of two tables. The PRODUCT operation can often produce unwanted side effects, however, requiring you to use the PROJECTION operation to clean them up.

As you can see, in a relational database data is perceived to exist in one or more two-dimensional tables. These tables are made up of rows and columns, where each record (row) is divided into fields (columns) that contain individual pieces of information. Although data is not actually stored this way, visualizing the data as a collection of two-dimensional tables makes it easier to describe data needs in easy-to-understand terms.

Relational Database Objects

A relational database system is more than just a collection of two-dimensional tables. Additional objects exist that aid in data storage and retrieval, database structure control, and database disaster recovery. In general, *objects* are defined as items about which DB2 retains information. With DB2, two basic types of objects exist: *data objects* and *support objects*.

Data objects are the database objects that are used to store and manipulate data. Data objects also control how user data (and some system data) is organized. Data objects include

- Databases
- Table Spaces
- Tables
- User-Defined Data Types (UDTs)
- User-Defined Functions (UDFs)
- Check Constraints
- Indexes
- Views
- Packages (access plans)
- Triggers
- Aliases
- Event Monitors

Databases

A *database* is simply a set of all DB2-related objects. When you create a DB2 database, you are establishing an administrative entity that provides an underlying structure for an eventual collection of tables, views, associated indexes, etc.—as well as the table spaces in which these items exist. Figure 1–1 illustrates a simple database object. The database structure also includes items such as system catalogs, transaction recovery logs, and disk storage directories. Data (or user) objects are always accessed from within the underlying structure of a database.

Table Spaces

A *table space* logically groups (or partitions) data objects such as tables, views, and indexes based on their data types. Up to three table spaces can be used per table. Typically, the first table space is used for table data (by default), while a second table space is used as a temporary storage area for *Structured Query Language* (SQL) operations (such as sorting, reorganizing tables, joining tables, and creating indexes). The third table space is typically used for *large object* (LOB) fields. Table spaces are designed to provide a level of indirection between user tables and the database in which they exist. Two basic types of table spaces exist: *database managed spaces* (DMSs) and *system managed spaces* (SMSs). For SMS-managed spaces, each storage space is a directory that is managed by the operating system's file manager system. For DMS-managed spaces, each storage space is either a fixed-size, pre-allocated file or a specific physical device (such as a disk) that is managed by the DB2 Database Manager. As mentioned earlier, table spaces can also allocate storage areas for LOBs and can control the device, file, or directory where both LOBs and table data are to be stored. Table spaces can span

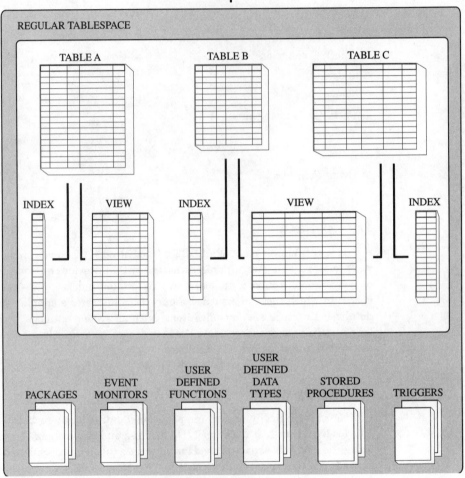

Figure 1–1   Database object and its related data objects

multiple physical disk drives, and their size can be extended at any time (stopping and restarting the database is not necessary). Figure 1–2 illustrates how you can use table spaces to direct a database object to store its table data on one physical disk drive—and store the table's corresponding indexes on another physical disk drive.

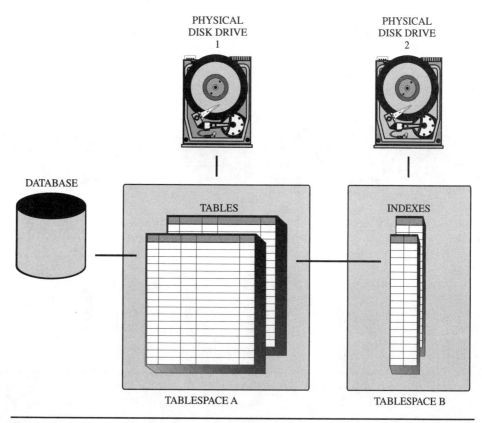

Figure 1–2   Using table spaces to separate the physical storage of tables and indexes

NOTE: *You should recognize that the table space concept implemented by DB2 Universal Database is different from the table space concept used by DB2 for OS/390.*

Tables

The *table* is the most fundamental data object of a DB2 database. All user data is stored in and retrieved from one or more tables in a database. Two types of tables can exist in a DB2 database: *base tables* and *result tables*. Tables that are created by the user to store user data are known as *base tables*. Temporary tables that are created (and deleted) by DB2 from one or more base tables to satisfy the result of a query are known as *result tables*. Each table contains an unordered collection of rows, and a fixed number of columns. The definition of the columns in the table makes up the table structure, and the rows contain the actual table data. The storage representation of a row is called a *record*, and the storage representation of a column is called a *field*. At each intersection of a row and column in a database table is a specific data item called a *value*. Figure 1–3 shows the structure of a simple database table.

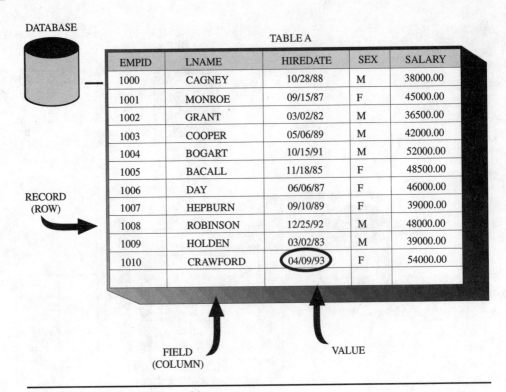

Figure 1–3 Simple database table

DATA TYPES Each column in a table is assigned a specific data type during its creation. This action ensures that only data of the correct type is stored in the table's columns. The following data types are available in DB2:

SMALLINT—A small integer is a binary integer with a precision of 15 bits. The range of a small integer is –32,768 to +32,767.

INTEGER (INT)—An integer is a large binary integer with a precision of 31 bits. The range of an integer is –2,147,483,648 to +2,147,483,647.

BIGINT—A big integer is a large binary integer with a precision of 63 bits.

FLOAT (REAL)—A single-precision, floating-point number is a 32-bit approximation of a real number. The range of a single-precision, floating-point number is $10.0 \ E^{-38}$ to $10.0 \ E^{+38}$.

DOUBLE—A double-precision, floating-point number is a 64-bit approximation of a real number. The number can be zero or can range from $-1.79769E^{+308}$ to $-2.225E^{-307}$ and $2.225E^{-307}$ to $1.79769E^{+308}$.

DECIMAL (DEC, NUMERIC, NUM)—A decimal value is a packed decimal number with an implicit decimal point. The position of the decimal point is determined by the precision and scale of the number. The range of a decimal variable or the numbers in a decimal column is -n to +n, where the absolute value of n is the largest number that can be represented with the applicable precision and scale.

CHARACTER (CHAR)—A character string is a sequence of bytes. The length of the string is the number of bytes in the sequence and must be between 1 and 254.

VARCHAR—A varying-length character string is a sequence of bytes in varying lengths, up to 4,000 bytes.

LONG VARCHAR—A long, varying-length character string is a sequence of bytes in varying lengths, up to 32,700 bytes.

GRAPHIC—A graphic string is a sequence of bytes that represents double-byte character data. The length of the string is the number of double-byte characters in the sequence and must be between 1 and 127.

VARGRAPHIC—A varying-length graphic string is a sequence of bytes in varying lengths, up to 2,000 double-byte characters.

LONG VARGRAPHIC—A long, varying-length graphic string is a sequence of bytes in varying lengths, up to 16,350 double-byte characters.

BLOB—A binary large object string is a varying-length string, measured in bytes, that can be up to 2GB (2,147,483,647 bytes) long. A BLOB is primarily intended to hold nontraditional data, such as pictures, voice, and mixed media. BLOBs can also hold structured data for user-defined types and functions.

CLOB—A character large object string is a varying-length string measured in bytes that can be up to 2GB long. A CLOB can store large, single-byte character strings or multibyte, character-based data, such as documents written with a single character set.

DBCLOB—A double-byte character large object string is a varying-length string of double-byte characters that can be up to 1,073,741,823 characters long. A DBCLOB can store large, double-byte, character-based data, such as documents written with a single character set. A DBCLOB is considered to be a graphic string.

DATE—A date is a three-part value (year, month, and day) designating a calendar date. The range of the year part is 0001 to 9999, the range of the month part is one to 12, and the range of the day part is one to n (28, 29, 30, or 31), where n depends on the month and whether the year value corresponds to a leap year.

TIME—A time is a three-part value (hour, minutes, and seconds) designating a time of day under a 24-hour clock. The range of the hour part is zero to 24, the range of the minutes part is 0 to 59, and the range of the seconds part is also 0 to 59. If the hour part is set to 24, the minutes and seconds must be 0.

TIMESTAMP—A timestamp is a seven-part value (year, month, day, hour, minutes, seconds, and microseconds) that designates a calendar date and time-of-day under a 24-hour clock. The ranges for each part are the same as defined for the previous two data types, while the range for the fractional specification of microseconds is 0 to 999,999.

DISTINCT TYPE—A distinct type is a user-defined data type that shares its internal representation (source type) with one of the previous data types—but is considered to be a separate, incompatible type for most SQL operations. For example, a user can define an AUDIO data type for referencing external .WAV files that use the BLOB data type for their internal source type. Distinct types do not automatically acquire the functions and operators of their source types, because these items might no longer be meaningful. However, user-defined functions and operators can be created and applied to distinct types to replace this lost functionality.

For more information about DB2 data types, refer to the *IBM DB2 Universal Database SQL Reference, Version 5.2* product manual.

CHECK CONSTRAINTS When you create or alter a table, you can also establish restrictions on data entry for one or more columns in the table. These restrictions, known as *check constraints*, exist to ensure that none of the data entered (or changed) in a table violates predefined conditions. Three types of check constraints exist, as shown in the following list:

Unique Constraint—A rule that prevents duplicate values from being stored in one or more columns within a table

Referential Constraint—A rule that ensures that values stored in one or more columns in a table can be found in a column of another table

Table Check Constraint—A rule that sets restrictions on all data that is added to a specific table

The conditions defined for a check constraint cannot contain any SQL queries, and they cannot refer to columns within another table. Tables can be defined with or without check constraints, and check constraints can define multiple restrictions on the data in a table. Check constraints are defined in the CREATE TABLE and ALTER TABLE SQL statements. If you define a check constraint in the ALTER TABLE SQL statement for a table that already contains data, the existing data will usually be checked against the new condition before the ALTER TABLE statement can be successfully completed. You can, however, place the table in a check-pending state with the SET CONSTRAINTS SQL statement, which enables the ALTER TABLE SQL statement to execute without checking existing data. If you place a table in a check-pending state, you must execute the SET CONSTRAINTS SQL statement again after the table has been altered to check the existing data and return the table to a normal state.

Indexes

An *index* is an ordered set of pointers to the rows of a base table. Each index is based on the values of data in one or more columns (refer to the definition of *key*, later in this section), and more than one index can be defined for a table. An index uses a balanced *binary tree* (a hierarchical data structure in which each element has at most one predecessor but can have many successors) to order the values of key columns in a table. When you index a table by one or more of its columns, DB2 can access data directly and more efficiently because the index is ordered by the columns to be retrieved. Also, because an index is stored separately from its associated table, the index provides a way to define keys outside of the table definition. Once you create an index, the DB2 Database Manager automatically builds the appropriate binary tree structure and maintains that structure. Figure 1–4 shows a simple table and its corresponding index.

DB2 uses indexes to quickly locate specific rows (records) in a table. If you create an index of frequently used columns in a table, you will see improved performance on row access and updates. A unique index (refer to the following paragraph) helps maintain data integrity by ensuring that each row of data in a table is unique. Indexes also provide greater concurrency when more than one transaction accesses the same table. Because row retrieval is faster, locks do not last as long. These benefits, however, are not without a price. Indexes increase actual disk-space requirements and cause a slight decrease in performance whenever an indexed table's data is updated, because all indexes defined for the table must also be updated.

A *key* is a column (or set of columns) in a table or index that is used to identify or access a particular row (or rows) of data. A key that is composed of more than one column is called a *composite key*. A column can be part of several composite keys. A key that is defined in such a way that the key identifies a single row of data within a table is called a *unique key*. A unique key that is part of the definition of a table is called a *primary key*. A table can have only one primary key, and the columns of a primary key cannot contain null (missing) values. A key that references (or points to) a primary key in another table is called a *foreign key*. A foreign key establishes a referential link to a primary key, and the columns defined in each key must match. In Figure 1–4, the EMPID column is the primary key for Table A.

TABLE A

			EMPID	LNAME	HIREDATE
	ROW 1	→	1004	CAGNEY	10/28/88
INDEX A	ROW 2	→	1001	MONROE	09/15/87
	ROW 3	→	1007	GRANT	03/02/82
KEY ROW	ROW 4	→	1010	COOPER	05/06/89
1000 8	ROW 5	→	1002	BOGART	10/15/91
1001 2	ROW 6	→	1005	BACALL	11/18/85
1002 5	ROW 7	→	1003	DAY	06/06/87
1003 7	ROW 8	→	1000	HEPBURN	09/10/89
1004 1	ROW 9	→	1008	ROBINSON	12/25/92
1005 6	ROW 10	→	1006	HOLDEN	03/02/83
1006 10	ROW 11	→	1009	CRAWFORD	03/02/83
1007 3					
1008 9					
1009 11					
1010 4					

Figure 1–4 *Simple database table and its corresponding index, where the EMPID column is the primary key*

Views

A *view* is an alternative way of representing data that exists in one or more tables. Essentially, a view is a named specification of a result table. The specification is a predefined data selection that occurs whenever the view is referenced in an SQL statement. For this reason, you can picture a view as having columns and rows, just like a base table. In fact, a view can be used just like a base table in most cases. Although a view looks like a base table, a view does not exist as a table in physical storage—so a view does not contain data. Instead, a view refers to data stored in other base tables. (Although a view might refer to another view, the reference is ultimately to data stored in one or more base tables.) Figure 1–5 illustrates the relationship between two base tables and a view.

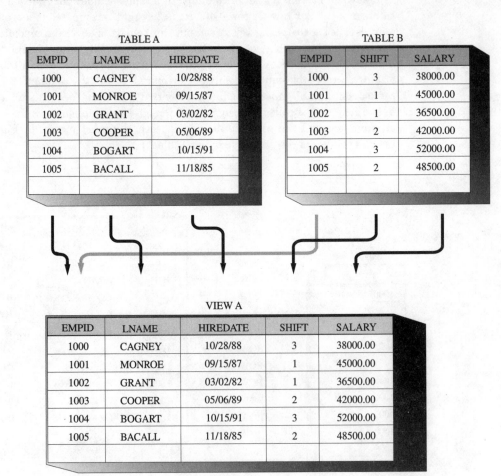

TABLE A

EMPID	LNAME	HIREDATE
1000	CAGNEY	10/28/88
1001	MONROE	09/15/87
1002	GRANT	03/02/82
1003	COOPER	05/06/89
1004	BOGART	10/15/91
1005	BACALL	11/18/85

TABLE B

EMPID	SHIFT	SALARY
1000	3	38000.00
1001	1	45000.00
1002	1	36500.00
1003	2	42000.00
1004	3	52000.00
1005	2	48500.00

VIEW A

EMPID	LNAME	HIREDATE	SHIFT	SALARY
1000	CAGNEY	10/28/88	3	38000.00
1001	MONROE	09/15/87	1	45000.00
1002	GRANT	03/02/82	1	36500.00
1003	COOPER	05/06/89	2	42000.00
1004	BOGART	10/15/91	3	52000.00
1005	BACALL	11/18/85	2	48500.00

Figure 1–5   In this figure, a view is created from two separate tables. Because the EMPID column is common in both tables, the EMPID column joins the tables to create a single view.

A view can include any number of columns from one or more base tables. A view can also include any number of columns from other views, so a view can be a combination of columns from both views and tables. When the column of a view comes from a column of a base table, that column inherits any constraints that apply to the column of the base table. For example, if a view includes a column that is a unique key for its base table, operations performed against that view are subject to the same constraint as operations performed against the underlying base table.

Packages (Access Plans)

A *package* (or *access plan*) is an object that contains control structures (known as *sections*) that are used to execute SQL statements. If an application program intends to access a database using static SQL, the application developer must embed the appropriate SQL statements in the program source code. When the program source code is converted to an executable object (static SQL) or executed (dynamic SQL), the strategy for executing each embedded SQL statement is stored in a package as a single section. Each section is the bound (or operational) form of the embedded SQL statement, and this form contains information such as which index to use and how to use the index.

When developing DB2 UDB database applications, you should hide package creation from users whenever possible. Packages and binding are discussed in more detail in Chapter 3, "Getting Started with DB2 Application Development."

Triggers

A *trigger* is a set of actions that are automatically executed (or triggered) when an INSERT, UPDATE, or DELETE SQL statement is executed against a specified table. Whenever the appropriate SQL statement is executed, the trigger is activated—and a set of predefined actions begin execution. You can use triggers along with foreign keys (referential constraints) and check constraints to enforce data integrity rules. You can also use triggers to apply updates to other tables in the database, to automatically generate and/or transform values for inserted or updated rows, and to invoke user-defined functions.

When creating a trigger, in order to determine when the trigger should be activated, you must first define and then later use the following criteria:

Subject table—The table for which the trigger is defined

Trigger event—A specific SQL operation that updates the subject table (could be an INSERT, UPDATE, or DELETE operation)

Activation time—Indicates whether the trigger should be activated before or after the trigger event is performed on the subject table

Set of affected rows—The rows of the subject table on which the INSERT, UPDATE, or DELETE SQL operation is performed

Trigger granularity—Defines whether the actions of the trigger will be performed once for the whole SQL operation or once for each of the rows in the set of affected rows

Triggered action—Triggered action is an optional search condition and a set of SQL statements that are to be executed whenever the trigger is activated. The triggered action is executed only if the search condition evaluates to TRUE.

At times, triggered actions might need to refer to the original values in the set of affected rows. This reference can be made with transition variables and/or transition tables. Transition variables are temporary storage variables that use the names of the columns in the subject table and are qualified by a specified name that identifies whether the reference is to the old value (prior to the SQL operation) or the new value (after the SQL operation). Transition tables also use the names of the columns of the subject table, but they have a specified name that enables the complete set of affected rows to be treated as a single table. As with transition variables, transition tables can be defined for both the old values and the new values.

Multiple triggers can be specified for a single table. The order in which the triggers are activated is based on the order in which they were created, so the most recently created trigger will be the last trigger to be activated. Activating a trigger that executes SQL statements may cause other triggers to be activated (or even the same trigger to be reactivated). This event is referred to as *trigger cascading*. When trigger cascading occurs, referential integrity delete rules can also be activated, thus a single operation can significantly change a database. Therefore, whenever you create a trigger, make sure to thoroughly examine the effects that the trigger's operation will have on all other triggers and referential constraints defined for the database.

Aliases

An *alias* is an alternate name for a table or view. Aliases can be referenced in the same way the original table or view is referenced. An alias can also be an alternate name for another alias. This process of aliases referring to each other is known as *alias chaining*. Because aliases are publicly referenced names, no special authority or privilege is needed to use them—unlike tables and views.

Event Monitors

An *event monitor* observes each event that happens to another specified object and records all selected events to either a named pipe or to an external file. Essentially, event monitors are "tracking" devices that inform other applications (either via named pipes or files) whenever specified event conditions occur. Event monitors allow you to observe the events that take place in a database whenever database applications are executing against it. Once defined, event monitors can automatically be started each time a database is opened.

Schemas

All data objects are organized (by the database administrator) into *schemas*, which provide a logical classification of the objects in the database. Object names consist of two parts. The first (leftmost) part is called the *qualifier*, or *schema*, and the second (right-most) part is called the *simple* (or *unqualified*) *name*. Syntactically, these two parts are concatenated as a single string of characters separated by a period. When an object such as a table space, table, index, view, alias, user-defined data type, user-defined function, package, event monitor, or trigger is created, that object is assigned to an appropriate schema based on its name. Figure 1–6 illustrates how a table is assigned to a particular schema during the table creation process.

NOTE: *If no schema is specified when an object is created, the DB2 Database Manager uses the creator's user ID as the default schema.*

This section completes the discussion of data objects. Now let's examine DB2 support objects. Support objects are database objects that contain descriptions of all objects in the database, provide transaction and failure support, and control system resource usage. Support objects include the following items:

- System catalog tables/views
- Log files and the Recovery History file
- DB2 Database Manager configuration files
- Database configuration files

System Catalog Views

DB2 creates and maintains a set of views and base tables for each database created. These views and base tables are collectively known as the *system catalog*. The system

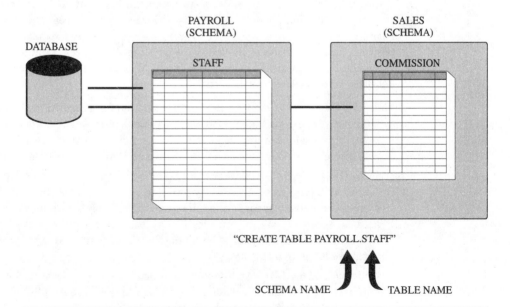

Figure 1–6 *Implementing schemas with the CREATE SQL statement*

catalog consists of tables that contain accurate descriptions of all objects in the database at all times. DB2 automatically updates the system catalog tables in response to SQL data definition statements, environment routines, and certain utility routines. The catalog views are similar to any other database views, with the exception that they cannot be explicitly created, updated (with the exception of some specific updateable views), or dropped. You can retrieve data in the catalog views in the same way that you retrieve data from any other view in the database. For a complete listing of the DB2 catalog views, refer to the *IBM DB2 Universal Database SQL Reference, Version 5.2* product manual.

Recovery Log Files and the Recovery History File

Database *recovery log files* keep a running record of all changes made to tables in a database, and these files serve two important purposes. First, they provide necessary support for transaction processing. Because an independent record of all database changes is written to the recovery log files, the sequence of changes making up a transaction can be removed from the database if the transaction is rolled back. Second, recovery log files ensure that a system power outage or application error will not leave the database in an inconsistent state. In the event of a failure, the changes that have been made, but that have not been made permanent (committed) are rolled back. Furthermore, all committed transactions, which might not have been physically written to disk, are redone. Database recovery logging is always active and cannot be deactivated. These actions ensure that the integrity of the database is always maintained.

You can also keep additional recovery log files to provide forward recovery in the event of disk (media) failure. The roll-forward database recovery utility uses these additional database recovery logs, called *archived logs*, to enable a database to be rebuilt to a specific point in time. In addition to using the information in the active database recovery log to rebuild a database, archived logs are used to reapply previous changes. For roll-forward database recovery to work correctly, you are required to have both a previous backup version of the database and a recovery log containing changes made to the database since that backup was made. The following list describes the types of database recovery logs that can exist:

Active log files—Active log files contain information for transactions whose changes have not yet been written to the database files. Active log files contain information necessary to roll back any active transaction not committed during normal processing. Active log files also contain transactions that are committed but are not yet physically written from memory (buffer pool) to disk (database files).

Online archived log files—An activity parallel to logging exists that automatically dumps the active transaction log file to an archive log file whenever transaction activity ceases, when the active log file is closed, or when the active log file gets full. An archived log is said to be "online" when the archived log is stored in the database log path directory.

Offline archived log files—Archived log files can be stored in locations other than the database log path directory. An archived log file is said to be "offline" when it is not stored in the database log path directory.

NOTE: *If an online archived log file does not contain any active transactions, the file will be overwritten the next time an archive log file is generated. On the other hand, if an archived log file contains active transactions, the file will not be overwritten by other active transaction log dumps until all active transactions stored in the file have been made permanent.*

If you delete an active log file, the database becomes unusable and must be restored before the database can be used again. If you delete an archived log file (either online or offline) roll-forward recovery will only be possible up to the point in time covered by the log file that was written to before the deleted log file was created.

The *recovery history file* contains a summary of the backup information that is used to recover part or all of the database to a specific point in time. A recovery history file is automatically created when a database is created, and the file is automatically updated whenever the database is backed up, restored, or populated with the LOAD operation.

Configuration Files

Similar to all computer software applications, DB2 UDB uses system resources both when it is installed and when it is running. In most cases, run time resource management (RAM and shared control blocks, for example) are managed by the *operating system* (OS). If, however, an application is greedy for system resources, problems can occur for both the application and for other concurrently running applications.

DB2 provides two sets of configuration parameters that can be used to control its consumption of system resources. One set of parameters that is used for the DB2 Database Manager itself exists in a DB2 Database Manager configuration file. This file contains values that are to be used to control resource usage when creating databases (database code page, collating sequence, and DB2 release level, for example). This file also controls system resources that are used by all database applications (as total shared RAM, for example).

A second set of parameters exists for each DB2 database created and is stored in a database configuration file. This file contains parameter values that are used to indicate the current state of the database (backup pending flag, database consistency flag, or roll-forward pending flag, for example) and parameter values that define the amount of system resources the database can use (buffer pool size, database logging, or sort memory size, for example). A database configuration file exists for each database, so a change to one database configuration does not have a corresponding effect on other databases. By fine-tuning these two configuration files, you can tailor DB2 for optimum performance in any number of OS environments. For more information about DB2 configuration file parameters, refer to the *IBM DB2 Universal Database Administration Guide, Version 5.2* product manual.

■ ■ DB2 Database Directories

DB2 UDB uses a set of directories for establishing an environment, storing data objects, and enabling data access to both local and other remote workstations (nodes) and databases. The set of directories used by DB2 contain the following items:

■ One or more physical database directories

■ One or more volume directories

- A system directory
- A workstation (node) directory
- A database connection services directory

These directories define the overall DB2 Database Manager operating environment. Figure 1–7 illustrates DB2's directory structure.

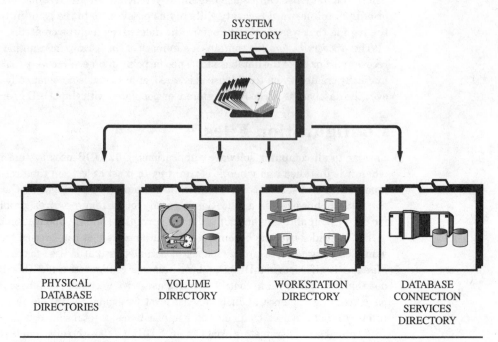

Figure 1–7　DB2's directory structure

Physical Database Directory

Each time a database is created, the DB2 Database Manager creates a separate subdirectory in which to store control files (such as log header files) and to allocate containers in which default table spaces are stored. Objects associated with the database are usually stored in the database subdirectory, but they can be stored in other various locations —including system devices. All database subdirectories are created within the instance defined in the DB2INSTANCE environment variable or within the instance to which the user application has been explicitly attached. The naming scheme used for a DB2 instance or UNIX Platforms is *install_ path*/$DB2INSTANCE/NODE*nnnn*. The naming scheme used on Intel platforms is *drive_letter*:\$DB2INSTANCE\NODE*nnnn*. In both cases, NODE*nnnn* is the node identifier in a partitioned database environment where NODE0000 is the first node, NODE0001 is the second node, and so on. The naming scheme for database subdirectories created within an instance is SQL00001 through SQL*nnnnn*, where the number for *nnnnn* increases each time a new database is created. For example, directory SQL00001 contains all objects associated with the first database created, SQL00002 contains all objects for the second database created, and so on. DB2 automatically creates and maintains these subdirectories.

Volume Directory

In addition to physical database directories, a volume directory exists on every logical disk drive available (on a single workstation) that contains one or more DB2 databases. This directory contains one entry for each database that is physically stored on that particular logical disk drive. The volume directory is automatically created when the first database is created on the logical disk drive, and DB2 updates its contents each time a database creation or deletion event occurs. Each entry in the volume directory contains the following information:

- The database name, as provided with the CREATE DATABASE command
- The database alias name (which is the same as the database name)
- The database comment, as provided with the CREATE DATABASE command
- The name of the root directory in which the database exists
- The product name and release number associated with the database
- Other system information, including the code page the database was created under and entry type (which is always HOME)
- The actual number of volume database directories that exist on the workstation, which is the number of logical disk drives on that workstation that contain one or more DB2 databases

System Directory

The system database directory is the master directory for a DB2 workstation. This directory contains one entry for each local and remote cataloged database that can be accessed by the DB2 Database Manager from a particular workstation. Databases are implicitly cataloged when the CREATE DATABASE command or API function is issued and can also be explicitly cataloged with the CATALOG DATABASE command or API function. The system directory exists on the logical disk drive where the DB2 product software is installed. Each entry in the system directory contains the following information:

- The database name provided with the CREATE DATABASE or CATALOG DATABASE command or API function
- The database alias name (which is usually the same as the database name)
- The database comment, as provided with the CREATE DATABASE or CATALOG DATABASE command or API function
- The logical disk drive on which the database exists, if it is local
- The node name on which the database exists, if it is remote
- Other system information, including where validation of authentication names (user IDs) and passwords will be performed

Workstation Directory

The workstation or node directory contains one entry for each remote database server workstation that can be accessed. The workstation directory also exists on the logical disk drive where the DB2 product software is installed. Entries in the workstation directory are used in conjunction with entries in the system directory to make connections to remote DB2 UDB database servers. Entries in the workstation directory are also used in conjunction with entries in the database connection services directory to make connections to hosts (OS/390, AS/400, etc.) database servers. Each entry in the workstation directory contains the following information:

- The node name of the remote server workstation where a DB2 database exists
- The node name comment
- The protocol that will be used to communicate with the remote server workstation
- The type of security checking that will be performed by the remote server workstation
- The hostname or address of the remote server
- The service name or port number for the remote server

Database Connection Services Directory

A database connection services directory only exists if the DB2 Connect product has been installed on the workstation. This directory exists on the logical disk drive where the DB2 Connect product software is installed. The database connection services directory contains one entry for each host (OS/390, AS/400, etc.) database that DB2 can access via the *distributed relational database architecture* (DRDA) services. Each entry in the connection services directory contains the following information:

- The local database name
- The target database name
- The database comment
- The application requester library file that executes the DRDA protocol to communicate with the host database
- The user-defined name or nickname for the remote server database
- The database system used on the remote server workstation
- Other system information, including a defaults override parameter string that defines SQLCODE mapping requirements, date and time formatting to use, etc.

NOTE: *To avoid potential problems, do not create directories that use the same naming scheme as the physical database directories, and do not manipulate the volume, system, node, and database connection services directories that have been created by DB2.*

SUMMARY

The goal of this chapter is to provide you with an overview of the underlying architecture of a DB2 Universal Database (UDB), Version 5.2 database. You should now understand the relational database model and be familiar with the following data objects and support objects:

- Data objects
  - Databases
  - Table spaces
  - Tables
  - User-Defined Data Types (UDTs)
  - User-Defined Functions (UDFs)
- Check constraints
  - Indexes
  - Views
  - Packages (access plans)
  - Triggers
  - Aliases
  - Event monitors
- Support objects
  - System catalog views
  - Recovery log files and the Recovery History file
  - DB2 Database Manager configuration file
  - Database configuration files

Finally, you should be aware of how DB2 UDB creates and uses the following directories and subdirectories on your storage media:

- Physical database directories
- Volume directories
- System directory
- Workstation directory
- Database Connection Services directory

You should be comfortable with these basic DB2 database concepts before you begin your database application design work (and especially before you actually begin writing the source code for your application). The next chapter continues to present these concepts by discussing the database consistency mechanisms available in DB2 Universal Database, Version 5.2.

2

Database Consistency Mechanisms

Once you understand the underlying architecture of DB2 Universal Database, you should become familiar with the mechanisms DB2 uses to provide and maintain data consistency. This chapter is designed to introduce you to the concepts of data consistency and to the three mechanisms DB2 uses to enforce consistency: *transactions*, *locking*, and *transaction logging*. The first part of this chapter defines database consistency and examines some of the requirements a database management system must meet to provide and maintain consistency. This part is followed by a close look at the heart of all data manipulation: the transaction. Next, DB2's locking mechanism is described and how that mechanism is used by multiple transactions working concurrently to maintain data integrity is discussed. Finally, this chapter concludes with a discussion of transaction logging and the data recovery process used by DB2 to restore data consistency if application or system failure occurs.

What Is Data Consistency?

The best way to define data consistency is by example. Suppose your company owns a chain of restaurants, and you have a database designed to keep track of supplies stored in each of those restaurants. To facilitate the supplies purchasing process, your database contains an inventory table for each restaurant in the chain. Whenever supplies are received or used by a restaurant, the inventory table for that restaurant is updated. Now, suppose some bottles of ketchup are physically moved from one restaurant to another. The ketchup bottle count value in the donating restaurant's inventory table needs to be lowered, and the ketchup bottle count value in the receiving restaurant's inventory table needs to be raised to accurately represent this inventory move. If a user lowers the ketchup bottle count from the donating restaurant's inventory table but fails to raise the ketchup bottle count in the receiving restaurant's inventory table, the data has become inconsistent. Now, the total ketchup bottle count for the entire chain of restaurants is incorrect.

Data can become inconsistent if a user fails to make all necessary changes (as in the previous example), if the system crashes while the user is in the middle of making changes, or if an application accessing data stops prematurely for some reason. Inconsistency can also occur when several users are accessing the same data at the same time. For example, one user might read another user's changes before the data has been properly updated and take some inappropriate action—or make an incorrect change based on the premature data values read.

To properly maintain data consistency, solutions must be provided for the following questions:

■ How can you maintain generic consistency of data if you do not know what each individual data owner or user wants?

■ How can you keep a single application from accidentally destroying data consistency?

■ How can you ensure that multiple applications accessing the same data at the same time will not destroy data consistency?

■ If the system fails while a database is in use, how can the database be returned to a consistent state?

DB2 provides solutions to these questions with its transaction support, locking, and logging mechanisms.

Transactions

A *transaction*, or a *unit of work*, is a recoverable sequence of one or more SQL operations grouped together as a single unit within an application process. The initiation and termination of a transaction define the points of data consistency within an application process. Either all SQL operations within a transaction are applied to the data source, or the effects of all SQL operations within a transaction are completely "undone."

Transactions and commitment control are relational database concepts that have been around for quite some time. They provide the capability to commit or recover from pending changes made to a database in order to enforce data consistency and integrity. With embedded SQL applications, transactions are automatically initiated when the application process is started. With *Open Database Connectivity* (ODBC) and *Call-Level Interface* (CLI), transactions are implicitly started whenever the application begins working with a data source.

Regardless of how transactions are initiated, they are terminated when they are either committed or rolled back. When a transaction is committed, all changes made to the data source since the transaction was initiated are made permanent. When a transaction is rolled back, all changes made to the data source since the transaction was initiated are removed, and the data in the data source is returned to its previous state (before the transaction began). In either case, the data source is guaranteed to be in a consistent state at the completion of each transaction.

A commit or roll back operation only affects the data changes made within the transaction they end. As long as data changes remain uncommitted, other application processes are usually unable to see them, and they can be removed with the roll back operation. However, once data changes are committed, they become accessible to other application processes and can no longer be removed by a roll back operation.

A database application program can do all of its work in a single transaction or spread its work over several sequential transactions. Data used within a transaction is protected from being changed or seen by other transactions through various isolation levels.

Transactions provide generic database consistency by ensuring that changes become permanent only when you issue a COMMIT SQL statement or via API calls defined within a Transaction Manager. Your responsibility, however, is to ensure that the sequence of SQL operations in each transaction results in a consistent database. DB2 then ensures that each transaction is either completed (committed) or removed (rolled back) as a single unit of work. If a failure occurs before the transaction is complete, DB2 will back out all uncommitted changes to restore the database consistency that DB2 assumes existed when the transaction was initiated. Figure 2–1 shows the effects of both a successful transaction and a transaction that failed.

Concurrency and Transaction Isolation Levels

So far, we have only looked at transactions from a single-user data source point-of-view. With single-user data sources, each transaction occurs serially and does not have to contend with interference from other transactions. With multi-user data sources, however, transactions can occur simultaneously, and each transaction has the potential to interfere with another transaction. Transactions that have the potential of interfering with one another are said to be *interleaved*, or parallel, transactions. Transactions that run isolated from each other are said to be *serializable*, which means that the results of running them

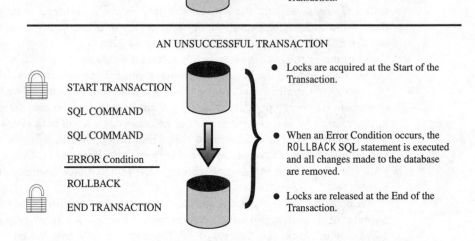

A SUCCESSFUL TRANSACTION

START TRANSACTION

SQL COMMAND

SQL COMMAND

SQL COMMAND

COMMIT

END TRANSACTION

- Locks are acquired at the Start of the Transaction.

- When the `COMMIT` SQL statement is executed, all changes are made permanent.

- Locks are released at the End of the Transaction.

AN UNSUCCESSFUL TRANSACTION

START TRANSACTION

SQL COMMAND

SQL COMMAND

ERROR Condition

ROLLBACK

END TRANSACTION

- Locks are acquired at the Start of the Transaction.

- When an Error Condition occurs, the `ROLLBACK` SQL statement is executed and all changes made to the database are removed.

- Locks are released at the End of the Transaction.

Figure 2–1   *Events that take place during the execution of a successful and an unsuccessful transaction*

simultaneously are the same as the results of running them one right after another (serially). Ideally, all transactions should be serializable.

So why should transactions be serializable? Consider the following problem. Suppose a salesman is entering orders on a database system at the same time a clerk is sending out bills. Now, suppose the salesman enters an order from Company X but does not commit the order (the salesman is still talking to the representative from Company X). While the salesman is on the phone, the clerk queries the database for a list of all outstanding orders, sees the order for Company X, and sends Company X a bill. Now, suppose the representative from Company X decides to cancel the order. The salesman rolls back the transaction, because the representative changed his mind and the order information was never committed. A week later, Company X receives a bill for a part it never ordered. If the salesman's transaction and the clerk's transaction had been isolated from each other (serialized), this problem would never have occurred. Either the salesman's transaction would have finished before the clerk's transaction started, or the clerk's transaction would have finished before the salesman's transaction started. In either case, Company X would not have received a bill.

When transactions are not isolated from each other in multi-user environments, the following three types of events (or phenomena) can occur as a result:

- **Dirty reads**—This event occurs when a transaction reads data that has not yet been committed. For example: Transaction 1 changes a row of data, and Transaction 2 reads the changed row before Transaction 1 commits the change. If Transaction 1 rolls back the change, then Transaction 2 will have read data that is considered never to have existed.

- **Nonrepeatable reads**—This event occurs when a transaction reads the same row of data twice but receives different data values each time. For example: Transaction 1 reads a row of data, and Transaction 2 changes or deletes that row and commits the change. If Transaction 1 attempts to reread the row, Transaction 1 retrieves different data values (if the row was updated) or discovers that the row no longer exists (if the row was deleted).

- **Phantoms**—This event occurs when a row of data matches a search criteria but initially is not seen. For example: Transaction 1 reads a set of rows that satisfy some search criteria, and Transaction 2 inserts a new row matching Transaction 1's search criteria. If Transaction 1 re-executes the query statement that produced the original set of rows, a different set of rows will be retrieved.

Maintaining database consistency and data integrity while enabling more than one application to access the same data at the same time is known as *concurrency*. DB2 enforces concurrency by using four different transaction isolation levels. An isolation level determines how data is locked or isolated from other processes while the data is being accessed. DB2 supports the following isolation levels:

- Repeatable read
- Read stability
- Cursor stability
- Uncommitted read

Repeatable Read

The *repeatable read* isolation level locks all the rows an application retrieves within a single transaction. If you use the repeatable read isolation level, SELECT SQL statements issued multiple times within the same transaction will yield the same result. A transaction running under the repeatable read isolation level can retrieve and operate on the same rows as many times as needed until the transaction completes. However, no other transactions can update, delete, or insert a row (which would affect the result table being accessed) until the isolating transaction terminates. Transactions running under the repeatable read isolation level cannot see uncommitted changes of other transactions. The repeatable read isolation level does not allow phantom rows to be seen.

Read Stability

The *read stability* isolation level locks only those rows that an application retrieves within a transaction. This feature ensures that any row read by a transaction is not changed by other transactions until the transaction holding the lock is terminated. Unfortunately, if a transaction using the read stability isolation level issues the same query more than once, the transaction can retrieve new rows that were entered by other transactions that now meet the search criteria. This event occurs because the read stability isolation level ensures that all data retrieved remains unchanged until the time that the transaction sees the data, even when temporary tables or row blocking is used. Thus, the read stability isolation level allows phantom rows to be seen and non-repeatable reads to occur.

Cursor Stability

The *cursor stability* isolation level locks any row being accessed by a transaction, as long as the cursor is positioned on that row. This lock remains in effect until the next row is retrieved (fetched)—or until the transaction is terminated. If a transaction running under the cursor stability isolation level has retrieved a row from a table, no other transactions can update or delete that row as long as the cursor is positioned on that row. Additionally, if a transaction running under the cursor stability isolation level changes the row it retrieved, no other application can update or delete that row until the isolating transaction is terminated. When a transaction has locked a row with the cursor stability isolation level, other transactions can insert, delete, or change rows on either side of the locked row—as long as the locked row is not accessed via an index. Therefore, the same SELECT SQL statement issued twice within a single transaction might not always yield the same results. Transactions running under the cursor stability isolation level cannot see uncommitted changes made by other transactions. With the cursor stability isolation level, both nonrepeatable reads and phantom reads are possible.

Uncommitted Read

The *uncommitted read* isolation level allows a transaction to access uncommitted changes made by other transactions (in either the same or in different applications). A transaction running under the uncommitted read isolation level does not lock other applications out of the row it is reading—unless another transaction attempts to drop or alter the table. If a transaction running under the uncommitted read isolation level accesses a read-only cursor, the transaction can access most uncommitted changes made by other transactions. The transaction cannot access tables, views, and indexes that are being created or dropped by other transactions, however, until those transactions are complete. All other changes made by other transactions can be read before they are committed or rolled back. If a transaction running under the uncommitted read isolation level accesses an updateable cursor, the transaction will behave as if the cursor stability isolation level were in effect. With the uncommitted read isolation level, both nonrepeatable reads and phantom reads are possible.

Table 2–1 shows the four transaction isolation levels that are supported by DB2 Universal Database, as well as the types of phenomena that can occur when each one is used.

Table 2–1 Transaction isolation levels supported by DB2 and the phenomena that can occur when each is used

DB2 Transaction Isolation Level	Dirty Reads	Nonrepeatable Reads	Phantoms
Uncommitted Read	Yes	Yes	Yes
Cursor Stability	No	Yes	Yes
Read Stability	No	No	Yes
Repeatable Read	No	No	No

Specifying the Isolation Level

You specify the isolation level for an embedded SQL application either at precompile time or when binding the application to a database. In most cases, you set the isolation level for embedded SQL applications with the ISOLATION option of the command line processor PREP or BIND commands. In other cases, you can set an embedded SQL application's isolation level by using the PREP or BIND API functions. The isolation level for a CLI application is set by CLI statement handle attributes. The default isolation level used for all applications is the cursor stability isolation level.

Locking

Along with isolation levels, DB2 uses locks to provide concurrency control and to control data access. A *lock* is a mechanism that associates a data resource with a single transaction, with the purpose of controlling how other transactions interact with that resource while the resource is associated with the transaction that acquired the lock. The transaction with which the resource is associated is said to "hold" or "own" the lock. When a data resource in the database is accessed by a transaction, that resource is locked according to the previously specified isolation level. This lock prevents other transactions from accessing the resource in a way that would interfere with the owning transaction. Once the owning transaction is terminated (either committed or rolled back), changes made to the resource are either made permanent or are removed, and the data resource is unlocked so it can be used by other transactions. Figure 2–2 illustrates the principles of data resource locking.

If one transaction tries to access a data resource in a way that is incompatible with a lock held by another transaction, that transaction must wait until the owning transaction has ended. This situation is known as a *lock wait*. When this event occurs, the transaction attempting to access the resource simply stops execution until the owning transaction has terminated and the incompatible lock is released. Locks are automatically provided by DB2 for each transaction, so applications do not need to explicitly request data resource locks.

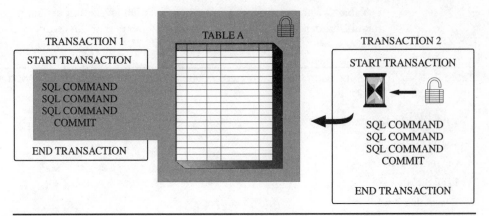

Figure 2–2 *DB2 prevents uncontrolled concurrent table access by using locks. In this example, Transaction 1 has locked table A, and Transaction 2 must wait until the lock is released before it can execute.*

Lock Attributes

All locks used by DB2 have the following basic attributes:

Object—The object attribute identifies the data resource being locked. Tables are the only data resource objects that can be explicitly locked by an application. DB2 can set locks on other types of resources, such as rows, tables, etc., but these locks are used for internal purposes only.

Size—The size attribute specifies the physical size of the portion of the data resource that is being locked. A lock does not always have to control an entire data resource. For example, rather than giving an application exclusive control over an entire table, DB2 can only give the lock exclusive control over the row that needs to be changed.

Duration—The duration attribute specifies the length of time a lock is held. The isolation levels described earlier control the duration of a lock.

Mode—The mode attribute specifies the type of access permitted for the lock owner, as well as the type of access permitted for concurrent users of the locked data resource. Mode is sometimes referred to as the "state" of the lock.

Lock States

As a transaction performs its operations, DB2 automatically acquires locks on the data resources it references. These locks are placed on a table, a row (or multiple rows), or both a table and a row (or rows). The only object a transaction can explicitly acquire a lock for is a table, and a transaction can only change the state of row locks by issuing a COMMIT or a ROLLBACK SQL statement. The locks that are placed on a data resource by a transaction can have one of the following states:

Next Key Share (NS)—If a lock is set in the Next Key Share state, the lock owner and all concurrent transactions can read—but cannot change—data in the locked row. Only individual rows can be locked in the Next Key Share state. This lock is acquired in place of a Share lock on data that is read using the read stability or cursor stability transaction isolation level.

Share (S)—If a lock is set in the Share state, the lock owner and any other concurrent transactions can read—but cannot change—data in the locked table or row. As long as a table is not Share locked, individual rows in that table can be Share locked. If, however, a table is Share locked, no row Share locks can be set in that table by the lock owner. If either a table or a row is Share locked, other concurrent transactions can read the data, but they cannot change the data.

Update (U)—If a lock is set in the Update state, the lock owner can update data in the locked data table. Furthermore, the Update operation automatically acquires Exclusive locks on the rows it updates. Other concurrent transactions can read—but not update—data in the locked table.

Next Key Exclusive (NX)—If a lock is set in the Next Key Exclusive state, the lock owner can read—but not change—the locked row. Only individual rows can be locked in the Next Key Exclusive state. This lock is acquired on the next row in a table when a row is deleted from or inserted into the index for a table.

Next Key Weak Exclusive (NW)—If a lock is set in the Next Key Weak Exclusive state, the lock owner can read—but not change—the locked row. Only individual rows can be locked in the Next Key Weak Exclusive state. This lock is acquired on the next row in a table when a row is inserted into the index of a non-catalog table.

Exclusive (X)—If a table or row lock is set in the Exclusive state, the lock owner can both read and change data in the locked table, but only transactions using the uncommitted read isolation level can access the locked table or row(s). Exclusive locks are best used with data resources that are to be manipulated with the INSERT, UPDATE, and/or DELETE SQL statements.

Weak Exclusive (W)—If a lock is set in the Weak Exclusive state, the lock owner can read and change the locked row. Only individual rows can be locked in the Weak Exclusive state. This lock is acquired on a row when the row is inserted into a non-catalog table.

Super Exclusive (Z)—If a lock is set in the Super Exclusive state, the lock owner can alter a table, drop a table, create an index, or drop an index. This lock is automatically acquired on a table whenever a transaction performs any one of these operations. No other concurrent transactions can read or update the table until this lock is removed.

In addition to these eight primary locks, there are four more special locks that are only used on tables. They are called intention locks and are used to signify that rows within the table may eventually become locked. These locks are always placed on the table before any rows within the table are locked. Intention locks can have one of the following states:

Intent None (IN)—If an intention lock is set in the Intent None state, the lock owner can read data in the locked data table, including uncommitted data, but cannot change this data. In this mode, no row locks are acquired by the lock owner, so other concurrent transactions can read and change data in the table.

Intent Share (IS)—If an intention lock is set in the Intent Share state, the lock owner can read data in the locked data table but cannot change the data. Again, because the lock owner does not acquire row locks, other concurrent transactions can both read and change data in the table. When a transaction owns an Intent Share lock on a table, the transaction acquires a Share lock on each row it reads. This intention lock is acquired when a transaction does not convey the intent to update any rows in the table.

Intent Exclusive (IX)—If an intention lock is set in the Intent Exclusive state, the lock owner and any other concurrent transactions can read and change data in the locked table. When the lock owner reads data from the data table, the lock owner acquires a Share lock on each row it reads and an Update and Exclusive lock on each row it updates. Other concurrent transactions can both read and update the locked table. This intent lock is acquired when a transaction conveys the intent to update rows in the table. The SELECT FOR UPDATE, UPDATE WHERE, and INSERT SQL statements convey the intent to update.

Share with Intent Exclusive (SIX)—If an intention lock is set in the Share with Intent Exclusive state, the lock owner can both read and change data in the locked table. The lock owner acquires Exclusive locks on the rows it updates but not on the rows it reads, so other concurrent transactions can read but not update data in the locked table.

As a transaction performs its operations, DB2 automatically acquires appropriate locks as data objects are referenced. Figure 2–3 illustrates the logic DB2 uses to determine the type of lock to acquire on a referenced data object.

Locks and Application Performance

When developing DB2 applications, you must be aware of several factors concerning the uses of locks and the effect they have on the performance of an application. The following factors can affect application performance:

- Concurrency versus lock size
- Deadlocks
- Lock compatibility
- Lock conversion
- Lock escalation

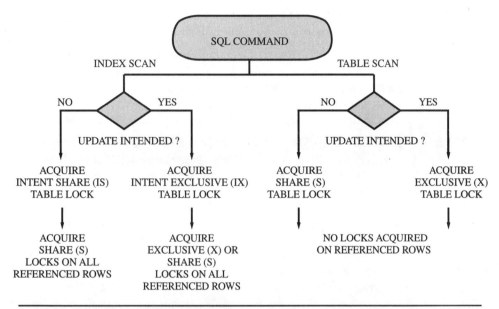

Figure 2–3 Logic used by DB2 to determine which type of lock(s) to acquire

CONCURRENCY VERSUS LOCK SIZE As long as multiple transactions access tables for the purpose of reading data, concurrency should be only a minor concern. What becomes more of an issue is the situation in which at least one transaction writes to a table. Unless an appropriate index is defined on a table, there is almost no concurrent write access to that table. Concurrent updates are only possible with Intent Share or Intent Exclusive locks. If no index exists for the locked table, the entire table must be scanned for the appropriate data row (table scan). In this case, the transaction must hold either a Share or an Exclusive lock on the table. Simply creating indexes on all tables does not guarantee concurrency. DB2's optimizer decides for you whether indexes are used in processing your SQL statements, so even if you have defined indexes, the optimizer might choose to perform a table scan for any of several reasons:

■ No index is defined for your search criteria (**WHERE** clause). The index key must match the columns used in the **WHERE** clause in order for the optimizer to use the index to help locate the desired rows. If you choose to optimize for high concurrency, make sure your table design includes a primary key for each table that will be updated. These primary keys should then be used whenever these tables are referenced with an **UPDATE** SQL statement.

■ Direct access might be faster than via an index. The table must be large enough so the optimizer thinks it is worthwhile to take the extra step of going through the index, rather than just searching all the rows in the table. For example, the optimizer would probably not use any index defined on a table with only four rows of data.

■ A large number of row locks will be acquired. If many rows in a table will be accessed by a transaction, the optimizer will probably acquire a table lock.

Any time one transaction holds a lock on a table or row, other transactions might be denied access until the owner transaction has terminated. To optimize for maximum concurrency, a small, row-level lock is usually better than a large table lock. Because locks require storage space (to keep) and processing time (to manage), you can minimize both of these factors by using one large lock—rather than many small ones.

DEADLOCKS   When two or more transactions are contending for locks, a situation known as a *deadlock* can occur. Consider the following example. Transaction 1 locks Table A with an Exclusive lock, and Transaction 2 locks Table B with an Exclusive lock. Now, suppose Transaction 1 attempts to lock Table B with an Exclusive lock, and Transaction 2 attempts to lock Table A with an Exclusive lock. Both transactions will be suspended until their second lock request is granted. Because neither lock request can be granted until one of the transactions performs a COMMIT or ROLLBACK operation—and because neither transaction can perform a COMMIT or ROLLBACK operation because they are both suspended (waiting on locks)—a deadlock situation has occurred. Figure 2–4 illustrates this scenario.

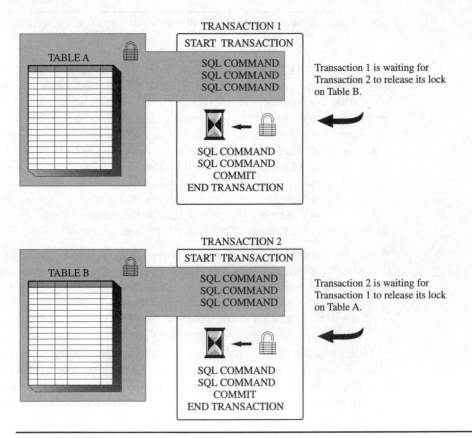

Figure 2–4   Deadlock cycle between two transactions

A deadlock is more precisely referred to as a "deadlock cycle," because the transactions involved in a deadlock form a circle of wait states. Each transaction in the circle is waiting for a lock held by one of the other transactions in the circle. When a deadlock cycle occurs, all the transactions involved in the deadlock will wait indefinitely—unless an outside agent performs some action to end the deadlock cycle. Because of this, DB2 contains an asynchronous system background process associated with each active database that is responsible for finding and resolving deadlocks in the locking subsystem. This background process is called the *deadlock detector*. When a database becomes active, the deadlock detector is started as part of the process that initializes the database for use. The deadlock detector stays "asleep" most of the time but "wakes up" at preset intervals to look for the presence of deadlocks between transactions using the database. Normally, the deadlock detector sees that there are no deadlocks on the database and goes back to sleep. If, however, the deadlock detector discovers a deadlock on the database, the detector selects one of the transactions in the cycle to roll back and terminate. The transaction that is rolled back receives an SQL error code, and all of its locks are released. The remaining transaction can then proceed, because the deadlock cycle is broken. The possibility exists (although unlikely) that more than one deadlock cycle exists on a database. If this is the case, the detector will find each remaining cycle and terminate one of the offending transactions in the same manner until all deadlock cycles are broken.

Because at least two transactions are involved in a deadlock cycle, you might assume that two data objects are always involved in the deadlock. This is not true. A certain type of deadlock, known as a *conversion deadlock*, can occur on a single data object. A conversion deadlock occurs when two or more transactions already hold compatible locks on an object, and then each transaction requests new, incompatible lock modes on that same object. A conversion deadlock usually occurs between two transactions searching for rows via an index (index scan). Using an index scan, each transaction acquires Share and Exclusive locks on rows. When each transaction has read the same row and then attempts to update that row, a conversion deadlock situation occurs.

Application designers need to watch out for deadlock scenarios when designing high-concurrency applications that are to be run by multiple concurrent users. In situations where the same set of rows will likely be read and then updated by multiple copies of the same application program, that program should be designed to roll back and retry any transactions that might be terminated as a result of a deadlock situation. As a general rule, the shorter the transaction, the less likely the transaction will be to get into a deadlock cycle. Setting the proper interval for the deadlock detector (in the database configuration file) is also necessary to ensure good concurrent application performance. An interval that is too short will cause unnecessary overhead, and an interval that is too long will enable a deadlock cycle to delay a process for an unacceptable amount of time. You must balance the possible delays in resolving deadlocks with the overhead of detecting the possible delays.

LOCK COMPATIBILITY   If the state of one lock placed on a data resource enables another lock to be placed on the same resource, the two locks (or states) are said to be *compatible*. Whenever one transaction holds a lock on a data resource and a second transaction requests a lock on the same resource, DB2 examines the two lock states to determine whether they are compatible. If the locks are compatible, the lock is granted to the second transaction (as long as no other transaction is waiting for the data resource). If the locks are incompatible, however, the second transaction must wait until the first transaction releases its lock. (In fact, the second transaction must wait until all existing incompatible locks are released.) Table 2–2 shows a lock compatibility matrix that identifies which locks are compatible and which are not.

Table 2–2 Lock compatibility matrix

	Lock Held By First Transaction												
Lock Type	none	IN	IS	NS	S	IX	SIX	U	NX	NW	X	W	Z
none	YES	YES	YES	YES	YES	YES	YES	YES	YES	YES	YES	YES	YES
IN	YES	YES	YES	YES	YES	YES	YES	YES	YES	YES	YES	YES	NO
IS	YES	YES	YES	YES	YES	YES	YES	YES	NO	NO	NO	NO	NO
NS	YES	YES	YES	YES	YES	NO	NO	YES	YES	YES	NO	NO	NO
S	YES	YES	YES	YES	YES	NO	NO	YES	NO	NO	NO	NO	NO
IX	YES	YES	YES	NO	NO	YES	NO	NO	NO	NO	NO	NO	NO
SIX	YES	YES	YES	NO	NO	NO	NO	NO	NO	NO	NO	NO	NO
U	YES	YES	YES	YES	YES	NO	NO	NO	NO	NO	NO	NO	NO
NX	YES	YES	NO	YES	NO	NO	NO	NO	NO	NO	NO	NO	NO
NW	YES	YES	NO	YES	NO	NO	NO	NO	NO	NO	NO	YES	NO
X	YES	YES	NO	NO	NO	NO	NO	NO	NO	NO	NO	NO	NO
W	YES	YES	NO	NO	NO	NO	NO	NO	NO	YES	NO	NO	NO
Z	YES	NO	NO	NO	NO	NO	NO	NO	NO	NO	NO	NO	NO

Lock Requested By Second Transaction

Adapted from *IBM DB2 Universal Database Embedded SQL Programming Guide*, page 143.

YES   Locks are compatible, therefore the lock requested is granted
NO   Locks are not compatible; therefore, the requesting transaction must wait for the held lock to be released or for a timeout to occur.

Lock Types
IN   Intent None
IS   Intent Share
NS   Next Key Share
S   Share
IX   Intent Exclusive
SIX   Share With Intent Exclusive
U   Update
NX   Next Key Exclusive
NW   Next Key Weak Exclusive
X   Exclusive
W   Weak Exclusive
Z   Super Exclusive

LOCK CONVERSION   When a transaction accesses a data resource on which the transaction already holds a lock—and the mode of access requires a more restrictive lock than the one the transaction already holds—the state of the lock is changed to the more restrictive state. The operation of changing the state of a lock already held to a more restrictive state is called a *lock conversion*. Lock conversion occurs because a transaction can only hold one lock on a data resource at a time. The conversion case for row locks is simple. A conversion only occurs if an Exclusive lock is needed and a Share or Update lock is held.

More distinct lock conversions exist for tables than for rows. In most cases, conversions result in the requested lock state becoming the new state of the lock currently held whenever the requested state is the higher state. Intent Exclusive and Share locks, however, are special cases, because neither is considered to be more restrictive than the other. If one of these locks is held and the other is requested, the resulting conversion is to a Share with Intent Exclusive lock. Lock conversion can cause locks only to increase restriction. Once a lock has been converted, the lock stays at the highest level obtained until the transaction is terminated.

LOCK ESCALATION   All locks require space for storage, and because this space is finite, DB2 limits the amount of space the system can use for locks. Furthermore, a limit is placed on the space each transaction can use for its own locks. A process known as lock escalation occurs when too many record locks are issued in the database and one of these space limitations is exceeded. *Lock escalation* is the process of converting several locks on individual rows in a table into a single, table-level lock. When a transaction requests a lock after the lock space is full, one of its tables is selected—and lock escalation takes place to create space in the lock list data structure. If enough space is not freed, another table is selected for escalation, and so on, until enough space has been freed for the transaction to continue. If there is still not enough space in the lock list after all the transaction's tables have been escalated, the transaction is asked to either commit or roll back all changes made since its initiation (i.e., the transaction receives an SQL error code, and the transaction is terminated).

An important point to remember is that an attempted escalation only occurs to the transaction that encounters a limit. This situation happens because, in most cases, the lock storage space will be filled when that transaction reaches its own transaction lock limit. If the system storage lock space limit is reached, however, a transaction that does not hold many locks might try to escalate, fail, and then be terminated. This event means that offending transactions holding many locks over a long period of time can cause other transactions to terminate prematurely. If escalation becomes objectionable, there are two ways to solve the problem:

- Increase the number of locks enabled in the database configuration file (with a corresponding increase in memory). This solution might be the best if concurrent access to the table by other processes is important. A point of diminishing returns exists on index access and record locking, even when concurrency is the primary concern. The overhead of obtaining record-level locks can impose more delays to other processes, which negates the benefits of concurrent access to the table.

- Locate and adjust the offending transaction(s), which might be the one(s) terminating prematurely, and explicitly issue LOCK TABLE SQL statements within the transaction(s). This choice might be the best if memory size is crucial, or if an extremely high percentage of rows are being locked.

■ Change the degree of transaction isolation being used.

■ Increase the frequency of commit operations.

Transaction Logging

Transaction logging is simply a method of keeping track of what changes have been made to a database. Every change made to a row of data in a database table is recorded in the active log file as an individual log record. Each log record enables DB2 to either remove or apply the data change to the database. To fully understand transaction logging operations, you should know what the transaction log contains, how transaction logging works, how the transaction log gets synchronized, and how to manage log file space.

HOW TRANSACTION LOGGING WORKS   Each change to a row in a table is made with an INSERT, UPDATE, or DELETE SQL statement. If you use the INSERT SQL statement, a transaction record containing the new row is written to the log file. If you use the UPDATE SQL statement, transaction records containing the old row information and the new row information are written to the log file (two separate records are written). If you use the DELETE SQL statement, a transaction record containing the old row information is written to the log file. These types of transaction log records make up the majority of the records in the transaction log file. Other transaction records also exist, which indicate whether a ROLLBACK or a COMMIT SQL statement was used to end a transaction. These records end a sequence of data log records for a single transaction.

Whenever a ROLLBACK or a COMMIT log record is written, the record is immediately forced out to the active log file. This action ensures that all the log records of a completed transaction are in the log file and will not be lost due to a system failure. Because more than one transaction might be using a database at any given time, the active log file contains the changes made by multiple transactions. To keep everything straight in the log, each log record contains an identifier of the transaction that created the record. In addition, all the log records for a single transaction are chained together.

Once a transaction is committed, all log records for that transaction are no longer needed (after all changes made by that transaction are physically written to the disk). If a ROLLBACK occurs, DB2 processes each log record written by the transaction in reverse order and backs out all changes made. Both "before" and "after" image UPDATE records are written to the log file for this reason.

LOG FILE AND DATABASE SYNCHRONIZATION   DB2 can maintain consistency only by keeping the log file and database synchronized. This synchronization is achieved with a write-ahead logging technique. When a transaction changes a row in a table, that change is actually made in a memory buffer contained in the database buffer pool and is written to the disk later. As a result, the most current data changes made to a working database are in the buffer pool, not on the disk. Write-ahead logging preserves consistency by writing the log record of a row change to the disk before the change itself is written from the memory buffer to the disk. Log records are written to disk whenever a transaction terminates—or whenever the buffer pool manager writes the memory buffer to the disk database.

If the system crashes, the log file and database will no longer be synchronized. Fortunately, the log file contains a record of every uncommitted change made to the database, because the log record of the change is forced to disk before the actual change is written. This event enables the recovery process to restore the database to a consistent state. The recovery process is discussed in more detail in the Database Recovery section later in this chapter.

MANAGING LOG FILE SPACE   It was mentioned earlier that DB2 writes records sequentially to the log file in order to support transactions. Because the log file grows until the file is reset, if no limits were imposed on the log file size, all free space on the system disk would eventually become full of log records. DB2's Log Manager controls the size of the log file, and whenever possible, the Log Manager resets the log to an empty state. The growth of the log is controlled by the initial size of the primary log files, the size limit for each secondary log file, and the number of primary and secondary log files being used. When the primary log file is filled, the Log Manager allocates space for a secondary log file, and the overflow is stored in that secondary file.

Whenever the primary log file becomes empty due to transaction inactivity (i.e., no transactions have uncommitted records in the log), the primary log file is reset and any secondary log files that have been allocated are released. If a transaction runs out of log space, either because the maximum primary log file size was reached and a secondary file was not used, or because there was too little disk space to allocate the next secondary log file, a roll back occurs and the transaction is terminated. Regardless of cause, this process continues until the log's inactive state is reached and the log is reset to its minimum size.

If two or more continuously overlapping transactions (e.g., high volume and high activity rate) are running, the primary log file might never be reset. Continuously overlapping transactions are not likely, but they can happen when two or more transactions starting at close intervals use the same database. When designing a database system in which the transaction arrival rate is high, you should increase the log file size to reduce the probability of transactions being rolled back due to insufficient log file space.

You can also prevent the primary log file from being reset if a lengthy transaction (one that causes many log records to be written before they are committed) is running. But first, you must consider how these transactions are used, as well as the amount of log file space needed to support them, when designing the database system. If other transactions are running concurrently with a lengthy transaction, the log file space requirement will increase. A lengthy transaction should probably run by itself, and the transaction should probably open the database for exclusive usage and fill up the log file before committing its changes. Any transaction that never ends execution (i.e., never performs a ROLLBACK or COMMIT) is a faulty application, because the transaction will eventually cause itself and possibly other transactions to fail.

DATABASE RECOVERY   *Database recovery* is the process of returning the data in a database to a consistent state after a system failure (such as a power failure in the middle of a work session) occurs. If a DB2 database is active when a system failure occurs, that database is left in an inconsistent state until the database is accessed again. At that time, a special recovery process is executed that restores the database to a new, consistent state. This new, consistent state is defined by the transaction boundaries of any applications that were using the database when the system failure occurred. This recovery process is made possible by the database log file (see *Recovery Log File* in Chapter 1, "DB2 Database Architecture"). Because the log file contains both a "before" and "after" image of every change made to a row, all transaction records stored in the log file can be either removed from or added to the database as necessary.

DB2 determines whether database recovery is needed by examining the recovery log file the first time a database is opened after a system failure occurs. If the log file shows that the database was not shut down normally, the disk image of the database could be inconsistent. That's because changes made by completed transactions (still in the memory buffers) might have been lost. To restore the database to a consistent state, DB2 does the following actions:

■ Any change made by a transaction that was in flight (had not been committed or rolled back) is removed from the database. DB2 works backward through the log file; if an uncommitted change is found, the record is restored to the "before" image retrieved from the log file.

■ Any change made by a committed transaction that is not found in the database is written to the database. As DB2 scans the log file, any committed log records found that are not in the database are written to the database.

■ If a transaction was in the process of being rolled back, the roll back operation is completed so that all changes made to the database by that transaction are removed.

Because DB2 knows that changes are only consistent when they are explicitly committed, all work done by in-flight transactions is considered inconsistent and must be backed out of the database to preserve database consistency.

As described previously, during the recovery process DB2 must scan the log file to restore the database to a consistent state. While scanning the log file, DB2 reads the database to determine whether the database contains the committed or uncommitted changes. If the log file is large, you could spend quite a while scanning the whole log and reading associated rows from the database. Fortunately, scanning the whole log is usually unnecessary, because the actions recorded at the beginning of the log file have been in the log file longer than the other actions. The chance is greater, then, that their transactions have been completed and that the data has already been written to the database; therefore, no recovery actions are required for the log records generated by these transactions.

If some way existed to skip these log records during the recovery process, the length of time necessary to recover the entire database could be shortened. This is the purpose of the *soft checkpoint*, which establishes a pointer in the log at which to begin database recovery. All log file records recorded before this checkpoint are the result of completed transactions, and their changes have already been written to the database. A soft checkpoint is most useful when log files are large, because the checkpoint can reduce the number of log records that are examined during database recovery; the more often the soft checkpoint is updated, the faster the database can be recovered.

SUMMARY

You will find it extremely important to understand the mechanisms DB2 uses to ensure database consistency before designing your database application. Unfortunately, this aspect is one of the more complicated topics of database application design. This chapter was designed to provide you with an overview of the database consistency mechanisms found in DB2 Universal Database, Version 5.2. You should now know what database consistency is and how to maintain it. You should also be familiar with transactions and how your application uses them to maintain data integrity. Furthermore, you should be familiar with the following transaction isolation levels:

- Repeatable read
- Read stability
- Cursor stability
- Uncommitted read

You should also understand the following lock attributes:

- Object
- Size
- Duration
- Mode

And you should understand the difference between the following lock states:

- Intent None (IN)
- Intent Share (IS)
- Next Key Share (NS)
- Share (S)
- Intent Exclusive (IX)
- Share with Intent Exclusive (SIX)
- Update (U)
- Next Key Exclusive (NX)
- Next Key Weak Exclusive (NW)
- Exclusive (X)

- Weak Exclusive (W)
- Super Exclusive (Z)

You should also be familiar with lock size, deadlocks, lock compatibility, lock conversion, and lock escalation. Finally, you should be aware of how transaction logging works and how transaction logs are used to restore database consistency in the event of a system failure.

As you build your database application, you will need to understand most of the information covered in this chapter. Incorporating this information in your application during the design and development process will help you catch and hopefully avoid potential problems in your application design.

Application Development Fundamentals

3

Getting Started with DB2 Application Development

The DB2 database application development process begins with the application design and continues with the actual source code development. This chapter is designed to introduce you to the elements that can be used to drive your application's design. The first part of this chapter defines a simple application program and explains how a DB2 database application differs. This is followed by an introduction to the four main elements that are used to develop DB2 applications. Next, directions for establishing a DB2 database application development and testing environment are discussed. Finally, a brief overview of transaction management and source code creation and preparation is provided. We will begin by answering the question, "What is a DB2 database application?"

What Is a DB2 Database Application?

Before identifying the basic elements of a DB2 database application, let's examine the basic elements of a simple application. Most simple applications contain five essential parts:

■ Input

■ Logic (decision control)

■ Memory (data storage and retrieval)

■ Arithmetic (calculation)

■ Output

Input is defined as the way an application receives the information it needs in order to produce solutions for the problems that it was designed to solve. Once input has been received, *logic* takes over and determines what information should be placed in or taken out of *memory* (data storage) and what *arithmetic* operations should be performed. Non-database applications use functions supplied by the operating system to store data in (and retrieve data from) simple, byte-oriented files. Once the application has produced a solution to the problem that it was designed to solve, it provides appropriate *output* in the form of either an answer or a specific action.

A DB2 database application contains these same five elements. The only real difference between a simple application program and a DB2 application program is the method of data storage/retrieval and decision control used. In DB2 applications, operating system file *input/output* (I/O) is replaced with DB2 database I/O, which provides more than just data storage and retrieval. DB2 database applications also require less decision control (logic); thanks to the nonprocedural nature of SQL, you can have DB2 applications retrieve only the data they need by restricting SELECT SQL statements with WHERE, GROUP BY, and HAVING clauses. In addition, you can eliminate data sorting routines by using the ORDER BY clause. Figure 3–1 illustrates the essential parts of both a simple application program and a DB2 database application program.

Designing a DB2 Database Application

Designing an efficient database application program requires a good understanding of how the production database is organized. If no written database design document exists, it is a good idea to produce one before you begin designing the actual database application. A good database design document should provide answers to the following questions:

■ What data will be stored in the database?

■ How will the data be stored?

■ What are the functional dependencies in the database?

■ How can the functional dependencies in the database be isolated?

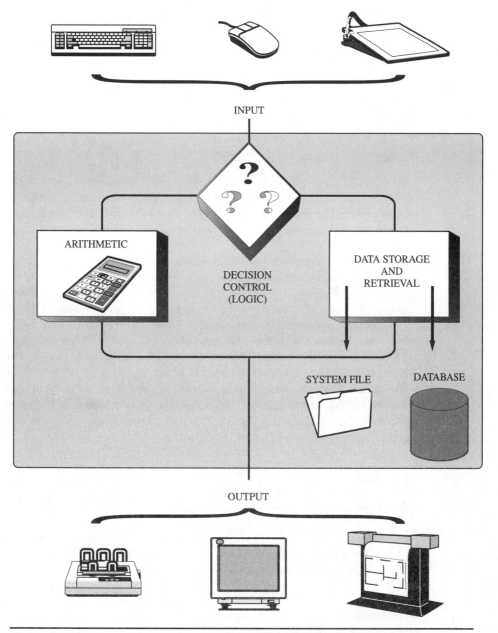

Figure 3–1   Elements of a simple application and a DB2 database application

■ How can data redundancy be reduced or eliminated?

■ What keys need to be created in order to establish referential data integrity?

Ideally, the best database design document will evolve around the requirements of the database applications that will access the database. Once the database design document has been prepared, the application designing process can begin. Application design considerations should include the following items:

- Transaction definitions
- Transaction management and logging
- Volatility and volume of data
- Security considerations
- *Remote Units of Work* (RUOW)
- *Distributed Units of Work* (DUOW)

Because DB2 provides you with a variety of application development capabilities, one of the most important design decisions that an application designer can make is, "Which capabilities of DB2 should be used in my application?" This question can be difficult to answer, because the capabilities that can be chosen and the extent to which they can be used can vary greatly.

The first and most fundamental decision to be made before this question can be answered is the determination of how much data logic (logic that is used to enforce business rules) to move into the database itself—and how much to keep in the application. The key advantage of transferring data logic from the application to the database is that the application becomes more independent from the data. This feature is beneficial when several applications access the same data. Data or data logic maintenance can be performed at one location—the database—and all applications accessing the database see the effects immediately. Although this advantage is powerful, you must take into consideration that when data logic is stored in a database, *all* users of that database are affected. If the data logic rules and constraints that you wish to impose should only apply to the users of your application, it is probably more appropriate to keep the data logic in the application and out of the database.

Elements of a DB2 Database Application

Now that you know the basic requirements of a DB2 database application design, let's examine the specific elements of a DB2 database application. The following elements are the major building blocks of DB2 database applications:

- A high-level programming language
- SQL statements
- CLI function calls (optional)
- *Application Programming Interface* (API) calls (optional)

Each of these elements accomplishes specific tasks in the overall design of a DB2 database application. You can accomplish almost any DB2 task by using a high-level programming language in conjunction with an SQL statement, a CLI function call, or an API call, although some tasks require several of these elements.

High-Level Programming Language

A *high-level programming language* provides the framework within which all SQL statements, CLI function calls, and API calls are contained. This framework enables you to control the sequence of your application's tasks (logic) and provides a way for your application to collect user input and produce appropriate output. A high-level programming language also enables you to use operating system calls and DB2 application elements (SQL statements, CLI function calls, and API calls) within the same application program. In essence, the high-level programming language can take care of everything except data storage and retrieval.

By combining OS calls and DB2 elements, you can develop DB2 database applications that incorporate OS-specific file I/O for referencing external data files. You can also use the high-level programming language to incorporate Presentation Manager functions, User Interface class library routines, and/or *Microsoft Foundation Class* (MFC) library routines in the application for both collecting user input and displaying application output. Additionally, by building a DB2 database application with a high-level language, you can exploit the capabilities of the computer hardware to enhance application performance (i.e., optimizing for high-level processors such as the Pentium III processor) and simplify user interaction (i.e., using special I/O devices such as light pens and scanners). DB2 Universal Database, Version 5.2, provides support for the following high-level languages:

- C
- C++
- COBOL
- FORTRAN
- REXX
- Visual BASIC (through the DB2 Stored Procedure Builder)

SQL Statements

SQL is a standardized language that is used to define, store, manipulate, and retrieve data in a relational database management system. SQL statements are executed by DB2, not by the operating system. Because SQL is nonprocedural by design, it is not an actual programming language; therefore, most database applications are a combination of the decision and sequence control of a high-level programming language and the data storage, manipulation, and retrieval capabilities of SQL statements. Two types of SQL statements can be embedded in an application program: *static* SQL statements and *dynamic* SQL statements. Each has its advantages and disadvantages.

STATIC SQL A static SQL statement is an SQL statement that is hard-coded in an application program when a source code file is written. Because high-level programming language compilers cannot interpret SQL statements, all source code files containing static SQL statements must be processed by an SQL *precompiler* before they can be compiled. Likewise, DB2 cannot work directly with high-level programming language variables. Instead, DB2 must work with host variables that are defined in a special place within an embedded SQL source code file (so the SQL precompiler can recognize them). The SQL precompiler is responsible for translating all SQL statements found in a source code file into their appropriate host-language function calls and for converting the actual SQL statements into host-language comments. The SQL precompiler is also responsible for evaluating the declared data types of host variables and determining which data conversion methods to use when moving data to-and-from the database. Additionally, the SQL precompiler performs error checking on each coded SQL statement and ensures that appropriate host-variable data types are used for their respective table column values.

Static SQL has one distinct advantage over dynamic SQL. Because the structure of the SQL statements used is known at precompile time, the work of analyzing the statement and creating a package containing a data access plan is done during the development phase. Thus, static SQL executes quickly, because its operational form already exists in the database at application run time. The down side to this property is that all static SQL statements must be prepared (i.e., their access plan must be stored in the database) before they can be executed, and they cannot be altered at run time. Because of this characteristic, if an application uses static SQL, its operational package(s) must be "bound" to each database the application will work with before the static SQL statements can be executed.

NOTE: *Because static SQL applications require prior knowledge of database, table, schema, and field names, changes made to these objects after the application is developed could produce undesirable results.*

DYNAMIC SQL   Although static SQL statements are fairly easy to use, they are limited because their format must be known in advance by the precompiler, and they can only use host variables. A dynamic SQL statement does not have a precoded, fixed format, so the data objects the statement uses can change each time the statement is executed. This feature is useful for an application that has an SQL requirement in which the format and syntax of the SQL statement is not known at the time the source code is written. Dynamic SQL statements do not have to be precompiled (although the overhead for dynamic SQL statements sometimes has to) and bound to the database they will access. Instead, they are combined with high-level programming language statements to produce an executable program, and all binding takes place at run time, rather than during compilation.

Because dynamic SQL statements are dynamically created according to the flow of application logic at execution time, they are more powerful than static SQL statements. Unfortunately, dynamic SQL statements are also more complicated to implement. Additionally, because dynamic SQL statements must be prepared at application run time, most will execute more slowly than their equivalent static SQL counterparts. However, because dynamic SQL statements use the most current database statistics during execution, there are some cases in which a dynamic SQL statement will execute faster than an equivalent static SQL statement. Dynamic SQL statements also enable the optimizer to see the real values of arguments, so they are not confined to the use of host variables. Figure 3–2 shows how both static SQL and dynamic SQL applications interact with a DB2 database.

STATIC SQL APPLICATIONS

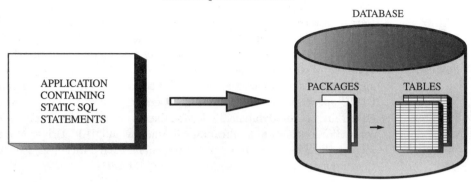

The operational form of static SQL statements are stored as packages in the database. Applications containing static SQL statements use these packages to access table data at application runtime.

DYNAMIC SQL APPLICATIONS

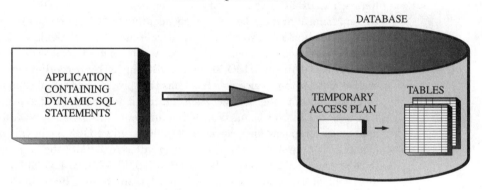

The operational form of dynamic SQL statements are automatically created at application run time. Temporary access plans, generated when dynamic SQL statements are prepared, are then used to access table data.

Figure 3–2   How SQL applications interact with a DB2 database

CLI Function Calls

DB2's *Call Level Interface* (CLI) is a collection of API function calls that were developed specifically for database access.

To understand the call level interface, you need to understand the basis of DB2's CLI and how it compares with existing, callable, SQL interfaces. In the early 1990s, the X/Open Company and the *SQL Access Group* (SAG), now a part of X/Open, jointly developed a standard specification for a callable SQL interface called the *X/Open Call-Level Interface*, or *X/Open CLI*. The goal of the X/Open CLI was to increase the portability of database applications by enabling them to become independent of any one database management system's programming interface. Most of the X/Open CLI specifications were later accepted as part of a new ISO CLI international standard. DB2's CLI is based on this ISO CLI standard interface specification.

In 1992, Microsoft Corporation developed a callable SQL interface, ODBC, for the Microsoft Windows operating system. ODBC is based on the X/Open CLI standards specification but provides extended functions that support additional capability. The ODBC specification also defines an operating environment where database-specific ODBC drivers are dynamically loaded (based on the database name provided with the connection request) at application run time by an ODBC Driver Manager. This Driver Manager provides a central point of control for each datasource-specific library (driver) that implements ODBC function calls and interacts with a specific *database management system* (DBMS). By using drivers, an application can be linked directly to a single ODBC driver library, rather than to each DBMS itself. When the application runs, the ODBC Driver Manager mediates its function calls and ensures that they are directed to the appropriate driver. Figure 3–3 shows how CLI applications interact with a DB2 database via the ODBC Driver Manager and the DB2 CLI driver.

Applications that incorporate DB2's CLI are linked directly to the DB2 CLI load library. The DB2 CLI load library can then be loaded as an ODBC driver by any ODBC Driver Manager or it can be used independently. DB2's CLI provides support for all ODBC 3.X Level 1 functions except `SQLBulkOperations()`; all ODBC Level 2 functions except `SQLDrivers()`; some X/Open CLI functions, and some DB2-specific functions. The CLI specifications defined for ISO, X/Open, ODBC, and DB2 are continually evolving in a cooperative manner to produce new functions that provide additional capabilities.

The important difference between embedded dynamic SQL statements and CLI function calls lies in how the actual SQL statements are invoked. With dynamic SQL, an application prepares and executes SQL for a single DBMS—in this case, DB2. For a dynamic SQL application to work with a different DBMS, the application would have to be precompiled and recompiled for that DBMS. With CLI, an application uses procedure calls at execution time to perform SQL operations. Because CLI applications do not have to be precompiled, they can be executed on a variety of database systems without undergoing any alteration.

API Function Calls

Application Programming Interface (API) function calls are a collection of DB2 product-specific function calls that provide services other than the data storage, manipulation, and retrieval services that are provided by SQL statements and CLI function calls. API calls are embedded within a high-level programming language and operate in a fashion similar to other host-language function calls. Each API function has both a call and a return interface, and the calling application must wait until a requested API function completes before it can continue. The services provided by DB2 API function calls can be divided into the following categories:

■ Database manager control APIs

■ Database manager configuration APIs

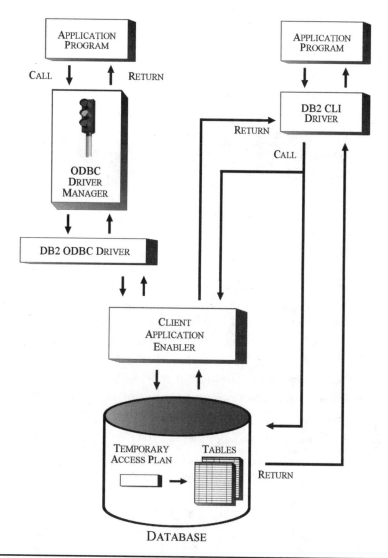

Figure 3–3 How CLI applications interact with a DB2 database

- Database control APIs
- Database configuration APIs
- Database directory management APIs
- Client/server directory management APIs
- Node management APIs
- Network support APIs
- Backup/recovery APIs

- Operational utility APIs
- Database monitoring APIs
- Data utility APIs
- General application programming APIs
- Application preparation APIs
- Remote server APIs
- Table space management APIs
- Transaction APIs
- Miscellaneous APIs

An application can use APIs to access DB2 facilities that are not available via SQL statements or CLI function calls. In addition, you can write applications containing only APIs that will perform the following functions:

- Manipulate the DB2 environment by cataloging and uncataloging databases and workstations (nodes), by scanning system database and workstation directories, and by creating, deleting, and migrating databases
- Perform routine database maintenance by backing up and restoring databases— and by exporting data to and importing data from external data files
- Manipulate the DB2 database manager configuration file and other DB2 database configuration files
- Perform specific client/server operations
- Provide a run-time interface for precompiled SQL statements
- Precompile embedded SQL applications
- Bulk load tables by importing data from external data files

Figure 3–4 illustrates how an application containing the BACKUP API interacts with the DB2 Database Manager to back up a DB2 database.

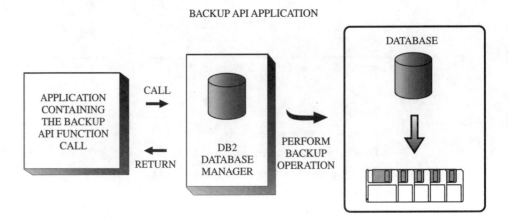

BACKUP API APPLICATION

Figure 3–4   *How a BACKUP API call is processed by DB2*

Establishing the DB2 Database Application Development Environment

Before you can begin developing DB2 database applications, you must establish the appropriate application development/operating system environment by performing the following steps:

1. Install the appropriate DB2 Universal Database software product on the workstation that will be used for application development. If the application will be developed in a client-server environment, you must install the DB2 Universal Database server software on the workstation that will act as the server and install the appropriate DB2 Universal Database *Client Application Enabler* (CAE) software on all client workstations. You also must install a communication protocol that is common to both client and server workstations.

2. Install and properly configure the DB2 Universal Database *Software Developer's Kit* (SDK) software on all workstations that will be used for application development.

3. Install and properly configure a high-level language compiler on all workstations that will be used for application development.

4. Make sure you can establish a connection to the appropriate database(s).

For additional information on how to accomplish these tasks, refer to the installation documentation for DB2 Universal Database, DB2 Universal Database SDK, the compiler being used, and the appropriate communications package.

You can develop DB2 database applications on any workstation that has the DB2 SDK installed. You can run DB2 database applications either at a DB2 server workstation or on any client workstation that has the appropriate DB2 CAE software installed. You can even develop applications in such a way that one part of the application runs on the client workstation and another part runs on the server workstation. When a DB2 database application is divided across workstations in this manner, the part that resides on the server workstation is known as a *stored procedure*.

To precompile, compile, and link DB2 database applications, your environment paths need to be properly set. If you follow the installation instructions that come with the DB2 Universal Database SDK and the supported high-level language compiler, your environment should automatically support application development. If, however, after installing the DB2 Universal Database SDK and your high-level language compiler you are unable to precompile, compile, and link your application, check the environment paths and make sure they point to the correct drives and directories.

NOTE: *Although environment paths are usually set appropriately during the installation process, the compiler/development interface being used may require that these paths are explicitly provided.*

Establishing the DB2 Database Application Testing Environment

As with any other application, the best way to ensure that a DB2 database application performs as expected is to thoroughly test it. You must perform this testing during both the actual development of the application and after the application coding phase has been completed. To thoroughly test your application, establish an appropriate testing environment that includes the following items:

- A testing database
- Appropriate testing tables
- Valid test data

Creating a Testing Database

If your application creates, alters, or drops tables, views, indexes, or any other data objects, you should create a temporary database for testing purposes. If your application inserts, updates, or deletes data from tables and views, you should also use a testing database to prevent your application from corrupting production-level data while it is being tested. You can create a testing database in any of the following ways:

- By writing a small application that calls the CREATE DATABASE API call, either with a high-level programming language (such as C) or as a command file with REXX
- By issuing the CREATE DATABASE command from the DB2 command-line processor
- By backing up the production database and restoring it on a dedicated application development and/or testing workstation

Creating Testing Tables and Views

To determine which testing tables and views you will need in the test database, you must first analyze the data needs of the application (or part of the application) being tested. You can perform this analysis by preparing a list of all data needed by the application and then describing how each data item in the list is going to be accessed. When the analysis is complete, you can construct the test tables and views that are necessary for testing the application in any of the following ways:

- By writing a small application in a high-level programming language that executes the CREATE TABLE or CREATE VIEW SQL statement and creates all necessary tables and views. (This application could be the same application that creates the testing database—provided static SQL is not used.)
- By issuing the CREATE TABLE or CREATE VIEW SQL statement from the DB2 command-line processor

■ By backing up the production database and restoring it on a dedicated application development and/or testing workstation

If you are developing the database schema along with the application, you may need to refine the definitions of the test tables repeatedly throughout the development process. Data objects such as tables and views usually cannot be created and accessed within the same database application, because the DB2 Database Manager cannot bind SQL statements to data objects that do not exist. To make the process of creating and changing data objects less time-consuming, and to avoid this type of binding problem, you can create a separate application that constructs all necessary data objects as you are developing the main application. When the main application development is complete, you can then use the application that creates the data objects to construct production databases. If appropriate, this application can then be incorporated into the main application's installation program.

Generating Test Data

The data an application uses during testing should represent all possible data input conditions. If the application is designed to check the validity of input data, the test data should include both valid and invalid data. This feature is necessary to verify that the valid data is processed appropriately—and the invalid data is detected and handled correctly. You can insert test data into tables in any of the following ways:

■ By writing a small application that executes the INSERT SQL statement. This statement will insert one or more rows into the specified table each time the statement is issued.

■ By writing a small application that executes the INSERT . . . SELECT SQL statement. This statement will obtain data from an existing table and insert the data into the specified table each time the statement is issued.

■ By writing a small application that calls the IMPORT API. You can use this API to load large amounts of new or existing data, or you can use this API in conjunction with the EXPORT API to duplicate one or more tables that have already been populated in a production database.

■ By writing a small application that calls the LOAD API. You can also use this API to bulk load large amounts of new or existing data into a database.

■ By backing up the production database and restoring it on a dedicated application development and/or testing workstation.

Managing Transactions

You might recall in Chapter 2, "Database Consistency Mechanisms," that transactions were described as the basic building blocks that DB2 uses to maintain database consistency. All data storage, manipulation, and retrieval must be performed within one or more transactions, and any application that successfully connects to a database automatically initiates a transaction. The application, therefore, must end the transaction by issuing either a COMMIT or a ROLLBACK SQL statement (or by calling the SQL EndTrans() CLI function), or by disconnecting from the database (which causes the DB2 Database Manager to automatically perform a COMMIT operation).

NOTE: *You should not disconnect from a database and allow the DB2 Database Manager to automatically end the transaction, because some database management systems behave differently than others (for example, DB2/400 will perform a ROLLBACK instead of a COMMIT).*

The COMMIT SQL statement makes all changes in the transaction permanent, while the ROLLBACK SQL statement removes all these changes from the database. Once a transaction has ended, all locks held by the transaction are freed—and another transaction can access the previously locked data. (Refer to Chapter 2, "Database Consistency Mechanisms," for more information.)

Applications should be developed in such a way that they end transactions on a timely basis, so other applications (or other transactions within the same application) are not denied access to necessary data resources for long periods of time. Applications should also be developed in such a way that their transactions do not inadvertently cause deadlock situations to occur. During the execution of an application program, you can issue explicit COMMIT or ROLLBACK SQL statements to ensure that transactions are terminated on a timely basis. Keep in mind, however, that once a COMMIT or ROLLBACK SQL statement has been issued, its processing cannot be stopped—and its effects cannot easily be reversed.

Creating and Preparing Source Code Files

The high-level programming language statements in an application program are usually written to a standard ASCII text file, known as a *source code file*, which can be edited with any text or source code editor. The source code files must have the proper file extension for the host language in which the code is written (i.e., C source files have a .C extension, and COBOL source files have a .COB extension) for the high-level language compiler to know what to do with them.

If your application is written in an interpreted language such as REXX, you can execute the application directly from the operating system command prompt by entering the program name after connecting to the required database. Applications written in interpreted host languages do not need to be precompiled, compiled, or linked. However, if your application was written in a compiled host language such as C, you must perform additional steps to build your application. Before you can compile your program, you must precompile it if it contains embedded SQL. Simply stated, *precompiling* is the process of converting embedded SQL statements into DB2 run-time API calls that a host compiler can process. The SQL calls are then stored in a package, in a bind file, or in both, depending upon the precompiler options specified. After the program is precompiled, compiled, and linked, the program must then be bound to the test or the production database. *Binding* is the process of creating a package from the source code or bind file and storing the package in the database for later use. If your application accesses more than one database, and if it contains embedded SQL, it must be bound to each database used before it can be executed. Precompiling and binding are only required if the source files contain embedded SQL statements; if they contain only CLI function calls and/or API calls, precompiling and binding are not necessary.

SUMMARY

The goal of this chapter was to provide you with an overview of the DB2 database application development process. You should now understand what a DB2 database application is, and you should be familiar with some of the issues that affect database application design.

You should also be familiar with the following application development building blocks:

- A high-level programming language
- SQL statements
- CLI function calls
- API calls

You should also be able to establish a DB2 database application development environment and create testing databases, testing tables, and test data. Finally, you should have some understanding about the way source code files are created and converted into executable programs. Chapter 4 continues to present DB2 database application development fundamentals by focusing on the development of CLI applications for DB2 Universal Database, Version 5.2.

Writing API Applications

DB2 Universal Database application programming interface (API) calls are a set of functions that are not part of the standard SQL sublanguage nor the *Call-Level Interface* (CLI) routines. Where SQL and CLI are used to add, modify, and retrieve data from a database, API calls provide an interface to the DB2 Database Manager. API calls are often included in embedded SQL or CLI applications to provide additional functionality that is not covered by SQL or CLI (for example, starting and stopping DB2's Database Manager). You can develop complete API applications that control database environments, modify database configurations, and perform administrative tasks. API applications can also be used to fine-tune database performance and perform routine database maintenance.

This chapter begins by describing the basic structure of an API database application source-code file. Then, the types of API calls available with DB2, their naming conventions, and the special data structures some API calls use is discussed. Next information on how to evaluate API return codes and display error messages is provided. Finally, this chapter concludes with a brief discussion on using the compiler and linker to convert an API application source-code file to an executable program.

NOTE: *When API calls are added to a CLI application, its portability is reduced because other database products will not know what to do when they encounter DB2-specific API calls.*

The Basic Structure of an API Source-Code File

An API application program source-code file can be divided into two main parts: the *header* and the *body*. The *header* contains, among other things, the host-language compiler preprocessor statements that are used to merge the contents of the appropriate DB2 API header file(s) with the host-language source-code file. These header files contain the API function prototype definitions and the structure templates for the special data structures that are required by some of the APIs. The *body* contains the local variable declaration statements, the variable assignment statements, and one or more API function calls. The body also contains additional processing statements and error-handling statements that may be required in order for the application to perform the desired task. The sample C programming language source code in Figure 4–1 illustrates these two parts, along with some of the C language statements that might be found in them.

Types of API Function Calls

DB2's rich set of API function calls can be divided into the following categories:

- Database Manager Control APIs
- Database Manager Configuration APIs
- Database Control APIs
- Database Configuration APIs
- Database Directory Management APIs
- Client/Server Directory Management APIs
- Node Management APIs
- Network Support APIs

API SOURCE CODE FRAMEWORK

```
/* Include Appropriate Header Files*/
#include <stdio.h>
#include <stdlib.h>
#include <string.h>
   •••
#include <sqljra.h>
#include <sqljacb.h>
#include <sqlenv.h>
/* Declare Function Prototypes */
int main(int argc, char *argv []);
   •••


/* Declare Procedure */
int main(int argc, char *argv[])
{
     /* Declare Local Variables */
     struct sqledinfo *pDB_DirInfo = NULL;
     unsigned short usHandle = 0;
     unsigned short usDBCount = 0;
     struct sqlca   sqlRetCode;
     •••
     /*Get The Database Directory Information */
     sqledosd(0, &usHandle, &usDBCount, &sqlRetCode);

     /*Scan The Directory Buffer And Print Info */
     for (; usDBCount !=0; usDBCount--)
         {
         sqledgne(usHandle, &pDB_DirInfo, &sqlRetCode)
         printf("%.8s\t", pDB_DirInfo->alias);
         printf("%.8s\t", pDB_DirInfo->alias);
         printf("%.30s\n", pDB_DirInfo->comment);
         }

     /* Free Resources (Directory Info Buffer) */
     sqledcls (usHandle, &sqlRetCode);
     •••
     /* Return To The Operating System */
     return((int) sqlRetCode.sqlcode);
}
```

HEADER

BODY

Figure 4–1   Parts of an API source-code file.

- Backup/Recovery APIs
- Operational Utility APIs
- Database Monitoring APIs
- Data Utility APIs
- General Application Programming APIs
- Application Preparation APIs
- Remote Server Connection APIs

■ Table Space Management APIs

■ Transaction APIs

■ Miscellaneous APIs

Each API function call falls into one of these categories according to its functionality. The following describes each of these categories in more detail.

DATABASE MANAGER CONTROL APIs.   Database Manager control APIs are a set of functions that start and stop the DB2 Database Manager background process. This background process must be running before any application can gain access to a DB2 database.

DATABASE MANAGER CONFIGURATION APIs.   The Database Manager configuration APIs are a set of functions that can be used to retrieve, change, or reset the information stored in the DB2 Database Manager configuration file. The DB2 Database Manager configuration file contains configuration parameters that affect the overall performance of DB2's Database Manager and its global resources. These APIs are rarely used in embedded SQL or CLI application programs; only API application programs that provide some type of generalized database utilities have a use for these functions.

DATABASE CONTROL APIs.   Database control APIs are a set of functions that can be used to create new databases, drop (delete) or migrate existing databases, and restart DB2 databases that were not stopped correctly (for example, databases that were open when a system failure occurred).

DATABASE CONFIGURATION APIs.   Every database has its own configuration file that is automatically created when the CREATE DATABASE API call (or command) is executed. Database configuration APIs are a set of functions that can be used to retrieve, change, or reset the information stored in these database configuration files. Each database configuration file contains configuration parameters that affect the performance of an individual database and its resource requirements. These APIs are rarely used in embedded SQL or CLI application programs; only API application programs that provide some type of generalized database utilities have a use for these functions.

DATABASE DIRECTORY MANAGEMENT APIs.   Database directory management APIs are a set of functions that can be used to catalog and uncatalog databases, change database comments (descriptions), and view the entries stored in the DB2 database directory.

CLIENT/SERVER DIRECTORY MANAGEMENT APIs.   Client/Server directory management APIs are a set of functions that can be used to catalog and uncatalog databases that are accessed via DB2 Connect. These APIs can also view the entries stored in the DB2 DCS directory.

NODE MANAGEMENT APIs.   Node management APIs are a set of functions that can be used to catalog and uncatalog remote workstations, and view the entries stored in the DB2 workstation directory.

NETWORK SUPPORT APIs.   Network support APIs are a set of functions that can be used to register and deregister a DB2 database server workstation's address in the NetWare bindery (on the network server).

BACKUP/RECOVERY APIs.   Backup/Recovery APIs are a set of functions that can be used to back up and restore databases, perform roll-forward recoveries on databases, and view the entries stored in a DB2 database recovery history file. Every database has its own recovery file, which is automatically created when the CREATE DATABASE API call (or command) is executed. Once created, this history file is automatically updated whenever the database or its table space(s) are backed up or restored. The recovery history file can be used to reset the database to the state it was in at any specific point in time.

OPERATIONAL UTILITY APIs.   Operational utility APIs are a set of functions that can be used to change lock states on table spaces, reorganize the data in database tables, update statistics on database tables, and force all users off a database (i.e., break all connections to a database).

DATABASE MONITORING APIs.   Database monitoring APIs are a set of functions that can be used to collect information about the current state of a DB2 database.

DATA UTILITY APIs.   Data utility APIs are a set of functions that can be used to import data from and export data to various external file formats.

GENERAL APPLICATION PROGRAMMING APIs.   General application programming APIs are a set of functions that can be used in conjunction with embedded SQL statements, CLI function calls, and/or other API function calls to develop robust database application programs. These APIs perform such tasks as retrieving SQL and API error messages, retrieving SQLSTATE values, installing signal and interrupt handlers, and copying and freeing memory buffers used by other APIs.

APPLICATION PREPARATION APIs.   Application preparation APIs are a set of functions that can be used to precompile, bind, and rebind embedded SQL source-code files.

REMOTE SERVER CONNECTION APIs.   Remote server connection APIs are a set of functions that can be used to attach to and detach from workstations (nodes) at which instance-level functions are executed. These functions essentially establish (and remove) a logical instance attachment to a specified workstation and start (or end) a physical communications connection to that workstation.

TABLE SPACE MANAGEMENT APIs.   Table space management APIs are a set of functions that can be used to create new table spaces and retrieve information about existing table spaces.

TRANSACTION APIs.   Transaction APIs are a set of functions that allow two-phase commit-compliant applications to execute problem-solving functions on transactions that are tying up system resources (otherwise known as *in doubt transactions*).

For DB2, these resources include locks on tables and indexes, log space, and transaction storage memory. Transaction APIs are used in applications that need to query, commit, roll back, or cancel in-doubt transactions. You can cancel indoubt transactions by removing log records and releasing log pages associated with the transaction.

MISCELLANEOUS APIs.   Miscellaneous APIs are a set of functions that do not fall into any of the categories previously listed. Some of these functions can be used to retrieve user authorization information, set and retrieve settings for connections made by application processes, and provide accounting information to DRDA servers.

API Naming Conventions

Although most embedded SQL statements and CLI functions are endowed with long and descriptive names, most DB2's API functions do not follow this pattern. Instead, many API function names creatively pack as much information as possible into eight characters. The conventions used by DB2 for naming most API functions are as follows:

■ Each API name begins with the letters *sql*.

■ The fourth character in each API name denotes the functional area to which the API call belongs:

-e   for C-specific environment services.

-u   for C-specific general utilities.

-f   for C-specific configuration services.

-a   for C-specific application services.

-m   for C-specific monitor services.

-b   for C-specific table and table-space query services.

-o   for C-specific SQLSTATE services.

-g   for a generic (language-independent) version of the above services.

■ The last four characters describe the function. As you might imagine, this four-letter limitation results in some strange abbreviations.

NOTE: In later versions of DB2 Universal Database, there is no limitation on the length of API function names. However, the first four characters continue following these naming conventions.

There is a C-language version of each API function that has been optimized for the C/C++ programming language. There is also a language-independent generic version that corresponds to almost every C-language API function available. If you are developing an API application program with C or C++, you should use the C-language specific version of the API function. However, if you are developing an API application program with another programming language, such as COBOL, REXX, or FORTRAN, you must use the generic API functions instead of their C-language counterparts.

API Data Structures

Often API application source-code files must contain declaration statements that create special data structure variables. These special data structure variables are used to either provide input information to or obtain return information from specific API functions. Table 4–1 lists the names of the data structure templates that are stored in the DB2 API header files, along with brief descriptions of what each data structure is used for.

API data structure templates are made available to C and C++ applications when the appropriate compiler preprocessor statements (#include <*xxxxxxx*.h>) are placed in the header portion of the source-code file. Once the structure templates are made available to the source-code file, a corresponding structure variable must be declared and initialized before it can be used in an API function call. In addition to API-specific structure templates, every source-code file that contains one or more API calls must, at a minimum, declare a variable of the SQLCA data structure type. This variable is used by almost every API function to return status information to the calling application after the API call completes execution.

Table 4–1   Data Structures Used by DB2's API Functions

Data Structure Name	Description
rfwd_input	Passes information needed for a roll forward recovery operation to the ROLLFORWARD DATABASE API.
rfwd_output	Returns information generated by a roll forward recovery operation to an application program.
sql_authorizations	Returns user authorization information to an application program.
sql_dir_entry	Transfers Database Connection Services directory information between an application program and DB2.
sqla_flaginfo	Holds flagger information.
sqlb_flagmsgs	Holds flagger messages.
sqlb_tbs_stats	Returns table space statistics information to an application program.
SQLB_TBSCONTQRY_DATA	Returns table space container data to an application program.
SQLB_TBSQRY_DATA	Returns table space data to an application program.
SQLB_QUESCER_DATA	Holds table space quescer information.
sqlca	Returns error and warning information to an application program.
sqlchar	Transfers variable length data between an application program and DB2.
sqlda	Transfers collections of data between an application program and DB2.
sqldcol	Passes column information to the IMPORT and EXPORT APIs.
sqle_addn_options	Passes tabel space information to the ADD NODE API.
sqle_client_info	Transfers client information between an application program and DB2.
sqle_conn_setting	Specifies connection setting types (Type 1 or Type 2) and values.
sqle_node_appc	Passes information for cataloging APPC nodes to the CATALOG NODE API.

Table 4–1   Data Structures Used by DB2's API Functions (Continued)

Data Structure Name	Description
sqle_node_appn	Passes information for cataloging APPN nodes to the **CATALOG NODE** API.
sqle_node_cpic	Passes information for cataloging CPIC nodes to the **CATALOG NODE** API.
sqle_node_ipxspx	Passes information for cataloging IPX/SPX nodes to the **CATALOG NODE** API.
sqle_node_local	Passes information for cataloging LOCAL nodes to the **CATALOG NODE** API.
sqle_node_netb	Passes information for cataloging NetBIOS nodes to the **CATALOG NODE** API.
sqle_node_npipe	Passes information for cataloging named pipes to the **CATALOG NODE** API.
sqle_node_struct	Passes information for cataloging all nodes to the **CATALOG NODE** API.
sqle_node_tcpip	Passes information for cataloging TCP/IP nodes to the **CATALOG NODE** API.
sqle_reg_nwbindery	Passes information for registering or deregistering the DB2 server in/from the bindery on the NetWare file server.
sqle_start_options	Passes start-up option infromation to the **START DATABASE MANAGER** API.
sqledbcountryinfo	Transfers country information between an application program and DB2.
sqledbdesc	Passes creation parameters to the **CREATE DATABASE** API.
SQLETSDESC	Passes table space description information to the **CREATE DATABASE** API.
SQLETSCDESC	Passes table space container description information to the **CREATE DATABASE** API.
sqledbstopopt	Passes stop information to the **STOP DATABASE MANAGER** API.
sqledinfo	Returns database directory information about a single entry in the system or local database directory to an application program.
sqleninfo	Returns node directory information about a single entry in the node directory to an application program.
sqlfupd	Passes database and Database Manager configuration file information between an application program and DB2.
sqlm_collected	Transfers Database System Monitor collection count information between an application program and DB2.
sqlm_recording_group	Transfers Database System Monitor monitor group information between an application program and DB2.
sqlm_timestamp	Holds Database System Monitor monitor group timestamp information.

Table 4–1   *Data Structures Used by DB2's API Functions (Continued)*

Data Structure Name	Description
sqlma	Sends database system monitor requests from an application program to DB2.
sqlm_obj_struct	Sends database system monitor requests from an application program to DB2.
sqlopt sqloptheader sqloptions	Passes bind options information to the **BIND** API and precompile options information to the **PRECOMPILE PROGRAM** API.
SQLU_LSN	Transfers log sequence number information between an application program and DB2.
sqlu_media_list sqlu_medialist_target sqlu_media_entry sqlu_vendor sqlu_location_entry	Holds a list of target media (**BACKUP**) or source media (**RESTORE**) for a backup image.
SQLU_RLOG_INFO	Transfers log status information between an application program and DB2.
sqlu_tablespace_bkrst_list sqlu_tablespace_entry	Passes a list of table-space names to an application program.
sqluexpt_out	Returns information generated by an export to an application program.
sqluhinfo sqluhtsp sqluhadm	Passes information from the recovery history file to an application program.
sqluimpt_in	Passes information needed for an import operation to the **IMPORT** API.
sqluimpt_out	Returns information generated by an import operation to an application program.
sqluload_in	Passes information needed for a bulk load operation to the **LOAD** API.
sqluload_out	Returns information generated by a bulk load operation to an application program.
sqlurf_newlogpath	Passes new log file directory information to the **ROLLFORWARD DATABASE** API.
sqlurf_info	Returns information generated by a rollforward database operation to an application program.
sqlupi sqlpart_key	Transfers partitioning information between an application program and DB2.
SQLXA_RECOVER	Provides a list of indoubt transactions to an application program.
SQLXA_XID	Used to identify a transaction to an application program.

Error Handling

You have already seen that error handling is an important part of every DB2 embedded SQL and CLI database application. The same holds true for DB2 API applications. Whenever an API call is executed, status information is returned to the calling application by the following:

■ The API function return code

■ The SQLCA data structure variable

Like embedded SQL and CLI applications, the best way to handle error conditions is with a common error-handling routine.

Evaluating Return Codes

Whenever an API function call is executed, a special value, known as a *return code*, is returned to the calling application. A common error-handling routine should first determine whether or not an error or warning condition has occurred by checking this return code value. If the error-handling routine discovers that an error or warning has occurred, it should examine the SQL code that is also returned and process the error accordingly. At a minimum, an error-handling routine should notify users that an error or warning has occurred —and provide enough information so the problem can be corrected.

Evaluating SQLCA Return Codes

It was mentioned earlier that each API application must declare a variable of the SQLCA data structure type. Whenever an API function is invoked from an application program, the address of this variable is always passed as an output parameter value. This variable is then used by DB2 to store status information when the API function completes execution.

If an error or warning condition occurs during the execution of an API function call, an error return-code value is returned to the calling application and additional information about the warning or error is placed in the SQLCA data structure variable. To save space, this information is stored in the form of a coded number. However, you can invoke the GET ERROR MESSAGE API, using this data structure variable, to translate the coded number into a more meaningful description, which can then be used to correct the problem. Incorporating the GET ERROR MESSAGE API call into your API application during the development phase will help you quickly determine when there is a problem in the way an API call was invoked. Incorporating the GET ERROR MESSAGE API call into your API application will also let the user know why a particular API function failed at application run time.

Evaluating SQLSTATEs

If an error or warning condition occurs during the execution of an API function call, a standardized error-code value is also placed in the SQLCA data structure variable. Like the SQLCA return-code value, the SQLSTATE information is stored in the form of a coded number. You can use the GET SQLSTATE API to translate this coded number into a more meaningful error-message description.

Creating Executable Applications

Once you have written your API application source-code file(s), you must convert them into an executable DB2 database application program. The steps used in this process are:

1. Compile the source-code files to create object modules.
2. Link the object modules to create an executable program.

After you have written an API source-code file, you must compile it with a high-level language compiler (such as VisualAge C++, Visual C++, and Borland C/C++). The high-level language compiler converts the source-code file into an object module that is then used by the linker to create the executable program. The linker combines specified object modules, high-level language libraries, and DB2 libraries to produce an executable application (provided no errors or unresolved external references occur). For most operating systems, the executable application can be either an *executable load module* (.EXE) a *shared library* or a *dynamic link library* (.DLL). Figure 4–2 illustrates the process of converting an API application source-code file to an executable application.

Running, Testing, and Debugging API Applications

Once your application program has been successfully compiled and linked, you can run the program and determine whether or not it performs as expected. You should be able to run your DB2 API application program as you would any other application program on your particular operating system. If problems occur, you can do the following to help test and debug your code:

■ When compiling and linking, specify the proper compiler and linker options so the executable program can be used with a symbolic debugger (usually provided with the high-level language compiler).

■ Make full use of the GET ERROR MESSAGE and GET SQLSTATE API function calls.

■ Display all error message and return codes generated whenever an API function call fails.

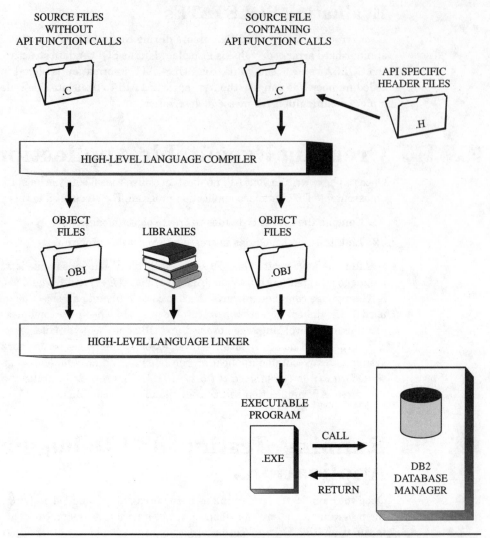

Figure 4–2   Process for converting API source-code files into executable DB2 application
                programs.

NOTE: *Because some APIs require a database connection before they can be executed,*
consider creating a temporary database to use while testing your API application to avoid
inadvertently corrupting a production database.

SUMMARY

The goal of this chapter was to provide you with an overview of how application programming interface (API) application source-code files are structured and to describe the processes involved in converting API application source-code files into executable database application programs. You should know that API functions are divided according to their functionality, into the following groups:

- Database Manager Control APIs
- Database Manager Configuration APIs
- Database Control APIs
- Database Configuration APIs
- Database Directory Management APIs
- Client/Server Directory Management APIs
- Node Directory Management APIs
- Network Support APIs
- Backup/Recovery APIs
- Operational Utility APIs
- Database Monitoring APIs
- Data Utility APIs
- General Application Programming APIs
- Application Preparation APIs
- Remote Server Connection APIs
- Table Space Management APIs
- Transaction APIs
- Miscellaneous APIs

You should also be familiar with the API routine naming conventions used by IBM and the special data structures that many of the DB2 APIs require. You should know how to detect errors by evaluating the API return codes and how to translate SQLCA-coded values into useful error messages with the GET ERROR MESSAGE API function call. You should also be familiar with the two-step process that is used to convert DB2 API source-code files to executable database applications:

- Compiling
- Linking

Finally, you should know how to run, test, and debug your DB2 API database application once it has been compiled and linked.

3

Application Programming Interface (API) Functions

5

Program Preparation and General Programming APIs

Before most DB2 applications can be compiled and executed, they must be prepared by the SQL precompiler, and the packages produced must be bound to one or more databases. This chapter is designed to introduce you to the set of DB2 API functions that are used to prepare applications and bind packages to DB2 databases and to the set of DB2 API functions that perform general tasks in an application program. The first part of this chapter provides a general discussion about embedded SQL application preparation. Then, the functions that are used to handle exceptions, signals, and interrupts are described. Next, information about accounting strings and the function used to set them is provided. This is followed by a brief discussion of the pointer manipulation and error message retrieval functions that are available. Finally, a detailed reference section covering each DB2 API function that can be used to prepare applications and perform general programming tasks is provided.

Embedded SQL Application Preparation

As discussed in Chapter 4, embedded SQL source-code files must always be precompiled. The precompile process converts a source-code file with embedded SQL statements into a high-level language source-code file that is made up entirely of high-level language statements. This process is important, because the high-level language compiler cannot interpret SQL statements, so it cannot create the appropriate object code files that are used by the linker to produce an executable program. The precompile process also creates a corresponding package that contains, among other things, one or more data access plans. Data access plans contain information about how the SQL statements in the source-code file are to be processed by DB2 at application run time.

Normally, the SQL precompiler is invoked from either the DB2 command-line processor or from a batch or make utility file. There may be times, however, when the SQL precompiler needs to be invoked from an application program (for example, when an embedded SQL source-code file is provided for a portable application and the application's installation program needs to precompile it in order to produce the corresponding execution package). In these cases, you can use the PRECOMPILE PROGRAM function to invoke the DB2 SQL precompiler.

When an embedded SQL source-code file is precompiled, the corresponding execution package produced can either be stored in a database immediately or written to an external bind file and bound to the database later (the process of storing this package in the appropriate database is known as *binding*). By default, packages are automatically bound to the database used for precompiling during the precompile process. By specifying the appropriate precompiler options, however, you can elect to store this package in a separate file and perform the binding process at a later time. Just as the SQL precompiler is normally invoked from either the DB2 command-line processor or from a batch or make utility file, the DB2 bind utility is normally invoked in the same manner. There may be times, however, when you need to invoke the bind utility from an application program (for example, when a bind file is provided for a portable application and the application's installation program needs to bind it to the database that the application will run against). You can use the BIND function to invoke the DB2 bind utility for cases such as these.

When producing execution packages for embedded SQL applications, the SQL precompiler determines the best access plan to use by evaluating the data objects available at package creation time. As more data objects, such as indexes, are added to the database, older packages need to be rebound so they can take advantage of new data objects (and possibly produce more efficient data access plans). If the bind files associated with an application are available, you can rebind older packages by re-invoking the DB2 bind utility. If the bind files are no longer available, you can still rebind existing packages by using the REBIND function. When the REBIND function is invoked, the specified package is recreated from the SQL statements that were stored in the SYSCAT.STATEMENTS system catalog table when the package was first created.

Exception, Signal, and Interrupt Handlers

A DB2 database application program must be able to shut down gracefully whenever an exception, signal, or interrupt occurs. Typically, this process is done through an exception, signal, or interrupt handler routine. The INSTALL SIGNAL HANDLER function can be used to install a default exception, signal, or interrupt handler routine in all DB2 applications. If this function is called before any other API functions or SQL statements are executed, any DB2 operations that are currently in progress will be ended gracefully whenever an exception, signal, or interrupt occurs (normally, a ROLLBACK SQL statement is executed in order to avoid the risk of inconsistent data).

The default exception, signal, or interrupt handler is adequate for most simple, single-task applications. However, if your application program is a multithread or multiprocess application, you might want to provide a customized exception, signal, or interrupt handler. If this situation is the case, the INTERRUPT function should be called from each custom exception, signal, or interrupt handler routine to ensure that all DB2 operations currently in progress are ended gracefully. This API function notifies DB2 that a termination has been requested. DB2 then examines which, if any, database operation is in progress and takes appropriate action to cleanly terminate that operation. Some database operations, such as the COMMIT and the ROLLBACK SQL statement, cannot be terminated and are allowed to complete, because their completion is necessary to maintain consistent data.

NOTE: *SQL statements other than* COMMIT *and* ROLLBACK *should never be placed in customized exception, signal, and interrupt handler routines.*

Pointer Manipulation and Memory Copy Functions

Because many DB2 API functions use pointers for either input or output parameters, some type of pointer manipulation is often required when API functions are included in application programs. Some host languages, such as C and C++, support pointer manipulation and provide memory copy functions. Other host languages, such as FORTRAN and COBOL, do not. The GET ADDRESS, COPY MEMORY, and DEREFERENCE ADDRESS functions are designed to provide pointer manipulation and memory copy functions for applications that are written in host languages that do not inherently provide this functionality.

Specifying Connection Accounting Strings

DB2 database applications designed to run in a distributed environment might need to connect to and retrieve data from a *Distributed Relational Database Architecture* (DRDA) application server (such as DB2 for OS/390). DRDA servers often use a process known as chargeback accounting to charge customers for their use of system resources. By using the SET ACCOUNTING STRING function, applications running on a DB2 Universal Database workstation (using DB2 Connect) can pass chargeback accounting information directly to a DRDA server when a connection is established. Accounting strings typically contain 56 bytes of system-generated data and up to 199 bytes of user-supplied data (suffix). Table 5–1 shows the fields and format of a typical accounting string. The following is an example accounting string:

```
X'3C'SQL050200S/2 CH14EX6A     ETPDD6Z    x'05'DEPT1
```

The SET ACCOUNTING STRING function combines system-generated data with a suffix, which is provided as one of its input parameters, to produce the accounting string that is to be sent to the specified server *at the next connect request*. Therefore, an application should call this function before attempting to connect to a DRDA application server. An application can also call this function any time it needs to change the accounting string (for example, to send a different string when a connection is made to a different DRDA database). If the SET ACCOUNTING STRING function is not called before a connection to a DRDA application server is made, the value stored in the DB2ACCOUNT environment variable will be used as the default. If no value exists for the DB2ACCOUNT environment variable, the value of the *dft_account_str* DB2 Database Manager configuration parameter will be used.

Table 5–1 *Accounting String Fields*

Field Name	Size (in Bytes)	Description
acct_str_len	1	A hexadecimal value representing the overall length of the accounting string minus 1. For example, this value would be 0x3C for a string containing 61 characters.
client_prdid	8	The product ID of the client's DB2 Client Application Enabler software. For example, the product ID for the DB2 Universal Database, Version 5.2 Client Application Enabler is "SQL05020."
client_platform	18	The platform (or operating system) on which the client application runs; for example, "OS/2," "AIX," "DOS," or "Windows."
client_appl_name	20	The first 20 characters of the application name; for example, "CH14EX6A."
client_authid	8	The authorization ID used to precompile and bind the application; for example, "ETPDD6Z."
suffix_len	1	A hexadecimal value representing the overall length of the user-supplied suffix string. This field should be set to 0x00 if no user-supplied suffix string is provided.
suffix	199	The user-supplied suffix string. This string can be a value specified by an application, the value of the DB2ACCOUNT environment variable, the value of the *dft_account_str* DB2 Database Manager configuration parameter, or a null string.

Adapted from IBM's *DB2 Connect Users Guide*, Table 5, p. 74.

Evaluating SQLCA Return Codes and SQLSTATE Values

Most DB2 API functions require a pointer to a SQL Communications Area (SQLCA) data structure variable as an output parameter. When an API function or an embedded SQL statement completes execution, this variable contains error, warning, or status information. To save on space, this information is stored in the form of a coded number. If the GET ERROR MESSAGE function is executed and the SQLCA data structure variable returned from another API function is provided as input, the coded number will be translated into more meaningful error message text. Standardized error code values or SQLSTATEs are also stored in the SQLCA data structure variable. Like the SQLCA return code value, the SQLSTATE information is stored in the form of a coded number. You can use the GET SQLSTATE MESSAGE function to translate this coded number into more meaningful error message text. By including either (or both) of these API functions in your DB2 database applications, you can return meaningful error and warning information to the end user whenever error and/or warning conditions occur.

The Program Preparation And General Application Programming Functions Table 5–2 lists the DB2 API functions that are used prepare applications, bind packages to

Table 5–2   Program Preparation and General Programming APIs

Function Name	Description
PRECOMPILE PROGRAM	Preprocesses a source-code file that contains embedded SQL statements and generates a corresponding package that is stored in either the database or an external file..
BIND	Prepares the SQL statements stored in a bind file and generates a corresponding package that is stored in the database.
REBIND	Recreates a package that is already stored in a database without using an external bind file.
GET INSTANCE	Retrieves the current value of the DB2INSTANCE environment variable.
INSTALL SIGNAL HANDLER	Installs the default interrupt signal handler in a DB2 database application program.
INTERRUPT	Safely stops execution of the current database request.
GET ADDRESS	Stores the address of one variable in another variable.
COPY MEMORY	Copies data from one memory storage area to another.
DEREFERENCE ADDRESS	Copies data from a buffer defined by a pointer to a variable that is directly accessible by an application.
SET ACCOUNTING STRING	Specifies accounting information that is to be sent to Distributed Relational Database Architecture (DRDA) servers along with connect requests.
GET ERROR MESSAGE	Retrieves the message text associated with an SQL Communications Area error code from a special DB2 error message file.
GET SQLSTATE MESSAGE	Retrieves the message text associated with a SQLSTATE value from a special DB2 error message file.
GET AUTHORIZATIONS	Retrieves the authorizations that have been granted to the current user.

DB2 databases, and perform general tasks in an application program. Each of these functions are described in detail in the remainder of this chapter.

■■ ■■ PRECOMPILE PROGRAM

Purpose   The PRECOMPILE PROGRAM function is used to precompile (preprocess) an application program source-code file that contains embedded SQL statements.

Syntax
```
SQL_API_RC SQL_API_FN sqlaprep (char        *ProgramName,
                                char        *MsgFileName,
                                struct sqlopt  *PrepOptions,
                                struct sqlca   *SQLCA);
```

Parameters   *ProgramName*   A pointer to a location in memory where the name of the source-code file to be precompiled is stored.

MsgFileName   A pointer to a location in memory where the name of the file or device that all error, warning, and informational messages generated are to be written to is stored.

PrepOptions   A pointer to a *sqlopt* structure that contains the precompiler options (if any) that should be used when precompiling the source-code file.

SQLCA   A pointer to a location in memory where a SQL Communications Area (SQLCA) data structure variable is stored. This variable returns either status information (if the function executed successfully) or error information (if the function failed) to the calling application.

Includes   `#include <sql.h>`

Description The PRECOMPILE PROGRAM function is used to precompile (preprocess) an application program source-code file that contains embedded SQL statements. When a source-code file containing embedded SQL statements is precompiled, a modified source file containing host language function calls for each SQL statement used is produced, and by default, a package for the SQL statements coded in the file is created and bound to the database to which a connection has been established. The name of the package to be created is, by default, the same as the first eight characters of the source-code file name (minus the file extension and converted to uppercase) from which the package was generated. However, you can overwrite bind file names and package names by using the SQL_BIND_OPT and the SQL_PKG_OPT options when this function is called.

A special structure (*sqlopt*) is used to pass different precompile options to the SQL precompiler when this function is called. The *sqlopt* structure is defined in *sql.h* as follows:

```
struct sqlopt
{

struct sqloptheader  header;      /* A Precompile/Bind options header   */
struct sqloptions    option[1];   /* An array of Precompile/Bind        */
                                  /* options                            */
};
```

This structure is composed of two or more additional structures: one *sqloptheader* structure and one or more *sqloptions* structures. The *sqloptheader* structure is defined in *sql.h* as follows:

```
struct sqloptheader
{
unsigned long  allocated;    /* Number of sqloptions structures that*/
                             /* have been allocated (the number of  */
                             /* elements in the array specified in   */
                             /* the option parameter of the          */
                             /* sqlopt structure)                    */
unsigned long  used;         /* The actual number of sqloptions      */
                             /* structures used (the actual          */
                             /* number of type and val option        */
                             /* pairs supplied)                      */
};
```

The *sqloptions* structure is defined in *sql.h* as follows:

```
struct sqloptions
{
unsigned long  type;    /* Precompile/Bind option type    */
unsigned long  val;     /* Precompile/Bind option value   */
};
```

Table 5–3 lists the values that can be used for the *type* and *val* fields of the *sqloptions* structure, as well as a description about what each *type/val* option causes the SQL precompiler (or the DB2 Bind utility) to do.

The PRECOMPILE PROGRAM function executes under the current transaction (which was initiated by a connection to a database), and upon completion, it automatically issues either a COMMIT or a ROLLBACK SQL statement to terminate the transaction.

Comments
- The *MsgFileName* parameter can contain the path and name of an operating system file or a standard device (such as standard error or standard out).
- If the *MsgFileName* parameter contains the path and name of a file that already exists, the existing file will be overwritten when this function is executed. If this parameter contains the path and name of a file that does not exist, a new file will be created.

Table 5–3   Precompile/Bind Options and Values

Precompile/Bind Option	Value	Currently Supported	Description
SQL_ACTION_OPT	SQL_ACTION_ADD	No	Specifies that the package does not already exist and is to be created.
	SQL_ACTION_REPLACE	No	Specifies that the package exists and is to be replaced. This value is the default value for the SQL_ACTION_OPT option.
SQL_BIND_OPT	NULL	Yes	Indicates that no bind file is to be generated by the precompiler. This option can only be used with the SQL precompiler.
	sqlchar structure value	Yes	Indicates that a bind file with the specified name is to be generated by the precompiler. This option can only be used with the SQL precompiler.
SQL_BLOCK_OPT	SQL_BL_ALL	Yes	Specifies that row blocking should be performed for read-only cursors, cursors not specified as FOR UPDATE OF, and cursors for which no static DELETE WHERE CURRENT OF statements are executed. In this case, ambiguous cursors are treated as read-only cursors.
	SQL_BL_NO	Yes	Specifies that row blocking is not to be performed for cursors. In this case, ambiguous cursors are treated as updateable cursors.
	SQL_BL_UNAMBIG	Yes	Specifies that row blocking should be performed for read-only cursors, cursors not specified as FOR UPDATE OF, cursors for which no static DELETE WHERE CURRENT OF statements are executed, and cursors that do not have dynamic statements associated with them. In this case, ambiguous cursors are treated as updateable cursors.
SQL_CCSIDG_OPT	unsigned long integer value	No	Specifies the coded character set identifier that is to be used for double-byte characters in character column definitions specified in CREATE TABLE and ALTER TABLE SQL statements.
SQL_CCSIDM_OPT	unsigned long integer value	No	Specifies the coded character set identifier that is to be used for

Table 5–3 Precompile/Bind Options and Values (Continued)

Precompile/Bind Option	Value	Currently Supported	Description
			mixed-byte characters in character column definitions specified in CREATE TABLE and ALTER TABLE SQL statements.
SQL_CCSIDS_OPT	unsigned long integer value	No	Specifies the coded character set identifier that is to be used for single-byte characters in character column definitions specified in CREATE TABLE and ALTER TABLE SQL statements.
SQL_CHARSUB_OPT	SQL_CHARSUB_BIT	No	Specifies that the FOR BIT DATA SQL character subtype is to be used in all new character column definitions specified in CREATE TABLE and ALTER TABLE SQL statements (unless otherwise explicitly specified).
	SQL_CHARSUB_DEFAULT	No	Specifies that the target system-defined default character subtype is to be used in all new character column definitions specified in CREATE TABLE and ALTER TABLE SQL statements (unless otherwise explicitly specified). This value is the default value for the SQL_CHARSUB_OPT option.
	SQL_CHARSUB_MIXED	No	Specifies that the FOR MIXED DATA SQL character subtype is to be used in all new character column definitions specified in CREATE TABLE and ALTER TABLE SQL statements (unless otherwise explicitly specified).
	SQL_CHARSUB_SBCS	No	Specifies that the FOR SBCS DATA SQL character subtype is to be used in all new character column definitions specified in CREATE TABLE and ALTER TABLE SQL statements (unless otherwise explicitly specified).
SQL_CNULREQD_OPT	SQL_CNULREQD_NO	No	Specifies that C/C++ NULL terminated strings are not NULL-terminated if truncation occurs.
	SQL_CNULREQD_YES	No	Specifies that C/C++ NULL-terminated strings are padded with blanks and always include a

Table 5–3   Precompile/Bind Options and Values (Continued)

Precompile/Bind Option	Value	Currently Supported	Description
			NULL-terminated character, even when if truncation occurs.
SQL_COLLECTION_OPT	*sqlchar* structure value	Yes	Specifies an eight-character collection identifier that is to be assigned to the package being created. If no collection identifier is specified, the authorization ID of the user executing the PRECOMPILE PROGRAM or BIND function will be used.
	SQL_CONNECT_2	Yes	Specifies that CONNECT SQL statements are to be processed as Type 2 Connects.
SQL_CONNECT_OPT	SQL_CONNECT_1	Yes	Specifies that CONNECT SQL statements are to be processed as Type 1 Connects.
	SQL_CONNECT_2	Yes	Specifies that CONNECT SQL statements are to be processed as Type 2 Connects.
SQL_DATETIME_OPT	SQL_DATETIME_DEF	Yes	Specifies that a date and time format that is associated with the country code of the database is to be used for date and time values.
	SQL_DATETIME_EUR	Yes	Specifies that the IBM standard for European date and time format is to be used for date and time values.
	SQL_DATETIME_ISO	Yes	Specifies that the *International Standards Organization* (ISO) date and time format is to be used for date and time values.
	SQL_DATETIME_JIS	Yes	Specifies that the Japanese Industrial Standard date and time format is to be used for date and time values.
	SQL_DATETIME_LOC	Yes	Specifies that the local date and time format that is associated with the country code of the database is to be used for date and time values.
	SQL_DATETIME_USA	Yes	Specifies that the IBM standard for the United States of America date and time format is to be used for date and time values.

Table 5–3 Precompile/Bind Options and Values (Continued)

Precompile/Bind Option	Value	Currently Supported	Description
SQL_DEC_OPT	SQL_DEC_15	No	Specifies that 15-digit precision is to be used in decimal arithmetic operations.
	SQL_DEC_31	No	Specifies that 31-digit precision is to be used in decimal arithmetic operations.
SQL_DECDEL_OPT	SQL_DECDEL_COMMA	No	Specifies that a comma is to be used as a decimal point indicator in decimal and floating point literals.
	SQL_DECDEL_PERIOD	No	Specifies that a period is to be used as a decimal point indicator in decimal and floating point literals.
SQL_DEFERRED_PREPARE_OPT	SQL_DEFERRED_PREPARE_NO	Yes	Specifies that **PREPARE** SQL statements are to be executed at the time they are issued.
	SQL_DEFERRED_PREPARE_YES	Yes	Specifies that the execution of **PREPARE** SQL statements is to be deferred until a corresponding **OPEN, DESCRIBE,** or **EXECUTE** statement is issued.
	SQL_DEFERRED_PREPARE_ALL	Yes	Specifies that all **PREPARE** SQL statements (other than **PREPARE INTO** statements which contain parameter markers) are to be executed at the time they are issued.
			If a **PREPARE** SQL statement uses an **INTO** clause to return information to an SQL Descriptor Area (SQLDA) data structure variable, the application must not reference the content of the SQLDA variable until the **OPEN, DESCRIBE,** or **EXECUTE** SQL statement has been executed.
SQL_DEGREE_OPT	SQL_DEGREE_ANY	Yes	Specifies that queries are to be executed using any degree of I/O parallel processing.
	unsigned long integer between 2 and 32767	Yes	Specifies the degree of parallel I/O processing that is to be used when executing queries.

Table 5–3   Precompile/Bind Options and Values (Continued)

Precompile/Bind Option	Value	Currently Supported	Description
	SQL_DEGREE_1	Yes	Specifies that I/O parallel processing cannot be used to execute SQL queries. This value is the default value for the SQL_DEGREE_OPT option.
SQL_DISCONNECT_OPT	SQL_DISCONNECT_AUTO	Yes	Specifies that all database connections are to be disconnected when a COMMIT SQL statement is executed.
	SQL_DISCONNECT_EXPL	Yes	Specifies that only database connections that have been explicitly marked for release by the RELEASE SQL statement are to be disconnected when a COMMIT SQL statement is executed.
	SQL_DISCONNECT_COND	Yes	Specifies that only database connections that have been explicitly marked for release by the RELEASE SQL statement or that do not have any cursors that were defined as WITH HOLD open are to be disconnected when a COMMIT SQL statement is executed.
SQL_DYNAMICRULES_OPT	SQL_DYNAMICRULES_BIND	No	Specifies that the package owner is to be used as the authorization identifier when executing dynamic SQL statements.
	SQL_DYNAMICRULES_DEFINE	No	Specifies that the definer of a user-defined function or stored procedure is to be used as the authorization identifier when executing dynamic SQL statements in the user-defined function or stored procedure.
	SQL_DYNAMICRULES_INVOKE	No	Specifies that the invoker of a user-defined function or stored procedure is to be used as the authorization identifier when executing dynamic SQL statements in the user-defined function or stored procedure.
	SQL_DYNAMICRULES_RUN	No	Specifies that the authorization ID of the user executing the package is to be used as the authorization identifier when executing dynamic SQL statements.
SQL_EXPLAIN_OPT	SQL_EXPLAIN_ALL	Yes	Specifies that Explain tables are to

Table 5–3 Precompile/Bind Options and Values (Continued)

Precompile/Bind Option	Value	Currently Supported	Description
			be populated with information about the access plans chosen for each eligible static SQL statement at precompile time and with each dynamic SQL statement at application run time.
	SQL_EXPLAIN_YES	No	Specifies that Explain tables are to be populated with information about the access plans chosen for each SQL statement in the package.
	SQL_EXPLAIN_NO	No	Specifies that Explain information about the access plans chosen for each SQL statement in the package is not to be stored in the Explain tables.
SQL_EXPLSNAP_OPT	SQL_EXPLSNAP_NO	No	Specifies that an Explain snapshot will not be written to the Explain tables for each eligible static SQL statement in the package.
	SQL_EXPLSNAP_YES	No	Specifies that an Explain snapshot is to be written to the Explain tables for each eligible static SQL statement in the package.
	SQL_EXPLSNAP_ALL	No	Specifies that an Explain snapshot is to be written to the Explain tables for each eligible static SQL statement in the package, and that Explain snapshot information is also to be gathered for eligible dynamic SQL statements at application runtime—even if the CURRENT EXPLAIN SNAPSHOT register is set to NO.
SQL_FLAG_OPT	SQL_SQL92E_SYNTAX	Yes	Specifies that SQL statements are to be checked against ISO/ANSI SQL92 standards, and all deviations are to be reported.
	SQL_MVSDB2V23_SYNTAX	Yes	Specifies that SQL statements are to be checked against MVS DB2 Version 2.3 SQL syntax, and all deviations are to be reported.
	SQL_MVSDB2V31_SYNTAX	Yes	Specifies that all SQL statements are to be checked against MVS DB2 Version 3.1 SQL syntax, and all deviations are to be reported.

Table 5–3   Precompile/Bind Options and Values (Continued)

Precompile/Bind Option	Value	Currently Supported	Description
	SQL_MVSDB2V41_SYNTAX	Yes	Specifies that SQL statements are to be checked against MVS DB2 Version 4.1 SQL syntax, and all deviations are to be reported.
SQL_FUNCTION_PATH	*sqlchar* structure value	No	Specifies the function path to be used when resolving user-defined distinct data types and functions referenced in static SQL statements.
SQL_GENERIC_OPT	*sqlchar* structure value	Yes	Provides a means of passing new bind options (as a single string) to target DRDA databases.
SQL_GRANT_GROUP_OPT	*sqlchar* structure value	Yes	Specifies that the EXECUTE and BIND authorizations are to be granted to a specific user ID. This option can only be used with the DB2 Bind utility.
SQL_GRANT_OPT	*sqlchar* structure value	Yes	Specifies that the EXECUTE and BIND authorizations are to be granted to a specified user ID or group ID (the group ID specified can be PUBLIC). This option can be used only with the DB2 Bind utility.
SQL_GRANT_USER_OPT	*sqlchar* structure value	Yes	Specifies that the EXECUTE and BIND authorizations are to be granted to a specific user ID. This option can only be used with the DB2 Bind utility.
SQL_INSERT_OPT	SQL_INSERT_BUF	Yes	Specifies that insert operations performed by an application should be buffered.
	SQL_INSERT_DEF	Yes	Specifies that insert operations performed by an application should not be buffered.
SQL_ISO_OPT	SQL_READ_STAB	Yes	Specifies that the Read Stability isolation level should be used to isolate the effects of other executing applications from the application using this package.
	SQL_NO_COMMIT	No	Specifies that commitment control is not to be used by this package
	SQL_CURSOR_STAB	Yes	Specifies that the Cursor Stability isolation level should be used to

Table 5-3   Precompile/Bind Options and Values (Continued)

Precompile/Bind Option	Value	Currently Supported	Description
			isolate the effects of other executing applications from the application using this package.
	SQL_REP_READ	Yes	Specifies that the Repeatable Read isolation level should be used to isolate the effects of other executing applications from the application using this package.
	SQL_UNCOM_READ	Yes	Specifies that the Uncommitted Read isolation level should be used to isolate the effects of other executing applications from the application using this package.
SQL_LEVEL_OPT	*sqlchar* structure value	No	Specifies the level consistency token that a module stored in a package is to use. This token verifies that the requesting application and the database package are synchronized. This option can only be used with the SQL precompiler.
SQL_LINEMACRO_OPT	SQL_NO_LINE_MACROS	Yes	Specifies that the generation of #line macros in the modified C/C++ file produced are to be suppressed.
	SQL_LINE_MACROS	Yes	Specifies that #line macros are to be embedded in the modified C/C++ file produced.
SQL_OPTIM_OPT	SQL_OPTIMIZE	Yes	Specifies that the precompiler is to optimize the initialization of internal SQLDA variables that are used when host variables are referenced in embedded SQL statements.
	SQL_DONT_OPTIMIZE	Yes	Specifies that the precompiler is not to optimize the initialization of internal SQLDA variables that are used when host variables are referenced in embedded SQL statements.
SQL_OWNER_OPT	*sqlchar* structure value	No	Specifies an eight-character authorization ID that identifies the package owner. By default, the authorization ID of the user performing the precompile or bind process is used to identify the package owner.

Table 5–3   Precompile/Bind Options and Values (Continued)

Precompile/Bind Option	Value	Currently Supported	Description
SQL_PKG_OPT	NULL	Yes	Specifies that a package is not to be created. This option can only be used with the SQL precompiler.
	sqlchar structure value	Yes	Specifies the name of the package that is to be created. If a package name is not specified, the package name is the uppercase name of the source-code file being precompiled (truncated to eight characters and minus the extension). This option can only be used with the SQL precompiler.
SQL_PREP_OUTPUT_OPT	*sqlchar* structure value	Yes	Specifies the name of the modified source-code file that is produced by the precompiler.
SQL_QUALIFIER_OPT	*sqlchar* structure value	No	Specifies an implicit qualifier name that is to used for all unqualified table names, views, indexes, and aliases contained in the package. By default, the authorization ID of the user performing the precompile or bind process is used as the implicit qualifier.
SQL_QUERYOPT_OPT	SQL_QUERYOPT_0 SQL_QUERYOPT_1 SQL_QUERYOPT_2 SQL_QUERYOPT_3 SQL_QUERYOPT_5 SQL_QUERYOPT_7 SQL_QUERYOPT_9	No	Specifies the level of optimization to use when precompiling the static SQL statements contained in the package. The default optimization level is SQL_QUERYOPT_5.
SQL_RELEASE_OPT	SQL_RELEASE_COMMIT	No	Specifies that resources acquired for dynamic SQL statements are to be released at each COMMIT point. This value is the default value for the SQL_RELEASE_OPT option.
	SQL_RELEASE_DEALLOCATE	No	Specifies that resources acquired for dynamic SQL statements are to be released when the application terminates.
SQL_REPLVER_OPT	*sqlchar* structure value	No	Identifies a specific version of a package to replace when the SQL_ACTION_REPLACE value is specified for the SQL_ACTION_OPT option. This option can only be used with the DB2 Bind utility.

Table 5–3 Precompile/Bind Options and Values (Continued)

Precompile/Bind Option	Value	Currently Supported	Description
SQL_RETAIN_OPT	SQL_RETAIN_NO	No	Specifies that EXECUTE authorizations are not to be preserved when a package is replaced. This option can only be used with the DB2 Bind utility.
	SQL_RETAIN_YES	No	Specifies that EXECUTE authorizations are to be preserved when a package is replaced. This option can only be used with the DB2 Bind utility. This value is the default value for SQL_RETAIN_OPT.
SQL_RULES_OPT	SQL_RULES_DB2	Yes	Specifies that the CONNECT SQL statement can be used to switch between established connections.
	SQL_RULES_STD	Yes	Specifies that the CONNECT SQL statement can only be used to establish new connections.
SQL_SAA_OPT	SQL_SAA_NO	Yes	Specifies that the modified FORTRAN source-code file produced by the precompiler is inconsistent with the SAA definition.
	SQL_SAA_YES	Yes	Specifies that the modified FORTRAN source-code file produced by the precompiler is consistent with the SAA definition.
SQL_SQLERROR_OPT	SQL_SQLERROR_CHECK	Yes	Specifies that the target system is to perform syntax and semantic checks on the SQL statements being bound to the database. If an error is encountered, a package will not be created.
	SQL_SQLERROR_CONTINUE	No	Specifies that the target system is to perform syntax and semantic checks on the SQL statements being bound to the database. If an error is encountered, a package will still be created.
	SQL_SQLERROR_NOPACKAGE	No	Specifies that the precompiler is to perform syntax and semantic checks on the SQL statements being precompiled. If an error is encountered, a package or a bind file will not be created. This value is the default value for the

Table 5–3   Continued

Precompile/Bind Option	Value	Currently Supported	Description
			SQL_SQLERROR_OPT option.
SQL_SQLWARN OPT	SQL_SQLWARN_NO	No	Specifies that warning messages will not be returned from the SQL precompiler.
	SQL_SQLWARN_YES	No	Specifies that warning messages will be returned from the SQL pre-compiler. This value is the default value for the SQL_SQLWARN_OPT option.
SQL_STANDARDS_OPT	SQL_SAA_COMP	Yes	Specifies that the IBM DB2 rules apply for both the syntax and semantics of static and dynamic SQL statements coded in an application.
	SQL_MIA_COMP	Yes	Specifies that the ISO/ANSI SQL92 rules apply for both the syntax and semantics of static and dynamic SQL statements coded in an application (SQLCA variables are used for error reporting).
	SQL_SQL92E_COMP	Yes	Specifies that the ISO/ANSI SQL92 rules apply for both the syntax and semantics of static and dynamic SQL statements coded in an application (SQLCODE and SQLSTATE variables are used for error reporting).
SQL_STRDEL_OPT	SQL_STRDEL_APOSTROPHE	No	Specifies that an apostrophe is to be used as the string delimiter within SQL statements.
	SQL_STRDEL_QUOTE	No	Specifies that double quotation marks are to be used as the string delimiter within SQL statements.
SQL_SYNCPOINT_OPT	SQL_SYNC_ONEPHASE	Yes	Specifies that a one-phase commit is to be used to commit the work done by each database in multiple database transactions.
	SQL_SYNC_TWOPHASE	Yes	Specifies that a Transaction Manager is to be used to perform two-phase commits to commit the work done by each database in multiple database transactions
	SQL_SYNC_NONE	Yes	Specifies that no Transaction Manager is to be used to perform two-

Table 5–3   Precompile/Bind Options and Values (Continued)

Precompile/Bind Option	Value	Currently Supported	Description
			phase commits, and that single updater–multiple reader operations are not enforced.
SQL_SYNTAX_OPT	SQL_NO_SYNTAX_CHECK	Yes	Specifies that the precompiler is to create a package or bind file along with a modified source code file, rather than performing SQL syntax checking only.
	SQL_SYNTAX_CHECK	Yes	Specifies that only SQL syntax checking is to be performed by the precompiler. No package or bind file is to be generated.
SQL_TARGET_OPT	*sqlchar* structure value		Instructs the precompiler to produce modified source code that is tailored to a specific compiler (on the current platform).
SQL_TEXT_OPT	*sqlchar* structure value	No	Specifies a description that is to be assigned to the package. The description can be up to 255 characters long.
SQL_VALIDATE_OPT	SQL_VALIDATE_BIND	No	Specifies that authorization validation is to be performed by the DB2 Database Manager at precompile/bind time.
	SQL_VALIDATE_RUN	No	Specifies that authorization validation is performed by the DB2 Database Manager at application run time. This value is the default value for the SQL_VALIDATE_OPT option.
SQL_VERSION_OPT	*sqlchar* structure value	No	Specifies the Version identifier for a package. This option can only be used with the SQL precompiler.
SQL_WCHAR_OPT	SQL_WCHAR_CONVERT	Yes	Specifies that data stored in host variables that were declared using the wchar_t base type are to be converted to DBCS format, using the ANSI C function wcstombs() (output DBCS data is converted to wchar_t format using the ANSI C function mbstowcs()).
	SQL_WCHAR_NOCONVERT	Yes	Specifies that data stored in host variables that were declared using the wchar_t base type are not to be converted to DBCS format (and vice-versa). This means that data

Table 5–3   Precompile/Bind Options and Values (Continued)

Precompile/Bind Option	Value	Currently Supported	Description
			stored in `wchar_t` format cannot be passed to the DB2 Database Manager.

Notes: When *sqlchar* structure option values are specified, the *sqlopt.sqloptions.val* field must contain a pointer to a valid *sqlchar* structure. This structure contains a character string that specifies the option value to be set, along with the length of the character string. In most cases, if an unsupported option is specified, the option will be ignored and a warning will be returned by the SQL precompiler or the DB2 bind utility.

Adapted from IBM's *DB2 Universal Database API Reference*, Table 4, pages 21 to 24 and Table 5, pages 14 and 15, and the PRECOMPILE PROGRAM and BIND commands documentation in IBM's DB2 *Universal Database Command Reference,* pages 305 to 324 and 98 to 110.

■ The SQL precompiler expects the following high-level language source-code file extensions:

.sqc   C applications

.sqx   C++ applications

.sqC   C++ applications (UNIX)

.sqb   COBOL applications

.sqf   FORTRAN applications

When the `SQL_TARGET_OPT` option is used, the input file does not have to use one of these predefined extensions.

■ The precompile process stops whenever a fatal error occurs or whenever more than 100 general errors occur. If the precompile process stops, DB2 will attempt to close all opened files and the package being produced will be discarded.

Connection Requirements   This function can only be called if a connection to a database exists.

Authorization   Only users with System Administrator (SYSADM) authority, Database Administrator (DBADM) authority, BINDADD authority (if the package that will be generated does not exist), or BIND authority (if the package that will be generated already exists) are allowed to execute this function.

The user also needs all authorizations that are required to compile any static SQL statements coded in the specified source-code file. Authorization privileges that have been granted to groups and to PUBLIC are not used when authorization checking is performed for static SQL statements.

NOTE: *If a user has SYSADM authority but not explicit authority to complete the bind process, the DB2 Database Manager will automatically give the user explicit DBADM authority.*

See Also   BIND

Example   The following C++ program illustrates how to use the PRECOMPILE PROGRAM function to precompile an embedded SQL source-code file:

```
/*————————————————————————————————————————————————————*/
/* NAME:      CH5EX1.SQC                                 */
/* PURPOSE: Illustrate How To Use The Following DB2 API Function */
/*          In A C++ Program:                            */
/*                                                       */
/*                 PRECOMPILE PROGRAM                    */
/*                                                       */
/*————————————————————————————————————————————————————*/

// Include The Appropriate Header Files
#include <windows.h>
#include <iostream.h>
#include <sqlutil.h>
#include <sql.h>

// Define The API_Class Class
class API_Class
{
    // Attributes
    public:
        struct sqlca   sqlca;

    // Operations
    public:
        long PrecompileProgram();
};

// Define The PrecompileProgram() Member Function
long API_Class::PrecompileProgram()
{
    // Declare The Local Memory Variables
    struct sqlopt                              *PrepOptions;
    struct sqloptions                          *OptionsPtr;
    struct sqlchar                             *BindFile;
    char                                       String[14];
    int                                        BuffSize;

    // Store The Bind File Name In A SQLCHAR Structure
    strcpy(String, "EXAMPLE.BND");
    BindFile = (struct sqlchar *) malloc (strlen(String) +
        sizeof(struct sqlchar));
    BindFile->length = strlen(String);
    strncpy(BindFile->data, String, strlen(String));
```

```
// Allocate And Initialize The Precompiler Options Structure
BuffSize = sizeof(struct sqlopt) + sizeof(struct sqloptheader) +
    (2 * sizeof(struct sqloptions));
PrepOptions = (struct sqlopt *) malloc(BuffSize);
PrepOptions->header.allocated = 2;
PrepOptions->header.used = 1;

OptionsPtr = (struct sqloptions *) PrepOptions->option;
OptionsPtr->type = SQL_BIND_OPT;
OptionsPtr->val = (unsigned long) BindFile;

// Precompile The Specified Source Code File
sqlaprep("EXAMPLE.SQC", "PREPINFO.DAT", PrepOptions, &sqlca);

// If The Source Code File Was Successfully Precompiled, Display
// A Success Message
if (sqlca.sqlcode == SQL_RC_OK)
{
    cout << "EXAMPLE.SQC has been precompiled. Check the file ";
    cout << "PREPINFO.DAT for" << endl;
    cout << "additional information." << endl;
}

// Return The SQLCA Return Code To The Calling Function
return(sqlca.sqlcode);
}

/*------------------------------------------------------------------*/
/* The Main Function                                                */
/*------------------------------------------------------------------*/
int main()
{
    // Declare The Local Memory Variables
    long         rc = SQL_RC_OK;
    struct sqlca  sqlca;

    // Create An Instance Of The API_Class Class
    API_Class  Example;

    // Connect To The SAMPLE Database
    EXEC SQL CONNECT TO SAMPLE USER userID USING password;

    // Precompile An Embedded SQL (.SQC) Program
    rc = Example.PrecompileProgram();

    // Issue A Rollback To Free All Locks
    EXEC SQL ROLLBACK;

    // Disconnect From The SAMPLE Database
    EXEC SQL DISCONNECT CURRENT;

    // Return To The Operating System
    return(rc);
}
```

■ ■ BIND

Purpose   The BIND function is used to invoke the bind utility, which prepares the SQL statements stored in a bind file that was generated by the SQL precompiler and creates a corresponding package that is stored in the database.

Syntax

```
SQL_API_RC SQL_API_FN  sqlabndx (char       *BindFileName,
                                 char       *MsgFileName,
                                 struct sqlopt *BindOptions,
                                 struct sqlca  *SQLCA);
```

Parameters   *BindFileName*   A pointer to a location in memory where the name of the bind file (or the name of a file containing a list of bind files) to be bound to the current connected database is stored.

MsgFileName   A pointer to a location in memory where the name of the file or device that all error, warning, and informational messages generated are to be written to is stored.

BindOptions   A pointer to a *sqlopt* structure that contains the bind options (if any) that should be used when the specified bind file(s) are bound to the current connected database.

SQLCA   A pointer to a location in memory where a SQL Communications Area (SQLCA) data structure variable is stored. This variable returns either status information (if the function executed successfully) or error information (if the function failed) to the calling application.

Includes   `#include <sql.h>`

Description   The BIND function is used to invoke the bind utility, which prepares the SQL statements stored in a bind file that was generated by the SQL precompiler and creates a corresponding package that is stored in the database. Binding can be performed as part of the precompile process or as a separate process at a later time—this function is only used when binding is performed as a separate process.

A special structure (*sqlopt*) is used to pass different bind options to the bind utility when this function is called. Refer to the PRECOMPILE PROGRAM function for a detailed description of the *sqlopt* structure and for more information about the bind options that are available.

The BIND function executes under the current transaction (which was initiated by a connection to a database) and, upon completion, it automatically issues either a COMMIT or a ROLLBACK SQL statement to terminate the current transaction.

Comments   ■ The *MsgFileName* parameter can contain the path and name of an operating system file or a standard device (such as standard error or standard out).

■ If the *MsgFileName* parameter contains the path and name of a file that already exists, the existing file will be overwritten when this function is executed. If this parameter contains the path and name of a file that does not exist, a new file will be created.

■ The bind utility expects all bind files to have the extension **.bnd**.

■ The *BindFileName* parameter can contain the name of a specific bind file or the name of a file that contains a list of bind file names. If the name of a file containing a list of bind file names is specified, it must be preceded with the at symbol (@), and the file itself must have the extension **.lst**. For example, a fully qualified bind list file name on Windows NT might be C:\@all.lst.

■ Path specifications can be supplied with bind file names in a bind list file. If the bind list file contains two or more bind file names, all but the last bind file name should be followed by a plus sign (+). The bind file paths and names can be placed on one or more lines in the bind list file. For example, on Windows NT, a bind list file might contain the following list:

```
mybind1.bnd+mybind2.bnd+
C:mybind3.bnd+
mybind4.bnd
```

■ By default, the name of the package to be created by this function is the same as the first eight characters of the source-code file name (minus the file extension and converted to uppercase) that was used to generate the bind file. However, you can overwrite bind file names and package names by using the SQL_BIND_OPT and SQL_PKG_OPT options with the PRECOMPILE PROGRAM function.

■ The bind process stops whenever a fatal error occurs or whenever more than 100 general errors occur. If the bind process stops, DB2 will attempt to close all opened files and the package(s) being produced will be discarded.

■ In a multi-node database environment, this function can be called from any node listed in the *db2nodes.cfg* configuration file. The node that this function is called from automatically updates the database catalog on the catalog node, and the changes are visible to all nodes.

Connection Requirements   This function can only be called if a connection to a database exists.

Authorization   Only users with System Administrator (SYSADM) authority, Database Administrator (DBADM) authority, BINDADD authority (if the package that will be generated does not exist), or BIND authority (if the package that will be generated already exists) are allowed to execute this function call.

The user also needs all authorizations required to compile any static SQL statements coded in the specified source-code file. Authorization privileges that have been granted to groups and to PUBLIC are not used when authorization checking is performed for static SQL statements.

NOTE: *If a user has SYSADM authority but not explicit authority to complete the bind process, the DB2 Database Manager will automatically give the user explicit DBADM authority.*

See Also   PRECOMPILE PROGRAM

Example   The following C++ program illustrates how to use the BIND function to bind the contents of an external bind file to the current connected database:

```
/*─────────────────────────────────────────────────────────*/
/* NAME:      CH5EX2.SQC                                     */
/* PURPOSE: Illustrate How To Use The Following DB2 API Function */
/*            In A C++ Program:                              */
/*                                                           */
/*                  BIND                                     */
/*                                                           */
/*─────────────────────────────────────────────────────────*/

// Include The Appropriate Header Files
#include <windows.h>
#include <iostream.h>
#include <sqlutil.h>
#include <sql.h>

// Define The API_Class Class
class API_Class
{
    // Attributes
    public:
        struct sqlca  sqlca;

    // Operations
    public:
        long BindProgram();
};

// Define The BindProgram() Member Function
long API_Class::BindProgram()
{
    // Declare The Local Memory Variables
    struct sqlopt       *BindOptions;
    struct sqloptions   *OptionsPtr;
    struct sqlchar      *Collection;
    char                String[14];
    int                 BuffSize;

    // Store The Collection Name In A SQLCHAR Structure
    strcpy(String, "BINDSAMP");
    Collection = (struct sqlchar *) malloc (strlen(String) +
        sizeof(struct sqlchar));
    Collection->length = strlen(String);
    strncpy(Collection->data, String, strlen(String));
```

```
    // Allocate And Initialize The Bind Options Structure
    BuffSize = sizeof(struct sqlopt) + sizeof(struct sqloptheader) +
        (2 * sizeof(struct sqloptions));
    BindOptions = (struct sqlopt *) malloc(BuffSize);
    BindOptions->header.allocated = 2;
    BindOptions->header.used = 1;

    OptionsPtr = (struct sqloptions *) BindOptions->option;
    OptionsPtr->type = SQL_COLLECTION_OPT;
    OptionsPtr->val = (unsigned long) Collection;

    // Bind The Specified Bind File To The SAMPLE Database
    sqlabndx("EXAMPLE.BND", "BINDINFO.DAT", BindOptions, &sqlca);

    // If The Bind File Was Successfully Bound To The SAMPLE
    // Database, Display A Success Message
    if (sqlca.sqlcode == SQL_RC_OK)
    {
        cout << "EXAMPLE.BND has been bound to the SAMPLE database. ";
        cout << "Check the file" << endl;
        cout << "BINDINFO.DAT for additional information." << endl;
    }

    // Return The SQLCA Return Code To The Calling Function
    return(sqlca.sqlcode);
}

/*─────────────────────────────────────────────────────────────*/
/* The Main Function                                            */
/*─────────────────────────────────────────────────────────────*/
int main()
{
    // Declare The Local Memory Variables
    long          rc = SQL_RC_OK;
    struct sqlca   sqlca;

    // Create An Instance Of The API_Class Class
    API_Class   Example;

    // Connect To The SAMPLE Database
    EXEC SQL CONNECT TO SAMPLE USER userID USING password;

    // Bind An Existing Bind File To The SAMPLE Database
    rc = Example.BindProgram();

    // Issue A Rollback To Free All Locks
    EXEC SQL ROLLBACK;

    // Disconnect From The SAMPLE Database
    EXEC SQL DISCONNECT CURRENT;

    // Return To The Operating System
    return(rc);
}
```

■ ■ REBIND

Purpose
The REBIND function is used to recreate a package that is already stored in the database without using a corresponding bind file.

Syntax
```
SQL_API_RC SQL_API_FN  sqlarbnd  (char       *PackageName,
                                  struct sqlca  *SQLCA,
                                  void         *Reserved);
```

Parameters

PackageName A pointer to a location in memory where the name (qualified or unqualified) of the package to be rebound is stored.

SQLCA A pointer to a location in memory where a SQL Communications Area (SQLCA) data structure variable is stored. This variable returns either status information (if the function executed successfully) or error information (if the function failed) to the calling application.

Reserved A pointer that is currently reserved for later use. For now, this parameter must always be set to NULL.

Includes
```
#include <sql.h>
```

Description
The REBIND function is used to re-create a package that is already stored in the database without using a corresponding bind file. When this function is executed, the DB2 Database Manager recreates the package from the SQL statements stored in the SYSCAT.STATEMENTS system catalog table. The REBIND function provides a user or an application with the following capabilities:

■ A quick way to recreate a package when the original bind file is not available (which enables a user to take advantage of changes in the system). For example, if an index is created for a table, you can use the REBIND function to recreate the package so SQL statements in the application can take advantage of the new index. Likewise, you can use this function to recreate packages after the RUN STATISTICS function is executed, so all access plans generated for the packages can take advantage of the new statistical information.

■ The ability to recreate inoperative packages. A package is marked inoperative (the VALID column of the SYSCAT.PACKAGES system catalog table is set to "X") when a function instance that the package depends on is dropped. Inoperative packages must be explicitly rebound to a database with either the bind or rebind utility before they can be used by any application that references them.

■ Control over the process of rebinding of invalid packages. Invalid packages are automatically (or implicitly) rebound by the DB2 Database Manager when they are executed. This process can result in a noticeable delay in the execution of the first SQL statement that requests an invalid package. A more desirable method might be to explicitly rebind invalid packages, rather than allow DB2 to implicitly rebind them, in order to eliminate this initial delay and to trap and process unexpected SQL error messages (which might be returned if the implicit rebind fails). For example, when an earlier version DB2 database is migrated, all packages stored in that database are invalidated by the migration process. This process might affect a large number of packages, so you might want to explicitly rebind all the invalid packages at one time.

Comments

■ If the package name specified in the *PackageName* parameter is not explicitly unqualified, it is implicitly qualified by the current authorization ID. Note that this default qualifier might be different from the authorization ID that was used when the package was originally bound to the database.

■ The bind options that were specified when a package was originally created and bound to the database are reused when the package is rebound.

■ This function does not automatically commit or roll back the current transaction after the rebind has occurred. Instead, the user must explicitly commit or roll back the transaction. This action allows the user to update different table statistics and then rebind the package to see what, if anything, changes. This action also allows a single transaction to perform multiple rebind operations.

■ During the rebind process, an exclusive lock is acquired and held on a package's record in the SYSIBM.SYSPLAN system table. Therefore, if the rebind utility attempts to rebind a package that is in use by another application, the utility must wait until the transaction that is using the package ends (so the utility can acquire the appropriate exclusive lock).

■ The rebind process will stop if a fatal or general error occurs. If the rebind process stops before the specified package is re-created, the corresponding package will be left in its original state.

■ The rebind utility will repopulate the Explain tables for packages that were created with the SQL_EXPLSNAP_OPT precompile/bind option set to SQL_EXPLAIN_YES or SQL_EXPLAIN_ALL when this function is called. However, the Explain facility will use the Explain tables of the user requesting the REBIND operation, not the Explain tables of the user who performed the original bind operation.

■ The REBIND function is supported by DB2 Connect.

■ Explicit rebinding can be done with the BIND function, the REBIND function, or the **db2rbind** tool (refer to the *IBM DB2 Universal Database Command Reference* for more information about the **db2rbind** tool). Because both the BIND and REBIND functions can explicitly rebind a package to a database, the choice of which function to use depends on the circumstances. Since the performance of the REBIND function is significantly better than that of the BIND function, use the REBIND function whenever the situation does not specifically require the use of the BIND function. The BIND function (and not the REBIND function) must be used to explicitly rebind a package when:

■ The embedded SQL application program has been modified (when SQL statements have been added or deleted, or when the package does not match the executable program image).

■ You want to modify any of the bind options as part of the rebind process.

The REBIND function does not allow the user to specify bind options.

■ The package does not currently exist in the database.

■ You want to detect all general bind errors. The REBIND function only returns the first error it detects (and then ends), whereas the BIND function returns the first 100 errors it encounters during the binding process.

Connection Requirements   This function can only be called if a connection to a database exists.

Authorization   Only users with System Administrator (SYSADM) authority, Database Administrator (DBADM) authority, or BIND authority for the package to be rebound can execute this function call.

NOTE: *The authorization ID stored in the BOUNDBY column of the SYSIBM.SYSPLAN system table, which is the authorization ID of the most recent binder of the package, is used as the binder authorization ID for the rebind operation and as the default schema for all table references in the package.*

See Also   BIND, RUN STATISTICS

Example   The following C++ program illustrates how to use the REBIND function to rebind a package that already exists in the current connected database:

```
/*————————————————————————————————————*/
/* NAME:       CH5EX3.SQC                                   */
/* PURPOSE: Illustrate How To Use The Following DB2 API Function */
/*          In A C++ Program:                               */
/*                                                          */
/*              REBIND                                      */
/*                                                          */
/*————————————————————————————————————*/

// Include The Appropriate Header Files
#include <windows.h>
#include <iostream.h>
#include <sqlutil.h>
#include <sql.h>

// Define The API_Class Class
class API_Class
{
    // Attributes
    public:
        struct sqlca  sqlca;

    // Operations
```

```
public:
    long DispPkgTimestamp();
    long Rebind();
};

// Define The DispPkgTimestamp() Member Function
long API_Class::DispPkgTimestamp()
{
    // Declare The SQL Host Memory Variables
    EXEC SQL BEGIN DECLARE SECTION;
        char    PackageName[9];
        char    BindTime[30];
    EXEC SQL END DECLARE SECTION;

    // Retrieve A Record From The SYSIBM.SYSPLAN Table
    EXEC SQL SELECT NAME,
                    CHAR(LAST_BIND_TIME)
        INTO :PackageName,
             :BindTime
        FROM SYSIBM.SYSPLAN
        WHERE NAME = 'EXAMPLE' AND BOUNDBY = 'USERID';

    // Print The Information Retrieved
    if (sqlca.sqlcode == SQL_RC_OK)
    {
        cout << "Package Name : ";
        cout.width(14);
        cout.setf(ios::left);
        cout << PackageName << "Last Bound : " << BindTime << endl;
    }

    // Return The SQLCA Return Code To The Calling Function
    return(sqlca.sqlcode);
}

// Define The Rebind() Member Function
long API_Class::Rebind()
{
    // Rebind The Specified Package
    sqlarbnd("EXAMPLE", &sqlca, NULL);

    // If The Bind File Was Successfully Rebound, Display A
    // Success Message
    if (sqlca.sqlcode == SQL_RC_OK)
        cout << "The EXAMPLE package has been rebound." << endl;

    // Return The SQLCA Return Code To The Calling Function
    return(sqlca.sqlcode);
}

/*-------------------------------------------------------------*/
/* The Main Function                                           */
/*-------------------------------------------------------------*/
int main()
{
```

```
                    // Declare The Local Memory Variables
                    long          rc = SQL_RC_OK;
                    struct sqlca  sqlca;

                    // Create An Instance Of The API_Class Class
                    API_Class  Example;

                    // Connect To The SAMPLE Database
                    EXEC SQL CONNECT TO SAMPLE USER userID USING password;

                    // Retrieve And Display The Timestamp For The Package Before
                    // It Is Rebound
                    rc = Example.DispPkgTimestamp();

                    // Bind An Existing Bind File To The SAMPLE Database
                    rc = Example.Rebind();

                    // Retrieve And Display The Timestamp For The Package After
                    // It Is Rebound (The Timestamp Should Be Different)
                    rc = Example.DispPkgTimestamp();

                    // Issue A Rollback To Free All Locks
                    EXEC SQL ROLLBACK;

                    // Disconnect From The SAMPLE Database
                    EXEC SQL DISCONNECT CURRENT;

                    // Return To The Operating System
                    return(rc);
                }
```

▮ ▮ GET INSTANCE

Purpose   The GET INSTANCE function is used to retrieve the current value of the DB2INSTANCE environment variable.

Syntax
```
SQL_API_RC SQL_API_FN sqlegins (char        *Instance,
                                struct sqlca *SQLCA);
```

Parameters   *Instance*   A pointer to a location in memory where this function is to store the current DB2 Database Manager instance name (the current value of the DB2INSTANCE environment variable).

SQLCA   A pointer to a location in memory where a SQL Communications Area (SQLCA) data structure variable is stored. This variable returns either status information (if the function executed successfully) or error information (if the function failed) to the calling application.

Includes   `#include <sqlenv.h>`

Description   The GET INSTANCE function is used to retrieve the current value of the DB2INSTANCE environment variable. This value usually identifies the instance-level node to which the application is currently attached.

Comments

- The buffer in which this function is to store the DB2 Database Manager instance name (the *Instance* parameter) must be at least eight bytes long.

- The value in the DB2INSTANCE environment variable is not necessarily the DB2 Database Manager instance to which the application is currently attached. To identify the DB2 Database Manager instance to which an application is currently attached, call the ATTACH function with all parameters except the *SQLCA* parameter set to NULL.

Connection Requirements   This function can be called at any time; a connection to a DB2 Database Manager instance or to a DB2 database does not have to be established first.

Authorization   No authorization is required to execute this function call.

Example   The following C++ program illustrates how to use the GET INSTANCE function to obtain the current value of the DB2INSTANCE environment variable:

```
/*------------------------------------------------------------*/
/* NAME:     CH5EX4.CPP                                       */
/* PURPOSE: Illustrate How To Use The Following DB2 API Function */
/*          In A C++ Program:                                 */
/*                                                            */
/*              GET INSTANCE                                  */
/*                                                            */
/*------------------------------------------------------------*/
// Include The Appropriate Header Files
#include <windows.h>
#include <iostream.h>
#include <sqlenv.h>
#include <sql.h>

// Define The API_Class Class
class API_Class
{
    // Attributes
    public:
        struct sqlca  sqlca;

    // Operations
    public:
        long GetInstance();
};

// Define The GetInstance() Member Function
long API_Class::GetInstance()
{
    // Declare The Local Memory Variables
```

```
        char   Instance[9];

        // Obtain The Current Value Of The DB2INSTANCE Environment
        // Variable
        sqlegins(Instance, &sqlca);
        Instance[8] = 0;

        // If The Current Value Of The DB2INSTANCE Environment Variable
        // Was Obtained, Display It
        if (sqlca.sqlcode == SQL_RC_OK)
        {
            cout << "Current value of the DB2INSTANCE environment ";
            cout << "variable : " << Instance << endl;
        }

        // Return The SQLCA Return Code To The Calling Function
        return(sqlca.sqlcode);
    }

/*—————————————————————————————————————*/
/* The Main Function                                             */
/*—————————————————————————————————————*/
int main()
{
    // Declare The Local Memory Variables
    long   rc = SQL_RC_OK;

    // Create An Instance Of The API_Class Class
    API_Class  Example;

    // Get The Current Value Of The DB2INSTANCE Environment Variable
    rc = Example.GetInstance();

    // Return To The Operating System
    return(rc);
}
```

INSTALL SIGNAL HANDLER

Purpose   The INSTALL SIGNAL HANDLER function is used to install the default interrupt signal handler provided with DB2.

Syntax   ```SQL_API_RC SQL_API_FN sqleisig (struct sqlca *SQLCA);```

Parameters   *SQLCA*   A pointer to a location in memory where a SQL Communications Area data structure variable is stored. This variable returns either status information (if the function executed successfully) or error information (if the function failed) to the calling application.

Includes   `#include <sqlenv.h>`

Description   The INSTALL SIGNAL HANDLER function is used to install the default interrupt signal handler that is provided with the *DB2 Software Development Kit* (SDK). When the default interrupt signal handler detects an interrupt signal (usually Ctrl-C and/or Ctrl-Break), it resets the signal and calls the INTERRUPT function to gracefully stop the processing of the current database request.

If an application has not installed an interrupt signal handler and an interrupt signal is received, the application will be terminated. This function provides simple interrupt signal handling and should always be used if an application does not have extensive interrupt handling requirements.

Comments   ■ If an application requires a more elaborate interrupt handling scheme, you can develop a signal handling routine that resets the signal, calls the INTERRUPT function, and then performs additional tasks.

■ You must call this API function before the default interrupt signal handler will function properly.

■ This function cannot be used in applications that run on the Windows or Windows NT operating system.

Connection   This function can be called at any time; a connection to a DB2 Database Manager
Requirements   instance or to a DB2 database does not have to be established first.

Authorization No authorization is required to execute this function call.

See Also   INTERRUPT

Example   The following C++ program illustrates how to use the INSTALL SIGNAL HANDLER function to install the default interrupt signal handling routine in an embedded SQL application:

```
/*---------------------------------------------------------------*/
/* NAME:    CH5EX5.SQC                                           */
/* PURPOSE: Illustrate How To Use The Following DB2 API Function */
/*          In A C++ Program:                                    */
/*                                                               */
/*              INSTALL SIGNAL HANDLER                           */
/*                                                               */
/*---------------------------------------------------------------*/

// Include The Appropriate Header Files
#include <windows.h>
#include <iostream.h>
#include <stdio.h>
#include <sqlenv.h>
#include <sql.h>

// Define The API_Class Class
class API_Class
```

```
    {
        // Attributes
        public:
            struct sqlca   sqlca;

        // Operations
        public:
            long SetSignalHandler();
    };

    // Define The SetSignalHandler() Member Function
    long API_Class::SetSignalHandler()
    {
        // Install DB2's Default Interrupt Signal Handler
        sqleisig(&sqlca);

        // If The Signal Handler Was Installed Successfully, Display
        // A Success Message
        if (sqlca.sqlcode == SQL_RC_OK)
        {
            cout << "The default interrupt signal handler has been ";
            cout << "installed." << endl;
        }

        // Return The SQLCA Return Code To The Calling Function
        return(sqlca.sqlcode);
    }

    /*----------------------------------------------------------------*/
    /* The Main Function                                              */
    /*----------------------------------------------------------------*/
    int main()
    {
        // Declare The Local Memory Variables
        long            rc = SQL_RC_OK;
        char            Commissions[20];
        struct sqlca    sqlca;

        // Declare The SQL Host Memory Variable
        EXEC SQL BEGIN DECLARE SECTION;
            long    TotalComm;
        EXEC SQL END DECLARE SECTION;

        // Create An Instance Of The API_Class Class
        API_Class   Example;

        // Install The Default Interrupt Signal Handler
        rc = Example.SetSignalHandler();

        // Set Up A Simple SQL Error Handler
        EXEC SQL WHENEVER SQLERROR GOTO EXIT;

        // Display A Message Telling The User To Generate An Interrupt
        // Signal By Pressing Ctrl-Break
```

```
        cout << "Press Ctrl-Break to terminate this program." << endl;

        // Connect To The SAMPLE Database
        EXEC SQL CONNECT TO SAMPLE USER userID USING password;

        // Retrieve The Total Amount Of Commissions Paid From The
        // EMPLOYEE Table
        EXEC SQL SELECT SUM(COMM)
            INTO :TotalComm
            FROM EMPLOYEE;

        // Print The Information Retrieved
        sprintf(Commissions, "$ %.21d.00", TotalComm);
        cout << "The company paid " << Commissions << " in commissions.";
        cout << endl;

EXIT:

        // If The Process Was Terminated By A Signal Interrupt, Display
        // An Error Message Saying So
        if (sqlca.sqlcode == -952)
            cout << "Processing was terminated due to an interrupt.";

        // Otherwise, If An Error Has Occurred, Display The SQL Return
        // Code
        else if (sqlca.sqlcode != SQL_RC_OK)
            cout << "ERROR : " << sqlca.sqlcode << endl;

        // Issue A Rollback To Free All Locks
        EXEC SQL ROLLBACK;

        // Disconnect From The SAMPLE Database
        EXEC SQL DISCONNECT CURRENT;

        // Return To The Operating System
        return(rc);
}
```

■ ■ INTERRUPT

Purpose   The INTERRUPT function is used to stop the processing of the current database request.

Syntax   `SQL_API_RC SQL_API_INTR sqleintr();`

Includes   `#include <sqlenv.h>`

Description The INTERRUPT function is used to stop the processing of the current database request. This function is normally the first function called in an interrupt signal handler routine. An application's interrupt signal handler can be the default signal handler installed by the INSTALL SIGNAL HANDLER function or a more elaborate interrupt handler routine supplied by the application developer and installed with the appropriate operating system call. In either case, when an interrupt handler detects an interrupt signal (usually Ctrl-C and/or Ctrl-Break), the handler takes control and performs one or more actions to ensure that all active processing is terminated gracefully.

When the INTERRUPT function is called while other DB2 API functions are executing, the executing functions are either interrupted or allowed to complete execution, depending on the work they are performing. Table 5–4 lists the effects the INTERRUPT function has on other API functions.

Table 5–4 Interrupt Effects on SQL and API Actions

Database Activity	Action
IMPORT	The import process is canceled, and all database updates are rolled back.
EXPORT	The export process is canceled, and all database updates are rolled back.
RUNSTATS	The run statistics process is canceled, and all database updates are rolled back.
REORGANIZE TABLE	The reorganize table process is canceled, and the table is left in its previous state.
BACKUP	The backup process is canceled, and the backup data stored on the specified media may be incomplete.
RESTORE	The restore process is canceled, and the database being restored is deleted (DROP DATABASE is performed). This action is not applicable to table space-level restore operations.
LOAD	The load process is canceled, and the data stored in table may be incomplete.
PRECOMPILE PROGRAM	The precompile process is canceled, and package creation is rolled back.
BIND	The bind process is canceled, and package creation is rolled back.
COMMIT	The COMMIT process runs to completion.
FORCE APPLICATION	The FORCE APPLICATION process runs to completion.
ROLLBACK	The ROLLBACK process runs to completion.
CREATE DATABASE	After a certain point, the CREATE DATABASE process cannot be terminated. If the interrupt signal is received before this point, the database is not created, and the database creation process is canceled. If the interrupt is received after this point, the CREATE DATABASE process runs to completion, and the database is created.
CREATE DATABASE AT NODE	After a certain point, the CREATE DATABASE AT NODE process cannot be terminated. If the interrupt signal is received before this point, the database is not created, and the database creation process is canceled. If the interrupt is received after this point, the CREATE DATABASE AT NODE process runs to completion, and the database is created.
ADD NODE	After a certain point, the ADD NODE process cannot be terminated. If the interrupt signal is received before this point, the node is not added, and the ADD NODE process is canceled. If the interrupt is received after this point,

Table 5–4   Interrupt Effects on SQL and API Actions (Continued)

Database Activity	Action
	the `ADD NODE` process runs to completion, and the node is added.
`DROP NODE VERIFY`	After a certain point, the `DROP NODE VERIFY` process cannot be terminated. If the interrupt signal is received before this point the `DROP NODE VERIFY` process is canceled. If the interrupt is received after this point, the `DROP NODE VERIFY` process runs to completion.
`DROP DATABASE`	The `DROP DATABASE` process runs to completion.
`DROP DATABASE AT NODE`	The `DROP DATABASE AT NODE` process runs to completion.
Directory Services	The specified directory is left in a consistent state. Utility functions may or may not be performed.
SQL Data Definition Statements	Database transactions are set to the state they were in before the SQL statement was executed.
Other SQL statements	Database transactions are set to the state they were in before the SQL statement was executed.

Adapted from IBM's DB2 *Universal Database API Reference*, Table 5, page 147.

Comments
- No DB2 function other than `INTERRUPT` should be called from a user-defined interrupt handler.
- When creating an interrupt handling routine, follow all operating system programming techniques and practices to ensure that all previously installed signal handlers continue to work properly.
- Any transaction that is in the process of being committed or rolled back cannot be interrupted.
- When a DB2 API function is interrupted, it places a return code that indicates it was interrupted in the appropriate SQLCA data structure variable.

Required Connection
This function can be called at any time; a connection to a DB2 Database Manager instance or to a DB2 database does not have to be established first.

Authorization
No authorization is required to execute this function call.

See Also
`INSTALL SIGNAL HANDLER`

Example
The following C++ program illustrates how to use the `INTERRUPT` function in a user-defined interrupt signal handling routine (Windows):

```
/*----------------------------------------------------------*/
/* NAME:    CH5EX6.SQC                                       */
/* PURPOSE: Illustrate How To Use The Following DB2 API Function */
/*          In A C++ Program:                                */
/*                                                           */
```

```
/*                    INTERRUPT                                    */
/*                                                                 */
/*---------------------------------------------------------------*/

// Include The Appropriate Header Files
#include <windows.h>
#include <iostream.h>
#include <stdio.h>
#include <sqlenv.h>
#include <sql.h>

// Define The API_Class Class
class API_Class
{
    // Attributes
    public:
        struct sqlca   sqlca;

    // Operations
    public:
        long GetCommission();
};

// Define The GetCommission() Member Function
long API_Class::GetCommission()
{
    // Declare The Local Memory Variables
    char   Commissions[20];

    // Declare The SQL Host Memory Variable
    EXEC SQL BEGIN DECLARE SECTION;
        long    TotalComm;
    EXEC SQL END DECLARE SECTION;

    // Retrieve The Total Amount Of Commissions Paid From The
    // EMPLOYEE Table
    EXEC SQL SELECT SUM(COMM)
        INTO :TotalComm
        FROM EMPLOYEE;

    // Print The Information Retrieved
    sprintf(Commissions, "$ %.21d.00", TotalComm);
    cout << "The company paid " << Commissions << " in commissions.";
    cout << endl;

    // Return The SQLCA Return Code To The Calling Function
    return(sqlca.sqlcode);
}

/*---------------------------------------------------------------*/
/* The Main Function                                             */
/*---------------------------------------------------------------*/
int main()
{
```

```
// Declare The Local Memory Variables
long            rc = SQL_RC_OK;
struct sqlca    sqlca;

// Create An Instance Of The API_Class Class
API_Class  Example;

// Connect To The SAMPLE Database
EXEC SQL CONNECT TO SAMPLE USER userID USING password;

// Display Commission Information
try
{
    rc = Example.GetCommission();
}

// If An Exception Occurs ...
catch(...)
{
    // Terminate All DB2 Database Requests That Are Currently
    // In Progress
    sqleintr();
}

// Issue A Rollback To Free All Locks
EXEC SQL ROLLBACK;

// Disconnect From The SAMPLE Database
EXEC SQL DISCONNECT CURRENT;

// Return To The Operating System
return(rc);
}
```

■ ■ GET ADDRESS

Purpose   The GET ADDRESS function is used to store the address of one variable into another variable in applications written in host languages that do not support pointer manipulation.

Syntax
```
SQL_API_RC SQL_API_FN sqlgaddr (char    *Variable,
                                char    *OutputAddress);
```

Parameters   *Variable*   A pointer to a location in memory where the variable whose address is to be returned is stored.

OutputAddress The address of a pointer to a location in memory where this function is to store the address retrieved of the variable specified in the *Variable* parameter.

Includes   `#include <sqlutil.h>`

Description   The GET ADDRESS function is used to store the address of one variable into another variable in applications written in host languages that do not support pointer manipulation. This function should only be used in applications written in either COBOL or FORTRAN. Applications written in host languages that support pointer manipulation (such as C and C++) should use the language-specific pointer manipulation elements provided.

Comments   ■ The buffer that this function is to store the retrieved address in (the *OutputAddress* parameter) must be four bytes long.

**Connection   This function can be called at any time; a connection to a DB2 Database Manager
Requirements** instance or to a DB2 database does not have to be established first.

Authorization   No authorization is required to execute this function call.

See Also   DEREFERENCE ADDRESS, COPY MEMORY

Example   Because this function should be used only in applications written in either the COBOL or the FORTRAN programming language, an example program is not provided. Refer to the *IBM DB2 Uninversal Database API Reference* for examples of how this function is used in COBOL and FORTRAN applications.

COPY MEMORY

Purpose   The COPY MEMORY function is used to copy data from one memory storage area to another in applications written in host languages that do not provide memory block copy functions.

Syntax
```
SQL_API_RC SQL_API_FN sqlgmcpy  (void         *Target,
                                 const void    *Source,
                                 unsigned long  NumBytes);
```

Parameters   *Target*   A pointer to a location in memory to which this function is to copy data.

Source   A pointer to a location in memory from which this function is to copy data.

NumBytes   The number of bytes of data that is to be copied from the *Source* memory storage area to the *Target* memory storage area.

Includes   `#include <sqlutil.h>`

Description   The COPY MEMORY function is used to copy data from one memory storage area to another in applications written in host languages that do not provide memory block copy functions. This function should be used only in applications written in either COBOL or FORTRAN. Applications written in host languages that provide memory copy functions (such as C and C++) should use the language memory block copy functions provided.

Comments   ■ The host programming language variable that contains the number of bytes of data to be copied (the *NumBytes* parameter) must be four bytes long.

Connection Requirements   This function can be called at any time; a connection to a DB2 Database Manager instance or to a DB2 database does not have to be established first.

Authorization   No authorization is required to execute this function call.

See Also   GET ADDRESS, DEREFERENCE ADDRESS

Example   Because this function should be used only in applications written in either the COBOL or the FORTRAN programming language, an example program is not provided. Refer to the *IBM DB2 Universal Database API Reference* for examples of how this function is used in COBOL and FORTRAN applications.

■ ■ DEREFERENCE ADDRESS

Purpose   The DEREFERENCE ADDRESS function is used to copy data from a buffer defined by a pointer to a local data storage variable in applications written in host languages that do not support pointer manipulation.

Syntax
```
SQL_API_RC SQL_API_FN sqlgdref (unsigned int   NumBytes,
                                char           *TargetVariable,
                                char           **SourceBuffer);
```

Parameters   *NumBytes*   The number of bytes of data to be copied from the *SourceBuffer* memory storage area to the *TargetVariable* variable.

   TargetVariable   A pointer to a local storage variable to which this function is to copy data.

   SourceBuffer   The address of a pointer to a location in memory where this function is to copy data from.

Includes   `#include <sqlutil.h>`

Description   The DEREFERENCE ADDRESS function is used to copy data from a buffer defined by a pointer to a local data storage variable in applications written in host languages that do not support pointer manipulation. This function should be used only in applications written in either COBOL or FORTRAN. Applications written in host languages that support pointer manipulation (such as C and C++) should use the language-specific pointer manipulation elements provided.

   You can use this function to obtain results from other API functions that return pointers to data storage areas that contain the data values retrieved, such as GET NEXT NODE DIRECTORY ENTRY.

Comments ■ The host programming language variable that contains the number of bytes of data to be copied (the *NumBytes* parameter) must be four bytes long.

Connection Requirements This function can be called at any time; a connection to a DB2 Database Manager instance or to a DB2 database does not have to be established first.

Authorization No authorization is required to execute this function call.

See Also GET ADDRESS, COPY MEMORY

Example Because this function should be used only in applications written in either COBOL or FORTRAN, an example program is not provided. Refer to the *IBM DB2 Universal Database API Reference* for examples of how this function is used in COBOL and FORTRAN applications.

■■ ■■ SET ACCOUNTING STRING

Purpose The SET ACCOUNTING STRING function is used to specify accounting information that is to be sent to a *Distributed Relational Database Architecture* (DRDA) server with the application's next connect request.

Syntax
```
SQL_API_RC SQL_API_FN sqlesact (char        *AccountingString,
                                struct sqlca *SQLCA);
```

Parameters *AccountingString* A pointer to a location in memory where the accounting information string is stored.

SQLCA A pointer to a location in memory where a SQL Communications Area (SQLCA) data structure variable is stored. This variable returns either status information (if the function executed successfully) or error information (if the function failed) to the calling application.

Includes `#include <sqlenv.h>`

Description The SET ACCOUNTING STRING function is used to specify accounting information that is to be sent to a DRDA server with the application's next connect request. An application should call this API function before attempting to connect to a DRDA database (DB2 for OS/390 or DB2 for OS/400). If an application contains multiple CONNECT SQL statements, you can use this function to change the accounting string before attempting to connect to each database. Refer to the beginning of this chapter for more information about the format and usage of accounting string information.

Comments ■ Once accounting string information has been set, it remains in effect until the application terminates.

■ The accounting string specified cannot exceed 199 bytes in length (this value is defined as SQL_ACCOUNT_STR_SZ in the file *sqlenv.h*); longer accounting strings will automatically be truncated.

■ To ensure that the accounting string is converted correctly when transmitted to the DRDA server, only use the characters A to Z, 0 to 9, and underscore (_).

Connection Requirements   This function can be called at any time; a connection to a DB2 Database Manager instance or to a DB2 database does not have to be established first.

Authorization   No authorization is required to execute this function call.

See Also   Refer to the *IBM DB2 Connect User's Guide* for more information about accounting strings and the DRDA servers that support them.

Example   The following C++ program illustrates how to use the SET ACCOUNTING STRING function to set accounting string information before a connection to a database is established:

```
/*------------------------------------------------------------*/
/* NAME:     CH5EX7.SQC                                        */
/* PURPOSE: Illustrate How To Use The Following DB2 API Function */
/*          In A C++ Program:                                  */
/*                                                             */
/*               SET ACCOUNTING STRING                         */
/*                                                             */
/*------------------------------------------------------------*/

// Include The Appropriate Header Files
#include <windows.h>
#include <iostream.h>
#include <sqlenv.h>
#include <sql.h>

// Define The API_Class Class
class API_Class
{
    // Attributes
    public:
        struct sqlca  sqlca;

    // Operations
    public:
        long SetAccount();
};

// Define The SetAccount() Member Function
long API_Class::SetAccount()
{
    // Declare The Local Memory Variables
    char  AccountingString[199];
```

```
// Initialize The Accounting String
strcpy(AccountingString, "DB2_EXAMPLES");

// Set The Accounting String
sqlesact(AccountingString, &sqlca);

// If The Accounting String Was Set, Display A Success Message
if (sqlca.sqlcode == SQL_RC_OK)
{
    cout << "The specified accounting string has been set.";
    cout << endl;
}

// Return The SQLCA Return Code To The Calling Function
return(sqlca.sqlcode);
}

/*———————————————————————————————————*/
/* The Main Function                                               */
/*———————————————————————————————————*/
int main()
{
    // Declare The Local Memory Variables
    long        rc = SQL_RC_OK;
    struct sqlca  sqlca;

    // Create An Instance Of The API_Class Class
    API_Class  Example;

    // Connect To The SAMPLE Database
    rc = Example.SetAccount();

    // Connect To The SAMPLE Database Using The Specified
    // Accounting String (In This Case The Accounting String
    // Will Be Ignored)
    EXEC SQL CONNECT TO SAMPLE USER userID USING password;

    // If The Connected, Display A Success Message
    if (sqlca.sqlcode == SQL_RC_OK)
        cout << "Connected to the SAMPLE database." << endl;

    // Issue A Rollback To Free All Locks
    EXEC SQL ROLLBACK;

    // Disconnect From The SAMPLE Database
    EXEC SQL DISCONNECT CURRENT;

    // Return To The Operating System
    return(rc);
}
```

GET ERROR MESSAGE

Purpose   The GET ERROR MESSAGE function is used to retrieve message text that is associated with an error or warning condition (specified by the current value of the *sqlcode* field of a *sqlca* data structure variable) from a special DB2 error message file.

Syntax
```
SQL_API_RC SQL_API_FN sqlaintp (char       *Buffer,
                                short       BufferSize,
                                short       MaxLineSize,
                                struct sqlca  *SQLCA);
```

Parameters   *Buffer*   A pointer to a location in memory where this function is to store the message text retrieved.

BufferSize   The size, in bytes, of the memory storage buffer that the message text retrieved is to be written to.

MaxLineSize The maximum number of characters that one line of message text should contain before a line break is inserted. A value of 0 indicates that the message text is to be returned without line breaks.

SQLCA   A pointer to a location in memory where a SQL Communications Area (SQLCA) data structure variable is stored. The value in the *sqlcode* field of this variable is used to locate the appropriate error message text.

Includes   #include <sql.h>

Description The GET ERROR MESSAGE function is used to retrieve message text that is associated with an error or warning condition from a special DB2 error message file. The DB2 error message file (*db2sql.mo*, located in the *misc* subdirectory of the *sqllib* directory where DB2 was installed) contains error message text corresponding to each error code value that can be generated by DB2. Each time this function is called, the value in the *sqlcode* field of a *sqlca* data structure variable is used to locate and retrieve appropriate error message text from this file. One error message is returned per GET ERROR MESSAGE function call.

Return Codes When this function has completed execution, it returns one of the following values:

+*i* A positive integer value indicating the number of bytes contained in the formatted message. If this value is greater than the value specified in the *BufferSize* parameter, the message text will be truncated. If the message must be truncated to fit in the buffer, the truncation will include room for the string NULL-termination character.

−1 Insufficient memory is available for the message formatting services to work properly. The requested message text is not returned.

−2 The specified SQLCA data structure variable did not contain an error or warning code (SQLCODE = 0).

−3 The message text file is inaccessible or incorrect.

−4 The value specified in the *MaxLineSize* parameter is less than zero.

−5 An invalid SQLCA data structure variable, bad buffer address, or bad buffer length (size) was specified.

If the return code −1 or −3 is returned, the message buffer will contain additional information about the problem.

Comments   ■ A new line (line feed or carriage return/line feed) sequence is automatically placed at the end of each message text string retrieved.

■ If a positive value is specified for the *MaxLineSize* parameter, new line sequences will be inserted between words so the lines of the message text string do not exceed the specified line length. If the last word in a line will cause that line to be longer than the specified line width, the line is filled with as many characters of the word that will fit, a new line sequence is inserted, and the remaining characters of the word are placed on the next line.

Connection Requirements   This function can be called at any time; a connection to a DB2 Database Manager instance or to a DB2 database does not have to be established first.

Authorization   No authorization is required to execute this function call.

See Also   GET SQLSTATE MESSAGE

Example   The following C++ program illustrates how to use the GET ERROR MESSAGE function to retrieve the error message text associated with the error code stored in a SQLCA data structure variable after another API function call fails:

```
/*-----------------------------------------------------------*/
/* NAME:     CH5EX8.CPP                                      */
/* PURPOSE:  Illustrate How To Use The Following DB2 API Function  */
/*           In A C++ Program:                               */
/*                                                           */
/*               GET ERROR MESSAGE                           */
/*                                                           */
/*-----------------------------------------------------------*/

// Include The Appropriate Header Files
#include <windows.h>
#include <iostream.h>
#include <sqlenv.h>
#include <sqlca.h>

// Define The API_Class Class
class API_Class
{
    // Attributes
    public:
        char  ErrorMsg[1024];
```

```
        // Operations
        public:
            void GetErrorMsg(struct sqlca  sqlca);
};

// Define The GetErrorMsg() Member Function
void API_Class::GetErrorMsg(struct sqlca  sqlca)
{
    // Declare The Local Memory Variables
    long  rc = SQL_RC_OK;

    // Retrieve The Error Message Text For The Error Code
    rc = sqlaintp(ErrorMsg, sizeof(ErrorMsg), 70, &sqlca);
    switch (rc)
    {
    case -1:
        cout << "ERROR : Insufficient memory." << endl;
        break;
    case -3:
        cout << "ERROR : Message file is inaccessable." << endl;
        break;
    case -5:
        cout << "ERROR : Invalid SQLCA, bad buffer, ";
        cout << "or bad buffer length specified." << endl;
        break;
    default:
        cout << ErrorMsg << endl;
        break;
    }

    // Return To The Calling Function
    return;
}

/*------------------------------------------------------------*/
/* The Main Function                                          */
/*------------------------------------------------------------*/
int main()
{
    // Declare The Local Memory Variables
    long          rc = SQL_RC_OK;
    struct sqlca  sqlca;

    // Create An Instance Of The API_Class Class
    API_Class  Example;

    // Attempt To Change The Comment Associated With An Invalid
    // Database - This Should Generate An Error
    sqledcgd("INVALID", "", "Invalid Database", &sqlca);

    // If The CHANGE DATABASE COMMENT Function Failed, Retrieve
    // The Error Message Text For The Error Code Returned
    if (sqlca.sqlcode != SQL_RC_OK)
        Example.GetErrorMsg(sqlca);
```

```
// Return To The Operating System
return(rc);
}
```

GET SQLSTATE MESSAGE

Purpose
The GET SQLSTATE MESSAGE function is used to retrieve message text that is associated with a SQLSTATE value (specified by the value of the *sqlstate* field of a *sqlca* data structure variable) from a special DB2 error message file.

Syntax
```
SQL_API_RC SQL_API_FN sqlogstt  (char    *Buffer
                                 short   BufferSize,
                                 short   MaxLineSize,
                                 char    *SQLSTATE);
```

Parameters

Buffer   A pointer to a location in memory where this function is to store the message text retrieved.

BufferSize   The size, in bytes, of the memory storage buffer that the message text retrieved is to be written to.

MaxLineSize   The maximum number of characters that one line of message text should contain before a line break is inserted. A value of 0 indicates that the message text is to be returned without line breaks.

SQLSTATE   A pointer to a location in memory where the SQLSTATE value that this function is to retrieve message text for is stored.

Includes
```
#include <sql.h>
```

Description
The GET SQLSTATE MESSAGE function is used to retrieve message text that is associated with a SQLSTATE value. Each time this function is called, the value in the *sqstate* field of a *sqlca* data structure variable is used to locate and retrieve the appropriate error message text. One message is returned per GET SQLSTATE MESSAGE function call.

Return Codes
When this function has completed execution, it returns one of the following values:

$+i$ A positive integer value indicating the number of bytes contained in the formatted message. If this value is greater than the value specified in the *BufferSize* parameter, the message text will be truncated. If the message must be truncated to fit in the buffer, the truncation will include room for the string NULL-termination character.

−1 Insufficient memory is available for the message formatting services to work properly. The requested message text is not returned.

−2 The specified SQLSTATE value is in the wrong format. This value must be alphanumeric and either two or five digits in length (and NULL-terminated if two digits long).

−3 The message text file is inaccessible or incorrect.

−4 The value specified in the *MaxLineSize* parameter is less than zero.

−5 An invalid SQLSTATE value, bad buffer address, or bad buffer length (size) was specified.

If the return code −1 or −3 is returned, the message buffer will contain additional information about the problem.

Comments

■ A new line (line feed or carriage return/line feed) sequence is automatically placed at the end of each message text string retrieved.

■ If a positive value is specified for the *MaxLineSize* parameter, new line sequences will be inserted between words so the lines of the message text string do not exceed the specified line length. If the last word in a line will cause that line to be longer than the specified line width, the line is filled with as many characters of the word that will fit, a new line sequence is inserted, and the remaining characters of the word are placed on the next line.

■ The value specified in the *SQLSTATE* parameter must be either a specific five-digit SQLSTATE value or a two-digit SQLSTATE class value (the first two digits of a SQLSTATE value). If the value provided for this parameter is a two-digit SQLSTATE class value, it must be NULL-terminated.

Connection Requirements

This function can be called at any time; a connection to a DB2 Database Manager instance or to a DB2 database does not have to be established first.

Authorization

No authorization is required to execute this function call.

See Also

GET ERROR MESSAGE

Example

The following C++ program illustrates how to use the GET SQLSTATE MESSAGE function to retrieve the error message text associated with the SQLSTATE value stored in a SQLCA data structure variable after another API function call fails:

```
/*------------------------------------------------------------------*/
/* NAME:     CH5EX9.CPP                                             */
/* PURPOSE: Illustrate How To Use The Following DB2 API Function    */
/*          In A C++ Program:                                       */
/*                                                                  */
/*              GET SQLSTATE MESSAGE                                */
/*                                                                  */
/*------------------------------------------------------------------*/

// Include The Appropriate Header Files
#include <windows.h>
#include <iostream.h>
#include <sqlenv.h>
#include <sqlca.h>
```

```
// Define The API_Class Class
class API_Class
{
    // Attributes
    public:
        char    ErrorMsg[1024];

    // Operations
    public:
        void GetSQLSTATEMsg(struct sqlca   sqlca);
};

// Define The GetSQLSTATEMsg() Member Function
void API_Class::GetSQLSTATEMsg(struct sqlca   sqlca)
{
    // Declare The Local Memory Variables
    long   rc = SQL_RC_OK;

    // Retrieve The SQLSTATE Message Text For The SQLSTATE Code
    rc = sqlogstt(ErrorMsg, sizeof(ErrorMsg), 70,
        (char *) &sqlca.sqlstate);
    switch (rc)
    {
    case -1:
        cout << "ERROR : Insufficient memory." << endl;
        break;
    case -3:
        cout << "ERROR : Message file is inaccessable." << endl;
        break;
    case -5:
        cout << "ERROR : Invalid SQLCA, bad buffer, ";
        cout << "or bad buffer length specified." << endl;
        break;
    default:
        cout << ErrorMsg << endl;
        break;
    }

    // Return To The Calling Function
    return;
}

/*-------------------------------------------------------------*/
/* The Main Function                                           */
/*-------------------------------------------------------------*/
int main()
{
    // Declare The Local Memory Variables
    long          rc = SQL_RC_OK;
    struct sqlca  sqlca;

    // Create An Instance Of The API_Class Class
    API_Class   Example;

    // Attempt To Change The Comment Associated With An Invalid
```

```
// Database - This Should Generate An Error
sqledcgd("INVALID", "", "Invalid Database", &sqlca);

// If The CHANGE DATABASE COMMENT Function Failed, Retrieve
// The Error Message Text For The SQLSTATE Code Returned
if (sqlca.sqlcode != SQL_RC_OK)
    Example.GetSQLSTATEMsg(sqlca);

// Return To The Operating System
return(rc);
}
```

■ ■ GET AUTHORIZATIONS

Purpose   The GET AUTHORIZATIONS function is used to retrieve the authorizations of the current user from both the database configuration file and the authorization system catalog view (SYSCAT.DBAUTH).

Syntax   ```
SQL_API_RC SQL_API_FN sqluadau (struct sql_authorizations *Authorizations,
                                struct sqlca   *SQLCA);
```

**Parameters**   *Authorizations*    A pointer to a *sql_authorizations* structure where this function is to store the authorization information retrieved.

                 *SQLCA*             A pointer to a location in memory where a SQL Communications Area (SQLCA) data structure variable is stored. This variable returns either status information (if the function executed successfully) or error information (if the function failed) to the calling application.

**Includes**     ```
#include <sqlutil.h>
```

Description The GET AUTHORIZATIONS function is used to retrieve the authorizations of the current user from both the database configuration file and the authorization system catalog view (SYSCAT.DBAUTH). The authorization information retrieved is stored in a *sql_authorizations* structure that contains short integer elements that indicate which authorizations the current user does and does not hold. The *sql_authorizations* structure is defined in *sqlutil.h* as follows:

```
struct sql_authorizations
{
short sql_authorizations_len;  /* The size of the                    */
                               /* sql_authorizations structure       */
short sql_sysadm_auth;         /* The user has System Administrator   */
                               /* authority                           */
short sql_dbadm_auth;          /* The user has Database Administrator  */
```

```
                                       /* authority                       */
       short sql_createtab_auth;       /* The user has CREATETAB authority */
       short sql_bindadd_auth;         /* The user has BINDADD authority   */
       short sql_connect_auth;         /* The user has CONNECT authority   */
       short sql_sysadm_grp_auth;      /* The user belongs to a group that */
                                       /* has System Administrator authority */
       short sql_dbadm_grp_auth;       /* The user belongs to a group that */
                                       /* has Database Administrator authority */
       short sql_createtab_grp_auth;   /* The user belongs to a group that */
                                       /* has CREATETAB authority          */
       short sql_bindadd_grp_auth;     /* The user belongs to a group that */
                                       /* has BINDADD authority            */
       short sql_connect_grp_auth;     /* The user belongs to a group that */
                                       /* has CONNECT authority            */
       short sql_sysctrl_auth;         /* The user has System Control authority */
       short sql_sysctrl_grp_auth;     /* The user belongs to a group that */
                                       /* has System Control authority     */
       short sql_sysmaint_auth;        /* The user has System Maintenance  */
                                       /* authority                        */
       short sql_sysmaint_grp_auth;    /* The user belongs to a group that */
                                       /* has SYSMAINT authority           */
       short sql_create_not_fenc_auth; /* The user has CREATE NOT          */
                                       /* FENCED authority                 */
       short sql_create_not_fenc_grp_auth;                                 */
                                       /* The user belongs to a group that has */
                                       /* CREATE NOT FENCED authority      */
       short sql_implicit_schema_auth;/* The user has IMPLICIT SCHEMA      */
                                       /* authority                        */
       short sql_implicit_schema_grp_auth;                                 */
                                       /* The user belongs to a group that has */
                                       /* IMPLICIT SCHEMA authority        */
       };
```

The first element in this structure, *sql_authorizations_len*, must be initialized to the size of the structure itself before the GET AUTHORIZATIONS function is called.

Comments ■ Explicit SQL commands can be used to grant direct authorities to a specific user. System Administrator, System Maintenance, and System Control are indirect authorities and therefore cannot be granted directly to a user. Instead, they are available only through the groups to which a user belongs. PUBLIC is a special group to which all users belong.

■ If this function executes without error, each field of the *sql_authorizations* structure variable will contain either a 0 or a 1. A value of 1 indicates that the current user holds the corresponding authorization, while a value of 0 indicates that the user does not.

Connection Requirements This function can only be called if a connection to a database exists.

Authorization No authorization is required to execute this function call.

Example

The following C++ program illustrates how to use the GET AUTHORIZATIONS function to determine whether or not the current user has been granted the authorizations needed to execute most of the DB2 API functions:

```
/*----------------------------------------------------------------*/
/* NAME:     CH5EX10.SQC                                          */
/* PURPOSE: Illustrate How To Use The Following DB2 API Function  */
/*          In A C++ Program:                                     */
/*                                                                */
/*              GET AUTHORIZATIONS                                */
/*                                                                */
/*----------------------------------------------------------------*/

// Include The Appropriate Header Files
#include <windows.h>
#include <iostream.h>
#include <sqlutil.h>
#include <sql.h>

// Define The API_Class Class
class API_Class
{
    // Attributes
    public:
        struct sqlca  sqlca;

    // Operations
    public:
        long GetAuthorizations();
};

// Define The GetAuthorizations() Member Function
long API_Class::GetAuthorizations()
{
    // Declare The Local Memory Variables
    struct sql_authorizations  AuthInfo;

    // Initialize The First Element Of The AuthInfo Structure
    AuthInfo.sql_authorizations_len = sizeof(struct sql_authorizations);

    // Retrieve The Current User's Authorizations
    sqluadau(&AuthInfo, &sqlca);

    // If The User's Authorization Information Was Retrieved, Display
    // A Message Stating Whether Or Not The User Has The
    // Authorizations Needed To Execute Most Of The DB2 APIs
    if (sqlca.sqlcode == SQL_RC_OK)
    {
        if (AuthInfo.sql_sysadm_auth                        == 1 ||
            AuthInfo.sql_sysmaint_auth                      == 1 ||
            AuthInfo.sql_sysctrl_auth                       == 1 ||
            AuthInfo.sql_dbadm_auth                         == 1)
        {
```

```
                    cout << "The current user has the authorizations ";
                    cout << "needed to execute most of" << endl;
                    cout << "the DB2 APIs." << endl;
            }

            else
            {
                    cout << "The current user does not have the authorizations ";
                    cout << "that are needed to execute many of" << endl;
                    cout << "the DB2 APIs." << endl;
            }
        }

        // Return The SQLCA Return Code To The Calling Function
        return(sqlca.sqlcode);
    }


/*──────────────────────────────────────────────────────────── */
/* The Main Function                                            */
/*──────────────────────────────────────────────────────────── */
int main()
{
    // Declare The Local Memory Variables
    long            rc = SQL_RC_OK;
    struct sqlca    sqlca;

    // Create An Instance Of The API_Class Class
    API_Class   Example;

    // Connect To The SAMPLE Database
    EXEC SQL CONNECT TO SAMPLE USER userID USING password;

    // Get The Current User's Authorizations
    rc = Example.GetAuthorizations();

    // Issue A Rollback To Free All Locks
    EXEC SQL ROLLBACK;

    // Disconnect From The SAMPLE Database
    EXEC SQL DISCONNECT CURRENT;

    // Return To The Operating System
    return(rc);
}
```

CHAPTER 6

DB2 Database Manager Control and Database Control APIs

DB2 applications communicate with DB2 databases through a set of background server processes know as the DB2 Database Manager. This chapter is designed to introduce you to the set of DB2 API functions that are used to start and stop the DB2 Database Manager background processes, interact with the DB2 Database Manager, and create and delete (drop) DB2 databases. The first part of this chapter provides a general discussion about the DB2 Database Manager background server processes. Then, the functions that are used to create and delete DB2 databases are described. Next, information about the functions that are used to control DB2 Database Manager instances is provided. Finally, a detailed reference section covering each DB2 API function that can be used to control the DB2 Database Manager and DB2 databases is provided.

The DB2 Database Manager Server Processes

Before a database connection or DB2 Database Manager instance attachment can be established by an embedded SQL or DB2 API application, the DB2 Database Manager server processes must first be started. DB2 Database Manager server processes are usually started when you issue the START DATABASE MANAGER command from the DB2 command-line processor. On DB2 server workstations, the DB2 Database Manager server processes are often started as part of the workstation boot-up sequence. You can also start the DB2 Database Manager server processes from within an application program by calling the START DATABASE MANAGER function.

Once started, these processes run in the background until they are explicitly stopped —when an application that started these processes terminates, the processes continue running. You can stop the DB2 Database Manager server processes by issuing the STOP DATABASE MANAGER command from the DB2 command-line processor or by calling the STOP DATABASE MANAGER function from within an application program.

Creating and Deleting DB2 Databases

A database is simply a set of all DB2-related objects. When you create a DB2 database, you are establishing an administrative entity that provides an underlying structure for an eventual collection of tables, views, associated indexes, etc., as well as the table spaces in which they reside.

You can create all the objects in a database through various embedded SQL statements. You must create the database itself, however, by some other means, and the database must exist before any of its objects can be created. You can create DB2 databases by issuing the CREATE DATABASE command from the DB2 command-line processor. In many cases, however, it is desirable to create one or more databases from an application program. This statement is especially true for applications that are designed to install database applications on new workstations where the necessary databases do not already exist. You can create databases from an application program by calling the CREATE DATABASE function.

When a database is no longer needed, you can delete it by issuing the DROP DATABASE command from the DB2 command-line processor. You can also delete databases from within an application program by calling the DROP DATABASE function. By using THE CREATE DATABASE and DROP DATABASE functions together, an application can create a temporary database when it starts execution and drop it when it is no longer needed.

Starting and Stopping DB2 Databases

When an application first issues a CONNECT SQL statement to establish a connection to a DB2 database, it must wait while the DB2 Database Manager starts up the appropriate database. In many cases, the application spends a significant amount of time initializing the database before it can do other work. However, once a database has been started, other applications can simply connect to and begin using it. To remove database start-up and initialization overhead from the first application that establishes a connection, database administrators can use the ACTIVATE DATABASE function to pre-start selected databases. Likewise, database adminstrators can remove the overhead of shutting down a database from an application by using the DEACTIVATE database function. When used together, these functions can improve the performance of embedded SQL applications, particularly when a database is partitioned across several workstations (nodes).

Retrieving and Setting Other Connection Setting Values

The type of connection an application makes to one or more databases is often determined by the precompiler options that were specified when the application was precompiled. An application can retrieve these values by calling the QUERY CLIENT function any time during its processing. You can leave these settings as they are or modify them by calling the SET CLIENT function before a connection to a database is established. This method of specifying connection options is particularly helpful when used by applications that contain no static embedded SQL statements (and therefore, do not need to be precompiled).

Controlling DB2 Database Manager Connection Instances

As long as an application executes against a local database, one or more connections to the background DB2 Database Manager server processes is sufficient for most processing needs. When an application is designed to execute against one or more remote databases, you must first establish a connection to the DB2 Database Manager server process instance that is controlling the remote database. The ATTACH function can be used to establish a logical instance attachment to the DB2 Database Manager server processes running at a remote workstation. When an application attaches to the remote DB2 Database Manager server processes, it starts a physical communications connection to the workstation if one does not already exist. When all remote processing is complete, the DETACH function can be used to close the physical communications connection to the workstation and detach from the remote DB2 Database Manager server processes.

The DB2 Database Manager and DB2 Database Control Functions

Table 6–1 lists the DB2 API functions that are used to interact with the DB2 Database Manager and that are used to create and delete DB2 databases.

Each of these functions are described in detail in the remainder of this chapter.

Table 6-1 DB2 Database Manager Control and Database Control APIs

Function Name	Description
START DATABASE MANAGER	Starts the DB2 Database Manager server processes.
STOP DATABASE MANAGER	Stops the DB2 Database Manager server processes.
FORCE APPLICATION	Forces all local and remote users and/or applications off a DB2 Database Manager instance.
CREATE DATABASE	Creates a new database and its associated support files.
DROP DATABASE	Deletes an existing database and all its associated support files.
ACTIVATE DATABASE	Activates a database and starts up all appropriate database services.
DEACTIVATE DATABASE	Deactivates a database and shuts down all appropriate database services.
ATTACH	Specifies the node at which DB2 Database Manager instance-level functions are to be executed.
ATTACH AND CHANGE PASSWORD	Specifies the node at which DB2 Database Manager instance-level functions are to be executed (and permits the user to change the password for the instance being attached).
DETACH	Removes a logical DB2 Database Manager instance attachment.
QUERY CLIENT	Retrieves the current connection setting values for an application.
SET CLIENT	Specifies connection setting values for an application.
QUERY CLIENT INFORMATION	Retrieves information about a client that is connected to a server.
SET CLIENT INFORMATION	Specifies information about a client that is connected to a server.

START DATABASE MANAGER

Purpose   The START DATABASE MANAGER function is used to start an instance of the DB2 Database Manager server background processes on a single node or on all nodes defined in a multi-node environment.

Syntax
```
SQL_API_RC SQL_API_FN sqlepstart (struct sqle_start_options *StartOptions,
                                  struct sqlca             *SQLCA);
```

Parameters   *StartOptions*   A pointer to a *sqle_start_options* data structure that contains information about how the DB2 Database Manager background processes are to be initialized when started.

              SQLCA   A pointer to a location in memory where a SQL Communications Area (SQLCA) data structure variable is stored. This structure returns either status information (if the function executed successfully) or error information (if the function failed) to the calling application.

Includes   `#include <sqlenv.h>`

Description   The START DATABASE MANAGER function is used to start an instance of the DB2 Database Manager server background processes on a single node or on all nodes defined in a multi-node environment. These processes must be started before any database connections or instance attachments to the DB2 Database Manager can be made. Once started, the DB2 Database Manager server processes run in the background until the STOP DATABASE MANAGER function or command is executed.

When this function is called, a special structure (*sqle_start_options*) is used to pass start-up options to the DB2 Database Manager. The *sqle_start_options* structure is defined in *sqlenv.h* as follows:

```
struct sqle_start_options
{
char               sqloptid[8];                                    */
                                  /* A structure identifier and      */
                                  /* eye-catcher for storage dumps. This */
                                  /* is a string, 8 bytes in length,  */
                                  /* that must be initialized with    */
                                  /* the value                        */
                                  /* SQLE_STARTOPTID_V51.             */
unsigned long      isprofile;                                     */
                                  /* Indicates whether or not a profile */
                                  /* file is specified. If no          */
                                  /* profile is specified, the file    */
                                  /* db2profile is used.              */
char               profile[237];                                  */
                                  /* The name of the profile file to be */
                                  /* executed at each node (to         */
```

```
                                   /* define the DB2 environment). This  */
                                   /* file is executed before the        */
                                   /* node is started.                   */
        unsigned long       isnodenum;                                   */
                                   /* Indicates whether or not a node     */
                                   /* number is specified                 */
        SQL_PDB_NODE_TYPE   nodenum;                                     */
                                   /* The node number that the START      */
                                   /* DATABASE MANAGER command is to be   */
                                   /* ran against. If no node number is   */
                                   /* specified, the command will be      */
                                   /* ran against all nodes stored in     */
                                   /* the file db2nodes.cfg.              */
        unsigned long       option;                                      */
                                   /* Indicates whether a normal start    */
                                   /* operation is to be performed        */
                                   /* (SQLE_NONE), a node is to be added  */
                                   /* when the start operation is         */
                                   /* performed (SQLE_ADDNODE), a         */
                                   /* database is to be restarted         */
                                   /* (SQLE_RESTART), or a node is to     */
                                   /* be started in stand-alone mode      */
                                   /* (SQLE_STANDALONE).                  */
        unsigned long       ishostname;                                  */
                                   /* Indicates whether or not a host     */
                                   /* name is specified                   */
        char hostname[257];                                              */
                                   /* The name of the system that the     */
                                   /* START DATABASE MANAGER command      */
                                   /* is to be ran against                */
        unsigned long       isport;                                      */
                                   /* Indicates whether or not a port     */
                                   /* number is specified                 */
        SQL_PDB_PORT_TYPE   port;                                       */
                                   /* The port number that the START      */
                                   /* DATABASE MANAGER command is to      */
                                   /* be ran against.                     */
        unsigned long       isnetname;                                   */
                                   /* Indicates whether or not a net      */
                                   /* name is specified                   */
        char netname[257];                                               */
                                   /* The net name that the START         */
                                   /* DATABASE MANAGER command is to be   */
                                   /* ran against                         */
        unsigned long       tblspace_type;                               */
                                   /* Indicates whether temporary table   */
                                   /* spaces are not to be crested        */
                                   /* when a node is added                */
                                   /* (SQLE_TABLESPACES_NONE),            */
                                   /* temporary table                     */
                                   /* space containers for an added       */
                                   /* node should be the same as those    */
                                   /* defined for the node                */
                                   /* (SQLE_TABLESPACES_LIKE_NODE),       */
```

```
                                     /* temporary                     */
                                     /* table space containers for an */
                                     /* added node should be the same as */
                                     /* those defined for the catalog */
                                     /* node of each database          */
                                     /* (SQLE_TABLESPACES_LIKE_CATALOG). */
        SQL_PDB_NODE_TYPE tblspace_node;  /*                           */
                                     /* Specifies the node number that */
                                     /* temporary table space definitions */
                                     /* should be obtained from. This node */
                                     /* number must exist in the       */
                                     /* db2nodes.cfg file, and is only */
                                     /* used if the tblspace_type field */
                                     /* is set to                      */
                                     /* SQLE_TABLESPACES_LIKE_NODE      */
        unsigned long       iscomputer;  /*                            */
                                     /* Indicates whether or not a     */
                                     /* computer name is specified     */
        char computer[17];           /*                                */
                                     /* The name of the computer that the */
                                     /* START DATABASE MANAGER          */
                                     /* command is to be ran against    */
        char *pUserName;             /*                                */
                                     /* Logon account user ID (OS/2 and */
                                     /* Windows only)                   */
        char *pPassword;             /*                                */
                                     /* Logon account password (OS/2 and */
                                     /* Windows only)                   */
        };
```

Comments   ■ This function does not need to be called on a client workstation if the applications running on that workstation only accesses databases on a server workstation (i.e., if no local databases stored on the client workstation are to be accessed).

■ If the DB2 Database Manager server processes are successfully started, a message will be sent to the standard output device. If the DB2 Database Manager server processes are not successfully started, processing will stop, and an error message will be sent to the standard output device. The standard output device is normally the display monitor, unless it has been redirected.

■ If this function is called while the DB2 Database Manager server processes are already running, an error will be generated. If this occurs, the application can ignore the error and continue execution (because the server processes are already running).

■ If no options are specified when this function is called in a multi-node database environment, the DB2 Database Manager is started on all parallel nodes specified in the node configuration file. Applications should ensure that all applicable nodes in a multi-node environment have been started before issuing a request to the database.

■ This function supports SIGINT and SIGALRM signals on Unix platforms. If either signal occurs, all in-process start operations are interrupted, and a message (SQL1044N for SIGINT and SQL6073N for SIGALRM) is returned to the error log from each interrupted node. Nodes that were already started are not affected. If the SIGINT signal is issued on a node that is just starting, the STOP DATABASE MANAGER function or command must be executed on that node before this function can be called again.

Connection Requirements
This function can be called at any time; a connection to a DB2 Database Manager instance or to a DB2 database does not have to be established first.

Authorization
Only users with either System Administrator (SYSADM) authority, System Control (SYSCTRL) authority, or System Maintenance (SYSMAINT) authority can execute this function call.

See Also
STOP DATABASE MANAGER

Example
The following C++ program illustrates how to use the START DATABASE MANAGER function to start the DB2 Database Manager server processes:

```
/*———————————————————————————————————*/
/* NAME:     CH6EX1.CPP                                      */
/* PURPOSE: Illustrate How To Use The Following DB2 API Function */
/*          In A C++ Program:                                */
/*                                                           */
/*                START DATABASE MANAGER                     */
/*                                                           */
/*———————————————————————————————————*/

// Include The Appropriate Header Files
#include <windows.h>
#include <iostream.h>
#include <sqlenv.h>
#include <sqlca.h>

// Define The API_Class Class
class API_Class
{
    // Attributes
    public:
        struct sqlca  sqlca;

    // Operations
    public:
        long StartDB2Mgr();
};

// Define The StartDB2Mgr() Member Function
long API_Class::StartDB2Mgr()
{
```

```
            // Declare The Local Memory Variables
            struct sqle_start_options   StartOptions;

            // Initialize The Start DB2 Database Manager Options
            // Structure
            strcpy(StartOptions.sqloptid, SQLE_STARTOPTID_V51);
            StartOptions.isprofile = 0;
            strcpy(StartOptions.profile, "");
            StartOptions.isnodenum = 0;
            StartOptions.nodenum = 0;
            StartOptions.option = SQLE_NONE;
            StartOptions.ishostname = 0;
            strcpy(StartOptions.hostname, "");
            StartOptions.isport = 0;
            StartOptions.port = 0;
            StartOptions.isnetname = 0;
            strcpy(StartOptions.netname, "");
            StartOptions.tblspace_type = SQLE_TABLESPACES_LIKE_CATALOG;
            StartOptions.tblspace_node = 0;
            StartOptions.iscomputer = 0;
            strcpy(StartOptions.computer, "");
            StartOptions.pUserName = NULL;
            StartOptions.pPassword = NULL;

            // Start The DB2 Database Manager Server Processes
            sqlepstart(&StartOptions, &sqlca);

            // If The DB2 Database Manager Server Processes Have Been
            // Started, Display A Success Message
            if (sqlca.sqlcode == SQL_RC_OK)
                cout << "The DB2 Database Manager has been started." << endl;

            // Return The SQLCA Return Code To The Calling Function
            return(sqlca.sqlcode);
}

/*------------------------------------------------------------------*/
/* The Main Function                                                */
/*------------------------------------------------------------------*/
int main()
{
      // Declare The Local Memory Variables
      long   rc = SQL_RC_OK;

      // Create An Instance Of The API_Class Class
      API_Class   Example;

      // Start The DB2 Database Manager Server Processes
      rc = Example.StartDB2Mgr();

      // Return To The Operating System
      return(rc);
}
```

■ ■ STOP DATABASE MANAGER

Purpose   The STOP DATABASE MANAGER function is used to stop all DB2 Database Manager server processes that are running in the background and to free all system resources held by the DB2 Database Manager.

Syntax

```
SQL_API_RC SQL_API_FN sqlepstp (struct sqledbstopopt  *StopOptions,
                                struct sqlca          *SQLCA);
```

Parameters   *StartOptions*   A pointer to a *sqledbstopopt* data structure that contains information about how the DB2 Database Manager background processes are to be stopped.

            SQLCA   A pointer to a location in memory where a SQL Communications Area (SQLCA) data structure variable is stored. This structure returns either status information (if the function executed successfully) or error information (if the function failed) to the calling application.

Includes   #include <sqlenv.h>

Description   The STOP DATABASE MANAGER function is used to stop all DB2 Database Manager server processes that are running in the background and to free all system resources held by the DB2 Database Manager. Unless explicitly stopped, the DB2 Database Manager server processes will continue running in the background, even after all application programs using the processes have ended.

      When this function is called, a special structure (*sqledbstopopt*) is used to pass shut-down options to the DB2 Database Manager. The *sqledbstopopt* structure is defined in *sqlenv.h* as follows:

```
struct sqledbstopopt
{
unsigned long      isprofile;
                              /* Indicates whether or not a profile */
                              /* file is specified. If no           */
                              /* profile is specified, the file     */
                              /* db2profile is used.                */
char               profile[237];
                              /* The name of the profile file that  */
                              /* was executed at each node          */
                              /* during start-up (to define the DB2 */
                              /* environment). This file must       */
                              /* be the same profile file that was  */
                              /* specified when the START           */
                              /* DATABASE MANAGER function was       */
                              /* called.                            */
```

```
    unsigned long        isnodenum;
                                    /* Indicates whether or not a node    */
                                    /* number is specified                */
    SQL_PDB_NODE_TYPE    nodenum;                                         */
                                    /* The node number that the STOP       */
                                    /* DATABASE MANAGER command is to be   */
                                    /* ran against. If no node number is   */
                                    /* specified, the command will be      */
                                    /* ran against all nodes stored in     */
                                    /* the file db2nodes.cfg.              */
    unsigned long        option;
                                    /* Indicates whether a normal stop     */
                                    /* operation is to be performed        */
                                    /* (SQLE_NONE), the FORCE APPLICATION  */
                                    /* (ALL) function is to be issued      */
                                    /* before the stop operation is        */
                                    /* performed (SQLE_FORCE), or a node   */
                                    /* is to be dropped when the stop      */
                                    /* operation is performed (SQLE_DROP)  */
    unsigned long        callerac;
                                    /* Indicates whether a node is to be   */
                                    /* dropped when the STOP DATABASE       */
                                    /* MANAGER function is first called    */
                                    /* (SQLE_DROP), dropped after the      */
                                    /* STOP DATABASE MANAGER function is   */
                                    /* called and all other processing     */
                                    /* is to continue (SQLE_CONTINUE), or  */
                                    /* dropped after the STOP              */
                                    /* DATABASE MANAGER function is         */
                                    /* called and all other processing is  */
                                    /* to terminate                        */
                                    /* (SQLE_TABLESPACES_LIKE_CATALOG).    */
                                    /* This field is only                  */
                                    /* used if the option SQLE_DROP.       */
    };
```

Comments   ■ This function does not need to be called on a client workstation if the applications running on that workstation only access databases on a server workstation (i.e., if no local databases stored on the client workstation are to be accessed).

■ The DB2 Database Manager instance to be stopped is determined by the value in the DB2INSTANCE environment variable. You can determine the current value of this environment variable by calling the GET INSTANCE function.

■ If the DB2 Database Manager server processes are successfully stopped, a successful completion message will be sent to the standard output device. If the DB2 Database Manager server processes are not successfully stopped, processing will stop, and an error message will be sent to the standard output device. The standard output device is normally the display monitor, unless it has been redirected.

■ The DB2 Database Manager server processes cannot be stopped if any DB2 application programs are currently connected to the DB2 Database Manager instance. The FORCE APPLICATION function can be used to disconnect all applications that are connected to a DB2 Database Manager instance.

■ If this function is called when the DB2 Database Manager server processes are not running, an error will be generated.

■ If this function is called while there are instance attachments but no database connections, the instance attachments are forced off, and the DB2 Database Manager background server processes are stopped.

■ In a multiple-node environment:

   ■ All nodes that have been added to the system since this function was last called will be included in the *db2nodes.cfg* configuration file. This function can be used to remove a node from this configuration file.

   ■ The file *db2cshrc* is not supported and cannot be specified as a profile file to use.

   ■ On UNIX platforms, if the SIGALRM signal is encountered, this function will interrupt all stops that are in progress and return SQL6037N for each interrupted node to the error log file. Nodes that have already been stopped are not affected.

Connection Requirements   This function can be called at any time; a connection to a DB2 Database Manager instance or to a DB2 database does not have to be established first.

Authorization   Only users with System Administrator (SYSADM) authority, System Control (SYSCTRL) authority, or System Maintenance (SYSMAINT) authority can execute this function call.

See Also   START DATABASE MANAGER, FORCE APPLICATION

Example   The following C++ program illustrates how to use the STOP DATABASE MANAGER function to stop the DB2 Database Manager server processes:

```
/*----------------------------------------------------------*/
/* NAME:    CH6EX2.CPP                                       */
/* PURPOSE: Illustrate How To Use The Following DB2 API Function */
/*            In A C++ Program:                              */
/*                                                           */
/*              STOP DATABASE MANAGER                        */
/*                                                           */
/*----------------------------------------------------------*/

// Include The Appropriate Header Files
#include <windows.h>
#include <iostream.h>
#include <sqlenv.h>
#include <sqlca.h>
```

```cpp
// Define The API_Class Class
class API_Class
{
    // Attributes
    public:
        struct sqlca   sqlca;

    // Operations
    public:
        long StopDB2Mgr();
};

// Define The StopDB2Mgr() Member Function
long API_Class::StopDB2Mgr()
{
    // Declare The Local Memory Variables
    struct sqledbstopopt  StopOptions;

    // Initialize The Stop DB2 Database Manager Options
    // Structure
    StopOptions.isprofile = 0;
    strcpy(StopOptions.profile, "");
    StopOptions.isnodenum = 0;
    StopOptions.nodenum = 0;
    StopOptions.option = SQLE_NONE;
    StopOptions.callerac = SQLE_DROP;

    // Stop The DB2 Database Manager Server Processes
    sqlepstp(&StopOptions, &sqlca);

    // If The DB2 Database Manager Server Processes Have Been
    // Stopped, Display A Success Message
    if (sqlca.sqlcode == SQL_RC_OK)
        cout << "The DB2 Database Manager has been stopped." << endl;

    // Return The SQLCA Return Code To The Calling Function
    return(sqlca.sqlcode);
}

/*------------------------------------------------------------------*/
/* The Main Function                                                */
/*------------------------------------------------------------------*/
int main()
{
    // Declare The Local Memory Variables
    long   rc = SQL_RC_OK;

    // Create An Instance Of The API_Class Class
    API_Class   Example;

    // Stop The DB2 Database Manager Server Processes
    rc = Example.StopDB2Mgr();

    // Return To The Operating System
    return(rc);
}
```

FORCE APPLICATION

Purpose The FORCE APPLICATION function is used to force both local and remote users and/or applications off a DB2 Database Manager instance.

Syntax
```
SQL_API_RC SQL_API_FN sqlefrce (long            NumAgentIDs,
                                unsigned long   *AgentIDs,
                                unsigned short  ForceMode,
                                struct sqlca    *SQLCA);
```

Parameters *NumAgentIDs*   The number of agent connections that are to be terminated. This value should be the same as the number of elements in the array specified in the *AgentIDs* parameter.

AgentIDs   A pointer to a location in memory where an array of unsigned long integers that contain the agent IDs of database users and/or applications to be forced off DB2 Database Manager instances is stored.

ForceMode   The operating mode in which the FORCE APPLICATION function is to execute. Because the asynchronous operating mode is currently the only mode supported, this parameter must always be set to SQL_ASYNCH.

SQLCA   A pointer to a location in memory where a SQL Communications Area (SQLCA) data structure variable is stored. This variable returns either status information (if the function executed successfully) or error information (if the function failed) to the calling application.

Includes   `#include <sqlenv.h>`

Description The FORCE APPLICATION function is used to force both local and remote users and/or applications off a DB2 Database Manager instance. Forcing a user or an application off a DB2 Database Manager instance will result in the loss of that user's or application's connections to all databases. To preserve database integrity, only users and applications that are either idle or executing interruptible database operations can be forced off a DB2 Database Manager instance.

Comments   ■ When this function is called with the *ForceMode* parameter set to SQL_ASYNCH (the only value permitted at this time), this function does not wait until all specified users and applications are terminated before returning. Instead, it returns as soon as its processing has completed or as soon as an error occurs. As a result, there might be a short interval between the time the FORCE APPLICATION completes and the time the specified connections are terminated.

■ The STOP DATABASE MANAGER function cannot be executed by another application while this function is executing. Instead, the DB2 Database Manager server remains active, so subsequent Database Manager operations can be handled without having to make a START DATABASE MANAGER function call.

■ Users and/or applications that are in the process of creating a database cannot be forced off a DB2 Database Manager instance.

■ After this function is called, the DB2 Database Manager will still accept database connect requests. Therefore, several FORCE APPLICATION function calls may be required to completely force all users off a DB2 Database Manager instance.

■ You can use the GET SNAPSHOT function to obtain a list of the agent IDs of all active applications currently connected to a database. You can use other database system monitor functions to gather additional information about the users and/or applications attached to the database.

■ Minimal validation is performed on the array of agent IDs specified in the *AgentIDs* parameter. Therefore, applications using this function must ensure that the value specified in the *AgentIDs* parameter points to an array that contains the same number of elements specified in the *NumAgentIDs* parameter.

■ If the value specified in the *NumAgentIDs* parameter is SQL_ALL_USERS, all users and applications will be forced off the DB2 Database Manager instance, and any values specified in the *AgentIDs* parameter will be ignored.

■ If the value specified in the *NumAgentIDs* parameter is 0, an error will be returned.

■ All users and applications that can be forced off a database connection instance will be forced off the connection instance. If one or more specified agent IDs cannot be found, an error will occur. (An agent ID might not be found, for instance, if the agent signs off between the time the agent ID information is collected and the time the FORCE APPLICATION function is called.)

■ The application that calls this function is not forced off the DB2 Database Manager instance.

■ When a user and/or application is terminated by the FORCE APPLICATION function, a ROLLBACK is performed to ensure that database consistency is maintained.

■ Agent IDs are recycled, so when one user signs off, another user might sign on and acquire the same agent ID. Because of this feature, if a significant period of time elapses between the time agent IDs are collected and the time the FORCE APPLICATION function is executed, the wrong user might be forced off the DB2 Database Manager instance.

■ If an operation that cannot be interrupted (such as BACKUP DATABASE or RESTORE DATABASE) is terminated because the application performing the operation was terminated by this function, that operation must be successfully reexecuted before the specified database will become available again.

■ In a partitioned database environment, this function can be issued from any node that is part of the partitioned database environment.

■ In a multi-node environment, this function affects all nodes that are listed in the *db2nodes.cfg* configuration file.

Connection Requirements   This function can only be called if a connection to a DB2 Database Manager instance exists. To force users and/or applications off a remote database server, an

application must first attach to that server. If no attachment exists, the FORCE
APPLICATION function is executed locally.

Authorization Only users with either System Administrator (SYSADM) authority or System Control
(SYSCTRL) authority are allowed to execute this function call.

See Also   STOP DATABASE MANAGER, ATTACH, DETACH

Example   The following C++ program illustrates how to use the FORCE APPLICATION function to
force all users and applications off a DB2 Database Manager instance:

```
/*-------------------------------------------------------------------*/
/* NAME:      CH6EX3.CPP                                             */
/* PURPOSE: Illustrate How To Use The Following DB2 API Function     */
/*          In A C++ Program:                                        */
/*                                                                   */
/*                  FORCE APPLICATION                                */
/*                                                                   */
/*-------------------------------------------------------------------*/

// Include The Appropriate Header Files
#include <windows.h>
#include <iostream.h>
#include <sqlenv.h>
#include <sqlca.h>

// Define The API_Class Class
class API_Class
{
    // Attributes
    public:
        struct sqlca  sqlca;

    // Operations
    public:
        long StartDB2Mgr();
        long StopDB2Mgr();
};

// Define The StartDB2Mgr() Member Function
long API_Class::StartDB2Mgr()
{
    // Declare The Local Memory Variables
    struct sqle_start_options  StartOptions;

    // Initialize The Start DB2 Database Manager Options
    // Structure
    strcpy(StartOptions.sqloptid, SQLE_STARTOPTID_V51);
    StartOptions.isprofile = 0;
    strcpy(StartOptions.profile, "");
    StartOptions.isnodenum = 0;
    StartOptions.nodenum = 0;
    StartOptions.option = SQLE_NONE;
```

```cpp
        StartOptions.ishostname = 0;
        strcpy(StartOptions.hostname, "");
        StartOptions.isport = 0;
        StartOptions.port = 0;
        StartOptions.isnetname = 0;
        strcpy(StartOptions.netname, "");
        StartOptions.tblspace_type = SQLE_TABLESPACES_LIKE_CATALOG;
        StartOptions.tblspace_node = 0;
        StartOptions.iscomputer = 0;
        strcpy(StartOptions.computer, "");
        StartOptions.pUserName = NULL;
        StartOptions.pPassword = NULL;

        // Start The DB2 Database Manager Server Processes
        sqlepstart(&StartOptions, &sqlca);

        // If The DB2 Database Manager Server Processes Have Been
        // Started, Display A Success Message
        if (sqlca.sqlcode == SQL_RC_OK)
            cout << "The DB2 Database Manager has been started." << endl;

        // Return The SQLCA Return Code To The Calling Function
        return(sqlca.sqlcode);
}

// Define The StopDB2Mgr() Member Function
long API_Class::StopDB2Mgr()
{
        // Declare The Local Memory Variables
        unsigned long          AgentID;
        struct sqledbstopopt   StopOptions;

        // Force All Applications Off The DB2 Database Manager Instance
        sqlefrce(SQL_ALL_USERS, &AgentID, SQL_ASYNCH, &sqlca);

        // If All Users Have Been Forced Off The DB2 Database Manager
        // Instance, Display A Success Message
        if (sqlca.sqlcode == SQL_RC_OK)
        {
            cout << "All users have been forced off the current DB2 ";
            cout << "Database Manager instance." << endl;
        }

        // Initialize The Stop DB2 Database Manager Options
        // Structure
        StopOptions.isprofile = 0;
        strcpy(StopOptions.profile, "");
        StopOptions.isnodenum = 0;
        StopOptions.nodenum = 0;
        StopOptions.option = SQLE_NONE;
        StopOptions.callerac = SQLE_DROP;

        // Stop The DB2 Database Manager Server Processes
        sqlepstp(&StopOptions, &sqlca);
```

```
    // If The DB2 Database Manager Server Processes Have Been
    // Stopped, Display A Success Message
    if (sqlca.sqlcode == SQL_RC_OK)
        cout << "The DB2 Database Manager has been stopped." << endl;

    // Return The SQLCA Return Code To The Calling Function
    return(sqlca.sqlcode);
}

/*—————————————————————————————————————————————*/
/* The Main Function                                            */
/*—————————————————————————————————————————————*/
int main()
{
    // Declare The Local Memory Variables
    long  rc = SQL_RC_OK;

    // Create An Instance Of The API_Class Class
    API_Class  Example;

    // Start The DB2 Database Manager Server Processes
    rc = Example.StartDB2Mgr();

    // Stop The DB2 Database Manager Server Processes
    rc = Example.StopDB2Mgr();

    // Return To The Operating System
    return(rc);
}
```

CREATE DATABASE

Purpose

The CREATE DATABASE function is used to create a new database (with an optional user-defined collating sequence), its three initial table spaces, its system tables, and its recovery log file.

Syntax

```
SQL_API_RC SQL_API_FN sqlecrea (char                       *DBName,
                                char                       *LocalDBAlias,
                                char                       *Path,
                                struct sqledbdesc          *DBDescriptor,
                                struct sqledbcountryinfo   *CountryInfo,
                                char                       Reserved1,
                                void                       *Reserved2,
                                struct sqlca               *SQLCA);
```

Parameters

DBName   A pointer to a location in memory where the name of the database to be created is stored.

LocalDBAlias   A pointer to a location in memory where the local alias of the database to be created is stored. This parameter can contain a NULL value.

Path	A pointer to a location in memory where the path name or the disk drive ID that specifies where the database is to be created is stored. This parameter can contain a NULL value.
DBDescriptor	A pointer to a *sqledbdesc* structure that contains database description information that is to be used when the database is created.
CountryInfo	A pointer to a *sqledbcountryinfo* structure that contains the locale and code set that is to be used when the database is created.
Reserved1	A character value that, at this time, is reserved for later use. For now, this parameter must always be set to '\0.'
Reserved2	A pointer that, at this time, is reserved for later use. For now, this parameter must always be set to NULL.
SQLCA	A pointer to a location in memory where a SQL Communications Area (SQLCA) data structure variable is stored. This variable will return either status information (if the function executed successfully) or error information (if the function failed) to the calling application.

Includes

```
#include <sqlenv.h>
```

Description   The CREATE DATABASE function is used to create a new database (with an optional user-defined collating sequence), its three initial table spaces, its system tables, and its recovery log file. When this function is executed, it performs the following actions:

1. Creates a database on the specified path or drive. In a multi-node system, the database is created on all nodes listed in the *db2nodes.cfg* configuration file and a **$DB2INSTANCE/NODExxxx** directory (where *xxxx* represents the local node number) is created under the default path at each node. This process ensures that all database objects associated with different nodes are stored in different directories—even if the subdirectory **$DB2INSTANCE** is shared by all nodes.

2. Creates the system catalog tables and recovery log for the new database.

3. Creates an entry in the server's local database directory on the path indicated by the value specified in the *Path* parameter (or on the default path, if no path is specified).

4. Creates an entry in the server's system database directory and sets the database alias equal to the database name (if no other alias was specified in the *LocalDBAlias* parameter).

5. Creates a second entry in the server's system database directory if a local alias was specified and if the function was issued locally; otherwise, creates an entry in the client's system database directory (if called from a remote client).

6. Creates a system or local database directory if neither exists. If a description is specified in the *DBDescriptor* parameter, the description (comment) is placed in both directories.

7. Assigns the code set and territory specified in the *CountryInfo* parameter to the database.

8. Assigns the collating sequence specified in the *DBDescriptor* parameter to the database. A flag is set in the database configuration file to indicate whether the collating sequence consists of unique weights or an identity sequence.

9. Creates the SYSIBM, SYSCAT, SYSFUN, and SYSSTAT schemas (with SYSIBM as the owner). Two node groups, IBMDEFAULTGROUP and IBMCATGROUP, are also created.

10. Binds previously defined DB2 Database Manager bind files to the database.

11. Creates the SYSCATSPACE, TEMPSPACE1, and USERSPACE1 table spaces (in a multi-node environment, the SYSCATSPACE table space is only created on the catalog node, and the TEMPSPACE1 and USERSPACE1 table spaces are created on all other nodes).

12. Performs a special system catalog step that creates extra views.

13. Grants the following database authorizations:

    – Database Administrator (DBADM) authority and CONNECT, CREATETAB, BINDADD, CREATE NOT FENCED, and IMPLICIT SCHEMA privileges to the database creator.

    – CONNECT, CREATETAB, BINDADD, and IMPLICIT SCHEMA database privileges to PUBLIC.

    – SELECT privilege on each system catalog to PUBLIC.

    – BIND and EXECUTE privilege to PUBLIC for each successfully bound utility.

Once the database has been successfully created in the database server's system database directory, it is automatically cataloged in the system database directory with a database alias set to the database name. Two special structures (*sqledbdesc* and *sqledbcountryinfo*) are used to pass characteristics about a database to the DB2 Database Manager when this function is called. The first structure, *sqledbdesc*, is defined in *sqlenv.h* as follows:

```
struct sqledbdesc
{
char        sqldbdid[8];    /* A structure identifier and       */
                            /* eye-catcher for storage dumps. It */
                            /* is a string of eight bytes that must */
                            /* be initialized with the value    */
                            /* "SQLE_DBDESC_2" (defined in sqlenv.h). */
                            /* The contents of this field are   */
                            /* validated for version control.   */
long        sqldbccp;       /* Code page value used for the     */
                            /* database comment                 */
long        sqldbcss;       /* Indicates whether the database is to */
                            /* use a collating sequence provided by */
```

```
                                    /* the system (SQL_CS_SYSTEM), a       */
                                    /* collating sequence provided by the  */
                                    /* user (SQL_CS_USER), a pre-Version 5  */
                                    /* collating sequence                   */
                                    /* (SQL_CS_COMPATIBILITY), or no collating*/
                                    /* sequence (SQL_CS_NONE).              */
        unsigned char sqldbudc[256]; /* User-defined collating sequence     */
                                    /* The nth byte of this field contains  */
                                    /* the sort weight of the code point    */
                                    /* whose underlying decimal             */
                                    /* representation is n in the code      */
                                    /* page of the database. If this field  */
                                    /* is not set to SQL_CS_USER, it is     */
                                    /* ignored.                             */
        char        sqldbcmt[31];   /* Optional database comment            */
        char        pad[1];         /* Reserved                             */
        unsigned long sqldbsgp;     /* Reserved; no longer used             */
        short       sqldbnsg;       /* The number of file segments to be    */
                                    /* created in the database. The         */
                                    /* minimum value for this field is 1    */
                                    /* and the maximum value is 256. If     */
                                    /* the value -1 is specified, this field */
                                    /* will default to 1. If the value 0 is */
                                    /* specified, a value for Version 1     */
                                    /* compatibility is provided.           */
        char        pad2[2];        /* Reserved                             */
        long        sqltsext;       /* The default extent size, in 4KB      */
                                    /* pages, for each table space in the   */
                                    /* database. The minimum value for      */
                                    /* this field is 2 and the maximum      */
                                    /* value is 256. If the value -1 is     */
                                    /* specified, this field will be set    */
                                    /* to 32.                               */
        struct SQLETSDESC *sqlcatts; /* A pointer to a table space          */
                                    /* description control block that       */
                                    /* defines the catalog table space.     */
                                    /* If NULL is specified, a catalog      */
                                    /* table space based on the values      */
                                    /* in sqltstext and sqldbnsg will be    */
                                    /* created.                             */
        struct SQLETSDESC *sqlusrts; /* A pointer to a table space          */
                                    /* description control block that       */
                                    /* defines a user table space. If       */
                                    /* NULL is specified, a user table      */
                                    /* space based on the values in         */
                                    /* sqltstext and sqldbnsg will be       */
                                    /* created.                             */
        struct SQLETSDESC *sqltmpts; /* A pointer to a table space          */
                                    /* description control block that       */
                                    /* defines a temporary table space.     */
                                    /* If NULL is specified, a temporary    */
                                    /* table space based on the values      */
                                    /* in sqltstext and sqldbnsg will be    */
                                    /* created.                             */
        };
```

This structure contains three pointers to an additional structure, *SQLETSDESC*, which holds various table space description information. The *SQLETSDESC* structure is defined in *sqlenv.h* as follows:

```
struct SQLETSDESC
{
char          sqltsdid[8];   /* A structure identifier and        */
                             /* eye-catcher for storage dumps. It */
                             /* is a string of eight bytes that must */
                             /* be initialized with the value     */
                             /* "SQLE_DBTSDESC_1" (defined in      */
                             /* sqlenv.h). The contents of         */
                             /* this field are validated for version */
                             /* control.                          */
long          sqlextnt;      /* The table space extent size, in   */
                             /* 4KB pages. If the value -1 is      */
                             /* specified, this field will be set  */
                             /* to the current value of the        */
                             /* dft_extent_sz database            */
                             /* configuration parameter.          */
long          sqlprftc;      /* The table space prefetch size, in */
                             /* 4KB pages. If the value -1 is      */
                             /* specified, this field will be set  */
                             /* be set to the current value of the */
                             /* dft_prefetch_sz database          */
                             /* configuration parameter.          */
double        sqlpovhd;      /* The table space I/O overhead, in  */
                             /* milliseconds. If the value -1 is   */
                             /* specified, this field will default to */
                             /* 24.1 ms (this value could change   */
                             /* in future releases of DB2).        */
double        sqltrfrt;      /* The table space I/O transfer rate, */
                             /* in milliseconds. If the value -1 is */
                             /* specified, this field will default to */
                             /* 0.9 ms (this value could change in */
                             /* future releases of DB2.           */
char          sqltstyp;      /* Indicates whether the table space  */
                             /* is system-managed (SQL_TBS_TYP_SMS) */
                             /* or database-managed (SQL_TBS_TYP_DMS). */
char          pad1;          /* Reserved                          */
short         sqlccnt;       /* The number of containers assigned  */
                             /* to the table space (the number of  */
                             /* elements in the containr array).   */
struct SQLETSCDESC containr[1];/* An array of SQLETSCDESC          */
                             /* structures that define table space */
                             /* containers to be assigned to the   */
                             /* tablespace.                       */
};
```

This structure contains an array of *SQLETSCDESC* structures that store table space container information. The *SQLETSCDESC* structure is defined in *sqlenv.h* as follows:

```
struct SQLETSCDESC
{
char            sqlctype;     /* Indicates whether the table space    */
                              /* container is a device                */
                              /* (SQL_TBSC_TYP_DEV), a file           */
                              /* (SQL_TBSC_TYP_FILE), or a            */
                              /* directory path                       */
                              /* (SQL_TBSC_TYP_PATH). Note: The value */
                              /* specified in this field cannot be    */
                              /* SQL_TBSC_TYP_PATH if the             */
                              /* sqltstyp field of the                */
                              /* SQLETSDESC structure is set to       */
                              /* SQL_TBS_TYP_DMS.                     */
char            pad1[3];      /* Reserved                             */
long            sqlcsize;     /* The size of the table space container,*/
                              /* specified                            */
                              /* in 4KB pages. The value in this      */
                              /* field is only valid when the sqltstyp*/
                              /* field of the SQLETSDESC structure    */
                              /* is set to  SQL_TBS_TYP_DMS.          */
short           sqlclen;      /* The length of the container name     */
char            sqlcontr[256];/* The container name                   */
char            pad2[2];      /* Reserved; 2 bytes of padding         */
                              /* between container descriptions.      */
};
```

If the database description block structure (*sqledbdesc*) is not set correctly when this function is called, an error message will be returned, and the database will not be created.

The second special structure used by this function, *sqledbcountryinfo*, is defined in *sqlenv.h* as follows:

```
struct sqledbcountryinfo
{
char      sqldbcodeset[10]; /* The code set that will be used by     */
                            /* the database                          */
char      sqldblocale[6];   /* The database territory                */
};
```

If this structure is not set correctly, or if no code set or territory values are specified, the locale of the application making the CREATE DATABASE function call will be used to determine the code set and territory values to use. For a list of valid locale and code set values, refer to the GET ROW PARTITIONING NUMBER function in Chapter 12.

Comments

■ If one or more of the previously defined Database Manager bind files are not successfully bound to the new database, this function will return a warning in the *sqlca* data structure variable (referenced by the *SQLCA* parameter), along with information about the bind operations that failed. If a bind operation fails, you can take corrective action by manually binding the bind file that failed to the new database after it is created. The failure to bind one or more predefined bind files does not prevent the database from being created.

■ When users have Database Administrator (DBADM) authority for a database, they can grant authorizations to (and revoke authorizations from) other users or the PUBLIC group. Another user with either System Administrator (SYSADM) authority or Database Administrator (DBADM) authority cannot revoke DBADM authority from the database creator.

■ This function will fail if the application calling it is connected to a database.

■ After a database is created, all character comparisons performed in that database use the collating sequence specified. This sequence affects the structure of indexes, as well as the results of queries. The following user-defined collating sequences are available in the C and C++ language header files:

sqle819a   If the code page of the database is 819 (ISO Latin/1), this sequence will sort according to the host CCSID 500 (EBCDIC International).

sqle819b   If the code page of the database is 819 (ISO Latin/1), this sequence will sort according to the host CCSID 037 (EBCDIC U.S. English).

sqle850a   If the code page of the database is 850 (ASCII Latin/1), this sequence will sort according to the host CCSID 500 (EBCDIC International).

sqle850b   If the code page of the database is 850 (ASCII Latin/1), this sequence will sort according to the host CCSID 037 (EBCDIC U.S. English).

sqle932a   If the code page of the database is 932 (ASCII Japanese), this sequence will sort according to the host CCSID 5035 (EBCDIC Japanese).

sqle932b   If the code page of the database is 932 (ASCII Japanese), this sequence will sort according to the host CCSID 5026 (EBCDIC Japanese).

■ You must specify a collating sequence when calling this function; this sequence cannot be changed once the database is created.

■ In a multi-node environment, this function affects all nodes that are listed in the *db2nodes.cfg* configuration file. The server node that this function is called on becomes the catalog node for the new database.

■ In multi-node environments, databases should not be created in NFS-mounted directories.

Connection   This function can only be called if no connection to a database exists. In order to

Requirements create a database at another node, you must first attach to that node; if necessary, a temporary database connection is established by this function while it executes.

Authorization Only users with either System Administrator (SYSADM) authority or System Control (SYSCTRL) authority can execute this function call.

See Also BIND, CATALOG DATABASE, DROP DATABASE

Example The following C++ program illustrates how to use the CREATE DATABASE function to create a new database and how to use the DROP DATABASE function to delete the database:

```cpp
/*-------------------------------------------------------------*/
/* NAME:      CH6EX4.CPP                                       */
/* PURPOSE: Illustrate How To Use The Following DB2 API Functions */
/*          In A C++ Program:                                  */
/*                                                             */
/*                CREATE DATABASE                              */
/*                DROP DATABASE                                */
/*                                                             */
/*-------------------------------------------------------------*/

// Include The Appropriate Header Files
#include <windows.h>
#include <iostream.h>
#include <sqlenv.h>
#include <sqlca.h>

// Define The API_Class Class
class API_Class
{
    // Attributes
    public:
        struct sqlca   sqlca;

    // Operations
    public:
        long CreateDB();
        long DropDB();
};

// Define The CreateDB() Member Function
long API_Class::CreateDB()
{
    // Declare The Local Memory Variables
    char              DBName[40];
    char              DBAlias[40];
    struct sqledbdesc    DBDescriptor;

    // Initialize The Local Memory Variables
    strcpy(DBName, "TEST_DB");
    strcpy(DBAlias, "TEST_DB");
```

```cpp
    // Initialize The Database Descriptor Variable
    strcpy(DBDescriptor.sqldbdid, SQLE_DBDESC_2);
    DBDescriptor.sqldbccp = 450;
    DBDescriptor.sqldbcss = SQL_CS_SYSTEM;
    DBDescriptor.sqldbudc[0] = 0;
    strcpy(DBDescriptor.sqldbcmt, "Test Database");
    DBDescriptor.pad[0] = 0;
    DBDescriptor.sqldbsgp = 0;
    DBDescriptor.sqldbnsg = -1;
    strcpy(DBDescriptor.pad2, " ");
    DBDescriptor.sqltsext = -1;
    DBDescriptor.sqlcatts = NULL;
    DBDescriptor.sqlusrts = NULL;
    DBDescriptor.sqltmpts = NULL;

    // Create A New Database
    sqlecrea(DBName, DBAlias, NULL, &DBDescriptor, NULL, '\0',
        NULL, &sqlca);

    // If The Database Was Created, Display A Success Message
    if (sqlca.sqlcode == SQL_RC_OK)
    {
        cout << "The database " << DBName;
        cout << " has been created." << endl;
    }

    // Return The SQLCA Return Code To The Calling Function
    return(sqlca.sqlcode);
}

// Define The DropDB() Member Function
long API_Class::DropDB()
{
    // Declare The Local Memory Variables
    char  DBAlias[40];

    // Initialize The Local Memory Variables
    strcpy(DBAlias, "TEST_DB");

    // Drop The Specified Database
    sqledrpd(DBAlias, &sqlca);

    // If The Database Was Dropped, Display A Success Message
    if (sqlca.sqlcode == SQL_RC_OK)
    {
        cout << "The database " << DBAlias;
        cout << " has been deleted." << endl;
    }

    // Return The SQLCA Return Code To The Calling Function
    return(sqlca.sqlcode);
}
```

```
/*————————————————————————————————————*/
/* The Main Function                                   */
/*————————————————————————————————————*/
int main()
{
    // Declare The Local Memory Variables
    long  rc = SQL_RC_OK;

    // Create An Instance Of The API_Class Class
    API_Class  Example;

    // Create A New Database
    rc = Example.CreateDB();

    // Drop The New Database
    rc = Example.DropDB();

    // Return To The Operating System
    return(rc);
}
```

■ ■ DROP DATABASE

Purpose   The DROP DATABASE function is used to uncatalog and delete the contents of a database, along with all files associated with the database.

Syntax
```
SQL_API_RC SQL_API_FN sqledrpd (char          *DBAlias,
                                struct sqlca  *SQLCA);
```

Parameters   *DBAlias*   A pointer to a location in memory where the alias of the database to be dropped is stored.

SQLCA   A pointer to a location in memory where a SQL Communications Area (SQLCA) data structure variable is stored. This variable returns either status information (if the function executed successfully) or error information (if the function failed) to the calling application.

Includes   `#include <sqlenv.h>`

Description   The DROP DATABASE function is used to uncatalog and delete the contents of a database, along with all log files associated with the database (and the database subdirectory). A database must be cataloged in the system database directory before it can be dropped. When the database is dropped, only the specified database alias is removed from the database directory. If other aliases with the same database name exist, their entries are not affected. If the database being dropped is the last entry in the local database directory, the local database directory is automatically deleted.

Comments

- Because this function deletes all user data and database log files, if you need the log files for a roll-forward recovery operation (after a database restore operation), save them before calling this function.

- The database to be dropped must not be in use (i.e., no application can be connected to the database) when this function is called. If necessary, the FORCE APPLICATION function can be used to disconnect all applications connected to the DB2 Database Manager instance that is controlling access to the specified database.

- If this function call is called from a remote client (or from a different instance on the same workstation), the alias specified will be removed from the client's system database directory, and the corresponding database name will be removed from the server's system database directory.

- When this function executes, it automatically unlinks any files that are linked through DATALINK columns. Because the unlink operation is performed asynchronously on the DB2 File Manager, its effects may not be seen immediately, and the unlinked files may be temporally unavailable for other operations.

- When this function is called, all DB2 File Managers that are configured to the specified database must be available.

Connection Requirements   This function can only be called if a connection to a DB2 Database Manager instance exists. It is not necessary to call the ATTACH function before dropping a remote database; however, if the database is cataloged as remote, an attachment to the DB2 Database Manager instance at the remote node will automatically be established for the duration of the function call.

Authorization   Only users with either System Administrator (SYSADM) authority or System Control (SYSCTRL) authority are allowed to execute this function call.

See Also   CREATE DATABASE, CATALOG DATABASE, UNCATALOG DATABASE

Example   See the example provided for the CREATE DATABASE function on page 157.

 # ACTIVATE DATABASE

Purpose   The ACTIVATE DATABASE function is used to start up all necessary database services so that a specific database is available for connection and use by any application.

Syntax
```
SQL_API_RC SQL_API_FN sqle_activate_db    (char        *DBAlias,
                                            char        *UserID,
                                            char        *Password,
                                            void        *Reserved,
                                            struct sqlca *SQLCA);
```

Parameters	*DBAlias*	A pointer to a location in memory where the alias of the database to be activated is stored.
	UserID	A pointer to a location in memory where the authorization name (user ID) of the user starting the database is stored. This parameter can contain a NULL value.
	Password	A pointer to a location in memory where the password for the authorization name specified is stored. This parameter can contain a NULL value unless an authorization name is specified in the *UserID* parameter.
	Reserved	A pointer that, at this time, is reserved for later use. For now, this parameter must always be set to NULL.
	SQLCA	A pointer to a location in memory where a SQL Communications Area (SQLCA) data structure variable is stored. This structure returns either status information (if the function executed successfully) or error information (if the function failed) to the calling application.

Includes   `#include <sqlenv.h>`

Description   The ACTIVATE DATABASE function is used to start up all necessary database services so that a specific database is available for connection and use by any application. If a database has not been started and a CONNECT SQL statement (or an implicit connect) is encountered in an application, that application must wait while the DB2 Database Manager starts and initializes the database. However, once the database has been started, other applications can simply connect to and use it. By using the ACTIVATE DATABASE function, a database administrator can start up selected databases in advance and eliminate the initialization overhead that would normally be incurred by the first application that established a connection.

Comments
- Databases that are started by this function can only be shut down by the DEACTIVATE DATABASE function or by the STOP DATABASE MANAGER function.
- If a database was started by a CONNECT SQL statement and was later activated by this function, the DEACTIVATE function must be used to shut it down.
- If this function is used to start a database that needs to be restarted, the database will either be restarted automatically or the RESTART DATABASE function will have to be executed before this function can be executed. The *autorestart* parameter of the database configuration file determines whether or not the database will be restarted automatically.
- This function activates the specified database on all nodes within the system. If one or more of these nodes encounters an error during activation of the database, a warning is returned (unless the error occurs on the coordinator node or the catalog node, in which case an error is returned). If a warning is returned, the database will remain active on all nodes where an error was not encountered.

Connection Requirements   This function can only be called when no database connection exists.

Authorization   Only users with either System Administrator (SYSADM) authority, System Control (SQLCTRL) authority, or System Maintenance (SYSMAINT) authority are allowed to execute this function call.

See Also   DEACTIVATE DATABASE

Example   The following C++ program illustrates how to use the ACTIVATE DATABASE function to activate the SAMPLE database:

```
/*─────────────────────────────────────────────────────────*/
/* NAME:    CH6EX5.CPP                                       */
/* PURPOSE: Illustrate How To Use The Following DB2 API Functions */
/*          In A C++ Program:                                */
/*                                                           */
/*              ACTIVATE DATABASE                            */
/*              DEACTIVATE DATABASE                          */
/*                                                           */
/*─────────────────────────────────────────────────────────*/

// Include The Appropriate Header Files
#include <windows.h>
#include <iostream.h>
#include <sqlenv.h>
#include <sqlca.h>

// Define The API_Class Class
class API_Class
{
    // Attributes
    public:
        struct sqlca  sqlca;

    // Operations
    public:
        long ActivateDB(char *DBAlias);
        long DeactivateDB(char *DBAlias);
};

// Define The ActivateDB() Member Function
long API_Class::ActivateDB(char *DBAlias)
{
    // Activate The Specified Database
    sqle_activate_db(DBAlias, "userID", "password", NULL, &sqlca);

    // If The Database Was Activated, Display A Success Message
    if (sqlca.sqlcode == SQL_RC_OK)
    {
        cout << "The database " << DBAlias;
        cout << " has been activated." << endl;
    }

    // Return The SQLCA Return Code To The Calling Function
    return(sqlca.sqlcode);
}
```

```
            // Define The DeactivateDB() Member Function
            long API_Class::DeactivateDB(char *DBAlias)
            {
                // Deactivate The Specified Database
                sqle_deactivate_db(DBAlias, "userID", "password", NULL, &sqlca);

                // If The Database Was Deactivated, Display A Success Message
                if (sqlca.sqlcode == SQL_RC_OK)
                {
                    cout << "The database " << DBAlias;
                    cout << " has been deactivated." << endl;
                }

                // Return The SQLCA Return Code To The Calling Function
                return(sqlca.sqlcode);
            }


            /*─────────────────────────────────────────────────────────*/
            /* The Main Function                                        */
            /*─────────────────────────────────────────────────────────*/
            int main()
            {
                // Declare The Local Memory Variables
                long  rc = SQL_RC_OK;
                char  DBAlias[40] = "SAMPLE";

                // Create An Instance Of The API_Class Class
                API_Class  Example;

                // Activate The DB2 SAMPLE Database
                rc = Example.ActivateDB(DBAlias);

                // Deactivate The DB2 SAMPLE Database
                rc = Example.DeactivateDB(DBAlias);

                // Return To The Operating System
                return(rc);
            }
```

■ ■ DEACTIVATE DATABASE

Purpose   The DEACTIVATE DATABASE function is used to shut down all necessary database services so that a specific database is no longer available for connection and use by an application.

Syntax   SQL_API_RC SQL_API_FN   sqle_deactivate_db (char   *DBAlias,
                                                          char   *UserID,
                                                          char   *Password,
                                                          void   *Reserved,
                                                          struct sqlca *SQLCA);

Parameters	*DBAlias*	A pointer to a location in memory where the alias of the database to deactivated is stored.
	UserID	A pointer to a location in memory where the authorization name (user ID) of the user stopping the database is stored. This parameter can contain a NULL value.
	Password	A pointer to a location in memory where the password for the authorization name specified is stored. This parameter can contain a NULL value, unless an authorization name is specified in the *UserID* parameter.
	Reserved	A pointer that, at this time, is reserved for later use. For now, this parameter must always be set to NULL.
	SQLCA	A pointer to a location in memory where a SQL Communications Area (SQLCA) data structure variable is stored. This structure returns either status information (if the function executed successfully) or error information (if the function failed) to the calling application.

Includes   `#include <sqlenv.h>`

Description   The DEACTIVATE DATABASE function is used to shut down all necessary database services so that a specific database is no longer available for connection and use by an application.

Comments
- ■ Databases that are started by the ACTIVATE DATABASE function can only be shut down by this function or by the STOP DATABASE MANAGER function.
- ■ If a database was started by a CONNECT SQL statement and was later activated by the ACTIVATE DATABASE function, this function must be used to stop it.
- ■ This function deactivates the specified database on all nodes within the system. If one or more of these nodes encounters an error during deactivation of the database, a warning is returned (unless the error occurs on the coordinator node or the catalog node, in which case an error is returned). The database will remain active on all nodes where a warning or an error occurs.

Connection Requirements   This function can only be called when no database connection exists.

Authorization   Only users with either System Administrator (SYSADM) authority, System Control (SYSCTRL) authority, or System Maintenance (SYSMAINT) authority are allowed to execute this function call.

See Also   ACTIVATE DATABASE, STOP DATABASE MANAGER

Example   See the example provided for the ACTIVATE DATABASE function on page 162.

■ ■ ATTACH

Purpose   The ATTACH function is used to specify the node at which instance-level functions (for example, CREATE DATABASE and FORCE APPLICATION) are to be executed.

Syntax

```
SQL_API_RC SQL_API_FN sqleatin (char      *NodeName,
                                char      *UserID,
                                char      *Password,
                                struct sqlca  *SQLCA);
```

Parameters   *NodeName*   A pointer to a location in memory where the name or alias of the DB2 Database Manager instance that the application is to attach to is stored. This parameter can contain a NULL value.

UserID   A pointer to a location in memory where the authorization name (user ID) of a user is stored. This name is the name under which the attachment is to be authenticated. This parameter can contain a NULL value.

Password   A pointer to a location in memory where the password for the authorization name specified is stored. This parameter can contain a NULL value.

SQLCA   A pointer to a location in memory where a SQL Communications Area (SQLCA) data structure variable is stored. This variable returns either status information (if the function executed successfully) or error information (if the function failed) to the calling application.

Includes   `#include <sqlenv.h>`

Description   The ATTACH function is used to specify the node at which instance-level API functions (for example, CREATE DATABASE and FORCE APPLICATION) are to be executed. This node might be the current DB2 Database Manager instance (as defined by the value of the DB2INSTANCE environment variable), another DB2 Database Manager instance on the same workstation, or a DB2 Database Manager instance on a remote workstation. When called, this function establishes a logical instance attachment to the specified node and starts a physical communications connection to the node if one does not already exist.

Comments   ■ If a logical instance attachment to a node is established when this function is called, the *sqlerrmc* field of the *sqlca* data structure variable (referenced by the *SQLCA* parameter) will contain nine tokens separated by the hexadecimal value **0xFF** (similar to the tokens returned when a CONNECT SQL statement is successful). These tokens will contain the following information:

   Token 1   The country code of the application server
   Token 2   The code page of the application server
   Token 3   The authorization ID

Token 4   The node name, as specified with the **ATTACH** function

Token 5   The identity and the platform type of the database server

Token 6   The agent ID of the agent that was started at the database server

Token 7   The agent index

Token 8   The node number of the server (always zero)

Token 9   The number of partitions on the server (if the server is a partitioned database server)

■ If the node name specified in the *NodeName* parameter is a zero-length string or the NULL value, information about the current state of attachment will be returned in the *sqlerrmc* field of the *sqlca* data structure variable (as previously outlined). If no attachment exists, an error will be returned.

■ The alias name specified in the *NodeName* parameter must have a matching entry in the local node directory. The only exception to this rule is the local DB2 Database Manager instance (as specified by the **DB2INSTANCE** environment variable), which can be specified as the object of an **ATTACH** function call but cannot be used as a node name in the node directory. A node name in the node directory can be regarded as an alias for a DB2 Database Manager instance.

■ If this function is never executed, all instance-level API functions are executed against the current DB2 Database Manager instance (which is specified by the **DB2INSTANCE** environment variable).

■ Certain functions (for example, **START DATABASE MANAGER**, **STOP DATABASE MANAGER**, and all directory services functions) are never executed remotely.

■ If an attachment already exists when this function is called with a node name specified, the current attachment will be dropped, and an attempt to attach to the new node will be made. If the attempt to attach to a new node fails, the application will be left in an "Unattached" state.

■ Where the *User ID/Password* pair is authenticated depends on the value of the *authentication* parameter in the Database Manager configuration file, located on the node to which the application is attempting to attach. If this configuration parameter contains the value **CLIENT**, the *User ID/Password* pair will be authenticated at the client machine from which the **ATTACH** function call is issued. If this configuration parameter contains the value **SERVER**, the *User ID/Password* pair will be authenticated at the node that the application is attempting to attach to. If a *User ID/Password* pair is not provided, the user ID associated with the current application process will be used for authentication.

Connection Requirements   This function establishes a DB2 Database Manager instance attachment (and possibly a physical database connection) when it is executed.

Authorization   No authorization is required to execute this function call.

See Also   ATTACH AND CHANGE PASSWORD, DETACH

Example   The following C++ program illustrates how to use the ATTACH function to obtain information about the current DB2 Database Manager instance attachment:

```
/*─────────────────────────────────────────────────*/
/* NAME:    CH6EX6.CPP                              */
/* PURPOSE: Illustrate How To Use The Following DB2 API Functions */
/*          In A C++ Program:                       */
/*                                                  */
/*                  ATTACH                          */
/*                  DETACH                          */
/*                                                  */
/*─────────────────────────────────────────────────*/

// Include The Appropriate Header Files
#include <windows.h>
#include <iostream.h>
#include <sqlenv.h>
#include <sqlca.h>

// Define The API_Class Class
class API_Class
{
    // Attributes
    public:
        struct sqlca   sqlca;

    // Operations
    public:
        long GetInstanceInfo();
};

// Define The GetInstanceInfo() Member Function
long API_Class::GetInstanceInfo()
{
    // Declare The Local Memory Variables
    int    Separator = 0xFF;
    int    Length;
    char   InfoString[71];
    char   *Buffer;
    char   Results[9][71];

    // Attach To The Default DB2 Database Manager Instance
    sqleatin("DB2", "userID", "password", &sqlca);

    // If Attached, Retrieve Information About The Current Attachment
    // And Parse It
    if (sqlca.sqlcode == SQL_RC_OK)
    {
        strncpy(InfoString, sqlca.sqlerrmc, 70);
        InfoString[69] = 0;
        Length = strlen(InfoString);
        Buffer = strrchr(InfoString, Separator);
        InfoString[Length - strlen(Buffer)] = '\0';
```

```
        for (int i = 8; i >= 0; i--)
        {
            Length = strlen(InfoString);
            Buffer = strrchr(InfoString, Separator);
            if (Buffer != NULL)
            {
                strcpy(Results[i], Buffer + 1);
                InfoString[Length - strlen(Buffer)] = '\0';
            }
            else
                strcpy(Results[i], InfoString);
        }

        // Display The Parsed Information
        cout << "Current Attachment Settings :" << endl << endl;
        cout << "Country Code              : " << Results[0] << endl;
        cout << "Server Code Page          : " << Results[1] << endl;
        cout << "Authorization ID          : " << Results[2] << endl;
        cout << "Node Name                 : " << Results[3] << endl;
        cout << "Server Platform           : " << Results[4] << endl;
        cout << "Agent ID                  : " << Results[5] << endl;
        cout << "Agent Index               : " << Results[6] << endl;
        cout << "Node Number               : " << Results[7] << endl;
        cout << "Number Of Partitions      : " << Results[8] << endl;

        // Detach From The Default DB2 Database Manager Instance
        sqledtin(&sqlca);
    }

    // Return The SQLCA Return Code To The Calling Function
    return(sqlca.sqlcode);
}

/*-----------------------------------------------------------------*/
/* The Main Function                                               */
/*-----------------------------------------------------------------*/
int main()
{
    // Declare The Local Memory Variables
    long   rc = SQL_RC_OK;

    // Create An Instance Of The API_Class Class
    API_Class  Example;

    // Attach To A DB2 Database Manager Instance And Obtain
    // Information About It
    rc = Example.GetInstanceInfo();

    // Return To The Operating System
    return(rc);
}
```

■ ■ ATTACH AND CHANGE PASSWORD

Purpose   The ATTACH AND CHANGE PASSWORD function is used to specify the node at which instance-level API functions (for example, CREATE DATABASE and FORCE APPLICATION) are to be executed and to change the user password for the instance being attached.

Syntax
```
SQL_API_RC SQL_API_FN sqleatcp(char          *NodeName,
                               char          *UserID,
                               char          *Password,
                               char          *NewPassword,
                               struct sqlca  *SQLCA);
```

Parameters *NodeName*   A pointer to a location in memory where the name or alias of the DB2 Database Manager instance that the application is to attach to is stored. This parameter can contain a NULL value.

UserID   A pointer to a location in memory where the authorization name (user ID) of a user is stored. This name is the name under which the attachment is to be authenticated. This parameter can contain a NULL value.

Password   A pointer to a location in memory where the password for the authorization name specified is stored. This parameter can contain a NULL value, unless an authorization name is specified in the *UserID* parameter.

NewPassword A pointer to a location in memory where the new password for the authorization name specified is stored. If this parameter contains a NULL value, the password for the authorization name specified in the *UserID* parameter remains unchanged.

SQLCA   A pointer to a location in memory where a SQL Communications Area (SQLCA) data structure variable is stored. This structure returns either status information (if the function executed successfully) or error information (if the function failed) to the calling application.

Includes   `#include <sqlenv.h>`

Description The ATTACH AND CHANGE PASSWORD function is used to specify the node at which instance-level API functions (for example, CREATE DATABASE and FORCE APPLICATION) are to be executed and to change the user password for the instance being attached. The node specified may be the current DB2 Database Manager instance (as defined by the value of the DB2INSTANCE environment variable), another DB2 Database Manager instance on the same workstation, or a DB2 Database Manager instance on a remote workstation. When called, this function establishes a logical instance attachment to the node specified and starts a physical communications connection to the node if one does not already exist.

Comments   ■ If a logical instance attachment to a node is established when this function is called, the *sqlerrmc* field of the *sqlca* data structure variable (referenced by the *SQLCA* parameter) will contain nine tokens separated by the hexadecimal value **0xFF** (similar to the tokens returned when a CONNECT SQL statement is successful). These tokens will contain the following information:

Token 1   The country code of the application server

Token 2   The code page of the application server

Token 3   The authorization ID

Token 4   The node name, as specified with the ATTACH AND CHANGE PASSWORD function

Token 5   The identity and the platform type of the database server

Token 6   The agent ID of the agent that was started at the database server

Token 7   The agent index

Token 8   The node number of the server (always zero)

Token 9   The number of partitions on the server (if the server is a partitioned database server)

■ If the node name specified in the *NodeName* parameter is a zero-length string or the NULL value, information about the current state of attachment will be returned in the *sqlerrmc* field of the *sqlca* data structure variable (as previously outlined). If no attachment exists, an error will be returned.

■ The alias name specified in the *NodeName* parameter must have a matching entry in the local node directory. The only exception to this is the local DB2 Database Manager instance (as specified by the DB2INSTANCE environment variable), which can be specified as the object of an ATTACH AND CHANGE PASSWORD function call but cannot be used as a node name in the node directory. A node name in the node directory can be regarded as an alias for a DB2 Database Manager instance.

■ If this function is never executed, all instance-level API functions are executed against the current DB2 Database Manager instance (which is specified by the DB2INSTANCE environment variable).

■ Certain functions (for example, START DATABASE MANAGER, STOP DATABASE MANAGER, and all directory services functions) are never executed remotely.

■ If an attachment already exists when this function is called with a node name specified, the current attachment will be dropped, and an attempt to attach to the new node will be made. If the attempt to attach to a new node fails, the application is left in an "Unattached" state.

■ Where the *UserID/Password* pair is authenticated depends on the value of the *authentication* parameter in the Database Manager configuration file, located on the node to which the application is attempting to attach. If this configuration parameter contains the value CLIENT, the *UserID/Password* pair is authenticated at the client machine from which the ATTACH AND CHANGE PASSWORD function call is issued. If this configuration parameter contains the value SERVER, the *UserID/*

Password pair is authenticated at the node to which the application is attempting to attach. If a *UserID / Password* pair is not provided, the user ID associated with the current application process will be used for authentication.

Connection Requirements   This function establishes a DB2 Database Manager instance attachment (and possibly a physical database connection) when it is executed.

Authorization   No authorization is required to execute this function call.

See Also   ATTACH, DETACH

Example   The following C++ program illustrates how the ATTACH AND CHANGE PASSWORD function is used to attach to, change the password at, and obtain information about a DB2 Database Manager instance:

```
/*------------------------------------------------------------*/
/* NAME:      CH6EX7.CPP                                      */
/* PURPOSE: Illustrate How To Use The Following DB2 API Functions */
/*          In A C++ Program:                                 */
/*                                                            */
/*              ATTACH AND CHANGE PASSWORD                    */
/*                                                            */
/* OTHER DB2 APIs SHOWN:                                      */
/*          DETACH                                            */
/*                                                            */
/*------------------------------------------------------------*/

// Include The Appropriate Header Files
#include <windows.h>
#include <iostream.h>
#include <sqlenv.h>
#include <sqlca.h>

// Define The API_Class Class
class API_Class
{
    // Attributes
    public:
        struct sqlca  sqlca;

    // Operations
    public:
        long GetInstanceInfo();
};

// Define The GetInstanceInfo() Member Function
long API_Class::GetInstanceInfo()
{
    // Declare The Local Memory Variables
    int    Separator = 0xFF;
    int    Length;
    char   InfoString[71];
    char   *Buffer;
    char   Results[9][71];
```

```cpp
// Attach To The Default DB2 Database Manager Instance
sqleatcp("DB2", "userID", "password", "newpass", &sqlca);

// If Attached, Retrieve Information About The Current Attachment
// And Parse It
if (sqlca.sqlcode == SQL_RC_OK)
{
    strncpy(InfoString, sqlca.sqlerrmc, 70);
    InfoString[69] = 0;
    Length = strlen(InfoString);
    Buffer = strrchr(InfoString, Separator);                /
    InfoString[Length - strlen(Buffer)] = '\0';
    for (int i = 8; i >= 0; i--)
    {
        Length = strlen(InfoString);
        Buffer = strrchr(InfoString, Separator);
        if (Buffer != NULL)
        {
            strcpy(Results[i], Buffer + 1);
            InfoString[Length - strlen(Buffer)] = '\0';
        }
        else
            strcpy(Results[i], InfoString);
    }

    // Display The Parsed Information
    cout << "Current Attachment Settings :" << endl << endl;
    cout << "Country Code              : " << Results[0] << endl;
    cout << "Server Code Page          : " << Results[1] << endl;
    cout << "Authorization ID          : " << Results[2] << endl;
    cout << "Node Name                 : " << Results[3] << endl;
    cout << "Server Platform           : " << Results[4] << endl;
    cout << "Agent ID                  : " << Results[5] << endl;
    cout << "Agent Index               : " << Results[6] << endl;
    cout << "Node Number               : " << Results[7] << endl;
    cout << "Number Of Partitions      : " << Results[8] << endl;

    // Detach From The Default DB2 Database Manager Instance
    sqledtin(&sqlca);
}

// Return The SQLCA Return Code To The Calling Function
return(sqlca.sqlcode);
}

/*------------------------------------------------------------*/
/* The Main Function                                          */
/*------------------------------------------------------------*/
int main()
{
```

```
        // Declare The Local Memory Variables
        long  rc = SQL_RC_OK;

        // Create An Instance Of The API_Class Class
        API_Class  Example;

        // Attach To A DB2 Database Manager Instance And Obtain
        // Information About It
        rc = Example.GetInstanceInfo();

        // Return To The Operating System
        return(rc);
    }
```

■ ■ DETACH

Purpose   The DETACH function is used to remove a logical DB2 Database Manager instance attachment and to terminate the physical communication connection if there are no other logical connections using the instance attachment being removed.

Syntax   SQL_API_RC SQL_API_FN sqledtin (struct sqlca *SQLCA);

Parameters   *SQLCA*   A pointer to a location in memory where a SQL Communications Area (SQLCA) data structure variable is stored. This variable returns either status information (if the function executed successfully) or error information (if the function failed) to the calling application.

Includes   #include <sqlenv.h>

Description   The DETACH function is used to remove a logical DB2 Database Manager instance attachment. If there are no other logical connections using the DB2 Database Manager instance attachment when the logical instance is removed, the physical communication connection will also be terminated.

Connection   This function can be called at any time; a connection to a DB2 Database Manager
Requirements instance or to a DB2 database does not have to be established first. When this function executes, an existing DB2 Database Manager instance attachment (and possibly a physical communications connection) will be removed.

Authorization No authorization is required to execute this function call.

See Also   ATTACH, ATTACH AND CHANGE PASSWORD

Example   See the example provided for the ATTACH function on page 167.

 # QUERY CLIENT

Purpose   The QUERY CLIENT function is used to retrieve the current connection setting values for an application process.

Syntax

```
SQL_API_RC SQL_API_FN sqleqryc(struct sqle_conn_setting *ConnectionSettings,
                               unsigned short            NumValues,
                               struct sqlca              *SQLCA);
```

Parameters   *ConnectionSettings*   A pointer to a *sqle_conn_setting* structure or an array of *sqle_conn_setting* structures where this function is to store the connection setting information retrieved.

NumValues   An integer value that specifies the number of connection information values to retrieve. The value for this parameter can be any number between 0 and 7.

SQLCA   A pointer to a location in memory where a SQL Communications Area data structure variable is stored. This variable returns either status information (if the function executed successfully) or error information (if the function failed) to the calling application.

Includes   #include <sqlenv.h>

Description   The QUERY CLIENT function is used to retrieve the current connection setting values for an application process. The information retrieved by this function is stored in a special structure (*sqle_conn_setting*) or an array of *sqle_conn_setting* structures that contain one or more connection options and their corresponding values. The *sqle_conn_setting* structure is defined in *sqlenv.h* as follows:

```
struct sqle_conn_setting
{
unsigned short          type;           /* Connection setting type */
unsigned short          value;          /* Connection setting value */
};
```

Table 6–2 lists each value that can be specified for the *type* field of the *sqle_conn_setting* structure, along with a description of each value that can be retrieved/specified for the corresponding *value* field of this structure.

Before this function can be executed, an *sqle_conn_setting* connection setting structure or an array of *sqle_conn_setting* connection setting structures must be allocated, and the *type* field of each structure used must be set to one of the seven possible connection setting options listed in Table 6–2. After this function has executed, the *value* field of each connection setting structure used will contain the current value (setting) of the option specified.

Comments
- The connection settings for an application can be retrieved at any time (as long as the application is executing).
- If this function is executed before the SET CLIENT function is called, the *sqle_conn_setting* structure will contain the values of the precompile options used (if a SQL statement has been processed); otherwise, it will contain the default values for the precompile options.

Connection Requirements
This function can be called at any time. A connection to a DB2 Database Manager instance or to a DB2 database does not have to be established first.

Authorization
No authorization is required to execute this function call.

See Also
SET CLIENT

Example
The following C++ program illustrates how to use the QUERY CLIENT function to obtain the current values of an application's connection settings:

```
/*————————————————————————————————————————————————*/
/* NAME:     CH6EX8.CPP                               */
/* PURPOSE: Illustrate How To Use The Following DB2 API Function */
/*          In A C++ Program:                         */
/*                                                    */
/*               QUERY CLIENT                         */
/*               SET CLIENT                           */
/*                                                    */
/*————————————————————————————————————————————————*/

// Include The Appropriate Header Files
#include <windows.h>
#include <iostream.h>
#include <sqlenv.h>
#include <sqlca.h>

// Define The API_Class Class
class API_Class
{
    // Attributes
    public:
        struct sqlca   sqlca;

    // Operations
```

Table 6–2 *Connection Settings*

Connection Setting Type	Connection Setting Value	Description
SQL_CONNECT_TYPE	SQL_CONNECT_1	Type 1 CONNECTs are supported. This characteristic enforces the single database per transaction semantics of older releases. Type 1 CONNECTs are also known as *Rules for Remote Unit of Work* (RUOW) connects.
	SQL_CONNECT_2	Type 2 CONNECTs (multiple databases per transaction semantics of RUOW) are supported.
SQL_RULES	SQL_RULES_DB2	Allows the CONNECT SQL statement to switch from the current connection to an established (dormant) connection
	SQL_RULES_STD	Allows the CONNECT SQL statement to only establish a new connection. The SET CONNECTION SQL statement must be used to switch from the current connection to an established (dormant) connection.
SQL_DISCONNECT	SQL_DISCONNECT_EXPL	Terminates all connections explicitly marked for release by the RELEASE SQL statement when the COMMIT SQL statement is executed.
	SQL_DISCONNECT_COND	Terminates all connections explicitly marked for release by the RELEASE SQL statement and all connections that do not contain WITHHOLD cursors when the COMMIT SQL statement is executed.
	SQL_DISCONNECT_AUTO	Terminates all connections when the COMMIT SQL statement is executed.
SQL_SYNCPOINT	SQL_SYNC_TWOPHASE	Uses two-phase commits to commit the work done by each database in multiple-database transactions. This setting requires a *Transaction Manager* (TM) to coordinate two-phase commits among databases that support this protocol.
	SQL_SYNC_ONEPHASE	Uses one-phase commits to commit the work done by each database in multiple-database transactions. Enforces single-updater, multiple-read behavior.

Table 6–2 Connection Settings (Continued)

Connection Setting Type	Connection Setting Value	Description
	SQL_SYNC_NONE	Uses one-phase commits to commit the work done by each database in multiple-database transactions but does not enforce single-updater, multiple-read behavior.
SQL_MAX_NETBIOS_CONNECTIONS	Any number between 1 and 254	Specifies the maximum number of concurrent connections that can be made in an application running on a workstation that is using the NETBIOS protocol.
SQL_DEFERRED_PREPARE_OPT	SQL_DEFERRED_PREPARE_NO	Specifies that PREPARE SQL statements are to be executed at the time they are issued.
	SQL_DEFERRED_PREPARE_YES	Specifies that the execution of PREPARE SQL statements is to be deferred until a corresponding OPEN, DESCRIBE, or EXECUTE statement is issued. A PREPARE statement will not be deferred if it contains the INTO clause (but no parameter markers).
	SQL_DEFERRED_PREPARE_ALL	Specifies that all PREPARE SQL statements (other than PREPARE INTO statements, which contain parameter markers) are to be executed at the time they are issued.
SQL_CONNECT_NODE	Any number between 0 and 999 or SQL_CONN_CATALOG_NODE	Specifies the node to which a connection is to be made. This setting overrides the value of the DB2NODE environment variable.
SQL_ATTACH_NODE	Any number between 0 and 999	Specifies the node to which an attachment is to be made. This setting overrides the value of the DB2NODE environment variable.

Adapted from IBM's *DB2 Universal Database API Reference*, Table 24, p. 388–390.

```cpp
    public:
        long QueryClient();
        long SetClient();
};

// Define The QueryClient() Member Function
long API_Class::QueryClient()
{
    // Declare The Local Memory Variables
    struct sqle_conn_setting  ConnInfo;

    // Initialize The Connection Information Structure
    ConnInfo.type = SQL_CONNECT_TYPE;

    // Obtain Information About The Current Connection
    sqleqryc(&ConnInfo, 1, &sqlca);

    // If The Connection Information Was Retrieved, Display It
    if (sqlca.sqlcode == SQL_RC_OK)
    {
        cout << "Current Connection Setting:" << endl << endl;
        cout << "Connection Type   : ";
        if (ConnInfo.value == SQL_CONNECT_1)
            cout << "Type 1" << endl << endl;
        else
            cout << "Type 2" << endl << endl;
    }

    // Return The SQLCA Return Code To The Calling Function
    return(sqlca.sqlcode);
}

// Define The SetClient() Member Function
long API_Class::SetClient()
{
    // Declare The Local Memory Variables
    struct sqle_conn_setting  ConnInfo;

    // Initialize The Connection Information Structure
    ConnInfo.type = SQL_CONNECT_TYPE;
    ConnInfo.value = SQL_CONNECT_2;

    // Set The Current Connection Type To "Type 2"
    sqlesetc(&ConnInfo, 1, &sqlca);

    // Return The SQLCA Return Code To The Calling Function
    return(sqlca.sqlcode);
}

/*-------------------------------------------------------------*/
/* The Main Function                                           */
/*-------------------------------------------------------------*/
int main()
{
```

```
// Declare The Local Memory Variables
long   rc = SQL_RC_OK;

// Create An Instance Of The API_Class Class
API_Class  Example;

// Retrieve Information About The Current Connection
// Settings
rc = Example.QueryClient();

// Set The Current Connection Type To "Type 2"
rc = Example.SetClient();

// Retrieve Information About The Current Connection Again
// To Verify That The Connection Type Has Been Changed
rc = Example.QueryClient();

// Return To The Operating System
return(rc);
}
```

SET CLIENT

Purpose   The SET CLIENT function is used to specify connection setting values for a DB2 application.

Syntax
```
SQL_API_RC SQL_API_FN sqlesetc (struct sqle_conn_setting *ConnectionSettings,
                                unsigned short            NumValues,
                                struct sqlca              *SQLCA);
```

Parameters   *ConnectionSettings*   A pointer to a *sqle_conn_setting* structure or an array of *sqle_conn_setting* structures that contain connection setting options and their corresponding values.

NumValues   An integer value that specifies the number of connection information values to set. The value for this parameter can be any number between 0 and 7.

SQLCA   A pointer to a location in memory where a SQL Communications Area (SQLCA) data structure variable is stored. This variable returns either status information (if the function executed successfully) or error information (if the function failed) to the calling application.

Includes   `#include <sqlenv.h>`

Description   The SET CLIENT function specifies connection setting values for a DB2 application.

Before this function can be executed, an array of special structures (*sqle_conn_setting* structures) must be allocated. Refer to the QUERY CLIENT function for a detailed description of this structure and for more information about the connection options available. Once an array of *sqle_conn_setting* structures has been allocated, the *type* field of each structure in this array must be set to one of seven possible connection setting options, and the corresponding value field must be set to the value desired for the specified connection option.

Once the SET CLIENT function has executed successfully, the connection settings are fixed, and the corresponding precompiler options used to precompile the application's source code modules are overridden. All connections made by subsequent transactions will use the new connection settings. You can change these new connection settings only by reexecuting the SET CLIENT function.

Comments

■ If this function is unsuccessful, the connection setting values for an application will remain unchanged.

■ The connection setting values for an application can only be changed when there are no active database connections associated with the application (i.e. before any connection is established or after a RELEASE ALL SQL statement, followed by a COMMIT SQL statement, is executed).

Connection Requirements

This function can only be called when no database connection exists.

Authorization   No authorization is required to execute this function call.

See Also   QUERY CLIENT

Example   See the example provided for the QUERY CLIENT function on page 175.

 # QUERY CLIENT INFORMATION

Purpose   The QUERY CLIENT INFORMATION function is used to retrieve client information that is associated with a specific database connection.

Syntax

```
SQL_API_RC SQL_API_FN sqleqryi(unsigned short        DBAliasLength,
                               char                  *DBAlias,
                               unsigned short        *NumValues,
                               struct sqle_client_info  *ClientInfo,
                               struct sqlca          *SQLCA);
```

Parameters   *DBAliasLength*   The length of the database alias name stored in the *DBAlias* parameter.

DBAlias   A pointer to a location in memory where the alias of the database to retrieve client information from is stored. This parameter can contain a NULL value.

NumValues	An integer value that specifies the number of client information values to retrieve. The value for this parameter can be any number between 1 and 4.
ClientInfo	A pointer to a *sqle_client_info* structure or an array of *sqle_client_info* structures where this function is to store the client information retrieved.
SQLCA	A pointer to a location in memory where an SQL Communications Area (SQLCA) data structure variable is stored. This structure returns either status information (if the function executed successfully) or error information (if the function failed) to the calling application.

Includes   `#include <sqlenv.h>`

Description   The QUERY CLIENT INFORMATION function is used to retrieve client information that is associated with a specific database connection. The information retrieved by this function is stored in a special structure (*sqle_client_info*) or an array of *sql_client_info* structures that contain one or more client information options. The *sqle_client_info* structure is defined in *sqlenv.h* as follows:

```
struct sqle_client_info
{
unsigned short    type;    /* Client information type                  */
unsigned short    length;  /* The length of the client information     */
                           /* value                                    */
char              *pValue; /* A pointer to a location in memory that   */
                           /* the client information value will either */
                           /* be written to (QUERY CLIENT INFORMATION) */
                           /* or read from (SET CLIENT INFORMATION)    */
};
```

Table 6–3 lists each value that can be specified for the *type* field of the *sqle_client_info* structure, along with a description of each value that can be retrieved/specified for the corresponding *pValue* field of this structure.

Before this function can be executed, an *sqle_client_info* client information structure or an array of *sqle_client_info* client information structures must be allocated, and the *type* field of each structure used must be set to one of the four possible client information values listed in Table 6–3. After this function has executed, the memory locations referenced by the *pValue* field of each client information structure used will contain the current value (setting) of the client information option specified.

Comments   ■ If this function is called with the *DBAlias* parameter set to NULL, client information will be retrieved for all connections (i.e., the values that were set when the SET CLIENT INFORMATION function was used to set client information for all connections).

Table 6–3   *Client Information Settings*

Connection Information Type	Data Type	Description
SQL_CLIENT_INFO_USERID	char[255][1]	Specifies the authorization (user ID) for the client. This ID is for identification purposes only; it is not used for authentication.
SQL_CLIENT_INFO_WRKSTNNAME	char[255][1]	Specifies the workstation name for the client
SQL_CLIENT_INFO_APPLNAME	char[255][1]	Specifies the application name for the client
SQL_CLIENT_INFO_ACCSTR	char[200][1]	Specifies the accounting string used by the client[2]

Adapted from IBM's *DB2 Universal Database API Reference*, Table 22, p. 386.

[1]Some servers may truncate this value.

[2]This information can also be set using the SET ACCOUNTING STRING function; however, that function does not allow the accounting string to be changed once a connection exists, whereas the SET CLIENT INFORMATION function does. Refer to Chapter 5 for information about the format of this string.

■ The client information returned by this function can be retrieved at any time.

■ If this function is used to retrieve the value of a client information option that has not been set, the *length* field of the corresponding *sqle_client_info* structure will be set to 0, and an empty, NULL-terminated string will be returned as the value.

Connection Requirements   This function can be called at any time; however, a connection to the DB2 database specified in the *DBAlias* parameter must exist if this function is used to obtain client information about a specific connection.

Authorization   No authorization is required to execute this function call.

See Also   SET CLIENT INFORMATION, QUERY CLIENT, SET CLIENT

Example   The following C++ program illustrates how to use the QUERY CLIENT INFORMATION function to obtain the current value of a client's application name:

```
/*-----------------------------------------------------------*/
/* NAME:    CH6EX9.SQC                                       */
/* PURPOSE: Illustrate How To Use The Following DB2 API Functions */
/*          In A C++ Program:                                */
/*                                                           */
/*              QUERY CLIENT INFORMATION                     */
/*              SET CLIENT INFORMATION                       */
/*                                                           */
/*-----------------------------------------------------------*/

// Include The Appropriate Header Files
#include <windows.h>
#include <iostream.h>
#include <sqlenv.h>
#include <sql.h>

// Define The API_Class Class
```

```
class API_Class
{
    // Attributes
    public:
        struct sqlca   sqlca;

    // Operations
    public:
        long QueryClientInfo();
        long SetClientInfo();
};

// Define The QueryClientInfo() Member Function
long API_Class::QueryClientInfo()
{
    // Declare The Local Memory Variables
    char                     DBAlias[8];
    struct sqle_client_info  ClientInfo;
    char                     ApplicationName[20];

    // Initialize The Local Variables
    strcpy(DBAlias, "SAMPLE");

    // Initialize The Client Information Structure
    ClientInfo.type = SQLE_CLIENT_INFO_APPLNAME;
    ClientInfo.length = 0;
    ClientInfo.pValue = ApplicationName;

    // Obtain Information About The Current Client Connection
    sqleqryi(strlen(DBAlias), DBAlias, 1, &ClientInfo, &sqlca);

    // If Information About The Current Client Connection Was
    // Retrieved, Display It
    if (sqlca.sqlcode == SQL_RC_OK)
        cout << "Application Name: " << ApplicationName << endl << endl;

    // Return The SQLCA Return Code To The Calling Function
    return(sqlca.sqlcode);
}

// Define The SetClientInfo() Member Function
long API_Class::SetClientInfo()
{
    // Declare The Local Memory Variables
    char                     DBAlias[8];
    struct sqle_client_info  ClientInfo;
    char                     ApplicationName[8];

    // Initialize The Local Variables
    strcpy(DBAlias, "SAMPLE");
    strcpy(ApplicationName, "APITest");

    // Initialize The Client Information Structure
```

```
        ClientInfo.type = SQLE_CLIENT_INFO_APPLNAME;
        ClientInfo.length = 7;
        ClientInfo.pValue = ApplicationName;

        // Set The Name Of The Client Application
        sqleseti(strlen(DBAlias), DBAlias, 1, &ClientInfo, &sqlca);

        // Return The SQLCA Return Code To The Calling Function
        return(sqlca.sqlcode);
}


/*────────────────────────────────────────────────────────────*/
/* The Main Function                                           */
/*────────────────────────────────────────────────────────────*/
int main()
{
    // Declare The Local Memory Variables
    long          rc = SQL_RC_OK;
    struct sqlca  sqlca;

    // Create An Instance Of The API_Class Class
    API_Class  Example;

    // Attempt To Connect To The SAMPLE Database
    EXEC SQL CONNECT TO SAMPLE USER userID USING password;

    // Retrieve Information About The Current Client Connection
    rc = Example.QueryClientInfo();

    // Set The Application Name For The Current Client Connection
    rc = Example.SetClientInfo();

    // Retrieve Information About The Current Client Connection
    // Again To Verify That The Application Name Has Been Set
    rc = Example.QueryClientInfo();

    // Issue A Rollback To Free All Locks
    EXEC SQL ROLLBACK;

    // Disconnect From The SAMPLE Database
    EXEC SQL DISCONNECT CURRENT;

    // Return To The Operating System
    return(rc);
}
```

SET CLIENT INFORMATION

Purpose   The SET CLIENT INFORMATION function is used to specify client information values that are associated with a specific database connection.

Syntax
```
SQL_API_RC SQL_API_FN sqleseti(unsigned short        DBAliasLength,
                               char                  *DBAlias,
                               unsigned short        *NumValues,
                               struct sqle_client_info *ClientInfo,
                               struct sqlca          *SQLCA);
```

Parameters *DBAliasLength* The length of the database alias name stored in the *DBAlias* parameter.

DBAlias A pointer to a location in memory where the alias of the database to set client information for is stored. This parameter can contain a NULL value.

NumValues An integer value that specifies the number of client information values to set. The value for this parameter can be any number between 0 and 4.

ClientInfo A pointer to a *sqle_client_info* structure or an array of *sqle_client_info* structures that contain client information options and their corresponding values.

SQLCA A pointer to a location in memory where an SQL Communications Area (SQLCA) data structure variable is stored. This structure returns either status information (if the function executed successfully) or error information (if the function failed) to the calling application.

Includes   `#include <sqlenv.h>`

Description The SET CLIENT INFORMATION function is used to specify client information values that are associated with a specific database connection. Often, in a Transaction Processing monitor or three-tier client/server environment, there is a need to obtain information about the client (not just the application server that is working on behalf of the client). By using this function, an application can pass information about the client itself to the DB2 server.

Before this function can be executed, a special structure (*sqle_client_info*), or an array of *sqle_client_info* client information structures must be allocated. Refer to the QUERY CLIENT INFORMATION function for a detailed description of this structure and for more information about the client information options available. Once one or more *sqle_client_info* structures have been allocated, the *type* field of each structure used must be set to one of the four client information options available. Also, the desired value for the option must be stored in the memory locations referenced by the *pValue* field, and the length (in bytes) of each value must be stored in the *length* field.

Comments

- This function can be used to set values prior to connecting to any database, or it can be used to set or modify values once a connection has been established.

- If this function is called with the *DBAlias* parameter set to NULL, client information will be set for all existing, as well as all future, connections.

- This function can only be used to set client information outside a transaction (i.e., either before a SQL statement is executed or after a transaction is committed or rolled back). If this function is successful, the new values will be sent to the DB server, grouped with the next SQL request sent on the specified connection.

- Client information values set for a specific connection by this function will remain in effect until the specified connection is broken. Client information values set for all connections by this function will remain in effect until the application that called this function terminates.

Connection Requirements

This function can be called at any time; however, a connection to the DB2 database specified in the *DBAlias* parameter must exist if this function is used to set client information values for a specific connection.

Authorization

No authorization is required to execute this function call.

See Also

QUERY CLIENT INFORMATION, QUERY CLIENT, SET CLIENT

Example

See the example provided for the QUERY CLIENT INFORMATION function on page 182.

7

DB2 Database Manager and Database Configuration APIs

DB2 uses an extensive array of configuration parameters to fine-tune the performance of both DB2 Database Manager and each DB2 database. This chapter is designed to introduce you to the set of DB2 API functions that are used to retrieve, modify, or reset DB2 Database Manager and DB2 database configuration parameters. The first part of this chapter provides a general overview of how configuration parameters affects application performance. Then, the DB2 Database Manager configuration file and individual DB2 database configuration files are discussed. Finally, a detailed reference section covering each DB2 API function that can be used to retrieve, modify, or reset DB2 configuration file parameters is provided.

Configuring DB2

The DB2 Database Manager uses the values stored in two sets of configuration parameters to determine how to allocate system resources (disk space and memory) for itself and for each open database. In many cases, the default values provided for the configuration parameters are sufficient to meet an application's needs. However, because the default values provided are oriented toward workstations that have relatively small amounts of memory and are dedicated database servers, you can improve overall system and application performance by changing one or more configuration parameter values.

DB2 database applications can range from modest data entry systems that contain one or two simple insert SQL statements to large data collection and management systems that contain hundreds of complex SQL queries for accessing dozens of tables within a single transaction. Different types of applications (and users) have different response time requirements and expectations. Additionally, each application's transaction processing environment contains one or more unique aspects. These differences can have a profound impact on the performance of the DB2 Database Manager, especially when the default configuration parameter values are used.

For this reason, it is strongly recommended that you fine-tune the DB2 configuration files to obtain the maximum performance from your particular operating environment. Configuration parameter values should always be modified if your database environment contains one or more of the following elements:

■ Large databases

■ Databases that normally service a large number of concurrent connections

■ One or more special applications that have high-performance requirements

■ A special hardware configuration

■ Unique query and/or transaction loads

■ Unique query and/or transaction types

DB2 Database Manager Configuration Parameters

DB2 Database Manager configuration parameter values are stored in the file *db2systm*, which is located in the *sqllib* subdirectory where DB2 was installed. This file is created along with DB2 Database Manager during the DB2 product installation process. Most of the parameter values in this file control the amount of system resources allocated to a single instance of the DB2 Database Manager. Other parameter values in this file contain information about the DB2 Database Manager itself and cannot be changed.

You can use any of the following methods to view, change, or reset the value of one or more DB2 Database Manager configuration parameters from an application program:

■ The DB2 database director

■ The **GET DATABASE MANAGER CONFIGURATION** command

■ The **GET DATABASE MANAGER CONFIGURATION** function

- The UPDATE DATABASE MANAGER CONFIGURATION command
- The UPDATE DATABASE MANAGER CONFIGURATION function
- The RESET DATABASE MANAGER CONFIGURATION command
- The RESET DATABASE MANAGER CONFIGURATION function
- The GET DATABASE MANAGER CONFIGURATION DEFAULTS function

DB2 Database Configuration Parameters

Configuration parameter values for an individual database are stored in the file *SQLDBCON*, which is located in the *SQLxxxxx* directory that is created when the database is created (*xxxxx* represents the number assigned by DB2 during the database creation process). This file is created along with the directory and other database control files whenever a new database is created. Most of the parameter values in this file control the amount of system resources that are allocated to the specified database. Other parameter values in this file contain information about the DB2 database itself and cannot be changed.

You can use any of the following methods to view, change, or reset the value of one or more DB2 database configuration parameters from an application program:

- The DB2 database director
- The GET DATABASE CONFIGURATION command
- The GET DATABASE CONFIGURATION function
- The UPDATE DATABASE CONFIGURATION command
- The UPDATE DATABASE CONFIGURATION function
- The RESET DATABASE CONFIGURATION command
- The RESET DATABASE CONFIGURATION function
- The GET DATABASE CONFIGURATION DEFAULTS function

The DB2 Database Manager and Database Configuration Functions

Table 7–1 lists the DB2 API functions that are used to retrieve, modify, or reset DB2 Database Manager and DB2 database configuration file parameters.

Each of these functions are described in detail in the remainder of this chapter.

Table 7–1   DB2 Database Manager and Database Configuration APIs

Function Name	Description
`GET DATABASE MANAGER CONFIGURATION`	Retrieves the current value of one or more DB2 Database Manager configuration file parameters.
`GET DATABASE MANAGER CONFIGURATION DEFAULTS`	Retrieves the system default value of one or more DB2 Database Manager configuration file parameters.
`UPDATE DATABASE MANAGER CONFIGURATION`	Changes the value of one or more DB2 Database Manager configuration file parameters.
`RESET DATABASE MANAGER CONFIGURATION`	Resets all DB2 Database Manager configuration file parameters to their system default values.
`GET DATABASE CONFIGURATION`	Retrieves the current value of one or more database configuration file parameters.
`GET DATABASE CONFIGURATION DEFAULTS`	Retrieves the system default value of one or more database configuration file parameters.
`UPDATE DATABASE CONFIGURATION`	Changes the value of one or more database configuration file parameters.
`RESET DATABASE CONFIGURATION`	Resets all database configuration file parameters to their system default values.

GET DATABASE MANAGER CONFIGURATION

Purpose   The GET DATABASE MANAGER CONFIGURATION function is used to retrieve the current value of one or more configuration parameters (entries) in a DB2 Database Manager configuration file.

Syntax
```
SQL_API_RC SQL_API_FN sqlfxsys (unsigned short   NumItems,
                                struct sqlfupd   *ItemList,
                                struct sqlca     *SQLCA);
```

Parameters   *NumItems*   The number of DB2 Database Manager configuration parameter values to retrieve. This value identifies the number of elements contained in the array of *sqlfupd* structures specified in the *ItemList* parameter.

ItemList   A pointer to an array of *sqlfupd* structures that specify which DB2 Database Manager configuration parameters values are to be retrieved.

SQLCA   A pointer to a location in memory where an SQL Communications Area (SQLCA) data structure variable is stored. This variable returns either status information (if the function executed successfully) or error information (if the function failed) to the calling application.

Includes   `#include <sqlutil.h>`

Description   The GET DATABASE MANAGER CONFIGURATION function is used to retrieve the current value of one or more configuration parameters (entries) in a DB2 Database Manager configuration file. DB2 Database Manager configuration parameter values are stored in a file named *db2systm*, which is located in the *sqllib* subdirectory. This file is automatically created along with the DB2 Database Manager when the DB2 Universal Database product is installed. Most of the values stored in this file control the amount of system resources that are allocated to a single instance of the DB2 Database Manager and can be modified to increase DB2's overall performance. Other parameter values in this file contain static information about the DB2 Database Manager instance itself and cannot be changed.

This function uses an array of special structures (*sqlfupd*) to retrieve the current

Table 7-2   DB2 Database Manager Configuration Parameters

Parameter Name	Description	Token	C Data Type
agent_stack_sz	Specifies the amount of memory allocated and committed by the operating system for each agent. This parameter specifies the number of pages for each agent stack on the server.	SQLF_KTN_AGENT_STACK_SZ	unsigned int

Table 7–2 DB2 Database Manager Configuration Parameters (Continued)

Parameter Name	Description	Token	C Data Type
agentpri	Specifies the execution priority assigned to DB2 Database Manager processes and threads on a particular workstation.	SQLF_KTN_AGENTPRI	int
aslheapsz	Specifies the size (in pages) of the memory shared between a local client application and a DB2 Database Manager agent.	SQLF_KTN_ASLHEAPSZ	unsigned long
audit_buf_sz	Specifies the size (in pages) of the buffer used when auditing a database.	SQLF_KTN_AUDIT_BUF_SZ	long
authentication	Specifies how and where authentication of a user takes place. A value of CLIENT indicates that all authentication takes place at the client workstation. A value of SERVER indicates that the user ID and password are sent from the client workstation to the server workstation, so authentication can take place at the server.	SQLF_KTN_AUTHENTICATION	unsigned int
backbufsz	Specifies the size (in pages) of the buffer that is used when backing up a database. This value is only used if the buffer size is not specified when the Backup utility is invoked.	SQLF_KTN_BACKBUFSZ	unsigned long
comm_bandwidth	Specifies the nominal communications bandwidth (in megabytes per second) that is used by the SQL optimizer to estimate the cost of performing certain operations between the database servers of a partitioned database.	SQLF_KTN_COMM_BANDWIDTH	float
conn_elapse	Specifies the number of seconds that a TCP/IP connection is to be established between two nodes in.	SQLF_KTN_CONN_ELAPSE	unsigned int
cpuspeed	Specifies the CPU speed (in milliseconds per instruction) that is used by the SQL optimizer to estimate the cost of performing certain operations.	SQLF_KTN_CPUSPEED	float
dft_account_str	Specifies the default accounting string that is to be used when connecting to DRDA servers.	SQLF_KTN_DFT_ACCOUNT_STR	char[25]
dft_client_adpt	Specifies the default client adapter number for the NetBIOS protocol whose server name is extracted from DCE Directory Services. This parameter is only used with the OS/2 operating system.	SQLF_KTN_DFT_CLIENT_ADPT	unsigned int

Table 7–2 DB2 Database Manager Configuration Parameters (Continued)

Parameter Name	Description	Token	C Data Type
dft_client_comm	Specifies the communication protocols that all client applications attached to a specific DB2 Database Manager instance can use for establishing remote connections.	SQLF_KTN_DFT_ CLIENT_COMM	char[31]
dft_monswitches	Specifies all default values for the snapshot monitor in a single value. You can manipulate the bits of this unsigned integer value, or you can use the individual tokens that make up this value (see the footnote for more information).	SQLF_KTN_DFT_ MONSWITCHES	unsigned int
dft_mon_bufpool	Specifies the default value of the snapshot monitor's buffer pool switch.	SQLF_KTN_DFT_MON_ BUFPOOL	unsigned int
dft_mon_lock	Specifies the default value of the snapshot monitor's lock switch.	SQLF_KTN_DFT_MON_ LOCK	unsigned int
dft_mon_sort	Specifies the default value of the snapshot monitor's sort switch.	SQLF_KTN_DFT_MON_ SORT	unsigned int
dft_mon_stmt	Specifies the default value of the snapshot monitor's statement switch.	SQLF_KTN_DFT_MON_ STMT	unsigned int
dft_mon_table	Specifies the default value of the snapshot monitor's table switch.	SQLF_KTN_DFT_MON_ TABLE	unsigned int
dft_mon_uow	Specifies the default value of the snapshot monitor's *Unit of Work* (UOW) switch.	SQLF_KTN_DFT_MON_ UOW	unsigned int
dftdbpath	Specifies the default drive or directory path to use to store new databases. If no path is specified when a database is created, the database is created in the location indicated by this parameter.	SQLF_KTN_DFTDBPATH	char[215]
diaglevel	Specifies the diagnostic error capture level used to determine the severity of diagnostic errors that get recorded in the error log file *(db2diag.log)*.	SQLF_KTN_DIAGLEVEL	unsigned int
diagpath	Specifies the fully qualified path that is to be used to locate DB2 diagnostic information.	SQLF_KTN_DIAGPATH	char[215]
dir_cache	Specifies whether directory cache support is enabled. If this parameter is set to YES, database, node, and DCS directory files are cached in memory. This process reduces connect overhead by eliminating directory file I/O and minimizing the directory searches	SQLF_KTN_DIR_CACHE	unsigned int

Table 7–2 DB2 Database Manager Configuration Parameters (Continued)

Parameter Name	Description	Token	C Data Type
	required to retrieve directory information.		
dir_obj_name	Specifies the object name that represents a DB2 Database Manager instance (or a database) in the DCE directory name space. The concatenation of this value and the *dir_path_name* value yields a global name that uniquely identifies the DB2 Database Manager instance or database in the name space governed by the directory services specified in the *dir_type* parameter.	SQLF_KTN_DIR_OBJ_ NAME	char[255]
dir_path_name	Specifies the directory path name in the DCE name space. The unique name of the DB2 Database Manager instance in the global name space is made up of this value and the value in the *dir_obj_name* parameter.	SQLF_KTN_DIR_PATH_ NAME	char[255]
dir_type	Specifies the type of directory services used (indicates whether the DB2 Database Manager instance uses the DCE global directory services).	SQLF_KTN_DIR_TYPE	unsigned int
discover	Specifies the type of discovery request that is supported on a client or server workstation. A value of SEARCH indicates that a DB2 client searches the network for DB2 databases. A value of KNOWN indicates that a DB2 client searches a specific DB2 Administration Server for DB2 databases. A value of DISABLE indicates that the client (or the server) does not support any type of discovery request.	SQLF_KTN_DISCOVER	unsigned int
discover_comm	Specifies the communications protocols that DB2 clients use to issue search discovery requests and that servers use to listen for search discovery requests. Cnly TCP/IP and NetBIOS are supported.	SQLF_KTN_DISCOVER_ COMM	char[35]
discover_inst	Specifies whether a DB2 client can discover a DB2 Database Manager instance.	SQLF_KTN_DISCOVER_ INST	unsigned int
dos_rqrioblk	Specifies the DOS requester I/O block size. This parameter controls the size of the I/O blocks allocated on both the client and the server workstations. This parameter is applicable only on	SQLF_KTN_DOS_ RQRIOBLK	unsigned int

Table 7–2 DB2 Database Manager Configuration Parameters (Continued)

Parameter Name	Description	Token	C Data Type
	DOS clients, including DOS clients running under OS/2.		
drda_heap_sz	Specifies the size, in pages, of the DRDA heap. This heap is used by the DRDA AS clause and by DB2 Connect.	SQLF_KTN_DRDA_ HEAP_SZ	unsigned int
fcm_num_anchors	Specifies the number of FCM message anchors that are to be used among the nodes of an instance to send messages among themselves.	SQLF_KTN_FCM_NUM_ ANCHORS	long
fcm_num_buffers	Specifies the number of 4KB buffers that are to be used for internal communications among the nodes of an instance.	SQLF_KTN_FCM_NUM_ BUFFERS	unsigned long
fcm_num_connect	Specifies the number of connection entries that are to be used among the nodes of an instance to pass data among themselves.	SQLF_KTN_FCM_NUM_ CONNECT	long
fcm_num_rqb	Specifies the number of FCM request blocks that are to be used to pass information between the FCM daemon and an agent.	SQLF_KTN_FCM_NUM_ RQB	unsigned long
fileserver	Specifies the IPX/SPX file server name (the name of the Novell NetWare file server) where the internetwork address of the DB2 Database Manager is registered. Note: The following characters are not valid: / \ : ; * ?	SQLF_KTN_FILESERVER	char[48]
indexrec	Specifies when invalid database indexes should be recreated. This parameter is used if the database configuration parameter *indexrec* is set to SYSTEM. A value of ACCESS indicates that invalid indexes should be recreated the next time they are accessed. A value of RESTART indicates that invalid indexes should be recreated when the database is restarted.	SQLF_KTN_INDEXREC	unsigned int
intra_parallel	Specifies whether the DB2 Database Manager can use intra-partition parallelism. In a *Symmetric Multiprocessor* (SMP) environment, the default for this parameter is YES. In a non-SMP environment, the default value for this parameter is NO. This	SQLF_KTN_INTRA_ PARALLEL	integer

Table 7–2   DB2 Database Manager Configuration Parameters (Continued)

Parameter Name	Description	Token	C Data Type
	parameter can be used on both partitioned and non-partitioned database systems.		
ipx_socket	Specifies a "well-known" IPX/SPX socket number and represents the connection end point in a DB2 server's NetWare internetwork address.	SQLF_KTN_IPX_SOCKET	char[4]
java_heap_sz	Specifies the maximum size (in bytes) of the heap that is used by the JAVA Interpreter. For non-partitioned database systems, one heap (of this size) is allocated for the instance; for partitioned database systems, however, one heap (of this size) is allocated for each database partition server.	SQLF_KTN_JAVA_HEAP_SZ	long
jdk11_path	Specifies the directory under which the JAVA Development Kit, Version 1.1, is installed.	SQLF_KTN_JDK11_PATH	char[255]
keepdari	Specifies whether to keep a *Database Application Remote Interface* (DARI) process after each DARI call. If this parameter is set to **NO**, a new DARI process will be created and terminated for each DARI invocation. If this parameter is set to **YES**, a DARI process will be reused for subsequent DARI calls and be terminated only when the associated user application exits.	SQLF_KTN_KEEPDARI	unsigned int
maxagents	Specifies the maximum number of DB2 Database Manager agents that can exist simultaneously on a node, regardless of which database is being used.	SQLF_KTN_MAXAGENTS	unsigned long
maxcagents	Specifies the maximum number of DB2 Database Manager agents that can be concurrently executing a Database Manager transaction. This parameter cannot exceed the *maxagents* parameter.	SQLF_KTN_MAXCAGENTS	long
max_connretries	Specifies the maximum number of connection retries (attempts) to make in order to establish a connection to a node.	SQLF_KTN_MAX_CONNRETRIES	unsigned int
max_coordagents	Specifies the maximum number of coordinating agents that can exist at one time on a single node.	SQLF_KTN_MAX_COORDAGENTS	long
maxdari	Specifies the maximum number of	SQLF_KTN_MAXDARI	long

Table 7–2 DB2 Database Manager Configuration Parameters (Continued)

Parameter Name	Description	Token	C Data Type
	DARI processes that can reside at the database server. The value of this parameter cannot exceed the value of the *maxagents* parameter.		
max_querydegree	Specifies the maximum degree of parallelism for an SQL statement to use when executing on this instance of the DB2 Database Manager. For multi-node systems, this parameter applies to the degree of parallelism to use within a single node.	SQLF_KTN_MAX_ QUERYDEGREE	long
max_time_diff	Specifies the maximum time difference, in minutes, that is permitted among the system clocks of the nodes listed in the nodes configuration file (*db2nodes.cfg*).	SQLF_KTN_MAX_TIME_ DIFF	unsigned int
maxtotfilop	Specifies the maximum number of files that can be open per OS/2 application. The value specified in this parameter defines the total number of database and application file handles that can be used by a specific process connected to a database (OS/2 only).	SQLF_KTN_MAXTOTFILOP	unsigned int
min_priv_mem	Specifies the number of pages that the database server process will reserve as private virtual memory when a DB2 Database Manager instance is started (OS/2 only).	SQLF_KTN_MIN_PRIV_ MEM	unsigned long
mon_heap_sz	Specifies the amount of memory to allocate (in 4KB pages) for database system monitor data (database system monitor heap size).	SQLF_KTN_MON_HEAP_ SZ	unsigned int
nname	Specifies the name of the node or workstation. Database clients use this value to access database server workstations using NetBIOS. If the database server workstation changes the name specified in *nname*, all clients that access the database server workstation must catalog it again and specify the new name (OS/2 only).	SQLF_KTN_NNAME	char[8]
nodetype	Specifies whether the node is con-figured as a server with local and remote clients, a client, or a server with local clients. This parameter is not updatable.	SQLF_KTN_NODETYPE	unsigned int

Table 7–2   DB2 Database Manager Configuration Parameters (Continued)

Parameter Name	Description	Token	C Data Type
numdb	Specifies the maximum number of local databases that can be concurrently active (i.e., that can have applications connected to them).	`SQLF_KTN_NUMDB`	unsigned int
num_initagents	Specifies the initial number of agents that are to be created in the agent pool when the DB2 Database Manager is started.	`SQLF_KTN_NUM_` `INITAGENTS`	unsigned long
num_poolagents	Specifies the size to which the agent pool is allowed to grow. The agent pool can contain both idle agents and MPP/SMP-associated subagents.	`SQLF_KTN_NUM_` `POOLAGENTS`	long
objectname	Specifies the IPX/SPX database manager object name of the DB2 Database Manager instance in a Novell NetWare network. Note: The following characters are not valid: / : ; , * ?	`SQLF_KTN_` `OBJECTNAME`	char[48]
priv_mem_thresh	Specifies a threshold below which a server will not release the memory associated with a client when that client's connection is terminated.	`SQLF_KTN_PRIV_MEM_` `THRESH`	long
query_heap_sz	Specifies the maximum amount of memory (in 4KB pages) that can be allocated for the query heap. A query heap stores each query in the agent's private memory.	`SQLF_KTN_QUERY_HEAP_` `SZ`	long
release	Specifies the release level of the DB2 Database Manager configuration file. This parameter is not updatable.	`SQLF_KTN_RELEASE`	unsigned int
restbufsz	Specifies the size (in 4KB pages) of the buffer that is used when restoring a database. This value is only used if the buffer size is not specified when the Restore utility is invoked.	`SQLF_KTN_RESTBUFSZ`	unsigned long
resync_interval	Specifies the time interval (in seconds) after which a *Transaction Manager* (TM) or *Resource Manager* (RM) retries the recovery of any outstanding, in-doubt transactions found in the TM or the RM. This parameter value is only used when transactions are running in a DUOW environment.	`SQLF_KTN_RESYNC_` `INTERVAL`	unsigned int
route_obj_name	Specifies the name of the default routing information object entry that is used by all client applications	`SQLF_KTN_ROUTE_` `OBJ_NAME`	char[255]

Table 7-2   DB2 Database Manager Configuration Parameters (Continued)

Parameter Name	Description	Token	C Data Type
	attempting to access a DRDA server (DCE only).		
rqrioblk	Specifies the size (in bytes) of the communication buffer that is used by remote applications and their database agents on the database server.	SQLF_KTN_RQRIOBLK	unsigned int
sheapthres	Specifies a limit on the total amount of memory (in 4KB pages) available for sorting across the entire DB2 Database Manager instance.	SQLF_KTN_SHEAPTHRES	unsigned long
spm_log_file_sz	Specifies the size (in 4KB pages) of the *Sync Point Manager* (SPM) log file. This log file is contained in the spmlog subdirectory of the *sqllib* subdirectory and is created the first time the Sync Point Manager is started.	SQL_KTN_LOG_FILE_SZ	long
spm_log_path	Specifies the directory where the SPM log files are written. By default, SPM log files are written to the *sqllib* subdirectory.	SQLF_KTN_SPM_LOG_PATH	char[226]
spm_max_resync	Specifies the number of simultaneous agents that can be used to perform resync operations.	SQLF_KTN_SPM_MAX_RESYNC	long
spm_name	Specifies the name of the SPM instance. The SPM name must be defined in the system database directory, and if remote, in the node directory.	SQLF_KTN_SPM_NAME	char[8]
ss_logon	Specifies whether a LOGON user ID and password are required to stop the DB2 Database Manager background processes (OS/2 only).	SQLF_KTN_SS_LOGON	unsigned int
start_stop_time	Specifies the time, in minutes, in which all nodes must respond to START DATABASE MANAGER and STOP DATABASE MANAGER requests.	SQLF_KTN_START_STOP_TIME	unsigned int
svcename	Specifies a service name that represents the DB2 Database Manager instance in a TCP/IP network.	SQLF_KTN_SVCENAME	char[14]
sysadm_group	Specifies the group name that has *System Administration* (SYSADM) authority for the DB2 Database Manager instance. This authority is the highest level of authority within the Database Manager and controls all database objects.	SQLF_KTN_SYSADM_GROUP	char[16]

Table 7–2   DB2 Database Manager Configuration Parameters (Continued)

Parameter Name	Description	Token	C Data Type
sysctrl_group	Specifies the group name that has *System Control* (SYSCTRL) authority for the DB2 Database Manager instance. This level allows operations that affect system resources but does not allow direct access to data.	SQLF_KTN_SYSCTRL_ GROUP	char[16]
sysmaint_group	Specifies the group name that has *System Maintenance* (SYSMAINT) authority for the DB2 Database Manager instance. This level allows maintenance operations on all databases associated with an instance but does not allow direct access to data.	SQLF_KTN_SYSMAINT_ GROUP	char[16]
tm_database	Specifies the name of the Transaction Manager (TM) database for each DB2 Database Manager instance.	SQLF_KTN_TM_ DATABASE	char[8]
tp_mon_name	Specifies the name of the Transaction Processing (TP) monitor product being used.	SQLF_KTN_TP_MON_ NAME	char[19]
tpname	Specifies the name of the remote transaction program that the database client must use when issuing an allocate request to the DB2 Database Manager instance using the APPC communication protocol.	SQLF_KTN_TPNAME	char[64]
trust_allclnts	Specifies whether all clients are trusted clients, in which case a level of security is available—and users can be validated at the client. This parameter, and the *trust_clntauth* parameter (see next paragraph), are used together to determine where users are validated.	SQLF_KTN_TRUST_ ALLCLNTS	unsigned int
trust_clntauth	Specifies whether all users of trusted clients are validated at the client. This parameter and the *trust_allclnts* parameter are used together to determine where users are validated.	SQLF_KTN_TRUST_ CLNTAUTH	unsigned int
udf_mem_sz	For a fenced User-Defined Function (UDF), this parameter specifies the default allocation for memory to be shared between the database process and the UDF. For an unfenced process, this parameter specifies the size of the private memory set. In both cases, this memory passes data to a UDF and back to a database.	SQLF_KTN_UDF_MEM_SZ	unsigned int

Table 7–2 *DB2 Database Manager Configuration Parameters (Continued)*

Parameter Name	Description	Token	C Data Type

Note: The bits of the **SQLF_KTN_DFT_MONSWITCHES** parameter value indicate the default monitor switch settings. The individual bits making up this composite parameter value are:

Bit 1 (xxxx xxxl): dft_mon_uow

Bit 2 (xxxx xxlx): dft_mon_stmt

Bit 3 (xxxx xlxx): dft_mon_table

Bit 4 (xxxx lxxx): dft_mon_buffpool

Bit 5 (xxxl xxxx): dft_mon_lock

Bit 6 (xxlx xxxx): dft_mon_sort

Adapted from *IBM DB2 Universal Database API Reference*, Tables 46 and 47, p. 425–428.

value of one or more configuration parameters. The *sqlfupd* structure is defined in *sqlutil.h* as follows:

```
struct sqlfupd
{
unsigned short  token;       /* A token that identifies the        */
                             /* configuration parameter whose      */
                             /* value is to be retrieved           */
char            *ptrvalue;   /* A pointer to a location in         */
                             /* memory where the configuration     */
                             /* parameter value is to be stored    */
};
```

Table 7–2 lists each DB2 Database Manager configuration parameter token that can be specified for the *token* field of a *sqlfupd* structure, a description of each corresponding DB2 Database Manager configuration parameter, and information about the C/C++ data type of the value retrieved.

Before this function can be executed, an array of *sqlfupd* structures must be allocated, the *token* field of each structure in this array must be set to one of the DB2 Database Manager configuration parameter tokens listed in Table 7–2, and the *ptrvalue* field must contain a pointer to a valid location in memory where the configuration parameter value retrieved is to be stored. When this function is executed, the current value (setting) of each DB2 Database Manager configuration parameter specified is placed in the memory storage areas (local variables) referred to by the *ptrvalue* field of each *sqlfupd* structure in the array.

Comments   ■ If an application is attached to a remote DB2 Database Manager instance (or to a different local DB2 Database Manager instance), the current values of the DB2 Database Manager configuration file parameters for the attached server will be returned; otherwise, the current values of the local DB2 Database Manager configuration file parameters will be returned.

■ The application that calls this function is responsible for allocating sufficient memory for each data value retrieved.

■ If an error occurs while this function is executing, the DB2 Database Manager configuration information retrieved will be invalid. If an error occurs because the DB2 Database Manager configuration file has been corrupted, an error message will be returned, and you must reinstall the DB2 product to correct the problem.

■ For detailed information about each DB2 Database Manager configuration file parameter, refer to the *IBM DB2 Universal Database Administration Guide*.

Connection Requirements   This function can be called at any time to retrieve DB2 Database Manager configuration file parameter values from the current DB2 Database Manager instance (as defined by the value of the `DB2INSTANCE` environment variable); a connection to the current DB2 Database Manager instance does not have to be established first.

In order to retrieve DB2 Database Manager configuration file parameter values for a DB2 Database Manager instance located at a remote node, an application must attach to that node before calling this function.

Authorization   No authorization is required to execute this function call.

See Also   `GET DATABASE MANAGER CONFIGURATION DEFAULTS`, `RESET DATABASE MANAGER CONFIGURATION`, `UPDATE DATABASE MANAGER CONFIGURATION`

Example   The following C++ program illustrates how to use the `GET DATABASE MANAGER CONFIGURATION` function to retrieve DB2 Database Manager configuration file parameter values:

```
/*———————————————————————————————————————————————————*/
/* NAME:    CH7EX1.CPP                                            */
/* PURPOSE: Illustrate How To Use The Following DB2 API Function  */
/*          In A C++ Program:                                     */
/*                                                                */
/*                GET DATABASE MANAGER CONFIGURATION              */
/*                                                                */
/*———————————————————————————————————————————————————*/
// Include The Appropriate Header Files
#include <windows.h>
#include <iostream.h>
#include <sqlutil.h>
#include <sqlca.h>

// Define The API_Class Class
class API_Class
{
    // Attributes
    public:
        struct sqlca   sqlca;

    // Operations
```

```
    public:
        long GetDBMgrInfo();
};

// Define The GetDBMgrInfo() Member Function
long API_Class::GetDBMgrInfo()
{
    // Declare The Local Memory Variables
    struct sqlfupd    DBManagerInfo[2];
    char              DBPath[216];
    unsigned int      NumDB = 0;

    // Initialize An Array Of DB2 Database Manager Configuration
    // Parameter Structures
    DBManagerInfo[0].token = SQLF_KTN_DFTDBPATH;
    DBManagerInfo[0].ptrvalue = DBPath;
    DBManagerInfo[1].token = SQLF_KTN_NUMDB;
    DBManagerInfo[1].ptrvalue = (char *) &NumDB;

    // Obtain The Current Value Of The DB2 Database Manager
    // Configuration Parameters Specified
    sqlfxsys(2, &DBManagerInfo[0], &sqlca);

    // If The Current Values Of The Configuration Parameters
    // Specified Were Retrieved, Display Them
    if (sqlca.sqlcode == SQL_RC_OK)
    {
        cout << "Max. number of local databases that can be active";
        cout << " : " << NumDB << endl;
        cout << "Path used to store all databases          ";
        cout << " : " << DBPath << endl;
    }

    // Return The SQLCA Return Code To The Calling Function
    return(sqlca.sqlcode);
}

/*-----------------------------------------------------------------*/
/* The Main Function                                               */
/*-----------------------------------------------------------------*/
int main()
{
    // Declare The Local Memory Variables
    long    rc = SQL_RC_OK;

    // Create An Instance Of The API_Class Class
    API_Class  Example;

    // Get The Current Values Of Specific DB2 Database Manager
    // Configuration File Parameters
    rc = Example.GetDBMgrInfo();

    // Return To The Operating System
    return(rc);
}
```

GET DATABASE MANAGER CONFIGURATION DEFAULTS

Purpose   The GET DATABASE MANAGER CONFIGURATION DEFAULTS function is used to retrieve the system default values for one or more parameters (entries) in a DB2 Database Manager configuration file.

Syntax
```
SQL_API_RC SQL_API_FN sqlfdsys  (unsigned short  NumItems,
                                 struct sqlfupd  *ItemList,
                                 struct sqlca    *SQLCA);
```

Parameters   *NumItems*   The number of DB2 Database Manager configuration parameter default values to retrieve. This value identifies the number of elements contained in the array of *sqlfupd* structures specified in the *ItemList* parameter.

ItemList   A pointer to an array of *sqlfupd* structures that specifies which DB2 Database Manager configuration parameter system default values are to be retrieved.

SQLCA   A pointer to a location in memory where a SQL Communications Area (SQLCA) data structure variable is stored. This variable returns either status information (if the function executed successfully) or error information (if the function failed) to the calling application.

Includes   `#include <sqlutil.h>`

Description   The GET DATABASE MANAGER CONFIGURATION DEFAULTS function is used to retrieve the system default values for one or more parameters (entries) in a DB2 Database Manager configuration file. This function uses an array of *sqlfupd* structures to retrieve the system default values for one or more configuration parameters. Refer to the GET DATABASE MANAGER CONFIGURATION function for a detailed description of this structure and for more information about the DB2 Database Manager configuration parameters available.

Before this function can be executed, an array of *sqlfupd* structures must be allocated, the *token* field of each structure in this array must be set to one of the DB2 Database Manager configuration parameter tokens listed in Table 7–2 (refer to the GET DATABASE MANAGER CONFIGURATION function), and the *ptrvalue* field must contain a pointer to a valid location in memory where the configuration parameter default value retrieved is to be stored. When this function is executed, the system default value for each DB2 Database Manager configuration parameter specified is placed in the memory storage areas (local variables) referred to by the *ptrvalue* field of each *sqlfupd* structure in the array.

Comments   ■ If an application is attached to a remote DB2 Database Manager instance (or to a different local DB2 Database Manager instance), the system default values of the DB2 Database Manager configuration file parameters for the attached server will be returned; otherwise, the system default values of the local DB2 Database Manager configuration file parameters will be returned.

■ The application that calls this function is responsible for allocating sufficient memory for each data value retrieved.

■ The current value of a non-updatable configuration parameter is returned as that parameter's system default value.

■ If an error occurs while this function is executing, the DB2 Database Manager default configuration information returned will be invalid. If an error occurs because the DB2 Database Manager configuration file has been corrupted, an error message will be returned, and you must reinstall the DB2 product to correct the problem.

■ For a brief description about each DB2 Database Manager configuration file parameter, refer to the **GET DATABASE MANAGER CONFIGURATION** function. For detailed information about each DB2 database manager configuration file parameter, refer to the *IBM DB2 Universal Database Administration Guide*.

Connection Requirements   This function may be called at any time to retrieve DB2 Database Manager configuration file parameter default values for the current DB2 Database Manager instance (as defined by the value of the **DB2INSTANCE** environment variable); a connection to the current DB2 Database Manager instance does not have to be established first.

In order to retrieve default DB2 Database Manager configuration file parameter default values for a DB2 Database Manager instance located at a remote node, an application must first attach to that node before calling this function.

Authorization   No authorization is required to execute this function call.

See Also   **GET DATABASE MANAGER CONFIGURATION, RESET DATABASE MANAGER CONFIGURATION, UPDATE DATABASE MANAGER CONFIGURATION**

Example   The following C++ program illustrates how to use the **GET DATABASE MANAGER CONFIGURATION DEFAULTS** function to retrieve DB2 Database Manager configuration file parameter system default values:

```
/*———————————————————————————————————————*/
/* NAME:      CH7EX2.CPP                                   */
/* PURPOSE: Illustrate How To Use The Following DB2 API Function */
/*          In A C++ Program:                              */
/*                                                         */
/*               GET DATABASE MANAGER CONFIGURATION DEFAULTS */
/*                                                         */
/*———————————————————————————————————————*/

// Include The Appropriate Header Files
#include <windows.h>
#include <iostream.h>
#include <sqlutil.h>
```

```cpp
#include <sqlca.h>

// Define The API_Class Class
class API_Class
{
    // Attributes
    public:
        struct sqlca   sqlca;

    // Operations
    public:
        long GetDBMgrInfo();
};

// Define The GetDBMgrInfo() Member Function
long API_Class::GetDBMgrInfo()
{
    // Declare The Local Memory Variables
    struct sqlfupd   DBManagerInfo[2];
    char             DBPath[216];
    unsigned int     NumDB = 0;

    // Initialize An Array Of DB2 Database Manager Configuration
    // Parameter Structures
    DBManagerInfo[0].token = SQLF_KTN_DFTDBPATH;
    DBManagerInfo[0].ptrvalue = DBPath;
    DBManagerInfo[1].token = SQLF_KTN_NUMDB;
    DBManagerInfo[1].ptrvalue = (char *) &NumDB;

    // Obtain The System Default Value Of The DB2 Database
    // Manager Configuration Parameters Specified
    sqlfdsys(2, &DBManagerInfo[0], &sqlca);

    // If The System Default Values Of The Configuration Parameters
    // Specified Were Retrieved, Display Them
    if (sqlca.sqlcode == SQL_RC_OK)
    {
        cout << "Max. number of local databases that can be active";
        cout << " : " << NumDB << endl;
        cout << "Path used to store all databases              ";
        cout << " : " << DBPath << endl;
    }

    // Return The SQLCA Return Code To The Calling Function
    return(sqlca.sqlcode);
}

/*------------------------------------------------------------*/
/* The Main Function                                          */
/*------------------------------------------------------------*/
int main()
{
    // Declare The Local Memory Variables
```

```
        long    rc = SQL_RC_OK;

        // Create An Instance Of The API_Class Class
        API_Class  Example;

        // Get The System Default Values Of Specific DB2 Database
        // Manager Configuration File Parameters
        rc = Example.GetDBMgrInfo();

        // Return To The Operating System
        return(rc);
    }
```

UPDATE DATABASE MANAGER CONFIGURATION

Purpose   The **UPDATE DATABASE MANAGER CONFIGURATION** function is used to change the value of one or more parameters (entries) in a DB2 Database Manager configuration file.

Syntax
```
SQL_API_RC SQL_API_FN sqlfusys (unsigned short  NumItems,
                                struct sqlfupd  *ItemList,
                                struct sqlca    *SQLCA);
```

Parameters   *NumItems*   The number of DB2 Database Manager configuration parameters values to update. This value identifies the number of elements contained in the array of *sqlfupd* structures specified in the *ItemList* parameter.

   ItemList   A pointer to an array of *sqlfupd* structures that specifies which DB2 Database Manager configuration parameters are to be updated, along with their corresponding values.

   SQLCA   A pointer to a location in memory where a SQL Communications Area (SQLCA) data structure variable is stored. This variable returns either status information (if the function executed successfully) or error information (if the function failed) to the calling application.

Includes   `#include <sqlutil.h>`

Description The **UPDATE DATABASE MANAGER CONFIGURATION** function is used to change the
value of one or more parameters (entries) in a DB2 Database Manager configuration file. This function uses an array of special structures (*sqlfupd*) to update the value of one or more DB2 Database Manager configuration parameters. The *sqlfupd* structure is defined in *sqlutil.h* as follows:

```
struct sqlfupd
{
unsigned short token;        /* A token that identifies the        */
                             /* configuration parameter whose       */
                             /* value is to be updated              */
char           *ptrvalue;    /* A pointer to a location in          */
                             /* memory where the new                */
                             /* configuration parameter value is    */
                             /* stored                              */
};
```

Before this function can be executed, an array of *sqlfupd* structures must be allocated, the *token* field of each structure in this array must be set to one of the DB2 Database Manager configuration parameter tokens listed in Table 7–2 (refer to the **GET DATABASE MANAGER CONFIGURATION** function), and the *ptrvalue* field must contain a pointer to a valid location in memory where the new configuration parameter value is stored. When this function is executed, the new DB2 Database Manager configuration parameter values are copied from the memory storage areas (local variables) referred to by the *ptrvalue* field of each *sqlfupd* structure in the array to the appropriate location in the DB2 Database Manager configuration file, provided the parameters specified can be updated.

NOTE: If a user attempts to edit a DB2 Database Manager configuration file using a method other than those provided by DB2, the database management system can become unusable. A DB2 Database Manager configuration file should only be updated with one of the following methods:

- *The DB2 Database Director*
- *The DB2 command-line processor (**UPDATE DATABASE MANAGER CONFIGURATION** and **RESET DATABASE MANAGER CONFIGURATION** commands)*
- *The appropriate DB2 API function calls (**UPDATE DATABASE MANAGER CONFIGURATION** and **RESET DATABASE MANAGER CONFIGURATION**)*

Comments
- If an application is attached to a remote DB2 Database Manager instance (or to a different local DB2 Database Manager instance), the current values of the DB2 Database Manager configuration file parameters for the attached server will be updated; otherwise, the current values of the local DB2 Database Manager configuration file parameters will be updated.
- Changes to DB2 Database Manager configuration file parameters only become effective when the modified configuration file is loaded into memory. This means that for database server workstations, the DB2 Database Manager must be stopped and restarted before new values take effect (refer to the **STOP DATABASE MANAGER** and **START DATABASE MANAGER** functions). For client workstations, new values will take effect the next time a client application connects to a server workstation. Although new configuration parameter values do not take effect

immediately, when configuration parameter values are retrieved, the most recent update values are always returned.

■ If an error occurs while this function is executing, the DB2 Database Manager configuration file will remain unchanged.

■ A DB2 Database Manager configuration file cannot be updated if its checksum is invalid. Checksums can become invalid if a configuration file is changed by something other than the tools provided with the DB2 product. If a DB2 Database Manager configuration file cannot be updated, an error message will be returned, and you must reinstall the DB2 product to correct the problem.

■ The values used for each DB2 Database Manager configuration parameter differ for each type of configured database node (server, client, or server with remote clients). For detailed information about the ranges and values that can be set for each node type, refer to the *IBM DB2 Universal Database Administration Guide*.

■ For a brief description about each DB2 Database Manager configuration file parameter, refer to the **GET DATABASE MANAGER CONFIGURATION** function. For detailed information about each DB2 database manager configuration file parameter, refer to the *IBM DB2 Universal Database Administration Guide*.

Connection Requirements
This function can be called at any time to update DB2 Database Manager configuration file parameter values for the current DB2 Database Manager instance (as defined by the value of the **DB2INSTANCE** environment variable); a connection to the current DB2 Database Manager instance does not have to be established first.

In order to update DB2 Database Manager configuration file parameter values for a DB2 Database Manager instance that is located at a remote node, an application must attach to that node before calling this function.

Authorization
Only users with System Administrator (SYSADM) authority are allowed to execute this function call.

See Also
GET DATABASE MANAGER CONFIGURATION DEFAULTS, GET DATABASE MANAGER CONFIGURATION, RESET DATABASE MANAGER CONFIGURATION

Example
The following C++ program illustrates how to use the **UPDATE DATABASE MANAGER CONFIGURATION** function to change the values of DB2 Database Manager configuration file parameters:

```
/*------------------------------------------------------------*/
/* NAME:     CH7EX3.CPP                                       */
/* PURPOSE:  Illustrate How To Use The Following DB2 API Functions */
/*           In A C++ Program:                                */
/*                                                            */
/*                UPDATE DATABASE MANAGER CONFIGURATION        */
/*                RESET DATABASE MANAGER CONFIGURATION         */
/*                                                            */
/* OTHER DB2 APIs SHOWN:                                      */
/*                GET DATABASE MANAGER CONFIGURATION           */
```

```
/*                                                                      */
/*--------------------------------------------------------------------- */

// Include The Appropriate Header Files
#include <windows.h>
#include <iostream.h>
#include <sqlutil.h>
#include <sqlca.h>

// Define The API_Class Class
class API_Class
{
    // Attributes
    public:
        struct sqlca   sqlca;

    // Operations
    public:
        long GetDBMgrInfo();
        long SetDBMgrInfo();
};

// Define The GetDBMgrInfo() Member Function
long API_Class::GetDBMgrInfo()
{
    // Declare The Local Memory Variables
    struct sqlfupd   DBManagerInfo[2];
    unsigned int     NumDB = 0;
    int              QueryHeapSize = 0;

    // Initialize An Array Of DB2 Database Manager Configuration
    // Parameter Structures
    DBManagerInfo[0].token = SQLF_KTN_NUMDB;
    DBManagerInfo[0].ptrvalue = (char *) &NumDB;
    DBManagerInfo[1].token = SQLF_KTN_QUERY_HEAP_SZ;
    DBManagerInfo[1].ptrvalue = (char *) &QueryHeapSize;

    // Obtain The Current Value Of The DB2 Database Manager
    // Configuration Parameters Specified
    sqlfxsys(2, &DBManagerInfo[0], &sqlca);

    // If The Current Values Of The Configuration Parameters
    // Specified Were Retrieved, Display Them
    if (sqlca.sqlcode == SQL_RC_OK)
    {
        cout << "Max. number of local databases that can be active ";
        cout << "at one time   : " << NumDB << endl;
        cout << "Max. amount of memory that can be allocated for ";
        cout << "the query heap : " << QueryHeapSize << endl;
    }

    // Return The SQLCA Return Code To The Calling Function
    return(sqlca.sqlcode);
}
```

```
// Define The SetDBMgrInfo() Member Function
long API_Class::SetDBMgrInfo()
{
    // Declare The Local Memory Variables
    struct sqlfupd   DBManagerInfo[2];
    unsigned int     NumDB = 0;
    int              QueryHeapSize = 0;

    // Initialize An Array Of DB2 Database Manager Configuration
    // Parameter Structures
    DBManagerInfo[0].token = SQLF_KTN_NUMDB;
    DBManagerInfo[0].ptrvalue = (char *) &NumDB;
    DBManagerInfo[1].token = SQLF_KTN_QUERY_HEAP_SZ;
    DBManagerInfo[1].ptrvalue = (char *) &QueryHeapSize;

    // Modify The Values Of The DB2 Database Manager
    // Configuration Parameters Specified
    NumDB = 4;
    QueryHeapSize = 1024;
    sqlfusys(2, &DBManagerInfo[0], &sqlca);

    // Return The SQLCA Return Code To The Calling Function
    return(sqlca.sqlcode);
}


/*————————————————————————————————————————————————————*/
/* The Main Function                                  */
/*————————————————————————————————————————————————————*/
int main()
{
    // Declare The Local Memory Variables
    long         rc = SQL_RC_OK;
    struct sqlca sqlca;

    // Create An Instance Of The API_Class Class
    API_Class   Example;

    // Get The Current Values Of Specific DB2 Database Manager
    // Configuration File Parameters
    cout << "Before Update:" << endl;
    rc = Example.GetDBMgrInfo();

    // Change The Values Of Specific DB2 Database Manager
    // Configuration File Parameters
    if (rc == SQL_RC_OK)
        rc = Example.SetDBMgrInfo();

    // Get The Current Values Of Specific DB2 Database Manager
    // Configuration File Parameters To See If They Were Changed
    if (rc == SQL_RC_OK)
    {
        cout << endl << "After Update:" << endl;
```

```
        rc = Example.GetDBMgrInfo();
}

// Reset The Values Of All DB2 Database Manager Configuration
// Parameters To Their System Default Values
sqlfrsys(&sqlca);

// Get The Current Values Of Specific DB2 Database Manager
// Configuration File Parameters To See If They Have Been Reset
if (rc == SQL_RC_OK)
{
    cout << endl << "After Reset:" << endl;
    rc = Example.GetDBMgrInfo();
}

// Return To The Operating System
return(rc);
}
```

RESET DATABASE MANAGER CONFIGURATION

Purpose   The RESET DATABASE MANAGER CONFIGURATION function is used to reset the values of all updatable configuration parameters (entries) in a DB2 Database Manager configuration file to their original system defaults.

Syntax   SQL_API_RC SQL_API_FN sqlfrsys (struct sqlca *SQLCA);

Parameters   *SQLCA*   A pointer to a location in memory where a SQL Communications Area (SQLCA) data structure variable is stored. This variable returns either status information (if the function executed successfully) or error information (if the function failed) to the calling application.

Includes   #include <sqlutil.h>

Description The RESET DATABASE MANAGER CONFIGURATION function is used to reset the values of all updatable configuration parameters (entries) in a DB2 Database Manager configuration file to their system defaults. When this function is executed, all non-updatable parameters in the configuration file remain unchanged.

Comments   ■ If an application is attached to a remote DB2 Database Manager instance (or a different local DB2 Database Manager instance), the values of the DB2 Database Manager configuration file parameters for the attached server will be reset; otherwise, the values of the local DB2 Database Manager configuration file parameters will be reset.

                 ■ Changes to DB2 Database Manager configuration file parameters only become effective when the modified configuration file is loaded into memory. This means that for database server workstations, the DB2 Database Manager must be stopped and restarted before the values take effect (refer to the **STOP DATABASE MANAGER** and **START DATABASE MANAGER** functions). For client workstations, new values will take effect the next time a client application connects to a server workstation. Although new configuration parameter values do not take effect immediately, when configuration parameter values are retrieved, the most recent update values are always returned.

■ If an error occurs while this function is executing, the DB2 Database Manager configuration file will remain unchanged.

■ A DB2 Database Manager configuration file cannot be updated if its checksum is invalid. Checksums can become invalid if a configuration file is changed by something other than the tools provided with the DB2 product. If a DB2 Database Manager configuration file cannot be reset, an error message will be returned, and you must reinstall the DB2 product to correct the problem.

■ For a brief description about each DB2 Database Manager configuration file parameter, refer to the **GET DATABASE MANAGER CONFIGURATION** function. For detailed information about each DB2 Database Manager configuration file parameter, refer to the *IBM DB2 Universal Database Administration Guide*.

Connection Requirements This function can be called at any time to reset DB2 Database Manager configuration file parameter values for the current DB2 Database Manager instance (as defined by the value of the **DB2INSTANCE** environment variable); a connection to the current DB2 Database Manager instance does not have to be established first.

To reset DB2 Database Manager configuration file parameter values for a DB2 Database Manager instance that is located at a remote node, an application must attach to that node before calling this function.

Authorization Only users with System Administrator (SYSADM) authority are allowed to execute this function call.

See Also **GET DATABASE MANAGER CONFIGURATION DEFAULTS, GET DATABASE MANAGER CONFIGURATION, UPDATE DATABASE MANAGER CONFIGURATION**

Example See the example provided for the **UPDATE DATABASE MANAGER CONFIGURATION** function on page 209.

GET DATABASE CONFIGURATION

Purpose The **GET DATABASE CONFIGURATION** function is used to retrieve the current value of one or more configuration parameters (entries) in a specific database configuration file.

Syntax
```
SQL_API_RC SQL_API_FN sqlfxdb (char          *DBAlias,
```

```
                                     unsigned short  NumItems,
                                     struct sqlfupd  *ItemList,
                                     struct sqlca    *SQLCA);
```

Parameters   *DBAlias*   A pointer to a location in memory where the alias name of the
                                database that parameter values are to be retrieved for is stored.

                 NumItems   The number of database configuration parameter values to retrieve.
                                This value identifies the number of elements contained in the array
                                of *sqlfupd* structures specified in the *ItemList* parameter.

                 ItemList   A pointer to an array of *sqlfupd* structures that specify which
                                database configuration parameter values are to be retrieved.

                 SQLCA   A pointer to a location in memory where a SQL Communications
                                Area (SQLCA) data structure variable is stored. This variable returns
                                either status information (if the function executed successfully) or
                                error information (if the function failed) to the calling application.

Includes   `#include <sqlutil.h>`

Description The GET DATABASE CONFIGURATION function is used to retrieve the current value
                 of one or more configuration parameters (entries) in a specific database
                 configuration file. Configuration parameter values for an individual database are
                 stored in the file *sqldbcon,* which is located in the *sqlxxxxx* directory that was
                 created when the database was created (*xxxxx* represents the number assigned by
                 DB2 during the database creation process). This file is automatically created
                 whenever a new database is created. Most of the values stored in this file control
                 the amount of system resources that are allocated to the corresponding database,
                 and can be modified to increase the database's overall performance. Other
                 parameter values in this file contain static information about the database itself
                 and cannot be changed.

                 This function uses an array of special structures (*sqlfupd*) to retrieve the current
                 value of one or more database configuration parameters. The *sqlfupd* structure is
                 defined in *sqlutil.h* as follows:

```
struct sqlfupd
{
unsigned short token;            /* A token that identifies the      */
                                 /* configuration parameter whose    */
                                 /* value is to be retrieved         */
char           *ptrvalue;        /* A pointer to a location in       */
                                 /* memory where the configuration   */
                                 /* parameter value is to be stored  */
};
```

Table 7–3 lists each database configuration parameter token that can be specified
for the *token* field of a *sqlfupd* structure, a description of each corresponding database
configuration parameter, and information about the C/C++ data type of the retrieved

Table 7–3   DB2 Database Configuration Parameters (Continued)

Parameter Name	Description	Token	C Data Type

value.

Before this function can be executed, an array of *sqlfupd* structures must be allocated, the *token* field of each structure in this array must be set to one of the database configuration parameter tokens listed in Table 7–3, and the *ptrvalue* field must contain a pointer to a valid location in memory where the configuration parameter value retrieved is to be stored. When this function is executed, the current value (setting) of each database configuration parameter specified is placed in the memory storage areas (local variables) referred to by the *ptrvalue* field of each *sqlfupd* structure in the array.

Comments
- Entries in the database configuration file that do not have a corresponding token value listed in Table 7–3 are not accessible to an application.
- The application that calls this function is responsible for allocating sufficient memory for each data value retrieved.
- If an error occurs while this function is executing, the database configuration information returned will be invalid. If an error occurs because the database configuration file has been corrupted, an error message will be returned and you must restore the database from a good backup image to correct the problem.
- For detailed information about each database configuration file parameter, refer to the *IBM DB2 Universal Database Administration Guide*.

Table 7–3   DB2 Database Configuration Parameters

Parameter Name	Description	Token	C Data Type
app_ctl_heap_sz	Specifies the maximum size, in 4KB pages, of the application control heap. The application control heap is required in order to share information among agents working on behalf of the same application at a node in an MPP or SMP database system.	`SQLF_DBTN_APP_CTL_HEAP_SZ`	unsigned int
applheapsz	Specifies the size, in pages, of the application heap that is available for each individual agent. Memory to be used for caching packages (specified by the *pckcachesz* parameter) is allocated from the application heap.	`SQLF_DBTN_APPLHEAPSZ`	unsigned int
asdm_mgmtclass	Specifies how the server should manage the backup versions or archive copies of objects being backed up. When performing any ASDM backup, the DB2 Database Manager uses this parameter	`SQLF_DBTN_ADSM_MGMTCLASS`	char[30]

Table 7–3 DB2 Database Configuration Parameters (Continued)

Parameter Name	Description	Token	C Data Type
	to pass the appropriate management class to ASDM.		
asdm_nodename	Specifies the node name that is associated with the ASDM product. This name is used when restoring databases that were backed up to ASDM from another node.	`SQLF_DBTN_ASDM_NODENAME`	char[64]
asdm_owner	Specifies the owner name that is associated with the ASDM product.	`SQLF_DBTN_ASDM_OWNER`	char[64]
adsm_password	Specifies the password that is associated with the ADSM product.	`SQLF_DBTN_ADSM_PASSWORD`	char[64]
autorestart	Specifies whether the DB2 Database Manager can automatically issue a `RESTART DATABASE` command when a connection is attempted, if the last database connection was disrupted, or if the database was not closed normally during the previous session. If this parameter is set to `ON`, the database is restarted automatically. If this parameter is set to `OFF`, the database must be restarted manually.	`SQLF_DBTN_AUTO_RESTART`	unsigned int
avg_appls	Specifies the average number of active applications that will access the database at a given time. This parameter is used by the SQL optimizer to help estimate how much buffer pool memory will be available for the chosen access plan at application run time.	`SQLF_DBTN_AVG_APPLS`	unsigned int
backup_pending	Specifies whether a database needs to be backed up. If this parameter is set to `NO`, the database is in a usable state. If this parameter is set to `YES`, an OFFLINE backup must be performed before the database can be used. This parameter is not updatable.	`SQLF_DBTN_BACKUP_PENDING`	unsigned int
buffpage	Specifies the size, in pages, of the buffer pool that stores and manipulates data read from the database.	`SQLF_DBTN_BUFF_PAGE`	unsigned long
catalogcache_sz	Specifies the size, in pages, of the internal catalog cache (allocated from the *dbheap*) that is used by the SQL precompiler to hold the packed descriptors for commonly referenced objects such as tables and constraints.	`SQLF_DBTN_CATALOGCACHE_SZ`	long

Table 7–3 DB2 Database Configuration Parameters (Continued)

Parameter Name	Description	Token	C Data Type
chngpgs_thresh	Specifies the level (percentage) of pages that must be changed before the asynchronous page cleaners will be started (if they are not already active).	SQLF_DBTN_CHNGPGS_THRESH	unsigned int
codepage	Specifies the code page of the database. This parameter is not updatable.	SQLF_DBTN_CODEPAGE	unsigned int
codeset	Specifies the code set of the database. This parameter is not updatable.	SQLF_DBTN_CODESET	char[9]
collate_info	Specifies the collate sequence that is used by the database when making character comparisons. This parameter is not updatable.	SQLF_DBTN_COLLATE_INFO	char[260]
none	Specifies all database attributes in a single value. You can manipulate the bits of this unsigned integer value or use the individual tokens making up this value (see the footnote for more information).	SQLF_DBTN_DETS	unsigned int
copyprotect	Enables or disables the database copy-protect attribute (OS/2 only).	SQLF_DBTN_COPY_PROTECT	unsigned int
country	Specifies the country code of the database. This parameter is not updatable.	SQLF_DBTN_COUNTRY	unsigned int
database_consistent	Specifies whether the database is in a consistent state. If this parameter is set to **YES**, all transactions have been committed or rolled back, and the data in the database is consistent. If this parameter is set to **NO**, a transaction or some other task is pending on the database, and the data in the database is not consistent at this time. This parameter is not updatable.	SQLF_DBTN_CONSISTENT	unsigned int
database_level	Specifies the release level of the DB2 Database Manager that can be used to access the database. This parameter is not updatable.	SQLF_DBTN_DATABASE_LEVEL	unsigned int
dbheap	Specifies the size, in pages, of the database heap that holds control information on all open cursors that are accessing the database. Both log buffers and catalog cache buffers are allocated from the database heap.	SQLF_DBTN_DBHEAP	unsigned int
dft_degree	Specifies the default value for the **CURRENT DEGREE** special register and the **DEGREE** bind option.	SQLF_DBTN_DFT_DEGREE	long

Table 7–3   DB2 Database Configuration Parameters (Continued)

Parameter Name	Description	Token	C Data Type
dft_extent_sz	Specifies the default extent size (in pages) of all table spaces.	SQLF_DBTN_DFT_EXTENT_SZ	unsigned long
dft_loadrec_ses	Specifies the default number of load recovery sessions that can be used during the recovery of a table load operation. This parameter is only applicable if roll-forward recovery is enabled.	SQLF_DBTN_DFT_LOADREC_SES	int
dft_prefetch_sz	Specifies the default prefetch size (in pages) of all table spaces.	SQLF_DBTN_DFT_PREFETCH_SZ	int
dft_queryopt	Specifies the default query optimization class that is to be used to direct the SQL optimizer to use different degrees of optimization when compiling SQL queries.	SQLF_DBTN_DFT_QUERYOPT	long
dft_sqlmathwarn	Specifies the default value that determines whether arithmetic errors and retrieval conversion problems are treated as errors or warnings during SQL statement compilation.	SQLF_DBTN_DFT_SQLMATHWARN	int
dir_obj_name	Specifies the object name in the DCE name space that represents a DB2 Database Manager instance (or database) in the directory.	SQLF_DBTN_DIR_OBJ_NAME	char[255]
discover_db	Specifies whether or not information about a database is returned to a client when a discovery request is issued against the server.	SQLF_DBTN_DISCOVER	unsigned int
dlchktime	Specifies the time interval frequency (in milliseconds) at which the DB2 Database Manager is to check for deadlocks among all the applications connected to a database.	SQLF_DBTN_DLCHKTIME	unsigned long
dl_expint	Specifies the interval of time, in seconds, for which a DB2 File Manager file access token generated is valid.	SQLF_DBTN_DL_EXPINT	long
dl_num_backup	Specifies the number of most recent database backups that the DB2 File Manager is to keep backup information for.	SQLF_DBTN_DL_NUM_BACKUP	unsigned int
dl_num_copies	Specifies the number of additional copies of a file that are to be made in the archive server (such as an ASDM server) when a file is linked to the database.	SQLF_DBTN_DL_NUM_COPIES	unsigned int
dl_time_drop	Specifies the interval of time (in days)	SQLF_DBTN_DL_TIME_	unsigned int

Table 7–3 DB2 Database Configuration Parameters (Continued)

Parameter Name	Description	Token	C Data Type
	that files are to be retained on an archive server (such as an ASDM server) after a **DROP TABLE**, **DROP TABLESPACE**, or **DROP DATABASE** SQL statement is issued.	DROP	
estore_seg_sz	Specifies the number of pages that are to be used in each extended memory segment of the database.	SQLF_DBTN_ESTORE_ SEG_SZ	long
indexrec	Specifies when invalid indexes are to be recreated. This parameter can be set to **SYSTEM (ACCESS)**, **SYSTEM (RESTART)**, **ACCESS**, or **RESTART**. The default setting is **SYSTEM**, which specifies that the value of the DB2 Database Manager configuration parameter *indexrec* is to be used.	SQLF_DBTN_INDEXREC	unsigned int
indexsort	Specifies whether or not index key sorting is to occur during index creation.	SQLF_DBTN_INDEXSORT	unsigned int
locklist	Specifies the maximum storage (in pages) that is to be allocated to the lock list.	SQLF_DBTN_LOCKLIST	unsigned int
locktimeout	Specifies the number of seconds an application will wait to obtain a lock before timing out.	SQLF_DBTN_ LOCKTIMEOUT	int
logbufsz	Specifies the number of pages used to buffer log records before they are written to disk. This buffer is allocated from the database heap.	SQLF_DBTN_LOGBUFSZ	unsigned int
logfilsiz	Specifies the amount of disk storage space (in pages) that is to be allocated to log files that are used for data recovery. This parameter defines the size of each primary and secondary log file.	SQLF_DBTN_LOGFIL_SIZ	unsigned int
loghead	Specifies the name of the log file that contains the head of the active log. The next log record written will start at the head of the active log file. This parameter is not updatable.	SQLF_DBTN_LOGHEAD	char[12]
logpath	Specifies the current path used to access log files. This parameter is not updatable.	SQLF_DBTN_LOGPATH	char[242]
logprimary	Specifies the number of primary log files that can be used for database recovery.	SQLF_DBTN_ LOGPRIMARY	unsigned int
logretain	Specifies whether active log files are to be retained as archived log files for use	SQLF_DBTN_LOG_ RETAIN	unsigned int

Table 7–3 DB2 Database Configuration Parameters (Continued)

Parameter Name	Description	Token	C Data Type
	in roll-forward recovery (also known as log retention logging).		
log_retain_status	Specifies whether or not log files are retained for use in roll-foward recovery. This parameter is not updatable.	`SQLF_DBTN_LOG_ RETAIN_STATUS`	unsigned int
logsecond	Specifies the number of secondary log files that are to be used for database recovery.	`SQLF_DBTN_LOGSECOND`	unsigned int
maxappls	Specifies the maximum number of application programs (both local and remote) that can be connected to the database at one time.	`SQLF_DBTN_MAXAPPLS`	unsigned int
maxfilop	Specifies the maximum number of database files an application program can have open at one time.	`SQLF_DBTN_MAXFILOP`	unsigned int
maxlocks	Specifies the maximum percentage of the lock list that any one application program can use.	`SQLF_DBTN_MAXLOCKS`	unsigned int
mincommit	Specifies the number of SQL commits that can be grouped for the database. You can achieve better control of I/O and log activity by grouping SQL commits.	`SQLF_DBTN_MINCOMMIT`	unsigned int
multipage_alloc	Specifies whether multipage file allocation is to be used to improve insert performance when working with SMS table spaces. This parameter is not updatable.	`SQLF_DBTN_ MULTIPAGE_ALLOC`	unsigned int
newlogpath	Specifies an alternate path to use when searching for recovery log files. Because this parameter accepts only fully qualified directories, you must specify the absolute path.	`SQLF_DBTN_ NEWLOGPATH`	char[242]
nextactive	Specifies the name of the next recovery log file to be used for logging. This parameter is not updatable.	`SQLF_DBTN_ NEXTACTIVE`	char[12]
num_estore_segs	Specifies the number of extended storage segments that are available for use by the database.	`SQLF_DBTN_NUM_ ESTORE_SEGS`	long
num_freqvalues	Specifies the number of most-frequent used values that will be collected when the `WITH DISTRIBUTION` option is specified in the `RUN STATISTICS` function (or command).	`SQLF_DBTN_NUM_ FREQVALUES`	unsigned int

Table 7–3 DB2 Database Configuration Parameters (Continued)

Parameter Name	Description	Token	C Data Type
num_iocleaners	Specifies the number of asynchronous page cleaners for the database.	SQLF_DBTN_NUM_ IOCLEANERS	unsigned int
num_ioservers	Specifies the number of I/O servers for the database. I/O servers are used on behalf of database agents to perform prefetch and asynchronous I/O that is needed by utilities such as BACKUP and RESTORE.	SQLF_DBTN_NUM_ IOSERVERS	unsigned int
num_quantiles	Specifies the number of quantiles (values in a column that satisfy a RANGE predicate) that will be collected when the WITH DISTRIBUTION option is specified in the RUN STATISTICS function or command.	SQLF_DBTN_NUM_ QUANTILES	unsigned int
numsegs	Specifies the number of containers that were created within the default SMS table spaces. This parameter is not updatable.	SQLF_DBTN_NUMSEGS	unsigned int
pckcachesz	Specifies the amount of application heap memory that is to be used for caching packages.	SQLF_DBTN_ PCKCACHE_SZ	unsigned int
rec_his_retentn	Specifies the number of days that historical information on backups is to be retained.	SQLF_DBTN_REC_HIS_ RETENTN	int
release	Specifies the release level of the database configuration file. This parameter is not updatable.	SQLF_DBTN_RELEASE	unsigned int
restore_pending	Specifies whether the database has a RESTORE PENDING status.	SQLF_DBTN_RESTORE_ PENDING	unsigned int
rollfwd_pending	Specifies whether a roll-forward recovery procedure needs to be performed before the database can be used. This parameter can be set to NO (neither the database nor any of its table spaces are in roll-forward pending state), DATABASE (the database needs to be rolled forward before it can be used), or TABLESPACES (one or more table spaces in the database needs to be rolled forward). This parameter is not updatable.	SQLF_DBTN_ROLLFWD_ PENDING	unsigned int
seqdetect	Specifies whether sequential detection for the database is enabled or disabled.	SQLF_DBTN_SEQDETECT	unsigned int
softmax	Specifies the maximum percentage of log file space to be consumed before a	SQLF_DBTN_SOFTMAX	unsigned int

Table 7–3 DB2 Database Configuration Parameters (Continued)

Parameter Name	Description	Token	C Data Type
	soft checkpoint is taken.		
sortheap	Specifies the number of private memory pages that are to be available for each sort operation in an application program.	SQLF_DBTN_SORT_HEAP	unsigned long
stat_heap_sz	Specifies the maximum size of the heap space (in pages) that is to be used for creating and collecting all table statistics when distribution statistics are being gathered.	SQLF_DBTN_STAT_HEAP_SZ	unsigned long
stmtheap	Specifies the heap size (in pages) that is to be used to compile SQL statements.	SQLF_DBTN_STMTHEAP	unsigned int
territory	Specifies the territory of the database. This parameter is not updatable.	SQLF_DBTN_TERRITORY	char[5]
userexit	Specifies whether a user exit function for archiving or retrieving log files can be called the next time the database is opened. If this parameter is set to OFF, a user exit function cannot be called. If this parameter is set to ON, a user exit function can be called.	SQLF_DBTN_USER_EXIT	unsigned int
user_exit_status	Specifies whether a user exit function can be called to store archive log files. If this parameter is set to OFF, a user exit function cannot be called to store archive log files. If this parameter is set to ON, a user exit function can be called to store archive log files. This parameter is not updatable.	SQLF_DBTN_USER_EXIT_STATUS	unsigned int
util_heap_sz	Specifies the maximum amount of shared memory that can be used simultaneously by the Backup, Restore, and Load utilities.	SQLF_DBTN_UTIL_HEAP_SZ	unsigned long
none	Specifies the database status in a single value. You may examine the bits of this unsigned integer value, or you can use the individual tokens that make up this value (see footnote for more information).	SQLF_DBTN_INTFLAGS	unsigned int

The bits of the SQLF_DBTN_DETS parameter value indicate the database attribute settings. The individual bits making up this composite parameter value are the following:

Bit 1 (xxxx xxxl): copyprotect

Bit 2 (xxxx xxlx): logretain

Bit 3 (xxxx xlxx): userexit

Bit 4 (xxxx lxxx): autorestart

The bits of the **SQLF_DBTN_INTFLAGS** parameter value indicate database status. The individual bits making up this composite parameter value are:

Bit 1 (xxxx xxxl): database_consistent

Bit 3 (xxxx xlxx): backup_pending

Bit 4 (xxxx 1xxx): rollfwd_pending

Bit 5 (xxx1 xxxx): log_retain_status

Bit 6 (xx1x xxxx): user_exit_status

Bit 7 (x1xx xxxx): tablespace roll-forward pending

The combination of bits 4 and 7 make up the rollfwd_pending parameter. If the rollfwd_pending bit (4) is on, the database needs to be rolled forward (rollfwd_pending = **DATABASE**). If the rollfwd_pending bit (4) is off and bit 7 is on, one or more table spaces need to be rolled forward (rollfwd_pending = **TABLESPACES**). If both bits are off, neither the database nor any of its table spaces need to be rolled forward (rollfwd_pending = **NO**).

Adapted from IBM's *DB2 Universal Database API Reference*, Tables 44 and 45, p. 422 to 424.

Connection Requirements This function can only be called if a connection to a DB2 Database Manager instance exists. In order to retrieve database configuration file parameter values for a DB2 database located at a remote node, an application must attach to that node. If necessary, a temporary connection is established by this function during its execution.

Authorization No authorization is required to execute this function call.

See Also **GET DATABASE CONFIGURATION DEFAULTS**, **RESET DATABASE CONFIGURATION**, **UPDATE DATABASE CONFIGURATION**

Example The following C++ program illustrates how to use the **GET DATABASE CONFIGURATION** function to retrieve database configuration file parameter values for the SAMPLE database:

```
/*————————————————————————————————— */
/* NAME:    CH7EX4.CPP                                   */
/* PURPOSE: Illustrate How To Use The Following DB2 API Function */
/*          In A C++ Program:                            */
/*                                                       */
/*             GET DATABASE CONFIGURATION                */
/*                                                       */
/*————————————————————————————————— */

// Include The Appropriate Header Files
#include <windows.h>
#include <iostream.h>
#include <sqlutil.h>
#include <sqlca.h>

// Define The API_Class Class
class API_Class
{
```

```
     // Attributes
     public:
          struct sqlca   sqlca;

     // Operations
     public:
          long GetDBaseInfo();
};

// Define The GetDBaseInfo() Member Function
long API_Class::GetDBaseInfo()
{
     // Declare The Local Memory Variables
     struct sqlfupd  DBaseInfo[4];
     unsigned int    AutoRestart = 0;
     unsigned int    AvgApplications = 0;
     unsigned int    DeadlockChkTime = 0;

     // Initialize An Array Of SAMPLE Database Configuration
     // Parameter Structures
     DBaseInfo[0].token = SQLF_DBTN_AUTO_RESTART;
     DBaseInfo[0].ptrvalue = (char *) &AutoRestart;
     DBaseInfo[1].token = SQLF_DBTN_AVG_APPLS;
     DBaseInfo[1].ptrvalue = (char *) &AvgApplications;
     DBaseInfo[2].token = SQLF_DBTN_DLCHKTIME;
     DBaseInfo[2].ptrvalue = (char *) &DeadlockChkTime;

     // Obtain The Current Value Of The SAMPLE Database
     // Configuration Parameters Specified
     sqlfxdb("SAMPLE", 3, &DBaseInfo[0], &sqlca);

     // If The Current Values Of The Configuration Parameters
     // Specified Were Retrieved, Display Them
     if (sqlca.sqlcode == SQL_RC_OK)
     {
          cout << "Automatically restart the database if necessary : ";
          if (AutoRestart == 0)
              cout << "No" << endl;
          else
              cout << "Yes" << endl;
          cout << "Avg. number of active applications allowed      : ";
          cout << AvgApplications << endl;
          cout << "Time interval between deadlock checks           : ";
          cout << DeadlockChkTime << " milliseconds" << endl;
     }

     // Return The SQLCA Return Code To The Calling Function
     return(sqlca.sqlcode);
}

/*--------------------------------------------------------------*/
/* The Main Function                                            */
/*--------------------------------------------------------------*/
int main()
{
```

```
    // Declare The Local Memory Variables
    long    rc = SQL_RC_OK;

    // Create An Instance Of The API_Class Class
    API_Class  Example;

    // Get The Current Values Of Specific SAMPLE Database
    // Configuration File Parameters
    rc = Example.GetDBaseInfo();

    // Return To The Operating System
    return(rc);
}
```

GET DATABASE CONFIGURATION DEFAULTS

Purpose   The GET DATABASE CONFIGURATION DEFAULTS function is used to retrieve the system default values for one or more configuration parameters (entries) in a database configuration file.

Syntax
```
SQL_API_RC SQL_API_FN sqlfddb (char          *DBAlias,
                               unsigned short NumItems,
                               struct sqlfupd *ItemList,
                               struct sqlca   *SQLCA);
```

Parameters *DBAlias*   A pointer to a location in memory where the alias name of the database that parameter values are to be retrieved for is stored.

NumItems   The number of database configuration parameter default values to retrieve. This value identifies the number of elements contained in the array of *sqlfupd* structures specified in the *ItemList* parameter.

ItemList   A pointer to an array of *sqlfupd* structures that specify which database configuration parameter system default values are to be retrieved.

SQLCA   A pointer to a location in memory where a SQL Communications Area (SQLCA) data structure variable is stored. This variable returns either status information (if the function executed successfully) or error information (if the function failed) to the calling application.

Includes   `#include <sqlutil.h>`

Description The GET DATABASE CONFIGURATION DEFAULTS function is used to retrieve the system default values of one or more configuration parameters (entries) in a database configuration file. This function uses an array of special structures (*sqlfupd*) to retrieve the system default values for one or more database configuration parameters. Refer to the GET DATABASE CONFIGURATION function for a detailed description of this structure and for more information about the database configuration parameters available.

Before this function can be executed, an array of *sqlfupd* structures must be allocated, the *token* field of each structure in this array must be set to one of the database configuration parameter tokens listed in Table 7–3 (refer to the GET DATABASE CONFIGURATION function), and the *ptrvalue* field must contain a pointer to a valid location in memory where the configuration parameter value retrieved is to be stored. When this function is executed, the system default value for each database configuration parameter specified is placed in the memory storage areas (local variables) referred to by the *ptrvalue* field of each *sqlfupd* structure in the array.

Comments
- The application that calls this function is responsible for allocating sufficient memory for each data value retrieved.
- The current value of a non-updatable configuration parameter is returned as that configuration parameter's system default value.
- If an error occurs while this function is executing, the database configuration information returned will be invalid. If an error occurs because the database configuration file has been corrupted, an error message will be returned, and you must restore the database from a good backup image to correct the problem.
- For a brief description about each database configuration file parameter, refer to the GET DATABASE CONFIGURATION function. For detailed information about each database configuration file parameter, refer to the *IBM DB2 Universal Database Administration Guide*.

Connection Requirements This function can only be called if a connection to a DB2 Database Manager instance exists. In order to retrieve default database configuration file parameter values for a DB2 database located at a remote node, an application must attach to that node. If necessary, a temporary connection is established by this function while it executes.

Authorization No authorization is required to execute this function call.

See Also RESET DATABASE CONFIGURATION, UPDATE DATABASE CONFIGURATION, GET DATABASE CONFIGURATION

Example The following C++ program illustrates how to use the GET DATABASE CONFIGURATION DEFAULTS function to retrieve the system default database configuration file parameter values for the SAMPLE database:

```
/*------------------------------------------------------------*/
/* NAME:    CH7EX5.CPP                                        */
/* PURPOSE: Illustrate How To Use The Following DB2 API Function */
/*          In A C++ Program:                                 */
/*                                                            */
/*              GET DATABASE CONFIGURATION DEFAULTS           */
/*                                                            */
/*------------------------------------------------------------*/
```

```cpp
// Include The Appropriate Header Files
#include <windows.h>
#include <iostream.h>
#include <sqlutil.h>
#include <sqlca.h>

// Define The API_Class Class
class API_Class
{
    // Attributes
    public:
        struct sqlca   sqlca;

    // Operations
    public:
        long GetDBaseInfo();
};

// Define The GetDBaseInfo() Member Function
long API_Class::GetDBaseInfo()
{
    // Declare The Local Memory Variables
    struct sqlfupd  DBaseInfo[4];
    unsigned int    AutoRestart = 0;
    unsigned int    AvgApplications = 0;
    unsigned int    DeadlockChkTime = 0;

    // Initialize An Array Of SAMPLE Database Configuration
    // Parameter Structures
    DBaseInfo[0].token = SQLF_DBTN_AUTO_RESTART;
    DBaseInfo[0].ptrvalue = (char *) &AutoRestart;
    DBaseInfo[1].token = SQLF_DBTN_AVG_APPLS;
    DBaseInfo[1].ptrvalue = (char *) &AvgApplications;
    DBaseInfo[2].token = SQLF_DBTN_DLCHKTIME;
    DBaseInfo[2].ptrvalue = (char *) &DeadlockChkTime;

    // Obtain The System Default Value Of The SAMPLE Database
    // Configuration Parameters Specified
    sqlfddb("SAMPLE", 3, &DBaseInfo[0], &sqlca);

    // If The System Default Values Of The Configuration Parameters
    // Specified Were Retrieved, Display Them
    if (sqlca.sqlcode == SQL_RC_OK)
    {
        cout << "Automatically restart the database if necessary : ";
        if (AutoRestart == 0)
            cout << "No" << endl;
        else
            cout << "Yes" << endl;
        cout << "Avg. number of active applications allowed    : ";
        cout << AvgApplications << endl;
        cout << "Time interval between deadlock checks          : ";
        cout << DeadlockChkTime << " milliseconds" << endl;
    }
```

```
    // Return The SQLCA Return Code To The Calling Function
    return(sqlca.sqlcode);
}

/*————————————————————————————————————————*/
/* The Main Function                                        */
/*————————————————————————————————————————*/
int main()
{
    // Declare The Local Memory Variables
    long    rc = SQL_RC_OK;

    // Create An Instance Of The API_Class Class
    API_Class   Example;

    // Get The System Default Values Of Specific SAMPLE Database
    // Configuration File Parameters
    rc = Example.GetDBaseInfo();

    // Return To The Operating System
    return(rc);
}
```

■■ ■■ UPDATE DATABASE CONFIGURATION

Purpose   The **UPDATE DATABASE CONFIGURATION** function is used to change the value of one or more parameters (entries) in a specific database configuration file.

Syntax
```
SQL_API_RC SQL_API_FN sqlfudb  (char            *DBAlias,
                                unsigned short  NumItems,
                                struct sqlfupd  *ItemList,
                                struct sqlca    *SQLCA);
```

Parameters *DBAlias*   A pointer to a location in memory where the alias name of the database that parameter values are to be updated for is stored.

NumItems   The number of database configuration parameters values to update. This value identifies the number of elements contained in the array of *sqlfupd* structures specified in the *ItemList* parameter.

ItemList   A pointer to an array of *sqlfupd* structures that specify which database configuration parameter values are to be updated, along with their corresponding values.

SQLCA   A pointer to a location in memory where an SQL Communications Area (SQLCA) data structure variable is stored. This variable returns

either status information (if the function executed successfully) or
error information (if the function failed) to the calling application.

Includes   #include <sqlutil.h>

Description   The UPDATE DATABASE CONFIGURATION function is used to change the value of one
or more configuration parameters (entries) in a specific database configuration file.
This function uses an array of special structures (*sqlfupd*) to update the value of one
or more database configuration parameters. The *sqlfupd* structure is defined in
sqlutil.h as follows:

```
struct sqlfupd
{
unsigned short token;          /* A token that identifies the       */
                               /* configuration parameter whose     */
                               /* value is to be updated            */
char          *ptrvalue;       /* A pointer to a location in        */
                               /* memory where the new              */
                               /* configuration parameter value is  */
                               /* stored                            */
};
```

Before this function can be executed, an array of *sqlfupd* structures must be
allocated, the *token* field of each structure in this array must be set to one of the
database configuration parameter tokens listed in Table 7–3 (refer to the GET
DATABASE CONFIGURATION function), and the *ptrvalue* field of each structure must
contain a pointer to a valid location in memory where the new configuration
parameter value is stored. When this function is executed, the new database
configuration parameter values are copied from the memory storage areas (local
variables) referred to by the *ptrvalue* field of each *sqlfupd* structure in the array to
the appropriate location in the database configuration file, provided the parameters
specified can be updated.

NOTE: *If a user attempts to edit a database configuration file using a method other than
those provided by DB2, the database can become unusable. A database configuration file
should only be updated with one of the following methods:*

■ *The DB2 Database Director*

■ *The DB2 command-line processor (UPDATE DATABASE CONFIGURATION and
RESET DATABASE CONFIGURATION commands)*

■ *The appropriate DB2 API function calls (UPDATE DATABASE CONFIGURATION and
RESET DATABASE CONFIGURATION function calls)*

Comments   ■ Changes to database configuration file parameters only become effective when the
modified configuration file is loaded into memory. This process will not occur until
all applications are disconnected from the database and a new connection is

established (when the first new connection to the database is established, the new values will take effect). Although new configuration parameter values do not take effect immediately, when configuration parameter values are retrieved, the most recent update values are always returned.

■ If an error occurs while this function is executing, the database configuration file will remain unchanged.

■ A database configuration file cannot be updated if its checksum is invalid. Checksums can become invalid if a configuration file is changed by something other than the tools provided with the DB2 product. If a database configuration file cannot be updated, an error message is returned, and you must restore the database from a good backup image to correct the problem.

■ The values used for each database configuration parameter differ for each type of configured database node (server, client, or server with remote clients). For detailed information about the ranges and values that can be set for each node type, refer to the *IBM DB2 Universal Database Administration Guide*.

■ For a brief description about each database configuration file parameter, refer to the GET DATABASE CONFIGURATION function. For detailed information about each database configuration file parameter, refer to the *IBM DB2 Universal Database Administration Guide*.

Connection Requirements This function can only be called if a connection to a DB2 Database Manager instance exists. In order to update database configuration file parameter values for a DB2 database located at a remote node, the application must attach to that node. If necessary, a temporary connection is established by this function while it executes.

Authorization Only users with System Administrator (SYSADM) authority, System Control (SYSCTRL) authority, or System Maintenance (SYSMAINT) authority can execute this function call.

Restrictions There are no restrictions associated with this function call.

See Also GET DATABASE CONFIGURATION DEFAULTS, GET DATABASE CONFIGURATION, RESET DATABASE CONFIGURATION

Example The following C++ program illustrates how to use the UPDATE DATABASE CONFIGURATION function to change the values of database configuration file parameters:

```
/*————————————————————————————————*/
/* NAME:    CH7EX6.CPP                                          */
/* PURPOSE: Illustrate How To Use The Following DB2 API Functions */
/*          In A C++ Program:                                   */
/*                                                              */
/*              UPDATE DATABASE CONFIGURATION                   */
/*              RESET DATABASE CONFIGURATION                    */
```

```
/*                                                                  */
/* OTHER DB2 APIs SHOWN:                                            */
/*            GET DATABASE CONFIGURATION                            */
/*                                                                  */
/*————————————————————————————————————————————————————————————————*/


// Include The Appropriate Header Files
#include <windows.h>
#include <iostream.h>
#include <sqlutil.h>
#include <sqlca.h>

// Define The API_Class Class
class API_Class
{
    // Attributes
    public:
        struct sqlca   sqlca;

    // Operations
    public:
        long GetDBaseInfo();
        long SetDBaseInfo();
};

// Define The GetDBaseInfo() Member Function
long API_Class::GetDBaseInfo()
{
    // Declare The Local Memory Variables
    struct sqlfupd   DBaseInfo[4];
    unsigned int     AutoRestart = 0;
    unsigned int     DeadlockChkTime = 0;

    // Initialize An Array Of SAMPLE Database Configuration
    // Parameter Structures
    DBaseInfo[0].token = SQLF_DBTN_AUTO_RESTART;
    DBaseInfo[0].ptrvalue = (char *) &AutoRestart;
    DBaseInfo[1].token = SQLF_DBTN_DLCHKTIME;
    DBaseInfo[1].ptrvalue = (char *) &DeadlockChkTime;

    // Obtain The Current Value Of The SAMPLE Database
    // Configuration Parameters Specified
    sqlfxdb("SAMPLE", 2, &DBaseInfo[0], &sqlca);

    // If The Current Values Of The Configuration Parameters
    // Specified Were Retrieved, Display Them
    if (sqlca.sqlcode == SQL_RC_OK)
    {
        cout << "Automatically restart the database if necessary : ";
        if (AutoRestart == 0)
            cout << "No" << endl;
        else
            cout << "Yes" << endl;
        cout << "Time interval between deadlock checks           : ";
```

```
        cout << DeadlockChkTime << " milliseconds" << endl;
    }

    // Return The SQLCA Return Code To The Calling Function
    return(sqlca.sqlcode);
}

// Define The SetDBaseInfo() Member Function
long API_Class::SetDBaseInfo()
{
    // Declare The Local Memory Variables
    struct sqlfupd  DBaseInfo[4];
    unsigned int    AutoRestart = 0;
    unsigned int    DeadlockChkTime = 0;

    // Initialize An Array Of SAMPLE Database Configuration
    // Parameter Structures
    DBaseInfo[0].token = SQLF_DBTN_AUTO_RESTART;
    DBaseInfo[0].ptrvalue = (char *) &AutoRestart;
    DBaseInfo[1].token = SQLF_DBTN_DLCHKTIME;
    DBaseInfo[1].ptrvalue = (char *) &DeadlockChkTime;

    // Modify The Values Of The Specified SAMPLE Database
    // Configuration Parameters
    AutoRestart = 0;
    DeadlockChkTime = 8000;
    sqlfudb("SAMPLE", 2, &DBaseInfo[0], &sqlca);

    // Return The SQLCA Return Code To The Calling Function
    return(sqlca.sqlcode);
}

/*---------------------------------------------------------------*/
/* The Main Function                                             */
/*---------------------------------------------------------------*/
int main()
{
    // Declare The Local Memory Variables
    long        rc = SQL_RC_OK;
    struct sqlca  sqlca;

    // Create An Instance Of The API_Class Class
    API_Class  Example;

    // Get The Current Values Of Specific SAMPLE Database
    // Configuration File Parameters
    cout << "Before Update:" << endl;
    rc = Example.GetDBaseInfo();

    // Change The Values Of Specific SAMPLE Database
    // Configuration File Parameters
    if (rc == SQL_RC_OK)
        rc = Example.SetDBaseInfo();
```

```
// Get The Current Values Of Specific SAMPLE Database
// Configuration File Parameters To See If They Were Changed
if (rc == SQL_RC_OK)
{
    cout << endl << "After Update:" << endl;
    rc = Example.GetDBaseInfo();
}

// Reset The Values Of All SAMPLE Database Configuration
// Parameters To Their System Default Values
sqlfrdb("SAMPLE", &sqlca);

// Get The Current Values Of Specific SAMPLE Database
// Configuration File Parameters To See If They Have Been Reset
if (rc == SQL_RC_OK)
{
    cout << endl << "After Reset:" << endl;
    rc = Example.GetDBaseInfo();
}

// Return To The Operating System
return(rc);
}
```

RESET DATABASE CONFIGURATION

Purpose   The RESET DATABASE CONFIGURATION function is used to reset the values of all
updatable configuration parameters (entries) in a database configuration file to their
original system defaults.

Syntax
```
SQL_API_RC SQL_API_FN sqlfrdb (char        *DBAlias,
                               struct sqlca *SQLCA);
```

Parameters *DBAlias*   A pointer to a location in memory where the alias name of the
database that parameter values are to be reset for is stored.

SQLCA   A pointer to a location in memory where a SQL Communications
Area (SQLCA) data structure variable is stored. This variable returns
either status information (if the function executed successfully) or
error information (if the function failed) to the calling application.

Includes   `#include <sqlutil.h>`

Description The RESET DATABASE CONFIGURATION function is used to reset the values of all
updatable configuration parameters (entries) in a database configuration file to their
original system defaults. When this function is executed, all nonupdatable
parameters in the configuration file remain unchanged.

Comments   ■ Changes to database configuration file parameters only become effective when the
modified configuration file is loaded into memory. This process will not occur until

all applications have disconnected from the database and a new connection is established (when the first new connection to the database is established, the new values will take effect). Although new configuration parameter values do not take effect immediately, when configuration parameter values are retrieved, the most recent update values are always returned.

■ If an error occurs while this function is executing, the database configuration file will remain unchanged.

■ A database configuration file cannot be updated if its checksum is invalid. Checksums can become invalid if a configuration file is changed by something other than the tools provided with the DB2 product. If a database configuration file cannot be reset, an error message is returned, and you must restore the database from a good backup image to correct the problem.

■ For a brief description about each database configuration file parameter, refer to the GET DATABASE CONFIGURATION function. For detailed information about each database configuration file parameter, refer to the *IBM DB2 Universal Database Administration Guide*.

Connection Requirements   This function can only be called if a connection to a DB2 Database Manager instance exists. In order to reset database configuration file parameter values for a DB2 database located at a remote node, an application must attach to that node. If necessary, a temporary connection is established by this function during its execution.

Authorization   Only users with System Administrator (SYSADM) authority, System Control (SYSCTRL) authority, or System Maintenance (SYSMAINT) authority can execute this function call.

See Also   GET DATABASE CONFIGURATION DEFAULTS, GET DATABASE CONFIGURATION, UPDATE DATABASE CONFIGURATION, RESTORE DATABASE

Example   See the example provided for the UPDATE DATABASE CONFIGURATION function on page 230.

CHAPTER 8

Database, Node, and DCS Directory Management APIs

DB2 uses a set of special directories to keep track of the workstations and databases that are available for use. This chapter is designed to introduce you to the set of DB2 API functions that are used to add entries to, remove entries from, and retrieve the contents of each of these directories. The first part of this chapter provides a general discussion about the various DB2 directories. Then, the functions that are used to retrieve and modify the contents of the various DB2 database directories are described. Next, information about the functions that are used to retrieve and modify the contents of the workstation directory is provided. This is followed by a discussion of the functions that are used to retrieve and modify the contents of the DRDA database directory. Then, the functions that are used to make a DB2 server visible and invisible to a Novell NetWare server are discussed. Finally, a detailed reference section covering each DB2 API function that can be used to add entries to, remove entries from, and retrieve the contents of the various DB2 directories is provided.

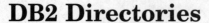

DB2 Directories

DB2 uses the following set of directories to access other remote workstations and both local and remote databases:

- A system database directory
- One or more volume (local) directories
- A workstation (node) directory
- A Database Connection Services (DCS) directory

Refer to the DB2 Database Directories section in Chapter 1 for detailed information about these directories.

The System Database Directory

Whenever a database is cataloged, an entry containing information that is needed in order for DB2 to establish a connection to that database is stored in the system database directory. Think of this directory as the master directory for a DB2 workstation, because it contains one entry for each local and remote cataloged database that can be accessed by that workstation.

Databases are implicitly cataloged in this directory when the **CREATE DATABASE** function or command is executed. You can explicitly catalog new databases and aliases for existing databases in this directory by calling the **CATALOG DATABASE** function in an application or by issuing the **CATALOG DATABASE** command from the DB2 command-line processor. You can remove (uncatalog) entries from this directory when they are no longer valid (or needed) by calling the **UNCATALOG DATABASE** function in an application or by issuing the **UNCATALOG DATABASE** command from the DB2 command-line processor. You can examine the entries in this directory by calling the **OPEN DATABASE DIRECTORY SCAN**, **GET NEXT DATABASE DIRECTORY ENTRY**, and **CLOSE DATABASE DIRECTORY SCAN** functions from within an application program.

Volume Directories

In addition to the system database directory, a volume directory exists on each logical disk drive on a workstation that contains one or more DB2 databases. The number of volume database directories that exist on a workstation is determined by the number of logical disk drives on that workstation that contain one or more DB2 databases. A volume directory contains one entry for each database that is physically stored on the logical disk drive.

Volume directories are automatically created the first time a database is created on a logical disk drive, and DB2 updates their contents (with implicit **CATALOG** and **UNCATALOG** commands) each time a database creation or deletion event occurs. You can explicitly catalog or uncatalog new databases and aliases for existing databases in a volume directory the same way you would explicitly catalog and uncatalog them in the system directory. Likewise, you can examine the entries stored in a volume directory the same way you would examine the entries in the system directory. However, the actual volume database directory where entries are to be added, deleted, or retrieved must be specified in the CATALOG DATABASE, UNCATALOG DATABASE, and OPEN DATABASE DIRECTORY SCAN function calls.

The Workstation (Node) Directory

The workstation or node directory contains one entry for each remote database server workstation that can be accessed. Entries in the workstation directory are used in conjunction with entries in the system directory to make connections to remote DB2 Universal Database database servers. Entries in the workstation directory are also used in conjunction with entries in the DCS directory for making connections to host (OS/390, AS/400, etc.) DB2 database servers. You can explicitly catalog new workstation nodes in this directory by calling the CATALOG NODE function in an application or by issuing the CATALOG NODE command from the DB2 command-line processor. You can uncatalog node directory entries when they are no longer valid (or needed) by calling the UNCATALOG NODE function in an application or by issuing the UNCATALOG NODE command from the DB2 command-line processor. You can examine the entries in this directory by calling the OPEN NODE DIRECTORY SCAN, GET NEXT NODE DIRECTORY ENTRY, and CLOSE NODE DIRECTORY SCAN functions from within an application program.

The Database Connection Services (DCS) Directory

A DCS directory only exists if the DB2 Connect product has been installed on the workstation. This directory contains one entry for each host (OS/390, AS/400, etc.) database that DB2 can access via the DRDA. You can explicitly catalog new DCS databases in this directory by calling the CATALOG DCS DATABASE function in an application or by issuing the CATALOG DCS DATABASE command from the DB2 command-line processor. You can remove entries from this directory when they are no longer valid (or needed) by calling the UNCATALOG DCS DATABASE function in an application or by issuing the UNCATALOG DCS DATABASE command from the DB2 command-line processor. You can examine an entry in this database directory by calling the OPEN DCS DIRECTORY SCAN, GET DCS DIRECTORY ENTRIES, GET DCS DIRECTORY ENTRY FOR DATABASE, and CLOSE DCS DIRECTORY SCAN functions from within an application program.

Registering/Deregistering DB2 Database Servers with NetWare

As long as DB2 database servers are serving clients in an environment that uses the Communications Manager to handle network processing, server workstations are always visible to their clients. However, if Novell NetWare handles the network processing, a DB2 server must be made visible to the network registry before clients can access the server. You can add DB2 servers to a Novell NetWare registry by calling the REGISTER function in an application or by issuing the REGISTER command from the DB2 command-line processor. You can remove DB2 servers from a NetWare registry by calling the DEREGISTER function in an application or by issuing the DEREGISTER command from the DB2 command-line processor.

The DB2 Database, Node, and DCS Directory Management Functions

Table 8–1 lists the DB2 API functions that are used to add, list, and delete entries stored in the various DB2 system directories.

Table 8–1   Database, Node, and DCS Directory Management APIs

Function Name	Description
CATALOG DATABASE	Stores information about a database in either the local or system database directory.
UNCATALOG DATABASE	Removes information about a database from either the local or system database directory.
CHANGE DATABASE COMMENT	Adds or changes the comment (description) associated with a database that is cataloged in either the local or system database directory.
OPEN DATABASE DIRECTORY SCAN	Stores a snapshot copy of the local or system database directory in memory.
GET NEXT DATABASE DIRECTORY ENTRY	Retrieves an entry from the snapshot copy of the database directory that was placed in memory by the OPEN DATABASE DIRECTORY SCAN function.
CLOSE DATABASE DIRECTORY SCAN	Frees system resources allocated by the OPEN DATABASE DIRECTORY SCAN function.
CATALOG NODE	Stores information about a remote workstation in the node directory.
UNCATALOG NODE	Removes information about a remote workstation from the node directory.
OPEN NODE DIRECTORY SCAN	Stores a snapshot copy of the node directory in memory.
GET NEXT NODE DIRECTORY ENTRY	Retrieves an entry from the snapshot copy of the node directory that was placed in memory by the OPEN NODE DIRECTORY SCAN function.
CLOSE NODE DIRECTORY SCAN	Frees system resources allocated by the OPEN NODE DIRECTORY SCAN function.
CATALOG DCS DATABASE	Stores information about a DRDA database in the DCS directory.
UNCATALOG DCS DATABASE	Removes information about a DRDA database from the DCS directory.

Table 8–1   Database, Node, and DCS Directory Management APIs (Continued)

Function Name	Description
OPEN DCS DIRECTORY SCAN	Returns the number of entries found in the DCS directory.
GET DCS DIRECTORY ENTRIES	Copies entries in the DCS directory to a user-allocated memory storage area.
GET DCS DIRECTORY ENTRY FOR DATABASE	Retrieves an entry from the copy of the DCS directory that was placed in memory by the GET DCS DIRECTORY ENTRIES function.
CLOSE DCS DIRECTORY SCAN	Frees system resources allocated by the OPEN DCS DIRECTORY SCAN function.
REGISTER	Registers a DB2 database server at a Novell NetWare file server registry.
DEREGISTER	Removes a DB2 database server registration from a Novell NetWare file server registry.

■ ■ CATALOG DATABASE

Purpose   The **CATALOG DATABASE** function is used to store information about a database in the system database directory.

Syntax

```
SQL_API_RC SQL_API_FN sqlecadb (char          *DBName,
                                char          *DBAlias,
                                unsigned char  Type,
                                char          *NodeName,
                                char          *Path,
                                char          *Comment,
                                unsigned short Authentication,
                                char          *DCEPrincipal,
                                struct sqlca  *SQLCA);
```

Parameters

DBName   A pointer to a location in memory where the name of the database to be cataloged is stored.

DBAlias   A pointer to a location in memory where the alias name of the database to be cataloged is stored.

Type   Designates whether the database is local (indirect), remote, or accessed via a *Distributed Computing Environment* (DCE). This parameter must be set to one of the following values:

    ■ **SQL_INDIRECT**
    Specifies that the database is local (i.e., that it resides at the same location as the DB2 Database Manager instance).

    ■ **SQL_REMOTE**
    Specifies that the database resides at another instance.

    ■ **SQL_DCE**
    Specifies that the database is accessed via DCE.

NodeName   A pointer to a location in memory where the name of the node where the database physically resides (if the database being cataloged is not a local database) is stored.

Path   A pointer to a location in memory where the letter of the drive OR the name of the path on which the database being cataloged resides (if the database being cataloged is a local database) is stored.

Comment   A pointer to a location in memory where a description of the database is stored. If this parameter contains a NULL value, no description (comment) will be stored for the database.

Authentication   Specifies where user authentication is to occur. Authentication is the process by which DB2 verifies that database users are who they claim to be. This parameter must be set to one of the following values:

    ■ **SQL_AUTHENTICATION_SERVER**
    Specifies that user authentication is to take place on the node containing the database.

■ **SQL_AUTHENTICATION_CLIENT**
Specifies that user authentication is to take place on the node where applications that access the cataloged database are invoked.

■ **SQL_AUTHENTICATION_DCS**
Specifies that user authentication is to take place on the node containing the database, except when DB2 Connect is used (when the **DRDA AS** option specifies that authentication is to takes place at the DRDA server).

■ **SQL_AUTHENTICATION_DCE**
Specifies that user authentication is to be performed by DCE Security Services.

■ **SQL_AUTHENTICATION_NOT_SPEC**
The location at which user authentication is to take place is not specified.

DCEPrincipal   A pointer to a location in memory where the DCE principal name of the DB2 server that the database resides on is stored.

SQLCA   A pointer to a location in memory where a SQL Communications Area (SQLCA) data structure variable is stored. This variable returns either status information (if the function executed successfully) or error information (if the function failed) to the calling application.

Includes   `#include <sqlenv.h>`

Description   The **CATALOG DATABASE** function is used to store information about a database in the system database directory. This function can catalog databases that are physically located on either the same physical workstation as the DB2 Database Manager instance or on a different remote workstation node. It can also recatalog databases that for some reason have been uncataloged. In addition, this function can catalog multiple aliases for a single database, regardless of its physical location.

DB2 automatically catalogs an entry in the local (volume) database directory and another entry in the system database directory whenever a new database is created. If a database is created from a remote client workstation (or from a client application executing from a different DB2 Database Manager instance on the same machine), an entry for the database will also be made in the system database directory that is stored at the client instance.

Comments   ■ The value specified for the *Path* parameter cannot exceed 215 characters in length. If a NULL value is specified for the *Path* parameter, the current value of the *dftdbpath* DB2 Database Manager configuration file parameter will be used to locate the database.

■ The value specified for the *Comment* parameter cannot exceed 30 characters in length.

■ This function can be used to recatalog a database that has been removed (uncataloged) from the system database directory, provided the database has not been deleted (dropped).

■ The value specified in the *DCEPrincipal* parameter must match the value stored in the server's keytab file.

■ If anything other than `SQL_AUTHENTICATION_DCE` is specified in the *Authentication* parameter, the *DCEPrincipal* parameter is ignored.

■ In a partitioned database environment, this function must be invoked from a node on the server where the database physically resides.

■ Access to all database objects is dependent upon user authentication. The *Authentication* parameter should always be set to `SQL_AUTHENTICATION_NOT_SPEC`, except when you are cataloging a database that resides on a DB2/2 Version 1.x or a DB2/6000 Version 1.x server.

■ If a NULL pointer is specified for both the *Path* and the *NodeName* parameters, DB2 will assume that the database is local and the location of the database is in the location specified in the DB2 Database Manager configuration file.

■ If a database is cataloged with the *Type* parameter set to `SQL_INDIRECT`, the value specified in the *Authentication* parameter will be ignored, and the authentication value in the system database directory will be set to `SQL_AUTHENTICATION_NOT_SPEC`.

■ Databases created at the current DB2 Database Manager instance (as defined by the value of the `DB2INSTANCE` environment variable) are cataloged as indirect (local). Databases created at other DB2 Database Manager instances are cataloged as remote (even if they physically reside on the same machine).

■ The `CATALOG DATABASE` function will automatically create a system database directory if one does not already exist. The system database directory is stored on the disk drive or path that contains the DB2 Database Manager instance currently being used.

■ The system database directory is maintained outside of the database. Each entry in this directory contains the following information:

–Database name

–Database alias

–Database comment (description)

–Database entry type

–Local database directory (if the database is a local database)

–Node name (if the database is a remote database)

–Authentication type

–DB2 release (version) information

■ You can use the `OPEN DATABASE DIRECTORY SCAN`, `GET NEXT DATABASE DIRECTORY ENTRY`, and `CLOSE DATABASE DIRECTORY SCAN` functions to list the contents of the system database directory. Together, these three functions work like a SQL cursor (i.e., they use the OPEN/FETCH/CLOSE paradigm).

■ If directory caching is enabled, database, node, and DCS directory files are cached in memory. An application's directory cache is created during the first directory lookup. Because the cache is only refreshed when an application modifies one of the directory files, directory changes made by other applications might not be effective until the application is restarted. To refresh DB2's shared cache (server only), an application should stop and then restart the database. To refresh an application's directory cache, the user should stop and then restart that application. For more information about directory caching, refer to the GET DATABASE MANAGER CONFIGURATION function.

Connection Requirements This function can be called at any time; a connection to a DB2 Database Manager instance or to a DB2 database does not have to be established first.

Authorization Only users with either System Administrator (SYSADM) authority or System Control (SYSCTRL) authority are allowed to execute this function call.

See Also UNCATALOG DATABASE, OPEN DATABASE DIRECTORY SCAN, GET NEXT DATABASE DIRECTORY ENTRY, CLOSE DATABASE DIRECTORY SCAN

Example The following C++ program illustrates how to use the CATALOG DATABASE function to catalog an alias for the SAMPLE database:

```
/*————————————————————————————————————*/
/* NAME:      CH8EX1.CPP                                        */
/* PURPOSE: Illustrate How To Use The Following DB2 API Function */
/*          In A C++ Program:                                  */
/*                                                             */
/*                CATALOG DATABASE                             */
/*                                                             */
/*————————————————————————————————————*/
// Include The Appropriate Header Files
#include <windows.h>
#include <iostream.h>
#include <sqlenv.h>
#include <sqlca.h>

// Define The API_Class Class
class API_Class
{
    // Attributes
    public:
        struct sqlca   sqlca;

    // Operations
    public:
        long CatalogDB();
};
```

```cpp
// Define The CatalogDB() Member Function
long API_Class::CatalogDB()
{
    // Declare The Local Memory Variables
    char   DBName[9];
    char   DBAlias[9];
    char   Comment[31];

    // Initialize The Local Memory Variables
    strcpy(DBName, "SAMPLE");
    strcpy(DBAlias, "SAMPLEDB");
    strcpy(Comment, "IBM Sample Database");

    // Catalog A New Alias For The SAMPLE Database
    sqlecadb(DBName, DBAlias, SQL_INDIRECT, NULL, NULL,
        Comment, SQL_AUTHENTICATION_NOT_SPEC, NULL, &sqlca);

    // If The New Alias Was Cataloged, Display A Success Message
    if (sqlca.sqlcode == SQL_RC_OK)
    {
        cout << "The alias " << DBAlias << " has been cataloged ";
        cout << "for the " << DBName << " database." << endl;
    }

    // Return The SQLCA Return Code To The Calling Function
    return(sqlca.sqlcode);
}

/*---------------------------------------------------------------*/
/* The Main Function                                             */
/*---------------------------------------------------------------*/
int main()
{
    // Declare The Local Memory Variables
    long  rc = SQL_RC_OK;

    // Create An Instance Of The API_Class Class
    API_Class  Example;

    // Catalog A New Alias For The SAMPLE Database
    rc = Example.CatalogDB();

    // Return To The Operating System
    return(rc);
}
```

UNCATALOG DATABASE

Purpose   The UNCATALOG DATABASE function is used to delete an entry from the system database directory.

Syntax
```
SQL_API_RC SQL_API_FN sqleuncd (char         *DBAlias,
                                struct sqlca *SQLCA);
```

Parameters   *DBAlias*   A pointer to a location in memory where the alias name of the database to be uncataloged is stored.

SQLCA   A pointer to a location in memory where a SQL Communications Area (SQLCA) data structure variable is stored. This variable returns either status information (if the function executed successfully) or error information (if the function failed) to the calling application.

Includes   `#include <sqlenv.h>`

Description   The **UNCATALOG DATABASE** function is used to delete an entry from the system database directory. This function can only delete entries in the system database directory. Entries in the local (volume) database directory must be deleted with the **DROP DATABASE** function.

Comments   ■ You can change the authentication type of a database when communicating with a down-level server by first uncataloging the database and then cataloging it again with a different authentication type. Refer to the **CATALOG DATABASE** function for more information about authentication types.

■ You can use the **OPEN DATABASE DIRECTORY SCAN, GET NEXT DATABASE DIRECTORY ENTRY,** and **CLOSE DATABASE DIRECTORY SCAN** functions to list the contents of the system database directory. Together, these three functions work like an SQL cursor (i.e., they use the OPEN/FETCH/CLOSE paradigm).

■ If directory caching is enabled, database, node, and DCS directory files are cached in memory. An application's directory cache is created during the first directory lookup. Because the cache is only refreshed when an application modifies one of the directory files, directory changes made by other applications might not be effective until the application has been restarted. To refresh DB2's shared cache (server only), an application should stop and then restart the database. To refresh an application's directory cache, the user should stop and then restart that application. For more information about directory caching, refer to the **GET DATABASE MANAGER CONFIGURATION** function.

Connection Requirements   This function can be called at any time; a connection to a DB2 Database Manager instance or to a DB2 database does not have to be established first.

Authorization   Only users with either System Administrator (SYSADM) authority or System Control (SYSCTRL) authority can execute this function call.

See Also   **CATALOG DATABASE, OPEN DATABASE DIRECTORY SCAN, GET NEXT DATABASE DIRECTORY ENTRY, CLOSE DATABASE DIRECTORY SCAN**

Example   The following C++ program illustrates how to use the **UNCATALOG DATABASE** function to remove an alias for the SAMPLE database from the system database directory:

```
/*------------------------------------------------------------*/
/* NAME:    CH8EX2.CPP                                         */
/* PURPOSE: Illustrate How To Use The Following DB2 API Function */
/*          In A C++ Program:                                  */
/*                                                             */
/*                UNCATALOG DATABASE                           */
/*                                                             */
/*------------------------------------------------------------*/
// Include The Appropriate Header Files
#include <windows.h>
#include <iostream.h>
#include <sqlenv.h>
#include <sqlca.h>

// Define The API_Class Class
class API_Class
{
    // Attributes
    public:
        struct sqlca  sqlca;

    // Operations
    public:
        long UncatalogDB();
};

// Define The UncatalogDB() Member Function
long API_Class::UncatalogDB()
{
    // Declare The Local Memory Variables
    char  DBAlias[9];

    // Initialize The Local Memory Variables
    strcpy(DBAlias, "SAMPLEDB");

    // Uncatalog An Alias For The SAMPLE Database
    sqleuncd(DBAlias, &sqlca);

    // If The Alias Was Uncataloged, Display A Success Message
    if (sqlca.sqlcode == SQL_RC_OK)
    {
        cout << "The alias " << DBAlias << " has been uncataloged.";
        cout << endl;
    }

    // Return The SQLCA Return Code To The Calling Function
    return(sqlca.sqlcode);
}

/*------------------------------------------------------------*/
/* The Main Function                                          */
/*------------------------------------------------------------*/
int main()
{
    // Declare The Local Memory Variables
```

```
long   rc = SQL_RC_OK;

// Create An Instance Of The API_Class Class
API_Class  Example;

// Uncatalog An Alias For The SAMPLE Database
rc = Example.UncatalogDB();

// Return To The Operating System
return(rc);
}
```

■ ■ CHANGE DATABASE COMMENT

Purpose   The **CHANGE DATABASE COMMENT** function is used to add or change the comment (description) associated with a database that has been cataloged in either the system database directory or the local (volume) database directory.

Syntax
```
SQL_API_RC SQL_API_FN sqledcgd (char      *DBAlias,
                                char      *Path,
                                char      *Comment,
                                struct sqlca  *SQLCA);
```

Parameters   *DBAlias*   A pointer to the location in memory where the alias name of the database whose comment is to be updated is stored.

Path   A pointer to a location in memory where the path to the local database directory is stored. If the value specified for this parameter is NULL, the system database directory is used.

Comment   A pointer to a location in memory where descriptive information (a comment) about the database is stored. This parameter can contain a NULL value.

SQLCA   A pointer to a location in memory where a SQL Communications Area (SQLCA) data structure variable is stored. This variable returns either status information (if the function executed successfully) or error information (if the function failed) to the calling application.

Includes   `#include <sqlenv.h>`

Description   The **CHANGE DATABASE COMMENT** function is used to add or change the comment (description) associated with a database that has been cataloged in either the system database directory or the local database directory. Only the comment associated with the database alias specified is modified by this function. Other entries in the system database directory or the local database directory that have the same database name but different aliases are not affected.

Comments
- The value specified for the *DBAlias* parameter cannot exceed eight characters in length.
- If a path name is specified in the *Path* parameter, the database alias specified in the *DBAlias* parameter must be cataloged in the local database directory. If no path name is specified, the database alias must be cataloged in the system database directory.
- The value specified for the *Comment* parameter cannot exceed 30 characters in length. If the *Comment* parameter is set to NULL, the database comment will be unchanged.
- If the *Comment* parameter contains text, the new text will replace any existing comment text when this function is executed. The comment is only changed in the local database directory or the system database directory on the node from which this function is invoked. To change the database comment on each node used by a partitioned database, this function must be executed from every node.
- To modify an existing database comment, an application should perform the following steps:

  1. Call the OPEN DATABASE DIRECTORY SCAN function.
  2. Call the GET NEXT DATABASE DIRECTORY ENTRY function to retrieve the existing database comment.
  3. Modify the retrieved comment.
  4. Call the CLOSE DATABASE DIRECTORY SCAN function.
  5. Call this function using the modified comment.

Connection Requirements This function can be called at any time; a connection to a DB2 Database Manager instance or to a DB2 database does not have to be established first.

Authorization Only users with either System Administrator (SYSADM) or System Control (SYSCTRL) authority are allowed to execute this function call.

See Also CREATE DATABASE, CATALOG DATABASE

Example The following C++ program illustrates how to use the CHANGE DATABASE COMMENT function to change the description (comment) associated with the SAMPLE database:

```
/*---------------------------------------------------------------*/
/* NAME:     CH8EX3.CPP                                          */
/* PURPOSE: Illustrate How To Use The Following DB2 API Function */
/*          In A C++ Program:                                    */
/*                                                               */
/*              CHANGE DATABASE COMMENT                          */
/*                                                               */
/*---------------------------------------------------------------*/
// Include The Appropriate Header Files
#include <windows.h>
#include <iostream.h>
```

```cpp
#include <sqlenv.h>
#include <sqlca.h>

// Define The API_Class Class
class API_Class
{
    // Attributes
    public:
        struct sqlca   sqlca;

    // Operations
    public:
        long ChangeComment();
};

// Define The ChangeComment() Member Function
long API_Class::ChangeComment()
{
    // Declare The Local Memory Variables
    char   DBAlias[9];
    char   Comment[31];

    // Initialize The Local Memory Variables
    strcpy(DBAlias, "SAMPLE");
    strcpy(Comment, "DB2 UDB Sample Database");

    // Change The Comment Associated With The SAMPLE Database Alias
    sqledcgd(DBAlias, "", Comment, &sqlca);

    // If The Comment Was Changed, Display A Success Message
    if (sqlca.sqlcode == SQL_RC_OK)
    {
        cout << "The comment associated with the " << DBAlias;
        cout << " database alias has been changed." << endl;
    }

    // Return The SQLCA Return Code To The Calling Function
    return(sqlca.sqlcode);
}

/*----------------------------------------------------------------*/
/* The Main Function                                              */
/*----------------------------------------------------------------*/
int main()
{
    // Declare The Local Memory Variables
    long   rc = SQL_RC_OK;

    // Create An Instance Of The API_Class Class
    API_Class   Example;

    // Change The Comment For The SAMPLE Database
    rc = Example.ChangeComment();
```

```
// Return To The Operating System
return(rc);
}
```

OPEN DATABASE DIRECTORY SCAN

Purpose   The OPEN DATABASE DIRECTORY SCAN function is used to store a copy of the system database directory or the local database directory in memory and to obtain a count of the number of entries found in the directory specified.

Syntax
```
SQL_API_RC SQL_API_FN sqledosd (char            *Path,
                                unsigned short  *Handle,
                                unsigned short  *NumEntries,
                                struct sqlca    *SQLCA);
```

Parameters   *Path*   A pointer to the location in memory where the path that identifies where the local database directory resides is stored. If the value specified for this parameter is NULL, the system database directory is used.

Handle   A pointer to a location in memory where this function is to store a directory scan buffer identifier that will be used in subsequent GET NEXT DATABASE DIRECTORY ENTRY and CLOSE DATABASE DIRECTORY SCAN function calls.

NumEntries A pointer to a location in memory where this function is to store a count of the number of entries found in the database directory specified.

SQLCA   A pointer to a location in memory where a SQL Communications Area (SQLCA) data structure variable is stored. This variable returns either status information (if the function executed successfully) or error information (if the function failed) to the calling application.

Includes   `#include <sqlenv.h>`

Description The OPEN DATABASE DIRECTORY SCAN function is used to store a copy of the system database directory or the local database directory in memory and to obtain a count of the number of entries found in the directory specified. The copy of the database directory that is placed in memory represents a snapshot of the directory when the directory scan is opened. This copy is never updated, even if the directory itself changes.

This function is normally followed by one or more GET NEXT DATABASE DIRECTORY ENTRY function calls and one CLOSE DATABASE DIRECTORY SCAN function call. Together, these three functions work like an SQL cursor (i.e., they use the OPEN/FETCH/CLOSE paradigm). The memory buffer that is used to store the database directory data obtained by the directory scan is automatically allocated by this function and a pointer to that buffer (the buffer identifier) is stored in the *Handle* parameter. This identifier is then used by subsequent GET NEXT DATABASE DIRECTORY ENTRY and CLOSE DATABASE DIRECTORY SCAN function calls to access information stored in the the memory buffer area.

Comments   ■ Multiple OPEN DATABASE DIRECTORY SCAN function calls can be issued against the same database directory. However, because the directory can change between each call, the directory entries copied into memory by each call might vary.

     ■ An application can have up to eight database directory scans open at one time.

Connection Requirements   This function can be called at any time; a connection to a DB2 Database Manager instance or to a DB2 database does not have to be established first.

Authorization   No authorization is required to execute this function call.

See Also   GET NEXT DATABASE DIRECTORY ENTRY, CLOSE DATABASE DIRECTORY SCAN

Example   The following C++ program illustrates how to use the OPEN DATABASE DIRECTORY SCAN, GET NEXT DATABASE DIRECTORY ENTRY, and CLOSE DATABASE DIRECTORY SCAN functions to retrieve the entries in the system database directory:

```
/*———————————————————————————————— */
/* NAME:    CH8EX4.CPP                                  */
/* PURPOSE: Illustrate How To Use The Following DB2 API Functions  */
/*          In A C++ Program:                           */
/*                                                      */
/*               OPEN DATABASE DIRECTORY SCAN           */
/*               GET NEXT DATABASE DIRECTORY ENTRY      */
/*               CLOSE DATABASE DIRECTORY SCAN          */
/*                                                      */
/*———————————————————————————————— */

// Include The Appropriate Header Files
#include <windows.h>
#include <iostream.h>
#include <sqlenv.h>
#include <sqlca.h>

// Define The API_Class Class
class API_Class
{
    // Attributes
    public:
        struct sqlca   sqlca;

    // Operations
    public:
        long ShowDatabases();
};
```

```
// Define The ShowDatabases() Member Function
long API_Class::ShowDatabases()
{
    // Declare The Local Memory Variables
    unsigned short    Handle;
    unsigned short    DBCount;
    struct sqledinfo  *DB_DirInfo = NULL;

    // Open The Database Directory Scan
    sqledosd(NULL, &Handle, &DBCount, &sqlca);

    // Scan The Database Directory Buffer And Retrieve All Database
    // Names And Descriptions Stored There
    if (sqlca.sqlcode == SQL_RC_OK)
    {
        cout << "Alias          Description" << endl;
        cout << "——————————————————————————————————————" << endl;
        for (;DBCount != 0; DBCount-)
        {
            // Retrieve The Next Database Directory Entry
            sqledgne(Handle, &DB_DirInfo, &sqlca);

            // Display Database Directory Entry Retrieved
            if (sqlca.sqlcode == SQL_RC_OK)
            {
                char  Alias[9];
                cout.width(14);
                cout.setf(ios::left);
                strncpy(Alias, DB_DirInfo->alias, 8);
                Alias[8] = 0;
                cout << Alias;
                cout.width(30);
                cout.setf(ios::left);
                cout << DB_DirInfo->comment << endl;
            }
        }

        // Close The Database Directory Scan And Free All Resources
        // Obtained By The Open Database Directory Scan API
        sqledcls(Handle, &sqlca);
    }

    // Return The SQLCA Return Code To The Calling Function
    return(sqlca.sqlcode);
}

/*————————————————————————————————————————————————————————————*/
/* The Main Function                                          */
/*————————————————————————————————————————————————————————————*/
int main()
{
    // Declare The Local Memory Variables
    long  rc = SQL_RC_OK;
```

```
        // Create An Instance Of The API_Class Class
        API_Class  Example;

        // Generate And Display A List OF Available Databases
        rc = Example.ShowDatabases();

        // Return To The Operating System
        return(rc);
    }
```

GET NEXT DATABASE DIRECTORY ENTRY

Purpose   The GET NEXT DATABASE DIRECTORY ENTRY function is used to retrieve the next entry from the copy of the system database directory or the local database directory that was placed in memory by the OPEN DATABASE DIRECTORY SCAN function.

Syntax
```
SQL_API_RC SQL_API_FN sqledgne (unsigned short    Handle,
                                struct sqledinfo  **DBDirEntry,
                                struct sqlca      *SQLCA);
```

Parameters   *Handle*   The directory scan buffer identifier that was returned by an associated OPEN DATABASE DIRECTORY SCAN function call.

DBDirEntry   A pointer to the address of an *sqledinfo* structure where this function is to store the database directory entry information retrieved.

SQLCA   A pointer to a location in memory where a SQL Communications Area (SQLCA) data structure variable is stored. This variable returns either status information (if the function executed successfully) or error information (if the function failed) bto the calling application.

Includes   `#include <sqlenv.h>`

Description   The GET NEXT DATABASE DIRECTORY ENTRY function is used to retrieve the next entry from the copy of the system database directory or the local database directory that was placed in memory by the OPEN DATABASE DIRECTORY SCAN function. The information retrieved is stored in a special structure, *sqledinfo*, that is defined in *sqlenv.h* as follows:

```
struct sqledinfo
{
char            alias[8];     /* The database alias (alternate) name    */
char            dbname[8];    /* The database name                      */
char            drive[215];   /* The path name or the disk drive ID     */
```

```
                                    /* that specifies where the database    */
                                    /* physically resides. A value is only   */
                                    /* returned for this field if the system */
                                    /* database directory was opened for      */
                                    /* scanning.                              */
        char        intname[8];     /* The subdirectory name where the        */
                                    /* database resides. A value is only      */
                                    /* returned for this field if the local   */
                                    /* database directory was opened for      */
                                    /* scanning.                              */
        char        nodename[8];    /* The name of the node where the         */
                                    /* database is physically located. A      */
                                    /* value is only returned for this field  */
                                    /* if the database is a remote database.  */
        char        dbtype[20];     /* DB2 Database Manager release            */
                                    /* information                            */
        char        comment[30];    /* The comment (description) that is       */
                                    /* associated with the database            */
        short       com_codepage;   /* The code page of comment. This field   */
                                    /* is no longer used.                     */
        char        type;           /* Indicates whether the database was      */
                                    /* was created by the current instance    */
                                    /* (SQL_INDIRECT), resides at a           */
                                    /* different instance (SQL_REMOTE),       */
                                    /* resides on this volume (SQL_HOME),     */
                                    /* or resides in a DCE directory          */
                                    /* (SQL_DCE).                             */
        unsigned short authentication; /* Indicates whether user ID and       */
                                    /* password authentication occurs at      */
                                    /* the database server workstation        */
                                    /* (SQL_AUTHENTICATION_SERVER),           */
                                    /* at the client workstation              */
                                    /* (SQL_AUTHENTICATION_CLIENT),           */
                                    /* at the DCS server                      */
                                    /* (SQL_AUTHENTICATION_DCS), by DCE       */
                                    /* Security Services                      */
                                    /* (SQL_AUTHENTICATION_DCE), or is        */
                                    /* unspecified                            */
                                    /* (SQL_AUTHENTICATION_NOT_SPEC)          */
        char        glbdbname[255]; /* The global name of the target          */
                                    /* database in the DCE directory if the   */
                                    /* type field of this structure is set    */
                                    /* to SQL_DCE                             */
        char        dceprincipal[1024]; /* The DCE principal name. A value is */
                                    /* only returned for this field if        */
                                    /* authentication is performed by DCE     */
                                    /* Security Services.                     */
        short       cat_nodenum;    /* The catalog node number                 */
        short       nodenum;        /* The node number                        */
        };
```

Comments   ■ All character fields in the database directory entry information buffer are right-padded with blanks.

■ When this function is executed, the value in the *DBDirEntry* parameter points to the next database directory entry in the copy of the database directory that resides in memory. Each subsequent GET NEXT DATABASE DIRECTORY ENTRY function call retrieves the database directory entry immediately following the current directory entry, unless there are no more directory entries available (in which case an error is returned).

■ You can use the value returned in the *NumEntries* parameter when the OPEN DATABASE DIRECTORY SCAN function is executed to set up a loop that scans through the entire database directory by issuing GET NEXT DATABASE DIRECTORY ENTRY function calls, one at a time, until the number of calls issued equals the number of entries found in the directory.

Prerequisites   The OPEN DATABASE DIRECTORY SCAN function must be executed before this function is called.

Connection   This function can be called at any time; a connection to a DB2 Database Manager
Requirements instance or to a DB2 database does not have to be established first.

Authorization   No authorization is required to execute this function call.

See Also   OPEN DATABASE DIRECTORY SCAN, CLOSE DATABASE DIRECTORY SCAN

Example   See the example provided for the OPEN DATABASE DIRECTORY SCAN function on page 251.

CLOSE DATABASE DIRECTORY SCAN

Purpose   The CLOSE DATABASE DIRECTORY SCAN function is used to free system resources that were allocated by the OPEN DATABASE DIRECTORY SCAN function.

Syntax
```
SQL_API_RC SQL_API_FN sqledcls (unsigned short  Handle,
                                struct sqlca    *SQLCA);
```

Parameters   *Handle*   The directory scan buffer identifier that was returned by an associated OPEN DATABASE DIRECTORY SCAN function call.

SQLCA   A pointer to a location in memory where a SQL Communications Area (SQLCA) data structure variable is stored. This variable returns either status information (if the function executed successfully) or error information (if the function failed) to the calling application.

Includes   `#include <sqlenv.h>`

Description   The CLOSE DATABASE DIRECTORY SCAN function is used to free system resources that were allocated by the OPEN DATABASE DIRECTORY SCAN function.

Connection   This function can be called at any time; a connection to a DB2 Database Manager
Requirements instance or to a DB2 database does not have to be established first.

Authorization   No authorization is required to execute this function call.

See Also   OPEN DATABASE DIRECTORY SCAN, GET NEXT DATABASE DIRECTORY ENTRY

Example   See the example provided for the OPEN DATABASE DIRECTORY SCAN function on page 251.

■■ ■■ CATALOG NODE

Purpose   The CATALOG NODE function is used to store information about the location of another DB2 Database Manager (server) instance and the associated communications protocol that is used to access that instance in the workstation node directory.

Syntax
```
SQL_API_RC SQL_API_FN sqlectnd (struct sqle_node_struct  *NodeInfo,
                                void                      *ProtocolInfo,
                                struct sqlca              *SQLCA);
```

Parameters   *NodeInfo*   A pointer to a *sqle_node_struct* structure that contains information about the node that is to be cataloged.

ProtocolInfo   A pointer to the appropriate protocol information structure that contains information about the communications protocol that will be used to access the specified node.

SQLCA   A pointer to a location in memory where a SQL Communications Area (SQLCA) data structure variable is stored. This variable returns either status information (if the function executed successfully) or error information (if the function failed) to the calling application.

Includes   `#include <sqlenv.h>`

Description   The CATALOG NODE function is used to store information about the location of another DB2 Database Manager (server) instance and the associated communications protocol that is to be used to access that instance in the workstation node directory. This information is needed in order for an application to establish a connection or an attachment to a remote DB2 database server.

Two special structures (*sqle_node_struct* and an appropriate protocol information structure) are used to pass characteristics about a node to the DB2 Database Manager when this function is called. The first of these structures, *sqle_node_struct*, is defined in *sqlenv.h* as follows:

```
struct sqle_node_struct
{
unsigned short   struct_id;      /* A unique structure identifier value.  */
                                 /* This field must always be set to      */
                                 /* SQL_NODE_STR_ID.                       */
unsigned short   codepage;       /* Code page value used for the node     */
```

```
                                     /* comment                           */
char            comment[31];         /* Optional description of the node  */
char            nodename[9];         /* Node name                         */
unsigned char   protocol;            /* Indicates whether the protocol that */
                                     /* communicates with the node is     */
                                     /* APPC (SQL_PROTOCOL_APPC),          */
                                     /* NetBIOS (SQL_PROTOCOL_NETB),       */
                                     /* APPN (SQL_PROTOCOL_APPN),          */
                                     /* TCP/IP (SQL_PROTOCOL_TCPIP),       */
                                     /* TCP/IP Using SOCKS (SQL_PROTOCOL_SOCKS)*/
                                     /* CPIC (SQL_PROTOCOL_CPIC),          */
                                     /* IPX/SPX (SQL_PROTOCOL_IPXSPX),     */
                                     /* LOCAL protocol for an instance on the */
                                     /* same workstation (SQL_PROTOCOL_LOCAL) */
                                     /* or a named pipe (SQL_PROTOCOL_NPIPE) */
};
```

The second special structure used by this function (the protocol information structure) is determined by the communications protocol that is to be used to communicate with the cataloged node. This structure can be any of the following DB2-defined structures:

- *sqle_node_appc*   *Advanced Program-to-Program Communications* (APPC) protocol

- *sqle_node_appc*   *Advanced Peer-to-Peer Networking* (APPN) protocol

- *sqle_node_netb*   NetBIOS protocol

- *sqle_node_tcpip*   TCP/IP

- *sqle_node_cpic*   *Common Programming Interface Communications* (CPIC) protocol

- *sqle_node_ipxspx*   *Internetwork Packet Exchange / Sequenced Packet Exchange* (IPX/SPX) protocol

- *sqle_node_local*   Local node

- *sqle_node_npipe*   Named pipe

The *sqle_node_appc* structure is defined in *sqlenv.h* as follows:

```
struct sqle_node_appc
{
char  local_lu[9];                   /* The logical unit (SNA port) name used */
                                     /* to establish the connection.        */
char  partner_lu[9];                 /* The logical unit (SNA port) name at  */
                                     /* the remote DB2 instance.             */
char  mode[9];                       /* The name of the transmission mode to */
                                     /* use. This field is usually set to    */
                                     /* "SQLL0001".                          */
};
```

The *sqle_node_appn* structure is defined in *sqlenv.h* as follows:

```
struct sqle_node_appn
{
char    networkid[9];       /* The network ID                   */
char    remote_lu[9];       /* The logical unit (SNA port) name */
                            /* at the remote DB2 instance       */
char    local_lu[9];        /* The logical unit (SNA port) name */
                            /* used to establish the connection */
char    mode[9];            /* The name of the transmission mode */
                            /* to use. This field is usually set */
                            /* to "SQLL0001".                   */
};
```

The *sqle_node_netb* structure is defined in *sqlenv.h* as follows:

```
struct sqle_node_netb
{
unsigned short  adapter;    /* The LAN adapter number. This parameter*/
                            /* can be set to any of the following   */
                            /* values:                              */
                            /* SQL_ADAPTER_0 (adapter number 0),    */
                            /* SQL_ADAPTER_1 (adapter number 1),    */
                            /* SQL_ADAPTER_MIN (the minimum         */
                            /* adapter number), or                  */
                            /* SQL_ADAPTER_MAX (the maximum         */
                            /* adapter number.                      */
char        remote_nname[9]; /* The workstation name that is stored */
                            /* in the nname parameter of the        */
                            /* Database Manager configuration file  */
                            /* on the remote workstation.           */
                            /* This field must be                   */
                            /* NULL-terminated or blank filled      */
                            /* up to 9 characters.                  */
};
```

The *sqle_node_tcpip* structure is defined in *sqlenv.h* as follows:

```
struct sqle_node_tcpip
{
char    hostname[256];      /* The name of the TCP/IP host that     */
                            /* the DB2 instance (server) resides on */
char    service_name[15];   /* The TCP/IP service name (or port     */
                            /* number) of the DB2 instance (server) */
};
```

The *sqle_node_cpic* structure is defined in *sqlenv.h* as follows:

```
struct sqle_node_cpic
{
```

```
char            sym_dest_name[9];/* The symbolic destination name of    */
                                 /* the remote partner                  */
unsigned short  security_type;   /* The security type used. This field  */
                                 /* must be set to                      */
                                 /* SQL_CPIC_SECURITY_NONE,             */
                                 /* SQL_CPIC_SECURITY_PROGRAM,          */
                                 /* or SQL_CPIC_SECURITY_SAME.          */
};
```

The *sqle_node_ipxspx* structure is defined in *sqlenv.h* as follows:

```
struct sqle_node_ipxspx
{
char   fileserver[49];           /* The name of the NetWare file server */
                                 /* where the DB2 server instance is    */
                                 /* registered                          */
char   objectname[49];           /* The name of a particular            */
                                 /* DB2 server instance that is stored   */
                                 /* in the NetWare file server bindery   */
};
```

The *sqle_node_local* structure is defined in *sqlenv.h* as follows:

```
struct sqle_node_local
{
char   instance_name[9];         /* The name of a DB2 Database Manager  */
                                 /* instance. This field must be NULL-  */
                                 /* terminated or blank filled up to 9  */
                                 /* characters.                         */
};
```

The *sqle_node_npipe* structure is defined in *sqlenv.h* as follows:

```
struct sqle_node_npipe
{
char        computername[16];    /* The name of the computer that a DB2 */
                                 /* Database Manager instance (server)  */
                                 /* resides on                          */
char        instance_name[9];    /* The name of a DB2 Database Manager  */
                                 /* instance                            */
};
```

Comments
- This function will automatically create a node directory if one does not already exist. On OS/2 and Windows, the node directory is stored on the disk drive that contains the DB2 Database Manager instance that is currently being used. On all other systems, the node directory is stored in the directory where the DB2 product was installed.

- You can use the OPEN NODE DIRECTORY SCAN, GET NEXT NODE DIRECTORY

ENTRY, and CLOSE NODE DIRECTORY SCAN functions to list the contents of the node directory. Together, these three functions work like an SQL cursor (i.e., they use the OPEN/FETCH/CLOSE paradigm).

■ If directory caching is enabled, database, node, and DCS directory files are cached in memory. An application's directory cache is created during the first directory lookup. Because the cache is only refreshed when an application modifies one of the directory files, directory changes made by other applications might not be effective until the application is restarted. To refresh DB2's shared cache (server only), an application should stop and then restart the database. To refresh an application's directory cache, the user should stop and then restart that application. For more information about directory caching, refer to the GET DATABASE MANAGER CONFIGURATION function.

Connection Requirements   This function can be called at any time; a connection to a DB2 Database Manager instance or to a DB2 database does not have to be established first.

Authorization   Only users with either System Administrator (SYSADM) authority or System Control (SYSCTRL) authority can execute this function call.

See Also   UNCATALOG NODE, OPEN NODE DIRECTORY SCAN, GET NEXT NODE DIRECTORY ENTRY, CLOSE NODE DIRECTORY SCAN

Example   The following C++ program illustrates how to use the CATALOG NODE function to catalog a remote workstation node:

```
/*————————————————————————————————————— */
/* NAME:     CH8EX5.CPP                                      */
/* PURPOSE: Illustrate How To Use The Following DB2 API Function */
/*          In A C++ Program:                                */
/*                                                           */
/*               CATALOG NODE                                */
/*                                                           */
/*————————————————————————————————————— */

// Include The Appropriate Header Files
#include <windows.h>
#include <iostream.h>
#include <sqlenv.h>
#include <sqlca.h>

// Define The API_Class Class
class API_Class
{
    // Attributes
    public:
        struct sqlca  sqlca;

    // Operations
    public:
```

```
                    long CatalogNode();
};

// Define The CatalogNode() Member Function
long API_Class::CatalogNode()
{
    // Declare The Local Memory Variables
    struct sqle_node_struct   NodeInfo;
    struct sqle_node_netb     Protocol;

    // Initialize The Node Information Data Structure
    NodeInfo.struct_id = SQL_NODE_STR_ID;
    strcpy(NodeInfo.comment, "Test Database Server");
    strcpy(NodeInfo.nodename, "TESTSVR");
    NodeInfo.protocol = SQL_PROTOCOL_NETB;

    // Initialize The NetBIOS Protocol Data Structure
    Protocol.adapter = SQL_ADAPTER_0;
    strcpy(Protocol.remote_nname, "TESTSVR");

    // Catalog A New Workstation Node
    sqlectnd(&NodeInfo, (void *) &Protocol, &sqlca);

    // If The New Workstation Was Cataloged, Display A Success Message
    if (sqlca.sqlcode == SQL_RC_OK)
    {
        cout << "The node " << NodeInfo.nodename;
        cout << " has been cataloged." << endl;
    }

    // Return The SQLCA Return Code To The Calling Function
    return(sqlca.sqlcode);
}

/*———————————————————————————————————*/
/* The Main Function                                                */
/*———————————————————————————————————*/
int main()
{
    // Declare The Local Memory Variables
    long  rc = SQL_RC_OK;

    // Create An Instance Of The API_Class Class
    API_Class  Example;

    // Catalog A New Workstation Node
    rc = Example.CatalogNode();

    // Return To The Operating System
    return(rc);
}
```

■ ■ UNCATALOG NODE

Purpose   The UNCATALOG NODE function is used to delete an entry from the node directory.

Syntax
```
SQL_API_RC SQL_API_FN sqleuncn (char          *NodeName,
                                struct sqlca  *SQLCA);
```

Parameters   *NodeName*   A pointer to a location in memory where the name of the node to be
                                uncataloged is stored.

                  SQLCA   A pointer to a location in memory where a SQL Communications
                                Area (SQLCA) ata structure variable is stored. This variable returns
                                either status information (if the function executed successfully) or
                                error information (if the function failed) to the calling application.

Includes   `#include <sqlenv.h>`

Description   The UNCATALOG NODE function is used to delete an entry from the node directory.

Comments
- The CATALOG NODE function can be used to recatalog a node that was removed
  (uncataloged) from the node directory.
- You can use the OPEN NODE DIRECTORY SCAN, GET NEXT NODE DIRECTORY
  ENTRY, and CLOSE NODE DIRECTORY SCAN functions to list the contents of the
  node directory. Together, these three functions work like a SQL cursor (i.e., they
  use the OPEN/FETCH/CLOSE paradigm).
- If directory caching is enabled, database, node, and DCS directory files are cached
  in memory. An application's directory cache is created during the first directory
  lookup. Because the cache is only refreshed when an application modifies one of
  the directory files, directory changes made by other applications might not take
  effect until the application is restarted. To refresh DB2's shared cache (server
  only), an application should stop and then restart the database. To refresh an
  application's directory cache, the user should stop and then restart that
  application. For more information about directory caching, refer to the GET
  DATABASE MANAGER CONFIGURATION function.

Connection   This function can be called at any time; a connection to a DB2 Database Manager
Requirements instance or to a DB2 database does not have to be established first.

Authorization Only users with either System Administrator (SYSADM) authority or System Control
                  (SYSCTRL) authority are allowed to execute this function call.

See Also   CATALOG NODE, OPEN NODE DIRECTORY SCAN, GET NEXT NODE DIRECTORY
                  ENTRY, CLOSE NODE DIRECTORY SCAN

Example   The following C++ program illustrates how to use the UNCATALOG NODE function to
                  uncatalog a remote workstation node:

```
/*------------------------------------------------------*/
/* NAME:      CH8EX6.CPP                                */
/* PURPOSE: Illustrate How To Use The Following DB2 API Function */
/*          In A C++ Program:                           */
/*                                                      */
/*                 UNCATALOG NODE                       */
/*                                                      */
/*------------------------------------------------------*/

// Include The Appropriate Header Files
#include <windows.h>
#include <iostream.h>
#include <sqlenv.h>
#include <sqlca.h>

// Define The API_Class Class
class API_Class
{
    // Attributes
    public:
        struct sqlca    sqlca;

    // Operations
    public:
        long UncatalogNode();
};

// Define The UncatalogNode() Member Function
long API_Class::UncatalogNode()
{
    // Declare The Local Memory Variables
    char   NodeName[9];

    // Initialize The Local Memory Variables
    strcpy(NodeName, "TESTSVR");

    // Uncatalog The Specified Node
    sqleuncn(NodeName, &sqlca);

    // If The Node Was Uncataloged, Display A Success Message
    if (sqlca.sqlcode == SQL_RC_OK)
    {
        cout << "The node " << NodeName << " has been uncataloged.";
        cout << endl;
    }

    // Return The SQLCA Return Code To The Calling Function
    return(sqlca.sqlcode);
}

/*------------------------------------------------------*/
/* The Main Function                                    */
/*------------------------------------------------------*/
int main()
```

```
{
        // Declare The Local Memory Variables
        long  rc = SQL_RC_OK;

        // Create An Instance Of The API_Class Class
        API_Class  Example;

        // Uncatalog A Workstation Node
        rc = Example.UncatalogNode();

        // Return To The Operating System
        return(rc);
}
```

■ ■ OPEN NODE DIRECTORY SCAN

Purpose   The OPEN NODE DIRECTORY SCAN function is used to store a copy of the node
                 directory in memory and to obtain a count of the number of entries found in the node
                 directory.

Syntax
```
SQL_API_RC SQL_API_FN sqlenops (unsigned short  *Handle,
                                unsigned short  *NumEntries,
                                struct sqlca    *SQLCA);
```

Parameters   *Handle*   A pointer to a location in memory where this function is to store a
                                directory scan buffer identifier that will be used in subsequent GET
                                NEXT NODE DIRECTORY ENTRY and CLOSE NODE DIRECTORY
                                SCAN function calls.

                 NumEntries   A pointer to a location in memory where this function is to store a
                                count of the number of entries found in the node directory.

                 SQLCA   A pointer to a location in memory where a SQL Communications
                                Area (SQLCA) data structure variable is stored. This variable returns
                                either status information (if the function executed successfully) or
                                error information (if the function failed) to the calling application.

Includes   `#include <sqlenv.h>`

Description The OPEN NODE DIRECTORY SCAN function is used to store a copy of the node
                 directory in memory and to obtain a count of the number of entries found in the node
                 directory. The copy of the node directory that is placed in memory represents a
                 snapshot of the directory when the directory scan is opened. This copy is never
                 updated, even if the directory itself changes.

                     This function is normally followed by one or more GET NEXT NODE DIRECTORY
                 ENTRY function calls and one CLOSE NODE DIRECTORY SCAN function call. Together,
                 these three functions work like a SQL cursor (i.e., they use the
                 OPEN/FETCH/CLOSE paradigm). The memory buffer that is used to store the node

directory data obtained by the directory scan is automatically allocated by this function and a pointer to that buffer (the buffer identifier) is stored in the *Handle* parameter. This identifier is then used by subsequent GET NEXT NODE DIRECTORY ENTRY and CLOSE NODE DIRECTORY SCAN function calls to access the information stored in the memory buffer area.

Comments
■ Multiple OPEN NODE DIRECTORY SCAN function calls can be issued against the same node directory. However, because the directory can change between each call, the directory entries copied into memory by each call may vary.

■ An application can have up to eight node directory scans open at one time.

Connection Requirements
This function can be called at any time; a connection to a DB2 Database Manager instance or to a DB2 database does not have to be established first.

Authorization
No authorization is required to execute this function call.

See Also
GET NEXT NODE DIRECTORY ENTRY, CLOSE NODE DIRECTORY SCAN

Example
The following C++ program illustrates how to use the OPEN NODE DIRECTORY SCAN, GET NEXT NODE DIRECTORY ENTRY, and CLOSE NODE DIRECTORY SCAN functions to retrieve entries in the node directory:

```
/*-----------------------------------------------------------*/
/* NAME:     CH8EX7.CPP                                      */
/* PURPOSE: Illustrate How To Use The Following DB2 API Functions */
/*          In A C++ Program:                                */
/*                                                           */
/*              OPEN NODE DIRECTORY SCAN                      */
/*              GET NEXT NODE DIRECTORY ENTRY                 */
/*              CLOSE NODE DIRECTORY SCAN                     */
/*                                                           */
/*-----------------------------------------------------------*/

// Include The Appropriate Header Files
#include <windows.h>
#include <iostream.h>
#include <sqlenv.h>
#include <sqlca.h>

// Define The API_Class Class
class API_Class
{
    // Attributes
    public:
        struct sqlca   sqlca;

    // Operations
    public:
        long ShowNodes();
};
```

```cpp
// Define The ShowNodes() Member Function
long API_Class::ShowNodes()
{
    // Declare The Local Memory Variables
    unsigned short    Handle;
    unsigned short    NodeCount;
    struct sqleninfo  *Node_DirInfo = NULL;

    // Open The Node Directory Scan
    sqlenops(&Handle, &NodeCount, &sqlca);

    // Scan The Node Directory Buffer And Retrieve All Node Names
    // And Descriptions Stored There
    if (sqlca.sqlcode == SQL_RC_OK)
    {
        cout << "Node Name      Description" << endl;
        cout << "————————————————————————————————" << endl;
        for (;NodeCount != 0; NodeCount—)
        {
            // Retrieve The Next Node Directory Entry
            sqlengne(Handle, &Node_DirInfo, &sqlca);

            // Display The Node Directory Entry Retrieved
            if (sqlca.sqlcode == SQL_RC_OK)
            {
                char  NodeName[9];
                cout.width(14);
                cout.setf(ios::left);
                strncpy(NodeName, Node_DirInfo->nodename, 8);
                NodeName[8] = 0;
                cout << NodeName;
                cout.width(30);
                cout.setf(ios::left);
                cout << Node_DirInfo->comment << endl;
            }
        }

        // Close The Node Directory Scan And Free All Resources
        // Obtained By The Open Node Directory Scan API
        sqlencls(Handle, &sqlca);
    }

    // Return The SQLCA Return Code To The Calling Function
    return(sqlca.sqlcode);
}

/*————————————————————————————————————————————————————————*/
/* The Main Function                                       */
/*————————————————————————————————————————————————————————*/
int main()
{
    // Declare The Local Memory Variables
    long  rc = SQL_RC_OK;
```

```
        // Create An Instance Of The API_Class Class
        API_Class  Example;

        // Generate And Display A List Of Available Nodes
        rc = Example.ShowNodes();

        // Return To The Operating System
        return(rc);
    }
```

■■ ■■ GET NEXT NODE DIRECTORY ENTRY

Purpose   The GET NEXT NODE DIRECTORY ENTRY function is used to retrieve the next entry from the copy of the node directory that was placed in memory by the OPEN NODE DIRECTORY SCAN function.

Syntax
```
SQL_API_RC SQL_API_FN sqlengne (unsigned short   Handle,
                                struct sqleninfo **NodeDirEntry,
                                struct sqlca     *SQLCA);
```

Parameters   *Handle*   The directory scan buffer identifier that was returned by an associated OPEN NODE DIRECTORY SCAN function call.

NodeDirEntry   A pointer to the address of an *sqleninfo* structure where this function is to store the node directory entry information retrieved.

SQLCA   A pointer to a location in memory where a SQL Communications Area (SQLCA) data structure variable is stored. This variable returns either status information (if the function executed successfully) or error information (if the function failed) to the calling application.

Includes   `#include <sqlenv.h>`

Description The GET NEXT NODE DIRECTORY ENTRY function is used to retrieve the next entry from the copy of the node directory that was placed in memory by the OPEN NODE DIRECTORY SCAN function. The information retrieved is stored in a special structure, *sqleninfo*, that is defined in *sqlenv.h* as follows:

```
struct sqleninfo
{
char            nodename[8];      /* Node name                          */
char            local_lu[8];      /* The logical unit (SNA port)        */
                                  /* name used to establish the connection*/
char            partner_lu[8];    /* The logical unit (SNA port) name at */
                                  /* the remote DB2 Database Manager    */
                                  /* instance                           */
char            mode[8];          /* The name of the transmission service */
                                  /* mode used                          */
char            comment[30];      /* Optional node comment (description) */
unsigned short  com_codepage;     /* Code page value used for the node  */
                                  /* comment                            */
```

```
unsigned short                                                            */
                adapter;          /* The NetBIOS LAN adapter number       */
char            networkid[8];     /* The APPN network ID                  */
char            protocol;         /* Identifies the protocol that is used */
                                  /* to communicate with the node. This   */
                                  /* field can be set to                  */
                                  /* SQL_PROTOCOL_APPC, SQL_PROTOCOL_NETB, */
                                  /* SQL_PROTOCOL_APPN, SQL_PROTOCOL_TCPIP,*/
                                  /* SQL_PROTOCOL_CPIC, SQL_PROTOCOL_SOCKS,*/
                                  /* SQL_PROTOCOL_IPXSPX,                  */
                                  /* SQL_PROTOCOL_LOCAL, or                */
                                  /* SQL_PROTOCOL_NPIPE.                   */
char            sym_dest_name[8]; /* The CPIC symbolic destination name of*/
                                  /* the remote partner                   */
unsigned short                                                            */
                security_type;    /* The CPIC security type. This field   */
                                  /* can be set to                        */
                                  /* SQL_CPIC_SECURITY_NONE,               */
                                  /* SQL_CPIC_SECURITY_PROGRAM,            */
                                  /* or SQL_CPIC_SECURITY_SAME.            */
char            hostname[255];    /* The TCP/IP host name at the DB2       */
                                  /* database manager instance (server)   */
char            service_name[14]; /* The TCP/IP service name of the DB2    */
                                  /* database manager instance (server)   */
char            fileserver[48];   /* The NetWare file server name where    */
                                  /* the DB2 server instance is            */
                                  /* registered                           */
char            objectname[48];   /* The name of a particular DB2 database*/
                                  /* manager instance (server) that is    */
                                  /* stored in the Novell NetWare file     */
                                  /* server bindery                       */
char            instance_name[8]; /* The LOCAL name of a DB2 database      */
                                  /* manager instance                     */
char            computername[15]; /* The server node's computer name       */
char            system_name[21];  /* The DB2 system name for the remote    */
                                  /* server                               */
char            remote_instname[8];/* The name of the DB2 server instance  */
char            catalog_node_type;/* The catalog node type                */
unsigned short                                                            */
                os_type;          /* The operating system used by the server*/
};
```

Comments   ■ All character fields in the node directory entry information buffer are right-padded with blanks.

■ When this function is executed, the value in the *NodeDirEntry* parameter points to the next node directory entry in the copy of the node directory that resides in memory. Each subsequent GET NEXT NODE DIRECTORY ENTRY function call retrieves the node directory entry immediately following the current directory entry, unless there are no more directory entries available (in which case an error is returned).

■ You can use the value returned in the *NumEntries* parameter when the OPEN NODE DIRECTORY SCAN function is executed to set up a loop that scans through the entire node directory by issuing GET NEXT NODE DIRECTORY ENTRY function calls, one at a time, until the number of calls issued equals the number of entries found in the directory.

Prerequisites The OPEN NODE DIRECTORY SCAN function must be executed before this function is called.

Connection Requirements This function can be called at any time; a connection to a DB2 Database Manager instance or to a DB2 database does not have to be established first.

Authorization No authorization is required to execute this function call.

See Also OPEN NODE DIRECTORY SCAN, CLOSE NODE DIRECTORY SCAN

Example See the example provided for the OPEN NODE DIRECTORY SCAN function on page 265.

■ ■ CLOSE NODE DIRECTORY SCAN

Purpose The CLOSE NODE DIRECTORY SCAN function is used to free system resources that were allocated by the OPEN NODE DIRECTORY SCAN function.

Syntax
```
SQL_API_RC SQL_API_FN sqlencls (unsigned short  Handle,
                                struct sqlca    *SQLCA);
```

Parameters *Handle* The directory scan buffer identifier that was returned by an associated OPEN NODE DIRECTORY SCAN function call.

SQLCA A pointer to a location in memory where a SQL Communications Area (SQLCA) data structure variable is stored. This variable returns either status information (if the function executed successfully) or error information (if the function failed) to the calling application.

Includes `#include <sqlenv.h>`

Description The CLOSE NODE DIRECTORY SCAN function is used to free system resources that were allocated by the OPEN NODE DIRECTORY SCAN function.

Connection Requirements This function can be called at any time; a connection to a DB2 Database Manager instance or to a DB2 database does not have to be established first.

Authorization No authorization is required to execute this function call.

See Also OPEN NODE DIRECTORY SCAN, GET NEXT NODE DIRECTORY ENTRY

Example See the example provided for the OPEN NODE DIRECTORY SCAN function on page 265.

CATALOG DCS DATABASE

Purpose

The **CATALOG DCS DATABASE** function is used to store information about a DRDA database in the DCS directory.

Syntax

```
SQL_API_RC SQL_API_FN sqlegdad (struct sql_dir_entry *DCSDirEntry,
                                struct sqlca        *SQLCA);
```

Parameters

DCSDirEntry   A pointer to an *sql_dir_entry* structure that contains information about the DCS database that is to be cataloged.

SQLCA   A pointer to a location in memory where a SQL Communications Area (SQLCA) data structure variable is stored. This variable returns either status information (if the function executed successfully) or error information (if the function failed) to the calling application.

Includes

```
#include <sqlenv.h>
```

Description

The **CATALOG DCS DATABASE** function is used to store information about a DRDA database in the DCS directory. Databases in this directory are accessed through an application requester, such as IBM's DB2 Connect product. When a DCS directory entry has a database name that matches a database name in the system database directory, the application requester associated with the DCS database forwards all SQL requests made against that database to the remote server where the DRDA database physically resides.

A special structure (*sql_dir_entry*) is used to pass characteristics about a DCS database to the DB2 Database Manager when this function is called. The *sql_dir_entry* structure is defined in *sqlenv.h* as follows:

```
struct sql_dir_entry
{
unsigned short   struct_id;       /* The structure identifier. This field */
                                  /* must always be set to SQL_DCS_STR_ID. */
unsigned short   release;         /* Release level of the DCS database entry*/
unsigned short   codepage;        /* Code page value used for the DCS      */
                                  /* database comment                      */
char             comment[31];     /* Optional DCS database comment         */
char             ldb[9];          /* Local database name                   */
char             tdb[19];         /* Actual host database name             */
char             ar[9];           /* Application client library name       */
char             parm[513];       /* Transaction program prefix, transaction */
                                  /* program name, SQLCODE mapping file    */
                                  /* name, disconnect option, and security */
                                  /* option                                */
};
```

 NOTE: *Each character field in this structure must be either NULL-terminated or blank, filled up to the specified length of the field.*

Comments
- This function will automatically create a DCS directory if one does not already exist. On OS/2 and Windows, the DCS directory is stored on the disk drive that contains the DB2 Database Manager instance currently being used. On all other systems, the DCS directory is stored in the directory where the DB2 product was installed.
- The DCS directory is maintained outside of the database.
- If a database is cataloged in the DCS directory, it must also be cataloged as a remote database in the system database directory.
- You can use the **OPEN DCS DIRECTORY SCAN, GET DCS DIRECTORY ENTRIES, GET DCS DIRECTORY ENTRY FOR DATABASE,** and **CLOSE DCS DIRECTORY SCAN** functions to obtain information about one or more entries in the DCS directory.
- If directory caching is enabled, database, node, and DCS directory files are cached in memory. An application's directory cache is created during the first directory lookup. Because the cache is only refreshed when an application modifies one of the directory files, directory changes made by other applications might not take effect until the application is restarted. To refresh DB2's shared cache (server only), an application should stop and then restart the database. To refresh an application's directory cache, the user should stop and then restart that application. For more information about directory caching, refer to the **GET DATABASE MANAGER CONFIGURATION** function.
- IBM's DB2 Connect product provides connections to DRDA application servers, such as:

—DB2 for OS/390 on System/370 and System/390 architecture host computers

—DB2 for VM and VSE on System/370 and System/390 architecture host computers

—OS/400 on Application System/400 (AS/400) host computers

Connection Requirements
This function can be called at any time; a connection to a DB2 Database Manager instance or to a DB2 database does not have to be established first.

Authorization
Only users with either System Administrator (SYSADM) authority or System Control (SYSCTRL) authority are allowed to execute this function call.

See Also
UNCATALOG DCS DATABASE, OPEN DCS DIRECTORY SCAN, GET DCS DIRECTORY ENTRIES, GET DCS DIRECTORY ENTRY FOR DATABASE, CLOSE DCS DIRECTORY SCAN, CATALOG DATABASE

Example
The following C++ program illustrates how to use the **CATALOG DCS DATABASE** function to catalog an alias for a DCS database:

```
/*———————————————————————————————————————— */
/* NAME:     CH8EX8.CPP                                    */
/* PURPOSE: Illustrate How To Use The Following DB2 API Function */
/*          In A C++ Program:                              */
```

```
/*                                                                   */
/*                    CATALOG DCS DATABASE                           */
/*                                                                   */
/*——————————————————————————————————————————————————————————————————*/

// Include The Appropriate Header Files
#include <windows.h>
#include <iostream.h>
#include <sqlenv.h>
#include <sqlca.h>

// Define The API_Class Class
class API_Class
{
    // Attributes
    public:
        struct sqlca  sqlca;

    // Operations
    public:
        long CatalogDCSDB();
};

// Define The CatalogDCSDB() Member Function
long API_Class::CatalogDCSDB()
{
    // Declare The Local Memory Variables
    struct sql_dir_entry  DCSInfo;

    // Initialize The DCS Database Information Data Structure
    DCSInfo.struct_id = SQL_DCS_STR_ID;
    DCSInfo.release = 0;
    DCSInfo.codepage = 450;
    strcpy(DCSInfo.comment, "DB2 For MVS Database");
    strcpy(DCSInfo.ldb, "SAMPLEDB");
    strcpy(DCSInfo.tdb, "SAMPLE");
    strcpy(DCSInfo.ar, "");
    strcpy(DCSInfo.parm, "");

    // Catalog A New DCS Database
    sqlegdad(&DCSInfo, &sqlca);

    // If The New DCS Database Was Cataloged, Display A Success
    // Message
    if (sqlca.sqlcode == SQL_RC_OK)
    {
        cout << "The DCS database " << DCSInfo.ldb;
        cout << " has been cataloged." << endl;
    }

    // Return The SQLCA Return Code To The Calling Function
    return(sqlca.sqlcode);
}

/*——————————————————————————————————————————————————————————————————*/
```

```
/* The Main Function                                              */
/*—————————————————————————————————————————*/
int main()
{
      // Declare The Local Memory Variables
      long  rc = SQL_RC_OK;

      // Create An Instance Of The API_Class Class
      API_Class  Example;

      // Catalog A New DCS Database
      rc = Example.CatalogDCSDB();

      // Return To The Operating System
      return(rc);
}
```

■ ■ UNCATALOG DCS DATABASE

Purpose   The **UNCATALOG DCS DATABASE** function is used to delete an entry from the DCS directory.

Syntax
```
SQL_API_RC SQL_API_FN sqlegdel (struct sql_dir_entry *DCSDirEntry,
                                struct sqlca         *SQLCA);
```

Parameters   *DCSDirEntry*   A pointer to an *sql_dir_entry* structure that contains information about the DCS database that is to be uncataloged.

                 SQLCA   A pointer to a location in memory where a SQL Communications Area (SQLCA) data structure variable is stored. This variable returns either status information (if the function executed successfully) or error information (if the function failed) to the calling application.

Includes   `#include <sqlenv.h>`

Description The **UNCATALOG DCS DATABASE** function is used to delete an entry from the DCS directory. Before this function can be executed, a special structure (*sql_dir_entry*) must be initialized with information about the DCS database that is to be uncataloged. Refer to the **CATALOG DCS DATABASE** function for a detailed description of this structure. Only two fields of this structure are used by the **UNCATALOG DCS DATABASE** function: *struct_id* and *ldb*. The database name stored in the *ldb* field of this structure specifies the local name of the DRDA database that is to be uncataloged.

Comments   ■ A DCS database should always be cataloged in the system database directory as a remote database. Therefore, when a DCS database is uncataloged, its corresponding entry in the system database directory should be uncataloged (with the **UNCATALOG DATABASE** function).

■ You can use the OPEN DCS DIRECTORY SCAN, GET DCS DIRECTORY ENTRIES, GET DCS DIRECTORY ENTRY FOR DATABASE, and CLOSE DCS DIRECTORY SCAN functions to obtain information about one or more entries in the DCS directory.

■ If directory caching is enabled, database, node, and DCS directory files are cached in memory. An application's directory cache is created during the first directory lookup. Because the cache is only refreshed when an application modifies one of the directory files, directory changes made by other applications might not be effective until the application is restarted. To refresh DB2's shared cache (server only), an application should stop and then restart the database. To refresh an application's directory cache, the user should stop and then restart that application. For more information about directory caching, refer to the GET DATABASE MANAGER CONFIGURATION function.

Connection Requirements This function can be called at any time; a connection to a DB2 Database Manager instance or to a DB2 database does not have to be established first.

Authorization Only users with either System Administrator (SYSADM) authority or System Control (SYSCTRL) authority can execute this function call.

See Also CATALOG DCS DATABASE, OPEN DCS DIRECTORY SCAN, GET DCS DIRECTORY ENTRIES, GET DCS DIRECTORY ENTRY FOR DATABASE, CLOSE DCS DIRECTORY SCAN, UNCATALOG DATABASE

Example The following C++ program illustrates how to use the UNCATALOG DCS DATABASE function to uncatalog an alias for a DCS database:

```
/*───────────────────────────────────────────────────────────────*/
/* NAME:     CH8EX9.CPP                                            */
/* PURPOSE:  Illustrate How To Use The Following DB2 API Function  */
/*           In A C++ Program:                                     */
/*                                                                 */
/*                 UNCATALOG DCS DATABASE                          */
/*                                                                 */
/*───────────────────────────────────────────────────────────────*/

// Include The Appropriate Header Files
#include <windows.h>
#include <iostream.h>
#include <sqlenv.h>
#include <sqlca.h>

// Define The API_Class Class
class API_Class
{
    // Attributes
    public:
        struct sqlca  sqlca;
```

```
        // Operations
        public:
            long UncatalogDCSDB();
};


// Define The UncatalogDCSDB() Member Function
long API_Class::UncatalogDCSDB()
{
    // Declare The Local Memory Variables
    struct sql_dir_entry  DCSInfo;

    // Initialize The DCS Database Information Data Structure
    DCSInfo.struct_id = SQL_DCS_STR_ID;
    DCSInfo.release = 0;
    DCSInfo.codepage = 450;
    strcpy(DCSInfo.comment, "DB2 For MVS Database");
    strcpy(DCSInfo.ldb, "SAMPLEDB");
    strcpy(DCSInfo.tdb, "SAMPLE");
    strcpy(DCSInfo.ar, "");
    strcpy(DCSInfo.parm, "");

    // Uncatalog The Specified DCS Database
    sqlegdel(&DCSInfo, &sqlca);

    // If The DCS Database Was Uncataloged, Display A Success Message
    if (sqlca.sqlcode == SQL_RC_OK)
    {
        cout << "The DCS database " << DCSInfo.ldb;
        cout <<     " has been uncataloged." << endl;
    }

    // Return The SQLCA Return Code To The Calling Function
    return(sqlca.sqlcode);
}


/*----------------------------------------------------------------*/
/* The Main Function                                              */
/*----------------------------------------------------------------*/
int main()
{
    // Declare The Local Memory Variables
    long  rc = SQL_RC_OK;

    // Create An Instance Of The API_Class Class
    API_Class  Example;

    // Uncatalog A DCS Database Node
    rc = Example.UncatalogDCSDB();

    // Return To The Operating System
    return(rc);
}
```

OPEN DCS DIRECTORY SCAN

Purpose   The OPEN DCS DIRECTORY SCAN function is used to obtain a count of the number of entries found in the DCS directory.

Syntax

```
SQL_API_RC SQL_API_FN sqlegdsc (short        *NumEntries,
                                struct sqlca *SQLCA);
```

Parameters   *NumEntries*   A pointer to a location in memory where this function is to store a count of the number of entries found in the DCS directory.

SQLCA   A pointer to a location in memory where a SQL Communications Area (SQLCA) data structure variable is stored. This variable returns either status information (if the function executed successfully) or error information (if the function failed) to the calling application.

Includes   `#include <sqlenv.h>`

Description   The OPEN DCS DIRECTORY SCAN function is used to obtain a count of the number of entries found in the DCS directory. An application can use this number to determine the amount of memory it needs to allocate in order to retrieve information about each DCS directory entry available. Once the correct amount of memory is allocated, you can use the GET DCS DIRECTORY ENTRIES function and the GET DCS DIRECTORY ENTRY FOR DATABASE function to retrieve information about each entry stored in the DCS directory.

Connection   This function can be called at any time; a connection to a DB2 Database Manager
Requirements instance or to a DB2 database does not have to be established first.

Authorization No authorization is required to execute this function call.

See Also   CLOSE DCS DIRECTORY SCAN, GET DCS DIRECTORY ENTRIES, GET DCS DIRECTORY ENTRY FOR DATABASE

Example   The following C++ program illustrates how to use the OPEN DCS DIRECTORY SCAN, GET DCS DIRECTORY ENTRIES, GET DCS DIRECTORY ENTRY FOR DATABASE, and CLOSE DCS DIRECTORY SCAN functions to retrieve the information associated with the DCS directory entry for a specified database:

```
/*-----------------------------------------------------------------*/
/* NAME:    CH8EX10.CPP                                            */
/* PURPOSE: Illustrate How To Use The Following DB2 API Functions  */
/*          In A C++ Program:                                      */
/*                                                                 */
/*              OPEN DCS DIRECTORY SCAN                            */
/*              GET DCS DIRECTORY ENTRIES                          */
/*              GET DCS DIRECTORY ENTRY FOR DATABASE               */
/*              CLOSE DCS DIRECTORY SCAN                           */
```

```
/*                                                                */
/*--------------------------------------------------------------*/

// Include The Appropriate Header Files
#include <windows.h>
#include <iostream.h>
#include <sqlenv.h>
#include <sqlca.h>

// Define The API_Class Class
class API_Class
{
    // Attributes
    public:
        struct sqlca    sqlca;

    // Operations
    public:
        long ShowDCSDBInfo();
};

// Define The ShowDCSDBInfo() Member Function
long API_Class::ShowDCSDBInfo()
{
    // Declare The Local Memory Variables
    short               DCSCount;
    struct sql_dir_entry  *DCS_DirInfo = NULL;
    char                Name[9];

    // Open The DCS Directory Scan
    sqlegdsc(&DCSCount, &sqlca);

    // Scan The DCS Database Directory Buffer And Retrieve Information
    // About A Specific DCS Database
    if (sqlca.sqlcode == SQL_RC_OK)
    {
        // Copy The DCS Directory Entries Into A User-Allocated Memory
        // Storage Buffer
        DCS_DirInfo = (struct sql_dir_entry *)
            malloc(DCSCount * sizeof(struct sql_dir_entry));
        sqlegdgt(&DCSCount, DCS_DirInfo, &sqlca);

        // Initialize The DCS Information Data Structure
        DCS_DirInfo->struct_id = SQL_DCS_STR_ID;
        strcpy(DCS_DirInfo->ldb, "SAMPLEDB");

        // Retrieve The DCS Directory Entry For The Specified DCS
        // Database From The Memory Storage Buffer
        sqlegdge(DCS_DirInfo, &sqlca);

        // Display The DCS Directory Entry Retrieved
        cout << "DCS Database Name    Database Name    Description";
        cout << endl;
        cout << "------------------------------";
        cout << "------" << endl;
```

```
                    cout.width(20);
                    cout.setf(ios::left);
                    strncpy(Name, DCS_DirInfo->ldb, 8);
                    Name[8] = 0;
                    cout << Name;
                    cout.width(16);
                    cout.setf(ios::left);
                    strncpy(Name, DCS_DirInfo->tdb, 8);
                    Name[8] = 0;
                    cout << Name;
                    cout << DCS_DirInfo->comment << endl;

                    // Close The DCS Directory Scan And Free The User-Allocated
                    // Memory Storage Buffer
                    sqlegdcl(&sqlca);
                    free(DCS_DirInfo);
                }

            // Return The SQLCA Return Code To The Calling Function
            return(sqlca.sqlcode);
        }

/*————————————————————————————————*/
/* The Main Function                                                     */
/*————————————————————————————————*/
int main()
{
        // Declare The Local Memory Variables
        long  rc = SQL_RC_OK;

        // Create An Instance Of The API_Class Class
        API_Class  Example;

        // Display Information About A DCS Database
        rc = Example.ShowDCSDBInfo();

        // Return To The Operating System
        return(rc);
}
```

GET DCS DIRECTORY ENTRIES

Purpose   The GET DCS DIRECTORY ENTRIES function is used to transfer a copy of the DCS directory to a user-allocated memory storage buffer that is supplied by the calling application.

Syntax
```
SQL_API_RC SQL_API_FN sqlegdgt (short              *NumEntries,
                                struct sql_dir_entry *DCSDirEntries,
                                struct sqlca         *SQLCA);
```

Parameters   *NumEntries*   A pointer to a location in memory where the number of *sql_dir_entry* structures contained in the user-allocated memory storage buffer is stored. When this function is executed, the number of entries actually copied from the DCS directory to the user-allocated memory storage buffer is stored in the location referred to by this parameter.

DCSDirEntries   A pointer to an array of *sql_dir_entry* structures where this function is to copy the DCS directory entry information retrieved.

SQLCA   A pointer to a location in memory where a SQL Communications Area (SQLCA) data structure variable is stored. This variable returns either status information (if the function executed successfully) or error information (if the function failed) to the calling application.

Includes   `#include <sqlenv.h>`

Description   The **GET DCS DIRECTORY ENTRIES** function is used to transfer a copy of the DCS directory to a user-allocated memory buffer. Before this function can be executed, a memory storage buffer containing an array of a *sql_dir_entry* structures must be allocated. Refer to the **CATALOG DCS DATABASE** function for a detailed description of this structure. You can determine the amount of memory needed for this storage buffer by multiplying the number of entries found in the DCS directory with the **OPEN DCS DIRECTORY SCAN** function by the size of a single *sql_dir_entry* structure.

Once a memory buffer is allocated, the number of DCS directory with entries that the buffer can hold (the number of elements in the array of *sql_dir_entry* structures) must be stored in the *NumEntries* parameter. When this function is executed, the number of DCS directory entries that are actually copied to the memory storage buffer is returned in the *NumEntries* parameter. By comparing the "before" function call and "after" function call values of this parameter, an application can determine whether all DCS directory entries were copied to the storage buffer area.

Comments   ■ If this function is executed when a copy of the DCS directory entries is already in memory, the previous copy will be replaced by a new copy of DCS directory entries.

■ If all DCS directory entries are copied to the user-allocated memory storage area, the DCS directory scan will automatically be closed, and all resources allocated by the **OPEN DCS DIRECTORY SCAN** function will be released.

■ If one or more DCS directory entries were not copied to the user-allocated memory storage area, you can make subsequent calls to this function to copy them. If these entries are not needed, you can call the **CLOSE DCS DIRECTORY SCAN** function to free system resources that were allocated by the **OPEN DCS DIRECTORY SCAN** function.

Prerequisites The **OPEN DCS DIRECTORY SCAN** function should be executed before this function is called (so the calling application can allocate a memory storage buffer that is large enough to hold the entries stored in the DCS directory).

Connection Requirements This function can be called at any time; a connection to a DB2 Database Manager instance or to a DB2 database does not have to be established first.

Authorization No authorization is required to execute this function call.

See Also OPEN DCS DIRECTORY SCAN, GET DCS DIRECTORY ENTRY FOR DATABASE, CLOSE DCS DIRECTORY SCAN

Example See the example provided for the OPEN DCS DIRECTORY SCAN function on page 276.

■ ■ GET DCS DIRECTORY ENTRY FOR DATABASE

Purpose The GET DCS DIRECTORY ENTRY FOR DATABASE function is used to retrieve an entry for a specified database from the copy of the DCS directory that was placed in memory by the GET DCS DIRECTORY ENTRIES function.

Syntax
```
SQL_API_RC SQL_API_FN sqlegdge (struct sql_dir_entry *DCSDirEntry,
                               struct sqlca         *SQLCA);
```

Parameters *DCSDirEntry* A pointer to the address of an *sql_dir_entry* structure where this function is to store the DCS directory entry information retrieved.

SQLCA A pointer to a location in memory where a SQL Communications Area (SQLCA) data structure variable is stored. This variable returns either status information (if the function executed successfully) or error information (if the function failed) to the calling application.

Includes `#include <sqlenv.h>`

Description The GET DCS DIRECTORY ENTRY FOR DATABASE function is used to retrieve an entry for a specified database from the copy of the DCS directory that was placed in memory by the GET DCS DIRECTORY ENTRIES function.

Before this function is executed, the local name of the database whose DCS directory entry is to be retrieved must be stored in the *ldb* field of a *sql_dir_entry* structure. Refer to the CATALOG DCS DATABASE function for a detailed description of this structure. The remaining fields of this structure are filled in when this function executes.

Connection Requirements This function can be called at any time; a connection to a DB2 Database Manager instance or to a DB2 database does not have to be established first.

Authorization No authorization is required to execute this function call.

See Also CATALOG DCS DATABASE, UNCATALOG DCS DATABASE, OPEN DCS DIRECTORY SCAN, GET DCS DIRECTORY ENTRIES, CLOSE DCS DIRECTORY SCAN

Example See the example provided for the OPEN DCS DIRECTORY SCAN function on page 276.

◼◼ CLOSE DCS DIRECTORY SCAN

Purpose The CLOSE DCS DIRECTORY SCAN function is used to free system resources that were allocated by the OPEN DCS DIRECTORY SCAN function.

Syntax `SQL_API_RC SQL_API_FN sqlegdcl (struct sqlca *SQLCA);`

Parameters *SQLCA* A pointer to a location in memory where a SQL Communications Area (SQLCA) data structure variable is stored. This variable returns either status information (if the function executed successfully) or error information (if the function failed) to the calling application.

Includes `#include <sqlenv.h>`

Description The CLOSE DCS DIRECTORY SCAN function is used to free system resources that were allocated by the OPEN DCS DIRECTORY SCAN function. This function should be called only if one or more DCS directory entries were not copied to the user-allocated memory storage area by the GET DCS DIRECTORY ENTRIES function.

Connection Requirements This function can be called at any time; a connection to a DB2 Database Manager instance or to a DB2 database does not have to be established first.

Authorization No authorization is required to execute this function call.

See Also OPEN DCS DIRECTORY SCAN, GET DCS DIRECTORY ENTRIES, GET DCS DIRECTORY ENTRY FOR DATABASE

Example See the example provided for the OPEN DCS DIRECTORY SCAN function on page 276.

◼◼ REGISTER

Purpose The REGISTER function is used to register a DB2 database server at a Novell NetWare file server.

Syntax
```
SQL_API_RC SQL_API_FN sqleregs (unsigned short  Registry,
                                void            *RegisterInfo,
                                struct sqlca    *SQLCA);
```

Parameters *Registry* Specifies where on the network file server to register the DB2 database server. For now, this parameter must be set to SQL_NWBINDERY.

RegisterInfo A pointer to a *sqle_reg_nwbindery* structure that contains a valid

NetWare user ID and password that can be used to access the
network file server.

SQLCA   A pointer to a location in memory where a SQL Communications
                   Area (SQLCA) data structure variable is stored. This variable returns
                   either status information (if the function executed successfully) or
                   error information (if the function failed) to the calling application.

Includes   `#include <sqlenv.h>`

Description   The **REGISTER** function is used to register a DB2 database server at a Novell
                   NetWare file server. When this function is executed, the DB2 database server's
                   network address is stored in a specified registry on the file server, where it can be
                   retrieved by any client application that uses the IPX/SPX communication protocol.
                   Before this function can be called, a valid user ID and password that can be used to
                   access the Novell network server must be stored in a special structure,
                   sql_reg_nwbindery, which is defined in *sqlenv.h* as follows:

```
struct sqle_reg_nwbindery
{
char            uid[49];           /* The user ID that is to be used to    */
                                   /* log into the Novell NetWare file      */
                                   /* server                                */
unsigned short reserved_len_1;     /* Reserved                              */
char            pswd[129];         /* The password that is to be used       */
                                   /* to validate the user ID               */
unsigned short reserved_len_2;     /* Reserved                              */
};
```

If the value specified in the *Registry* parameter is **SQL_NWBINDERY** (this is the
only value currently supported), the NetWare user ID and password stored in the
sql_reg_nwbindery structure is used to log onto the network server specified in the
fileserver parameter of the DB2 Database Manager configuration file. This function
determines the IPX/SPX address of the workstation to register (which is the
workstation from which it was invoked), and then creates an object in the specified
fileserver bindery using the DB2 Database Manager object name specified in the
objectname parameter of the DB2 Database Manager configuration file. The IPX/SPX
address of the server is stored as an attribute in that object. In order for a client to
connect or attach to the registered DB2 server using this information, it must first
catalog an IPX/SPX node (using the same *fileserver* and *objectname* values) in its
node directory.

Comments   ■ The Novell NetWare user ID and password specified in the *sqle_reg_nwbindery*
                   structure must have supervisory or equivalent authority.

                   ■ This function can only be issued locally from a DB2 database server workstation.
                   Remote execution of this function is not supported.

                   ■ After IPX/SPX support software is installed and configured, the DB2 database
                   server should be registered on the network server (unless IPX/SPX clients will only

be using *direct addressing* to connect to this DB2 server).

■ Once a DB2 database server is registered on the network server, if you need to reconfigure IPX/SPX or change the DB2 server's network address, deregister the DB2 server from the network server (with the **DEREGISTER** function) and then register it again (using this function) after the changes have been made.

■ This function cannot be used in applications that run on the Windows or the Windows NT operating system.

Connection Requirements This function can be called at any time; a connection to a DB2 Database Manager instance or to a DB2 database does not have to be established first.

Authorization No authorization is required to execute this function call.

See Also DEREGISTER

Example The following C++ program illustrates how to use the **REGISTER** function and the **DEREGISTER** function to register and deregister the current DB2 database server at a NetWare file server:

```
/*————————————————————————————————*/
/* NAME:     CH8EX11.CPP                                  */
/* PURPOSE: Illustrate How To Use The Following DB2 API Function */
/*          In A C++ Program:                             */
/*                                                        */
/*                   REGISTER                             */
/*                   DEREGISTER                           */
/*                                                        */
/*————————————————————————————————*/

// Include The Appropriate Header Files
#include <windows.h>
#include <iostream.h>
#include <sqlenv.h>
#include <sqlutil.h>
#include <sqlca.h>

// Define The API_Class Class
class API_Class
{
    // Attributes
    public:
        struct sqlca   sqlca;

    // Operations
    public:
        long RegisterServer();
        long DeregisterServer();
};

// Define The RegisterServer() Member Function
```

```
long API_Class::RegisterServer()
{
    // Declare The Local Memory Variables
    struct sqle_reg_nwbindery    NWInfo;
    struct sqlfupd               DBManagerInfo;
    struct sqle_start_options     StartOptions;
    struct sqledbstopopt          StopOptions;
    char                         FileServer[10];

    // Initialize The DB2 Database Manager Configuration
    // Parameter Structure
    strcpy(FileServer, "PCHOST");
    DBManagerInfo.token = SQLF_KTN_FILESERVER;
    DBManagerInfo.ptrvalue = (char *) FileServer;

    // Store The Novell NetWare File Server Name In The DB2
    // Database Manager Configuration File
    sqlfusys(1, &DBManagerInfo, &sqlca);

    // Initialize The Stop DB2 Database Manager Options
    // Structure
    StopOptions.isprofile = 0;
    strcpy(StopOptions.profile, "");
    StopOptions.isnodenum = 0;
    StopOptions.nodenum = 0;
    StopOptions.option = SQLE_NONE;
    StopOptions.callerac = SQLE_DROP;

    // Stop The DB2 Database Manager Server Processes
    sqlepstp(&StopOptions, &sqlca);

    // Initialize The Start DB2 Database Manager Options
    // Structure
    strcpy(StartOptions.sqloptid, SQLE_STARTOPTID_V51);
    StartOptions.isprofile = 0;
    strcpy(StartOptions.profile, "");
    StartOptions.isnodenum = 0;
    StartOptions.nodenum = 0;
    StartOptions.option = SQLE_NONE;
    StartOptions.ishostname = 0;
    strcpy(StartOptions.hostname, "");
    StartOptions.isport = 0;
    StartOptions.port = 0;
    StartOptions.isnetname = 0;
    strcpy(StartOptions.netname, "");
    StartOptions.tblspace_type = SQLE_TABLESPACES_LIKE_CATALOG;
    StartOptions.tblspace_node = 0;
    StartOptions.iscomputer = 0;
    strcpy(StartOptions.computer, "");
    StartOptions.pUserName = NULL;
    StartOptions.pPassword = NULL;

    // Re-Start The DB2 Database Manager Server Processes (This
    // Will Make DB2 See The Changes Made To The Configuration
```

```
        // File
        sqlepstart(&StartOptions, &sqlca);

        // Initialize The NetWare Registry Information Data Structure
        strcpy(NWInfo.uid, "userid");
        strcpy(NWInfo.pswd, "password");

        // Register The Current DB2 Server On A NetWare File Server
        sqleregs(SQL_NWBINDERY, &NWInfo, &sqlca);

        // If The DB2 Server Was Registered On A NetWare File Server,
        // Display A Success Message
        if (sqlca.sqlcode == SQL_RC_OK)
        {
            cout << "The DB2 Server has been registered at the ";
            cout << "NetWare file server." << endl;
        }

        // Return The SQLCA Return Code To The Calling Function
        return(sqlca.sqlcode);
}

// Define The DeregisterServer() Member Function
long API_Class::DeregisterServer()
{
        // Declare The Local Memory Variables
        struct sqle_reg_nwbindery  NWInfo;

        // Initialize The NetWare Registry Information Data Structure
        strcpy(NWInfo.uid, "userid");
        strcpy(NWInfo.pswd, "password");

        // Deregister The Current DB2 Server From A NetWare File Server
        sqledreg(SQL_NWBINDERY, &NWInfo, &sqlca);

        // If The DB2 Server Was Deregistered On A NetWare File Server,
        // Display A Success Message
        if (sqlca.sqlcode == SQL_RC_OK)
        {
            cout << "The DB2 Server has been un-registered at the ";
            cout << "NetWare file server." << endl;
        }

        // Return The SQLCA Return Code To The Calling Function
        return(sqlca.sqlcode);
}

/*------------------------------------------------------------*/
/* The Main Function                                          */
/*------------------------------------------------------------*/
int main()
{
    // Declare The Local Memory Variables
    long            rc = SQL_RC_OK;
```

```
                    // Create An Instance Of The API_Class Class
                    API_Class  Example;

                    // Register A DB2 Server With A NetWare File Server
                    rc = Example.RegisterServer();

                    // Unregister A DB2 Server With A NetWare File Server
                    if (rc == SQL_RC_OK)
                        rc = Example.DeregisterServer();

                    // Return To The Operating System
                    return(rc);
                }
```

■ ■ DEREGISTER

Purpose   The DEREGISTER function is used to deregister a DB2 server (remove a DB2 server's network address) from a registry at a Novell NetWare file server.

Syntax
```
SQL_API_RC SQL_API_FN sqledreg  (unsigned short  Registry,
                                 void            *RegisterInfo,
                                 struct sqlca    *SQLCA);
```

Parameters   *Registry*   Indicates where on the network file server to deregister the DB2 database server. For now, this parameter must be set to SQL_NWBINDERY.

RegisterInfo   A pointer to a *sqle_reg_nwbindery* structure that contains a valid NetWare user ID and password that can be used to access the network server.

SQLCA   A pointer to a location in memory where a SQL Communications Area (SQLCA) data structure variable is stored. This variable returns either status information (if the function executed successfully) or error information (if the function failed) to the calling application.

Includes   `#include <sqlenv.h>`

Description   The DEREGISTER function is used to deregister a DB2 server from a registry at a Novell NetWare file server. Before calling this function, you must store a valid user ID and password that can be used to access the Novell network server in a special *sql_reg_nwbindery* structure. Refer to the REGISTER function for a detailed description of this structure.

Comments   ■ The Novell NetWare user ID and password specified in the *sqle_reg_nwbindery* structure must have supervisory or equivalent authority.

                  ■ This function can only be issued locally from a DB2 database server workstation.

Remote execution of this function is not supported.

■ Once a DB2 database server is registered on the network server, if you need to reconfigure IPX/SPX or change the DB2 server's network address, deregister the DB2 server from the network server (using this function), and then register it again (with the **REGISTER** function) after the changes have been made.

■ This function cannot be used in applications that run on the Windows or the Windows NT operating system.

Connection Requirements   This function can be called at any time; a connection to a DB2 Database Manager instance or to a DB2 database does not have to be established first.

Authorization   No authorization is required to execute this function call.

See Also   **REGISTER**

Example   See the example provided for the **REGISTER** function on page 283.

9

Table and Table Space Management APIs

DB2 uses tables to store data and table spaces to logically group tables and other data objects. This chapter is designed to introduce you to the set of DB2 API functions that are used to obtain information about database table spaces and to reorganize data in and update statistics for database tables. The first part of this chapter provides a general overview of table spaces and table space containers. Then, information is provided on reorganizing and updating the statistics for a database table. Finally, a detailed reference section covering each DB2 API function that can be used to manage table spaces and tables is provided.

Table Spaces and Table Space Containers

Table spaces are designed to provide a level of direction between user tables and the database in which they reside. Two basic types of table spaces exist: *Database-Managed Space* (DMS) table spaces, which support raw devices and files, and *System-Managed Space* (SMS) table spaces, which support directories.

You can retrieve information about all table spaces that have been defined for a particular database by calling the **TABLESPACE QUERY** function. This function retrieves information about all table spaces that have been defined for a single database and copies it into a large memory storage buffer. If several table spaces have been defined for a database, you can retrieve this information in smaller pieces by calling the **OPEN TABLESPACE QUERY**, **FETCH TABLESPACE QUERY**, and **CLOSE TABLESPACE QUERY** functions. Together, these three functions work like an SQL cursor (i.e., they use the OPEN/FETCH/CLOSE pardigm).

A single table space can consist of one or more containers; for example, a DMS table space can reference many different drives and/or directories. You can retrieve information about all containers that have been defined for a specific table space by calling the **TABLESPACE CONTAINER QUERY** function. This function retrieves information about all table space containers that have been defined for a single table space and copies it into a large memory storage buffer. If a table space consists of many table space containers, you might want to retrieve this information in smaller pieces. You can do this by calling the **OPEN TABLESPACE CONTAINER QUERY**, **FETCH TABLESPACE CONTAINER QUERY**, and **CLOSE TABLESPACE CONTAINER QUERY** functions. These three functions work in a manner similar to their **OPEN/FETCH/CLOSE TABLESPACE QUERY** counterparts.

Reorganizing Table Data

Database tables that undergo many updates and deletes will, in time, become fragmented (i.e., the table and its indexes will contain empty space). As a table becomes fragmented, its performance drops. DB2 provides a utility that can reorganize the data in a table in order to reclaim this lost space. You can invoke this utility from within an application by calling the **REORGANIZE TABLE** function.

Table reorganization exports data (in some particular order) to an external file, deletes all entries in the table, and then imports the data back. This process can be a time-consuming operation and can require a large amount of disk space as tables grow in size. Unfortunately, while a database table is being reorganized, no other applications and/or users can access it. This restriction makes table reorganization a difficult task to add to the normal flow of an application. Therefore, applications that call the **REORGANIZE TABLE** function should only be executed when they will not significantly affect other users and applications.

Updating Table Statistics

The system catalog tables that are created as a part of a database contain, among other things, statistics on all user-defined tables and indexes. Database statistics include items such as the number of rows in a table, information about indexes that have been created for a table, and the overall size of a table. These statistics are important, because they are used by the SQL optimizer to build the most optimal access plans for each SQL statement used in an embedded SQL application.

Unfortunately, these statistics are not automatically kept up to date. This means that if you develop an application that accesses a particular database table, and you later create an index for that table, the static SQL statements in your application will not be able to take advantage of the new index (i.e., performance will not be increased). An application can update statistics for a specified table by calling the **RUN STATISTICS** function. Once a table's statistic information is updated, you need to rebind all packages that access the table so they can take full advantage of the updated statistical information.

The DB2 Table and Table Space Management Functions

Table 9–1 lists the DB2 API functions that are used to manage tables and table spaces.

Each of these functions are described in detail in the remainder of this chapter.

Table 9–1   Table and Table Space Management APIs

Function Name	Description
OPEN TABLESPACE QUERY	Obtains a count of the number of table spaces that have been defined for the current connected database.
FETCH TABLESPACE QUERY	Retrieves and copies a specified number of rows of table space information to a user-allocated memory storage buffer.
CLOSE TABLESPACE QUERY	Ends a table space query request that was made by the **OPEN TABLESPACE QUERY** function.
TABLESPACE QUERY	Stores a copy of all table space information available for the current connected database in a large DB2-allocated memory storage buffer.
SINGLE TABLESPACE QUERY	Retrieves information about a single, currently defined table space.
GET TABLESPACE STATISTICS	Retrieves information about the space utilization of a table space.
OPEN TABLESPACE CONTAINER QUERY	Obtains a count of the number of table space containers that have been defined for either a specified table space or for the current connected database.

Table 9–1   Table and Table Space Management APIs (Continued)

Function Name	Description
FETCH TABLESPACE CONTAINER QUERY	Retrieves and copies a specified number of rows of table space container information to a user-allocated memory storage buffer.
CLOSE TABLESPACE CONTAINER QUERY	Ends a table space container query request that was made by the OPEN TABLESPACE CONTAINER QUERY function.
TABLESPACE CONTAINER QUERY	Stores a copy of all table space container information available for either a specified table space or for the current connected database in a large DB2-allocated memory storage buffer.
FREE MEMORY	Frees memory that was allocated by either the TABLESPACE QUERY or the TABLESPACE CONTAINER QUERY function.
REORGANIZE TABLE	Reorganizes a table so that fragmented data is eliminated and information is compacted.
RUN STATISTICS	Updates statistical information about a table and any or all of its associated indexes.

OPEN TABLESPACE QUERY

Purpose   The OPEN TABLESPACE QUERY function is used to obtain a count of the number of table spaces that have been defined for the current connected database.

Syntax
```
SQL_API_RC SQL_API_FN sqlbotsq (struct sqlca    *SQLCA,
                                unsigned long   QueryOptions,
                                unsigned long   *NumTableSpaces);
```

Parameters   *SQLCA*   A pointer to a location in memory where a SQL Communications Area (SQLCA) data structure variable is stored. This variable returns either status information (if the function executed successfully) or error information (if the function failed) to the calling application.

QueryOptions   Specifies the type of table space information that is to be retrieved. This parameter must be set to one the following values:

■ SQLB_OPEN_TBS_ALL
Retrieve information about all table spaces that have been defined for the database.

■ SQLB_OPEN_TBS_RESTORE
Only retrieve information about table spaces that are being restored by the user's agent.

NumTableSpaces   A pointer to a location in memory where this function is to store the actual number of table spaces found in the current connected database that meet the specified criteria *(QueryOptions)*.

Includes   `#include <sqlutil.h>`

Description   The OPEN TABLESPACE QUERY function is used to obtain a count of the number of table spaces that have been defined for the current connected database.

This function is normally followed by one or more FETCH TABLESPACE QUERY functions calls and one CLOSE TABLESPACE QUERY function call. Together, these three functions work like an SQL cursor (i.e., they use the OPEN/FETCH/CLOSE paradigm). An application can use these three functions to scan a list of table spaces and search for specific information.

Comments   ■ Only one table space query can be active at one time.

■ The first time this function is called, a snapshot of the table space information available is buffered in the agent that is servicing the application. If the application calls this function again, this snapshot is replaced with refreshed information.

■ Because locking is not performed by this function, the information returned in the snapshot buffer may not reflect recent changes made by another application.

Connection Requirements   This function can only be called if a connection to a database exists.

Authorization   Only users with System Administrator (SYSADM) authority, Database Administrator (DBADM) authority, System Control (SYSCTRL) authority, or System Maintenance (SYSMAINT) authority can execute this function call.

See Also   FETCH TABLESPACE QUERY, CLOSE TABLESPACE QUERY, TABLESPACE QUERY, SINGLE TABLESPACE QUERY

Example   The following C++ program illustrates how to use the OPEN TABLESPACE QUERY, FETCH TABLESPACE QUERY, and CLOSE TABLESPACE QUERY functions to retrieve information about the table spaces defined for a database:

```
/*─────────────────────────────────────────────────────────────*/
/* NAME:     CH9EX1.SQC                                          */
/* PURPOSE: Illustrate How To Use The Following DB2 API Functions */
/*          In A C++ Program:                                    */
/*                                                               */
/*                   OPEN TABLESPACE QUERY                       */
/*                   FETCH TABLESPACE QUERY                      */
/*                   CLOSE TABLESPACE QUERY                      */
/*                                                               */
/*─────────────────────────────────────────────────────────────*/

// Include The Appropriate Header Files
#include <windows.h>
#include <iostream.h>
#include <sqlutil.h>
#include <sql.h>

// Define The API_Class Class
class API_Class
{
    // Attributes
    public:
        struct sqlca  sqlca;

    // Operations
    public:
        long GetTSpaceInfo();
};

// Define The GetTSpaceInfo() Member Function
long API_Class::GetTSpaceInfo()
{
    // Declare The Local Memory Variables
    unsigned long            TSCount;
    struct SQLB_TBSPQRY_DATA  *TableSpaceHead;
    struct SQLB_TBSPQRY_DATA  *TableSpaceData;
```

```
        unsigned long                NumRows;

        // Open The Table Space Query
        sqlbotsq(&sqlca, SQLB_OPEN_TBS_ALL, &TSCount);
        if (sqlca.sqlcode != SQL_RC_OK)
            return(sqlca.sqlcode);

        // Allocate A Memory Storage Buffer
        TableSpaceData = (struct SQLB_TBSPQRY_DATA *)
            malloc(TSCount * sizeof(struct SQLB_TBSPQRY_DATA));

        // Initialize The Memory Storage Buffer And Store Its
        // Address (So It Can Be Freed Later)
        strcpy(TableSpaceData->tbspqver, SQLB_TBSPQRY_DATA_ID);
        TableSpaceHead = TableSpaceData;

        // Copy The Table Space Data Into The Memory Storage Buffer
        // (Fetch Table Space Data)
        sqlbftpq(&sqlca, TSCount, TableSpaceData, &NumRows);
        if (sqlca.sqlcode != SQL_RC_OK)
            return(sqlca.sqlcode);

        // Display The Table Space Data Retrieved
        cout << "Table Spaces Defined For The SAMPLE Database" << endl;
        cout << "ID   Name            Type" << endl;
        cout << "————————————————————————————————————————————————" <<
endl;
    for (int i = 0; i < (int) NumRows; i++, TableSpaceData++)
    {
        cout.width(4);
        cout.setf(ios::left);
        cout << TableSpaceData->id;
        cout.width(14);
        cout.setf(ios::left);
        cout << TableSpaceData->name;
        switch (TableSpaceData->flags)
        {
        case SQLB_TBS_SMS:
            cout << "System Managed Space" << endl;
            break;
        case SQLB_TBS_DMS:
            cout << "Database Managed Space" << endl;
            break;
        case SQLB_TBS_ANY:
            cout << "Regular Contents" << endl;
            break;
        case SQLB_TBS_LONG:
            cout << "Long Field Data" << endl;
            break;
        case SQLB_TBS_TMP:
            cout << "Temporary Data" << endl;
            break;
        default:
            cout << endl;
        }
```

```
        }

        // Close The Table Space Query And Free All Resources Used
        sqlbctsq(&sqlca);
        free(TableSpaceHead);

        // Return The SQLCA Return Code To The Calling Function
        return(sqlca.sqlcode);
}

/*──────────────────────────────────────────────────────────*/
/* The Main Function                                         */
/*──────────────────────────────────────────────────────────*/
int main()
{
    // Declare The Local Memory Variables
    long          rc = SQL_RC_OK;
    struct sqlca  sqlca;

    // Create An Instance Of The API_Class Class
    API_Class  Example;

    // Connect To The SAMPLE Database
    EXEC SQL CONNECT TO SAMPLE USER userID USING password;

    // Get Information About The Table Spaces That Are Defined For
    // The SAMPLE Database
    rc = Example.GetTSpaceInfo();

    // Issue A Rollback To Free All Locks
    EXEC SQL ROLLBACK;

    // Disconnect From The SAMPLE Database
    EXEC SQL DISCONNECT CURRENT;

    // Return To The Operating System
    return(rc);
}
```

■ ■ FETCH TABLESPACE QUERY

Purpose   The FETCH TABLESPACE QUERY function is used to retrieve (fetch) and transfer a specified number of rows of table space information to a user-allocated memory storage buffer that is supplied by the calling application.

Syntax
```
SQL_API_RC SQL_API_FN  sqlbftpq (struct sqlca            *SQLCA,
                                 unsigned long           MaxTableSpaces,
                                 struct SQLB_TBSQRY_DATA *TableSpaceData,
                                 unsigned long           *NumTableSpaces);
```

Parameters   *SQLCA*   A pointer to a location in memory where a SQL Communications Area (SQLCA) data structure variable is stored. This variable returns either status information (if the function executed successfully) or error information (if the function failed) to the calling application.

                      MaxTableSpaces   The maximum number of rows of table space data that the user-allocated memory storage buffer can hold.

                      TableSpaceData   A pointer to a user-allocated array of *SQLB_TBSPQRY_DATA* structures where this function is to store the table space data retrieved.

                      NumTableSpaces   A pointer to a location in memory where this function is to store the actual number of rows of table space data retrieved.

Includes   `#include <sqlutil.h>`

Description   The `FETCH TABLESPACE QUERY` function is used to retrieve (fetch) and transfer a specified number of rows of table space information to a user-allocated memory storage buffer that is supplied by the calling application. The copy of table space data that is placed in memory represents a snapshot of the table space information at the time this function was executed. Because no locking is performed, the information in this snapshot may not reflect recent changes made by other applications. Before this function can be executed, an array of *SQLB_TBSPQRY_DATA* structures must be allocated, and the number of elements in this array must be stored in the *MaxTableSpaces* parameter. The *SQLB_TBSPQRY_DATA* structure is defined in *sqlutil.h* as follows:

```
struct SQLB_TBSPQRY_DATA
{
char          tbspqver[8];    /* The structure version identifier      */
unsigned long id;             /* The internal ID for the table space   */
unsigned long nameLen;        /* The length of the table space name    */
                              /* (for languages other than C and C++   */
char          name[128];      /* The table space name (NULL-terminated) */
unsigned long totalPages;     /* The total number of pages occupied by */
                              /* the table space (DMS table spaces only */
unsigned long useablePages;   /* The total number of 4KB pages occupied */
                              /* by the table space (DMS table spaces only */
unsigned long flags;          /* Bit attributes for the table space    */
unsigned long pageSize;       /* The size (in bytes) of one page of memory */
                              /* - currently fixed at 4K               */
unsigned long extSize;        /* The extent size (in pages) of the table */
                              /* space                                 */
unsigned long prefetchSize;   /* The table space prefetch buffer size  */
unsigned long nContainers;    /* The number of containers in the table */
                              /* space                                 */
unsigned long tbsState;       /* The state of the table space          */
char          lifeLSN[6];     /* The date and time that the table space */
                              /* was created                           */
char          pad[2];         /* Reserved; used for alignment          */
```

```
unsigned long    flags2;           /* Additional bit attributes for the table */
                                   /* space                                    */
char                                                                          */
          minimumRecTime[27];
                                   /* The earliest point in time that may be */
                                   /* specified for a point-in-time           */
                                   /* roll-forward recovery                    */
char             pad1[1];          /* Reserved; used for alignment            */
unsigned long    StateChngObj;     /* The object ID in table space StateChngID */
                                   /* that caused the table space state to be */
                                   /* set to SQLB_LOAD_PENDING or             */
                                   /* SQLB_DELETE_PENDING                      */
unsigned long    StateChngID;      /* The table space ID of object StateChngObj */
                                   /* that caused the table space state to be */
                                   /* set to SQLB_LOAD_PENDING or             */
                                   /* SQLB_DELETE_PENDING                      */
unsigned long    nQuiescers;       /* The number of quiescers of the table    */
                                   /* space (if the table space state is set to */
                                   /* SQLB_LOAD_PENDING or SQLB_DELETE_PENDING */
struct SQLB_QUIESCER_DATA                                                     */
          quiescer[5];                                                        */
                                   /* Quiescer Information                     */
char             reserved[32];     /* Reserved for future use                 */
};
```

This structure contains a pointer to an array of *SQLB_QUIESCER_DATA* structures that provide additional information about any quiescers of the table space. The *SQLB_QUIESCER_DATA* structure is defined in *sqlutil.h* as follows:

```
SQL_STRUCTURE SQLB_QUIESCER_DATA
{
unsigned long   quiesceId;       /* The table space ID of quiesceObject   */
unsigned long   quiesceObject;   /* The table space object in quiesceId   */
}
```

Comments   ■ The *flags* field of the SQLB_TBSPQRY_DATA structure can contain one of the following values:

   ■ **SQLB_TBS_SMS**   *System-Managed Space* (SMS) table space

   ■ **SQLB_TBS_DMS**   *Database-Managed Space* (DMS) table space

   ■ **SQLB_TBS_ANY**   Regular data table space

   ■ **SQLB_TBS_LONG**   Long field data table space

   ■ **SQLB_TBS_TMP**   Temporary data table space

   ■ The *tbsState* field of the *SQLB_TBSQRY_DATA* structure can contain one of the following values:

   ■ **SQLB_NORMAL**   *Normal*

   ■ **SQLB_QUIESCED_SHARE**   *Quiesced: SHARE*

   ■ **SQLB_QUIESCED_UPDATE**   *Quiesced: UPDATE*

   ■ **SQLB_QUIESCED_EXCLUSIVE** *Quiesced: EXCLUSIVE*

- SQLB_LOAD_PENDING   *Load pending*
- SQLB_DELETE_PENDING   *Delete pending*
- SQLB_BACKUP_PENDING   *Backup pending*
- SQLB_ROLLFORWARD_IN_PROGRESS   *Roll-forward recovery in progress*
- SQLB_ROLLFORWARD_PENDING   *Roll-forward recovery pending*
- SQLB_RESTORE_PENDING   *Restore pending*
- SQLB_DISABLE_PENDING   *Disable pending*
- SQLB_REORG_IN_PROGRESS   *Table reorganization in progress*
- SQLB_BACKUP_IN_PROGRESS   *Backup in progress*
- SQLB_STORDEF_PENDING   *Storage must be defined*
- SQLB_RESTORE_IN_PROGRESS   *Restore in progress*
- SQLB_STORDEF_ALLOWED   *Storage can be defined*
- SQLB_STORDEF_FINAL_VERSION   *Storage definition in final state*
- SQLB_STORDEF_CHANGED   *Storage definition changed prior to roll-forward recovery*
- SQLB_REBAL_IN_PROGRESS   *DMS rebalancer active*
- SQLB_PSTAT_DELETION   *Table space deletion in progress*
- SQLB_PSTAT_CREATION   *Table space creation in progress*

- When the array of *SQLB_TBSPQRY_DATA* structures that was allocated for this function is no longer needed, it must be freed by the application that allocated it.

- If this function is executed when a snapshot of table space information is already in memory, the previous snapshot will be replaced with refreshed table space information.

- One snapshot buffer storage area is used for table space queries and another snapshot buffer storage area is used for table space container queries. These buffers are independent of one another.

Prerequisites   The OPEN TABLESPACE QUERY function must be executed before this function is called.

Connection Requirements   This function can only be called if a connection to a database exists.

Authorization   Only users with System Administrator (SYSADM) authority, System Control (SYSCTRL) authority, System Maintenance (SYSMAINT) authority, or Database Administrator (DBADM) authority can execute this function call.

See Also   OPEN TABLESPACE QUERY, CLOSE TABLESPACE QUERY, TABLESPACE QUERY, SINGLE TABLESPACE QUERY, GET TABLESPACE STATISTICS

Example   See the example provided for the OPEN TABLESPACE QUERY function on page 294.

CLOSE TABLESPACE QUERY

Purpose   The CLOSE TABLESPACE QUERY function is used to terminate a table space query request made by the OPEN TABLESPACE QUERY function.

Syntax   `SQL_API_RC SQL_API_FN sqlbctsq (struct sqlca *SQLCA);`

Parameters   *SQLCA*   A pointer to a location in memory where a SQL Communications Area (SQLCA) data structure variable is stored. This variable returns either status information (if the function executed successfully) or error information (if the function failed) to the calling application.

Includes   `#include <sqlutil.h>`

Description   The CLOSE TABLESPACE QUERY function is used to end a table space query request made by the OPEN TABLESPACE QUERY function and to free all associated resources.

Connection Requirements   This function can only be called if a connection to a database exists.

Authorization   Only users with System Administrator (SYSADM) authority, System Control (SYSCTRL) authority, System Maintenance (SYSMAINT) authority, or Database Administrator (DBADM) authority are allowed to execute this function call.

See Also   OPEN TABLESPACE QUERY, FETCH TABLESPACE QUERY, TABLESPACE QUERY, SINGLE TABLESPACE QUERY, GET TABLESPACE STATISTICS

Example   See the example provided for the OPEN TABLESPACE QUERY function on page 294.

TABLESPACE QUERY

Purpose   The TABLESPACE QUERY function is used to retrieve a copy of the table space information that is available for the current connected database into a large DB2-allocated memory storage buffer.

Syntax
```
SQL_API_RC SQL_API_FN sqlbmtsq (struct sqlca          *SQLCA,
                                unsigned long          *NumTableSpaces,
                                struct SQLB_TBSPQRY_DATA **TableSpaceData);
```

Parameters   *SQLCA*   A pointer to a location in memory where a SQL Communications Area (SQLCA) data structure variable is stored. This variable returns either status information (if the function executed successfully) or error information (if the function failed) to the calling application.

    NumTableSpaces   A pointer to a location in memory where this function is to store the actual number of table spaces found in

	the current connected database.
TableSpaceData	A pointer to the address of an array of *SQLB_TBSPQRY_DATA* structures where this function is to store the table space information retrieved.

Includes   `#include <sqlutil.h>`

Description   The **TABLESPACE QUERY** function is used to retrieve a copy of the table space information that is available for the current connected database into a large DB2-allocated memory storage buffer. When called, this function also returns the number of table spaces that have been defined for the current connected database to the application. This function provides a one-call interface to the **OPEN TABLESPACE QUERY**, **FETCH TABLESPACE QUERY**, and **CLOSE TABLESPACE QUERY** functions (which can also be used to retrieve the table space information for a connected database).

When this function is executed, a memory storage buffer that is used to hold all of the table space information retrieved is automatically allocated, a pointer to that buffer is stored in the *TableSpaceData* parameter, and the number of table spaces found in the current connected database is stored in the *NumTableSpaces* parameter. The memory storage buffer that holds the table space information is actually an array of *SQLB_TBSPQRY_DATA* structures and the value returned in this *NumTableSpaces* parameter identifies the number of elements in this array. Refer to the **FETCH TABLESPACE QUERY** function for a detailed description of the *SQLB_TBSPQRY_DATA* structure.

Comments
- When this function is executed, if a sufficient amount of free memory is available, a memory storage buffer will automatically be allocated. This memory storage buffer can only be freed by calling the **FREE MEMORY** function. It is up to the application to ensure that all memory allocated by this function is freed when it is no longer needed. If sufficient memory is not available, this function simply returns the number of table spaces found in the connected database, and no memory is allocated.

- If there is not enough free memory available to retrieve the complete set of table space information available at one time, you can use the **OPEN TABLESPACE QUERY**, **FETCH TABLESPACE QUERY**, and **CLOSE TABLESPACE QUERY** functions to retrieve the same table space information in smaller pieces.

Connection Requirements   This function can only be called if a connection to a database exists.

Authorization   Only users with System Administrator (SYSADM) authority, System Control (SYSCTRL) authority, System Maintenance (SYSMAINT) authority, or Database Administrator (DBADM) authority are allowed to execute this function call.

See Also   OPEN TABLESPACE QUERY, FETCH TABLESPACE QUERY, CLOSE TABLESPACE QUERY, SINGLE TABLESPACE QUERY, GET TABLESPACE STATISTICS, FREE

MEMORY

Example   The following C++ program illustrates how to use the **TABLESPACE QUERY** function to retrieve information about the table spaces that have been defined for the SAMPLE database:

```
/*———————————————————————————————————————————————*/
/* NAME:    CH9EX2.SQC                                  */
/* PURPOSE: Illustrate How To Use The Following DB2 API Functions */
/*          In A C++ Program:                           */
/*                                                      */
/*                 TABLESPACE QUERY                     */
/*                 FREE MEMORY                           */
/*                                                      */
/*———————————————————————————————————————————————*/

// Include The Appropriate Header Files
#include <windows.h>
#include <iostream.h>
#include <sqlenv.h>
#include <sqlutil.h>
#include <sql.h>

// Define The API_Class Class
class API_Class
{
    // Attributes
    public:
        struct sqlca    sqlca;

    // Operations
    public:
        long GetTSpaceInfo();
};

// Define The GetTSpaceInfo() Member Function
long API_Class::GetTSpaceInfo()
{
    // Declare The Local Memory Variables
    unsigned long           TSCount;
    struct SQLB_TBSPQRY_DATA   **TableSpaceData;

    // Retrieve Table Space Data
    sqlbmtsq(&sqlca, &TSCount, &(TableSpaceData), SQLB_RESERVED1,
        SQLB_RESERVED2);
    if (sqlca.sqlcode != SQL_RC_OK)
        return(sqlca.sqlcode);

    // Display The Table Space Data Retrieved
    cout << "Table Spaces Defined For The SAMPLE Database" << endl;
    cout << "ID   Name            Type" << endl;
    cout << "———————————————————————————————————————————" << endl;
    for (int i = 0; i < (int) TSCount; i++)
```

```
    {
        cout.width(4);
        cout.setf(ios::left);
        cout << TableSpaceData[i]->id;
        cout.width(14);
        cout.setf(ios::left);
        cout << TableSpaceData[i]->name;
        switch (TableSpaceData[i]->flags)
        {
        case SQLB_TBS_SMS:
            cout << "System Managed Space" << endl;
            break;
        case SQLB_TBS_DMS:
            cout << "Database Managed Space" << endl;
            break;
        case SQLB_TBS_ANY:
            cout << "Regular Contents" << endl;
            break;
        case SQLB_TBS_LONG:
            cout << "Long Field Data" << endl;
            break;
        case SQLB_TBS_TMP:
            cout << "Temporary Data" << endl;
            break;
        default:
            cout << endl;
        }
    }

    // Free All Resources Associated With The Table Space Query
    sqlefmem(&sqlca, TableSpaceData);

    // Return The SQLCA Return Code To The Calling Function
    return(sqlca.sqlcode);
}

/*————————————————————————————————————————————— */
/* The Main Function                             */
/*————————————————————————————————————————————— */
int main()
{
    // Declare The Local Memory Variables
    long        rc = SQL_RC_OK;
    struct sqlca  sqlca;

    // Create An Instance Of The API_Class Class
    API_Class  Example;

    // Connect To The SAMPLE Database
    EXEC SQL CONNECT TO SAMPLE USER userID USING password;

    // Get Information About The Table Spaces That Are Defined For
    // The SAMPLE Database
    rc = Example.GetTSpaceInfo();
```

```
// Issue A Rollback To Free All Locks
EXEC SQL ROLLBACK;

// Disconnect From The SAMPLE Database
EXEC SQL DISCONNECT CURRENT;

// Return To The Operating System
return(rc);
}
```

■ ■ SINGLE TABLESPACE QUERY

Purpose   The SINGLE TABLESPACE QUERY function is used to retrieve information about a single, currently defined table space.

Syntax
```
SQL_API_RC SQL_API_FN sqlbstpq (struct sqlca            *SQLCA,
                                unsigned long           TableSpaceID,
                                struct SQLB_TBSQRY_DATA *TableSpaceData);
```

Parameters   *SQLCA*   A pointer to a location in memory where a SQL
                                              Communications Area (SQLCA) data structure variable
                                              is stored. This variable returns either status information
                                              (if the function executed successfully) or error
                                              information (if the function failed) to the calling
                                              application.

                 TableSpaceID   The ID of the table space that information is to be
                                              retrieved for.

                 TableSpaceData   A pointer to a *SQLB_TBSPQRY_DATA* structure
                                              where this function is to store the table space
                                              information retrieved.

Includes   `#include <sqlutil.h>`

Description The SINGLE TABLESPACE QUERY function is used to retrieve information about a single, currently defined table space. The information retrieved is stored in a special structure, *SQLB_TBSPQRY_DATA*, that is defined in *sqlutil.h*. Refer to the FETCH TABLESPACE QUERY function for a detailed description of this structure.

                 The SINGLE TABLESPACE QUERY function provides an alternative to the more expensive combination of OPEN TABLESPACE QUERY, FETCH TABLESPACE QUERY, and CLOSE TABLESPACE QUERY function calls when the table space identifier of a table space is already known.

Comments   ■ Table space IDs for table spaces can be found in the SYSCAT.TABLESPACES system catalog table.

■ No agent snapshot is taken when this function is executed. Because there is only one table space entry to return, the entry is returned directly.

■ When the table space identifier is not known in advance, you must use either the OPEN TABLESPACE QUERY, FETCH TABLESPACE QUERY, and CLOSE TABLESPACE QUERY functions or the TABLESPACE QUERY to retrieve information about the desired table space.

Connection Requirements This function can only be called if a connection to a database exists.

Authorization Only users with System Administrator (SYSADM), System Control (SYSCTRL) authority, System Maintenance (SYSMAINT) authority, or Database Administrator (DBADM) authority are allowed to execute this function call.

See Also OPEN TABLESPACE QUERY, FETCH TABLESPACE QUERY, CLOSE TABLESPACE QUERY, TABLESPACE QUERY, GET TABLESPACE STATISTICS

Example The following C++ program illustrates how to use the SINGLE TABLESPACE function to retrieve information about a table space whose ID is already known:

```
/*————————————————————————————————————*/
/* NAME:     CH9EX3.SQC                                        */
/* PURPOSE: Illustrate How To Use The Following DB2 API Function */
/*          In A C++ Program:                                  */
/*                                                             */
/*              SINGLE TABLESPACE QUERY                        */
/*                                                             */
/*————————————————————————————————————*/

// Include The Appropriate Header Files
#include <windows.h>
#include <iostream.h>
#include <sqlutil.h>
#include <sql.h>

// Define The API_Class Class
class API_Class
{
    // Attributes
    public:
        struct sqlca   sqlca;

    // Operations
    public:
        long GetTSpaceInfo();
};

// Define The GetTSpaceInfo() Member Function
long API_Class::GetTSpaceInfo()
{
    // Declare The Local Memory Variables
```

```
struct SQLB_TBSPQRY_DATA   TableSpaceData;

// Initialize The Memory Variable
strcpy(TableSpaceData.tbspqver, SQLB_TBSPQRY_DATA_ID);

// Retrieve The Table Space Data Into A Local Variable
sqlbstpq(&sqlca, 2, &TableSpaceData, SQLB_RESERVED1);

// Display The Table Space Data Retrieved
if (sqlca.sqlcode == SQL_RC_OK)
{
    cout << "Table Spaces Defined For The SAMPLE Database" << endl;
    cout << "ID   Name            Type" << endl;
    cout << "————————————————————————————————————" << endl;
    cout.width(4);
    cout.setf(ios::left);
    cout << TableSpaceData.id;
    cout.width(14);
    cout.setf(ios::left);
    cout << TableSpaceData.name;
    switch (TableSpaceData.flags)
    {
    case SQLB_TBS_SMS:
        cout << "System Managed Space" << endl;
        break;
    case SQLB_TBS_DMS:
        cout << "Database Managed Space" << endl;
        break;
    case SQLB_TBS_ANY:
        cout << "Regular Contents" << endl;
        break;
    case SQLB_TBS_LONG:
        cout << "Long Field Data" << endl;
        break;
    case SQLB_TBS_TMP:
        cout << "Temporary Data" << endl;
        break;
    default:
        cout << endl;
    }
}

// Return The SQLCA Return Code To The Calling Function
return(sqlca.sqlcode);
}

/*————————————————————————————————————————————————————*/
/* The Main Function                                    */
/*————————————————————————————————————————————————————*/
int main()
{
    // Declare The Local Memory Variables
    long         rc = SQL_RC_OK;
    struct sqlca  sqlca;
```

```
            // Create An Instance Of The API_Class Class
            API_Class   Example;

            // Connect To The SAMPLE Database
            EXEC SQL CONNECT TO SAMPLE USER userID USING password;

            // Get Information About The Table Spaces That Are Defined For
            // The SAMPLE Database
            rc = Example.GetTSpaceInfo();

            // Issue A Rollback To Free All Locks
            EXEC SQL ROLLBACK;

            // Disconnect From The SAMPLE Database
            EXEC SQL DISCONNECT CURRENT;

            // Return To The Operating System
            return(rc);
        }
```

GET TABLESPACE STATISTICS

Purpose   The GET TABLESPACE STATISTICS function is used to retrieve information about the space utilization of a specific table space.

Syntax
```
SQL_API_RC SQL_API_FN sqlbgtss  (struct sqlca         *SQLCA,
                                 unsigned long         TableSpaceID,
                                 struct SQLB_TBS_STATS *TableSpaceStats);
```

Parameters   *SQLCA*   A pointer to a location in memory where a SQL Communications Area (SQLCA) data structure variable is stored. This variable returns either status information (if the function executed successfully) or error information (if the function failed) to the calling application.

TableSpaceID   The ID of the table space that space usage information is to be retrieved for.

TableSpaceStats A pointer to the address of a *SQLB_TBS_STATS* structure where this function is to store the table space usage information retrieved.

Includes   `#include <sqlutil.h>`

Description The GET TABLESPACE STATISTICS function is used to retrieve information about the space utilization of a specific table space. The information retrieved is stored in a special structure, *SQLB_TBS_STATS*, that is defined in *sqlutil.h* as follows:

```
struct SQLB_TBS_STATS
{
unsigned long  totalPages;       /* The total amount of operating    */
                                 /* system space (in 4KB pages)      */
                                 /* needed by the table space. For   */
                                 /* DMS table spaces, this is the sum */
                                 /* of the table space container sizes */
                                 /* (including overhead). For SMS     */
                                 /* table spaces, this is the sum of all */
                                 /* file space used for the tables   */
                                 /* stored in this table space.      */
unsigned long  usablePages;      /* The total amount of operating    */
                                 /* system space (in 4KB pages)      */
                                 /* needed by the table space minus  */
                                 /* overhead (for DMS table spaces). */
                                 /* For SMS table spaces, this value is */
                                 /* equal to the totalPages value.   */
unsigned long  usedPages;        /* The total number of 4KB pages    */
                                 /* currently being used by the table */
                                 /* space (for DMS table spaces).    */
                                 /* For SMS table spaces, this value is */
                                 /* equal to the totalPages value.   */
unsigned long  freePages;        /* The total number of 4KB pages    */
                                 /* that are available for a DMS table */
                                 /* space (usablePages value minus   */
                                 /* usedPages value). This field is not */
                                 /* applicable for SMS table spaces. */
unsigned long  highWaterMark;    /* The current "end" of the DMS     */
                                 /* table space address space, in other */
                                 /* words, the page number of the    */
                                 /* first free 4KB page following the */
                                 /* last allocated extent of the table */
                                 /* space. This field is not applicable */
                                 /* for SMS table spaces. Note: this is */
                                 /* not really a "high-water mark" but */
                                 /* rather a "current-water mark"     */
                                 /* since the value can increase or  */
                                 /* decrease.                        */
};
```

Connection Requirements   This function can only be called if a connection to a database exists.

Authorization   Only users with System Administrator (SYSADM) authority, System Control (SYSCTRL) authority, System Maintenance (SYSMAINT) authority, or Database Administrator (DBADM) authority can execute this function call.

See Also   OPEN TABLESPACE QUERY, FETCH TABLESPACE QUERY, CLOSE TABLESPACE QUERY, TABLESPACE QUERY, SINGLE TABLESPACE QUERY

Example   The following C++ program illustrates how to use the GET TABLESPACE STATISTICS function to retrieve space usage information for the SYSCATSPACE table space (of the SAMPLE database):

```
/*-----------------------------------------------------------------*/
/* NAME:     CH9EX4.SQC                                            */
/* PURPOSE: Illustrate How To Use The Following DB2 API Function   */
/*          In A C++ Program:                                      */
/*                                                                 */
/*               GET TABLESPACE STATISTICS                         */
/*                                                                 */
/*-----------------------------------------------------------------*/

// Include The Appropriate Header Files
#include <windows.h>
#include <iostream.h>
#include <sqlutil.h>
#include <sql.h>

// Define The API_Class Class
class API_Class
{
    // Attributes
    public:
        struct sqlca   sqlca;

    // Operations
    public:
        long GetTSpaceStats();
};

// Define The GetTSpaceStats() Member Function
long API_Class::GetTSpaceStats()
{
    // Declare The Local Memory Variables
    struct SQLB_TBS_STATS  TableSpaceStats;

    // Retrieve The Table Space Statistics
    sqlbgtss(&sqlca, 0, &TableSpaceStats);

    // Display The Table Space Statistical Data Retrieved
    if (sqlca.sqlcode == SQL_RC_OK)
    {
        cout << "Statistics for SYSCATSPACE Table Space :" << endl;
        cout << "Total Number Of Pages          : ";
        cout <<   TableSpaceStats.totalPages << endl;
        cout << "Total Number Of Usable Pages  : ";
        cout <<   TableSpaceStats.useablePages << endl;
        cout << "Total Number Of Used Pages    : ";
        cout <<   TableSpaceStats.usedPages << endl;
        cout << "Total Number Of Free Pages    : ";
        cout <<   TableSpaceStats.freePages << endl;
        cout << "Current End Of Address Space  : ";
        cout <<   TableSpaceStats.highWaterMark << endl;
    }
```

```
                    // Return The SQLCA Return Code To The Calling Function
                    return(sqlca.sqlcode);
          }

          /*————————————————————————————————————*/
          /* The Main Function                                              */
          /*————————————————————————————————————*/
          int main()
          {
                    // Declare The Local Memory Variables
                    long          rc = SQL_RC_OK;
                    struct sqlca  sqlca;

                    // Create An Instance Of The API_Class Class
                    API_Class  Example;

                    // Connect To The SAMPLE Database
                    EXEC SQL CONNECT TO SAMPLE USER userID USING password;

                    // Get Statistics About The First Table Space Defined For
                    // The SAMPLE Database
                    rc = Example.GetTSpaceStats();

                    // Issue A Rollback To Free All Locks
                    EXEC SQL ROLLBACK;

                    // Disconnect From The SAMPLE Database
                    EXEC SQL DISCONNECT CURRENT;

                    // Return To The Operating System
                    return(rc);
          }
```

OPEN TABLESPACE CONTAINER QUERY

Purpose   The OPEN TABLESPACE CONTAINER QUERY function is used to obtain a count of the number of table space containers that have been defined for either a specified table space or for the current connected database.

Syntax
```
SQL_API_RC SQL_API_FN sqlbotcq (struct sqlca    *SQLCA,
                                unsigned long    TableSpaceID,
                                unsigned long    *NumContainers);
```

Parameters   *SQLCA*   A pointer to a location in memory where a SQL
                                          Communications Area (SQLCA) data structure variable
                                          is stored. This variable returns either status

	information (if the function executed successfully) or error information (if the function failed) to the calling application.
TableSpaceID	The ID of the table space that container information is to be retrieved for. If the value specified for this parameter is **SQLB_ALL_TABLESPACES**, a count of table space containers for the entire database will be returned.
NumContainers	A pointer to a location in memory where this function is to store the actual number of containers found in the specified table space (or database).

Includes   `#include <sqlutil.h>`

Description   The **OPEN TABLESPACE CONTAINER QUERY** function is used to obtain a count of the number of table space containers that have been defined for either a specified table space or for the current connected database.

This function is normally followed by one or more **FETCH TABLESPACE CONTAINER QUERY** function calls and one **CLOSE TABLESPACE CONTAINER QUERY** function call. Together, these three functions work like an SQL cursor (i.e., they use the OPEN/FETCH/CLOSE paradigm). An application can use these three functions to scan a list of table space containers and search for specific information.

Comments   ■ Only one table space container query can be active at one time.

■ The first time this function is called, a snapshot of the table space information is buffered in the agent that is servicing the application. If the application calls this function again, this snapshot is replaced with refreshed information.

■ Because locking is not performed by this function, the information returned in the snapshot buffer may not reflect recent changes made by another application.

Connection Requirements   This function can only be called if a connection to a database exists.

Authorization   Only users with System Administrator (SYSADM) authority, System Control (SYSCTRL) authority, System Maintenance (SYSMAINT) authority, or Database Administrator (DBADM) authority can execute this function call.

See Also   **FETCH TABLESPACE CONTAINER QUERY**, **CLOSE TABLESPACE CONTAINER QUERY**, **TABLESPACE CONTAINER QUERY**

Example   The following C++ program illustrates how to use the **OPEN TABLESPACE CONTAINER QUERY**, **FETCH TABLESPACE CONTAINER QUERY**, and **CLOSE TABLESPACE CONTAINER QUERY** functions to retrieve a list of containers for a specified table space:

```
/*-----------------------------------------------------------------*/
/* NAME:     CH9EX5.SQC                                            */
/* PURPOSE: Illustrate How To Use The Following DB2 API Functions  */
/*          In A C++ Program:                                      */
/*                                                                 */
/*              OPEN TABLESPACE CONTAINER QUERY                    */
/*              FETCH TABLESPACE CONTAINER QUERY                   */
/*              CLOSE TABLESPACE CONTAINER QUERY                   */
/*                                                                 */
/*-----------------------------------------------------------------*/
// Include The Appropriate Header Files
#include <windows.h>
#include <iostream.h>
#include <sqlutil.h>
#include <sql.h>

// Define The API_Class Class
class API_Class
{
    // Attributes
    public:
        struct sqlca   sqlca;

    // Operations
    public:
        long GetTSCInfo();
};

// Define The GetTSCInfo() Member Function
long API_Class::GetTSCInfo()
{
    // Declare The Local Memory Variables
    unsigned long              TSCCount;
    struct SQLB_TBSCONTQRY_DATA   *TSContainerData = NULL;
    struct SQLB_TBSCONTQRY_DATA   *TSCDataHead = NULL;
    unsigned long              NumRows;

    // Open The Table Space Container Query
    sqlbotcq(&sqlca, 2, &TSCCount);
    if (sqlca.sqlcode != SQL_RC_OK)
        return(sqlca.sqlcode);

    // Allocate A Memory Storage Buffer
    TSContainerData = (struct SQLB_TBSCONTQRY_DATA *)
        malloc(TSCCount * sizeof(struct SQLB_TBSCONTQRY_DATA));

    // Store The Memory Storage Buffer's Address (So It Can Be
    // Freed Later)
    TSCDataHead = TSContainerData;

    // Copy The Table Space Container Data Into The Memory Storage
    // Buffer
    // (Fetch Table Space Container Data)
    sqlbftcq(&sqlca, TSCCount, TSContainerData, &NumRows);
```

```
           if (sqlca.sqlcode != SQL_RC_OK)
               return(sqlca.sqlcode);

           // Display The Table Space Container Data Retrieved
           cout << "Containers Defined For The USERSPACE1 Table Space";
           cout << endl << "ID   Name" << endl;
           cout << "─────────────────────────────────" << endl;
           for (int i = 0; i < (int) NumRows; i++, TSContainerData++)
           {
               cout.width(4);
               cout.setf(ios::left);
               cout << TSContainerData->id;
               cout.width(14);
               cout.setf(ios::left);
               cout << TSContainerData->name;
           }

           // Close The Table Space Container Query And Free All Resources
           // Used
           sqlbctcq(&sqlca);
           free(TSCDataHead);

           // Return The SQLCA Return Code To The Calling Function
           return(sqlca.sqlcode);
   }


   /*──────────────────────────────────────────────────────*/
   /* The Main Function                                     */
   /*──────────────────────────────────────────────────────*/
   int main()
   {
       // Declare The Local Memory Variables
       long        rc = SQL_RC_OK;
       struct sqlca  sqlca;

       // Create An Instance Of The API_Class Class
       API_Class  Example;

       // Connect To The SAMPLE Database
       EXEC SQL CONNECT TO SAMPLE USER userID USING password;

       // Get Information About The Table Space Containers
       // That Are Defined For The SAMPLE Database
       rc = Example.GetTSCInfo();

       // Issue A Rollback To Free All Locks
       EXEC SQL ROLLBACK;

       // Disconnect From The SAMPLE Database
       EXEC SQL DISCONNECT CURRENT;

       // Return To The Operating System
       return(rc);
   }
```

FETCH TABLESPACE CONTAINER QUERY

Purpose   The FETCH TABLESPACE CONTAINER QUERY function is used to retrieve (fetch) and transfer a specified number of rows of table space container information to a user-allocated memory buffer that is supplied by the calling application.

Syntax
```
SQL_API_RC SQL_API_FN sqlbftcq (struct sqlca                *SQLCA,
                                unsigned long                MaxContainers,
                                struct SQLB_TBSCONTQRY_DATA *ContainerData
                                unsigned long               *NumContainers);
```

Parameters   *SQLCA*   A pointer to a location in memory where a SQL Communications Area (SQLCA) data structure variable is stored. This variable returns either status information (if the function executed successfully) or error information (if the function failed) to the calling application.

MaxContainers   The maximum number of rows of table space container information that the user-allocated memory storage buffer can hold.

ContainerData   A pointer to the address of an array of *SQLB_TBSCONTQRY_DATA* structures where this function is to store the table space container information retrieved.

NumContainers   A pointer to a location in memory where this function is to store the actual number of rows of table space container information retrieved.

Includes   `#include <sqlutil.h>`

Description   The FETCH TABLESPACE CONTAINER QUERY function is used to retrieve (fetch) and transfer a specified number of rows of table space container information to a user-allocated memory storage buffer that is supplied by the calling application. The copy of table space container data that is placed in memory represents a snapshot of the table space container information at the time this function was executed. Because no locking is performed, the information in this snapshot might not reflect recent changes made by other applications. Before this function can be executed, an array of *SQLB_TBSCONTQRY_DATA* structures must be allocated, and the number of elements in this array must be stored in the *MaxContainers* parameter. The *SQLB_TBSCONTQRY_DATA* structure is defined in *sqlutil.h* as follows:

```
struct SQLB_TBSCONTQRY_DATA
{
unsigned long    id;         /* The container identifier            */
unsigned long    nTbs;       /* The number of table spaces sharing this*/
                             /* container. The value for this parameter*/
                             /* is always 1 (DMS table spaces can have*/
                             /* only 1 container space at this time). */
unsigned long    tbsID;      /* The table space identifier          */
unsigned long    nameLen;    /* The length of the container name (for */
```

```
                                   /* languages other than C and C++)   */
        char           name[256];  /* The container name (NULL-terminated) */
        unsigned long  underDBDir; /* Indicates whether the table space  */
                                   /* container is under the database    */
                                   /* directory (1) or not (0).          */
        unsigned long  contType;   /* Indicates whether the table space  */
                                   /* container specifies a directory path */
                                   /* (SQLB_CONT_PATH), a raw device     */
                                   /* (SQLB_CONT_DISK), or a file        */
                                   /* (SQLB_CONT_FILE). Note: the value   */
                                   /* SQLB_CONT_PATH is only valid for   */
                                   /* SMS table spaces.                  */
        unsigned long  totalPages; /* Total number of 4KB pages occupied by */
                                   /* the table space container (DMS table */
                                   /* spaces only)                       */
        unsigned long  usablePages;/* Total number of 4KB pages occupied by the*/
                                   /* table space container overhead (DMS */
                                   /* table spaces only)                 */
        unsigned long  ok;         /* Indicates whether the table space  */
                                   /* container is accessible (1) or     */
                                   /* inaccessible (0). A value of 0 indicates */
                                   /* an abnormal situation that might require */
                                   /* the database administrator's attention. */
        };
```

Comments   ■ When the array of *SQLB_TBSCONTQRY_DATA* structures that was allocated for this function is no longer needed, it must be freed by the application that allocated it.

■ If this function is executed when a snapshot of table space container information is already in memory, the previous snapshot will be replaced with refreshed table space container information.

■ One snapshot buffer storage area is used for table space queries and another snapshot buffer storage area is used for table space container queries. These buffers are independent of one another.

Prerequisites   The OPEN TABLESPACE CONTAINER QUERY function must be executed before this function is called.

Connection Requirements   This function can only be called if a connection to a database exists.

Authorization   Only users with System Administrator (SYSADM) authority, System Control (SYSCTRL) authority, System Maintenance (SYSMAINT) authority, or Database Administrator (DBADM) authority can execute this function call.

See Also   OPEN TABLESPACE CONTAINER QUERY, CLOSE TABLESPACE CONTAINER QUERY, TABLESPACE CONTAINER QUERY

Example   See the example provided for the OPEN TABLESPACE CONTAINER QUERY function on page 312.

CLOSE TABLESPACE CONTAINER QUERY

Purpose   The CLOSE TABLESPACE CONTAINER QUERY function is used to terminate a table
space container query request that was made by the OPEN TABLESPACE CONTAINER
QUERY function.

Syntax   SQL_API_RC SQL_API_FN sqlbctcq (struct sqlca *SQLCA);

Parameters   *SQLCA*   A pointer to a location in memory where a SQL Communications
                                  Area data structure variable is stored. This variable returns either
                                  status information (if the function executed successfully) or error
                                  information (if the function failed) to the calling application.

Includes   #include <sqlutil.h>

Description The CLOSE TABLESPACE CONTAINER QUERY function is used to end a table space
container query request that was made by the OPEN TABLESPACE CONTAINER
QUERY function and to free all associated resources.

Connection   This function can only be called if a connection to a database exists.
Requirements

Authorization Only users with System Administrator (SYSADM) authority, System Control
(SYSCTRL) authority, System Maintenance (SYSMAINT) authority, or Database
Administrator (DBADM) authority can execute this function call.

See Also   OPEN TABLESPACE CONTAINER QUERY, FETCH TABLESPACE CONTAINER QUERY,
TABLESPACE CONTAINER QUERY

Example   See the example provided for the OPEN TABLESPACE CONTAINER QUERY function on
page 312.

TABLESPACE CONTAINER QUERY

Purpose   The TABLESPACE CONTAINER QUERY function is used to retrieve a copy of the table
space container information that is available for a table space (or for all table spaces
in the current connected database) into a large DB2-allocated memory storage buffer.

Syntax   SQL_API_RC SQL_API_FN sqlbtcq (struct sqlca   *SQLCA,
                                               unsigned long   TableSpaceID,
                                               unsigned long   *NumContainers,
                                               struct SQLB_TBSCONTQRY_DATA **ContainerData);

Parameters   *SQLCA*   A pointer to a location in memory where a SQL Communications Area (SQLCA) data structure variable is stored. This variable returns either status information (if the function executed successfully) or error information (if the function failed) to the calling application.

TableSpaceID   The ID of the table space that container information is to be retrieved for. If the value specified for this parameter is SQLB_ALL_TABLESPACES, a composite list of table space container information for all table spaces in the entire database will be returned.

NumContainers   A pointer to a location in memory where this function is to store the actual number of table space containers found for the table space specified.

ContainerData   A pointer to the address of an array of *SQLB_TBSCONTQRY_DATA* structures where this function is to store the table space container information retrieved.

Includes   `#include <sqlutil.h>`

Description   The TABLESPACE CONTAINER QUERY function is used to retrieve a copy of the table space container information that is available for a table space (or for all table spaces in the current connected database) into a large DB2-allocated memory storage buffer. When called, this function also returns the number of table space containers that have been defined for a specified table space (or for all table spaces in the current connected database) to the application. This function provides a one-call interface to the OPEN TABLESPACE CONTAINER QUERY, FETCH TABLESPACE CONTAINER QUERY, and CLOSE TABLESPACE CONTAINER QUERY functions (which can also be used to retrieve the table space container information for one or more table spaces).

When this function is executed, a memory storage buffer that is used to hold all of the table space container information retrieved is automatically allocated, a pointer to that buffer is stored in the *ContainerData* parameter, and the number of table space containers found in either the specified table space or in the current connected database is stored in the *NumContainers* parameter. The memory storage buffer that holds the table space container information is actually an array of *SQLB_TBSCONTQRY_DATA* structures, and the value returned in the *NumContainers* parameter identifies the number of elements in this array. Refer to the FETCH TABLESPACE CONTAINER QUERY function for a detailed description of the *SQLB_TBSCONTQRY_DATA* structure.

Comments   ■ When this function is executed, if a sufficient amount of free memory is available, a memory storage buffer will automatically be allocated. This memory storage buffer can only be freed by calling the FREE MEMORY function. It is up to the application to ensure that all memory allocated by this function is freed when it is no longer needed. If sufficient memory is not available, this function will simply return the number of table space containers found, and no memory is allocated.

■ If there is not enough free memory available to retrieve the complete set of table space container information available at one time, you can use the OPEN TABLESPACE CONTAINER QUERY, FETCH TABLESPACE CONTAINER QUERY, and

CLOSE TABLESPACE CONTAINER QUERY functions to retrieve the same table space container information in smaller pieces.

Connection Requirements This function can only be called if a connection to a database exists.

Authorization Only users with System Administrator (SYSADM) authority, System Control (SYSCTRL) authority, System Maintenance (SYSMAINT) authority, or Database Administrator (DBADM) authority are allowed to execute this function call.

See Also OPEN TABLESPACE CONTAINER QUERY, FETCH TABLESPACE CONTAINER QUERY, CLOSE TABLESPACE CONTAINER QUERY, FREE MEMORY

Example The following C++ program illustrates how to use the TABLESPACE CONTAINER QUERY function to retrieve information about the table space containers defined for the SYSCATSPACE table space:

```
/*————————————————————————————————————*/
/* NAME:    CH9EX6.SQC                                        */
/* PURPOSE: Illustrate How To Use The Following DB2 API Functions */
/*          In A C++ Program:                                 */
/*                                                            */
/*              TABLESPACE CONTAINER QUERY                    */
/*              FREE MEMORY                                   */
/*                                                            */
/*————————————————————————————————————*/

// Include The Appropriate Header Files
#include <windows.h>
#include <iostream.h>
#include <sqlenv.h>
#include <sqlutil.h>
#include <sql.h>

// Define The API_Class Class
class API_Class
{
    // Attributes
    public:
        struct sqlca   sqlca;

    // Operations
    public:
        long GetTSCInfo();
};

// Define The GetTSCInfo() Member Function
long API_Class::GetTSCInfo()
{
    // Declare The Local Memory Variables
    unsigned long              TSCCount;
```

```
                struct SQLB_TBSCONTQRY_DATA   *TSContainerData;

                // Retrieve The Table Space Container Data
                sqlbtcq(&sqlca, 2, &TSCCount, &(TSContainerData));
                if (sqlca.sqlcode != SQL_RC_OK)
                    return(sqlca.sqlcode);

                // Display The Table Space Container Data Retrieved
                cout << "Containers Defined For The USERSPACE1 Table Space";
                cout << endl << "ID   Name" << endl;
                cout << "--------------------------------" << endl;
                for (int i = 0; i < (int) TSCCount; i++)
                {
                    cout.width(4);
                    cout.setf(ios::left);
                    cout << TSContainerData->id;
                    cout.width(14);
                    cout.setf(ios::left);
                    cout << TSContainerData->name;
                }

                // Free All Resources Associated With The Table Space
                // Container Query
                sqlefmem(&sqlca, TSContainerData);

                // Return The SQLCA Return Code To The Calling Function
                return(sqlca.sqlcode);
}

/*----------------------------------------------------------------*/
/* The Main Function                                              */
/*----------------------------------------------------------------*/
int main()
{
    // Declare The Local Memory Variables
    long         rc = SQL_RC_OK;
    struct sqlca  sqlca;

    // Create An Instance Of The API_Class Class
    API_Class  Example;

    // Connect To The SAMPLE Database
    EXEC SQL CONNECT TO SAMPLE USER userID USING password;

    // Get Information About The Table Space Containers
    // That Are Defined For The SAMPLE Database
    rc = Example.GetTSCInfo();

    // Issue A Rollback To Free All Locks
    EXEC SQL ROLLBACK;

    // Disconnect From The SAMPLE Database
    EXEC SQL DISCONNECT CURRENT;
```

```
                    // Return To The Operating System
                    return(rc);
          }
```

FREE MEMORY

Purpose   The FREE MEMORY function is used to free memory that has been allocated by either
                 the TABLESPACE QUERY function or the TABLESPACE CONTAINER QUERY function.

Syntax
```
SQL_API_RC SQL_API_FN sqlefmem (struct sqlca   *SQLCA,
                                void           *Buffer);
```

Parameters   *SQLCA*   A pointer to a location in memory where a SQL Communications
                                Area (SQLCA) data structure variable is stored. This variable
                                returns either status information (if the function executed
                                successfully) or error information (if the function failed) to the
                                calling application.

                 Buffer   A pointer to a location in memory that contains the starting address
                                of the DB2-allocated memory storage buffer that this function is to
                                free.

Includes   ```#include <sqlenv.h>```

Description The FREE MEMORY function is used to free memory that has been allocated by either
                 the TABLESPACE QUERY function or the TABLESPACE CONTAINER QUERY function.

Comments   ■ Because the TABLESPACE CONTAINER QUERY and TABLESPACE QUERY functions
                 do not release the memory they allocate, this function should be called whenever
                 either of these two functions are used.

Connection   This function can be called at any time; a connection to a DB2 Database Manager
Requirements instance or to a DB2 database does not have to be established first.

Authorization No authorization is required to execute this function call.

Example   See the examples provided for the TABLESPACE QUERY function on page 302 and the
                 TABLESPACE CONTAINER QUERY function on page 318.

REORGANIZE TABLE

Purpose   The REORGANIZE TABLE function is used to reorganize a table by reconstructing the
                 rows in that table so that fragmented data is eliminated and information is

compacted.

Syntax

```
SQL_API_RC SQL_API_FN sqlureot_api (char        *TableName,
                                    char        *IndexName,
                                    char        *TableSpace,
                                    struct sqlca *SQLCA);
```

Parameters   *TableName*   A pointer to a location in memory where the name of the table to be reorganized is stored. The table name specified can be an alias, except in the case of down-level servers, in which case a fully qualified table name must be used.

IndexName   A pointer to a location in memory where the fully qualified name of the index to be used when reorganizing the table is stored. If this parameter is set to NULL, the data will not be reorganized in any specific order.

TableSpace   A pointer to a location in memory where the name of a temporary table space (if a secondary work area is to be used) is stored. This parameter can contain a NULL value.

SQLCA   A pointer to a location in memory where a SQL Communications Area (SQLCA) data structure variable is stored. This variable returns either status information (if the function executed successfully) or error information (if the function failed) to the calling application.

Includes   `#include <sqlutil.h>`

Description   The **REORGANIZE TABLE** function is used to reorganize a table by reconstructing the rows in that table so fragmented data is eliminated and information is compacted. Tables that have been modified so often that they contain fragmented data, which noticeably slows down access performance, are excellent candidates for reorganization.

After a table is reorganized, the **RUN STATISTICS** function should be executed to update the table's statistics, and packages that reference the table should be rebound (with either the **BIND** or the **REBIND** function or command), so that new and possibly more efficient access plans will be generated.

Comments
- You must complete all database operation and release all acquired locks (by issuing either **COMMIT** or **ROLLBACK** SQL statements from all active transactions) before this function can be called.
- You can use the **REORGCHK** command to determine whether or not a table needs to be reorganized.
- If an index name is specified in the *IndexName* parameter, the DB2 Database Manager will reorganize the data according to the order of the index. To maximize DB2 and application performance, specify indexes that are used often in SQL queries.
- This function cannot be used to reorganize views.
- This function cannot be used on a table while an online backup of the table space in

which the table resides is being performed (if the table space is a DMS table space).

■ To complete a table space roll-forward recovery operation following a table reorganization, all data and LOB table spaces used must be enabled for roll-forward recovery.

■ If a table contains LOB columns that do not use the COMPACT option, the LOB data storage object can be significantly larger following table reorganization. This increase in size can result from the order in which the rows were reorganized and from the types of table spaces used (SMS or DMS).

■ DB2 for Common Servers, Version 2.x, does not support down-level client requests to reorganize a table. If a Version 2 client requests to reorganize a table on a Version 2 server, and if that request specifies a path instead of a temporary table space name in the *TableSpace* parameter, the **REORGANIZE TABLE** function will choose a temporary table space in which to place the work files on behalf of the user.

■ A temporary table space name containing a path separator character (/ or \) should not be specified; rather, it will be interpreted as a temporary path (a request before Version 2) and the **REORGANIZE TABLE** function will choose a temporary table space on behalf of the user.

■ If the specified table is not successfully reorganized when this function is executed, do not delete any temporary files that are created. The DB2 Database Manager will need these files in order to recover the database.

Connection Requirements   This function can only be called if a connection to a database exists.

Authorization   Only users with System Administrator (SYSADM) authority, System Control (SYSCTRL) authority, System Maintenance (SYSMAINT) authority, or Database Administrator (DBADM) authority (or CONTROL authority for the specified table) are allowed to execute this function call.

See Also   RUN STATISTICS, REBIND

Example   The following C++ program illustrates how to use the **REORGANIZE TABLE** function to reorganize the EMPLOYEE table in the SAMPLE database:

```
/*————————————————————————————————————————————*/
/* NAME:    CH9EX7.SQC                                    */
/* PURPOSE: Illustrate How To Use The Following DB2 API Function */
/*          In A C++ Program:                             */
/*                                                        */
/*              REORGANIZE TABLE                          */
/*                                                        */
/*————————————————————————————————————————————*/

// Include The Appropriate Header Files
#include <windows.h>
#include <iostream.h>
```

```
#include <sqlenv.h>
#include <sqlutil.h>
#include <sql.h>

// Define The API_Class Class
class API_Class
{
    // Attributes
    public:
        struct sqlca    sqlca;

    // Operations
    public:
        long ReorgTable();
};

// Define The ReorgTable() Member Function
long API_Class::ReorgTable()
{
    // Create An Index On The EMPLOYEE Table
    EXEC SQL CREATE INDEX USERID.EMP_NUM ON USERID.EMPLOYEE(EMPNO);
    if (sqlca.sqlcode == SQL_RC_OK)
    {
        cout << "Index EMP_NUM has been created for ";
        cout << "the EMPLOYEE table." << endl;
    }

    // Reorganize The EMPLOYEE Table, Using The EMP_NUM Index
    sqlureot("USERID.EMPLOYEE", "USERID.EMP_NUM", NULL, &sqlca);
    if (sqlca.sqlcode == SQL_RC_OK)
    {
        cout << "The EMPLOYEE table has been organized by Employee ";
        cout << "Number." << endl;
    }

    // Delete The Index On The EMPLOYEE Table
    EXEC SQL DROP INDEX USERID.EMP_NUM;
    if (sqlca.sqlcode == SQL_RC_OK)
        cout << "Index EMP_NUM has been deleted." << endl;

    // Return The SQLCA Return Code To The Calling Function
    return(sqlca.sqlcode);
}

/*----------------------------------------------------------------*/
/* The Main Function                                              */
/*----------------------------------------------------------------*/
int main()
{
    // Declare The Local Memory Variables
    long            rc = SQL_RC_OK;
    struct sqlca    sqlca;

    // Create An Instance Of The API_Class Class
    API_Class   Example;
```

```
        // Connect To The SAMPLE Database
        EXEC SQL CONNECT TO SAMPLE USER userID USING password;

        // Reorganize The EMPLOYEE Table In The SAMPLE Database
        rc = Example.ReorgTable();

        // Issue A Rollback To Free All Locks
        EXEC SQL ROLLBACK;

        // Disconnect From The SAMPLE Database
        EXEC SQL DISCONNECT CURRENT;

        // Return To The Operating System
        return(rc);
    }
```

RUN STATISTICS

Purpose   The RUN STATISTICS function is used to update statistical information about the characteristics of a table and any or all of its associated indexes.

Syntax
```
SQL_API_RC SQL_API_FN sqlustat (char          *TableName,
                                unsigned short NumIndexes,
                                char           **IndexList,
                                unsigned char  StatsOption,
                                unsigned char  ShareLevel,
                                struct sqlca   *SQLCA);
```

Parameters *TableName*   A pointer to a location in memory where the name of the table that statistics are to be updated for is stored. The table name specified can be an alias, except in the case of down-level servers, in which case a fully qualified table name must be used.

NumIndexes   The number of indexes that statistics are to be updated for. If this parameter is set to 0, statistics will be calculated for all indexes that have been defined for the table.

IndexList   A pointer to a location in memory where an array of fully qualified index names is stored.

StatsOption   Specifies which statistical calculations are to be updated. This parameter must be set to one of the following values:

■ SQL_STATS_TABLE
Update basic table statistics only.

■ SQL_STATS_EXTTABLE_ONLY
Update basic table statistics with extended (distribution) statistics.

■ **SQL_STATS_BOTH**
Update both basic table statistics and basic statistics for indexes.

■ **SQL_STATS_EXTTTABLE_INDEX**
Update both basic table statistics (with distribution statistics) and basic statistics for indexes.

■ **SQL_STATS_INDEX**
Update basic statistics for indexes only.

■ **SQL_STATS_EXTINDEX_ONLY**
Update extended statistics for indexes only.

■ **SQL_STATS_EXTINDEX_TABLE**
Update extended statistics for indexes and basic table statistics.

■ **SQL_STATS_ALL**
Update extended statistics for indexes and basic table statistics (with distribution statistics).

ShareLevel   Specifies how the statistics are to be gathered with respect to other users. This parameter must be set to one of the following values:

■ **SQL_STATS_REF**
Allow other users to have read-only access while the statistics are being gathered.

■ **SQL_STATS_CHG**
Allow other users to have both read and write access while the statistics are being gathered.

SQLCA   A pointer to a location in memory where a SQL Communications Area (SQLCA) data structure variable is stored. This variable returns either status information (if the function executed successfully) or error information (if the function failed) to the calling application.

Includes   `#include <sqlutil.h>`

Description   The **RUN STATISTICS** function is used to update statistical information about the characteristics of a table and any or all of its associated indexes. This information includes, among other things, the number of records in the table, the number of pages used to store the table, and the average record length. The SQL optimizer uses these statistics to determine the best access path to use when preparing SQL statements. You should call this function whenever any of the following situations occur:

■ When a table has been modified many times (for example, if a large number of updates have been made, or if a significant amount of data has been inserted or deleted).

■ When a table has been reorganized.

■ When one or more new indexes have been created.

After a table's statistics are updated, you should rebind all packages that reference the table (with either the BIND or the REBIND function or command), so new and possibly more efficient access plans will be generated.

Comments   ■ Each string stored in the index list array (referenced by the *IndexList* parameter) should contain a fully qualified index name, and the value stored in the *NumIndexes* parameter should be equivalent to the number of index names stored in this index list (unless the *NumIndexes* parameter is set to 0, in which case the index list array is ignored).

■ If this function is to be called with the *StatsOption* parameter set to SQL_STATS_TABLE or SQL_STATS_EXTTTABLE, make the call before creating any indexes on the table. This guarantees that statistics gathered during index creation will not be overlaid by estimates gathered during the calculation of the table statistics.

■ If index statistics are requested and statistics have never been run on the table containing the index, statistics for both the table and the indexes will be collected.

■ After calling this function, an application should issue a COMMIT SQL statement to release all locks acquired.

■ All statistics collected are based on the table data that is physically located on the database partition where this function is executed. Complete statistics for a partitioned table can be derived by multiplying the values obtained at the database partition where this function is executed by the number partitions in the nodegroup over which the table is partitioned.

■ If this function is called from a database partition that does not contain a table partition, the request is sent to the first database partition in the nodegroup that contains a partition for the table (and is executed there).

■ If inconsistencies are found while this function is executing (usually caused by activity on the table after this function was called), a warning message is returned. When this situation occurs, this function should be called again to refresh the table and/or index statistics.

Connection Requirements   This function can only be called if a connection to a database exists.

Authorization   Only users with System Administrator (SYSADM) authority, System Control (SYSCTRL) authority, System Maintenance (SYSMAINT) authority, or Database Administrator (DBADM) authority (or CONTROL authority for the specified table) are allowed to execute this function call.

See Also   GET DATABASE CONFIGURATION, REORGANIZE TABLE, BIND, REBIND

Example   The following C++ program illustrates how to use the RUN STATISTICS function to update the statistics for the EMPLOYEE table in the SAMPLE database after a new index is created:

/*——*/

```
/* NAME:    CH9EX8.SQC                                                    */
/* PURPOSE: Illustrate How To Use The Following DB2 API Function          */
/*          In A C++ Program:                                             */
/*                                                                        */
/*              RUN STATISTICS                                            */
/*                                                                        */
/*——————————————————————————————————————————————————————————————————————*/


// Include The Appropriate Header Files
#include <windows.h>
#include <iostream.h>
#include <sqlenv.h>
#include <sqlutil.h>
#include <sql.h>

// Define The API_Class Class
class API_Class
{
    // Attributes
    public:
        struct sqlca   sqlca;

    // Operations
    public:
        long RunStats();
};

// Define The RunStats() Member Function
long API_Class::RunStats()
{
    // Declare The Local Memory Variables
    char   *IndexArray = "USERID.EMP_NUM";

    // Create An Index On The EMPLOYEE Table
    EXEC SQL CREATE INDEX USERID.EMP_NUM ON USERID.EMPLOYEE(EMPNO);
    if (sqlca.sqlcode == SQL_RC_OK)
    {
        cout << "Index EMP_NUM has been created for ";
        cout << "the EMPLOYEE table." << endl;
    }

    // Update The Statistics For The EMPLOYEE Table, So That The
    // EMP_NUM Index Will Be Used When Creating Access Plans
    sqlustat("USERID.EMPLOYEE", 1, &IndexArray, SQL_STATS_ALL,
             SQL_STATS_REF, &sqlca);
    if (sqlca.sqlcode == SQL_RC_OK)
    {
        cout << "The statistical information for the EMPLOYEE table ";
        cout << "has been updated." << endl;
    }

    // Delete The Index On The EMPLOYEE Table
    EXEC SQL DROP INDEX USERID.EMP_NUM;
    if (sqlca.sqlcode == SQL_RC_OK)
        cout << "Index EMP_NUM has been deleted." << endl;

    // Return The SQLCA Return Code To The Calling Function
```

10

Database Migration and Disaster Recovery APIs

When working with DB2 databases, it is important to keep in mind that problems can and will occur. Most problems are directly related to some type of media or storage failure, power interruptions, and/or application failures. Because database problems can never be eliminated, it is imperative that a database administrator in charge of a DB2 Universal Database database become familiar with the different recovery mechanisms that are available with DB2. This chapter is designed to introduce you to the set of DB2 API functions that are used to migrate, restart, back up, and restore DB2 databases and to work with a database's recovery history file (which keeps track of backup, restore, and bulk load operations). The first part of this chapter provides a general discussion of the database migration process. Then, information about the database recovery mechanisms available with DB2 is provided. Next, the recovery history file that is automatically created and associated with each DB2 database is discussed. Finally, a detailed reference section covering each DB2 API function that can be used to migrate, back up, and restore DB2 databases—and manipulate recovery history files—is provided.

Database Migration

DB2 Universal Database Version 5.2 is the seventh form of the Database 2 software product released for microcomputers. Each version of DB2 released has its own unique internal format for creating and storing database information. Because of significant differences between each internal format, databases created under one version of the DB2 product cannot be directly accessed by another version of DB2. However, databases created under earlier versions of DB2 can be converted to a more recent version's format. The MIGRATE DATABASE function can be used by an application to convert databases created under earlier versions of DB2 to DB2 Universal Database Version 5.2 format. Unfortunately, the database conversion process only performs upward compatibility conversions. You cannot convert DB2 Universal Database Version 5.2 databases to an earlier DB2 version format.

Recovering from an "Inconsistent" State

Whenever one or more transactions (also known as units of work) are unexpectedly interrupted, all databases being accessed at the time the transaction was interrupted are placed in an inconsistent or unstable state. Once placed in an inconsistent state, a database must be returned to a consistent state before it can be used again. A database notifies an application that it is in an inconsistent state via a specific return code that gets generated when the application attempts to establish a connection to the database. Any DB2 database can be returned to a consistent state by issuing the RESTART DATABASE command from the DB2 command line processor—or by invoking the RESTART DATABASE API function from an application program. When the RESTART DATABASE command or function call is executed, all incomplete or indoubt transactions that were still in memory when the transaction was interrupted are rolled back, and all completed transactions that were still in memory when the transaction was interrupted are committed. Figure 10–1 illustrates how a database is placed in and removed from an inconsistent state.

The *autorestart* parameter in a DB2 database's configuration file can also be used to return an inconsistent database to a consistent state. By default, this parameter is set so that the RESTART DATABASE command is automatically executed whenever the DB2 Database Manager determines that a database is in an inconsistent state.

NOTE: *DB2 Database Manager checks the state of a database when it attempts to establish the first connection to the database.*

The RESTART DATABASE function is designed to handle database problems that are caused by power interruptions and application failure. However, the RESTART DATABASE function cannot handle database problems that occur because of media or storage failure. To handle these types of problems, the Database Administrator must establish some type of backup/restore program.

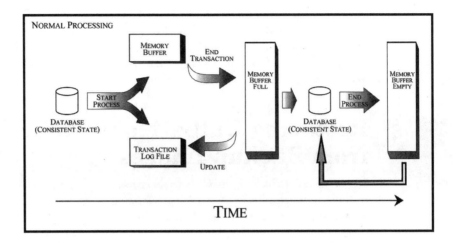

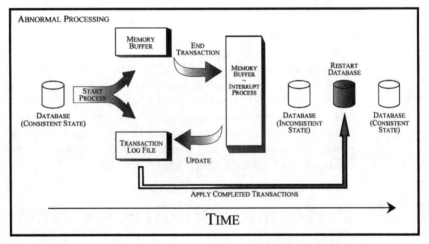

Figure 10–1   Normal processing—As transactions are executed, they are written to a memory buffer and to a transaction log file. When transactions are ended (with ROLLBACK or COMMIT), the transaction log file is updated. When the memory buffer is full, all transactions stored there are written to the database.

Abnormal processing—As transactions are executed, they are written to a memory buffer and to a transaction log file. When the transaction is unexpectedly interrupted, the database is placed in an inconsistent state. When the database is restarted, all completed transactions stored in the transaction log file are applied to the database; all incomplete or indoubt transactions are rolled back.

Creating Backup Images

DB2 provides a utility for creating backup images of a database or of one or more individual table spaces within a database. Backup images can be created by issuing the **BACKUP DATABASE** command from the DB2 command line processor—or by incorporating the BACKUP DATABASE API function in an application program. After one or more backup images are created, they can be used to rebuild a database or a table space if either become damaged or corrupted. A special file, known as the database recovery file, is automatically created when the first backup image is created. Once created, this file is updated with summary information each time a new backup image is made.

Restoring Datbase and Table Spaces from Backup Images

Whenever a database or one of its table spaces becomes damaged or corrupt, it can be restored to its state *when the last backup image was made* by executing the RESTORE DATABASE function or command. Because the database recovery history file contains summary information about each backup image created, the file is used as a tracking mechanism during a recovery (restore) operation. Each backup image file contains special information in its header that is checked against the records in the recovery history file to verify that the backup image being used corresponds to the database being restored.

Each backup image also contains a copy of the database's recovery history file. When a backup image is used to restore an existing database, its recovery history file is not overwritten. If, however, a backup image is used to create a new database (a backup image can be used to create an exact duplicate of the database that the backup image was created from), the recovery history file stored in the backup image becomes the recovery history file for that database. If the current database is unstable, and if its recovery history file is damaged or has been deleted, just the recovery history file itself can be restored from a backup image.

Performing Redirected Restore Operations

Backup images contain a list of all table space containers that were being used at the time the backup image was made. During a restore operation, all table space containers listed in the backup image are checked to see if they still exist and are accessible. If one or more of these table space containers no longer exists or is no longer accessible, the restore operation will fail. When this condition exists, table space containers can be redefined during a special restore operation known as a *redirected restore*. The SET TABLESPACE CONTAINERS API function is used to define new table spaces during a redirected restore operation. Because there is no SET TABLESPACE CONTAINERS command, redirected restore operations can only be performed by an application program. When new table space containers are defined during a redirected restore operation, all previous table space containers defined for the specified table space become invalid. Unfortunately, DB2 does not automatically release the media storage used by invalid table space containers. This task must be performed by the Database Administrator after the redirected restore operation has completed.

Using Roll-Forward Recovery

When a database is restored from a backup image, all changes made to the database *since the backup image was created* will be discarded unless roll-forward recovery has been enabled. Roll-forward is enabled by setting the *logretain* and/or the *userexit* parameter in the database configuration file to the appropriate value. Roll-forward recovery uses a database's transaction log files to reapply some or all changes recorded since the last backup image was made to the database.

The Roll-Forward Recovery Utility is invoked by issuing the ROLLFORWARD DATABASE command from the DB2 command line processor—or by incorporating the ROLLFORWARD DATABASE API function in an application program. A roll-forward recovery operation can follow the completion of a full database restore operation, or it can be performed on any table space that is in a "Rollforward Pending" state. However, if a roll-forward recovery operation is to follow a full database restore, all database log files must be copied to a separate directory before the restore operation is performed (otherwise, they will be replaced with the log files stored in the backup image during the restore operation). These log files must then be copied to the appropriate log file path (as specified in the database configuration file) after the restore operation executes and before the ROLLFORWARD DATABASE function is called or the directory that they are stored in must be specified when the ROLLFORWARD DATABASE command or function is invoked. If the database transaction log files cannot be accessed by the Roll-Forward Recovery Utility, the roll-forward recovery operation will fail. Figure 10–2 illustrates how roll-forward recovery is used in conjunction with the backup and restore utilities to return a database to the state it was in at a specified point in time.

If a roll-forward recovery operation is to follow a redirected restore, it may not be desirable to reapply table space container changes recorded in the database's transaction log files (for example, if the specified table spaces no longer exist). When an application invokes the SET TABLESPACE CONTAINERS function to redefine table space containers during a redirected restore operation, it can specify whether table space container transactions found in the database's transaction log files are to be reapplied or ignored.

Recovery History Files

As mentioned earlier, a recovery history file is created when a database is created and is automatically updated in the following situations:

■ When the database or one of its table spaces is backed up
■ When the database or one of its table spaces is restored
■ When one of the database's tables is loaded

The recovery history file contains a summary of backup information that is used in case all or part of the database must be recovered to a specific point in time (roll-forward

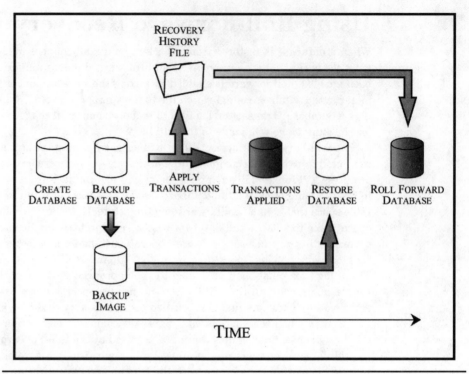

Figure 10–2 *As transactions are applied to the database, they are also written to the recovery history file. When the database is restored from the backup image, all changes made to the database since the backup image was created are lost. When roll-forward recovery is applied to the database (using the recovery history file), the database is left in the same state as it was before the restore operation began.*

recovery). The information stored in this file includes the following:

■ The tables and table spaces of the database that were backed up, restored, or loaded

■ How the backup, restore, or load operation was performed

■ The time the backup image was made (if a backup operation was performed)

■ The location of the backup or copy image that was created (stating both the device information and the logical way to access the image)

■ The last time a restore operation was performed

Each backup image contains a copy of the database's recovery history file. When a backup image is restored to a database that already has a recovery history file, the existing recovery history file is not overwritten. However, if a backup image is restored to a new database, the recovery history file stored in the backup image becomes the recovery history file for that database. If the current database is unstable or unavailable and if its recovery history file is damaged or has been deleted, just the recovery history file itself can be restored from a backup image.

An application can retrieve records (entries) stored in a database recovery history file by performing the following steps:

1. Call the OPEN RECOVERY HISTORY FILE SCAN function to copy select recovery history file records to a function-allocated memory storage buffer.

2. Allocate a *sqluhinfo* structure with space for *x* number of table spaces, where *x* is the value returned in the *NumEntries* parameter after the OPEN RECOVERY HISTORY FILE SCAN function is called. This number is normally the number of table spaces that have been defined for the specified database. You can use the macro SQLUHINFOSIZE(*x*), defined in *sqlutil.h*, to determine how much memory is required for a *sqluhinfo* structure with *x* table space fields.

3. Set the *sqln* field of the allocated *sqluhinfo* structure to *x*

4. In a loop, performing the following steps:

   a. Call the GET NEXT RECOVERY FILE HISTORY ENTRY function to retrieve records from the history file.

   b. Check the *sqlca.sqlcode* value returned by the GET NEXT RECOVERY FILE HISTORY ENTRY function call. If the *sqlca.sqlcode* value is SQL_RC_OK, use the *sqld* field of the *sqluhinfo* structure to determine the number of table space entries returned. If the *sqlca.sqlcode* value is SQLUH_SQLUHINFO_VARS_WARNING (meaning not enough space is allocated for all the table spaces that DB2 is trying to return), free and reallocate the *sqluhinfo* structure with enough space for *sqld* table space entries—and set *sqln* to *sqld*. If the *sqlca.sqlcode* value is SQLE_RC_NOMORE, all records have been retrieved.

   c. Display or process the information retrieved.

5. When all recovery history file records are retrieved, call the CLOSE RECOVERY HISTORY FILE SCAN function to free the resources allocated by the OPEN RECOVERY HISTORY FILE SCAN function.

You can change entries in a database recovery history file by call the UPDATE RECOVERY HISTORY FILE function and you can remove entries in a recovery history file that are no longer valid (or needed) by calling the PRUNE RECOVERY HISTORY FILE function.

The DB2 Database Migration And Disaster Recovery Functions

Table 10-1 lists the DB2 API functions that are used to migrate, restart, backup, and restore DB2 databases, and that are used to manipulate a database's recovery history file.

Each of these functions are described in detail in the remainder of this chapter.

Table 10–1 Database Migration and Recovery APIs

Function name	Description
MIGRATE DATABASE	Converts databases created under previous versions of DB2/2 and DB2/6000 to DB2 for Common Servers, version 2.1.
RESTART DATABASE	Restarts a database that has been left in an inconsistent state.
BACKUP DATABASE	Creates a backup image of a database or of one or more table spaces.
RESTORE DATABASE	Rebuilds a database (or one or more table spaces) by restoring them from a backup image.
RECONCILE	Validates all references to external files that are made by DATALINK data columns in a specific database table.
SET TABLESPACE CONTAINERS	Allows a database to be restored into a different set of table space storage containers.
ROLLFORWARD DATABASE	Restores a database (or one or more table spaces) by applying transactions recorded in the database log files to it after it has been restored from a backup image.
ASYNCHRONOUS READ LOG	Extracts specific log records from a DB2 Universal Database transaction log file OR queries the Log Manager for current log state information.
OPEN RECOVERY HISTORY FILE SCAN	Stores a copy of selected records retrieved from a database recovery history file in memory.
GET NEXT RECOVERY HISTORY FILE ENTRY	Retrieves a record from the copy of recovery history file records that was placed in memory by the OPEN RECOVERY HISTORY FILE SCAN function.
CLOSE RECOVERY HISTORY FILE SCAN	Frees system resources allocated by the OPEN RECOVERY HISTORY FILE SCAN function.
UPDATE RECOVERY HISTORY FILE	Changes the location, device type, or comment associated with a record in a recovery history file.
PRUNE RECOVERY HISTORY FILE	Removes one or more records from a recovery history file.

■ ■ MIGRATE DATABASE

Purpose   The MIGRATE DATABASE function is used to convert databases created under previous versions of DB2 to DB2 Universal Database Version 5.2 format.

Syntax
```
SQL_API_RC SQL_API_FN sqlemgdb (char      *DBAlias,
                                char      *UserID,
                                char      *Password,
                                struct sqlca  *SQLCA);
```

Parameters   *DBAlias*   A pointer to a location in memory where the alias of a database that was created with an earlier version of DB2 is stored.

UserID   A pointer to a location in memory where the user's authorization name (user identifier) is stored. This name is the name under which the attachment is authenticated. This parameter can contain a NULL value.

Password   A pointer to a location in memory where the password for the authorization name specified is stored. This parameter can contain a NULL value.

SQLCA   A pointer to a location in memory where a SQL Communications Area (SQLCA) data structure variable is stored. This variable returns either status information (if the function executed successfully) or error information (if the function failed) to the calling application.

Includes   `#include <sqlenv.h>`

Description   The MIGRATE DATABASE function is used to convert databases created under previous versions of DB2 to DB2 Universal Database Version 5.2 format. Databases created under the following DB2 products can be converted by the DB2 Universal Database Version 5.2 database migration process:

■ DB2 for OS/2, Version 1.x

■ DB2 for OS/2, Version 2.x

■ DB2 for AIX, Version 1.x

■ DB2 for AIX, Version 2.x

■ DB2 for HP-UX, Version 2.x

■ DB2 for Solaris, Version 2.x

■ DB2 for Windows NT, Version 2.x

■ DB2 Parallel Edition, Version 1.x

Once a database has been converted (migrated) to DB2 Universal Database Version 5.2 format, it cannot be returned to its original format. Because of this, it is a good idea to create a backup image of a database before it is migrated.

Comments   ■ A database must be cataloged in the system database directory before it can be migrated.

                 ■ You can use the Database Pre-Migration Tool (*db2ckmig* command) to determine whether or not a DB2 database can be migrated (refer to the *IBM DB2 Command Reference* for more information about this tool).

Connection   This function can be called at any time; a connection to a DB2 Database Manager
Requirements instance or to a DB2 database does not have to be established first. When this function is called, it establishes a connection to the specified database.

Authorization Only users with System Administrator (SYSADM) authority can execute this function call.

See Also   BACKUP DATABASE

Example   The following C++ program illustrates how to use the MIGRATE DATABASE function to convert a DB2 for Windows NT Version 2.0 database to the DB2 Universal Database Version 5.2 format:

```
/*────────────────────────────────────────────────────────────*/
/* NAME:     CH10EX1.CPP                                        */
/* PURPOSE:  Illustrate How To Use The Following DB2 API Function */
/*           In A C++ Program:                                  */
/*                                                              */
/*                    MIGRATE DATABASE                          */
/*                                                              */
/*────────────────────────────────────────────────────────────*/

// Include The Appropriate Header Files
#include <windows.h>
#include <iostream.h>
#include <sqlenv.h>
#include <sqlca.h>

// Define The API_Class Class
class API_Class
{
    // Attributes
    public:
        struct sqlca  sqlca;

    // Operations
    public:
        long MigrateDB();
};

// Define The MigrateDB() Member Function
long API_Class::MigrateDB()
{
    // Migrate The DB2 Database To DB2 UDB Version 5.2
    sqlemgdb ("SAMPLE", "userID", "password", &sqlca);
```

```
        // If The DB2 Database Was Migrated Successfully, Display
        // A Success Message
        // Note: The Return Code 1103 Will Be Returned If The Database
        // Is Already At The Current Level
        if (sqlca.sqlcode == SQL_RC_OK || sqlca.sqlcode == 1103)
            cout << "The SAMPLE database has been migrated." << endl;

        // Return The SQLCA Return Code To The Calling Function
        return(sqlca.sqlcode);
}

/*------------------------------------------------------------------*/
/* The Main Function                                                */
/*------------------------------------------------------------------*/
int main()
{
        // Declare The Local Memory Variables
        long   rc = SQL_RC_OK;

        // Create An Instance Of The API_Class Class
        API_Class   Example;

        // Migrate The SAMPLE Database
        rc = Example.MigrateDB();

        // Return To The Operating System
        return(rc);
}
```

■■ ■■ RESTART DATABASE

Purpose   The RESTART DATABASE function is used to restart a database that has been abnormally terminated and left in an inconsistent state.

Syntax
```
SQL_API_RC SQL_API_FN sqlerstd (char         *DBAlias,
                                char         *UserID,
                                char         *Password,
                                struct sqlca *SQLCA);
```

Parameters   *DBAlias*   A pointer to a location in memory where the alias of the database to be restarted is stored.

                UserID   A pointer to a location in memory where the user's authorization name (user identifier) is stored. This name is the name under which the attachment is authenticated. This parameter can contain a NULL value.

                Password   A pointer to a location in memory where the password for the

	authorization name specified is stored. This parameter can contain a NULL value.
SQLCA	A pointer to a location in memory where a SQL Communications Area (SQLCA) data structure variable is stored. This variable returns either status information (if the function executed successfully) or error information (if the function failed) to the calling application.

Includes   `#include <sqlenv.h>`

Description   The RESTART DATABASE function is used to restart a database that was abnormally terminated and left in an inconsistent state. This function should be called whenever an attempt to connect to a database produces an error message that indicates that the database must be restarted. This error message will only be generated if the previous session with the specified database was terminated abnormally.

Comments
- Upon successful completion of this function, a shared connection to the specified database is maintained if the user who called the function has CONNECT authorization.
- Whenever a database is restarted, a SQL warning is generated if one or more indoubt transactions exist (in this case, the database is usable). If the indoubt transactions are not resolved before the last connection to the database is terminated, however, another RESTART DATABASE function call must be issued before the database can be used again. The transaction APIs discussed in Chapter 13 can be used to generate a list of and correctly process indoubt transactions.

Connection Requirements   When this function is called, it establishes a connection to the specified database.

Authorization   No authorization is required to execute this function call.

See Also   CONNECT (SQL statement)

Example   The following C++ program illustrates how to use the RESTART DATABASE function to restart a database that has been left in an inconsistent state:

```
/*———————————————————————————————————————————————————————————————— */
/* NAME:    CH10EX2.SQC                                              */
/* PURPOSE: Illustrate How To Use The Following DB2 API Function     */
/*          In A C++ Program:                                        */
/*                                                                   */
/*              RESTART DATABASE                                     */
/*                                                                   */
/*———————————————————————————————————————————————————————————————— */

// Include The Appropriate Header Files
#include <windows.h>
#include <iostream.h>
#include <sqlenv.h>
```

```
#include <sql.h>

// Define The API_Class Class
class API_Class
{
    // Attributes
    public:
        struct sqlca   sqlca;

    // Operations
    public:
        long RestartDB();
};

// Define The RestartDB() Member Function
long API_Class::RestartDB()
{
    // If Necessary, Restart The Specified Database
    cout << "Restarting the database. Please wait." << endl;
    sqlerstd("SAMPLE", "userID", "password", &sqlca);

    // If Unable To Restart The Database, Display An Error
    // Message
    if (sqlca.sqlcode != SQL_RC_OK)
    {
        cout << "ERROR : Unable to restart the SAMPLE database.";
        cout << endl;
    }

    // Return The SQLCA Return Code To The Calling Function
    return(sqlca.sqlcode);
}

/*————————————————————————————————————————*/
/* The Main Function                       */
/*————————————————————————————————————————*/
int main()
{
    // Declare The Local Memory Variables
    long         rc = SQL_RC_OK;
    struct sqlca  sqlca;

    // Create An Instance Of The API_Class Class
    API_Class   Example;

    // Attempt To Connect To The SAMPLE Database
    EXEC SQL CONNECT TO SAMPLE USER userID USING password;

    // If Necessary, Restart The Specified Database
    // Note: The Return Code -1015 Will Be Returned If The
    // Database Needs To Be Restarted
    if (sqlca.sqlcode == -1015)
        rc = Example.RestartDB();
```

```
// Issue A Rollback To Free All Locks
EXEC SQL ROLLBACK;

// Disconnect From The SAMPLE Database
EXEC SQL DISCONNECT CURRENT;

// Return To The Operating System
return(rc);
}
```

BACKUP DATABASE

Purpose

The BACKUP DATABASE function is used to create a backup copy of a database or of one or more table spaces.

Syntax

```
SQL_API_RC SQL_API_FN sqlubkup (char                 *DBAlias,
                                unsigned long         BufferSize,
                                unsigned long         BackupMode,
                                unsigned long         BackupType,
                                unsigned long         CallerAction,
                                char                 *ApplicationID,
                                char                 *TimeStamp,
                                unsigned long         NumBuffers,
                                struct sqlu_tablespace_bkrst_list
                                                     *TableSpaceList,
                                struct sqlu_media_list
                                                     *MediaTargetList,
                                char                 *UserName,
                                char                 *Password,
                                void                 *Reserved1,
                                unsigned long        *VendorOptionsSize,
                                void                 *VendorOptions,
                                unsigned long         Parallelism,
                                unsigned long        *BackupSize,
                                void                 *Reserved2,
                                void                 *Reserved3
                                struct sqlca         *SQLCA);
```

Parameters

DBAlias   A pointer to a location in memory where the alias name of the database to back up is stored.

BufferSize   The size, in 4KB pages, that all temporary buffers created and used during the backup operation should be. Temporary backup buffers must be at least eight 4KB pages in size.

BackupMode   Specifies how the backup utility is to be run. This parameter must be set to one of the following values:

■ SQLUB_OFFLINE

The backup utility is to be run off-line (i.e., no other applications can connect to the database while the backup operation is in progress).

■ SQLUB_ONLINE

The backup utility is to be run online (i.e., other applications can connect to and access the database while the backup operation occurs).

BackupType   Specifies the type of backup image to create. This parameter must be set to one of the following values:

■ SQLUB_FULL

A full database backup image is to be created.

■ SQLUB_TABLESPACE

A backup image containing one or more table spaces is to be created. If this value is specified, a list of the appropriate table spaces must be provided in the *TableSpaceList* parameter.

CallerAction   Specifies the action this function is to take when it is executed. This parameter must be set to one of the following values:

■ SQLUB_BACKUP

The backup operation is to be started.

■ SQLUB_NOINTERRUPT

The backup operation is to be started, and it is to run unattended. When this caller action is specified, scenarios that normally require user intervention will be attempted without returning to the calling application (if they fail, they will generate an error).

■ SQLUB_CONTINUE

The backup operation is to be continued after the user has performed some action that was requested by the Backup utility (inserting a diskette, mounting a new tape, etc.).

■ SQLUB_TERMINATE

The backup operation is to be terminated because the user failed to perform some action that was requested by the Backup utility.

■ SQLUB_DEVICE_TERMINATE

A particular device is to be removed from the list of devices used by Backup utility. When a particular medium is full, the Backup utility returns a warning to the caller (while continuing to process using the remaining devices). By calling the BACKUP DATABASE function again with this caller action specified, you can remove the device that generated the warning condition from the list of devices being used.

■ SQLUB_PARAM_CHECK

The parameter values specified for the BACKUP DATABASE function are to be checked for validity. This caller action does not terminate the database connection, nor does it invoke the Backup utility. After using this caller action to validate parameters, the BACKUP DATABASE function can be called again with the SQLUB_CONTINUE caller action specified to start the backup utility.

■ SQLUB_PARAM_CHECK_ONLY

The parameter values specified for the BACKUP DATABASE function are to be checked for validity. This caller action does not invoke the backup utility, and it causes the BACKUP DATABASE function to terminate the database connection upon completion.

ApplicationID	A pointer to a location in memory where this function is to store a string that identifies the agent that is servicing the application. (You can use the application ID string to obtain information about the progress of the backup operation via the database monitor).
TimeStamp	A pointer to a location in memory where this function is to store the time stamp (in ISO format) that identifies when the backup image was created. This value is also stored in the backup image.
NumBuffers	The number of temporary buffers that are to be created and used by the Backup utility.
TableSpaceList	A pointer to a *sqlu_tablespace_bkrst_list* structure that contains a list of table space names that are to be used when creating a table space backup image. If a full database backup is to be performed, this parameter will be ignored.
MediaTargetList	A pointer to a *sqlu_media_list* structure that contains a list of destination devices that are to be used for storing the backup image.
UserName	A pointer to a location in memory where the authorization name (user identifier) that is to be used to connect to the database is stored.
Password	A pointer to a location in memory where the password for the authorization name specified is stored. This parameter can contain a NULL value.
Reserved1	A pointer that is reserved for later use. For now, this parameter must always be set to NULL.

VendorOptionsSize	The size, in bytes, of the data stored in the structure referenced by the *VendorOptions* parameter.
VendorOptions	A pointer to a *sqlu_vendor* structure that contains vendor specific information that is to be passed from the application calling the **BACKUP DATABASE** function to one or more vendor-supplied functions.
Parallelism	The number of buffer manipulators that are to be used by the Backup utility (i.e., the degree of parallelism used by the database).
BackupSize	A pointer to a location in memory where this function is to store the size (in megabytes) of the backup image that was created.
Reserved2	A pointer that is currently reserved for later use. For now, this parameter must always be set to NULL.
Reserved3	A pointer that is reserved for later use. For now, this parameter must always be set to NULL.
SQLCA	A pointer to a location in memory where a SQL Communications Area (SQLCA) data structure variable is stored. This variable returns either status information (if the function executed successfully) or error information (if the function failed) to the calling application.

Includes   `#include <sqlutil.h>`

Description   The **BACKUP DATABASE** function is used to create a backup copy of a database or of one or more table spaces. If you have a database backup image available and the database becomes damaged or corrupted, it can be returned to the state it was in the last time it was backed up. Furthermore, if the database is enabled for roll-forward recovery, it can be restored to the state it was in just before the damage occurred. Table space level backup images can also be made for a database. You can use table space backup images to repair problems that only affect specific table spaces.

Two special structures (*sqlu_tablespace_bkrst_list* and *sqlu_media_list*) are used to pass table space names and backup device information to the Backup utility when this function is called. The first of these structures, *sqlu_tablespace_bkrst_list*, is defined in *sqlutil.h* as follows:

```
typedef struct sqlu_tablespace_bkrst_list
{
long                             num_entry;   /* The number of entries      */
                                              /* in the list of table space */
                                              /* names stored in the        */
                                              /* the tablespace field       */
struct sqlu_tablespace_entry *tablespace;    /* A pointer to an array of    */
                                              /* sqlu_tablespace_entry       */
                                              /* structures that contains a  */
sqlu_tablespace_bkrst_list;                   /* list of table space names   */
}
```

This structure contains a pointer to an array of additional *sqlu_tablespace_entry* structures that are used to hold table space names. The *sqlu_tablespace_entry* structure is defined in *sqlutil.h* as follows:

```
typedef struct sqlu_tablespace_entry
{
unsigned long    reserve_len;          /* The length of the table       */
                                       /* space name stored in the      */
                                       /* tablespace_entry field.        */
                                       /* This field is only used if    */
                                       /* the table space name is not   */
                                       /* NULL-terminated.              */
char             tablespace_entry[19]; /* The table space name          */
char             filler[1];            /* Reserved                      */
} sqlu_tablespace_entry;
```

The second special structure used by the BACKUP DATABASE function, the *sqlu_media_list* structure, is used to describe the type(s) of media that the backup image is to be written to. The *sqlu_media_list* structure is defined in *sqlutil.h* as follows:

```
typedef struct sqlu_media_list
{
char                        media_type;  /* Indicates that the media    */
                                         /* type is one or more         */
                                         /* local devices               */
                                         /* (SQLU_LOCAL_MEDIA), a        */
                                         /* DB2 ASDM shared library      */
                                         /* (SQLU_ASDM_MEDIA),           */
                                         /* a vendor product             */
                                         /* shared library               */
                                         /* (SQLU_OTHER_MEDIA),          */
                                         /* or a user exit routine       */
                                         /* (SQLU_USER_EXIT). Local      */
                                         /* devices can be any           */
                                         /* combination of tapes,        */
                                         /* disks, or diskettes.         */
char                        filler[3];   /* Reserved                    */
long                        sessions;    /* The number of entries in    */
                                         /* the list of devices         */
                                         /* stored in the target        */
                                         /* field                       */
union sqlu_media_list_targets target;                                   
                                         /* A pointer to an array       */
                                         /* of one of two types of      */
                                         /* structures that contains    */
                                         /* additional device           */
                                         /* information. The type       */
                                         /* of structure used is        */
                                         /* determined by the value     */
                                         /* specified in the            */
                                         /* media_type field.           */
} sqlu_media_list;
```

This structure contains a pointer to an array of structures that provide additional information about the specific media devices to be used. This array can contain either of the following DB2-defined structures:

- *sqlu_media_entry* Local media information (SQLU_LOCAL_MEDIA)
- *sqlu_vendor* Other vendor specific media information (SQLU_OTHER_MEDIA)

The *sqlu_media_entry* structure is defined in *sqlutil.h* as follows:

```
typedef struct sqlu_media_entry
{
unsigned long   reserve_len;      /* The length of the path name       */
                                  /* stored in the media_entry field.  */
                                  /* This field is only used if the path*/
                                  /* name is not NULL-terminated.      */
char            media_entry[216]; /* A valid path name                 */
} sqlu_media_entry;
```

The *sqlu_vendor* structure is defined in *sqlutil.h* as follows:

```
typedef struct sqlu_vendor
{
unsigned long   reserve_len1;     /* The length of the shared library  */
                                  /* name stored in the shr_lib field. */
                                  /* This field is only used if the shared */
                                  /* library name is not null-terminated. */
char            shr_lib[256];     /* The name of a vendor-supplied     */
                                  /* shared library that is used for   */
                                  /* storing and retrieving data       */
unsigned long   reserve_len2;     /* The length of the load input      */
                                  /* source-file name stored in the    */
                                  /* filename field. This field is only used */
                                  /* if the source-file name is not    */
                                  /* NULL-terminated.                  */
char            filename[256];    /* The name of an input source file  */
                                  /* that is to be used for providing  */
                                  /* information to a shared library   */
} sqlu_vendor;
```

The type of structure used to provide additional information about specific media devices is determined by the value specified in the *media_type* field of the *sqlu_media_list* structure as follows:

- SQLU_LOCAL_MEDIA One or more *sqlu_media_entry* structures.

- SQLU_ADSM_MEDIA No structure is needed (if the *ADSTAR Distributed Storage Manager* (ADSM) shared library provided with DB2 Universal Database is used). If a different version of an ADSM shared library is used, the SQLU_OTHER_MEDIA value should be used.

- SQLU_OTHER_MEDIA One or more *sqlu_vendor* structures.

■ SQLU_USER_EXIT   No structure is needed. (Note that this value can only be
                        specified with OS/2.)

Refer to the *IBM DB2 Administration Guide* for a general discussion of DB2
Universal Database's backup and restore utilities.

Comments

■ If the *BackupType* parameter is set to SQLUB_TABLESPACE, the *TableSpaceList*
parameter must contain a pointer to a list of valid table space names.

■ The *CallerAction* parameter must be set to SQLUB_BACKUP, SQLUB_NOINTERRUPT,
SQLUB_PARAM_CHECK or SQLUB_PARAM_CHECK_ONLY the first time this function is
called.

■ The *CallerAction* parameter should be set to SQLUB_NOINTERRUPT whenever all media
needed for the backup operation is available and user interaction is not needed.

■ The application ID string returned by this function can be up to 33 characters in
length (including the NULL-terminator character).

■ The time stamp string returned by this function can be up to 15 characters in
length (including the NULL-terminator character).

■ The *sqlu_vendor* structure that the *VendorOptions* parameter references must be
flat (i.e., it must not contain any level of indirection). Byte reversal is not
performed on this structure and code page values are not compared.

■ Online backups are only permitted if roll-forward recovery is enabled. An online
backup can be performed while the database is being accessed and modified by
other applications.

■ In order to perform an offline backup, the Backup utility must be able to connect to
the specified database in exclusive mode. Therefore, this function will fail if any
application, including the application calling the BACKUP DATABASE function, is
connected to the specified database. If the Backup utility can connect to the
specified database in exclusive mode, it will lock out all other applications until
the backup operation is complete. Because the time required to create a database
backup image can be significant (especially for large databases), offline backups
should only be performed when a database will not be needed by other
applications for an extended period of time.

■ An offline backup operation will fail if the specified database or table space(s) are
not in a consistent state. If the specified database is not in a consistent state, it
must be restarted with the RESTART DATABASE function (to bring it back to a
consistent state) before this function can be executed.

■ Backup images can be directed to fixed disks, diskettes, tapes, ADSM, or other
vendor products that are enabled for DB2. In order to direct backup images to
tapes in OS/2, a unique device driver for the tape drive being used must be
installed (there is no native tape support in OS/2), and this function must be called
with SQLU_USER_EXIT specified as the media type (in the *media_type* field of the
sqlu_media_list data structure stored in the *MediaTargetList* parameter).

■ Although you can use the BACKUP DATABASE function to back up databases located at remote sites, the backup image itself must be directed to devices that are local to the machine on which the database resides (unless ADSM or another DB2-enabled vendor product is used). With ADSM and other DB2-enabled vendor products, the interface for the backup is local, but the location of the storage media to which the backup image is to be written can be remote.

■ If a database that has been enabled for roll-forward recovery is backed up, it can be returned to the state it was in at a specific point in time (refer to the RESTORE DATABASE and ROLLFORWARD DATABASE functions for more information).

■ If a database is left in a partially restored state because of a system failure during restoration, the restore operation must be successfully rerun before this function can be executed. If the database is placed in the "Rollforward-Pending" state after a successful restoration, the database must also be rolled forward to a consistent state before this function can be executed.

■ If a database is changed from the "Rollforward Disabled" to the "Rollforward Enabled" state, either the *logretain* or *userexit* database configuration parameter must be set appropriately before this function can be executed (refer to Chapter 7 for more information about retrieving and setting database configuration parameters).

■ A table space level backup image can contain one or more table spaces.

■ While one table space is being restored, all other table spaces are available for processing.

■ To ensure that restored table spaces are synchronized with the rest of the database, they must be rolled forward to the end of the recovery history log file (or to the point where the table spaces were last used). Because of this, table space level backup images can only be made if roll-forward recovery is enabled.

■ A user might choose to store data, indexes, long field (LONG) data, and large object (LOB) data in different table spaces. If LONG and LOB data do not reside in the same table space, a table space backup cannot be performed.

■ You can back up and restore each component of a table by independently backing up and restoring each table space in which the table components reside.

■ Temporary table spaces cannot be backed up. If a list of table spaces to be backed up contains one or more temporary table space names, the backup operation will fail.

■ Table space level backups and restores cannot be run concurrently.

Connection Requirements This function can be called at any time; a connection to a DB2 Database Manager instance or to a DB2 database does not have to be established first. When this function is called, it establishes a connection to the database specified.

Authorization Only users with System Administrator (SYSADM) authority, System Control (SYSCTRL) authority, or System Maintenance (SYSMAINT) authority can execute this function call.

See Also RESTORE DATABASE, ROLLFORWARD DATABASE, RESTART DATABASE

Example The following C++ program illustrates how to use the BACKUP DATABASE function to back up the SAMPLE database to a subdirectory on the D: drive:

```
/*─────────────────────────────────────────────────────────────*/
/* NAME:    CH10EX3.CPP                                          */
/* PURPOSE: Illustrate How To Use The Following DB2 API Function */
/*          In A C++ Program:                                    */
/*                                                               */
/*               BACKUP DATABASE                                 */
/*                                                               */
/*─────────────────────────────────────────────────────────────*/

// Include The Appropriate Header Files
#include <windows.h>
#include <iostream.h>
#include <conio.h>
#include <sqlutil.h>
#include <sqlca.h>

// Define The API_Class Class
class API_Class
{
    // Attributes
    public:
        struct sqlca   sqlca;

    // Operations
    public:
        long BackupDB();
};

// Define The BackupDB() Member Function
long API_Class::BackupDB()
{
    // Declare The Local Memory Variables
    struct sqlu_media_list    Media_List;
    struct sqlu_media_entry   Media_Entry;
    char                      ApplicationID[33];
    char                      TimeStamp[27];

    // Initialize The Media List Information Data Structure
    Media_List.media_type = SQLU_LOCAL_MEDIA;
    Media_List.sessions = 1;
    strcpy(Media_Entry.media_entry, "D:\\Backup");
    Media_List.target.media = &Media_Entry;

    // Tell The User That The Backup Process Is Being Started
    cout << "Starting Backup ..." << endl << endl;

    // Start Backing Up The SAMPLE Database
    sqlubkup("SAMPLE", 16, SQLUB_OFFLINE, SQLUB_FULL,
        SQLUB_BACKUP, ApplicationID, TimeStamp, 4, NULL,
```

```
                &Media_List, "userID", "password", NULL, 0, NULL,
                NULL, &sqlca);

        // If The Database Could Not Be Backed Up, Display An Error
        // Message And Terminate The Backup Process
        if (sqlca.sqlcode != SQL_RC_OK)
        {
            cout << "ERROR : " << sqlca.sqlcode << endl;
            sqlubkup ("SAMPLE", 16, SQLUB_OFFLINE, SQLUB_FULL,
                SQLUB_TERMINATE, ApplicationID, TimeStamp, 4,
                NULL, &Media_List, "userID", "password", NULL, 0,
                NULL, NULL, &sqlca);
        }

        // If The SAMPLE Database Was Successfully Backed Up, Display A
        // Message Saying So
        else
        {
            cout << "The SAMPLE database was successfully backed up.";
            cout << endl;
        }

        // Return The SQLCA Return Code To The Calling Function
        return(sqlca.sqlcode);
}

/*------------------------------------------------------------------*/
/* The Main Function                                                */
/*------------------------------------------------------------------*/
int main()
{
    // Declare The Local Memory Variables
    long  rc = SQL_RC_OK;

    // Create An Instance Of The API_Class Class
    API_Class  Example;

    // Back Up The SAMPLE Database
    rc = Example.BackupDB();

    // Return To The Operating System
    return(rc);
}
```

■ ■ RESTORE DATABASE

Purpose   The RESTORE DATABASE function is used to rebuild a damaged or corrupted database
(or one or more damaged or corrupted table spaces) by restoring it from a backup
image (created with the BACKUP DATABASE command or function).

Syntax

```
SQL_API_RC SQL_API_FN sqlurestore (char            *SourceDBAlias,
                                   char            *TargetDBAlias,
                                   unsigned long   BufferSize,
                                   unsigned long   RollForwardMode,
                                   unsigned long   DatalinkMode,
                                   unsigned long   RestoreType,
                                   unsigned long   RestoreMode,
                                   unsigned long   CallerAction,
                                   char            *ApplicationID,
                                   char            *TimeStamp,
                                   char            *TargetPath,
                                   unsigned long   NumBuffers,
                                   char            *ReportFile,
                                   struct sqlu_tablespace_bkrst_list
                                                   *TableSpaceList,
                                   struct sqlu_media_list
                                                   *MediaSourceList,
                                   char            *UserName,
                                   char            *Password,
                                   void            *Reserved1,
                                   unsigned long   VendorOptionsSize,
                                   void            *VendorOptions,
                                   unsigned long   Parallelism,
                                   void            *RestoreInfo,
                                   void            *ContainerPageList,
                                   void            *Reserved2,
                                   struct sqlca    *SQLCA);
```

Parameters

SourceDBAlias   A pointer to a location in memory where the alias name of the database that was used to create the backup image (source) is stored.

TargetDBAlias   A pointer to a location in memory where the alias name of the target database that the backup image is to be restored to is stored. If this parameter is set to NULL, the backup image is restored to the database alias specified in the *SourceDBAlias* parameter.

BufferSize   The size, in 4KB pages, that all temporary buffers created and used during the restore operation should be. Temporary restore buffers must be at least sixteen 4KB pages in size.

RollForwardMode   Specifies whether or not the database should be placed in "Rollforward Pending" state after the database is restored. This parameter must be set to one of the following values:

■ SQLUD_ROLLFWD
The database is to be placed in "Rollforward Pending" state after it has been successfully restored.

■ SQLUD_NOROLLFWD
The database is not to be placed in "Rollforward Pending" state after it has been successfully restored.

DatalinkMode   Specifies whether or not tables with DATALINK columns are to be placed in "Datalink Reconcile Pending" state and validation (reconciliation) of linked files is to be performed (provided the table has the RECOVERY YES option specified). This parameter must be set to one of the following values:

■ **SQLUD_DATALINK**
Linked file validation (reconciliation) is to be performed by the restore utility.

■ **SQLUD_NODATALINK**
Linked file validation (reconciliation) is not to be performed by the restore utility.

RestoreType   Specifies the type of restore operation to perform. This parameter must be set to one of the following values:

■ **SQLUD_FULL**
Everything found in the backup image is to be restored. If this value is specified, the restore utility will be run offline.

■ **SQLUD_ONLINE_TABLESPACE**
Only table space level information found in the backup image is to be restored. If this value is specified, the restore utility will be run online.

■ **SQLUD_HISTORY**
Only the database's recovery history file is to be restored.

RestoreMode   Specifies how the restore utility is to be run. This parameter must be set to one of the following values:

■ **SQLUD_OFFLINE**
The restore utility is to be run offline (i.e., no other applications can connect to the database while the restore operation is in progress).

■ **SQLUD_ONLINE**
The restore utility is to be run online (i.e., other applications can connect to and access the database while the restore operation is in progress).

CallerAction   Specifies the action this function is to take when it is executed. This parameter must be set to one of the following values:

■ **SQLUD_RESTORE**
The restore operation is to be started.

■ **SQLUD_NOINTERRUPT**
The restore operation is to be started and is to run unattended. When this caller action is specified, scenarios

that normally require user intervention will be attempted without returning to the calling application (if the attempt fails, an error will be generated).

■ SQLUD_CONTINUE
The restore operation is to be continued after the user has performed some action that was requested by the Restore utility (for example, inserting a diskette or mounting a new tape).

■ SQLUD_TERMINATE
The restore operation is to be terminated because the user failed to perform some action that was requested by the Restore utility.

■ SQLUD_DEVICE_TERMINATE
A particular device is to be removed from the list of devices used by the Restore utility. When a particular device has exhausted its input, the Restore utility returns a warning to the caller (while continuing to process using the remaining devices). By calling the RESTORE DATABASE function again with this caller action specified, you can remove the device that generated the warning condition from the list of devices being used.

■ SQLUD_PARAM_CHECK
The parameter values specified for the RESTORE DATABASE function call are to be checked for validity. This caller action does not invoke the Restore utility.

■ SQLUD_RESTORE_STORDEF
One or more table space redefinitions are to be performed during the restore operation.

ApplicationID   A pointer to a location in memory where this function is to store a string that identifies the agent that is servicing the application. (You can use this application ID string to obtain information about the progress of the restore operation via the database monitor).

TimeStamp   A pointer to a location in memory that contains a time stamp that identifies when the backup image to be used was created. This value is not needed if there is only one backup image on the backup image source media specified.

TargetPath   A pointer to a location in memory where the relative or fully qualified name of the target database is stored. This parameter is only used if a new database is to be created from the backup image being used.

NumBuffers	The number of temporary buffers that are to be created and used by the Restore utility.
ReportFile	A pointer to a location in memory where the name of the file in which the names of all DATALINK files that become unlinked during the restore operation are to be reported is stored.
TableSpaceList	A pointer to an *sqlu_tablespace_bkrst_list* structure that is currently reserved for later use. For now, this parameter must always be set to NULL.
MediaSourceList	A pointer to an *sqlu_media_list* structure that contains a list of devices that are to be used when restoring the database or one or more table spaces from a backup image created by the Backup utility.
UserName	A pointer to a location in memory where the authorization name (user identifier) that is to be used to connect to the database is stored.
Password	A pointer to a location in memory where the password for the authorization name specified is stored. This parameter can contain a NULL value.
Reserved1	A pointer that is currently reserved for later use. For now, this parameter must always be set to NULL.
VendorOptionsSize	The size, in bytes, of the data stored in the structure referenced by the *VendorOptions* parameter.
VendorOptions	A pointer to an *sqlu_vendor* structure that contains vendor-specific information that is to be passed from the application calling the RESTORE DATABASE function to one or more vendor-supplied functions.
Parallelism	The number of buffer manipulators that are to be used by the restore utility (i.e., the degree of parallelism used by the database).
RestoreInfo	A pointer that is currently reserved for later use. For now, this parameter must always be set to NULL.
ContainerPageList	A pointer that is currently reserved for later use. For now, this parameter must always be set to NULL.
Reserved2	A pointer that is currently reserved for later use. For now, this parameter must always be set to NULL.
SQLCA	A pointer to a location in memory where a SQL Communications Area (SQLCA) data structure variable is stored. This variable returns either status information (if the function executed successfully) or error information (if the function failed) to the calling application.

Includes   `#include <sqlutil.h>`

Description   The RESTORE DATABASE function is used to rebuild a damaged or corrupted database (or one or more damaged or corrupted table spaces) by restoring it from a backup image that was created with the BACKUP DATABASE command or function. Backup images of databases or table spaces must have been created with the BACKUP DATABASE command or function in order to be used by the RESTORE DATABASE function.

When a database is restored, it is placed in the same state it was in when the backup copy image was made. If the database was enabled for roll-forward recovery before the backup image was made, you can return it to the state it was in just before the damage occurred by executing the ROLLFORWARD DATABASE function after the RESTORE DATABASE function is successfully executed.

> **NOTE:** *Database log files must be copied to a separate directory before a database is restored if they are to be used to roll a database forward. Otherwise, they will be replaced with the log files stored in the backup image during the restore operation. These log files must then be copied to the appropriate log file path (as specified in the database configuration file) after the restore operation executes and before the ROLLFORWARD DATABASE function is called—or the directory they are stored in must be specified in the* **OverflowLogPath** *parameter of the ROLLFORWARD DATABASE function. If these log files cannot be accessed by the roll-forward recovery utility, the roll-forward recovery operation will fail (refer to the ROLLFORWARD DATABASE function for more information).*

A database backup image can be restored as a new database if the original database from which the backup image was made no longer exists (the new database will have the same name). Also, because a database backup image can be restored to a database with a different name, the RESTORE DATABASE function essentially provides a method for copying entire databases. You can also use the RESTORE DATABASE function to restore one or more table spaces from a table space level backup image that was created with the BACKUP DATABASE function. Table space backup images can be used to repair problems that only affect specific table spaces.

Two special structures (*sqlu_tablespace_bkrst_list* and *sqlu_media_list*) are used to pass table space names and restore device information to the Restore utility when this function is called. Refer to the BACKUP DATABASE function for a detailed description of each of these structures and for more information about how they are initialized.

Comments   ■ If a database is left in the "Rollforward Pending" state after it has been successfully restored, the ROLLFORWARD DATABASE function must be executed before it can be used by other applications.

■ The *CallerAction* parameter must be set to SQLUD_RESTORE, SQLUD_NOINTERRUPT, SQLUD_RESTORE_STORDEF, or SQLUD_PARM_CHECK the first time this function is called.

■ The *CallerAction* parameter should be set to SQLUD_NOINTERRUPT whenever all media needed for the restore operation is available and user interaction is not needed.

■ The *CallerAction* parameter should be set to SQLUD_DEVICE_TERMINATE to close a device when it is no longer needed. For example, if a user is restoring a database from a backup image stored on three tape volumes using two tape devices, and all the data on one of the tapes has been restored, the application calling the RESTORE DATABASE function will receive control from the function, along with a SQL return code that indicates that the end of the tape was reached. The application can then prompt the user to mount another tape, and if the user indicates that there are no more tapes, the application can call the RESTORE DATABASE function again with the *CallerAction* parameter set to SQLUD_DEVICE_TERMINATE to signal that there is no more media available. The device driver will be terminated, but the rest of the devices involved in the restore operation will continue to have their input processed until all segments of the backup image are restored (the number of segments in the backup image is placed on the last media device during the backup process).

■ The application ID string returned by this function can be up to 33 characters in length (including the NULL-terminator character).

■ The time stamp string specified in the *TimeStamp* parameter can be up to 15 characters in length (including the NULL-terminator character).

■ The *sqlu_vendor* structure that the *VendorOptions* parameter references must be flat (i.e., it must not contain any level of indirection). Byte reversal is not performed on this structure and code page values are not compared.

■ In order to perform an offline restore, the Restore utility must be able to connect to the specified database in exclusive mode. Therefore, this function will fail if any application, including the application calling the RESTORE DATABASE function, is connected to the specified database. If the Restore utility can connect to the specified database in exclusive mode, it will lock out all other applications until the restore operation is complete. Because the time required to restore a database from a backup image can be significant (especially for large databases), offline restores should only be performed when a database will not be needed by other applications for an extended period of time.

■ When restoring an existing database, if a system failure occurs during a crucial stage of the restore operation, the database will be left in a partially restored state, and the restore operation must be successfully rerun before any users and/or applications can connect to the database. Unfortunately, this condition may not be detected until an application or user attempts to connect to the partially restored database.

■ When restoring to a nonexistent or new database, if a system failure occurs during a crucial stage of the restore operation, the restored database will be deleted (dropped).

■ If a database was not configured for roll-forward recovery when its backup image was made, and if the current database configuration file has roll-forward recovery enabled, the user must either make a new backup image of the database or disable the *logretain* and *userexit* database configuration file parameters immediately after the restore operation is completed. No user or application can connect to the database until one of these actions is performed.

■ If the *RestoreType* parameter is set to SQLUD_HISTORY, the recovery history file stored in the backup image will be restored over the existing recovery history file for the database, effectively erasing any changes that were made to the recovery history file after the backup image was created. If this action is undesirable, restore the recovery history file to a new database so you can view its contents without destroying any changes that have taken place since the backup image was made. Refer to the OPEN RECOVERY HISTORY FILE SCAN, GET NEXT RECOVERY HISTORY FILE ENTRY, and CLOSE RECOVERY HISTORY FILE SCAN functions for information on how to view the contents of a recovery history file.

■ If roll-forward recovery is disabled for a database after a table space level backup image was made, you cannot restore the table space(s) from the backup table space image and then roll the table space(s) forward to the current point in time. Instead, all table space level backup images made prior to the time roll-forward recovery was disabled can no longer be used (the RESTORE DATABASE function will fail if the user attempts to restore from such a backup image). In cases where you cannot determine whether or a backup image is invalid, the restore operation might appear to be successful. The invalid backup image will only be detected during the roll-forward recovery operation.

■ In order to perform a redirected restore (a restore operation in which a database is restored and a different set of operating system storage containers are desired or required), the *CallerAction* parameter must be set to SQLUD_RESTORE_STORDEF and the SET TABLESPACE CONTAINERS function must be used to identify the new system storage locations. Refer to the SET TABLESPACE CONTAINERS function for more information.

■ The current configuration file for the database being restored will not be replaced by the configuration file stored in the backup image unless the file is no longer usable. If the configuration file is replaced, a warning message will be returned to the calling application.

Connection Requirements   The connection requirements for this function are dependent upon the type of restore operation being performed:

■ When restoring a backup image to an existing database, this function can be called at any time. A connection to a DB2 Database Manager instance or to a DB2 database does not have to be established first. When this function is called, it establishes a connection to the database specified.

■ When restoring a backup image to a new database, this function cannot be called unless a connection to both a DB2 Database Manager instance and a DB2 database exists (an instance attachment is required to create the new database).

■ When restoring a backup image to a new database at a remote DB2 Database Manager instance, an instance attachment must exist before this function is called.

Authorization   Only users with System Administrator (SYSADM) authority, System Control (SYSCTRL) authority, or System Maintenance (SYSMAINT) authority can execute this function to restore a backup image to an existing database. Only users with either SYSCTRL or SYSADM authority can execute this function to restore a backup image to a new database.

See Also   BACKUP DATABASE, ROLLFORWARD DATABASE, MIGRATE DATABASE, SET TABLESPACE CONTAINERS, GET DATABASE CONFIGURATION

Example   The following C++ program illustrates how to use the RESTORE DATABASE function to restore the SAMPLE database from a backup image stored in a subdirectory on the D: drive:

```
/*————————————————————————————————————*/
/* NAME:     CH10EX4.CPP                                        */
/* PURPOSE:  Illustrate How To Use The Following DB2 API Function */
/*           In A C++ Program:                                  */
/*                                                              */
/*               RESTORE DATABASE                               */
/*                                                              */
/*————————————————————————————————————*/

// Include The Appropriate Header Files
#include <windows.h>
#include <iostream.h>
#include <conio.h>
#include <sqlutil.h>
#include <sqlca.h>

// Define The API_Class Class
class API_Class
{
    // Attributes
    public:
        struct sqlca   sqlca;

    // Operations
    public:
        long RestoreDB();
};

// Define The RestoreDB() Member Function
long API_Class::RestoreDB()
{
    // Declare The Local Memory Variables
    struct sqlu_media_list    Media_List;
    struct sqlu_media_entry   Media_Entry;
    char                      ApplicationID[33];

    // Initialize The Media List Information Data Structure
    Media_List.media_type = SQLU_LOCAL_MEDIA;
    Media_List.sessions = 1;
```

```
strcpy(Media_Entry.media_entry, "D:\\Backup");
Media_List.target.media = &Media_Entry;

// Tell The User That The Restore Process Is Being Started
cout << "Starting Restore ..." << endl << endl;

// Start Restoring The SAMPLE Database
sqlurestore("SAMPLE", "SAMPLE", 16, SQLUD_NOROLLFWD,
    SQLUD_NODATALINK, SQLUD_FULL, SQLUD_OFFLINE,
    SQLUD_RESTORE, ApplicationID, 0, "D:", 4,
    NULL, NULL, &Media_List, "userID", "password", NULL, 0,
    NULL, 4, NULL, NULL, NULL, &sqlca);

// Ignore The Warning Message Stating That The Existing
// Database Will Be Overwritten
if (sqlca.sqlcode == 2529 || sqlca.sqlcode == 2539)
{
    sqlurestore("SAMPLE", "SAMPLE", 16, SQLUD_NOROLLFWD,
        SQLUD_NODATALINK, SQLUD_FULL, SQLUD_OFFLINE,
        SQLUD_CONTINUE, ApplicationID, 0, "D:", 4,
        NULL, NULL, &Media_List, "userID", "password", NULL, 0,
        NULL, 4, NULL, NULL, NULL, &sqlca);
}

// If The Database Could Not Be Restored, Display An Error
// Message And Terminate The Restore Process
if (sqlca.sqlcode != SQL_RC_OK)
{
    cout << "ERROR : " << sqlca.sqlcode << endl;
    sqlurestore("SAMPLE", "SAMPLE", 16, SQLUD_NOROLLFWD,
        SQLUD_NODATALINK, SQLUD_FULL, SQLUD_OFFLINE,
        SQLUD_TERMINATE, ApplicationID, 0, "D:", 4,
        NULL, NULL, &Media_List, "userID", "password", NULL, 0,
        NULL, 4, NULL, NULL, NULL, &sqlca);
}

// If The SAMPLE Database Was Restored Successfully, Display A
// Message Saying So
else
{
    cout << "The SAMPLE database was successfully restored.";
    cout << endl;
}

// Return The SQLCA Return Code To The Calling Function
return(sqlca.sqlcode);
}
```

```
/*————————————————————————————————————————————————————————*/
/* The Main Function                                        */
/*————————————————————————————————————————————————————————*/
int main()
{
    // Declare The Local Memory Variables
    long  rc = SQL_RC_OK;

    // Create An Instance Of The API_Class Class
    API_Class  Example;

    // Restore The SAMPLE Database From A Backup Image
    rc = Example.RestoreDB();

    // Return To The Operating System
    return(rc);
}
```

RECONCILE

Purpose   The RECONCILE function is used to validate any references to files that are stored in DATALINK columns of a specific database table.

Syntax
```
SQL_API_RC SQL_API_FN sqlurcon (char      *TableName,
                                char      *Reserved1,
                                char      *DLFMServerName,
                                char      *ReportFile,
                                void      *Reserved2,
                                struct sqlca  *SQLCA);
```

Parameters *TableName*

A pointer to a location in memory where the name of the table that DATALINK file validation is to be performed for is stored.

Reserved1

A pointer that is currently reserved for later use. For now, this parameter must always contain a blank string (" ").

DLFMServerName

A pointer to a location in memory where the name of a DATALINK File Server that was preconfigured for use with the database that the specified table resides in is stored.

ReportFile

A pointer to a location in memory where the name of the file in which information about all DATALINK files that have become unlinked will be written to is stored.

Reserved2

A pointer that is currently reserved for later use. For now, this parameter must always be set to NULL.

SQLCA

A pointer to a location in memory where a SQL Communications Area (SQLCA) data structure variable is stored. This structure returns either status information (if the function executed successfully) or error information (if the function failed) to the calling application.

Includes   `#include <sqlutil.h>`

Description   The RECONCILE function is used to validate any references to files that are stored in DATALINK columns of a specific database table. During reconciliation (validation), DB2 attempts to link DATALINK files that are referenced by table data but that no longer exist according to DLFM server metadata (provided no other conflict is found). If, during reconciliation, a file reference link cannot be established, the violating rows remain in the table, and the offending DATALINK values are set to NULL. If the DATALINK column is defined as NOT NULL, the URL part of the DATALINK value is replaced by a zero length string, and the comment remains untouched.

Comments   ■ If no DLFM server name is specified in the *DLFMServerName* parameter when this function is called, reconciliation is performed with respect to all DATALINK data found in the table. If a DLFM server name is specified, reconciliation is performed with respect to all DATALINK data found in the table that references the specified DLFM server. Other servers are not contacted.

■ Before this function can be executed, the table specified must be in the "Datalink Reconcile Pending" state. If reconciliation is performed with respect to all DLFM servers, the table is taken out of the "Datalink Reconcile Pending" state when this function completes execution. If reconciliation is performed with respect to a single DLFM server, the table is only taken out of the "Datalink Reconcile Pending" state when this function completes execution if no other DLFM servers are referenced by DATALINK data.

■ If the integrity of the data is certain (after reconciliation has been performed in respect to one or more servers referenced by DATALINK data), a table can be taken out of "Datalink Reconcile Pending" state by issuing the SET CONSTRAINTS...IMMEDIATE UNCHECKED SQL statement.

Connection Requirements   This function can only be called if a connection to a database exists.

Authorization Only users with System Administrator (SYSADM) authority, System Control (SYSCTRL) authority, System Maintenance (SYSMAINT) authority, Database Administrator (DBADM) authority, or CONTROL authority on the table specified are allowed to execute this function call.

See Also   RESTORE DATABASE

Example   The following C++ program illustrates how to use the RECONCILE function to validate a DATALINK file reference in a database table:

```
/*————————————————————————————————————————————————————————————————*/
/* NAME:     CH10EX5.SQC                                            */
/* PURPOSE: Illustrate How To Use The Following DB2 API Function    */
/*          In A C++ Program:                                       */
/*                                                                  */
/*              RECONCILE                                           */
/*                                                                  */
/*————————————————————————————————————————————————————————————————*/

// Include The Appropriate Header Files
#include <windows.h>
#include <iostream.h>
#include <sqlutil.h>
#include <sqlenv.h>
#include <sql.h>

// Define The API_Class Class
class API_Class
{
    // Attributes
    public:
        struct sqlca   sqlca;

    // Operations
    public:
        long Reconcile();
};

// Define The Reconcile() Member Function
long API_Class::Reconcile()
{
    // Declare The Local Memory Variables
    char    TableName[20];
    char    ServerName[20];
    char    RecInfoFileName[80];

    // Initialize The Local Variables
    strcpy(TableName, "EXTERNAL_SITES");
    strcpy(ServerName, "");
    strcpy(RecInfoFileName, "C:\\REC_INFO.DAT");

    // Validate All DATALINK References
    sqlurcon(TableName, "", ServerName, RecInfoFileName, NULL,
        &sqlca);

    // If DATALINK Reference Information Was Obtained, Display A
    // Success Message
    if (sqlca.sqlcode == SQL_RC_OK)
    {
        cout << "Information about all DATALINK references used ";
        cout << "in the EXTERNAL_SITES table were" << endl;
        cout << "collected and placed in the file C:\\REC_INFO.DAT.";
        cout << endl;
    }
```

```
    // Return The SQLCA Return Code To The Calling Function
    return(sqlca.sqlcode);
}

/*------------------------------------------------------------------*/
/* The Main Function                                                */
/*------------------------------------------------------------------*/
int main()
{
    // Declare The Local Memory Variables
    long        rc = SQL_RC_OK;
    struct sqlca  sqlca;

    // Declare The SQL Host Memory Variable
    EXEC SQL BEGIN DECLARE SECTION;
        char    CTString[255];
        char    IString[180];
    EXEC SQL END DECLARE SECTION;

    // Create An Instance Of The API_Class Class
    API_Class  Example;

    // Connect To The SAMPLE Database
    EXEC SQL CONNECT TO SAMPLE USER userID USING password;

    // Create The EXTERNAL_SITES Table
    strcpy((char *) CTString, "CREATE TABLE EXTERNAL_SITES (        ");
    strcat((char *) CTString, "  SITE_ID    CHAR(2) NOT NULL,       ");
    strcat((char *) CTString, "  URL          DATALINK(200)         ");
    strcat((char *) CTString, "    LINKTYPE URL NO LINK CONTROL)    ");

    // Prepare The Create Table SQL Statement
    EXEC SQL PREPARE SQL_STMNT1 FROM :CTString;
    if (sqlca.sqlcode == SQL_RC_OK)
    {
        // Execute The Insert Statement
        EXEC SQL EXECUTE SQL_STMNT1;

        // Tell The User That The New Table Was Created
        if (sqlca.sqlcode == SQL_RC_OK)
        {
            cout << "New table has been added to the SAMPLE database.";
            cout << endl << endl;
        }
    }

    // Commit The Transaction
    EXEC SQL COMMIT;

    // Build An Insert SQL Statement String
    strcpy(IString, "INSERT INTO EXTERNAL_SITES VALUES ('01',       ");
    strcat(IString, "DLVALUE('http://dlfs.almaden.ibm.com/a.b',     ");
    strcat(IString, "'URL', 'IBM Data'))                            ");
```

```
// Prepare The Insert SQL Statement
EXEC SQL PREPARE SQL_STMNT FROM :IString;
if (sqlca.sqlcode == SQL_RC_OK)
{
    // Execute The Insert Statement
    EXEC SQL EXECUTE SQL_STMNT;

    // Tell The User That The New Record Was Added
    if (sqlca.sqlcode == SQL_RC_OK)
    {
        cout << "New data has been added to the SAMPLE database.";
        cout << endl << endl;
    }
}

// Commit The Transaction
EXEC SQL COMMIT;

// Validate The DATALINK Reference
rc = Example.Reconcile();

// Disconnect From The SAMPLE Database
EXEC SQL DISCONNECT CURRENT;

// Return To The Operating System
return(rc);
}
```

■ ■ SET TABLESPACE CONTAINERS

Purpose   The SET TABLESPACE CONTAINERS function is used to facilitate a redirected restore operation (a restore operation in which a database is restored and a different set of table space storage containers are desired or required).

Syntax
```
SQL_API_RC SQL_API_FN  sqlbstsc  (struct sqlca            *SQLCA,
                                  unsigned long           RecoveryOption,
                                  unsigned long           TableSpaceID,
                                  unsigned long           NumContainers,
                                  struct SQLB_TBSCONTQRY_DATA
                                                          *ContainerData);
```

Parameters   *SQLCA*   A pointer to a location in memory where a SQL Communications Area (SQLCA) data structure variable is stored. This variable returns either status information (if the function executed successfully) or error information (if the function failed) to the calling application.

RecoveryOption	Specifies how ALTER TABLESPACE operations found in a recovery log file are to be handled when a roll-forward database recovery operation is performed. This parameter must be set to one of the following values:

■ SQLB_SET_CONT_INIT_STATE
   ALTER TABLESPACE operations found in the recovery log file(s) are to be redone when performing a roll-forward recovery operation

■ SQLB_SET_CONT_FINAL_STATE
   ALTER TABLESPACE operations found in the recovery log file(s) are to be ignored when performing a roll-forward recovery operation

TableSpaceID	The ID of the table space that one or more storage containers are to be redefined for.
NumContainers	The number of table space container definitions (elements) stored in the array of *SQLB_TBSCONTQRY_DATA* structures referenced by the *ContainerData* parameter.
ContainerData	A pointer to an array of *SQLB_TBSCONTQRY_DATA* structures that contain one or more table space container definitions.

Includes   #include <sqlutil.h>

Description   The SET TABLESPACE CONTAINERS function is used to facilitate a *redirected* restore operation (a restore operation in which a database is restored and a different set of table space storage containers is desired or required). Before this function is executed, an array of special structures (*SQLB_TBSCONTQRY_DATA*) must first be allocated and initialized with table space container definitions. Refer to the FETCH TABLESPACE CONTAINER QUERY function for a detailed description of the *SQLB_TBSCONTQRY_DATA* structure. Although an array of *SQLB_TBSCONTQRY_DATA* structures must be provided, only the *contType*, *totalPages*, *name*, and *nameLen* fields of each structure must be initialized. All other fields in this structure are ignored.

This function is used in conjunction with the RESTORE DATABASE function to restore a database or one or more table spaces that were backed up with the BACKUP DATABASE command or function. A backup image of a database, or of one or more table spaces, contains information about all table space containers that were defined for the database or table space(s) when the backup operation took place. During a restore operation, all containers identified in the backup image are checked to see if they exist and are accessible. If one or more of these containers no longer exists or for some reason has become inaccessible, the restore operation will fail. This function can be used to add, change, or remove table space containers during a restore operation, thereby getting around this problem and allowing a backup image to be successfully restored.

The following steps illustrate how to use this function in a redirected restore operation:

1. Call the RESTORE DATABASE function with the *CallerAction* parameter set to SQLUD_RESTORE_STORDEF.

2. Wait for the RESTORE DATABASE function to return a SQL return code indicating that one or more of the required table space containers is inaccessible.

3. Call the SET TABLESPACE CONTAINER function with the appropriate table space container definitions and the *RecoveryOption* parameter set to the appropriate state (SQLB_SET_CONT_FINAL_STATE is the recommended state to use).

4. Call the RESTORE DATABASE function again, this time with the *CallerAction* parameter set to SQLUD_CONTINUE.

This will allow the restore operation to use the new table space container definitions. Any table space container referenced in recovery log file(s) will be ignored when the ROLLFORWARD DATABASE function is called (if the SQLB_SET_CONT_FINAL_STATE state was specified).

Comments   ■ Only use this function when a table space is in a "Storage Definition Pending" or a "Storage Definition Allowed" state. These states occur during a restore operation, immediately prior to the restoration of database or table space pages.

■ When creating the table space container list, keep in mind that there must be sufficient disk space to allow for the restore and roll-forward operations to place all the original data into these new containers. If there is not enough disk space available, one or more table spaces will be left in the "Recovery Pending" state until sufficient disk space is made available. It is a good idea to keep records of disk usage on a regular basis. Then, when a restore and roll-forward operation needs to be performed, you can determine in advance how much disk space will be required.

■ When new containers are defined for an existing table space, they will replace containers that currently exist for the table space when the redirected restore operation is performed. When new containers replace existing containers, the existing containers are not automatically removed from the storage media on which they reside. Therefore, it is the user's responsibility to remove unused containers after a redirected restore operation is performed.

Connection Requirements   This function can only be called if a connection to a database exists.

Authorization   Only users with either System Administrator (SYSADM) authority or System Control (SYSCTRL) authority are allowed to execute this function call.

See Also   BACKUP DATABASE, RESTORE DATABASE, ROLLFORWARD DATABASE

Example   The following C++ program illustrates how to use the SET TABLESPACE CONTAINERS function to redefine table space containers during a restore operation:

```
/*------------------------------------------------------------*/
/* NAME:    CH10EX6.SQC                                       */
/* PURPOSE: Illustrate How To Use The Following DB2 API Function */
/*          In A C++ Program:                                 */
/*                                                            */
/*              SET TABLESPACE CONTAINERS                     */
/*                                                            */
/*------------------------------------------------------------*/

// Include The Appropriate Header Files
#include <windows.h>
#include <iostream.h>
#include <sqlutil.h>
#include <sqlenv.h>
#include <sql.h>

// Define The API_Class Class
class API_Class
{
    // Attributes
    public:
        struct sqlca   sqlca;

    // Operations
    public:
        long BackupDB();
        long RestoreDB();
};

// Define The BackupDB() Member Function
long API_Class::BackupDB()
{
    // Declare The Local Memory Variables
    struct sqlu_media_list    Media_List;
    struct sqlu_media_entry   Media_Entry;
    char                      ApplicationID[33];
    char                      TimeStamp[27];

    // Initialize The Media List Information Data Structure
    Media_List.media_type = SQLU_LOCAL_MEDIA;
    Media_List.sessions = 1;
    strcpy(Media_Entry.media_entry, "D:\\Backup");
    Media_List.target.media = &Media_Entry;

    // Tell The User That The Backup Process Is Being Started
    cout << "Starting Backup ..." << endl << endl;
```

```
        // Start Backing Up The SAMPLE Database
        sqlubkup("SAMPLE", 16, SQLUB_OFFLINE, SQLUB_FULL,
            SQLUB_BACKUP, ApplicationID, TimeStamp, 4, NULL,
            &Media_List, "userID", "password", NULL, 0, NULL,
            NULL, &sqlca);

        // If The Database Could Not Be Backed Up, Display An Error
        // Message And Terminate The Backup Process
        if (sqlca.sqlcode != SQL_RC_OK)
        {
            cout << "ERROR : " << sqlca.sqlcode << endl;
            sqlubkup ("SAMPLE", 16, SQLUB_OFFLINE, SQLUB_FULL,
                SQLUB_TERMINATE, ApplicationID, TimeStamp, 4,
                NULL, &Media_List, "userID", "password", NULL, 0,
                NULL, NULL, &sqlca);
        }

        // If The SAMPLE Database Was Successfully Backed Up, Display A
        // Message Saying So
        else
        {
            cout << "The SAMPLE database was successfully backed up.";
            cout << endl;
        }

        // Return The SQLCA Return Code To The Calling Function
        return(sqlca.sqlcode);
}

// Define The RestoreDB() Member Function
long API_Class::RestoreDB()
{
        // Declare The Local Memory Variables
        struct sqlu_media_list      Media_List;
        struct sqlu_media_entry     Media_Entry;
        char                        ApplicationID[33];
        struct SQLB_TBSCONTQRY_DATA TSContainers[3];

        // Initialize The Media List Information Data Structure
        Media_List.media_type = SQLU_LOCAL_MEDIA;
        Media_List.sessions = 1;
        strcpy(Media_Entry.media_entry, "D:\\Backup");
        Media_List.target.media = &Media_Entry;

        // Tell The User That The Restore Process Is Being Started
        cout << "Starting Restore ..." << endl << endl;

        // Start Restoring The SAMPLE Database
        sqlurestore("SAMPLE", "SAMPLE", 16, SQLUD_NOROLLFWD,
            SQLUD_NODATALINK, SQLUD_FULL, SQLUD_OFFLINE,
            SQLUD_RESTORE_STORDEF, ApplicationID, 0, "D:", 4,
            NULL, NULL, &Media_List, "userID", "password", NULL, 0,
            NULL, 4, NULL, NULL, NULL, &sqlca);
```

```
// Ignore The Warning Message Stating That The Existing
// Database Will Be Overwritten
if (sqlca.sqlcode == 2529 || sqlca.sqlcode == 2539)
{
    sqlurestore("SAMPLE", "SAMPLE", 16, SQLUD_NOROLLFWD,
        SQLUD_NODATALINK, SQLUD_FULL, SQLUD_OFFLINE,
        SQLUD_CONTINUE, ApplicationID, 0, "D:", 4,
        NULL, NULL, &Media_List, "userID", "password", NULL, 0,
        NULL, 4, NULL, NULL, NULL, &sqlca);
}

// If The Error Message Stating That A Table Space Container
// No Longer Exists Is Generated, Define New Table Space
// Containers
if (sqlca.sqlcode == 1277)
{
    // Tell The User That New Table Space Containers Are Being
    // Defined
    cout << "Defining New Table Spaces ..." << endl << endl;

    // Define A New List Of Table Space Containers
    TSContainers[0].contType = SQLB_CONT_PATH;
    strcpy(TSContainers[0].name, "D:\\NEW_TSP1.1");
    TSContainers[1].contType = SQLB_CONT_PATH;
    strcpy(TSContainers[1].name, "D:\\NEW_TSP1.2");

    // Set The New Table Space Containers
    sqlbstsc(&sqlca, SQLB_SET_CONT_INIT_STATE, 3, 2,
        (struct SQLB_TBSCONTQRY_DATA *) &TSContainers[0]);

    // If The New Table Space Containers Could Not Be Set,
    // Display An Error Message
    if (sqlca.sqlcode != SQL_RC_OK)
    {
        cout << "ERROR : " << sqlca.sqlcode << endl << endl;
        return(sqlca.sqlcode);
    }

    // Continue The Restore Operation
    sqlurestore("SAMPLE", "SAMPLE", 16, SQLUD_NOROLLFWD,
        SQLUD_NODATALINK, SQLUD_FULL, SQLUD_OFFLINE,
        SQLUD_CONTINUE, ApplicationID, 0, "D:", 4,
        NULL, NULL, &Media_List, "userID", "password", NULL, 0,
        NULL, 4, NULL, NULL, NULL, &sqlca);
}

// If The Database Could Not Be Restored, Display An Error
// Message And Terminate The Restore Process
if (sqlca.sqlcode != SQL_RC_OK)
{
    cout << "ERROR : " << sqlca.sqlcode << endl;
    sqlurestore("SAMPLE", "SAMPLE", 16, SQLUD_NOROLLFWD,
        SQLUD_NODATALINK, SQLUD_FULL, SQLUD_OFFLINE,
        SQLUD_TERMINATE, ApplicationID, 0, "D:", 4,
```

```
                NULL, NULL, &Media_List, "userID", "password", NULL, 0,
                NULL, 4, NULL, NULL, NULL, &sqlca);
    }

    // If The SAMPLE Database Was Restored Successfully, Display A
    // Message Saying So
    else
    {
        cout << "The SAMPLE database was successfully restored.";
        cout << endl;
    }

    // Return The SQLCA Return Code To The Calling Function
    return(sqlca.sqlcode);
}

/*--------------------------------------------------------------------*/
/* The Main Function                                                  */
/*--------------------------------------------------------------------*/
int main()
{
    // Declare The Local Memory Variables
    long        rc = SQL_RC_OK;
    struct sqlca  sqlca;

    // Create An Instance Of The API_Class Class
    API_Class   Example;

    // Connect To The SAMPLE Database
    EXEC SQL CONNECT TO SAMPLE USER userID USING password;

    // Create A Temporary SMS Table Space
    EXEC SQL CREATE TEMPORARY TABLESPACE MY_SPACE
        MANAGED BY SYSTEM
        USING ('D:\TMPTBSP1.TSP', 'D:\TMPTBSP2.TSP')
        EXTENTSIZE 256;

    // Tell The User That The Table Space Was Created
    if (sqlca.sqlcode == SQL_RC_OK)
    {
        cout << "The SMS Table Space MY_SPACE has been created.";
        cout << endl;
    }

    // Commit The Transaction
    EXEC SQL COMMIT;

    // Disconnect From The SAMPLE Database
    EXEC SQL DISCONNECT CURRENT;

    // Backup The SAMPLE Database
    rc = Example.BackupDB();
```

```
// Re-Connect To The SAMPLE Database
EXEC SQL CONNECT TO SAMPLE USER userID USING password;

// Delete The Table Space Created Earlier
EXEC SQL DROP TABLESPACE MY_SPACE;

// Commit The Transaction
EXEC SQL COMMIT;

// Re-Create The Temporary SMS Table Space (Minus 1 Container)
EXEC SQL CREATE TEMPORARY TABLESPACE MY_SPACE
    MANAGED BY SYSTEM
    USING ('D:\TMPTBSP1.TSP')
    EXTENTSIZE 256;

// Tell The User That The Table Space Was Modified
if (sqlca.sqlcode == SQL_RC_OK)
{
    cout << "The SMS Table Space MY_SPACE has been modified.";
    cout << endl;
}

// Commit The Transaction
EXEC SQL COMMIT;

// Disconnect From The SAMPLE Database
EXEC SQL DISCONNECT CURRENT;

// Restore The SAMPLE Database
rc = Example.RestoreDB();

// Return To The Operating System
return(rc);
}
```

ROLLFORWARD DATABASE

Purpose

The ROLLFORWARD DATABASE function is used to return a damaged or corrupted database (or one or more damaged or corrupted table spaces) to the state it was in just before the damage occurred.

Syntax

```
SQL_API_RC SQL_API_FN sqluroll (struct rfwd_input   *RfwdInput,
                                struct rfwd_output  *RfwdOutput,
                                struct sqlca        *SQLCA);
```

Parameters   *RfwdInput*   A pointer to a *rfwd_input* structure that contains information about the type of roll-forward recovery operation to perform.

RfwdOutput		A pointer to a *rfwd_output* structure where this function is to store information about the status of the roll-forward recovery operation just performed.
SQLCA	/	A pointer to a location in memory where a SQL Communications Area (SQLCA) data structure variable is stored. This structure returns either status information (if the function executed successfully) or error information (if the function failed) to the calling application.

Includes

```
#include <sqlutil.h>
```

Description

The ROLLFORWARD DATABASE function is used to return a damaged or corrupted database (or one or more damaged or corrupted table spaces) to the state it was in just before the damage occurred by applying transactions recorded in the database log files to it after a successful restore operation. When this function is called, the DB2 Database Manager uses information stored in both archived and active log files to reconstruct the transactions performed on the database since the last backup image was made.

The ROLLFORWARD DATABASE function is normally called after the RESTORE DATABASE function has been used to restore a database or one or more table spaces, or when one or more table spaces have been taken offline by the database due to a media error. A database must be enabled for roll-forward recovery (that is, either the *logretain* parameter and/or the *userexit* parameter in the database configuration file must be set appropriately) before it can be used with this function.

Two special structures (*rfwd_input* and *rfwd_output*) are used to pass information to and obtain status information from the Roll-Forward Recovery utility. The first of these structures, *rfwd_input*, is defined in *sqlutil.h* as follows:

```
SQL_STRUCTURE rfwd_input
{
unsigned long    version;       /* Identifies the version of the      */
                                /* ROLLFORWARD DATABASE function       */
                                /* parameters being used. This field   */
                                /* should always be set to             */
                                /* SQLUM_RFWD_VERSION.                  */
char             *pDbAlias;     /* A pointer to a location in memory   */
                                /* where the alias name of the         */
                                /* database to be rolled forward is    */
                                /* stored.                             */
unsigned short   CallerAction;  /* Specifies the action the            */
                                /* ROLLFORWARD DATABASE function is     */
                                /* to take when it is executed. This    */
                                /* field must be set to one of the     */
                                /* values shown in Table 10-2.         */
char             *pStopTime;    /* A pointer to a location in memory   */
                                /* where a time stamp value is stored   */
                                /* (in ISO format). This value is used  */
                                /* to specify a point in time to which the */
```

```
                             /* database is to be rolled forward.  */
                             /* If the value                       */
                             /* SQLUM_INFINITY_TIMESTAMP is used,   */
                             /* the database will be rolled forward */
                             /* as far as possible.                 */
char          *pUserName;    /* A pointer to a location in memory   */
                             /* where the authorization name (user  */
                             /* ID) of the person performing the    */
                             /* roll-forward recovery operation is  */
                             /* stored.                             */
char          *pPassword;    /* A pointer to a location in memory   */
                             /* where the password for the          */
                             /* authorization name specified in the */
                             /* pUserName field is stored. This     */
                             /* field can contain a NULL value.     */
char          *pOverflowLogPath;
                             /* A pointer to a location in memory   */
                             /* where an alternate log file path    */
                             /* (that is to be used when searching  */
                             /* for active and archived log files)  */
                             /* is stored. This field can contain a */
                             /* NULL value.                         */
unsigned short  NumChngLgOvrflw;
                             /* The number of overflow log paths    */
                             /* changed in a multi-node database    */
                             /* environment (MPP only).             */
struct sqlurf_newlogpath  *pChngLogOvrflw;
                             /* A pointer to an array of structures */
                             /* that contain fully qualified names  */
                             /* of changed overflow log paths.      */
                             /* These overflow log paths only       */
                             /* override the default overflow log   */
                             /* path for the node specified. (MPP   */
                             /* only).                              */
unsigned short  ConnectionMode;
                             /* Specifies that the roll-forward     */
                             /* recovery utility is to be run       */
                             /* offline (SQLUM_OFFLINE), or online  */
                             /* (SQLUM_ONLINE). The roll-forward    */
                             /* recovery utility must be run offline */
                             /* if a database is being rolled       */
                             /* forward; it can be run offline or   */
                             /* online if a table space is being   */
                             /* rolled forward.                     */
struct sqlu_tablespace_bkrst_list pTablespaceList;
                             /* A pointer to a structure that       */
                             /* contains a list of table space names */
                             /* that identify specific table spaces */
                             /* that are to be rolled forward. If no */
                             /* list of table space names is        */
                             /* provided (i.e., if this field is set */
                             /* to NULL), all table spaces that need */
                             /* to be rolled forward will be.       */
```

```
short          AllNodeFlag;   /* Indicates whether the roll-forward  */
                              /* operation is to be performed at all */
                              /* nodes defined in the db2nodes.cfg   */
                              /* configuration file                  */
                              /* (SQLURF_ALL_NODES), at the catalog  */
                              /* node only (SQLURF_CAT_NODE_ONLY), at */
                              /* all nodes identified in the node    */
                              /* list that the pNodeList field of    */
                              /* this structure references           */
                              /* (SQLURF_NODE_LIST), or at all nodes */
                              /* except those identified in the node */
                              /* list that the pNodeList field of    */
                              /* this structure references           */
                              /* (SQLURF_ALL_EXCEPT).                */
             short NumNodes;  /* The number of nodes stored in the   */
                              /* node list that the pNodeList field  */
                              /* of this structure references.       */
SQL_PDB_NODE_TYPE             *pNodeList;
                              /* A pointer to a location in memory   */
                              /* where an array of node numbers is   */
                              /* stored.                             */
             short NumNodeInfo;
                              /* Identifies the number nodes that are */
                              /* being rolled forward. In a single    */
                              /* node environment, this field must be */
                              /* set to 1.                            */
unsigned short DlMode;        /* Currently, this field is not used    */
                              /* and should always be set to 0.       */
char           *pReportFile;  /* A pointer to a location in memory    */
                              /* where the name of the file in which  */
                              /* information about all DATALINK files */
                              /* that become unlinked during the roll- */
                              /* forward recovery operation will be   */
                              /* written to is stored.                */
};
```

NOTE: SQL_PDB_NODE_TYPE *is a type definition for* signed short.

The *rfwd_input* structure contains a pointer to an array *sqlurf_newlogpath* data structures and a pointer to a *sqlu_tablespace_bkrst_list* data structure. The first of these, the *sqlurf_newlogpath* structure, is defined in *sqlutil.h* as follows:

```
SQL_STRUCTURE sqlurf_newlogpath
{
SQL_PDB_NODE_TYPE     nodenum;  /* A number that identifies a specific node*/
                               /* (within a multi-node environment).    */
unsigned short        pathlen;  /* The length of the overflow log path   */
                               /* specified in the logpath field of this */
                               /* structure.                             */
```

Table 10–2 ROLLFORWARD DATABASE Function Actions

Caller Action	Description
SQLUM_ROLLFWD	The database is to be rolled forward to the point in time specified by the value stored in the *pStopTime* field of the *rfwd_input* structure. If this caller action is specified, the database will be placed in "Rollforward Pending" state.
SQLUM_STOP	The roll-forward operation is to be terminated. If this caller action is specified, the database will be taken out of the "Rollforward Pending" state, no new log records will be processed, and all uncommitted transactions will be backed out.
SQLUM_ROLLFWD_STOP	The database is to be rolled forward to the point in time specified by the value stored in the *pStopTime* field of the *rfwd_input* structure, and the roll-forward operation is to be terminated. If this caller action is specified, the database will be taken out of the "Rollforward Pending" state when the roll-forward operation terminates.
SQLUM_QUERY	Values for the *nextarclog*, *firstarcdel*, *lastarcdel*, and *lastcommit* fields of the *sqlurf_info* structure are to be obtained from the recovery log files. This caller action does not invoke the Roll-Forward Recovery utility.
SQLUM_PARAM_CHECK	Specifies that all parameter/structure values specified for the ROLLFORWARD DATABASE function call are to be checked for validity. This caller action does not invoke the Roll-Forward Recovery utility.
SQLUM_CANCEL	The roll-forward recovery operation that is currently running is to be terminated. If this caller action is specified, the database will be left in the "Recovery Pending" state.
SQLUM_LOADREC_CONTINUE	The roll-forward operation is to be continued after the user has performed some action that was requested by the Roll-Forward Recovery utility (for example, mounting a new tape).
SQLUM_LOADREC_DEVICE_TERMINATE	A particular device is to be removed from the list of devices used by the Roll-Forward Recovery utility. When a particular device has exhausted its input, the Roll-Forward Recovery utility returns a warning to the application (while continuing to process using the remaining devices). By calling the ROLLFORWARD DATABASE function again with this caller action specified, you can remove the device that generated the warning condition from the list of devices being used.
SQLUD_LOADREC_TERMINATE	All devices being used by roll-forward recovery are to be terminated.

```
char      logpath[255];       /* A pointer to a location in memory where  */
                              /* an alternate log file path (that is to   */
                              /* be used when searching for active and    */
                              /* archived log files) is stored.           */
};
```

Refer to the BACKUP DATABASE function for a detailed description of the *sqlu_tablespace_bkrst_list* structure.

The second structure used by this function, the *rfwd_output* structure, is defined in *sqlutil.h* as follows:

```
SQL_STRUCTURE rfwd_output
{
char            *pApplicationId; /* A pointer to a location in memory  */
                                 /* where the ROLLFORWARD DATABASE     */
                                 /* function is to store a string that */
                                 /* identifies the agent that is       */
                                 /* servicing the application. This    */
                                 /* ID can be used to obtain           */
                                 /* information about the progress of  */
                                 /* a roll-forward recovery operation. */
                                 /* This field can contain a NULL      */
                                 /* value.                             */
long            *pNumReplies;    /* A pointer to a location in memory  */
                                 /* where the ROLLFORWARD DATABASE     */
                                 /* function is to store the number of */
                                 /*  node replies received. Each node  */
                                 /* that replies fills in a sqlurf_info*/
                                 /* sqlurf_info structure. In a        */
                                 /* single-node environment, the value */
                                 /* 1 is always returned.              */
struct sqlurf_info *pNodeInfo;   /* A pointer to a user-defined array  */
                                 /* of structures that the ROLLFORWARD */
                                 /* DATABASE                           */
                                 /* function is to store information   */
                                 /* about each node involved in a      */
                                 /* roll-forward recovery operation.   */
};
```

This structure contains a pointer to an array of *sqlurf_info* structures. The *sqlurf_info* structure is defined in *sqlutil.h* as follows:

```
SQL_STRUCTURE sqlurf_info
{
long state;                      /* The current state of a node.       */
unsigned char   nextarclog[13];  /* The name of the next recovery log  */
                                 /* file needed by the Roll-Rorward    */
                                 /*  Recovery utility.                 */
unsigned char   firstarcdel[13];
                                 /* The name of the first recovery log */
                                 /* file used (and no longer needed) by */
                                 /* the Roll-Forward Recovery utility. */
unsigned char   lastarcdel[13];  /* The name of the last recovery log file*/
                                 /* used (and no longer needed) by the */
                                 /* Roll-Forward Recovery utility.     */
unsigned char   lastcommit[27];  /* A time stamp (in ISO format) that  */
                                 /* identifies when the last transaction */
                                 /* was committed. This value is provided */
                                 /* after the Roll-Forward Recovery    */
                                 /* operation terminates.              */
};
```

NOTE: Log files must be copied to a separate directory before a database is restored if they are to be used to roll a database forward (otherwise, they will be replaced with the log files stored in the backup image during the restore operation). These log files must then be copied to the appropriate log file path (as specified in the database configuration file) after the restore operation executes and before the ROLLFORWARD DATABASE function is called (or the directory in which they are stored must be specified in the OverflowLogPath parameter). If these log files cannot be accessed by the Roll-Forward Recovery utility, the roll-forward recovery operation will fail.

Once roll-forward recovery is started, it will not stop until one of the following events occurs:

- No more recovery log files are found in the specified directories.

- A time stamp in the current recovery log file being used exceeds the completion time stamp specified in the *pStopTime* field of the *rfwd_input* structure.

- An error occurs while reading a recovery log file.

Comments

- The *CallerAction* field of the *rfwd_input* structure must be set to SQLUM_ROLLFWD, SQLUM_QUERY, or SQLUM_PARM_CHECK the first time this function is called.

- The application ID string returned by this function can be up to 33 characters in length (including the NULL terminator).

- If the *CallerAction* field of the *rfwd_input* structure is set to anything other than SQLUM_ROLLFWD, SQLUM_STOP, or SQLUM_ROLLFWD_STOP, the *pStopTime* field can be set to NULL.

- The *pStopTime* field of the *rfwd_input* structure must be set to SQLUM_INFINITY_TIMESTAMP, for table space roll-forward recovery operations.

- If the *CallerAction* field of the *rfwd_input* structure is set to anything other than SQLUM_QUERY and a filename is returned in the *nextarclog* field of the *sqlurf_info* structure, an error occurred while attempting to access that file. Possible causes of this type of error include the following:

  —The file was not found in the database log directory nor in the path specified in the *pOverflowLogPath* field of the *rfwd_input* structure.

  —The user exit program failed to return the archived recovery log file.

- All log files up to and including the log file (name) returned in the *lastarcdel* field of the *sqlurf_info* structure parameter can be removed from the storage media to make room for other files. For example, if the recovery log file name returned in the *firstarcdel* field of the *sqlurf_info* parameter is S0000001.LOG, and the recovery log file name returned in the *lastarcdel* field is S0000005.LOG, the following recovery log files can be deleted: S0000001.LOG, S0000002.LOG, S0000003.LOG, S0000004.LOG, and S0000005.LOG.

- During roll-forward recovery, all recovery log files are searched for, first in the directory specified in the *logpath* parameter of the database configuration file and then in the overflow log path specified in the *pOverflowLogPath* field of the *rfwd_input* structure. If no overflow log path is specified, all active log files and archived log files need to be located in the *logpath* directory. This means that one or more log files might have to be physically moved from one location to another before they can be used by the Roll-Forward Recovery utility. With this approach, problems can occur if there is not sufficient space in the *logpath* directory. If you store the location of archived recovery log files in the *pOverflowLogPath* field of the rfwd_input structure, recovery log files do not have to be moved—and potential problems can be avoided.

- In a multi-node environment, the overflow log path specified must be a valid, fully qualified path. The default path used is the default overflow log path for each node. In a single-node environment, the overflow log path can be a valid, fully qualified path or a valid, relative path if the server is local.

- For table space roll-forward recovery operations, the SQLM_ROLLFWD, SQLM_STOP, and SQLM_ROLLFWD_STOP caller actions have the same effect, which is rolling forward all table spaces that are in the "Rollforward Pending" (SQLB_ROLLFORWARD_PENDING) or "Rollforward in Progress" (SQLB_ROLLFORWARD_IN_PROGRESS) states.

- The action performed when this function is executed depends on the current value of the database's *rollforward_pending* configuration file parameter (you can determine the value of this parameter by executing the GET DATABASE CONFIGURATION function). If the database is in the "Rollforward Pending" state (SQLB_ROLLFORWARD_PENDING), this parameter will be set to DATABASE. If one or more table spaces are in the "Rollforward Pending" state (SQLB_ROLLFORWARD_PENDING) or "Rollforward in Progress" state (SQLB_ROLLFORWARD_IN_PROGRESS), this parameter will be set to TABLESPACE. If neither the database nor any of its table spaces needs to be rolled forward, this parameter will be set to NO.

- If the database is in the "Rollforward Pending" state (the *rollforward_pending* configuration file parameter is set to DATABASE) when this function is called, the entire database (and all of its table spaces that are not in an abnormal state) will be rolled forward. If one or more table spaces are in the "Rollforward Pending" state (the *rollforward_pending* configuration file parameter is set to TABLESPACE), only the table spaces in the "Rollforward Pending" state will be rolled forward. If a table space roll-forward recovery operation terminates abnormally, table spaces that were being rolled forward will be put in the "Rollforward in Progress" state (the *rollforward_pending* configuration file parameter is set to TABLESPACE), and the next time the ROLLFORWARD DATABASE function is executed, only the table spaces in the "Rollforward in Progress" state will be processed. If the set of table space names specified does not include all table spaces that are in the "Rollforward in Progress" state, the table spaces that are rolled forward will be placed in the "Restore Pending" (SQLB_RESTORE_PENDING) state.

■ If the specified database is not in the "Rollforward Pending" state, no action will be taken when this function is called.

■ More information must be stored in a database's recovery log files for LOB data and LONG VARCHAR fields if roll-forward recovery is enabled (less information has to be retained if the database is not enabled for roll-forward recovery).

■ The ROLLFORWARD DATABASE function reads recovery log files, starting with the log file that is matched with the backup image that was used to restore the database. You can determine the name of this log file by calling this function with the *CallerAction* field of the *rfwd_input* structure set to SQLUM_QUERY before the roll-forward recovery operation is started.

■ All transactions contained in recovery log files are reapplied to the database, if possible, as they are read. Recovery log files are processed as far forward in time as information is available, unless an earlier time is specified. If an earlier time is specified, the *lastcommit* field of the *sqlrf_info* structure will contain the time stamp of the last committed transaction that was applied to the database.

■ If a database recovery was necessary because of application or human error, a time stamp value can be specified in the *pStopTime* field of the *rfwd_input* structure so roll-forward recovery processing will end before the application or human error occurred. Also, if a time stamp value is specified for the *pStopTime* field, you can stop the roll-forward recovery process before a recovery log file read error occurs (if this type of error occurred during an earlier roll-forward recovery attempt). This process only applies to full database roll-forward recovery operations.

■ When the *rollforward_pending* configuration file parameter is set to DATABASE, the database specified is not available for use by other applications until the roll-forward recovery process terminates. You can terminate the process by calling this function with the *CallerAction* field of the *rfwd_input* set to SQLUM_STOP or SQLUM_ROLLFORWARD_STOP; either of these values will bring the database out of "Rollforward Pending" state. If the *rollforward_pending* configuration file parameter is set to TABLESPACE, the database is available for use by other applications during the roll-forward recovery process, but table spaces in the "Rollforward Pending" and "Rollforward in Progress" states will not be available until this function is called to perform the necessary table space roll-forward recovery operation.

■ The SQLUM_CANCEL caller action cannot be used while the roll-forward recovery operation is in progress. Instead, it can only be used if the roll-forward recovery operation is paused (that is, waiting for input), or if a system failure occurs. In either case, this caller action should be used with caution.

■ In a multi-node database environment, this function can only be called from the catalog node. The roll-forward recovery operation itself only affects the nodes that are listed in the *db2nodes.cfg* configuration file, unless specific nodes are specified. If no roll-forward recovery operation is needed on a particular node, that node is ignored.

■ Rolling databases forward might involve prerequisites and restrictions that are beyond the scope of this reference. Refer to the *IBM DB2 Universal Database Administration Guide* for more information about roll-forward recovery.

Connection Requirements This function can be called at any time; a connection to a DB2 Database Manager instance or to a DB2 database does not have to be established first. When this function is called, it establishes a connection to the database specified.

Authorization Only users with System Administrator (SYSADM) authority, System Control (SYSCTRL) authority, or System Maintenance (SYSMAINT) authority can execute this function call.

See Also BACKUP DATABASE, RESTORE DATABASE, LOAD

Example The following C++ program illustrates how to use the ROLLFORWARD DATABASE function to bring the SAMPLE database to the state it was in just before a crucial error occurred:

```
/*------------------------------------------------------------*/
/* NAME:     CH10EX7.SQC                                      */
/* PURPOSE:  Illustrate How To Use The Following DB2 API Function */
/*           In A C++ Program:                                */
/*                                                            */
/*                ROLLFORWARD DATABASE                        */
/*                                                            */
/*------------------------------------------------------------*/

// Include The Appropriate Header Files
#include <windows.h>
#include <iostream.h>
#include <stdlib.h>
#include <sqlutil.h>
#include <sqlenv.h>
#include <sql.h>

// Define The API_Class Class
class API_Class
{
    // Attributes
    public:
        struct sqlca  sqlca;

    // Operations
    public:
        long BackupDB();
        long RestoreDB();
        long RollforwardDB();
};

// Define The BackupDB() Member Function
long API_Class::BackupDB()
{
```

```cpp
// Declare The Local Memory Variables
struct sqlu_media_list      Media_List;
struct sqlu_media_entry     Media_Entry;
char                        ApplicationID[33];
char                        TimeStamp[27];

// Initialize The Media List Information Data Structure
Media_List.media_type = SQLU_LOCAL_MEDIA;
Media_List.sessions = 1;
strcpy(Media_Entry.media_entry, "D:\\Backup");
Media_List.target.media = &Media_Entry;

// Tell The User That The Backup Process Is Being Started
cout << "Starting Backup ..." << endl << endl;

// Start Backing Up The SAMPLE Database
sqlubkup("SAMPLE", 16, SQLUB_OFFLINE, SQLUB_FULL,
    SQLUB_BACKUP, ApplicationID, TimeStamp, 4, NULL,
    &Media_List, "userID", "password", NULL, 0, NULL,
    NULL, &sqlca);

// If The Database Could Not Be Backed Up, Display An Error
// Message And Terminate The Backup Process
if (sqlca.sqlcode != SQL_RC_OK)
{
    cout << "ERROR : " << sqlca.sqlcode << endl;
    sqlubkup ("SAMPLE", 16, SQLUB_OFFLINE, SQLUB_FULL,
        SQLUB_TERMINATE, ApplicationID, TimeStamp, 4,
        NULL, &Media_List, "userID", "password", NULL, 0,
        NULL, NULL, &sqlca);
}

// If The SAMPLE Database Was Successfully Backed Up, Display A
// Message Saying So
else
{
    cout << "The SAMPLE database was successfully backed up.";
    cout << endl;
}

// Return The SQLCA Return Code To The Calling Function
return(sqlca.sqlcode);
}

// Define The RestoreDB() Member Function
long API_Class::RestoreDB()
{
    // Declare The Local Memory Variables
    struct sqlu_media_list      Media_List;
    struct sqlu_media_entry     Media_Entry;
    char                        ApplicationID[33];
```

```
// Initialize The Media List Information Data Structure
Media_List.media_type = SQLU_LOCAL_MEDIA;
Media_List.sessions = 1;
strcpy(Media_Entry.media_entry, "D:\\Backup");
Media_List.target.media = &Media_Entry;

// Tell The User That The Restore Process Is Being Started
cout << "Starting Restore ..." << endl << endl;

// Start Restoring The SAMPLE Database - Note That The
// Database Will Be Left In A Rollforward-Pending State
sqlurestore("SAMPLE", "SAMPLE", 16, SQLUD_ROLLFWD,
    SQLUD_NODATALINK, SQLUD_FULL, SQLUD_OFFLINE,
    SQLUD_RESTORE, ApplicationID, 0, "D:", 4,
    NULL, NULL, &Media_List, "userID", "password", NULL, 0,
    NULL, 4, NULL, NULL, NULL, &sqlca);

// Ignore The Warning Message Stating That The Existing
// Database Will Be Overwritten
if (sqlca.sqlcode == 2529 || sqlca.sqlcode == 2539)
{
    sqlurestore("SAMPLE", "SAMPLE", 16, SQLUD_ROLLFWD,
        SQLUD_NODATALINK, SQLUD_FULL, SQLUD_OFFLINE,
        SQLUD_CONTINUE, ApplicationID, 0, "D:", 4,
        NULL, NULL, &Media_List, "userID", "password", NULL, 0,
        NULL, 4, NULL, NULL, NULL, &sqlca);
}

// If The Database Could Not Be Restored, Display An Error
// Message And Terminate The Restore Process
if (sqlca.sqlcode != SQL_RC_OK)
{
    cout << "ERROR : " << sqlca.sqlcode << endl;
    sqlurestore("SAMPLE", "SAMPLE", 16, SQLUD_ROLLFWD,
        SQLUD_NODATALINK, SQLUD_FULL, SQLUD_OFFLINE,
        SQLUD_TERMINATE, ApplicationID, 0, "D:", 4,
        NULL, NULL, &Media_List, "userID", "password", NULL, 0,
        NULL, 4, NULL, NULL, NULL, &sqlca);
}

// If The SAMPLE Database Was Restored Successfully, Display A
// Message Saying So
else
{
    cout << "The SAMPLE database was successfully restored.";
    cout << endl;
}

// Return The SQLCA Return Code To The Calling Function
return(sqlca.sqlcode);
}
```

```cpp
// Define The RollforwardDB() Member Function
long API_Class::RollforwardDB()
{
    // Declare The Local Memory Variables
    int                     rc = 0;
    char                    Command[50];
    struct rfwd_input       Input;
    struct rfwd_output      Output;
    char                    DBAlias[10];
    char                    UserID[10];
    char                    Password[10];
    char                    LogDir[12];
    char                    ApplicationID[33];
    long                    NumReplies;
    struct sqlurf_info      NodeInfo;

    // Create A Temporary Directory And Copy The SAMPLE Database's
    // Transaction Log Files To It
    rc = CreateDirectory("D:\\LOGDIR", NULL);
    if (rc != 0)
    {
        strcpy(Command, "copy ");
        strcat(Command, "D:\\DB2\\NODE0000\\SQL00001\\SQLOGDIR\\");
        strcat(Command, "*.* D:\\LOGDIR");
        rc = system(Command);
        if (rc != -1)
        {
            cout << "The log files directory has been relocated.";
            cout << endl;
        }
    }

    // Restore The SAMPLE Database - This Will Overwrite The
    // Existing Log Files (Which Is Why They Were Copied To
    // A New Location Before The Restore Operation Was Started)
    // And Leave The Database In A Rollforward-Pending State
    rc = RestoreDB();

    // Initialize The Local Variables
    strcpy(DBAlias, "SAMPLE");
    strcpy(UserID, "userID");
    strcpy(Password, "password");
    strcpy(LogDir, "D:\\LOGDIR");

    // Initialize The Roll-Forward Recovery Input Structure
    Input.version = SQLUM_RFWD_VERSION;
    Input.pDbAlias = DBAlias;
    Input.CallerAction = SQLUM_ROLLFWD_STOP;
    Input.pStopTime = SQLUM_INFINITY_TIMESTAMP;
    Input.pUserName = UserID;
```

```
    Input.pPassword = Password;
    Input.pOverflowLogPath = LogDir;
    Input.NumChngLgOvrflw = 0;
    Input.pChngLogOvrflw =  NULL;
    Input.ConnectMode = SQLUM_OFFLINE;
    Input.pTablespaceList = NULL;
    Input.AllNodeFlag = SQLURF_ALL_NODES;
    Input.NumNodes = 0;
    Input.pNodeList = NULL;
    Input.NumNodeInfo = 1;
    Input.DlMode = 0;
    Input.pReportFile = NULL;

    // Initialize The Roll-Forward Recovery Output Structure
    Output.pApplicationId = ApplicationID;
    Output.pNumReplies = &NumReplies;
    Output.pNodeInfo = &NodeInfo;

    // Perform Roll-Forward Recovery For The SAMPLE Database
    cout << "Starting the database roll-forward recovery process.";
    cout << endl << endl;
    sqluroll(&Input, &Output, &sqlca);

    // If The SAMPLE Database Was Rolled Forwarded Successfully,
    // Display A Message Saying So
    if (rc == SQL_RC_OK)
    {
        cout << "The SAMPLE database was successfully rolled ";
        cout << "forward." << endl;
    }

    // Return The SQLCA Return Code To The Calling Function
    return(sqlca.sqlcode);
}

/*------------------------------------------------------------*/
/* The Main Function                                          */
/*------------------------------------------------------------*/
int main()
{
    // Declare The Local Memory Variables
    long                    rc = SQL_RC_OK;
    struct sqlfupd          DBaseInfo[2];
    unsigned int            LogRetain = 1;
    unsigned int            UserExit = 0;
    unsigned long           AgentID;
    struct sqlca            sqlca;
```

```
// Declare The SQL Host Memory Variable
EXEC SQL BEGIN DECLARE SECTION;
    char      InsertString[180];
EXEC SQL END DECLARE SECTION;

// Create An Instance Of The API_Class Class
API_Class  Example;

// Turn On Roll-Forward Recovery For The SAMPLE Database
DBaseInfo[0].token = SQLF_DBTN_LOG_RETAIN;
DBaseInfo[0].ptrvalue = (char *) &LogRetain;
DBaseInfo[1].token = SQLF_DBTN_USER_EXIT;
DBaseInfo[1].ptrvalue = (char *) &UserExit;
sqlfudb("SAMPLE", 2, &DBaseInfo[0], &sqlca);

// Force All Applications Off The DB2 Database Manager Instance
sqlefrce(SQL_ALL_USERS, &AgentID, SQL_ASYNCH, &sqlca);

// Backup The SAMPLE Database
rc = Example.BackupDB();

// Connect To The SAMPLE Database
EXEC SQL CONNECT TO SAMPLE USER userID USING password;

// Build An Insert SQL Statement String
strcpy(InsertString, "INSERT INTO DEPARTMENT VALUES ( ");
strcat(InsertString, "'K50', 'TESTING', '000500', 'A00', ");
strcat(InsertString, "'NC')");

// Prepare The Insert SQL Statement
EXEC SQL PREPARE SQL_STMNT FROM :InsertString;
if (sqlca.sqlcode == SQL_RC_OK)
{
    // Execute The Insert Statement
    EXEC SQL EXECUTE SQL_STMNT;

    // Tell The User That The New Record Was Added
    if (sqlca.sqlcode == SQL_RC_OK)
    {
        cout << "Data has been added to the SAMPLE database.";
        cout << endl << endl;
    }
}

// Commit The Transaction
EXEC SQL COMMIT;

// Disconnect From The SAMPLE Database
EXEC SQL DISCONNECT CURRENT;
```

```
// Force All Applications Off The DB2 Database Manager Instance
sqlefrce(SQL_ALL_USERS, &AgentID, SQL_ASYNCH, &sqlca);

// Restore And Roll Forward The SAMPLE Database
rc = Example.RollforwardDB();

// Return To The Operating System
return(rc);
}
```

ASYNCHRONOUS READ LOG

Purpose   The ASYNCHRONOUS READ LOG function is used to query the Log Manager for current log state information and to extract specific records from a database's log files.

Syntax
```
SQL_API_RC  SQL_API_FN  sqlurlog  (unsigned long      CallerAction,
                                    SQLU_LSN           StartingLSN
                                    SQLU_LSN           EndingLSN,
                                    char               *LogBuffer,
                                    unsigned long      LogBufferSize,
                                    SQLU_RLOG_INFO     LogInfo,
                                    struct sqlca       *SQLCA);
```

Parameters *CallerAction*   Specifies the action this function is to take when it is executed. This parameter must be set to one of the following values:

■ SQLU_RLOG_QUERY
Query the Log Manager for current log state information.

■ SQLU_RLOG_READ
Read the database log, beginning at the starting log sequence number specified (*StartingLSN*) and continuing to the ending log sequence number specified (*EndingLSN*), and return all propagatable log records found within this range.

■ SQLU_RLOG_READ_SINGLE
Read a single record, which is identified by the starting log sequence number specified (*StartingLSN*).

StartingLSN   A pointer to a *SQLU_LSN* structure where a valid starting log sequence number is stored.

EndingLSN   A pointer to a *SQLU_LSN* structure where a valid ending log sequence number or ending relative byte address is stored.

LogBuffer   A pointer to a location in memory where all propagatable log records read from the database's recoverable log file are to be stored (sequentially).

LogBufferSize	The length of the memory storage buffer where this function is to store all log records retrieved (*LogBuffer*).
LogInfo	A pointer to a *SQLU_RLOG_INFO* structure where this function is to store current log state information.
SQLCA	A pointer to a location in memory where a SQL Communications Area (SQLCA) data structure variable is stored. This structure returns either status information (if the function executed successfully) or error information (if the function failed) to the calling application.

Includes

```
#include <sqlutil.h>
```

Description

The ASYNCHRONOUS READ LOG function is used to query the Log Manager for current log state information and to extract specific records from a database's log files.

To query the Log Manager for state information, an application calls this function with the *CallerAction* parameter set to SQLU_RLOG_QUERY. When this function executes, current active log information is returned in an *SQLU_RLOG_INFO* structure.

To extract specific records from a database's log files, an application calls this function with the *CallerAction* parameter set to SQLU_RLOG_READ or SQLU_RLOG_READ_SINGLE. When this function executes, one or more log records are returned in the user-allocated buffer pointed to by the *LogBuffer* parameter and current active log information is returned in an *SQLU_RLOG_INFO* structure.

Typically, an application will query the Log Manager to obtain a valid starting log sequence number, then it will use that number to read one or more records from the database log files.

The *SQLU_RLOG_INFO* structure is defined in *sqlutil.h* as follows:

```
typedef SQL_STRUCTURE SQLU_RLOG_INFO
{
SQLU_LSN        initialLSN;    /* The log sequence number of the first    */
                               /* log record written to the database      */
                               /* after the first connection was          */
                               /* established                             */
SQLU_LSN        firstReadLSN;  /* The log sequence number of the first    */
                               /* log record read                         */
SQLU_LSN        lastReadLSN;   /* The log sequence number of the log      */
                               /* record that corresponds to the last     */
                               /* byte read                               */
SQLU_LSN        curActiveLSN;  /* The log sequence number of the          */
                               /* current active log record               */
unsigned long logRecsWritten;  /* The number of log records written to    */
                               /* the user-allocated buffer (referenced   */
                               /* in the LogBuffer parameter)             */
unsigned long logBytesWritten; /* The number of bytes written to the      */
                               /* user-allocated buffer (referenced in    */
                               /* the LogBuffer parameter).               */
} SQLU_RLOG_INFO;
```

This structure contains four fields that use another structure, the *SQLU_LSN* structure to store log sequence numbers. The *SQLU_LSN* structure is defined in *sqlutil.h* as follows:

```
typedef union SQLU_LSN
{
unsigned char  lsnChar[6];    /* 6-byte character representation    */
unsigned short lsnWord[3];    /* 6-byte short integer representation */
} SQLU_LSN;
```

The structure of the actual log record information returned to the user-allocated buffer (referenced by the *LogBuffer* parameter) by this function is dependant upon the log record itself. Refer to Appendix B for more information about the structure of each log record that can be returned.

Comments
- The starting log sequence number specified in the *StartingLSN* parameter must correspond to the start of an actual log record.
- The ending log sequence number specified in the *EndingLSN* parameter can be one of the following:

  - The value of the *curActiveLSN* field of a *SQLU_RLOG_INFO* structure that was populated when the Log Manager was queried.

  - A value that is greater than the value of the *initialLSN* field of a *SQLU_RLOG_INFO* structure that was populated when the Log Manager was queried.

  - `0xFFFF  0xFFFF  0xFFFF` (which is interpreted as the end of the current log file)

- The ending log sequence number specified in the *EndingLSN* parameter must be greater than the starting log sequence number specified in the *StartingLSN* parameter.

- The buffer that this function is to store all propagatable log records read in (whose address is stored in the *LogBuffer* parameter) must be large enough to hold at least one log record. At a minimum, this buffer should be at least 32 bytes in length (the size of the log record header). Its maximum size is dependent upon the requested log sequence number range.

- Each log record returned in the log record buffer is prefixed by a six-byte log sequence number that is used to identify the log record itself.

- To read the next sequential log record in a file (after this function has been called once), add 1 to the log sequence number of the last log record returned and call this function again with this value specified as the new starting log sequence number (*StartingLSN*).

- If this function returns the SQL return code `SQLU_RLOG_READ_TO_CURRENT` (stored in the *sqlcode* field of the *sqlca* data structure), the log reader has read to the end of the current active log file.

- This function can only be used on databases that have roll-forward recovery

enabled (i.e the database configuration parameters *logretain* and/or *userexit* must
be enabled).

Connection   This function can only be called if a connection to a database exists.
Requirements

Authorization   Only users with System Administrator (SYSADM) authority or Database
                        Administrator (DBADM) are allowed to execute this function call.

See Also   ROLLFORWARD DATABASE

Example   The following C++ program illustrates how to use the ASYNCHRONOUS READ LOG
                        function to view a record stored in the SAMPLE database's recoverable log file:

```
/*─────────────────────────────────────────────────────────────*/
//* NAME:     CH10EX8.SQC                                        */
/* PURPOSE: Illustrate How To Use The Following DB2 API Function */
/*          In A C++ Program:                                    */
/*                                                               */
/*               ASYNCHRONOUS READ LOG                           */
/*                                                               */
/*─────────────────────────────────────────────────────────────*/
// Include The Appropriate Header Files
#include <windows.h>
#include <iostream.h>
#include <stdlib.h>
#include <sqlutil.h>
#include <sqlenv.h>
#include <sql.h>

// Define The API_Class Class
class API_Class
{
    // Attributes
    public:
        struct sqlca    sqlca;

    // Operations
    public:
        long BackupDB();
        long ReadLogFile();
};

// Define The BackupDB() Member Function
long API_Class::BackupDB()
{
    // Declare The Local Memory Variables
    struct sqlu_media_list    Media_List;
    struct sqlu_media_entry   Media_Entry;
    char                      ApplicationID[33];
    char                      TimeStamp[27];

    // Initialize The Media List Information Data Structure
    Media_List.media_type = SQLU_LOCAL_MEDIA;
```

```
      Media_List.sessions = 1;
      strcpy(Media_Entry.media_entry, "D:\\Backup");
      Media_List.target.media = &Media_Entry;

      // Tell The User That The Backup Process Is Being Started
      cout << "Starting Backup ..." << endl << endl;

      // Start Backing Up The SAMPLE Database
      sqlubkup("SAMPLE", 16, SQLUB_OFFLINE, SQLUB_FULL,
          SQLUB_BACKUP, ApplicationID, TimeStamp, 4, NULL,
          &Media_List, "userID", "password", NULL, 0, NULL,
          NULL, &sqlca);

      // If The Database Could Not Be Backed Up, Display An Error
      // Message And Terminate The Backup Process
      if (sqlca.sqlcode != SQL_RC_OK)
      {
          cout << "ERROR : " << sqlca.sqlcode << endl;
          sqlubkup ("SAMPLE", 16, SQLUB_OFFLINE, SQLUB_FULL,
              SQLUB_TERMINATE, ApplicationID, TimeStamp, 4,
              NULL, &Media_List, "userID", "password", NULL, 0,
              NULL, NULL, &sqlca);
      }

      // If The SAMPLE Database Was Successfully Backed Up, Display A
      // Message Saying So
      else
      {
          cout << "The SAMPLE database was successfully backed up.";
          cout << endl;
      }

      // Return The SQLCA Return Code To The Calling Function
      return(sqlca.sqlcode);
}

// Define The ReadLogFile() Member Function
long API_Class::ReadLogFile()
{
      // Declare The Local Memory Variables
      SQLU_LSN        StartLSN;
      SQLU_LSN        EndLSN;
      char            *LogBuffer;
      SQLU_RLOG_INFO  LogInfo;
      char            *BuffPtr;
      long            *LongVal;
      char            *CharVal;

      // Allocate Memory For The Log Record Buffer
      LogBuffer = new char[1024];
      BuffPtr = LogBuffer;

      // Query The Database Log To Obtain A Valid Starting Log Sequence
      // Number
```

```cpp
    sqlurlog(SQLU_RLOG_QUERY, &StartLSN, &EndLSN, LogBuffer,
        1024, &LogInfo, &sqlca);

    // If The Database Log Query Was Successful, Display The
    // Information Obtained
    if (sqlca.sqlcode == SQL_RC_OK)
    {
        // Initialize The Starting And Ending Log Sequence Numbers
        StartLSN.lsnWord[0] = LogInfo.initialLSN.lsnWord[0];
        StartLSN.lsnWord[1] = LogInfo.initialLSN.lsnWord[1];
        StartLSN.lsnWord[2] = LogInfo.initialLSN.lsnWord[2];

        EndLSN.lsnWord[0] = 0xFFFF;
        EndLSN.lsnWord[1] = 0xFFFF;
        EndLSN.lsnWord[2] = 0xFFFF;

        // Retrieve The First Record Stored In The Log File
        sqlurlog(SQLU_RLOG_READ_SINGLE, &StartLSN, &EndLSN, LogBuffer,
            1024, &LogInfo, &sqlca);

        // Print Information About The Record Retrieved
        BuffPtr += 6;
        LongVal = (long *) BuffPtr;
        cout << "Length of record : " << *LongVal << endl;
        BuffPtr += 4;
        CharVal = (char *) BuffPtr;
        cout << "Type of record   : " << CharVal << endl;
    }

    // Free Allocated Memory
    delete[] LogBuffer;

    // Return The SQLCA Return Code To The Calling Function
    return(sqlca.sqlcode);
}

/*------------------------------------------------------------------*/
/* The Main Function                                                */
/*------------------------------------------------------------------*/
int main()
{
    // Declare The Local Memory Variables
    long           rc = SQL_RC_OK;
    struct sqlfupd DBaseInfo[2];
    unsigned int   LogRetain = 1;
    unsigned int   UserExit = 1;
    struct sqlca   sqlca;

    // Declare The SQL Host Memory Variable
    EXEC SQL BEGIN DECLARE SECTION;
        char    InsertString[180];
    EXEC SQL END DECLARE SECTION;

    // Create An Instance Of The API_Class Class
```

```
API_Class   Example;

// Turn On Roll-Forward Recovery For The SAMPLE Database
DBaseInfo[0].token = SQLF_DBTN_LOG_RETAIN;
DBaseInfo[0].ptrvalue = (char *) &LogRetain;
DBaseInfo[1].token = SQLF_DBTN_USER_EXIT;
DBaseInfo[1].ptrvalue = (char *) &UserExit;
sqlfudb("SAMPLE", 2, &DBaseInfo[0], &sqlca);

// Backup The SAMPLE Database
rc = Example.BackupDB();

// Connect To The SAMPLE Database
EXEC SQL CONNECT TO SAMPLE USER userID USING password;

// Build An Insert SQL Statement String
strcpy(InsertString, "INSERT INTO DEPARTMENT VALUES ( ");
strcat(InsertString, "'K50', 'TESTING', '000500', 'A00', ");
strcat(InsertString, "'NC')");

// Prepare The Insert SQL Statement
EXEC SQL PREPARE SQL_STMNT FROM :InsertString;
if (sqlca.sqlcode == SQL_RC_OK)
{
    // Execute The Insert Statement
    EXEC SQL EXECUTE SQL_STMNT;

    // Tell The User That The New Record Was Added
    if (sqlca.sqlcode == SQL_RC_OK)
    {
        cout << "New data has been added to the SAMPLE database.";
        cout << endl << endl;
    }
}

// Commit The Transaction
EXEC SQL COMMIT;

// Retrieve And Display The First Record Found In The SAMPLE
// Database's Recoverable Log File
rc = Example.ReadLogFile();

// Disconnect From The SAMPLE Database
EXEC SQL DISCONNECT CURRENT;

// Return To The Operating System
return(rc);
}
```

OPEN RECOVERY HISTORY FILE SCAN

Purpose

The OPEN RECOVERY HISTORY FILE SCAN function is used to store a copy of selected records retrieved from a database recovery history file in memory and to return the number of records found in the recovery history file that meet specified selection criteria to the calling application.

Syntax

```
SQL_API_RC SQL_API_FN sqluhops (char           *DBAlias,
                                char           *TimeStamp,
                                char           *ObjectName,
                                unsigned short *NumEntries,
                                unsigned short *Handle,
                                unsigned short RecordType,
                                void           *Reserved,
                                struct sqlca   *SQLCA);
```

Parameters

DBAlias   A pointer to a location in memory where the alias name of a database is stored.

TimeStamp   A pointer to a location in memory where a string that specifies a time stamp that is to be used for selecting recovery history file records is stored. Records whose time stamp value is equal to or greater than the time stamp value specified are retrieved. This parameter can contain a NULL value.

ObjectName   A pointer to a location in memory where the table name or table space name that is to be used for selecting recovery history file records is stored. This parameter can contain a NULL value.

NumEntries   A pointer to a location in memory where this function is to store the number of records found in the recovery history file that match the selection criteria specified.

Handle   A pointer to a location in memory where this function is to store a recovery history file scan buffer identifier that is to be used in subsequent GET NEXT RECOVERY HISTORY FILE ENTRY and CLOSE RECOVERY HISTORY FILE SCAN function calls.

RecordType   Specifies which records in the recovery history file (that meet the selection criteria) are to be retrieved. This parameter must be set to one of the following values:

■ SQLUH_LIST_ADM_HISTORY
All records in the recovery history file that meet the selection criteria specified are to be retrieved.

■ SQLUH_LIST_ADM_BACKUP
Only backup and restore records that meet the selection criteria specified are to be retrieved.

■ SQLUH_LIST_ADM_ROLLFORWARD
Only roll forward database records that meet the selection criteria specified are to be retrieved.

■ SQLUH_LIST_ADM_RUNSTATS
Only run statistics (RUNSTATS) records that meet the selection criteria specified are to be retrieved.

■ SQLUH_LIST_ADM_REORG
Only reorganize table records that meet the selection criteria specified are to be retrieved.

■ SQLUH_LIST_ADM_ALTER_TABLESPACE
Only ALTER TABLESPACE records that meet the selection criteria specified are to be retrieved.

■ SQLUH_LIST_ADM_DROPPED_TABLE
Only DROP TABLE records that meet the selection criteria specified are to be retrieved.

■ SQLUH_LIST_ADM_LOAD
Only load records that meet the selection criteria specified are to be retrieved.

Reserved   A pointer that is currently reserved for later use. For now, this parameter must always be set to NULL.

SQLCA   A pointer to a location in memory where a SQL Communications Area (SQLCA) data structure variable is stored. This variable returns either status information (if the function executed successfully) or error information (if the function failed) to the calling application.

Includes   #include <sqlutil.h>

Description The OPEN RECOVERY HISTORY FILE SCAN function is used to store a copy of selected records retrieved from a database recovery history file in memory and to return the number of records found in the recovery history file that meet the selection criteria specified to the calling application. The copy of the recovery history file records placed in memory represents a snapshot of the recovery history file at the time the recovery history file scan is opened. This copy is never updated, even if the recovery history file itself changes.

This function is normally followed by one or more GET NEXT RECOVERY HISTORY FILE ENTRY functions calls and one CLOSE RECOVERY HISTORY FILE SCAN function call. Together, these three functions work like a SQL cursor (i.e., they use the OPEN/FETCH/CLOSE paradigm). The memory buffer that is used to store the recovery history file records obtained by the recovery history file scan is automatically allocated by DB2 and a pointer to that buffer (the buffer identifier) is stored in the *Handle* parameter. This identifier is then used by subsequent GET NEXT RECOVERY HISTORY FILE ENTRY and CLOSE RECOVERY HISTORY FILE SCAN function calls to access the information stored in memory buffer area.

Comments
■ The values specified in the *TimeStamp*, *ObjectName*, and *CallerAction* parameters are combined to define the selection criteria that filters the records in the recovery history file. Only records that meet the specified selection criteria are copied to the memory storage buffer.

■ If the *TimeStamp* parameter is set to NULL (or to the address of a local variable that contains the value 0), time stamp information will not be a part of the recovery history file record (entry) selection criteria.

■ If the *ObjectName* parameter is set to NULL (or to the address of a local variable that contains the value 0), the object name will not be a part of the recovery history file record (entry) selection criteria.

■ The filtering effect of the *ObjectName* parameter depends on the type of object name specified:

—If a table name is specified, only records for loads can be retrieved, because this is the only information kept for tables in the recovery history file.

—If a table space name is specified, all records can be retrieved.

■ If the *ObjectName* parameter refers to a database table name, the fully qualified table name must be specified.

■ If both the *TimeStamp* parameter and the *ObjectName* parameter are set to NULL and the *CallerAction* parameter is set to SQLU_LIST_HISTORY, every record found in the recovery history file will be copied to the memory storage buffer.

■ An application can have up to eight recovery history file scans open at one time.

Connection Requirements
This function can only be called if a connection to a DB2 Database Manager instance exists. In order to open a recovery history file scan for a database at another node, you must first attach to that node. If necessary, this function can establish a temporary attachment to a DB2 Database Manager instance while it is executing.

Authorization
No authorization is required to execute this function call.

See Also
GET NEXT RECOVERY HISTORY FILE ENTRY, CLOSE RECOVERY HISTORY FILE SCAN, UPDATE RECOVERY HISTORY FILE, PRUNE RECOVERY HISTORY FILE

Example
The following C++ program illustrates how the OPEN RECOVERY HISTORY FILE SCAN, GET NEXT RECOVERY HISTORY FILE ENTRY, and CLOSE RECOVERY HISTORY FILE SCAN functions are used to retrieve records from the SAMPLE database's recovery history file:

```
/*─────────────────────────────────────────────────────────── */
/* NAME:    CH10EX9.CPP                                         */
/* PURPOSE: Illustrate How To Use The Following DB2 API Functions */
/*          In A C++ Program:                                   */
/*                                                              */
/*              OPEN RECOVERY HISTORY FILE SCAN                 */
/*              GET NEXT RECOVERY HISTORY FILE ENTRY            */
```

```
/*                      CLOSE RECOVERY HISTORY FILE SCAN                      */
/*                                                                            */
/*--------------------------------------------------------------------------*/

// Include The Appropriate Header Files
#include <windows.h>
#include <iostream.h>
#include <sqlutil.h>
#include <sqlca.h>

// Define The API_Class Class
class API_Class
{
    // Attributes
    public:
        struct sqlca   sqlca;

    // Operations
    public:
        long ShowHistory();
};

// Define The ShowHistory() Member Function
long API_Class::ShowHistory()
{
    // Declare The Local Memory Variables
    unsigned short              Handle;
    short                       Size;
    unsigned short              NumRows;
    struct sqluhinfo            *HistoryInfo;
    struct sqluhadm             AdminInfo;

    // Open The Recovery History File Scan
    sqluhops("SAMPLE", NULL, NULL, &NumRows, &Handle,
        SQLUH_LIST_ADM_HISTORY, NULL, &sqlca);

    // Allocate Memory For A Recovery History File Record Using
    // The Three Default Table Spaces
    HistoryInfo = (struct sqluhinfo *) malloc (SQLUHINFOSIZE(3));
    HistoryInfo->sqln = 3;

    // Scan The Recovery History File Buffer And Retrieve The
    // Information Stored There
    if (sqlca.sqlcode == SQL_RC_OK)
    {
        cout << endl << "    Object                    Comment (Truncated)";
        cout << endl;
        cout << "-----------------------------------------";
        cout << "------------------------" << endl;
        for (;NumRows != 0; NumRows--)
        {
            // Retrieve The Next Recovery History File Entry
            sqluhget(Handle, SQLUH_GET_NEXT_ENTRY, 0, HistoryInfo,
                &AdminInfo, NULL, &sqlca);
```

```
                    // If The Memory Area Allocated For Recovery History File
                    // Records Was To Small, Reallocate It
                    if (sqlca.sqlcode == SQLUH_SQLUHINFO_VARS_WARNING)
                    {
                        Size = HistoryInfo->sqld;
                        free(HistoryInfo);
                        HistoryInfo = (struct sqluhinfo *)
                            malloc (SQLUHINFOSIZE(Size));
                        HistoryInfo->sqln = Size;
                        sqluhgne(Handle, NULL, HistoryInfo, &sqlca);
                    }

                    // Display The Recovery History File Entry Retrieved
                    if (sqlca.sqlcode == SQL_RC_OK)
                    {
                        cout.width(3);
                        cout.setf(ios::left);
                        cout << HistoryInfo->operation;
                        cout.width(20);
                        cout.setf(ios::left);
                        cout << HistoryInfo->object_part;
                        cout.width(30);
                        cout.setf(ios::left);
                        cout << HistoryInfo->comment << endl;
                    }
                }

            // Close The Recovery History File Scan And Free All
            // Resources Obtained By The Open Recovery History File
            // Scan API
            sqluhcls(Handle, NULL, &sqlca);
            free(HistoryInfo);
        }

    // Return The SQLCA Return Code To The Calling Function
    return(sqlca.sqlcode);
}

/*-----------------------------------------------------------------------*/
/* The Main Function                                                     */
/*-----------------------------------------------------------------------*/
int main()
{
    // Declare The Local Memory Variables
    long  rc = SQL_RC_OK;

    // Create An Instance Of The API_Class Class
    API_Class  Example;

    // Generate And Display Recovery History File Information
    rc = Example.ShowHistory();

    // Return To The Operating System
    return(rc);
}
```

GET NEXT RECOVERY HISTORY FILE ENTRY

Purpose   The GET NEXT RECOVERY HISTORY FILE ENTRY function is used to retrieve the next record from the copy of recovery history file records that was placed in memory by the OPEN RECOVERY HISTORY FILE SCAN function.

Syntax
```
SQL_API_RC SQL_API_FN sqluhget (unsigned short    Handle,
                                unsigned short    EntryType,
                                unsigned long     Reserved1,
                                struct sqluhinfo  *HistoryInfo,
                                struct sqluhadm   *AdminInfo,
                                void              *Reserved2,
                                struct sqlca      *SQLCA);
```

Parameters   *Handle*   The recovery history file scan buffer identifier that was returned by an associated OPEN RECOVERY HISTORY FILE SCAN function call.

EntryType   Specifies the type of recovery history file entry to retrieve. This parameter must be set to one of the following values:

■ SQLUH_GET_NEXT_ENTRY
Retrieve the next matching entry in the recovery history file.

■ SQLUH_GET_DDL
Retrieve the DDL data associated with the last matching entry retrieved from the recovery history file.

Reserved1   A pointer that is currently reserved for later use. For now, this parameter must always be set to NULL.

HistoryInfo   A pointer to a *sqluhinfo* structure where this function is to store the recovery history file entry (record) information retrieved.

AdminInfo   A pointer to a *sqluhadm* structure where this function is to store administration information associated with the recovery history file entry (record) retrieved.

Reserved2   A pointer that is currently reserved for later use. For now, this parameter must always be set to NULL.

SQLCA   A pointer to a location in memory where a SQL Communications Area (SQLCA) data structure variable is stored. This variable returns either status information (if the function executed successfully) or error information (if the function failed) to the calling application.

Includes   `#include <sqlutil.h>`

Description   The GET NEXT RECOVERY HISTORY FILE ENTRY function is used to retrieve the next record from the copy of recovery history file records that was placed in memory by the OPEN RECOVERY HISTORY FILE SCAN function. The information retrieved is stored in two special structures: *sqluhinfo* and *sqluhadm*. The first of these structures, *sqluhinfo*, is defined in *sqlutil.h* as follows:

```
struct sqluhinfo
{
        char      sqluhinfoid[8];     /* A structure identifier and      */
                                      /* eye-catcher for storage dumps. It */
                                      /* is a string of eight bytes that must */
                                      /* be initialized with the value   */
                                      /* "SQLUHINF" or "SQLUHADM".         */
        long      sqluhinfobc;        /* The size of the sqluhinfo structure */
        short     sqln;               /* The total number of table space  */
                                      /* elements referenced              */
        short     sqld;               /* The total number of table space  */
                                      /* elements used                    */
        char      operation[2];       /* Indicates whether the recovery   */
                                      /* operation is a backup operation  */
                                      /* (B), a restore operation (R), a  */
                                      /* load operation (L), or a drop table */
                                      /* operation (D),                   */
                                      /* a roll-forward operation (F),    */
                                      /* a reorganize table operation, (G), */
                                      /* a run statistics operation (S),  */
                                      /* or an alter tablespace operation (T). */
        char      object[2];          /* Indicates whether the recovery   */
                                      /* operation is a full operation (D), */
                                      /* a table space operation (P), or a */
                                      /* table operation (T). This field  */
                                      /* specifies the granularity used in the */
                                      /* recovery operation.              */
        char      object_part[18];    /* The recovery history file record */
                                      /* identifier. The first 14 characters */
                                      /* of this identifier are a time stamp */
                                      /* value (with the format           */
                                      /* yyyymmddhhnnss) that indicates   */
                                      /* when the operation was performed. */
                                      /* The last three characters of this */
                                      /* identifier are a unique operation */
                                      /* sequence number.                 */
        char      optype[2];          /* Specifies additional qualification */
                                      /* information about the operation. */
                                      /* If the operation was a full level */
                                      /* database or table space backup,  */
                                      /* F indicates offline backup and   */
                                      /* N indicates online backup. If    */
                                      /* the operation was a load         */
                                      /* operation, R indicates replace, A */
                                      /* indicates append, and C indicates */
                                      /* copy. For all other operations, this */
                                      /* field is left blank.             */
        char      device_type[2];     /* Indicates how information in the */
                                      /* location field is to be interpreted. */
                                      /* Information in this field can be */
                                      /* interpreted to mean a disk (D), a */
```

```
                                    /* diskette (K), a tape (T), an        */
                                    /* ADSTAR distributed storage          */
                                    /* manager (A), a user exit routine    */
                                    /* (U), or something else (O).         */
char        first_log[13];          /* The most recent log file ID used    */
                                    /* Values for this field range from    */
                                    /* S0000000 to S9999999.                */
char        last_log[13];           /* The latest log file ID used. Values  */
                                    /* for this field range from S0000000   */
                                    /* to S9999999.                         */
char        backup_id[15];          /* A time stamp value with the          */
                                    /* format yyyymmddhhnnss that           */
                                    /* refers to one or more file entries    */
                                    /* that represent backup operations.    */
                                    /* For a full database restore, the     */
                                    /* value stored in this field refers to  */
                                    /* the full database backup image       */
                                    /* that was restored. For a table        */
                                    /* space restore, the value in this      */
                                    /* field refers to the table space       */
                                    /* backup image or the full              */
                                    /* database backup image that was        */
                                    /* used to restore the specified table   */
                                    /* spaces. For any other operation,      */
                                    /* this field is left blank.             */
char        table_creator[9]        /* The authorization ID of the user     */
                                    /* who created the table. This field is  */
                                    /* only filled in for load operations.   */
char        table_name[19];         /* The name of the table. This field is  */
                                    /* only filled in for load operations.   */
char        num_of_tablespaces[6];
                                    /* The number of table spaces           */
                                    /* involved in a backup or restore       */
                                    /* operation                             */
char        location[256];          /* For backups and copies for            */
                                    /* loads, this field indicates where the */
                                    /* data has been saved. For backup       */
                                    /* entries in the file, this field        */
                                    /* contains the sequence number          */
                                    /* that identifies which part            */
                                    /* of the backup is found in the         */
                                    /* specified location. For restore and    */
                                    /* load operations, the field identifies  */
                                    /* where the first part of the data       */
                                    /* restored or loaded (sequence           */
                                    /* number 001) has been saved.            */
                                    /* Otherwise, the value stored in this     */
                                    /* field contains different information,   */
                                    /* depending on the value stored in       */
                                    /* the device_type field. For disk or     */
                                    /* diskette (D or K) values, this field    */
                                    /* contains a fully qualified filename;   */
                                    /* for tape (T) values, this field         */
                                    /* contains a volume label; for           */
```

```
                               /* ADSM (A) values, this field        */
                               /* contains the server name; and      */
                               /* for user exit or other (U or O)    */
                               /* values, this field contains free-  */
                               /* form text.                         */
char        comment[31];       /* A free-form comment that           */
                               /* describes the recovery history file */
                               /* record (entry).                    */
char        filler;            /* Reserved; Used to define the size  */
                               /* of this structure.                 */
struct sqluhtsp tablespace[1];
                               /* An array of sqluhtsp structures     */
                               /* that contain the table space names  */
                               /* that are associated with the       */
                               /* recovery operation.                */
};
```

This structure contains an array of *sqluhtsp* structures that are used to store table space name information. The *sqluhtsp* structure is defined in *sqlutil.h* as follows:

```
struct sqluhtsp
{
char        tablespace_name[19]; /* The name of a table space        */
char        filler;            /* Reserved; Used to define the size of */
                               /* this structure.                    */
};
```

The second structure used by this function, the *sqluhadm* structure, is defined in *sqlutil.h* as follows:

```
SQL_STRUCTURE sqluhadm
{
char             end_time[15]; /* A time stamp value (with the format */
                               /* yyyymmddhhnnss) that identifies when the */
                               /* operation was completed            */
char             id[25];       /* Unique object identifier for a dropped */
                               /* table                              */
struct sqlca     event_sqlca;  /* SQLCA results for the operation    */
struct sqlchar   command;      /* Command text for the operation     */
};
```

Comments   ■ The recovery history file records that reside in memory are selected from a recovery history file based upon the selection criteria specified when the OPEN RECOVERY HISTORY FILE SCAN function was executed.

■ When this function is executed, the value in the *HistoryInfo* parameter points to the next recovery history file record in the copy of recovery history file records that reside in memory. Each subsequent GET NEXT RECOVERY HISTORY FILE ENTRY function call obtains the recovery history file record immediately following the current recovery history file record, unless there are no more records to retrieve (in which case, an error is returned).

■ If this function is called with the *EntryType* parameter set to SQLUH_GET_DDL immediately after a recovery history file entry (record) has been retrieved, the DDL data associated with that entry will be returned. Currently, only dropped table events contain DDL information that can be retrieved by this function. If this function is called with the *EntryType* parameter set to SQLUH_GET_DDL after any other type of record has been retrieved, no additional data will be returned.

■ You can use the value stored in the *NumEntries* parameter after the OPEN RECOVERY HISTORY FILE SCAN function is executed to set up a loop that scans through all of the recovery history file records by issuing GET NEXT RECOVERY HISTORY FILE ENTRY function calls, one at a time, until the number of calls issued equals the number of records copied from the recovery history file.

■ Each backup operation can produce multiple records in a recovery history file (when the backup image is saved in multiple files or on multiple tapes). The sequence number used in the recovery history file record identifier (returned in the *object_part* field of the *sqluhinfo* structure) enables you to specify multiple locations during a backup operation. Because restore and load operations produce only one record in a recovery history file, the sequence number 001 is always used for these types of operations.

■ The value stored in the *first_log* field of the *sqluhinfo* structure is:

—Required to apply roll-forward recovery for an online backup.

—Required to apply roll-forward recovery for an offline backup.

—Applied after restoring a full database or table space level backup that was current when the load operation started.

■ The value stored in the *last_log* field of the *sqluhinfo* structure is:

—Required to apply roll-forward recovery for an online backup.

—Required to apply roll-forward recovery to the current point in time for an offline backup.

—Applied after restoring a full database or table space level backup that was current when the load finished (this value will be the same as the *first_log* value if roll-forward recovery is not applied).

■ Each table space backup image can contain one or more table spaces, and each table space restore operation replaces one or more table spaces. If the *num_of_tablespaces* field of the *sqluhinfo* structure is not zero (indicating a table space level backup or restore operation), subsequent records in the recovery history file will contain the name(s) of the table space(s) backed up or restored, (represented by an 18-character string). One record is written to the recovery history file for each table space contained in the backup image.

Prerequisites   The OPEN RECOVERY HISTORY FILE SCAN function must be executed before this function is called.

Connection Requirements This function can only be called if a connection to a DB2 Database Manager instance exists. If necessary, this function will establish a temporary attachment to a DB2 Database Manager instance while it is executing.

Authorization No authorization is required to execute this function call.

See Also OPEN RECOVERY HISTORY FILE SCAN, CLOSE RECOVERY HISTORY FILE SCAN, UPDATE RECOVERY HISTORY FILE, PRUNE RECOVERY HISTORY FILE

Example See the example provided for the OPEN RECOVERY HISTORY FILE SCAN function on page 396.

■ ■ CLOSE RECOVERY HISTORY FILE SCAN

Purpose The CLOSE RECOVERY HISTORY FILE SCAN function is used to free system resources that were allocated by the OPEN RECOVERY HISTORY FILE SCAN function.

Syntax
```
SQL_API_RC SQL_API_FN sqluhcls (unsigned short   Handle,
                                void             *Reserved,
                                struct sqlca     *SQLCA);
```

Parameters *Handle* The recovery history file scan buffer identifier that was returned by an associated OPEN RECOVERY HISTORY FILE SCAN function call.

Reserved A pointer that is currently reserved for later use. For now, this parameter must always be set to NULL.

SQLCA A pointer to a location in memory where a SQL Communications Area (SQLCA) data structure variable is stored. This variable returns either status information (if the function executed successfully) or error information (if the function failed) to the calling application.

Includes `#include <sqlutil.h>`

Description The CLOSE RECOVERY HISTORY FILE SCAN function is used to free system resources that were allocated by the OPEN RECOVERY HISTORY FILE SCAN function.

Connection Requirements This function can only be called if a connection to a DB2 Database Manager instance exists. If necessary, this function will establish a temporary attachment to a DB2 Database Manager instance while it is executing.

Authorization No authorization is required to execute this function call.

See Also OPEN RECOVERY HISTORY FILE SCAN, GET NEXT RECOVERY HISTORY FILE ENTRY, UPDATE RECOVERY HISTORY FILE, PRUNE RECOVERY HISTORY FILE

Example   See the example provided for the OPEN RECOVERY HISTORY FILE SCAN function on
                     page 396.

■ ■ UPDATE RECOVERY HISTORY FILE

Purpose   The UPDATE RECOVERY HISTORY FILE function is used to change the location, device
                     type, or comment associated with a record in a database's recovery history file.

Syntax
```
SQL_API_RC SQL_API_FN sqluhupd (char          *RHFEntryID,
                                char           *NewLocation,
                                char           *NewDeviceType,
                                char           *NewComment,
                                void           *Reserved,
                                struct sqlca   *SQLCA);
```

Parameters   *RHFEntryID*   A pointer to a location in memory where the identifier for the
                                   backup, restore, or load copy recovery history file record to update is
                                   stored. This identifier has the form of a time stamp, followed by a
                                   sequence number ranging from 001 to 999.

                 NewLocation   A pointer to a location in memory where the new location for the
                                   backup, restore, or load copy image associated with a specific
                                   recovery history file record is stored. This parameter can contain a
                                   NULL value.

                 NewDeviceType   A pointer to a location in memory where a new device type for
                                   storing the backup, restore, or load copy image associated with a
                                   specific recovery history file record is stored. This parameter can
                                   contain a NULL value.

                 NewComment   A pointer to a location in memory where a new comment describing
                                   a specific recovery history file record is stored. This parameter can
                                   contain a NULL value.

                 Reserved   A pointer that is currently reserved for later use. For now, this
                                   parameter must always be set to NULL.

                 SQLCA   A pointer to a location in memory where a SQL Communications
                                   Area (SQLCA) data structure variable is stored. This variable
                                   returns either status information (if the function executed
                                   successfully) or error information (if the function failed) to the
                                   calling application.

Includes   `#include <sqlutil.h>`

Description   The UPDATE RECOVERY HISTORY FILE function is used to change the location, device
                     type, or comment associated with a record in a database's recovery history file. When
                     a record in a recovery history file is updated, all information associated with the

record that existed prior to the update operation is replaced with the new information. Unfortunately, all original information is lost, because changes made to the recovery history file are not written to the transaction log.

The recovery history file is only used for activity recording purposes and is not used directly by the RESTORE DATABASE or ROLL FORWARD DATABASE functions. During a restore operation, you can specify the location of the backup image of a database and use the recovery history file to keep track of this location. You can then provide this location information to additional BACKUP DATABASE function calls, so other backup images are stored in the same location.

Comments   ■ If the *NewLocation* parameter is set to NULL (or to the address of a local variable that contains the value 0), the location information for the recovery history file record will remain unchanged.

■ If the *NewDeviceType* parameter is set to NULL (or to the address of a local variable that contains the value 0), the device type information for the recovery history file record will remain unchanged.

■ If the *NewComment* parameter is set to NULL (or to the address of a local variable that contains the value 0), the comment that describes the recovery history file record will remain unchanged.

■ If the location of a load copy image is moved, subsequent roll-forward recovery operations must be informed of the new location and storage media.

Connection Requirements   This function can only be called if a database connection exists. In order to update records in the recovery history file for a database other than the default database, an application must first establish a connection to that database before this function is called.

Authorization   Only users with System Administrator (SYSADM), System Control (SYSCTRL), System Maintenance (SYSMAINT), or Database Administrator (DBADM) authority can execute this function call.

See Also   OPEN RECOVERY HISTORY FILE SCAN, GET NEXT RECOVERY HISTORY FILE ENTRY, CLOSE RECOVERY HISTORY FILE SCAN, PRUNE RECOVERY HISTORY FILE

Example   The following C++ program illustrates how to use the UPDATE RECOVERY HISTORY FILE function to change the comment associated with a record stored in the SAMPLE database's recovery history file:

```
/*————————————————————————————————————————————*/
/* NAME:    CH10EX10.SQC                                      */
/* PURPOSE: Illustrate How To Use The Following DB2 API Function  */
/*          In A C++ Program:                                 */
/*                                                            */
/*               UPDATE RECOVERY HISTORY FILE                 */
/*                                                            */
/*————————————————————————————————————————————*/

// Include The Appropriate Header Files
```

```
#include <windows.h>
#include <iostream.h>
#include <sqlutil.h>
#include <sql.h>

// Define The API_Class Class
class API_Class
{
    // Attributes
    public:
        struct sqlca    sqlca;

    // Operations
    public:
        long ShowHistory();
};

// Define The ShowHistory() Member Function
long API_Class::ShowHistory()
{
    // Declare The Local Memory Variables
    unsigned short      Handle;
    short               Size;
    unsigned short      NumRows;
    struct sqluhinfo    *HistoryInfo;

    // Open The Recovery History File Scan
    sqluhops("SAMPLE", NULL, NULL, &NumRows, &Handle,
        SQLUH_LIST_ADM_HISTORY, NULL, &sqlca);

    // Allocate Memory For A Recovery History File Record Using
    // The Three Default Table Spaces
    HistoryInfo = (struct sqluhinfo *) malloc (SQLUHINFOSIZE(3));
    HistoryInfo->sqln = 3;

    // Scan The Recovery History File Buffer And Retrieve The
    // Information Stored There
    if (sqlca.sqlcode == SQL_RC_OK)
    {
        cout << endl << "    Object                 Comment (Truncated)";
        cout << endl;
        cout << "————————————————————————————";
        cout << "——————————————————" << endl;
        for (;NumRows != 0; NumRows—)
        {
            // Retrieve The Next Recovery History File Entry
            sqluhgne(Handle, NULL, HistoryInfo, &sqlca);

            // If The Memory Area Allocated For Recovery History File
            // Records Was To Small, Reallocate It
            if (sqlca.sqlcode == SQLUH_SQLUHINFO_VARS_WARNING)
            {
```

```
                    Size = HistoryInfo->sqld;
                    free(HistoryInfo);
                    HistoryInfo = (struct sqluhinfo *)
                        malloc (SQLUHINFOSIZE(Size));
                    HistoryInfo->sqln = Size;
                    sqluhgne(Handle, NULL, HistoryInfo, &sqlca);
                }

                // Display The Recovery History File Entry Retrieved
                if (sqlca.sqlcode == SQL_RC_OK)
                {
                    cout.width(3);
                    cout.setf(ios::left);
                    cout << HistoryInfo->operation;
                    cout.width(20);
                    cout.setf(ios::left);
                    cout << HistoryInfo->object_part;
                    cout.width(30);
                    cout.setf(ios::left);
                    cout << HistoryInfo->comment << endl;
                }
            }

            // Close The Recovery History File Scan And Free All
            // Resources Obtained By The Open Recovery History File
            // Scan API
            sqluhcls(Handle, NULL, &sqlca);
            free(HistoryInfo);
        }

        // Return The SQLCA Return Code To The Calling Function
        return(sqlca.sqlcode);
}

/*-------------------------------------------------------------------*/
/* The Main Function                                                 */
/*-------------------------------------------------------------------*/
int main()
{
    // Declare The Local Memory Variables
    long           rc = SQL_RC_OK;
    struct sqlca   sqlca;

    // Create An Instance Of The API_Class Class
    API_Class  Example;

    // Attempt To Connect To The SAMPLE Database
    EXEC SQL CONNECT TO SAMPLE USER userID USING password;

    // Display The Contents Of The Recovery History File
    rc = Example.ShowHistory();
```

```
                // Change The Comment Associated With The Recovery History
                // File Entry For The Last Backup Operation
                sqluhupd("19990204130435001", NULL, NULL, "Last Backup",
                         NULL, &sqlca);

                // Display The Contents Of The Recovery History File Again
                // To See The Change
                rc = Example.ShowHistory();

                // Issue A Rollback To Free All Locks
                EXEC SQL ROLLBACK;

                // Disconnect From The SAMPLE Database
                EXEC SQL DISCONNECT CURRENT;

                // Return To The Operating System
                return(rc);
          }408
```

■ ■ ■ PRUNE RECOVERY HISTORY FILE

Purpose   The PRUNE RECOVERY HISTORY FILE function is used to remove one or more records from a database's recovery history file.

Syntax
```
SQL_API_RC SQL_API_FN sqluhprn (char            *TimeStamp,
                                unsigned short  ForceOption,
                                void            *Reserved,
                                struct sqlca    *SQLCA);
```

Parameters   *TimeStamp*   A pointer to a location in memory that contains a string that specifies a time stamp that is to be used for selecting recovery history file records that are to be deleted. Records whose time stamp value is equal to or greater than the time stamp value specified are deleted. This parameter can contain a NULL value.

ForceOption   Specifies whether or not history file records for the most recent full backup and its corresponding restore set should be kept. A restore set includes all table space backups and load copies taken since the last (most recent) full database backup operation was performed. This parameter must be set to one of the following values:

■ SQLUH_NO_FORCE
All recent restore set records are to be kept, even if the time stamp is less than or equal to the time stamp specified.

■ SQLUH_FORCE
All records in the recovery history file are to be pruned according to the time stamp specified. Recent restore set records with time stamps less than or equal to the time stamp specified are to be deleted from the file.

Reserved	A pointer that is currently reserved for later use. For now, this parameter must always be set to NULL.
SQLCA	A pointer to a location in memory where a SQL Communications Area (SQLCA) data structure variable is stored. This variable returns either status information (if the function executed successfully) or error information (if the function failed) to the calling application.

Includes

```
#include <sqlutil.h>
```

Description

The PRUNE RECOVERY HISTORY FILE function is used to remove one or more records from a database's recovery history file. When records in a recovery history file are deleted, the actual backup images and load copy files that the records refer to remain untouched. The application that calls this function must manually delete these files to free up the disk storage space they consume.

Comments

■ If the latest full database backup records need to be pruned from a recovery history file (and their corresponding files need to be deleted from the media (disk storage) where they are stored), the user must ensure that all table spaces, including the system catalog table space and all user table spaces on which the database resides, are backed up first. Failure to back up these table spaces may result in a database that cannot be recovered or the loss of some portion of user data previously stored in the database.

Connection Requirements

This function can only be called if a database connection exists. In order to delete records in the recovery history file for a database other than the default database, an application must first establish a connection to that database before calling this function is called.

Authorization

Only users with System Administrator (SYSADM) authority, System Control (SYSCTRL) authority, System Maintenance (SYSMAINT) authority, or Database Administrator (DBADM) authority are allowed to execute this function call.

See Also

OPEN RECOVERY HISTORY FILE SCAN, GET NEXT RECOVERY HISTORY FILE ENTRY, CLOSE RECOVERY HISTORY FILE SCAN, UPDATE RECOVERY HISTORY FILE

Example

The following C++ program illustrates how to use the PRUNE RECOVERY HISTORY FILE function to remove records from the SAMPLE database's recovery history file:

```
/*-----------------------------------------------------------------*/
/* NAME:    CH10EX11.SQC                                           */
/* PURPOSE: Illustrate How To Use The Following DB2 API Function   */
/*          In A C++ Program:                                      */
/*                                                                 */
/*              PRUNE RECOVERY HISTORY FILE                        */
/*                                                                 */
/*-----------------------------------------------------------------*/

// Include The Appropriate Header Files
```

```
#include <windows.h>
#include <iostream.h>
#include <sqlutil.h>
#include <sql.h>

// Define The API_Class Class
class API_Class
{
    // Attributes
    public:
        struct sqlca  sqlca;

    // Operations
    public:
        long ShowHistory();
};

// Define The ShowHistory() Member Function
long API_Class::ShowHistory()
{
    // Declare The Local Memory Variables
    unsigned short      Handle;
    short               Size;
    unsigned short      NumRows;
    struct sqluhinfo    *HistoryInfo;

    // Open The Recovery History File Scan
    sqluhops("SAMPLE", NULL, NULL, &NumRows, &Handle,
            SQLUH_LIST_ADM_HISTORY, NULL, &sqlca);

    // Allocate Memory For A Recovery History File Record Using
    // The Three Default Table Spaces
    HistoryInfo = (struct sqluhinfo *) malloc (SQLUHINFOSIZE(3));
    HistoryInfo->sqln = 3;

    // Scan The Recovery History File Buffer And Retrieve The
    // Information Stored There
    if (sqlca.sqlcode == SQL_RC_OK)
    {
        cout << endl << "    Object                  Comment (Truncated)";
        cout << endl;
        cout << "—————————————————————————————";
        cout << "———————————————————" << endl;
        for (;NumRows != 0; NumRows—)
        {
            // Retrieve The Next Recovery History File Entry
            sqluhgne(Handle, NULL, HistoryInfo, &sqlca);

            // If The Memory Area Allocated For Recovery History File
            // Records Was To Small, Reallocate It
            if (sqlca.sqlcode == SQLUH_SQLUHINFO_VARS_WARNING)
            {
```

```
            Size = HistoryInfo->sqld;
            free(HistoryInfo);
            HistoryInfo = (struct sqluhinfo *)
                malloc (SQLUHINFOSIZE(Size));
            HistoryInfo->sqln = Size;
            sqluhgne(Handle, NULL, HistoryInfo, &sqlca);
        }

        // Display The Recovery History File Entry Retrieved
        if (sqlca.sqlcode == SQL_RC_OK)
        {
            cout.width(3);
            cout.setf(ios::left);
            cout << HistoryInfo->operation;
            cout.width(20);
            cout.setf(ios::left);
            cout << HistoryInfo->object_part;
            cout.width(30);
            cout.setf(ios::left);
            cout << HistoryInfo->comment << endl;
        }
    }

    // Close The Recovery History File Scan And Free All
    // Resources Obtained By The Open Recovery History File
    // Scan API
    sqluhcls(Handle, NULL, &sqlca);
    free(HistoryInfo);
    }

    // Return The SQLCA Return Code To The Calling Function
    return(sqlca.sqlcode);
}

/*------------------------------------------------------------*/
/* The Main Function                                          */
/*------------------------------------------------------------*/
int main()
{
    // Declare The Local Memory Variables
    long        rc = SQL_RC_OK;
    char        Timestamp[SQLU_TIME_STAMP_LEN + 1];
    struct sqlca sqlca;

    // Create An Instance Of The API_Class Class
    API_Class  Example;

    // Attempt To Connect To The SAMPLE Database
    EXEC SQL CONNECT TO SAMPLE USER userID USING password;

    // Display The Contents Of The Recovery History File
    rc = Example.ShowHistory();
```

```
// Delete All Entries In The Recovery History File
strcpy(Timestamp, "19990204130435");
sqluhprn(Timestamp, SQLUH_FORCE, NULL, &sqlca);

// Display The Contents Of The Recovery History File Again
// To See The Change
rc = Example.ShowHistory();

// Issue A Rollback To Free All Locks
EXEC SQL ROLLBACK;

// Disconnect From The SAMPLE Database
EXEC SQL DISCONNECT CURRENT;

// Return To The Operating System
return(rc);
}
```

Data Handling APIs

Although a database is normally a self-contained entity, there are times when it is necessary for a database to exchange data with the outside world. This chapter is designed to introduce you to the set of DB2 API functions that are used to move data between a DB2 database and external files. The first part of this chapter describes how data can be copied from a DB2 database to an external file. Then, information about the various methods of moving data stored in external files into database tables is provided. Finally, a detailed reference section covering each DB2 API function that can be used to transfer data between databases and external files is provided.

Exporting Data

There are times when you need to make some or all of a database's data available to the outside world. On these occasions, an application can make select portions of database data available to other applications by calling the EXPORT function (which, in turn, invokes the Export facility). The EXPORT function can:

- Copy the contents of a table, along with its indexes, to an external file (using a format that other DB2 products can access).
- Make a backup copy of a database table.
- Copy select data to an external file and put the data in a format that other applications recognize.

A SELECT SQL statement is used to identify the data that is to be exported. When large object (LOB) columns are included in this SELECT statement, the first 32KB of data are written to the file by default. However, by specifying different values in one of the EXPORT function's input parameters, you can store LOB data, in its entirety, in different external files.

Importing Data

Just as there may be times that you need to export data to an external file, occasionally you may need to make data stored in an external file available to a DB2 database. An application can make data in an external file available to a database by calling the IMPORT function (which invokes the Import facility) or by calling the LOAD function (which invokes the Load facility). The IMPORT function can:

- Create a table, along with its indexes, from an external data file (provided the file is stored in a format that DB2 products can access).
- Restore a database table from a backup copy made by the Export facility.
- Copy data from an external data file produced by another application into a database table.

When data is imported, if the table or updateable view receiving the data already contains data, the new data can either replace or be appended to the existing data—as long as the base table receiving the data does not contain a primary key that is referenced by a foreign key of another table. (If the base table contains a primary key that is referenced by a foreign key, imported data can only be appended to the existing table.) LOB data can reside either in the file being imported or in a separate external file that is referenced by the imported file. If LOB data resides in external files, DB2 expects there to be a separate file for each LOB data value needed.

The import facility can also create new tables from the external file being imported, provided that the file was created by another DB2 product, using the DB2 product standard file format.

 # Loading Data

The Load facility works similarly to the Import facility, but some functional differences do exist. These differences are outlined in Table 11–1.

Table 11–1   Differences Between IMPORT and LOAD

IMPORT	LOAD
Significantly slower than **LOAD** on large amounts of data.	Significantly faster than **IMPORT** on large amounts of data.
Tables, hierarchies, and indexes can be created from IXF format files.	Tables and indexes must exist before data can be loaded into them.
Files formatted in Work Sheet Format (WSF) are supported.	Files formatted in WSF are not supported.
Data can be imported into tables and views (aliases are supported).	Data can only be loaded into tables (aliases are not supported).
Table spaces in which the table and its indexes reside remain online during an Import operation.	Table spaces in which the table and its indexes reside are taken offline during a Load operation.
All row transactions are written to the log file.	Minimal logging is performed.
Triggers can be fired during the import process.	Triggers are not supported.
If an Import operation is interrupted and a commit frequency value is specified, the table will remain usable and will contain all rows that were inserted up to the last commit operation. The user can restart the Import operation or leave the table as it is.	If a Load operation is interrupted and a consistency point (commit frequency) value is specified, the table remains in a "Load Pending" state and cannot be used until either the load process is restarted in order to continue the Load operation or the table space in which the table resides is restored from a backup image that was created before the Load operation was started.
The amount of free disk space needed to import data is approximately the size of the largest index being imported, plus about 10 percent. This space is allocated from the temporary table spaces defined for the database.	The amount of free disk space needed to load data is approximately as large as the sum of all indexes for the database. This space is temporarily allocated outside the database.
All constraint checking is performed during an Import operation.	Only uniqueness checking is performed during a Load operation. All other constraint checking must be performed after the load operation has completed (with the **SET CONSTRAINTS** SQL statement).
The keys of each row are inserted into the appropriate index during an Import operation.	All keys are sorted during a Load operation, and the indexes are rebuilt when the Load operation is complete.
The **RUN STATISTICS** function or command must be executed after an Import operation, so the statistics for the affected table are updated.	Statistics are collected and updated during a Load operation.
Data can be imported into a host database through DB2 Connect.	Data cannot be loaded into a host database.

Table 11–1   Differences Between IMPORT and LOAD (Continued)

IMPORT	LOAD
Data files to be imported must reside on the same workstation from which the Import facility is invoked.	Data files and named pipes to be loaded must reside on the same workstation on which the database receiving the data resides.
A backup image is not created during an Import operation.	A backup image can be created during a Load operation.
The Import utility makes limited use of intra-partition parallelism.	The Load utility takes full advantage of intra-partition parallelism on symmetric multiprocessor (SMP) machines.
Full referential integrity checking and constraints checking is performed on user-supplied data.	Referential integrity checking and constraints checking on user-supplied data can be reduced.
Data conversion between code pages is not performed during an Import operation.	Character data (and numeric data expressed in characters) can be converted from one code page to another during a Load operation.
Hierarchical data is supported.	Hierarchical data is not supported.
Numeric data to be imported must be stored as character representations.	Numeric data (other than DECIMAL) can be stored and loaded in either binary form or as character representations.
Decimal data to be imported must be stored as character representations.	Decimal data can be stored and loaded in either packed-decimal form or as character representations.

Adapted from IBM's *DB2 Universal Database Administration Guide*, pp. 247–248

The Load facility is intended to be used for an initial load of a base table when large amounts of data need to be moved. The Load facility is significantly faster than the Import facility, because it writes formatted data pages directly to the database, as opposed to executing multiple INSERT SQL statements. The Load facility also eliminates almost all transaction logging that is normally associated with the loading of data. Instead of logging transactions, the Load facility optionally stores a copy of the data being loaded in an external file. The load process consists of three separate phases:

Load   Data is written to the table.

Build   Indexes are created for the table.

Delete   Any data that caused a unique key violation is removed from the table.

During the Load phase, data is loaded into the specified database table, then index key and table statistics information is collected. Save points (also known as points of consistency) are established when the Load process is started and a specified number of rows are committed as data is loaded. If a failure occurs during the Load phase, you can skip the number of rows that were successfully committed at the last save point when the load process is restarted.

During the Build phase, indexes are created based on the index key information that was collected during the Load phase. Index keys are automatically sorted during the

Load phase, and index statistics are collected. If a failure occurs during the Build phase, it is restarted from when the Load operation is restarted. Rows containing values that cause unique key violations to occur are placed in an exception table (if one is specified), and messages about the rows are written to a message file, so they can be manually corrected after the Load process has completed.

During the Delete phase, all rows containing values that caused unique key violations to occur are removed from the table, and information about these rows is stored in a temporary file. If a failure occurs during the Delete phase, the Load operation must be manually restarted. When a Load operation is restarted beginning at the Delete phase, violating rows are removed from the table based on information stored in the temporary file. If no temporary files exist, the Load operation should be restarted at the beginning of the Build phase. You must not modify temporary files in any way, and you must call the LOAD function with the same parameter values that were used when the load facility was originally started—or the restart of the Delete phase will fail.

It is always a good idea to restrict access to the table spaces associated with a table that is receiving load data. You can restrict table space access by calling the QUIESCE TABLESPACES FOR TABLE function before the Load operation is started, and you can call this function again to restore the table spaces to their original state after the Load process has completed.

Supported Export, Import, and Load File Formats

Four types of file formats are supported by the Import facility, and three types of formats are supported by the Export and Load facilities. File formats determine how data is physically stored in a file. The file formats that are supported are:

Delimited ASCII	This format consists of data values (variable in length) that are separated by a delimiting (field separator) character. Because commas are typically used as the field separator character, this format is sometimes referred to as *comma-separated variable* (CSV) format. This format is used for exchanging data with a wide variety of application products, especially other database products.
Nondelimited ASCII	This format consists of data values (with the same length) that are column-aligned. This format is also used for exchanging data with a wide variety of application products, especially spreadsheet products.
Work Sheet Format	This format is specifically intended to define data stored in a file format that is compatible with Lotus Development Corporation's Lotus 1-2-3 and

Lotus Symphony products. The Load utility does not support this file format.

PC Integrated Exchange Format   This format defines data that is stored in a file format that is compatible with DB2 products. When this format is used, tables in the database do not have to exist before data can be imported into them.

Refer to the IBM *DB2 Universal Database Administration Guide* for more information about the Export, Import, and Load facilities—and for more information about their supported file formats.

The DB2 Data Handling Functions

Table 11-2 lists the DB2 API functions that are used to move data between database tables and external files.

Each of these functions are described in detail in the remainder of this chapter.

Table 11-2   Data Handling APIs

Function Name	Description
EXPORT	Copies data from a DB2 database to an external file.
IMPORT	Copies data from an external file to a DB2 database.
LOAD	Loads data from files, tapes, or named pipes into a DB2 database table.
LOAD QUERY	Queries the DB2 database server for the current status of a Load operation.
QUIESCE TABLESPACES FOR TABLE	Places all table spaces associated with a particular database table in a quiesced (restricted access) state.

██ ██ EXPORT

Purpose   The EXPORT function is used to export (copy) data from a database to one of several external file formats.

Syntax
```
SQL_API_RC SQL_API_FN sqluexpr (char              *DataFileName,
                                sqlu_media_list   *LOBPathList,
                                sqlu_media_list   *LOBFileList,
                                struct sqldcol    *DataDescriptor,
                                struct sqlchar    *SelectStatement,
                                char              *FileType,
                                struct sqlchar    *FileTypeMod,
                                char              *MsgFileName,
                                short             CallerAction,
                                struct sqluexpt_out *NumRows,
                                void              *Reserved,
                                struct sqlca      *SQLCA);
```

Parameters   *DataFileName*   A pointer to a location in memory where the path and name of the external file that data is to be exported into is stored.

LOBPathList   A pointer to a *sqlu_media_list* structure that contains a list of local paths on the client workstation that identify where LOB data files are to be stored.

LOBFileList   A pointer to a *sqlu_media_list* structure that contains a list of base LOB filenames that are to be generated.

DataDescriptor   A pointer to a *sqldcol* structure that contains the column names that are to be written to the external file.

SelectStatement   A pointer to a *sqlchar* structure that contains a valid dynamic SELECT SQL statement that specifies which data is to be extracted from the database and written to the external file.

FileType   A pointer to a location in memory where a string that specifies the format to use when writing data to the external file is stored. This parameter must be set to one of the following values:

■ SQL_DEL
   Data is to be written to the external file using delimited ASCII format.

■ SQL_WSF
   Data is to be written to the external file using a worksheet (Lotus Symphony and Lotus 1-2-3) format.

■ SQL_IXF
   Data is to be written to the external file using the PC/Integrated Exchange format.

FileTypeMod   A pointer to a *sqlchar* structure that contains additional information (unique to the format being used) that is to be to used to write data to the external file.

MsgFileName   A pointer to a location in memory where the name of the file that all

EXPORT error, warning, and informational messages are to be written to is stored.

CallerAction Specifies the action that this function is to take when it executes. This parameter must be set to one of the following values:

- **SQLU_INITIAL**
  The EXPORT operation is to be started.

- **SQLU_CONTINUE**
  The EXPORT operation is to be continued after the user has performed some action that was requested by the Export utility (for example, inserting a diskette or mounting a new tape).

- **SQLU_TERMINATE**
  Specifies that the EXPORT operation is to be terminated because the user failed to perform some action that was requested by the Export utility.

NumRows A pointer to a *sqluexpt_out* structure where this function is to store a count of the number of rows that were exported (written) to the external file.

Reserved A pointer that is currently reserved for later use. For now, this parameter must always be set to NULL.

SQLCA A pointer to a location in memory where a SQL Communications Area (SQLCA) data structure variable is stored. This variable returns either status information (if the function executed successfully) or error information (if the function failed) to the calling application.

Includes   `#include <sqlutil.h>`

Description The EXPORT function is used to export (copy) data from a database to an external file. The data to be copied is specified by a SELECT SQL statement and can be written to an external file in one of three internal formats:

- Delimited ASCII
- Lotus Worksheet
- PC Integrated Exchange Format (IXF)

NOTE: *IXF is the preferred format to use when exporting data from a table. Files created in this format can later be imported or loaded much easier into the same table or into another database table.*

Three special structures (*sqldcol, sqlu_media_list,* and *sqlchar*) are used to pass general information to the DB2 Export utility when this function is called. An additional structure, *sqluexpt_out*, is used to determine how many records were actually copied to an external file by the Export utility. The first of these structures, *sqldcol*, is defined in *sqlutil.h* as follows:

```
struct sqldcol
{
short            dcolmeth;        /* A value indicating the method to    */
                                  /* use to select and name columns      */
                                  /* within the data file                */
short            dcolnum;         /* The number of columns specified     */
                                  /* in the dcolname array               */
struct sqldcoln dcolname[1];      /* A pointer to an array of sqldcoln    */
                                  /* structures that contain a list of    */
                                  /* column names                        */
};
```

This structure contains a pointer to an array of *sqldcoln* structures that are used to build a list of column names that are to be written to the external file during the Export process. The *sqldcoln* structure is defined in *sqlutil.h* as follows:

```
struct sqldcoln
{
short   dcolnlen;        /* The size of the data element pointed to */
                         /* by the dcolnptr field                   */
char    *dcolnptr;       /* A pointer to a location in memory where */
                         /* the data element specified by the dcolmeth*/
                         /* field of the sqldcol structure is stored*/
};
```

The second special structure used by this function, *sqluexpt_out*, is used to obtain a count of the number of records that were written to the external file after the Export operation is completed. The *sqluexpt_out* structure is defined in *sqlutil.h* as follows:

```
struct sqluexpt_out
{
unsigned  long sizeOfStruct;    /* The size of the sqluexpt_out        */
                                /* structure                           */
unsigned  long rowsExported;    /* The number of records copied        */
                                /* from the database to the target     */
                                /* file                                */
};
```

Another structure, the *sqlu_media_list* structure, is used to describe the type of media that the external file is to be written to. Refer to the BACKUP DATABASE function in Chapter 10 for a detailed description of the *sqlu_media_list* structure and for more information about how it is initialized.

Comments
- If a list of local paths that identify where LOB data files are to be stored is specified in the *LOBPathList* parameter, LOB data will be written to the first path in this list until file space is exhausted, then to the second path, and so on.
- When LOB data files are created during an Export operation, DB2 constructs the filenames by combining the current base name in the list of base LOB file names

specified in the *LOBFileList* parameter with the current path (obtained from the list of paths provided in the *LOBFilePath* parameter), and then appending a three-digit sequence number to it. For example, if the current LOB path is the directory `/usr/local/LOB/empdata`, and the current base LOB filename is `resume`, then the LOB files produced will be named `/usr/local/LOB/empdata/resume.001`, `/usr/local/LOB/emp-data/resume.002`, and so on.

■ The *dcolmeth* field of the *sqldcol* structure specified in the *DataDescriptor* parameter defines how column names are to be provided for the exported data file. This parameter can be set to either of the following values:

  ■ `SQL_METH_N`
  Specifies that column names in the external file are provided via the *sqldcol* structure.

  ■ `SQL_METH_D` (or NULL)
  Specifies that column names in the external file are to be derived from the `SELECT` statement specified in *SelectStatement* parameter (the column names specified in the `SELECT` statement become the names of the columns in the external file).

■ If the *DataDescriptor* parameter is set to NULL or if the *dcolmeth* field of the *sqldcol* structure specified in the *DataDescriptor* parameter is set to `SQL_METH_D`, the *dcolnum* and *dcolname* fields of the *sqldcol* structure are ignored.

■ A warning message is issued whenever the number of columns specified in the external column name array (stored in the *DataDescriptor* parameter) does not equal the number of columns that were generated by the `SELECT` SQL statement that was used to retrieve the data from the database. When these numbers do not match, the number of columns written to the external file is the lesser of the two numbers. Excess database columns or external file column names are not used to generate the external file.

■ The *sqlca* structure specified in the *SelectStatement* parameter must contain a valid dynamic `SELECT` SQL statement. This statement specifies how data is to be extracted from the database and written to the external file. The columns for the external file (specified in the *DataDescriptor* parameter) and the database columns returned from the `SELECT` statement are matched according to their respective list/structure positions. When this function is executed, the `SELECT` statement is passed to the database for processing, and the first column of data retrieved is placed in the first column of the external file, the second column retrieved is placed in the second column, and so on.

■ A warning message is issued whenever a character column with a length greater than 254 is selected as part of the data that is to be exported to a delimited ASCII (`SQL_DEL`) file.

■ If the *MsgFileName* parameter contains the path and the name of a file that already exists, the existing file will be overwritten when this function is executed. If this parameter contains the path and the name of a file that does not exist, a new file will be created. Messages placed in the external message file include information returned from the message retrieval service. Each message begins on a new line.

■ The *CallerAction* parameter must be set to SQLUB_INITIAL the first time this function is called.

■ All table operations need to be completed and all locks must be released before this function is called. You can accomplish this by issuing either a ROLLBACK or a COMMIT SQL statement after closing all cursors that were opened with the WITH HOLD option. One or more COMMIT SQL statements are automatically issued during the export process.

■ You can use delimited ASCII format files to exchange data with many other Database Manager and File Manager programs.

■ If character data containing row separators is exported to a delimited ASCII (SQL_DEL) file that is later processed by a text transfer program, fields that contain row separators will either shrink or expand in size.

■ Use the PC/IXF (SQL_IXF) file format when exporting data to files that will be imported into other databases, because PC/IXF file format specifications permit the migration of data between different DB2 products. You can perform data migration by executing the following steps:

1. Export the data from one database to a file.

2. Binary copy the files between operating systems. This step is not necessary if the source and target databases are both accessible from the same workstation.

3. Import the data from the file into the other database.

■ You can use DB2 Connect to export tables from DRDA servers such as DB2 for OS/390, DB2 for UM/USE, and DB2 for OS/400. In this case, only the PC/IXF file format is supported.

■ Index definitions and NOT NULL WITH DEFAULT attributes for a table are included in PC/IXF format files when a SELECT * FROM <tablename> statement is specified in the *SelectStatement* parameter, and the *DataDescriptor* parameter is set so that default column names are generated. Indexes are not saved if the SELECT statement specified in the *SelectStatement* parameter contains a join—or if the SELECT statement references views. WHERE, GROUP BY, and HAVING clauses do not affect the saving of indexes.

■ The EXPORT utility cannot create multiple-part PC/IXF format files when executed on an AIX system.

■ The *data* field of the *sqlchar* structure specified in the *FileTypeMod* parameter can contain any of the following values:

"dldelx"

"lobsinfile"

"coldelx"

"chardelx"

"decptx"

"decplusblank"

"datesiso"

"nodoubledel"

"1"

"2"

"3"

"4"

"L"

"S"

These values provide additional information about the chosen file format. Only a portion of these values are used with a particular file format. If the *FileTypeMod* parameter is set to NULL or if the *length* field of the *sqlchar* structure is set to 0, default information is provided for the file format specified.

■ If data is being exported to either a delimited ASCII (SQL_DEL) or PC/IXF (SQL_IXF) format file, the *FileTypeMod* parameter can specify where LOB data is to be stored. If this parameter is set to "lobsinfile," LOB data will be stored in separate files; otherwise, all LOB data will be truncated to 32KB and stored in the exported file. When "lobsinfile" is specified for PC/IXF files, the original length of the LOB data is lost, and the LOB file length is stored in the exported file. If the IMPORT function is later used to import the file—and if the CREATE option is specified—the LOB value created will be 267 bytes in size.

■ If data is exported to a delimited ASCII (SQL_DEL) format file, the *FileTypeMod* parameter can be used to specify characters that override the following options:

Datalink delimiters	By default, the inter-field separator for a DATALINK value is a semicolon (;). Specifying "dldel" followed by a character will cause the specified character to be used in place of a semicolon as the inter-field separator. The character specified must be different from the characters used as row, column, and character string delimiters.
Double character delimiters	Specifying "nodoubledel" will cause recognition of all double-byte character delimiters to be suppressed.
Column delimiters	By default, columns are delimited with commas. Specifying "coldel" followed by a character will cause the specified character to be used in place of a comma to signal the end of a column.
Character string delimiters	By default, character strings are delimited with double quotation marks. Specifying "chardel"

followed by a character will cause the specified character to be used in place of double quotation marks to enclose a character string.

Decimal point characters   By default, decimal points are specified with periods. Specifying "`decpt`" followed by a character will cause the specified character to be used in place of a period as a decimal point character.

Plus sign character   By default, positive decimal values are prefixed with a plus sign. Specifying "`decplusblank`" will cause positive decimal values to be prefixed with a blank space instead of a plus sign.

Date format   Specifying "`datesiso`" will cause all date data values to be exported in ISO format.

- ■ If two or more delimiters are specified, they must be separated by blank spaces. Blank spaces cannot be used as delimiters.

- ■ Each delimiter character specified must be different from all other delimiter characters being used, so it can be uniquely identified. Table 11–3 lists the characters that can be used as delimiter overrides.

- ■ If data is being exported to a worksheet (`SQL_WSF`) format file, the *FileTypeMod* parameter can be used to specify which release (version) of Lotus 1-2-3 or Lotus Symphony the file is compatible with (only one product designator can be specified for a worksheet format file):

  1   Causes a worksheet format file that is compatible with Lotus 1-2-3 Release 1 or Lotus 1-2-3 Release 1a to be created. This is the default version used if no version is specified.

  2   Causes a worksheet format file that is compatible with Lotus Symphony Release 1.0 to be created.

  3   causes a worksheet format file that is compatible with Lotus 1-2-3 Version 2 or Lotus Symphony Release 1.1 to be created.

  4   Causes a worksheet format file that contains DBCS characters to be created.

  L   Causes a worksheet format file that is compatible with Lotus 1-2-3 Version 2 to be created.

  S   Causes a worksheet format file that is compatible with Lotus Symphony Release 1.1 to be created.

- ■ This function will not issue a warning if you attempt to specify options that are not supported by the file type specified in the *FileType* parameter. Instead, this function will fail, and an error will be generated.

Table 11–3 Delimiter Characters for Use with Delimited ASCII Files

Character	Decimal Value	Hex Value	Description
"	34	0x22	Double quotation marks
%	37	0x25	Percent sign
&	38	0x26	Ampersand
'	39	0x27	Apostrophe
(	40	0x28	Left parenthesis
)	41	0x29	Right parenthesis
*	42	0x2A	Asterisk
,	44	0x2C	Comma
.	46	0x2E	Period (not valid as a character string delimiter)
/	47	0x2F	Slash or forward slash
:	58	0x3A	Colon
;	59	0x3B	Semicolon
<	60	0x3C	Less-than sign
=	61	0x3D	Equal sign
>	62	0x3E	Greater-than sign
?	63	0x3F	Question mark
_	95	0x5F	Underscore (valid only in single-byte character systems)
|	124	0x7C	Vertical bar

These characters are the same for all code page values.
Adapted from IBM's *DB2 Universal Database Command Reference*, Table 6, pp. 166 and 167.

■ If any of the bind files (particularly *db2uexpm.bnd*) that are shipped with DB2 have to be manually bound to a database, do not use the FORMAT option during the bind operation. If you do, this function will not work correctly.

Connection Requirements   This function can only be called if a connection to a database exists.

Authorization   Only users with System Administrator (SYSADM) authority, Database Administrator (DBADM) authority, or CONTROL or SELECT authority for each table and/or view specified can execute this function call.

See Also   IMPORT, LOAD

Example   The following C++ program illustrates how to use the EXPORT function to copy data from the DEPARTMENT table in the SAMPLE database to a PC/IXF formatted external file:

```
/*————————————————————————————————————————————— */
/* NAME:     CH11EX1.SQC                                    */
/* PURPOSE: Illustrate How To Use The Following DB2 API Function */
/*          In A C++ Program:                               */
/*                                                          */
/*              EXPORT                                      */
/*                                                          */
/*————————————————————————————————————————————— */

// Include The Appropriate Header Files
#include <windows.h>
#include <iostream.h>
#include <sqlutil.h>
#include <sql.h>

// Define The API_Class Class
class API_Class
{
    // Attributes
    public:
        struct sqlca   sqlca;

    // Operations
    public:
        long ExportData();
};

// Define The ExportData() Member Function
long API_Class::ExportData()
{
    // Declare The Local Memory Variables
    char                 DataFileName[80];
    char                 MsgFileName[80];
    char                 String[80];
    struct sqlchar       *SelectString;
    struct sqluexpt_out  OutputInfo;

    // Initialize The Local Variables
    strcpy(DataFileName, "C:\\DEPT.IXF");
    strcpy(MsgFileName, "C:\\EXP_MSG.DAT");
    OutputInfo.sizeOfStruct = SQLUEXPT_OUT_SIZE;

    // Define The SELECT Statement That Will Be Used To Select The
    // Data To Be Exported
    strcpy(String, "SELECT * FROM DEPARTMENT");
    SelectString = (struct sqlchar *)
        malloc (strlen(String) + sizeof(struct sqlchar));
    strncpy(SelectString->data, String, strlen(String));
    SelectString->length = strlen(String);

    // Export The Data To An IXF Format File
    sqluexpr(DataFileName, NULL, NULL, NULL, SelectString,
        SQL_IXF, NULL, MsgFileName, SQLU_INITIAL, &OutputInfo,
        NULL, &sqlca);
```

```
        // If The Data Was Exported Successfully, Display A Success
        // Message
        if (sqlca.sqlcode == SQL_RC_OK)
        {
            cout << OutputInfo.rowsExported << " ";
            cout << "rows of data in the DEPARTMENT table were ";
            cout << "exported to the file C:/DEPT.IXF." << endl;
        }

        // Free All Allocated Memory
        if (SelectString != NULL)
            free(SelectString);

        // Return The SQLCA Return Code To The Calling Function
        return(sqlca.sqlcode);
    }

/*------------------------------------------------------------*/
/* The Main Function                                          */
/*------------------------------------------------------------*/
int main()
{
    // Declare The Local Memory Variables
    long          rc = SQL_RC_OK;
    struct sqlca  sqlca;

    // Create An Instance Of The API_Class Class
    API_Class  Example;

    // Connect To The SAMPLE Database
    EXEC SQL CONNECT TO SAMPLE USER userID USING password;

    // Export Data In The DEPARTMENT Table (In The SAMPLE Database)
    // To An External File
    rc = Example.ExportData();

    // Issue A Rollback To Free All Locks
    EXEC SQL ROLLBACK;

    // Disconnect From The SAMPLE Database
    EXEC SQL DISCONNECT CURRENT;

    // Return To The Operating System
    return(rc);
}
```

IMPORT

Purpose   The IMPORT function is used to copy data stored in an external file (of a supported file format) into a database table or view.

Syntax	SQL_API_RC SQL_API_FN sqluimpr	(char	*DataFileName,
		sqlu_media_list	*LOBPathList,
		struct sqldcol	*DataDescriptor,
		struct sqlchar	*ActionString,
		char	*FileType,
		struct sqlchar	*FileTypeMod,
		char	*MsgFileName,
		short	CallerAction,
		struct sqluimpt_in	*ImportInfoIn,
		struct sqluimpt_out	*ImportInfoOut,
		long	*NullIndicators,
		void	*Reserved,
		struct sqlca	*SQLCA);

Parameters

DataFileName A pointer to a location in memory where the path and name of the external file that data is to be imported from is stored.

LOBPathList A pointer to a *sqlu_media_list* structure that contains a list of local paths on the client workstation that identify where LOB data files are to be imported from.

DataDescriptor A pointer to a *sqldcol* structure that contains information about the columns in the external data file that are to be imported. The value of the *dcolmeth* field of this structure determines how columns will be selected from the external file.

ActionString A pointer to a *sqlchar* structure that contains a valid dynamic SQL statement that identifies the action to be taken when importing data into tables that already contain data.

FileType A pointer to a location in memory where a string that specifies the format of the external data file is stored. This parameter must be set to one of the following values:

▨ SQL_DEL
   Data in the external file is stored in delimited ASCII format.

▨ SQL_ASC
   Data in the external file is stored in nondelimited ASCII format.

▨ SQL_WSF
   Data in the external file is stored in worksheet (Lotus Symphony and Lotus 1-2-3) format.

▨ SQL_IXF
   Data in the external file is stored in PC/Integrated Exchange format.

FileTypeMod A pointer to a *sqlchar* structure that contains additional information (unique to the format used) about the data stored in the external file.

MsgFileName A pointer to a location in memory where the name of the file that all

IMPORT error, warning, and informational messages are to be written to is stored.

CallerAction   Specifies the action that this function is to take when it executes. This parameter must be set to one of the following values:

■ SQLU_INITIAL
The IMPORT operation is to be started.

■ SQLU_CONTINUE
The IMPORT operation is to be continued after the user has performed some action that was requested by the Import utility (for example, inserting a diskette or mounting a new tape).

■ SQLU_TERMINATE
The IMPORT operation is to be terminated because the user failed to perform some action that was requested by the Import utility.

ImportInfoIn   A pointer to a *sqluimpt_in* structure that contains information about the number of records to skip and the number of records to retrieve before committing changes to the database.

ImportInfoOut   A pointer to a *sqluimpt_out* structure where this function is to store summary information about the IMPORT operation.

NullIndicators   A pointer to an array of integers that indicates whether or not each column of data retrieved can contain NULL values. This parameter is only used if the *FileType* parameter is set to SQL_DEL.

Reserved   A pointer that is currently reserved for later use. For now, this parameter must always be set to NULL.

SQLCA   A pointer to a location in memory where a SQL Communications Area (SQLCA) data structure variable is stored. This variable returns either status information (if the function executed successfully) or error information (if the function failed) to the calling application.

Includes   `#include <sqlutil.h>`

Description The IMPORT function is used to copy data stored in an external file (of a supported file format) into a database table or view. Data can be imported from any file that uses one of the following internal file formats:

■ Delimited ASCII

■ Nondelimited ASCII

■ Lotus Worksheet

■ PC Integrated Exchange Format (IXF)

NOTE: *IXF is the preferred format to use when exporting data from and importing data to a DB2 database table.*

Three special structures (*sqldcol*, *sqlu_media_list*, and *sqlchar*) are used to pass general information to the DB2 Import utility when this function is called. Refer to the **EXPORT** function for a detailed description of the *sqldcol* structure, and refer to the **BACKUP DATABASE** function for a detailed description of the *sqlu_media_list* structure.

A special structure (the *sqlloctab* structure) may also be used by the *sqldcol* structure (if the *dcolmeth* field is set to SQL_METH_L) when this function is executed. The *sqlloctab* structure is defined in *sqlutil.h* as follows:

```
struct sqlloctab
{
struct sqllocpair locpair[1];  /* A pointer to an array of sqllocpair  */
                               /* structures that contains a list of   */
                               /* column starting and ending           */
                               /* positions                            */
};
```

This structure contains a pointer to an array of *sqllocpair* structures that are used to build a list of starting and ending column positions that identify how data is stored in an external file. The *sqllocpair* structure is defined in *sqlutil.h* as follows:

```
struct sqllocpair
{
        short   begin_loc;  /* The starting position of the    */
                            /* column data in the external file */
        short   end_loc;    /* The ending position of the column */
                            /* data in the external file         */
};
```

Two additional structures, *sqluimpt_in* and *sqluimpt_out*, are used to pass IMPORT-specific information to and receive IMPORT-specific information from the DB2 Import facility when this function is called. The first of these structures, *sqluimpt_in*, passes information about when data is to be committed to the database to the Import facility and is defined in *sqlutil.h* as follows:

```
struct sqluimpt_in
{
unsigned long   sizeOfStruct;  /* The size of the sqluimpt_in structure */
unsigned long   commitcnt;     /* The number of records to import before */
                               /* a COMMIT SQL statement is executed.    */
```

```
                                 /* A COMMIT statement is executed each   */
                                 /* time this number of records are imported*/
                                 /* to make the additions permanent.     */
      unsigned long    restartcnt;    /* The number of records to skip in the file*/
                                 /* before starting the Import process. This */
                                 /* field can be used if a previous attempt to*/
                                 /* import records failed after n number of */
                                 /* rows of data were already committed   */
                                 /* to the database.                      */
      };
```

The second of these structures, *sqluimpt_out*, is used to return statistical
information about the import operation to the application after all data has been
copied to the table. The *sqluimpt_out* structure is defined in *sqlutil.h* as follows:

```
struct sqluimpt_out
{
unsigned long    sizeOfStruct;    /* The size of the sqluimpt_out    */
                                 /* structure                       */
unsigned long    rowsRead;        /* The number of records read from */
                                 /* the external file               */
unsigned long    rowsSkipped;     /* The number of records skipped   */
                                 /* before the import process was   */
                                 /* started                         */
unsigned long    rowsInserted;    /* The number of rows inserted into */
                                 /* the specified database table    */
unsigned long    rowsUpdated;     /* The number of rows updated in   */
                                 /* the specified table. Indicates the */
                                 /* number of records in the file that */
                                 /* have matching primary key values */
                                 /* in the table.                   */
unsigned long    rowsRejected;    /* The number of records in the file */
                                 /* that, for some reason, could not */
                                 /* be imported                     */
unsigned long    rowsCommitted;   /* The number of rows successfully */
                                 /* imported and committed          */
};
```

NOTE: *Data that has minor incompatibility problems will usually be accepted by the
Import facility (for example, you can import character data by using padding or truncation
and numeric data by using a different numeric data type). Data that has major
incompatibility problems will be rejected.*

Comments ■ The *dcolmeth* field of the *sqldcol* structure specified in the *DataDescriptor*
parameter defines how columns are to be selected for import from the external
data file. This parameter can be set to any of the following values:

  ■ SQL_METH_N
    Specifies that column names provided in the *sqldcol* structure identify the data

that is to be imported from the external file. This method cannot be used if the external file is in delimited ASCII format.

■ **SQL_METH_P**
Specifies that starting column positions provided in the *sqldcol* structure identify the data that is to be imported from the external file. This method cannot be used if the external file is in delimited ASCII format.

■ **SQL_METH_L**
Specifies that starting and ending column positions provided in the *sqldcol* structure identify the data that is to be imported from the external file. This method is the only method that can be used if the external file is in delimited ASCII format.

■ **SQL_METH_D**
Specifies that the first column in the external file is to be imported into the first column of the table, the second column in the external file into the second column of the table, and so on.

■ If the *DataDescriptor* parameter is set to NULL or if the *dcolmeth* field of the *sqldcol* structure specified in the *DataDescriptor* parameter is set to **SQL_METH_D**, the *dcolnum* and *dcolname* fields of the *sqldcol* structure are ignored.

■ If the *dcolmeth* field of the *sqldcol* structure in the *DataDescriptor* parameter is set to **SQL_METH_N**, the *dcolnptr* pointer of each element of the *dcolname* array must point to a string, *dcolnlen* characters in length, that contains the name of a valid column in the external file that is to be imported.

■ If the *dcolmeth* field of the *sqldcol* structure in the *DataDescriptor* parameter is set to **SQL_METH_P**, the *dcolnptr* pointer of each element of the *dcolname* array is ignored and the *dcolnlen* field of each element of the *dcolname* array must contain a valid column position in the external file that is to be imported. The lowest column (byte) position value that can be specified is 1 (indicating the first column or byte), and the largest column (byte) position value that can be specified is determined by the number bytes contained in one row of data in the external file.

■ If the *dcolmeth* field of the *sqldcol* structure in the *DataDescriptor* parameter is set to **SQL_METH_L**, the *dcolnptr* pointer of the first element of the *dcolname* array points to a *sqlloctab* structure that consists of an array of *sqllocpair* structures. The number of elements in this array must be stored in the *dcolnum* field of the *sqldcol* structure. Each element in this array must contain a pair of integer values that indicates the positions in the file where a column begins and ends. The first integer value is the byte position (in a row) in the file where the column begins, and the second integer value is the byte position (in the same row) where the column ends. The first byte position value that can be specified is 1 (indicating the first byte in a row of data), and the largest byte position value that can be specified is determined by the number of bytes contained in one row of data in the external file. Columns defined by starting and ending byte positions can overlap.

■ If the *dcolmeth* field of the *sqldcol* structure in the *DataDescriptor* parameter is set to SQL_METH_L, the DB2 Database Manager will reject an IMPORT call if a location pair is invalid because of any of the following conditions:

— Either the beginning or the ending location specified is not valid.

— The ending location value is smaller than the beginning location value.

— The input column width defined by the beginning/end location pair is not compatible with the data type and length of the target database table column.

■ Beginning/end location pairs that have both values set to 0 indicate that a column is nullable and that it is to be filled with NULL values.

■ If the *DataDescriptor* parameter is set to NULL or if the *dcolmeth* field of the *sqldcol* structure specified in the *DataDescriptor* parameter is set to SQL_METH_D, the first *n* columns (where *n* is the number of database columns into which the data is to be imported) of data found in the external file will be imported in their natural order.

■ Columns in external files can be specified more than once, but anything that is not a valid specification of an external column (i.e., a name, position, location, or default) will cause an error to be generated. Every column found in an external file does not have to be imported.

■ The SQL statement specified in the *ActionString* parameter must be in the following format:

```
[Action] INTO [TableName <(ColumnName,...)>|<ALL TABLES|(TableName
<(ColumnName,...)> <IN> HIERARCHY [STARTING TableName,...)]
<UNDER SubTableName|AS ROOT TABLE>
```

where:

Action   Specifies how the data is to be imported into the database table. The action can be any of the following values:

■ INSERT
Specifies that imported data rows are to be added to a table that already exists in the database—and that any data previously stored in the table should not be changed.

■ INSERT_UPDATE
Specifies that imported data rows are to be added to a table if their primary keys do not match existing table data—and that they are to be used to update data in a table if matching primary keys are found. This option is only valid when the target table has a primary key and when the specified (or implied) list of target columns being imported includes all columns for the primary key. This *Action* cannot be applied to views.

■ REPLACE
Specifies that all existing data in a table is to be deleted before data is imported. When existing data is deleted, table and index definitions remain undisturbed unless otherwise specified

(indexes are deleted and replaced if the *FileTypeMod* parameter is set to "indexixf" and if the *FileType* parameter is set to SQL_IXF). If the table is not already defined, an error will be returned. If an error occurs after existing data is deleted, that data will be lost and can only be recovered if the database was backed up before the IMPORT function was called.

■ CREATE
Specifies that if the table does not already exist, it will be created using the table definition stored in the specified PC/IXF format data file. If the PC/IXF file was exported from a DB2 database, indexes will also be created. If the specified table name is already defined, an error will be returned. This *Action* is only valid for PC/IXF format files.

■ REPLACE_CREATE
Specifies that if the table already exists, any data previously stored in it will be replaced with the data imported from the PC/IXF format file. If the table does not already exist, the table will be created using the table definition stored in the specified PC/IXF format data file. If the PC/IXF file was exported from a DB2 database, indexes will also be created when the table is created. This *Action* is only valid for PC/IXF format files. If an error occurs after existing data is deleted from the table, that data will be lost and can only be recovered if the database was backed up before the IMPORT function was called.

TableName   Specifies the name of the table or updatable view that the data is to be inserted into. A alias name can be used if the REPLACE, INSERT_UPDATE, or INSERT *Action* is specified, except in the case of a down-level server. In this case, a table name (either qualified or unqualified) should always be used.

ColumnName   Specifies one or more column names within the table or view into which data from the external file is to be inserted. Commas must separate each column name in this list. If no column names are specified, the column names defined for the table will be used.

ALL TABLES   Specifies to import all tables specified in the traversal order list when importing a hierarchy.

HIERARCHY   Specifies that hierarchical data is to be imported.

STARTING   Specifies that the default order of a hierarchy, starting at a given sub-table name, is to be used when importing hierarchical data.

UNDER   Specifies that the new hierarchy, sub-hierarchy, or sub-table is to be created under a given sub-table.

SubTableName   Specifies the parent table to use when creating one or more sub-tables in a hierarchy.

AS ROOT TABLE   Specifies that the new hierarchy, sub-hierarchy, or sub-table is to be created as a stand-alone hierarchy.

■ The *TableName* and the *ColumnName* list parameters correspond to the *TableName* and *ColName* list parameters of the INSERT SQL statement that is used to import the data, and they have the same restrictions.

■ The columns in the *ColumnName* list and the columns (either specified or implied) in the external file are matched according to their position in the list or in the *sqldcol* structure (data from the first column specified in the *sqldcol* structure is inserted into the table or view column that corresponds to the first element of the *ColumnName* list). If unequal numbers of columns are specified, the number of columns actually processed is the lesser of the two numbers. This situation could cause an error message (because there might not be values to place in some NOT NULL table columns) or an informational message (because some external file columns are ignored) to be generated.

■ If the *MsgFileName* parameter contains the path and the name of a file that already exists, the existing file will be overwritten when this function is executed. If this parameter contains the path and name of a file that does not exist, a new file will be created. Messages placed in the message file include information returned from the message retrieval service. Each message begins on a new line.

■ The *CallerAction* parameter must be set to SQLU_INITIAL the first time this function is called.

■ The caller action *repeat call* facility provides support for importing data from multiple PC/IXF (SQL_IXF) format files that have been created on platforms that support diskettes.

■ The number of elements in the *NullIndicators* array must match the number of columns in the input file (the number of elements must equal the *dcolnum* field of the *sqldcol* structure in the *DataDescriptor* parameter). There is a one-to-one ordered correspondence between the elements of this array and the columns being imported from the data file. Each element of this array must either contain a number that identifies a column in the external data file to be used as a null indicator field, or a 0 to indicate that the table column is not nullable. If the element contains a number that identifies a column in the external data file, the column identified must contain either a "Y" or an "N" (a "Y" value indicates that the table column data is NULL, and an "N" value indicates that the table column data is not NULL).

■ All table operations need to be completed and all locks must be released before this function is called. You can accomplish this task by issuing either a ROLLBACK or a COMMIT SQL statement after closing all cursors that were opened with the WITH HOLD option. One or more COMMIT SQL statements are automatically issued during the Import process.

■ Whenever a COMMIT SQL statement is executed, two messages are written to the message file. One message identifies the number of records that are to be committed, and the other identifies whether or not the COMMIT SQL statement was successfully executed. When restarting IMPORT after a system failure has occurred, specify the number of records to skip, as determined from the last messages generated by the last successful COMMIT.

- When importing PC/IXF (SQL_IXF) format files to a remote database, the performance can be greatly improved if the external PC/IXF file resides on a hard drive, rather than on diskettes.

- Specifying non-default column values in the *DataDescriptor* parameter or an explicit list of table columns in the *ActionString* parameter makes importing to a remote database slower.

- When importing to a remote database, make sure there is enough disk space on the server workstation for a copy of the input data file, the output message file, and the potential growth in the size of the database.

- If this function is run against a remote database and the output message file generated is large (more than 60KB in size), the actual message file returned to the user on the client workstation may be missing messages from the middle of the Import process. This result occurs is because the first and last 30KB of message information is always retained.

- A COMMIT SQL statement is automatically issued after old rows of data are deleted during a REPLACE or REPLACE_CREATE import. Consequently, if a system failure occurs or if an application interrupts the DB2 Database Manager after the records are deleted, part or all of the original data will be lost. Ensure that the original data is no longer needed before using either of these options.

- When the recovery log becomes full during a CREATE, REPLACE, or REPLACE_CREATE import, a COMMIT SQL statement is automatically issued to commit all records inserted. If a system failure occurs or if the application interrupts the DB2 Database Manager after the COMMIT statement executes, a table that is partially filled with data will remain in the database. If this situation occurs, perform a REPLACE or a REPLACE_CREATE import to import the whole file again, or perform an INSERT import with the number of rows that have already been imported specified in the *restartcount* field of the *sqluimpt_in* structure.

- By default, automatic commits are not performed if the INSERT or INSERT_UPDATE option is specified. However, they are performed if the *commitcnt* field of the *sqluimpt_in* structure contains anything other than 0.

- If the recovery log file becomes full during an INSERT or INSERT_UPDATE import, all changes will be removed (rolled back).

- The Import utility adds rows to the target database table using an INSERT SQL statement. This utility issues one INSERT statement for each row of data found in the external data file. If an INSERT statement fails, one of two actions will result:

—If it is likely that subsequent INSERT statements can be successful, a warning message will be written to the message file and processing will continue.

—If it is likely that subsequent INSERT statements will fail and that there is potential for database damage, an error message will be written to the message file, and processing will stop.

■ Data from external files cannot be imported to system catalog tables.

■ Views cannot be created with a CREATE import.

■ REPLACE and REPLACE_CREATE imports cannot be performed on object tables that have other dependents (other than themselves) or on object views whose base tables have other dependents (including themselves). To replace such a table or a view, perform the following steps:

1. Drop all foreign keys in which the table is a parent.

2. Execute the IMPORT function.

3. Alter the table to recreate the foreign keys. If an error occurs while recreating the foreign keys, modify the data so that it maintains referential integrity.

■ Referential constraints and key definitions are not preserved when tables are created (CREATE *Action*) from PC/IXF (SQL_IXF) format files.

■ You can use the IMPORT function to recover a previously exported table if the PC/IXF (SQL_IXF) format was used. When the IMPORT function is executed, the table returns to the state it was in when the table was exported. This operation is similar to but distinct from a backup and restore operation.

■ The *data* field of the *sqlchar* structure specified in the *FileTypeMod* parameter can contain any of the following values:

"compound=*x*"

"dldel*x*"

"lobsinfile"

"no_type_id"

"nodefaults"

"usedefaults"

"implieddecimal"

"noeofchar"

"nullindchar=*x*"

"reclen=*x*"

"striptblanks"

"striptnulls"

"chardel*x*"

"coldel*x*"

"datesiso"

"decplusblank"

"decpt*x*"

"nodoubledel"

"defer_import"

"forcein"

"indexixf"

"indexschema=*schema*"

"nochecklengths"

These values provide additional information about the chosen file format. Only a portion of these values are used with a particular file format. If the *FileTypeMod* parameter is set to NULL or if the *length* field of the *sqlchar* structure is set to 0, default information is provided for the file format specified.

- If the *FileTypeMod* parameter is set to "no_type_id," all imported data will be converted into a single sub-table.

- If the source column in an external file is not explicitly specified, and if the corresponding table column that the data is to be loaded into is not nullable, the *FileTypeMod* parameter can be set to "nodefaults" to keep default values from being substituted. Otherwise, a default value is substituted if the table column is nullable and if a default value exists. A NULL is substituted if the table column is nullable and no default exists — or an error occurs if the table column is not nullable.

- If the source column in an external file has been explicitly specified, and if it does not contain data for one or more rows, the *FileTypeMod* parameter can be set to "usedefaults" to ensure that default values are substituted. Otherwise, a NULL is substituted if the table column is nullable—or the row is not loaded if the table column is not nullable.

- If data is being imported from either a delimited ASCII (SQL_DEL) or PC/IXF (SQL_IXF) format file, the *FileTypeMod* parameter can specify where LOB data is stored. If this parameter is set to "lobsinfile," LOB data is stored in separate external files; otherwise, all LOB data is assumed to be truncated to 32KB and stored in the same file.

- If the *FileTypeMod* parameter is set to "lobsinfile" and the CREATE option is used, the original LOB length is lost, and the LOB value stored in the database is truncated to 32KB.

- If the *FileTypeMod* parameter is set to "compound=*x*" (where *x* is any number between 1 and 100 or 7 on DOS/Windows platforms), nonatomic compound SQL is used to insert the imported data (i.e., *x* number of statements will be processed as a single compound SQL statement).

- If data is being imported from a delimited ASCII (SQL_DEL) format file, the *FileTypeMod* parameter can be set to "noeofchar" to specify that the optional end-of-file character (0x1A) is not to be recognized as the end-of-file character. If this option is set, the end-of-file character (0x1A) is treated as a normal character.

■ If data is being imported from a delimited ASCII (`SQL_DEL`) format file, the *FileTypeMod* parameter can be set to `reclen=xxxx` (where *xxxx* is a number no larger than 32767) to specify that *xxxx* characters are to be read in for each row. In this case, a new-line character does not indicate the end of a row.

■ If data is being imported from a delimited ASCII (`SQL_DEL`) format file, you can use the *FileTypeMod* parameter to specify characters that override the following options:

Datalink delimiters	By default, the inter-field separator for a DATALINK value is a semicolon (;). Specifying "`dldel`" followed by a character will cause the specified character to be used in place of a semicolon as the inter-field separator. The character specified must be different from the characters used as row, column, and character string delimiters.
Double character delimiters	Specifying "`nodoubledel`" will cause recognition of all double-byte character delimiters to be suppressed.
Column delimiters	By default, columns are delimited with commas. Specifying "`coldel`" followed by a character will cause the specified character to be used in place of a comma to signal the end of a column.
Character string delimiters	By default, character strings are delimited with double quotation marks. Specifying "`chardel`" followed by a character will cause the specified character to be used in place of double quotation marks to enclose a character string.
Decimal point characters	By default, decimal points are specified with periods. Specifying "`decpt`" followed by a character will cause the specified character to be used in place of a period as a decimal point character.
Plus sign character	By default, positive decimal values are prefixed with a plus sign. Specifying "`decplusblank`" will cause positive decimal values to be prefixed with a blank space instead of a plus sign.
Date format	Specifying "`datesiso`" will cause all date values to be imported in ISO format.

■ If two or more delimiters are specified, they must be separated by blank spaces. Blank spaces cannot be used as delimiters. Each delimiter character specified must be different from the delimiter characters already being used so all delimiters can be uniquely identified. Table 11–3 (refer to the `EXPORT` function) lists the characters that can be used as delimiter overrides.

■ If data is being imported from an ASCII (SQL_DEL or SQL_ASC) format file, the *FileTypeMod* parameter can be set to "implieddecimal" to specify that the location of an implied decimal point is to be determined by the table column definition (for example, if the value 12345 were to be loaded into a DECIMAL(8,2) column, it would be loaded as 123.45, not as 12345.00—which would otherwise be the case).

■ If data is being imported from a non-delimited ASCII (SQL_ASC) format file, the *FileTypeMod* parameter can be set to "nullindchar=x" (where *x* equals a character) to specify that a NULL value is to be replaced with a specific character. The character specified is case-sensitive for EBCDIC data files, except when the character is an English character.

■ If data is being imported from a non-delimited ASCII (SQL_ASC) format file, the *FileTypeMod* parameter can be set to "striptblanks" to specify that trailing blank spaces (after the last nonblank character) are to be removed (truncated) when data is imported. If this option is not set, trailing blanks are kept.

■ If data is being imported from a non-delimited ASCII (SQL_ASC) format file, the *FileTypeMod* parameter can be set to "striptnulls" to specify that trailing NULLs (after the last nonblank character) are to be removed (truncated) when data is imported into variable length fields. If this option is not set, NULLs (0x00 characters) are kept.

■ The "striptblanks" and the "striptnulls" options are mutually exclusive. If one is specified, the other cannot be used.

■ If data is being imported from a PC/IXF (SQL_IXF) format file, the *FileTypeMod* parameter can be set to "defer_import" to specify that the tables/sub-tables stored in the file are to be created, but the data is not to be imported. This setting can only be used with a CREATE import.

■ If data is being imported from a PC/IXF (SQL_IXF) format file, the *FileTypeMod* parameter can be set to "forcein" to tell the import utility to accept data in spite of code page mismatches and to suppress all translations between code pages.

■ If data is being imported from a PC/IXF (SQL_IXF) format file, the *FileTypeMod* parameter can be set to "nochecklengths" to specify that checking to ensure that fixed length target fields are large enough to hold the imported data is not to be performed. This option is used in conjunction with the "forcein" option.

■ If data is being imported from a PC/IXF (SQL_IXF) format file, the *FileTypeMod* parameter can be set to "indexixf" to tell the import utility to drop all indexes currently defined on the existing table and create new ones from the index definitions found in the PC/IXF format file being imported. This option can only be used when the contents of a table are being replaced. This option cannot be used with a view.

■ If data is being imported from a PC/IXF (SQL_IXF) format file, the *FileTypeMod* parameter can be set to "indexschema=*schema*" (where *schema* is a valid schema name) to indicate that the specified schema is to be used for the index name whenever indexes are created. If no schema is specified, the authorization ID that was used to establish the current database connection will be used as the default schema.

■ This function will not issue a warning if you attempt to specify options that are not supported by the file type specified in the *FileType* parameter. Instead, this function will fail, and an error will be generated.

■ If data is being imported from a WSF (sql_wsf) format file, the *FileTypeMod* parameter is ignored.

■ The LOAD function is a faster alternative to the IMPORT function.

Connection Requirements This function can only be called if a connection to a database exists.

Authorization Only users with System Administrator (SYSADM) authority, Database Administrator (DBADM) authority, or CONTROL, INSERT, or SELECT authority for the specified table or view can execute this function with the INSERT action (*ActionString* parameter) specified. Only users with SYSADM authority, DBADM authority, or CONTROL authority for the specified table or view can execute this function with the INSERT_UPDATE, REPLACE, or REPLACE_CREATE action (*ActionString* parameter) specified. Only users with SYSADM authority, DBADM authority, or CREATETAB authority for the specified table or view can execute this function with the CREATE or the REPLACE_CREATE action (*ActionString* parameter) specified.

See Also EXPORT, LOAD

Example The following C++ program illustrates how to use the IMPORT function to insert data from an external file into the DEPARTMENT table of the SAMPLE database:

```
/*—————————————————————————————————————————— */
/* NAME:    CH11EX2.SQC                                      */
/* PURPOSE: Illustrate How To Use The Following DB2 API Function */
/*          In A C++ Program:                                */
/*                                                           */
/*              IMPORT                                       */
/*                                                           */
/*—————————————————————————————————————————— */

// Include The Appropriate Header Files
#include <windows.h>
#include <iostream.h>
#include <sqlutil.h>
#include <sql.h>

// Define The API_Class Class
class API_Class
{
    // Attributes
    public:
```

```
                    struct sqlca    sqlca;

        // Operations
        public:
            long ImportData();
    };


    // Define The ImportData() Member Function
    long API_Class::ImportData()
    {
        // Declare The Local Memory Variables
        char                    DataFileName[80];
        char                    MsgFileName[80];
        char                    String[80];
        struct sqlchar          *ActionString;
        struct sqluimpt_in      InputInfo;
        struct sqluimpt_out     OutputInfo;

        // Initialize The Local Variables
        strcpy(DataFileName, "C:\\DEPT.IXF");
        strcpy(MsgFileName, "C:\\IMP_MSG.DAT");

        // Initialize The Import Input Structure
        InputInfo.sizeOfStruct = SQLUIMPT_IN_SIZE;
        InputInfo.commitcnt = 20;
        InputInfo.restartcnt = 0;

        // Initialize The Import Output Structure
        OutputInfo.sizeOfStruct = SQLUIMPT_OUT_SIZE;

        // Define The Action String That Will Be Used To Control How
        // Data Is Imported
        strcpy(String, "REPLACE INTO DEPARTMENT");
        ActionString = (struct sqlchar *)
            malloc (strlen(String) + sizeof(struct sqlchar));
        ActionString->length = strlen(String);
        strncpy(ActionString->data, String, strlen(String));

        // Import Data Into The DEPARTMENT Table From An IXF Format
        // File (This File Was Created By The EXPORT Example)
        sqluimpr(DataFileName, NULL, NULL, ActionString, SQL_IXF, NULL,
            MsgFileName, SQLU_INITIAL, &InputInfo, &OutputInfo,
            NULL, NULL, &sqlca);

        // If The Data Was Imported Successfully, Display A Success
        // Message
        if (sqlca.sqlcode == SQL_RC_OK)
        {
            cout << OutputInfo.rowsInserted << " ";
            cout << "rows of data were inserted into the DEPARTMENT ";
            cout << "table from the " << endl;
            cout << "file C:/DEPT.IXF." << endl;
        }

        // Free All Allocated Memory
```

```
    if (ActionString != NULL)
        free(ActionString);

    // Return The SQLCA Return Code To The Calling Function
    return(sqlca.sqlcode);
}

/*────────────────────────────────────────────────────────────── */
/* The Main Function                                              */
/*────────────────────────────────────────────────────────────── */
int main()
{
    // Declare The Local Memory Variables
    long         rc = SQL_RC_OK;
    struct sqlca  sqlca;

    // Create An Instance Of The API_Class Class
    API_Class  Example;

    // Connect To The SAMPLE Database
    EXEC SQL CONNECT TO SAMPLE USER userID USING password;

    // Import Data Stored In An External File Into The DEPARTMENT
    // Table (In The SAMPLE Database)
    rc = Example.ImportData();

    // Issue A Rollback To Free All Locks
    EXEC SQL ROLLBACK;

    // Disconnect From The SAMPLE Database
    EXEC SQL DISCONNECT CURRENT;


    // Return To The Operating System
    return(rc);
}
```

■ ■ **LOAD**

Purpose   The LOAD function is used to bulk load data from external files, tapes, or named pipes into DB2 database tables.

Syntax
```
SQL_API_RC SQL_API_FN sqluload (sqlu_media_list   *DataFileList,
                                sqlu_media_list   *LOBPathList,
                                struct sqldcol    *DataDescriptor,
                                struct sqlchar    *ActionString,
                                char              *FileType,
                                struct sqlchar    *FileTypeMod,
                                char              *LocalMsgFileName,
                                char              *RemoteMsgFileName,
                                short             CallerAction,
                                struct sqluload_in   *LoadInfoIn,
                                struct sqluload_out  *LoadInfoOut,
```

```
                                sqlu_media_list    *WorkDirectoryList,
                                sqlu_media_list    *CopyTargetList,
                                long               *NullIndicators,
                                void               *Reserved,
                                struct sqlca       *SQLCA);
```

Parameters   *DataFileList*   A pointer to a *sqlu_media_list* structure that contains a list of external data files, devices, vendors, or named pipes that identify where data is to be loaded from.

LOBPathList   A pointer to a *sqlu_media_list* structure that contains a list of local paths on the client workstation that identify where LOB data files are to be loaded from.

DataDescriptor   A pointer to a *sqldcol* structure that contains information about the columns in the external data file(s) that are to be loaded. The value of the *dcolmeth* field of this structure determines how columns are selected from the external file(s).

ActionString   A pointer to a *sqlchar* structure that contains a valid dynamic SQL statement that identifies the action to be taken when loading data into tables that already contain data.

FileType   A pointer to a location in memory where a string that specifies the format of the external data file(s) is stored. This parameter must be set to one of the following values:

- SQL_DEL
  Data in the external file(s) is stored in delimited ASCII format.

- SQL_ASC
  Data in the external file(s) is stored in nondelimited ASCII format.

- SQL_IXF
  Data in the external file(s) is stored in PC/Integrated Exchange format.

FileTypeMod   A pointer to a *sqlchar* structure that contains additional information (unique to the format used) about the data stored in the external file.

LocalMsgFileName   A pointer to a location in memory where the name of the file that all LOAD error, warning, and informational messages are to be written to is stored.

RemoteMsgFileName   A pointer to a location in memory where the base name that is to be used for naming temporary files created by the

Load operation currently in progress is stored.

CallerAction   Specifies the action that this function is to take when it executes. This parameter must be set to one of the following values:

- SQLU_INITIAL
  The LOAD operation is to be started.

- SQLU_CONTINUE
  The LOAD operation is to be continued after the user has performed some action that was requested by the Load utility (for example, inserting a diskette or mounting a new tape).

- SQLU_TERMINATE
  The LOAD operation is to be terminated because the user failed to perform some action that was requested by the Load utility.

- SQLU_NOINTERRUPT
  The LOAD operation is to run without suspending processing.

- SQLU_ABORT
  The LOAD operation is to be terminated.

- SQLU_RESTART
  The LOAD operation is to be restarted.

- SQLU_DEVICE_TERMINATE
  A particular device should be removed from the list of devices used by the LOAD utility. When a particular device has exhausted its input, the LOAD utility returns a warning to the caller (while continuing to use the remaining devices). By calling the LOAD function again with this caller action specified, you can remove the device that generated the warning condition from the list of devices being used.

LoadInfoIn   A pointer to an *sqluload_in* structure that contains information about the number of records to skip, number of records to load, sizes of internal buffers, and load fail conditions.

LoadInfoOut   A pointer to an *sqluload_out* structure where this function is to store summary information about the LOAD operation.

WorkDirectoryList   A pointer to an *sqlu_media_list* structure that contains a list of optional work directories that are to be used for sorting index keys during the LOAD operation. This

	parameter can be set to NULL.
CopyTargetList	A pointer to an *sqlu_media_list* structure that contains a list of external data files, devices, or shared libraries where copy images of the data (if created) are to be written.
NullIndicators	A pointer to an array of integers that indicates whether or not each column of data retrieved can contain NULL values. This parameter is only used if the *FileType* parameter is set to SQL_DEL.
Reserved	A pointer that is currently reserved for later use. For now, this parameter must always be set to NULL.
SQLCA	A pointer to a location in memory where a SQL Communications Area (SQLCA) data structure variable is stored. This variable returns either status information (if the function executed successfully) or error information (if the function failed) to the calling application.

Includes   `#include <sqlutil.h>`

Description   The LOAD function is used to bulk load data from external files, tapes, or named pipes into DB2 database tables. Data can be loaded from any file that uses one of the following internal file formats:

- Delimited ASCII
- Nondelimited ASCII
- PC Integrated Exchange Format IXF

Three special structures (*sqldcol, sqlu_media_list,* and *sqlchar*) are used to pass general information to the DB2 Load utility when this function is called. Refer to the EXPORT function for a detailed description of the *sqldcol* structure, and refer to the BACKUP DATABASE function for a detailed description of the *sqlu_media_list* structure. A special structure (the *sqlloctab* structure) may also be used by the *sqldcol* structure (if the *dcolmeth* field is set to SQL_METH_L) when this function is executed. Refer to the IMPORT function for a detailed description of this structure.

Two additional structures, *sqluload_in* and *sqluload_out*, are used to pass LOAD-specific information to and receive LOAD-specific information from the DB2 Load facility when this function is called. The first of these structures, *sqluload_in*, passes information such as when data is to be committed and the number of records to skip before starting the load operation to the Load facility and is defined in *sqlutil.h* as follows:

```
struct sqluload_in
{
unsigned long   sizeOfStruct;   /* The size of the sqluload_in structure */
unsigned long   savecnt;        /* The number of records to load before  */
                                /* a COMMIT SQL statement is executed     */
```

```
                                 /* A COMMIT statement is executed each   */
                                 /* time this number of records are loaded */
                                 /* to make the additions permanent        */
        unsigned long   restartcnt;      /* The number of records to skip in the file*/
                                 /* before starting the load process. This */
                                 /* field can be used if a previous attempt to*/
                                 /* load records failed after n number of   */
                                 /* rows of data had already been committed*/
                                 /* to the database.                        */
        unsigned long   rowcnt;          /* The number of rows of data to load      */
        unsigned long   warningcnt;      /* The number of warning conditions to     */
                                 /* ignore before failing                   */
        unsigned long   data_buffer_size;/* The size, in 4KB pages, of the buffer to */
                                 /* be used when loading data               */
        unsigned long   sort_buffer_size;/* The size, in 4KB pages, of the buffer to*/
                                 /* be used when sorting data               */
        unsigned short  hold_quiesce;    /* A flag indicating whether or not the table*/
                                 /* spaces for the table being loaded are   */
                                 /* in a quiesced state                     */
        char            restartphase;    /* Indicates that an interrupted load      */
                                 /* operation is to be restarted at the load*/
                                 /* phase (SQLU_LOAD_PHASE), at the         */
                                 /* build phase (SQLU_BUILD_PHASE),         */
                                 /* or at the delete phase                  */
                                 /* (SQLU_DELETE_PHASE)                     */
        char            statsopt;        /* Specifies the granularity to use when   */
                                 /* collecting statistical information during */
                                 /* the load operation. This field can contain*/
                                 /* any of the following values:            */
                                 /* SQLU_STATS_NONE                         */
                                 /* SQL_STATS_TABLE,                        */
                                 /* SQL_STATS_EXTTABLE_ONLY,                */
                                 /* SQL_STATS_BOTH,                         */
                                 /* SQL_STATS_EXTTTABLE_INDEX,              */
                                 /* SQL_STATS_INDEX,                        */
                                 /* SQL_STATS_EXTINDEX_ONLY,                */
                                 /* SQL_STATS_EXTINDEX_TABLE,               */
                                 /* SQL_STATS_ALL. Refer to the RUN         */
                                 /* STATISTICS function for more            */
                                 /* information about statistic granularity. */
        unsigned short  cpu_parallelism; /* The number of processes or threads that*/
                                 /* the load utility is to spawn for parsing,*/
                                 /* converting, and formatting records when */
                                 /* building table objects. If this field   */
                                 /* will automatically be set to 1 if loading*/
                                 /* tables containing either LOB or LONG    */
                                 /* VARCHAR fields.                         */
        unsigned short  disk parallelism;/* The number of processes or threads that */
                                 /* the load utility is to spawn for writing*/
                                 /* data to table space containers         */
        unsigned short  non_recoverable; /* Indicates that the load transaction is to*/
                                 /* be marked non-recoverable               */
                                 /* (SQLU_NON_RECOVERABLE_LOAD) or          */
                                 /* recoverable (SQLU_RECOVERABLE_LOAD).    */
                                 /* This field identifies whether or not it */
```

```
                                     /* will be possible to recover the LOAD  */
                                     /* operation with a roll-forward recovery */
                                     /* operation                              */
  } ;
```

The second of these structures, *sqluload_out*, is used to return statistical information about the load operation to the application after all data has been loaded. The *sqluload_out* structure is defined in *sqlutil.h* as follows:

```
struct sqluload_out
{
unsigned long   sizeOfStruct;   /* The size of the sqluload_out    */
                                /* structure                       */
unsigned long   rowsRead;       /* The number of records read from */
                                /* the external file               */
unsigned long   rowsSkipped;    /* The number of records skipped   */
                                /* before the load process was     */
                                /* started                         */
unsigned long   rowsLoaded;     /* The number of rows inserted into*/
                                /* the specified database table    */
unsigned long   rowsRejected;   /* The number of records in the file*/
                                /* that, for some reason, could not*/
                                /* be loaded                       */
unsigned long   rowsDeleted;    /* The number of duplicate rows that*/
                                /* were deleted                    */
unsigned long   rowsCommitted;  /* The number of rows successfully */
                                /* loaded and committed            */
};
```

NOTE: *Data that has minor incompatibility problems will usually be accepted by the load facility (for example, you can load character data by using padding or truncation and numeric data by using a different numeric data type). Data with major incompatibility problems will be rejected.*

Comments

■ The type of structure used to provide information about where data is to be loaded from is determined by the value specified in the *media_type* field of the *sqlu_media_list* structure (stored in the *DataFileList* parameter) as follows:

■ SQLU_SERVER_LOCATION
One or more *sqlu_location_entry* structures. The *sessions* field of the *sqlu_media_list* structure should indicate the number of *sqlu_location_entry* structures used.

■ SQLU_ADSM_MEDIA
One *sqlu_vendor* structure. The *filename* field of the *sqlu_vendor* structure should contain a unique identifier for the data source to be loaded. The Load utility will start each session with a different sequence number, but with the same data specified in the *sqlu_vendor* structure.

■ SQLU_OTHER_MEDIA
One *sqlu_vendor* structure. The *shr_lib* field of the *sqlu_vendor* structure should

contain a valid shared library name, and the *filename* field of the *sqlu_vendor* structure should contain a unique identifier for the data to be loaded. The Load utility will start each session with a different sequence number but with the same data specified in the *sqlu_vendor* structure.

■ Data files that were created with the EXPORT function or command will have LOB data filenames stored in them if the specified data set contained LOB data and if the "lobsinfile" option was specified. These names are appended to the paths specified in the *sqlu_media_list* structure during the Load process to provide a reference to LOB data.

■ The type of structure used to provide information about external LOB data file paths is determined by the value specified in the *media_type* field of the *sqlu_media_list* structure stored in the *LOBPathList* parameter as follows:

■ SQLU_LOCAL_MEDIA

One or more *sqlu_media_entry* structures. The *sessions* field of the *sqlu_media_list* structure should indicate the number of *sqlu_media_entry* structures used.

■ SQLU_ADSM_MEDIA

One *sqlu_vendor* structure. The *filename* field of the *sqlu_vendor* structure should contain a unique identifier for the data to be loaded. The Load utility will start each ADSM session with a different sequence number but with the same data specified in the *sqlu_vendor* structure.

■ SQLU_OTHER_MEDIA

One *sqlu_vendor* structure. The *shr_lib* field of the *sqlu_vendor* structure should contain a valid shared library name, and the *filename* field of the *sqlu_vendor* structure should contain a unique identifier for the data to be loaded. The Load utility will start each session with a different sequence number but with the same data specified in the *sqlu_vendor* structure.

■ The *dcolmeth* field of the *sqldcol* structure specified in the *DataDescriptor* parameter defines how columns are selected for loading from the external data file. This parameter can be set to any of the following values:

■ SQL_METH_N

Specifies that column names provided in the *sqldcol* structure identify the data that is to be loaded from the external file. This method cannot be used if the external file is in delimited ASCII format.

■ SQL_METH_P

Specifies that starting column positions provided in the *sqldcol* structure identify the data that is to be loaded from the external file. This method cannot be used if the external file is in delimited ASCII format.

■ SQL_METH_L

Specifies that starting and ending column positions provided in the *sqldcol* structure identify the data that is to be loaded from the external file. This method is the only method that can be used if the external file is in delimited ASCII format.

■ **SQL_METH_D**

Specifies that the first column in the external file is to be loaded into the first column of the table, the second column in the external file is to be loaded into the second column of the table, and so on.

■ If the *DataDescriptor* parameter is set to NULL or if the *dcolmeth* field of the *sqldcol* structure specified in the *DataDescriptor* parameter is set to SQL_METH_D, the *dcolnum* field and the *dcolname* field of the *sqldcol* structure are ignored.

■ If the *dcolmeth* field of the *sqldcol* structure in the *DataDescriptor* parameter is set to SQL_METH_N, the *dcolnptr* pointer of each element of the *dcolname* array must point to a string, *dcolnlen* characters in length, that contains the name of a valid column in the external file that is to be loaded.

■ If the *dcolmeth* field of the *sqldcol* structure in the *DataDescriptor* parameter is set to SQL_METH_P, the *dcolnptr* pointer of each element of the *dcolname* array is ignored and the *dcolnlen* field of each element of the *dcolname* array must contain a valid column position in the external file that is to be loaded. The lowest column (byte) position value that can be specified is 1 (indicating the first column or byte), and the largest column (byte) position value that can be specified is determined by the number bytes contained in one row of data in the external file.

■ If the *dcolmeth* field of the *sqldcol* structure in the *DataDescriptor* parameter is set to SQL_METH_L, the *dcolnptr* pointer of the first element of the *dcolname* array points to a *sqlloctab* structure that consists of an array of *sqllocpair* structures. The number of elements in this array must be stored in the *dcolnum* field of the *sqldcol* structure. Each element in this array must contain a pair of integer values that indicate the position in the file where a column begins and ends. The first integer value is the byte position (in a row) in the file where the column begins, and the second integer value is the byte position (in the same row) where the column ends. The first byte position value that can be specified is 1 (indicating the first byte in a row of data), and the largest byte position value that can be specified is determined by the number of bytes contained in one row of data in the external file. Columns defined by starting and ending byte positions can overlap.

■ If the *dcolmeth* field of the *sqldcol* structure in the *DataDescriptor* parameter is set to SQL_METH_L, the DB2 Database Manager will reject a LOAD call if a location pair is invalid because of any of the following conditions:

— Either the beginning or the ending location specified is not valid.

— The ending location value is smaller than the beginning location value.

— The input column width defined by the beginning/end location pair is not compatible with the data type and length of the target database table column.

■ Location pairs that have both values set to 0 indicate that a column is nullable and that it is to be filled with NULL values.

■ If the *DataDescriptor* parameter is set to NULL or if the *dcolmeth* field of the *sqldcol* structure specified in the *DataDescriptor* parameter is set to SQL_METH_D, the first *n* columns (where *n* is the number of database columns into which the data is to be loaded) of data found in the external file will be loaded in their natural order.

■ Columns in external files can be specified more than once, but anything that is not a valid specification of an external column (a name, position, location, or default) will cause an error to be generated. Every column found in an external file does not have to be loaded.

■ The SQL statement specified in the *ActionString* parameter must be in the following format:

```
[Action] INTO [TableName <(ColumnName,...)> <FOR EXCEPTION ETableName>
```

where:

Action   Specifies how the data is to be loaded into the database table. The action can be any of the following values:

    ■ INSERT
    Specifies that loaded data rows are to be added to a table that already exists in the database—and that any data previously stored in the table should not be changed.

    ■ REPLACE
    Specifies that all existing data in a table is to be deleted before data is loaded. When existing data is deleted, table and index definitions remain undisturbed unless otherwise specified (indexes are deleted and replaced if the *FileTypeMod* parameter is set to "indexixf" and if the *FileType* parameter is set to SQL_IXF). If the table is not already defined, an error is returned. If an error occurs after existing data is deleted, that data is lost and can only be recovered if the database was backed up before the LOAD function was called.

    ■ RESTART
    Specifies that a load operation that was started and was later interrupted is to be restarted. The last commit point of the interrupted load must be provided in the LOAD call that specifies the RESTART action. The LOAD QUERY function can be used to obtain this value.

    ■ TERMINATE
    Specifies that a previously interrupted load operation is to be terminated. When this action is specified, all table spaces in which the table being loaded resides are changed from "Load Pending" to "Recovery Pending" state and they cannot be used until they are restored and rolled forward. This option is not

recommended for general use and should only be used if an unrecoverable error has occurred. Attempt to restart an interrupted load whenever possible.

TableName   Specifies the name of the table that the data is to be loaded into. A alias name, a fully qualified name, or an unqualified name can be specified. If an unqualified name is specified, the authorization ID of the current user will be used as the default qualifier.

ColumnName   Specifies one or more column names within the table into which data from the external file is to be loaded. Commas must separate each column name in this list. If no column names are specified, the column names defined for the table are used. If a column name contains spaces or lower-case characters, the name must be enclosed by a quotation.

ETableName   Specifies the name of the exception table to which all data that causes an error to occur during the load operation is to be copied. Data that violates a unique index or a primary key index of the specified table is stored here.

■ The *TableName* and the *ColumnName* list parameters correspond to the *TableName* and *ColName* list parameters of the INSERT SQL statement that is used to load the data, and they have the same restrictions.

■ The columns in the *ColumnName* list and the columns (either specified or implied) in the external file are matched according to their position in the list or in the *sqldcol* structure (data from the first column specified in the *sqldcol* structure is inserted into the table column that corresponds to the first element of the *ColumnName* list). If unequal numbers of columns are specified, the number of columns actually processed is the lesser of the two numbers. This situation could cause an error message (because there might not be values to place in some NOT NULL table columns) or an informational message (because some external file columns are ignored) to be generated.

■ The Load utility builds indexes according to existing definitions. The exception tables handle duplicate values found in unique keys. The load utility does not perform referential integrity or constraint checking. If referential integrity and constraint checks are included in the table definition, the tables are placed in "Check Pending" state, and the user must either force the check flag or execute the SET CONSTRAINTS SQL statement.

■ If the *LocalMsgFileName* parameter contains the path and name of a file that already exists, the existing file will be overwritten when this function is executed. If this parameter contains the path and name of a file that does not exist, a new file will be created. Messages placed in the message file include information returned from the message retrieval service. Each message begins on a new line.

■ The *CallerAction* parameter must be set to SQLU_INITIAL the first time this function is called.

- If a list of work directories to use for sorting index keys during the load operation is not specified in the *WorkDirectoryList* parameter, the *tmp* subdirectory of the *sqllib* directory will be used.

- The type of structure used to provide information about paths, devices, or shared libraries where copy images of loaded data are to be stored is determined by the value specified in the *media_type* field of the *sqlu_media_list* structure (stored in the *CopyTargetList* parameter) as follows:

  - SQLU_LOCAL_MEDIA

    One or more *sqlu_media_entry* structures. The *sessions* field of the *sqlu_media_list* structure should indicate the number of *sqlu_media_entry* structures used.

  - SQLU_ADSM_MEDIA

    No other structure is needed.

  - SQLU_OTHER_MEDIA

    One *sqlu_vendor* structure. The *shr_lib* field of the *sqlu_vendor* structure should contain the shared library name of the vendor product being used. The Load utility will start each session with a different sequence number but with the same data specified in the *sqlu_vendor* structure.

- The number of elements in the *NullIndicators* array must match the number of columns in the external data file (i.e., the number of elements must equal the *dcolnum* field of the *sqldcol* structure in the *DataDescriptor* parameter). There is a one-to-one ordered correspondence between the elements of this array and the columns being loaded from the data file. Each element of this array must contain either a number identifying a column in the data file that is to be used as a null indicator field or a 0 to indicate that the table column is not nullable. If the element contains a number identifying a column in the data file, the identified column must contain either a "Y" or an "N" (a "Y" value indicates that the table column data is NULL, and an "N" value indicates that the table column data is not NULL).

- The *data* field of the *sqlchar* structure specified in the *FileTypeMod* parameter can contain any of the following values:

  "anyorder"

  "dldel$x$"

  "fastparse"

  "indexfreespace=x"

  "lobsinfile"

  "noheader"

  "norowwarnings"

  "pagefreespace=x"

  "totalfreespace=x"

  "usedefaults"

"codepage=*x*"

"dumpfile=*x*"

"implieddecimal"

"noeofchar"

"binarynumerics"

"nullindchar=*x*"

"packeddecimal"

"reclen=*x*"

"striptblanks"

"striptnulls"

"chardel*x*"

"coldel*x*"

"dateiso"

"decplusblank"

"decpt*x*"

"nodoubledel"

"forcein"

"nochecklengths"

These values provide additional information about the chosen file format. Only a portion of these values is used with a particular file format. If the *FileTypeMod* parameter is set to NULL or if the *length* field of the *sqlchar* structure is set to 0, default information is provided for the file format specified.

- If data is being loaded from either a delimited ASCII (SQL_DEL) or PC/IXF (SQL_IXF) format file the *FileTypeMod* parameter can specify where LOB data is stored. If this parameter is set to "lobsinfile," LOB data is stored in separate external files; otherwise, all LOB data is assumed to be truncated to 32KB and stored in the same file.

- If the *FileTypeMod* parameter is set to "norowwarnings," all warnings that are generated because rows of data were rejected are ignored.

- If the *FileTypeMod* parameter is set to "pagefreespace=*x*" (where *x* is an integer between 0 and 100), the value specified for *x* is interpreted as the percentage of each data page that is to be left as free storage space.

- If the *FileTypeMod* parameter is set to "totalpagefreespace=*x*" (where *x* is an integer between 0 and 100), the value specified for *x* is interpreted as the percentage of the total number of pages in the table that are to be appended to the end of the table as free storage space. For example, if *x* is 20 and the table contains 100 data pages, 20 additional empty pages will be appended to the table. If a value of 100 is specified for *x*, each row of data will be placed on a separate page.

- If data is being loaded from a delimited ASCII (SQL_DEL) format file, the

FileTypeMod parameter can be set to "`noeofchar`" to specify that the optional end-of-file character (0x1A) is not to be recognized as the end-of-file character. If this option is set, the end-of-file character is treated as a normal character.

■ If data is being loaded from a delimited ASCII (`SQL_DEL`) format file, the *FileTypeMod* parameter can be set to "`reclen=xxxx`" (where *xxxx* is an number no larger than 32,767) to specify that *xxxx* characters are to be read in for each row. In this case, a new-line character does not indicate the end of a row.

■ If data is being loaded from a delimited ASCII (`SQL_DEL`) format file, you can use the *FileTypeMod* parameter to specify characters that override the following options:

Datalink delimiters	By default, the inter-field separator for a DATALINK value is a semicolon (;). Specifying "`dldel`" followed by a character will cause the specified character to be used in place of a semicolon as the inter-field separator. The character specified must be different from the characters used as row, column, and character string delimiters.
Double character delimiters	Specifying "`nodoubledel`" will cause recognition of all double byte character delimiters to be suppressed.
Column delimiters	By default, columns are delimited with commas. Specifying "`coldel`" followed by a character causes the specified character to be used in place of a comma to signal the end of a column.
Character string delimiters	By default, character strings are delimited with double quotation marks. Specifying "`chardel`" followed by a character causes the specified character to be used in place of double quotation marks to enclose a character string.
Decimal point characters	By default, decimal points are specified with periods. Specifying "`decpt`" followed by a character causes the specified character to be used in place of a period as a decimal point character.
Plus sign character	By default, positive decimal values are prefixed with a plus sign. Specifying "`decplusblank`" will cause positive decimal values to be prefixed with a blank space instead of a plus sign.
Date format	Specifying "`datesiso`" will cause all date values to be imported in ISO format.

■ If two or more delimiters are specified, they must be separated by blank spaces. Blank spaces cannot be used as delimiters. Each delimiter character specified must be different from the delimiter characters already being used, so all delimiters can be uniquely identified. Table 11–3 (refer to the EXPORT function) lists the characters that can be used as delimiter overrides.

■ If the *FileTypeMod* parameter is set to "anyorder", the order of the source data does not have to be preserved. If this option is specified, significant performance gains can be seen on SMP systems.

■ If the *FileTypeMod* parameter is set to "fastparse", less data checking is performed on user-supplied column values. This option does not affect referential integrity checking or constraints checking; instead, it reduces syntax checking to improve overall performance.

■ If the *FileTypeMod* parameter is set to "indexfreespace=*x*" (where *x* is an integer between 0 and 99), the value specified for *x* is interpreted as the percentage of each index page that is to be left as free storage space when loading the index.

■ If the *FileTypeMod* parameter is set to "noheader", the header verification code that is written to files by the Data Declustering Tool (**db2split**) is ignored. This option should only be used when loading files into a table that exists on a single-node nodegroup.

■ If the source column in an external file has been explicitly specified, and if it does not contain data for one or more rows, the *FileTypeMod* parameter can be set to "usedefaults" to ensure that default values are substituted. Otherwise, a NULL is substituted if the table column is nullable—or the row is not loaded if the table column is not nullable.

■ If data is being loaded from an ASCII (SQL_DEL or SQL_ASC) format file, the *FileTypeMod* parameter can be set to "codepage=*xxx*" (where *xxx* equals a character string) to specify the code page of the data in the external file.

■ If data is being loaded from an ASCII (SQL_DEL or SQL_ASC) format file, the *FileTypeMod* parameter can be set to "dumpfile=*x*" (where *x* equals a valid file name) to specify the name of an exception file that exception rows of data will be written to.

■ If data is being loaded from an ASCII (SQL_DEL or SQL_ASC) format file, the *FileTypeMod* parameter can be set to "implieddecimal" to specify that the location of an implied decimal point is to be determined by the table column definition (for example, if the value 12,345 were to be loaded into a DECIMAL(8,2) column, it would be loaded as 123.45, not as 12345.00—which would otherwise be the case).

■ If data is being loaded from a non-delimited ASCII (SQL_ASC) format file, the *FileTypeMod* parameter can be set to "binarynumerics" to specify that numeric data (other than DECIMAL) is stored and is to be loaded in binary format (not a character representation).

■ If data is being loaded from a non-delimited ASCII (SQL_ASC) format file, the *FileTypeMod* parameter can be set to "nullindchar=*x*" (where *x* equals a character) to specify that a NULL value is to be replaced with a specific character. The character specified is case-sensitive for EBCDIC data files, except when the character is an English character.

■ If data is being loaded from a non-delimited ASCII (sQL_ASC) format file, the *FileTypeMod* parameter can be set to "packeddecimal" to specify that DECIMAL numeric data is stored and is to be loaded in packed-decimal format (not a character representation).

■ If data is being loaded from a non-delimited ASCII (sQL_ASC) format file, the *FileTypeMod* parameter can be set to "striptblanks" to specify that trailing blank spaces (after the last nonblank character) are to be removed (truncated) when data is imported. If this option is not set, trailing blanks are kept.

■ If data is being loaded from a non-delimited ASCII (sQL_ASC) format file, the *FileTypeMod* parameter can be set to "striptnulls" to specify that trailing NULLs (after the last nonblank character) are to be removed (truncated) when data is imported into variable length fields. If this option is not set, NULLs (0x00 characters) are kept.

■ The "striptblanks" and the "striptnulls" options are mutually exclusive. If one is specified, the other cannot be used.

■ If data is being loaded from a PC/IXF (sQL_IXF) format file, the *FileTypeMod* parameter can be set to "forcein" to tell the import utility to accept data in spite of code page mismatches—and to suppress all translations between code pages.

■ If data is being loaded from a PC/IXF (sQL_IXF) format file, the *FileTypeMod* parameter can be set to "nochecklengths" to specify that checking to ensure that fixed length target fields are large enough to hold the imported data is not to be performed. This option is used in conjunction with the "forcein" option.

■ Data cannot be loaded into system catalog tables.

■ Data is loaded in the same sequence (order) it is stored in. If you want a particular data sequence, make sure the data is sorted before it is loaded.

■ This function will not issue a warning if you attempt to specify options that are not supported by the file types specified in the *FileType* parameter. Instead, the LOAD function will fail, and an error will be generated.

■ The LOAD utility builds indexes by using existing definitions.

■ The LOAD utility does not enforce referential constraints, check constraints, or update summary tables that are dependent upon the table being loaded. Tables that have referential or check constraints are placed in the "Check Pending" state after a load operation. Summary tables that are dependent on the tables being loaded are also placed in the "Check Pending" state.

■ If clustering is required, the data should be sorted on a clustering index before it is loaded.

■ The remote file name specified in the *RemoteMsgFileName* parameter resides on the server workstation and is accessed exclusively by DB2. Therefore, it is imperative that any file name qualification given to this file correspond to the directory structure of the server—not the client—and that the DB2 instance has read/write permission on this file.

■ Two different LOAD operations that use the same fully qualified remote message file name cannot run at the same time.

Authorization Only users with either System Administrator (SYSADM) authority or Database Administrator (DBADM) authority can execute this function call.

See Also IMPORT, EXPORT, LOAD QUERY, QUIESCE TABLESPACES FOR TABLE

Example The following C++ program illustrates how to use the LOAD function to load data into the DEPARTMENT table of the SAMPLE database:

```
/*─────────────────────────────────────────────────────────*/
/* NAME:     CH11EX3.SQC                                     */
/* PURPOSE:  Illustrate How To Use The Following DB2 API Functions */
/*           In A C++ Program:                               */
/*                                                           */
/*                LOAD                                       */
/*                QUIESCE TABLESPACES FOR TABLE              */
/*                                                           */
/*─────────────────────────────────────────────────────────*/

// Include The Appropriate Header Files
#include <windows.h>
#include <iostream.h>
#include <sqlenv.h>
#include <sqlutil.h>
#include <sql.h>

// Define The API_Class Class
class API_Class
{
    // Attributes
    public:
        struct sqlca   sqlca;

    // Operations
    public:
        long LoadData();
};

// Define The LoadData() Member Function
long API_Class::LoadData()
{
    // Declare The Local Memory Variables
    char                      String[80];
    char                      MsgFileName[80];
    char                      TempFileName[80];
    struct sqlu_media_list    DataFiles;
    struct sqlu_location_entry Location_Entry;
    struct sqlchar            *ActionString;
    struct sqldcol            DataDescriptor;
    struct sqluload_in        InputInfo;
    struct sqluload_out       OutputInfo;
```

```
// Initialize The Local Variables
strcpy(MsgFileName, "C:\\LOAD_MSG.DAT");
strcpy(TempFileName, "C:\\TEMP");
DataDescriptor.dcolmeth = SQL_METH_D;

// Initialize The Load Input Structure
InputInfo.sizeOfStruct = SQLULOAD_IN_SIZE;
InputInfo.savecnt = 0;
InputInfo.restartcnt = 0;
InputInfo.rowcnt = 0;
InputInfo.warningcnt = 20;
InputInfo.data_buffer_size = 0;
InputInfo.sort_buffer_size = 0;
InputInfo.hold_quiesce = FALSE;
InputInfo.restartphase = SQLU_LOAD_PHASE;
InputInfo.statsopt = SQL_STATS_ALL;
InputInfo.cpu_parallelism = 5;
InputInfo.disk_parallelism = 5;
InputInfo.non_recoverable = SQLU_RECOVERABLE_LOAD;

// Initialize The Load Output Structure
OutputInfo.sizeOfStruct = SQLULOAD_OUT_SIZE;

// Define The Action String That Will Be Used To Control How
// Data Is Loaded
strcpy(String, "REPLACE INTO DEPARTMENT");
ActionString = (struct sqlchar *)
    malloc (strlen(String) + sizeof(struct sqlchar));
ActionString->length = strlen(String);
strncpy(ActionString->data, String, strlen(String));

// Initialize The Media List Information Data Structure
DataFiles.media_type = SQLU_SERVER_LOCATION;
DataFiles.sessions = 1;
strcpy(Location_Entry.location_entry, "C://DEPT.IXF");
DataFiles.target.location = &Location_Entry;

// Restrict Access To The Table Spaces That Are Associated With
// The DEPARTMENT Table (Quiesce The Table Spaces)
sqluvqdp("DEPARTMENT", SQLU_QUIESCEMODE_EXCLUSIVE, NULL, &sqlca);

// If The Table Spaces Were Quiesced, Display A Message
if (sqlca.sqlcode == SQL_RC_OK)
{
    cout << "Table spaces for the DEPARTMENT table have been ";
    cout << "quiesced." << endl << endl;
}

// Load Data Into The DEPARTMENT Table From An IXF Format File
// (This File Was Created By The EXPORT Example)
sqluload(&DataFiles, NULL, &DataDescriptor, ActionString, SQL_IXF,
    NULL, MsgFileName, TempFileName, SQLU_INITIAL, &InputInfo,
    &OutputInfo, NULL, NULL, NULL, NULL, &sqlca);
```

```
    // If The Data Was Loaded Successfully, Display A Success
    // Message
    if (sqlca.sqlcode == SQL_RC_OK)
    {
        cout << OutputInfo.rowsLoaded << " ";
        cout << "rows of data were loaded into the DEPARTMENT ";
        cout << "table from the " << endl;
        cout << "file C:/DEPT.IXF." << endl << endl;
    }

    // Remove The Access Restriction That Was Placed On The Table
    // Spaces That Are Associated With The DEPARTMENT Table
    sqluvqdp("DEPARTMENT", SQLU_QUIESCEMODE_RESET, NULL, &sqlca);

    // If The Quiesced Table Spaces Were Released, Display A Message
    if (sqlca.sqlcode == SQL_RC_OK)
    {
        cout << "Table spaces for the DEPARTMENT table have been ";
        cout << "released." << endl << endl;
    }

    // Free All Allocated Memory
    if (ActionString != NULL)
        free(ActionString);

    // Return The SQLCA Return Code To The Calling Function
    return(sqlca.sqlcode);
}

/*-----------------------------------------------------------*/
/* The Main Function                                         */
/*-----------------------------------------------------------*/
int main()
{
    // Declare The Local Memory Variables
    long         rc = SQL_RC_OK;
    struct sqlca sqlca;

    // Create An Instance Of The API_Class Class
    API_Class  Example;

    // Connect To The SAMPLE Database
    EXEC SQL CONNECT TO SAMPLE USER userID USING password;

    // Load Data Stored In An External File Into The DEPARTMENT
    // Table (In The SAMPLE Database)
    rc = Example.LoadData();

    // Issue A Rollback To Free All Locks
    EXEC SQL ROLLBACK;

    // Disconnect From The SAMPLE Database
    EXEC SQL DISCONNECT CURRENT;
```

```
                  // Return To The Operating System
                  return(rc);
              }
```

■■ ■■ LOAD QUERY

Purpose   The LOAD QUERY function is used to query a DB2 Database Manager instance for the
                 current status of a Load operation.

Syntax   SQL_API_RC SQL_API_FN sqluqry (char   *LocalMsgFileName,
                                                char   *RemoteMsgFileName,
                                                struct sqlca *SQLCA);

Parameters   *LocalMsgFileName*   A pointer to a location in memory where the name of the
                                        local file that all load status messages are to be written to
                                        is stored.

                 RemoteMsgFileName   A pointer to a location in memory where the name of the
                                        remote message file that all load error, warning, and
                                        informational messages are written to is stored.

                 SQLCA   A pointer to a location in memory where a SQL
                                        Communications Area (SQLCA) data structure variable is
                                        stored. This variable returns either status information (if
                                        the function executed successfully) or error information (if
                                        the function failed) to the calling application.

Includes   #include <sqlutil.h>

Description The LOAD QUERY function is used to query a DB2 Database Manager instance for the
                 current status of a load operation. This function retrieves the status of a Load
                 operation from the remote message file that is created and used by the Load
                 operation that is currently in progress, and places the results in the file specified by
                 the *LocalMsgFileName* parameter.

Comments   ■ The remote file name specified must be the same as the file name specified in the
                 RemoteMsgFileName parameter of the LOAD function call.

**Connection   This function can only be called if a connection to a DB2 Database Manager instance
Requirements**   exists.

Authorization No authorization is required to execute this function call.

See Also   LOAD

Example   The following C++ program illustrates how the LOAD QUERY function is used to obtain
                 the status of a Load operation:

```
/*-----------------------------------------------------------------*/
/* NAME:     CH11EX4.SQC                                           */
/* PURPOSE: Illustrate How To Use The Following DB2 API Function   */
/*          In A C++ Program:                                      */
/*                                                                 */
/*                  LOAD QUERY                                     */
/*                                                                 */
/*-----------------------------------------------------------------*/

// Include The Appropriate Header Files
#include <windows.h>
#include <iostream.h>
#include <sqlutil.h>
#include <sql.h>

// Define The API_Class Class
class API_Class
{
    // Attributes
    public:
        struct sqlca   sqlca;

    // Operations
    public:
        long GetLoadStatus();
};

// Define The GetLoadStatus() Member Function
long API_Class::GetLoadStatus()
{
    // Declare The Local Memory Variables
    char    MsgFileName[80];
    char    StatsFileName[80];

    // Initialize The Local Variables
    strcpy(MsgFileName, "C:\\TEMP");
    strcpy(StatsFileName, "C:\\L_STATS.DAT");

    // Query The Status Of The Current Load Process
    sqluqry(StatsFileName, MsgFileName, &sqlca);

    // If Load Status Information Was Obtained, Display A Success
    // Message
    if (sqlca.sqlcode == SQL_RC_OK)
    {
        cout << "The status of the current load process has been ";
        cout << "collected and placed in" << endl;
        cout << "the file C:\\L_STATS.DAT." << endl;
    }

    // Return The SQLCA Return Code To The Calling Function
    return(sqlca.sqlcode);
}
```

```
/*————————————————————————————————————————————*/
/* The Main Function                                              */
/*————————————————————————————————————————————*/
int main()
{
    // Declare The Local Memory Variables
    long          rc = SQL_RC_OK;
    struct sqlca  sqlca;

    // Create An Instance Of The API_Class Class
    API_Class  Example;

    // Connect To The SAMPLE Database
    EXEC SQL CONNECT TO SAMPLE USER userID USING password;

    // Get Information About The Status Of A Load Operation
    rc = Example.GetLoadStatus();

    // Issue A Rollback To Free All Locks
    EXEC SQL ROLLBACK;

    // Disconnect From The SAMPLE Database
    EXEC SQL DISCONNECT CURRENT;

    // Return To The Operating System
    return(rc);
}
```

QUIESCE TABLESPACES FOR TABLE

Purpose   The QUIESCE TABLESPACES FOR TABLE function is used to place all table spaces that
are associated with a particular database table in a quiesced (restricted access) state.

Syntax
```
SQL_API_RC SQL_API_FN sqluvqdp (char          *TableName,
                                long          QuiesceMode,
                                void          *Reserved,
                                struct sqlca *SQLCA);
```

Parameters   *TableName*   A pointer to a location in memory where the name of the table, as it
is defined in the system catalog, is stored.

QuiesceMode   Specifies the quiesce mode to be used. This parameter must be set to
one of the following values:

■ SQLU_QUIESCEMODE_SHARE
The Table space(s) are to be placed in the "Quiesced Share" state.

■ SQLU_QUIESCEMODE_INTENT_UPDATE
Table space(s) are to be placed in the "Quiesce Intent to Update"
state.

- **SQLU_QUIESCEMODE_EXCLUSIVE**
  Table space(s) are to be placed in the "Quiesce Exclusive" state.

- **SQLU_QUIESCEMODE_RESET**
  Table space(s) are to be returned to their normal state if the caller owns the quiesce—or if the caller who originally set the quiesce disconnects.

- **SQLU_QUIESCEMODE_RESET_OWNED**
  Table space(s) are to be returned to their normal state if the caller owns the quiesce.

Reserved   A pointer that is currently reserved for later use. For now, this parameter must always be set to NULL.

SQLCA   A pointer to a location in memory where a SQL Communications Area (SQLCA) data structure variable is stored. This variable returns either status information (if the function executed successfully) or error information (if the function failed) to the calling application.

Includes   `#include <sqlutil.h>`

Description The QUIESCE TABLESPACES FOR TABLE function is used to place all table spaces that are associated with a particular database table in a quiesced (restricted access) state. When this function is executed, only transactions that are holding the table space in a quiesced state are granted access to the table space. All other transactions are "locked out" of the table space until it is returned to its normal state. Table spaces can be placed one of the following quiesce states:

"Quiesced Share"

"Quiesced Update"

"Quiesced Exclusive"

These states determine how other transactions that currently hold a quiesce state on the table space or that attempt to set a quiesce state for the table space can access the table space.

Comments
- The table name specified in the *TableName* parameter can be a two-part name with the schema and table name separated by a period. If the schema is not provided, the authorization ID that was used to establish the database connection will be used as the default schema.

- The table name specified in the *TableName* parameter cannot be a system catalog table.

- When the SQLU_QUIESCEMODE_SHARE value is specified in the *QuiesceMode* parameter, the transaction requests a Share lock for the specified table and Intent Share locks for all associated table spaces. When the transaction obtains the locks, the state of the table spaces is changed to "Quiesced Share." This state is only granted to the application that quiesced the table space (the quiescer) if there is no conflicting state held by other applications. The state of the table spaces is recorded in the table space table, along with the authorization ID and the database agent ID of the quiescer, so the state is persistent. The table specified cannot be changed while the table spaces for that table are in the "Quiesced Share" state. However, other share mode requests to the table and table spaces are allowed. When the transaction is committed or rolled back, the locks are released, but the table spaces for the table remain in the "Quiesced Share" state until the state is explicitly reset (by another call to this function).

■ When the SQLU_QUIESCEMODE_EXCLUSIVE value is specified in the *QuiesceMode* parameter, the transaction requests a Super-Exclusive lock for the table specified and Super-Exclusive locks for all associated table spaces. When the transaction obtains the locks, the state of the table spaces changes to "Quiesced Exclusive," and the state of the table spaces, along with the authorization ID and the database agent ID of the quiescer, are recorded in the table space table. Since the table spaces are held in super-exclusive mode, no other access to the table spaces is allowed. The transaction that invokes this function, however, has exclusive access to the table and the table spaces.

■ When the SQLU_QUIESCEMODE_INTENT_UPDATE value is specified in the *QuiesceMode* parameter, the transaction requests an Update lock for the table specified and Intent Exclusive locks for all associated table spaces. When the transaction obtains the locks, the state of the table spaces changes to the "Quiesced Update" and the state of the table spaces, along with the authorization ID and the database agent ID of the quiescer, are recorded in the table space table. Because the table spaces are held in exclusive mode, no other access to the table spaces is allowed. The transaction that invokes this function, however, has exclusive access to the table and the table spaces.

■ There is a limit of five quiescers on a table space at any given time. Because the "Quiesced Exclusive" state is incompatible with any other state, and a "Quiesced Update" state is incompatible with another "Quiesced Update" state, the five-quiescer limit, if reached, must consist of at least four "Quiesced Share" states and, at most, one "Quiesced Update" or one "Quiesced Exclusive" state.

■ A quiescer can upgrade the state of a table space from a less restrictive state to a more restrictive one (for example, SHARE to UPDATE or UPDATE to EXCLUSIVE). If a user requests a state lower than one that is already held, the original state will be returned. Quiesce states cannot be downgraded.

■ Once changed, you must explicitly reset the quiesced state of a table space by executing this function with the SQLU_QUIESCEMODE_RESET value specified in the *QuiesceMode* parameter.

■ In a multi-node environment, this function acts locally on a single node; i.e., it only quiesces that portion of one or more table spaces that belong to the node that this function is called from.

Connection Requirements   This function can only be called if a connection to a database exists.

Authorization   Only users with System Administrator (SYSADM) authority, System Control (SYSCTRL) authority, System Maintenance (SYSMAINT) authority, or Database Administrator (DBADM) authority can execute this function call.

See Also   LOAD

Example   See the example provided for the LOAD function on page 461.

12

DB2 Database Partition Management Functions

DB2 Universal Database has been designed to run on a wide variety of hardware configurations. Unlike earlier versions, DB2 UDB Version 5.0 and later can exploit the power of parallel multi-node environments. This chapter is designed to introduce you to the set of DB2 API functions that are used to manage database partitions and nodegroups in multi-node environments. The first part of this chapter provides a general discussion about nodegroups and database partitioning. Then, the types of parallelism that are available with DB2 Universal Database are discussed. Finally, a detailed reference section covering each DB2 API function that can be used to manage nodegroups and database partitions is provided.

Nodegroups And Data Partitioning

As mentioned earlier, the DB2 Database Manager controls what can be done to data in a database and manages any system resources that have been assigned to it. DB2 Universal Database 5.0 and later enables the Database Manager to operate in a parallel, multi-node (workstation) environment by allowing a database to be broken into several different partitions.

A *database partition* is a part of a single database that contains its own indexes, configuration files, and transaction log files. You can define a named subset of one or more database partitions; each named subset is referred to as a *nodegroup*, and each node-group that contains more than one database partition is known as a *multi-partition nodegroup*. However, each database partition defined in a multi-partition nodegroup must belong to the same DB2 Database Manager instance.

Each nodegroup is associated with a *partitioning map*, which is an array of 4096 partition numbers. The partitioning index that is automatically created for each row of a partitioned table is used as an index into the partitioning map. This index is used to determine which partition a particular row of data is stored on. The GET TABLE PARTITIONING INFORMATION and GET ROW PARTITIONING NUMBER functions can be used to view partitioning map and index information. The REDISTRIBUTE NODEGROUP function can be used to rearrange the contents of a partitioning map/index.

A *single-partition* database is a database that has only one partition; all of the database's data is stored in that partition. In this case, a nodegroup is present; however, the nodegroup does not provide any additional capability. A *partitioned database* is a database that has been divided into two or more partitions. Data (i.e. tables) in a partitioned database can reside in one, several, or all available partitions. When a table is in a multi-partition nodegroup, some of its rows are stored in one partition, and the rest of its rows are stored in other partitions.

Usually, a single database partition exists on each physical node (workstation) in a multi-node system, and the processors located at each node are used by the Database Manager to manage that partition's part of the database's data. This process allows an application to utilize the power of multiple processors to satisfy large data manipulation requests. Data retrieval and update requests are divided into sub-requests that are executed in parallel on the applicable partitions. The fact that the database is split across multiple partitions is transparent to users. That's because user interaction is always performed through a single partition, which is known as the *coordinator node*. The coordinator runs on the same database partition as the application, or in the case of a remote application, the partition to which the application is connected. Any database partition can be used as a coordinator node.

Types Of Parallelism

There are different ways that a task can be performed in parallel. Three factors—the nature of the task, the database configuration, and the hardware environment—determine how DB2 will perform a task in parallel. Using these factors, DB2 can initiate one of the following types of parallelism:

- I/O parallelism
- Query parallelism

I/O Parallelism

For situations in which multiple storage containers exist for a single table space, the DB2 Database Manager can initiate *I/O parallelism*. I/O parallelism refers to the process of reading from or writing to two or more *input/output* (I/O) devices at the same time. I/O parallelism can cause significant improvements to I/O throughput.

Query Parallelism

Query parallelism controls how database operations are performed. DB2 Universal Database supports two types of query parallelism: *inter-query parallelism* and *intra-query parallelism*. Inter-query parallelism refers to the ability to allow multiple applications to query a database at the same time. With this type of query parallelism, each application's query will execute independently of the others, but all queries will be executed at the same time.

Intra-query parallelism refers to the ability to break large database operations such as index creation, loads, and complex SQL queries into multiple parts that are then executed simultaneously, using either *intra-partition parallelism*, *inter-partition parallelism*, or both.

INTRA-PARTITION PARALLELISM

With intra-partition parallelism, database operations are subdivided into multiple parts which are then executed in parallel within a single database partition. Figure 12–1 shows how a large SQL query might be executed faster using intra-partition parallelism. In this example, the query is broken into three parts—which are then executed at the same time in the same partition. All four parts are essentially a copy of each other.

Whether or not intra-partition parallelism will be utilized is determined by the database configuration file. The degree of parallelism specified controls the number of parts that a query can be broken into for executing.

INTER-PARTITION PROCESSING

With inter-partition parallelism, database operations are subdivided into multiple parts, which are then executed in parallel across one or more partitions of a partitioned database (which may reside on one machine or on multiple machines). Figure 12–2 shows how a large SQL query might be executed faster using inter-partition parallelism. In this example, the query is broken into three parts, which are then executed at the same time across multiple partitions.

With inter-partition parallelism, the degree of parallelism used is largely determined by the number of partitions created and by the way nodegroups have been defined.

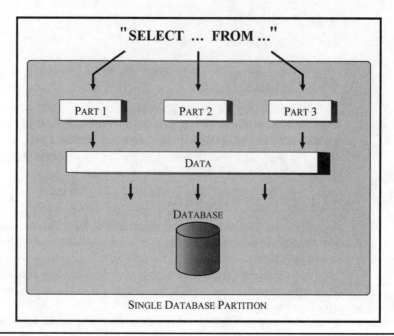

Figure 12–1   Intra-Partition Parallelism.

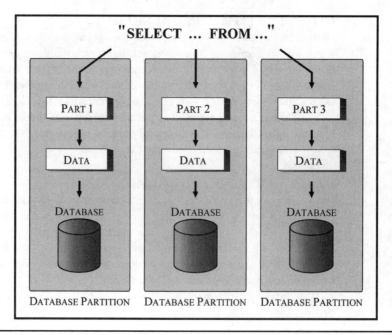

Figure 12–2   Inter-Partition Parallelism.

USING BOTH INTRA-PARTITION PARALLELISM AND INTER-PARTITION PARALLELISM

Intra-partition parallelism and inter-partition parallelism are not mutually exclusive. Both can be used at the same time. This characteristic, in effect, provides two dimensions of parallelism. When used together, an even more dramatic increase in the speed at which database operations are performed can be achieved.

Enabling Query Parallelism

In order to take advantage of parallelism within a database partition or within a non-partitioned database, you must modify the parameters in the DB2 Database Manager configuration file (and in some cases the parameters in one or more database configuration files).

For example, the configuration file parameters that affect intra-partition parallelism include the DB2 Database Manager configuration file parameters *max_querydegree* and *intra_parallel* and the database configuration file parameter *dft_degree*. Refer to the GET DATABASE MANAGER CONFIGURATION function and the GET DATABASE CONFIGURATION function in Chapter 9 for more information about configuration file parameters.

Enabling Data Partitioning

Before creating a partitioned database, you must decide whether your workstation will be a local or a remote client to the DB2 Database Manager instance where the database will be created. Then, you must decide which partition will serve as the catalog node for the database. The workstation on which you execute the CREATE DATABASE command or function will become the catalog node for that particular database (the catalog node is the partition on which all system catalog tables are stored). All access to the system tables must go through this partition.

When you execute the CREATE DATABASE command or function, the new database is automatically created across all database partitions that are defined in the *db2nodes.cfg* configuration file. In addition, the following three nodegroups are defined:

- IBMCATGROUP (for the SYSCATSPACE table space, to hold all system tables)
- IBMTEMPGROUP (for the TEMPSPACE1 table space, to hold all temporary tables that are created during database processing)
- IBMDEFAULTGROUP (for the USERSPACE1 table space, to hold user-defined tables and indexes)

Once the database has been created, parameters in both the DB2 Database Manager configuration file and in the new database's configuration file have to be modified in order to take advantage of data partitioning. Specifically, the *conn_elapse*, *fcm_num_anchors*, *fcm_num_buffers*, *fcm_num_connect*, *fcm_num_rqb*, *max_connretries*, *max_coordagents*, *max_time_diff*, *num_poolagents*, and *stop_start_time* DB2 Database Manager configuration parameters affect database partitioning. Refer to the

GET DATABASE MANAGER CONFIGURATION function and the GET DATABASE CONFIGURA-TION function in Chapter 9 for more information about configuration file parameters.

The DB2 Database Partition Management Functions

Table 12–1 lists the DB2 API functions that are used to manage nodegroups and database partitions.

Each of these functions is described in detail in the remainder of this chapter.

Table 12–1   DB2 Database Partition Management Functions

Function Name	Description
ADD NODE	Adds a new node to a parallel database system.
DROP NODE VERIFY	Identifies whether or not a specific node is currently being used by a database.
CREATE DATABASE AT NODE	Creates a database at a specific node in a parallel database system.
DROP DATABASE AT NODE	Removes (drops) a database from a specific node in a parallel database system.
SET RUNTIME DEGREE	Sets the run-time degree of intra-partition parallelism that is to be used to process SQL statements.
GET TABLE PARTITIONING INFORMATION	Obtains the partitioning information for a database table.
GET ROW PARTITIONING NUMBER	Obtains the partition number and node number at which a specific row of data in a table is stored (in a parallel database system).
REDISTRIBUTE NODEGROUP	Redistributes data across the nodes in a nodegroup.

ADD NODE

Purpose   The ADD NODE function is used to add a new node to a parallel database system.

Syntax
```
SQL_API_RC SQL_API_FN sqleaddn (unsigned short    NodeOptionsSize,
                                void              *NodeOptions,
                                struct sqlca      *SQLCA);
```

Parameters *NodeOptionsSize*   The length, in bytes, of the *sqle_addn_options* structure stored in the *NodeOptions* parameter.

NodeOptions   A pointer to a location in memory where an *sqle_addn_options* structure that contains information about the node to be added is stored.

SQLCA   A pointer to a location in memory where a SQL Communications Area (SQLCA) data structure variable is stored. This structure returns either status information (if the function executed successfully) or error information (if the function failed) to the calling application.

Includes   `#include <sqlenv.h>`

Description The ADD NODE function is used to add a new node to a parallel database system. When this function is called, database partitions are automatically created (on the new node) for each database that is currently defined in the MPP server instance, and the configuration parameters for each new database partition are set to the system default values. However, these partitions cannot be used to store user data until the ALTER NODEGROUP SQL statement has been used to add the new node to an existing nodegroup.

This function uses a special structure, the *sqle_addn_options* structure, to specify information about the node (if any) in which the temporary table space definitions for all database partitions to be created is stored. The *sqle_addn_options* structure is defined in *sqlenv.h* as follows:

```
struct sqle_addn_options
{
char              sqladdid[8];   /* An "eye catcher" value that is used  */
                                 /* to identify the structure. This field*/
                                 /* must be set to SQLE_ADDOPTID_V51.    */
unsigned long     tblspace_type; /* Indicates that temporary table       */
                                 /* spaces should be the same as those   */
                                 /* found at the specified node          */
                                 /* (SQLE_TABLESPACES_LIKE_NODE), the     */
                                 /* same as those found at the catalog    */
                                 /* node of each database                */
                                 /* (SQLE_TABLESPACES_LIKE_CATALOG),      */
                                 /* or not created at all                */
                                 /* (SQLE_TABLESPACES_NONE).              */
```

```
SQL_PDB_NODE_TYPE tblspace_node; /* Specifies the node number that     */
                                 /* tablespace definitions should be   */
                                 /* obtained from (provided the        */
                                 /* tblspace_type field is set         */
                                 /* to SQLE_TABLESPACES_LIKE_NODE).     */
                                 /* Note: The node number specified must */
                                 /* exist in the file db2nodes.cfg.    */
        };
```

Comments

■ This function must be called from the node that is to be added, and it can only be issued against an MPP server.

■ Before a new node can be added, sufficient disk space must exist for each storage container that will be created (for each existing database) on the system.

■ If an add node operation fails while creating a database partition locally, a clean-up phase is initiated, and all database partitions that have already been created are dropped (i.e. database partitions are removed from the node being added—the local node). If the clean-up phase is initiated, existing database partitions on other nodes are not affected.

■ If this function is called while a database creation (CREATE DATABASE) or a database deletion (DROP DATABASE) operation is in progress, an error will be returned.

■ If temporary table spaces are to be created within the database partitions that are automatically created when this function is called, this function may communicate with another node in the MPP system to retrieve existing table space definitions. In this case, the *start_stop_time* DB2 Database Manager configuration file parameter is used to specify the time, in minutes, in which the other node must respond. If this time is exceeded, an error will be returned.

Connection
Database Manager
Requirements
first.

This function can be called at any time; a connection to a DB2 instance or to a DB2 database does not have to be established

Authorization

Only users with either System Administrator (SYSADM) authority or System Control (SYSCTRL) authority are allowed to execute this function call.

See Also

DROP NODE VERIFY

Example

The following C++ program illustrates how to use the ADD NODE function to add a new node to an MPP system:

```
/*------------------------------------------------------------------*/
/* NAME:     CH12EX1.CPP                                            */
/* PURPOSE:  Illustrate How To Use The Following DB2 API Function   */
/*           In A C++ Program:                                      */
/*                                                                  */
```

```
/*                      ADD NODE                              */
/*                                                            */
/*————————————————————————————————————————————————————————————*/

// Include The Appropriate Header Files
#include <windows.h>
#include <iostream.h>
#include <sqlenv.h>
#include <sqlca.h>

// Define The API_Class Class
class API_Class
{
    // Attributes
    public:
        struct sqlca   sqlca;

    // Operations
    public:
        long AddNode();
};

// Define The AddNode() Member Function
long API_Class::AddNode()
{
    // Declare The Local Memory Variables
    struct sqle_addn_options   NodeOptions;

    // Initialize The Add Node Options Structure
    strcpy(NodeOptions.sqladdid, SQLE_ADDOPTID_V51);
    NodeOptions.tblspace_type = SQLE_TABLESPACES_NONE;
    NodeOptions.tblspace_node = 0;

    // Add The New Node
    sqleaddn(&NodeOptions, &sqlca);

    // If The New Node Has Been Added, Display A Success Message
    if (sqlca.sqlcode == SQL_RC_OK)
        cout << "The new node has been added." << endl;

    // Return The SQLCA Return Code To The Calling Function
    return(sqlca.sqlcode);
}

/*————————————————————————————————————————————————————————————*/
/* The Main Function                                          */
/*————————————————————————————————————————————————————————————*/
int main()
{
    // Declare The Local Memory Variables
    long   rc = SQL_RC_OK;

    // Create An Instance Of The API_Class Class
    API_Class   Example;
```

```
// Add A New Node To A Parallel Database System
rc = Example.AddNode();

// Return To The Operating System
return(rc);
}
```

■■ ■■ DROP NODE VERIFY

Purpose   The DROP NODE VERIFY function is used to identify whether or not a specific node in a parallel database system is currently being used by a database.

Syntax

```
SQL_API_RC SQL_API_FN sqledrpn  (unsigned short   Action,
                                 void             *Reserved,
                                 struct sqlca     *SQLCA);
```

Parameters   *Action*   Specifies the action that this function is to perform. This parameter must be set to the following value:

              ■ SQL_DROPNODE_VERIFY

        Reserved   A pointer that, at this time, is reserved for later use. For now, this parameter must always be set to NULL.

        SQLCA   A pointer to a location in memory where a SQL Communications Area (SQLCA) data structure variable is stored. This structure returns either status information (if the function executed successfully) or error information (if the function failed) to the calling application.

Includes   `#include <sqlenv.h>`

Description   The DROP NODE VERIFY function is used to identify whether or not a specific node in a parallel database system is currently being used by a database. If this function indicates that a node is not being used by one or more databases, the STOP DATABASE MANAGER command or function can be used to remove the node from the database system (by removing its corresponding entry in the *db2nodes.cfg* file). However, if this function indicates that a node is being used by one or more databases, the following steps must be performed before the node can be removed from the database system:

1. If the node contains data, call the REDISTRIBUTE NODEGROUP function to move the data to other nodes within the database system.

2. Call the REDISTRIBUTE NODEGROUP function or execute the ALTER NODEGROUP SQL statement to remove the node from any node groups that the node has been assigned to. Note that this step must be done for each database that has the node defined in a node group.

3. Delete (drop) any event monitors that have been defined for the node.

4. Call the DROP NODE VERIFY function again to ensure that the node is no longer being used by one or more databases.

5. Call the STOP DATABASE MANAGER function to remove the node from the database system.

Comments ■ This function must be called from the node that is to be verified/removed from the database system, and the function can only be issued against an MPP server.

Connection Requirements This function can be called at any time; a connection to a DB2 Database Manager instance or to a DB2 database does not have to be established first.

Authorization Only users with either System Administrator (SYSADM) authority or System Control (SYSCTRL) authority are allowed to execute this function call.

See Also ADD NODE, STOP DATABASE MANAGER, REDISTRIBUTE NODEGROUP

Example The following C++ program illustrates how to use the DROP NODE VERIFY function to determine whether or not specific node in a parallel database system is currently being used by a database:

```
/*----------------------------------------------------------*/
/* NAME:     CH12EX2.CPP                                     */
/* PURPOSE:  Illustrate How To Use The Following DB2 API Function */
/*           In A C++ Program:                               */
/*                                                           */
/*              DROP NODE VERIFY                             */
/*                                                           */
/*----------------------------------------------------------*/

// Include The Appropriate Header Files
#include <windows.h>
#include <iostream.h>
#include <sqlenv.h>
#include <sqlca.h>

// Define The API_Class Class
class API_Class
{
    // Attributes
    public:
        struct sqlca   sqlca;

    // Operations
    public:
        long CheckNode();
};

// Define The CheckNode() Member Function
long API_Class::CheckNode()
{
    // Declare The Local Memory Variables
    char   Message[1024];
```

```
// Determine Whether Or Not The Current Node Is Being Used By
// A Database
sqledrpn(SQL_DROPNODE_VERIFY, NULL, &sqlca);

// Display The Message Returned
sqlaintp(Message, 1024, 70, &sqlca);
cout << Message << endl;

// Return The SQLCA Return Code To The Calling Function
return(sqlca.sqlcode);
}

/*-------------------------------------------------------------------*/
/* The Main Function                                                 */
/*-------------------------------------------------------------------*/
int main()
{
// Declare The Local Memory Variables
long  rc = SQL_RC_OK;

// Create An Instance Of The API_Class Class
API_Class  Example;

// Determine Whether Or Not The Current Node Is Being Used By A
// Database
rc = Example.CheckNode();

// Return To The Operating System
return(rc);
}
```

CREATE DATABASE AT NODE

Purpose   The CREATE DATABASE AT NODE function is used to create a database at a specific node in a parallel database system.

Syntax
```
SQL_API_RC SQL_API_FN sqlecran (char        *DBName,
                                void        *Reserved,
                                struct sqlca *SQLCA);
```

Parameters   *DBName*   A pointer to location in memory where the name of the database to create is stored.

                   Reserved   A pointer that, at this time, is reserved for later use. For now, this parameter must always be set to NULL.

                   SQLCA   A pointer to a location in memory where a SQL Communications Area (SQLCA) data structure variable is stored. This structure returns either status information (if the function executed successfully) or error information (if the function failed) to the calling application.

Includes   `#include <sqlenv.h>`

Description The CREATE DATABASE AT NODE function is used to create a database at a specific node in a parallel database system. This function should only be used to recreate a database partition (at a node) that has been damaged and is unusable.

NOTE: Improper use of this function can cause inconsistencies in a database system. Therefore, this function should be used with extreme caution.

Comments
- This function must be called from the node that the database is to be created on and it can only be issued against an MPP server.
- When a database is created at a specific node, the database is placed in the "Restore Pending" state and must be restored before it can be used.

Connection Requirements This function can only be called when a connection to a DB2 Database Manager instance exists. To create a database at another node, an attachment to that node must first be established. A database connection is temporarily established by this function for the duration of the call.

Authorization Only users with either System Administrator (SYSADM) authority or System Control (SYSCTRL) authority are allowed to execute this function call.

See Also   DROP DATABASE AT NODE

Example The following C++ program illustrates how to use the CREATE DATABASE AT NODE function to recreate a database at a specific node in a parallel database system:

```
/*————————————————————————————————————*/
/* NAME:     CH12EX3.CPP                                    */
/* PURPOSE: Illustrate How To Use The Following DB2 API Function */
/*          In A C++ Program:                               */
/*                                                          */
/*              CREATE DATABASE AT NODE                     */
/*                                                          */
/*————————————————————————————————————*/

// Include The Appropriate Header Files
#include <windows.h>
#include <iostream.h>
#include <sqlenv.h>
#include <sqlca.h>

// Define The API_Class Class
class API_Class
{
    // Attributes
    public:
        struct sqlca  sqlca;
```

```
    // Operations
    public:
        long CreateDBAtNode();
};


// Define The CreateDBAtNode() Member Function
long API_Class::CreateDBAtNode()
{
    // Declare The Local Memory Variables
    char  Instance[9];

    // Obtain The Current Value Of The DB2INSTANCE Environment
    // Variable
    sqlegins(Instance, &sqlca);
    Instance[8] = 0;

    // Attach To The Current DB2 Database Manager Instance
    sqleatin(Instance, "userid", "password", &sqlca);

    // Create The TEST Database At The Current Node
    sqlecran("TEST", NULL, &sqlca);

    // If The TEST Database Has Been Created, Display A Success
    // Message
    if (sqlca.sqlcode == SQL_RC_OK)
    {
        cout << "The TEST database has been created ";
        cout << "at this node." << endl;
    }

    // Detach From The Current DB2 Database Manager Instance
    sqledtin(&sqlca);

    // Return The SQLCA Return Code To The Calling Function
    return(sqlca.sqlcode);
}

/*———————————————————————————————————————————————————*/
/* The Main Function                                 */
/*———————————————————————————————————————————————————*/
int main()
{
    // Declare The Local Memory Variables
    long  rc = SQL_RC_OK;

    // Create An Instance Of The API_Class Class
    API_Class  Example;

    // Create The TEST Database At The Current Node
    rc = Example.CreateDBAtNode();

    // Return To The Operating System
    return(rc);
}
```

 **DROP DATABASE AT NODE**

Purpose   The DROP DATABASE AT NODE function is used to remove (drop) a database from a specific node in a parallel database system.

Syntax
```
SQL_API_RC  SQL_API_FN  sqledpan (char        *DBAlias,
                                  void         *Reserved,
                                  struct sqlca *SQLCA);
```

Parameters   *DBAlias*   A pointer to location in memory where the alias of the database to be removed (dropped) is stored.

                 Reserved   A pointer that, at this time, is reserved for later use. For now, this parameter must always be set to NULL.

                 SQLCA   A pointer to a location in memory where a SQL Communications Area (SQLCA) data structure variable is stored. This structure returns either status information (if the function executed successfully) or error information (if the function failed) to the calling application.

Includes   `#include <sqlenv.h>`

Description The DROP DATABASE AT NODE function is used to remove (drop) a database from a specific node in a parallel database system. This function is used by utilities that are supplied with DB2 Universal Database Extended Enterprise Edition and is not intended for general use.

 NOTE: Improper use of this function can cause inconsistencies in a database system. Therefore, this function should be used with extreme caution.

Comments   ■ This function must be called from the node that the database is to be dropped from, and it can only be issued against an MPP server.

Connection Requirements This function can be called at any time; a connection to a DB2 Database Manager instance or to a DB2 database does not have to be established first. An attachment to a DB2 Database Manager instance is implicitly established for the duration of the call.

Authorization Only users with either System Administrator (SYSADM) authority or System Control (SYSCTRL) authority are allowed to execute this function call.

See Also   CREATE DATABASE AT NODE

Example   The following C++ program illustrates how to use the DROP DATABASE AT NODE function to remove a database from a specific node in a parallel database system:

```
/*-------------------------------------------------------------------*/
/* NAME:     CH12EX4.CPP                                             */
/* PURPOSE: Illustrate How To Use The Following DB2 API Function     */
/*          In A C++ Program:                                        */
/*                                                                   */
/*              DROP DATABASE AT NODE                                */
/*                                                                   */
/*-------------------------------------------------------------------*/

// Include The Appropriate Header Files
#include <windows.h>
#include <iostream.h>
#include <sqlenv.h>
#include <sqlca.h>

// Define The API_Class Class
class API_Class
{
    // Attributes
    public:
        struct sqlca    sqlca;

    // Operations
    public:
        long DropDBAtNode();
};

// Define The DropDBAtNode() Member Function
long API_Class::DropDBAtNode()
{
    // Drop The TEST Database At The Current Node
    sqledpan("TEST", NULL, &sqlca);

    // If The TEST Database Has Been Dropped, Display A Success
    // Message
    if (sqlca.sqlcode == SQL_RC_OK)
    {
        cout << "The TEST database has been dropped ";
        cout << "at this node." << endl;
    }

    // Return The SQLCA Return Code To The Calling Function
    return(sqlca.sqlcode);
}


/*-------------------------------------------------------------------*/
/* The Main Function                                                 */
/*-------------------------------------------------------------------*/
int main()
{
    // Declare The Local Memory Variables
    long   rc = SQL_RC_OK;

    // Create An Instance Of The API_Class Class
    API_Class  Example;
```

```
                  // Drop The TEST Database At The Current Node
                  rc = Example.DropDBAtNode();

                  // Return To The Operating System
                  return(rc);
         }
```

■■ ■■ SET RUNTIME DEGREE

Purpose   The SET RUNTIME DEGREE function is used to set the run-time degree of intra-partition parallelism that is to be used to process SQL statements for one or more active applications.

Syntax
```
SQL_API_RC SQL_API_FN sqlesdeg  (long          NumAgentIDs,
                                 unsigned long *AgentIDs,
                                 long          Degree,
                                 struct sqlca  *SQLCA);
```

Parameters   *NumAgentIDs*   The total number of active applications to which the new degree of intra-parallelism is to apply (i.e., the number of elements in the array of agent IDs specified in the *AgentIDs* parameter).

              AgentIDs   A pointer to a location in memory where an array of active application agent IDs are stored.

              Degree   The maximum run-time degree of intra-partition parallelism that is to be used to process SQL statements.

              SQLCA   A pointer to a location in memory where a SQL Communications Area (SQLCA) data structure variable is stored. This structure returns either status information (if the function executed successfully) or error information (if the function failed) to the calling application.

Includes   `#include <sqlenv.h>`

Description   The SET RUNTIME DEGREE function is used to set the run-time degree of intra-partition parallelism that is to be used to process SQL statements for one or more active applications. This function has no effect on the run-time degree of intra-partition parallelism that is used by the CREATE INDEX SQL statement.

Comments   ■ If the *NumAgentIDs* parameter is set to SQL_ALL_USERS, the new degree value specified in the *Degree* parameter will be applied to all active applications, and the value specified in the *AgentIDs* parameter is ignored.

        ■ The value specified in the *Degree* parameter must be in the range of 1 to 32767.

■ The database system monitor functions described in Chapter 13 (specifically, the GET SNAPSHOT function) can be used to generate a list of agent IDs (and run-time degrees) of all active applications.

■ A limited amount of validation is performed when an array of agent IDs is referenced by the *AgentIDs* parameter. The application must ensure that the number of elements found in the array of agent IDs referenced is the same as the value specified in the *NumAgentIDs* parameter.

■ If one or more of the agent IDs specified in the *AgentIDs* parameter cannot be found when this function is executed, they are ignored—and no error is returned. For example, an agent ID may not be found if a user signs off (an application terminates) between the time its agent ID was collected and the time this function is called.

■ Agent IDs are recycled. When one user signs off, another user may sign on and acquire the same agent ID. Therefore, if this function is not called immediately after agent IDs are collected, the run-time degree of intra-partition parallelism that is to be used to process SQL statements may be modified for the wrong application.

■ This function affects all nodes that are identified in the *db2nodes.cfg* configuration file.

Connection Requirements   This function can only be called when a connection to a DB2 Database Manager instance exists. In order to change the run-time degree of intra-partition parallelism on a remote server, an attachment must first be made to that server.

Authorization   Only users with either System Administrator (SYSADM) authority or System Control (SYSCTRL) authority are allowed to execute this function call.

See Also   GET SNAPSHOT

Example   The following C++ program illustrates how to use the SET RUNTIME DEGREE function to set the run-time degree of intra-partition parallelism that is to be used to process SQL statements for all active applications:

```
/*------------------------------------------------------------*/
/* NAME:     CH12EX5.CPP                                      */
/* PURPOSE: Illustrate How To Use The Following DB2 API Function  */
/*          In A C++ Program:                                 */
/*                                                            */
/*                SET RUNTIME DEGREE                          */
/*                                                            */
/*------------------------------------------------------------*/

// Include The Appropriate Header Files
#include <windows.h>
#include <iostream.h>
#include <sqlenv.h>
#include <sqlca.h>

// Define The API_Class Class
```

```
class API_Class
{
    // Attributes
    public:
        struct sqlca   sqlca;

    // Operations
    public:
        long SetRuntimeDegree();
};

// Define The SetRuntimeDegree() Member Function
long API_Class::SetRuntimeDegree()
{
    // Declare The Local Memory Variables
    char   Instance[9];

    // Obtain The Current Value Of The DB2INSTANCE Environment
    // Variable
    sqlegins(Instance, &sqlca);
    Instance[8] = 0;

    // Attach To The Current DB2 Database Manager Instance
    sqleatin(Instance, "userid", "password", &sqlca);

    // Set The Maximum Runtime Degree Of Intra-Partition Parallelism
    // To Be Used To Process SQL Statements (By All Active
    // Applications)
    sqlesdeg(SQL_ALL_USERS, NULL, 16384, &sqlca);

    // If The TEST Database Has Been Created, Display A Success
    // Message
    if (sqlca.sqlcode == SQL_RC_OK)
    {
        cout << "The runtime degree of intra-partition ";
        cout << "parallelism is now 16K " << endl;
        cout << "(for all applications)." << endl;
    }

    // Detach From The Current DB2 Database Manager Instance
    sqledtin(&sqlca);

    // Return The SQLCA Return Code To The Calling Function
    return(sqlca.sqlcode);
}

/*—————————————————————————————————————————*/
/* The Main Function                        */
/*—————————————————————————————————————————*/
int main()
{
    // Declare The Local Memory Variables
    long   rc = SQL_RC_OK;

    // Create An Instance Of The API_Class Class
```

```
API_Class   Example;

// Set The Maximum Runtime Degree Of Intra-Partition Parallelism
// That Is To Be Used To Process SQL Statements
rc = Example.SetRuntimeDegree();

// Return To The Operating System
return(rc);
}
```

GET TABLE PARTITIONING INFORMATION

Purpose   The GET TABLE PARTITIONING INFORMATION function is used to obtain the partitioning information for a database table.

Syntax
```
SQL_API_RC SQL_API_FN sqlugtpi (unsigned char   *TableName,
                                struct sqlupi   *PartionInfo,
                                struct sqlca    *SQLCA);
```

Parameters *TableName*   A pointer to location in memory where the name of the table that partitioning information is to be retrieved for is stored.

PartitionInfo A pointer to a location in memory where an *sqlupi* structure that this function is to return partitioning information to is stored.

SQLCA   A pointer to a location in memory where a SQL Communications Area (SQLCA) data structure variable is stored. This structure returns either status information (if the function executed successfully) or error information (if the function failed) to the calling application.

Includes   `#include <sqlutil.h>`

Description The GET TABLE PARTITIONING INFORMATION function is used to obtain the partitioning information for a table (for example, the partitioning map and the column definitions of the partitioning key) in a partitioned database. This function returns partitioning information in a special structure, *sqlupi*, which is defined in *sqlutil.h* as follows:

```
struct sqlupi
{
unsigned short    pmaplen;        /* The length, in bytes, of the      */
                                  /* partitioning map. For a single-   */
                                  /* node table, this value is equal to*/
                                  /* sizeof(SQL_PDB_NODE_TYPE). For a   */
                                  /* multi-node table, this value is    */
```

```
                                          /* equal to 4096 *            */
                                          /* sizeof(SQL_PDB_NODE_TYPE).  */
        SQL_PDB_NODE_TYPE pmap[4096];
                                          /* The partitioning map        */
        unsigned short     sqld;          /* The number of columns in a  */
                                          /* partitioning key (i.e. the number */
                                          /* of elements in the sqlpartkey */
                                          /* array).                     */
        struct sqlpartkey sqlpartkey[500];
                                          /* The description of the partitioning*/
                                          /* columns in a partitioning key */

        };
```

Table 12–2   SQL Data Types and Lengths for the SQLUPI Data Structure

Data Type	SQL Data Type (NULLs Not Allowed)	SQL Data Type (NULLs Allowed)	Length
Date	384	385	Ignored
Time	388	389	Ignored
Timestamp	392	393	Ignored
Variable-length character string	448	449	Length of the string
Fixed-length character string	452	453	Length of the string
Long character string	456	457	Ignored
NULL-terminated character string	460	461	Length of the string
Floating point	480	481	Ignored
Decimal	484	485	Byte 1 equals Precision Byte 2 equals Scale
Large integer	496	497	Ignored
Small integer	500	501	Ignored
Variable length graphic string	464	465	Length in double-byte characters

Adapted from IBM's *DB2 Universal Database API Reference*, Table 75, page 463.

This structure references an additional structure, *sqlpartkey*. The *sqlpartkey* structure is defined in *sqlutil.h* as follows:

```
struct sqlpartkey
{
unsigned short     sqltype;   /* The SQL data type of a column in a */
                              /* partitioning key (See Table 12-2)  */
unsigned short     sqllen;    /* The length of the data stored in a */
                              /* column in a partitioning key (See  */
                              /* Table 12-2)                        */
};
```

Table 12–2 lists the SQL data types and column length values that can be returned for each column in a partitioning key when this function is called.

Comments   ■ Information returned by this function can be used as input to the GET ROW PARTITIONING NUMBER function.

■ This function affects all nodes that are identified in the *db2nodes.cfg* configuration file.

Connection   This function can only be called if a connection to a database exists.
Requirements

Authorization Only users with either System Administrator (SYSADM) authority, Database Administrator (DBADM) authority, CONTROL authority for the table specified, or SELECT authority for the table specified are allowed to execute this function call.

See Also   GET ROW PARTITIONING NUMBER, REDISTRIBUTE NODEGROUP

Example   The following C++ program illustrates how to use the GET TABLE PARTITIONING INFORMATION function to retrieve partition information for a table in the SAMPLE database:

```
/*————————————————————————————————————————————————*/
/* NAME:     CH12EX6.SQC                                      */
/* PURPOSE: Illustrate How To Use The Following DB2 API Function */
/*          In A C++ Program:                                 */
/*                                                            */
/*              GET TABLE PARTITIONING INFORMATION            */
/*                                                            */
/*————————————————————————————————————————————————*/

// Include The Appropriate Header Files
#include <windows.h>
#include <iostream.h>
#include <sqlutil.h>
#include <sqlca.h>

// Define The API_Class Class
class API_Class
{
    // Attributes
    public:
        struct sqlca  sqlca;

    // Operations
    public:
        long GetTablePartitionInfo();
};

// Define The GetTablePartitionInfo() Member Function
long API_Class::GetTablePartitionInfo()
{
```

```
        // Declare The Local Memory Variables
        unsigned char   *TableName;
        sqlupi          PartitionInfo;

        // Initialize The Local Memory variables
        TableName = new unsigned char[20];
        strcpy((char *) TableName, "EMPLOYEE");

        // Get The Partitioning Information For The EMPLOYEE Table
        // In The SAMPLE Database
        sqlugtpi(TableName, &PartitionInfo, &sqlca);
        if (sqlca.sqlcode != SQL_RC_OK)
            return(sqlca.sqlcode);

        // Display The Partitioning Information Retrieved
        cout << "Partitioning Key Information For The EMPLOYEE Table";
        cout << endl << endl;
        for (int i = 0; i < (int) PartitionInfo.sqld; i++)
        {
            cout << "Data Type : ";
            cout.width(4);
            cout.setf(ios::left);
            cout << PartitionInfo.sqlpartkey[i].sqltype;

            cout << "Data Length : ";
            cout.width(4);
            cout.setf(ios::left);
            cout << PartitionInfo.sqlpartkey[i].sqllen;
        }

        // Free Previously Allocated Memory
        delete[] TableName;

        // Return The SQLCA Return Code To The Calling Function
        return(sqlca.sqlcode);
}
/*─────────────────────────────────────────────────────────────*/
/* The Main Function                                             */
/*─────────────────────────────────────────────────────────────*/
int main()
{
        // Declare The Local Memory Variables
        long   rc = SQL_RC_OK;
        struct sqlca   sqlca;

        // Create An Instance Of The API_Class Class
        API_Class   Example;

        // Connect To The SAMPLE Database
        EXEC SQL CONNECT TO SAMPLE USER sasrys USING Pdr793;

        // Get The Table Partition Information For The EMPLOYEE Table
        rc = Example.GetTablePartitionInfo();
```

```
// Issue A Rollback To Free All Locks
EXEC SQL ROLLBACK;

// Disconnect From The SAMPLE Database
EXEC SQL DISCONNECT CURRENT;

// Return To The Operating System
return(rc);
}
```

■■ ■■ GET ROW PARTITIONING NUMBER

Purpose   The GET ROW PARTITIONING NUMBER function is used to obtain the partition number and node number at which a specific row of data in a table (in a parallel database system) is stored.

Syntax

```
SQL_API_RC SQL_API_FN sqlugrpn (unsigned short      NumKeys,
                                unsigned char       **PartitionKeys,
                                unsigned short      *KeyLengths,
                                unsigned short      CountryCode,
                                unsigned short      CodePage,
                                struct sqlupi       *PartitionInfo,
                                short               *PartitionNumber,
                                SQL_PDB_NODE_TYPE   *NodeNumber,
                                unsigned short      CheckLevel,
                                struct sqlca        *SQLCA,
                                short               KeyFormat,
                                void                *Reserved1,
                                void                *Reserved2);
```

Parameters

NumKeys   The number of partition keys stored in the array of partition keys stored in the *PartitionKeys* parameter.

PartitionKeys   A pointer to location in memory where an array of character representations of values for each part of the partitioning key identified in the *PartitionInfo* parameter is stored.

KeyLengths   A pointer to location in memory where an array of lengths for each partition key value stored in the *PartitionKeys* parameter is stored.

CountryCode   Specifies the country code of the target database. This parameter must be set to one of the following values:

1	(United States of America/Canada)
3	(Latin America)
7	(Russia)
27	(South Africa)

30	(Greece)
31	(Netherlands)
32	(Belgium)
33	(France)
34	(Spain)
36	(Hungary)
39	(Italy)
40	(Romania)
41	(Switzerland)
42	(Czech Republic)
43	(Austria)
44	(United Kingdom)
45	(Denmark)
46	(Sweden)
47	(Norway)
48	(Poland)
49	(Germany)
55	(Brazil)
61	(Australia)
64	(New Zealand)
66	(Thailand)
81	(Japan)
82	(South Korea)
86	(China)
88	(Taiwan)
90	(Turkey)
351	(Portugal)
353	(Ireland)
354	(Iceland)
358	(Finland)
359	(Bulgaria)
370	(Lithuania)
371	(Latvia)
372	(Estonia)
375	(Belarus)

380	(Ukraine)
381	(Serbia/Montenegro)
385	(Albania/Croatia)
386	(Slovenia)
389	(Former Yugoslav Republic of Macedonia)
785	(Arabic Countries)
938	(Slovakia)
972	(Israel)

CodePage   Specifies the code page of the target database. This parameter must be set to one of the following values:

37	273	277	278	280
284	285	297	420	423
424	437	500	737	813
819	850	852	855	857
860	862	863	864	866
869	870	871	874	875
912	915	916	920	921
922	930	932	933	935
937	938	939	942	943
948	949	950	954	964
970	1025	1026	1046	1051
1089	1112	1122	1131	1140
1141	1142	1143	1144	1145
1146	1147	1148	1149	1250
1251	1252	1253	1254	1255
1256	1275	1280	1281	1282
1283	1363	1364	1381	1383
1386	1388	5026	5035	5039

PartitionInfo   A pointer to a location in memory where an *sqlupi* structure that this function is to obtain partition key and partitioning map information from is stored.

PartitionNumber   A pointer to a location in memory where this function is to store the partition number where the specified row of data resides.

NodeNumber   A pointer to a location in memory where this function is to store the node number where the specified row of data resides.

CheckLevel	Specifies the level of checking that is to be performed on all input parameters before this function is executed. For now, if this parameter is set to 0, no checking is performed; and, if this parameter is set to any non-zero number, all input parameters are checked.
SQLCA	A pointer to a location in memory where a SQL Communications Area (SQLCA) data structure variable is stored. This structure returns either status information (if the function executed successfully) or error information (if the function failed) to the calling application.
KeyFormat	Specifies the data type that is used to represent partitioning key values. This parameter must be set to one of the following values:

- SQL_CHARSTRING_FORMAT
  All partitioning key values are represented by character strings.

- SQL_PACKEDDECIMAL_FORMAT
  All decimal partitioning key values are stored in packed decimal format.

- SQL_BINARYNUMERICS_FORMAT
  All numeric partitioning key values are stored in binary format.

Reserved1	A pointer that, at this time, is reserved for later use. For now, this parameter must always be set to NULL.
Reserved2	A pointer that, at this time, is reserved for later use. For now, this parameter must always be set to NULL.

Includes   `#include <sqlutil.h>`

Description   The GET ROW PARTITIONING NUMBER function is used to obtain the partition number and node number at which a specific row of data in a table (in a parallel database system) is stored. This information can be useful when analyzing how data is distributed in a partitioned database environment.

Either the contents of an *sqlupi* structure that has been populated by the GET TABLE PARTITIONING INFORMATION function, or a set of partitioning key values, must be available before this function can be executed. Refer to the GET TABLE PARTITIONING INFORMATION function for a detailed description of the *sqlupi* structure.

Comments   ■ If partitioning map information is not provided as input, only the partition number is returned when this function is executed.

■ If this function is called with the *NodeNumber* parameter set to something other than NULL, partitioning map information must be provided (i.e., the *pmaplen* field of the *sqlupi* structure provided in the *PartitionInfo* parameter must equal 2 or 8,192).

■ If a NULL value is assigned to a non-nullable partitioning key column when this function is called, an error will occur.

■ If this function is called before the partitioning key has been defined (i.e., the *sqld* field of the *sqlupi* structure provided in the *PartitionInfo* parameter equals 0), an error will occur.

■ Any data type that is supported by the operating system can be used to define a partitioning key.

■ CHAR, VARCHAR, GRAPHIC, and VARGRAPHIC data values must be converted to the code page specified before they can be used as partitioning key values.

■ The character representations of numeric and datetime data values must use the same code page as that of the operating system in use where this function is invoked.

■ All leading and trailing blanks found in the character representations of partitioning key values (provided in the *PartitionKey* parameter) are removed, unless the data type of the partitioning key is CHAR, VARCHAR, GRAPHIC, or VARGRAPHIC; in which case, only trailing blanks are removed.

■ This function can be called from any node that is identified in the *db2nodes.cfg* configuration file.

Connection Requirements   This function can only be called if a connection to a database exists.

Authorization   No authorization is required to execute this function call.

See Also   GET DATABASE CONFIGURATION, GET TABLE PARTITIONING INFORMATION, REDISTRIBUTE NODEGROUP

Example   The following C++ program illustrates how to use the GET ROW PARTITIONING NUMBER function to obtain the partition number and node number at which a specific row of data in a table (in a parallel database system) is stored:

```
/*————————————————————————————————————————————————————— */
/* NAME:     CH12EX7.SQC                                  */
/* PURPOSE: Illustrate How To Use The Following DB2 API Function */
/*          In A C++ Program:                             */
/*                                                        */
/*          GET ROW PARTITIONING NUMBER                   */
/*                                                        */
/*————————————————————————————————————————————————————— */

// Include The Appropriate Header Files
#include <windows.h>
#include <iostream.h>
#include <sqlutil.h>
#include <sqlca.h>
```

```
// Define The API_Class Class
class API_Class
{
    // Attributes
    public:
        struct sqlca   sqlca;

    // Operations
    public:
        long GetRowPartitionNumber();
};

// Define The GetRowPartitionNumber() Member Function
long API_Class::GetRowPartitionNumber()
{
    // Declare The Local Memory Variables
    unsigned char       *TableName;
    sqlupi              PartitionInfo;
    short               PartitionNumber;
    SQL_PDB_NODE_TYPE   NodeNumber;

    // Initialize The Local Memory Variables
    TableName = new unsigned char[20];
    strcpy((char *) TableName, "EMPLOYEE");

    // Get The Partitioning Information For The EMPLOYEE Table
    // In The SAMPLE Database
    sqlugtpi(TableName, &PartitionInfo, &sqlca);
    if (sqlca.sqlcode != SQL_RC_OK)
        return(sqlca.sqlcode);

    // Get The Row Partitioning Number For The EMPLOYEE Table
    sqlugrpn(PartitionInfo.sqld, NULL, NULL, 1, 1252, &PartitionInfo,
        &PartitionNumber, &NodeNumber, 0, &sqlca,
        SQL_CHARSTRING_FORMAT, NULL, NULL);

    // If The Row Partitioning Number Was Retrieved, Display It
    if (sqlca.sqlcode == SQL_RC_OK)
    {
        cout << "The row partitioning number for the EMPLOYEE ";
        cout << "table is : " << PartitionNumber << endl;
    }

    // Free Previously Allocated Memory
    delete[] TableName;

    // Return The SQLCA Return Code To The Calling Function
    return(sqlca.sqlcode);
}

/*---------------------------------------------------------------*/
/* The Main Function                                             */
/*---------------------------------------------------------------*/
int main()
```

```
{
     // Declare The Local Memory Variables
     long  rc = SQL_RC_OK;
     struct sqlca   sqlca;

     // Create An Instance Of The API_Class Class
     API_Class   Example;

     // Connect To The SAMPLE Database
     EXEC SQL CONNECT TO SAMPLE USER userid USING password;

     // Get The Row Partitioning Number For The EMPLOYEE Table
     rc = Example.GetRowPartitionNumber();

     // Issue A Rollback To Free All Locks
     EXEC SQL ROLLBACK;

     // Disconnect From The SAMPLE Database
     EXEC SQL DISCONNECT CURRENT;

     // Return To The Operating System
     return(rc);
}
```

■ ■ REDISTRIBUTE NODEGROUP

Purpose   The REDISTRIBUTE NODEGROUP function is used to redistribute data across the nodes in a nodegroup.

Syntax
```
SQL_API_RC SQL_API_FN sqlurdt (char              *NodeGroup,
                               char              *PartitionMapFile,
                               char              *DataDistributionFile,
                               SQL_PDB_NODE_TYPE AddNodeList,
                               unsigned short    AddNodeCount,
                               SQL_PDB_NODE_TYPE DropNodeList,
                               unsigned short    DropNodeCount,
                               unsigned char     *CallerAction,
                               struct sqlca       *SQLCA);
```

Parameters   *NodeGroup*   A pointer to location in memory where the name of the nodegroup to be redistributed is stored.

PartitionMapFile   A pointer to location in memory where the name of the file that contains the target partitioning map is stored. This parameter can contain a NULL value.

DataDistributionFile A pointer to a location in memory where the name of the file that contains data distribution information is stored. This parameter can contain a NULL value.

AddNodeList   A list of nodes that are to be added to the nodegroup during data redistribution. This parameter can contain a NULL value.

AddNodeCount	The number of nodes defined in the *AddNodeList* parameter.
DropNodeList	A list of nodes that are to be removed from the nodegroup during data redistribution. This parameter can contain a NULL value.
DropNodeCount	The number of nodes defined in the *DropNodeList* parameter.
CallerAction	Specifies the action this function is to take when the function is executed. This parameter must be set to one of the following values:

■ U

Data in the nodegroup is to be redistributed to achieve a balanced distribution. If a data distribution file is provided (the *DataDistributionFile* parameter does not equal NULL), it is assumed that the values in this file represent the way data is to be distributed. If a data distribution file is not provided (the *DataDistributionFile* parameter equals NULL), it is assumed that the data is to be distributed uniformly (that is, each has partition is to represent the same amount of data).

■ T

Data in the nodegroup is to be redistributed according to the contents of a target partitioning map file (referenced by the *PartitionMapFile* parameter).

■ C

A nodegroup redistribution operation that failed earlier is to be continued.

■ R

A nodegroup redistribution that failed is to be rolled back.

SQLCA	A pointer to a location in memory where a SQL Communications Area (SQLCA) data structure variable is stored. This structure returns either status information (if the function executed successfully) or error information (if the function failed) to the calling application.

Includes `#include <sqlutil.h>`

Description The REDISTRIBUTE NODEGROUP function is used to redistribute data across the nodes in a nodegroup. When this function is called, a redistribution algorithm selects any partitions that are to be moved according to how data is currently distributed. Nodegroups that contain replicated summary tables or tables that have been defined with DATA CAPTURE CHANGES constraints cannot be redistributed.

Comments ■ This function can only be called from a database's catalog node. The GET NEXT

DATABASE DIRECTORY ENTRY function can be used to determine which node is the catalog node for a database.

- If a directory path is not included in the file name specified in the *PartitionMapFile* or *DataDistributionFile* parameter, this function assumes that the file is located in the current directory.

- The partition map file referenced by the *PartitionMapFile* parameter must be in character format, and the file must contain either one entry (for a single-node nodegroup) or 4,096 entries (for a multi-node nodegroup). Each entry must identify a valid node number.

- The data distribution file referenced by the *DataDistributionFile* parameter must be in character format and must contain 4,096 positive integer entries. Each entry must indicate the weight of the corresponding partition, and the sum of all entries should be less than or equal to 4,294,967,295.

- If the *CallerAction* parameter is set to U, nodes listed in the *AddNodeList* parameter are added to the nodegroup, and nodes listed in the *DropNodeList* parameter are removed from the nodegroup during the data redistribution operation. Otherwise, these parameters, along with the *AddNodeCount* and *DropNodeCount* parameters, are ignored.

- If the *CallerAction* parameter is set to U, the *PartitionMapFile* parameter should contain a NULL pointer. The *DataDistributionFile* parameter may or may not contain a NULL pointer.

- If the *CallerAction* parameter is set to T, the *DataDistributionFile*, *AddNodeList*, and *DropNodeList* parameters should contain NULL pointers. The *AddNodeCount* and *DropNodeCount* parameters should be set to 0, and the *PartitionMapFile* parameter must contain a valid file reference.

- If the *CallerAction* parameter is set to C or R, the *PartitionMapFile*, *DataDistributionFile*, *AddNodeList*, and *DropNodeList* parameters should contain NULL pointers, and the *AddNodeCount* and *DropNodeCount* parameters should be set to 0.

- This function performs intermittent commits while executing.

- The ALTER NODEGROUP SQL statement can be used to add nodes to a nodegroup.

NOTE: The ADD NODE and DROP NODE SQL statements that were provided in DB2 Parallel Edition for AIX Version 1 are supported for users with SYSADM or SYSCTRL authority. When the ADD NODE SQL statement is processed, containers are created like the containers found on the lowest node number of existing nodes within the nodegroup.

- When this function executes, all packages that have a dependency on a table that has been redistributed are invalidated. Therefore, it is important to explicitly rebind all packages that were affected immediately after a redistribute nodegroup operation has completed. Explicit rebinding eliminates the initial delay that will result the first time an SQL request attempts to use an invalid package. It is also a good idea to update table statistics for all tables that have been redistributed.

■ When a redistribution operation is performed, a message file is written to:

■ The *$HOME/sqllib/redist* directory on UNIX based systems, using the following format:

database-name.nodegroup-name.timestamp, where *timestamp* is the time at which this function was called

■ The *$HOME\sqllib\redist* directory on other operating systems, using the following format:

database-name\first-eight-characters-of-nodegroup-name\date\time, where *date* and *time* are the date and time at which this function was called

Connection Requirements This function can only be called if a connection to a database exists.

Authorization Only users with either System Administrator (SYSADM) authority, System Control (SYSCTRL) authority, or Database Administrator (DBADM) authority are allowed to execute this function call.

See Also DROP NODE VERIFY, REBIND, RUNSTATS

Example The following C++ program illustrates how to use the REDISTRIBUTE NODEGROUP function to activate the SAMPLE database:

```
/*-------------------------------------------------- */
/* NAME:      CH12EX8.SQC                            */
/* PURPOSE: Illustrate How To Use The Following DB2 API Function  */
/*          In A C++ Program:                        */
/*                                                   */
/*                 REDISTRIBUTE NODEGROUP            */
/*                                                   */
/*-------------------------------------------------- */

// Include The Appropriate Header Files
#include <windows.h>
#include <iostream.h>
#include <sqlutil.h>
#include <sqlca.h>

// Define The API_Class Class
class API_Class
{
    // Attributes
    public:
        struct sqlca   sqlca;

    // Operations
    public:
```

```
          long RedistributeNodegroup();
};


// Define The RedistributeNodegroup() Member Function
long API_Class::RedistributeNodegroup()
{
     // Declare The Local Memory Variables
     char   NodeGroup[20];

     // Initialize The Local Memory Variables
     strcpy(NodeGroup, "IBMTEMPGROUP");

     // Redistribute The Nodegroup Uniformly
     sqludrdt(NodeGroup, NULL, NULL, NULL, 0, NULL, 0, 'U', &sqlca);

     // If The Nodegroup Has Been Redistributed, Display A Success
     // Message
     if (sqlca.sqlcode == SQL_RC_OK)
         cout << "The nodegroup has been redistributed." << endl;

     // Return The SQLCA Return Code To The Calling Function
     return(sqlca.sqlcode);
}


/*------------------------------------------------------------------*/
/* The Main Function                                                */
/*------------------------------------------------------------------*/
int main()
{
     // Declare The Local Memory Variables
     long   rc = SQL_RC_OK;
     struct sqlca  sqlca;

     // Create An Instance Of The API_Class Class
     API_Class  Example;

     // Connect To The SAMPLE Database
     EXEC SQL CONNECT TO SAMPLE USER userid USING password;

     // Redistribute The Specified Nodegroup
     rc = Example.RedistributeNodegroup();

     // Issue A Rollback To Free All Locks
     EXEC SQL ROLLBACK;

     // Disconnect From The SAMPLE Database
     EXEC SQL DISCONNECT CURRENT;

     // Return To The Operating System
     return(rc);
}
```

13

Database Monitor and Indoubt Transaction Processing APIs

DB2 has a Database System Monitor utility that can be used to monitor activity on one or more databases. DB2 also provides a mechanism that breaks the commit process into two phases to better ensure data integrity when working with multiple databases. This chapter is designed to introduce you to the set of DB2 API functions that are used to set database monitor switches and retrieve database monitor data—and to the set of API functions that are used to list and process indoubt transactions (partially committed transactions that have been executed in a two-phase commit environment). The first part of this chapter provides a general overview of the DB2 Database System Monitor and of the APIs that are used to interact with it. Then, the two-phase commit process is described in detail, and the APIs that are used to list and process indoubt transactions are discussed. Finally, a detailed reference section covering each DB2 API function that can be used to set/reset database monitor switches, collect database monitor data, and list, commit, roll back, and forget indoubt transactions is provided.

The DB2 Database System Monitor

The DB2 Database System monitor is a facility that can collect information about database activity and performance at a given point in time. Specifically, the Database System Monitor can collect the following types of information:

- Status information at the DB2 Database Manager instance, database, table, and table space levels. Status information contains counters, status indicators, and other data that is specific to each level.

- Application-level information. This information includes transaction status, lock status, numerous counters, and information about the current SQL statement being processed.

- Locking details, such as lock waits and deadlock cycles.

- Status information on distributed database connection services (DDCS) applications (if an application is using DB2 Connect to access a DRDA database server).

The DB2 Database System Monitor can also collect SQL statement information. When this type of information is collected, information for the SQL statement being processed when the snapshot was taken is returned. If no SQL statement is being processed at the time the snapshot is taken, information for the last SQL statement processed is returned. You can specify what information a snapshot monitor collects and access collected snapshot monitor information by using the commands provided with the DB2 command-line processor interface—or by including the database system monitor APIs in an application program.

Database System Monitor Switches

The information collected by a database system monitor snapshot is divided into six separate groups (to simplify data collection and interpretation). Table 13–1 lists these six groups along with a description of some of the information that is collected for each group.

Table 13–1   Database Monitor Groups

Monitor Group	Information Collected
Sorts	Number of heaps used, overflows, and number of sorts performed
Locks	Number of locks held and number of deadlocks detected
Tables	Amount of activity (number of rows read and written)
Buffer pools	Number of reads and writes and the time taken for each read and write operation
Units of work (transactions)	Transaction start times, transaction end times, and transaction completion status
SQL statements	Start time, stop time, and statement identification

You can determine whether or not information is being collected for any of the monitor groups listed in Table 13–1 by calling the GET/UPDATE MONITOR SWITCHES function. Information about when the monitoring of these different groups was started (that is, when the group switch was turned on), along with the current state of each monitor group switch is returned when this function is executed. The GET/UPDATE MONITOR SWITCHES function can also be used to turn one or more monitor group switches ON or OFF (which, in turn, starts or stops data collection for the specified monitor group). If the SQL statement monitor switch is turned on while an SQL statement is being processed, the database system monitor will start collecting information when the next SQL statement is executed. As a result, the snapshot monitor will not return information about SQL statements that the DB2 Database Manager is in the process of executing when the SQL statement monitor group switch is turned on. The same applies to unit of work (transaction) information and the unit of work (transaction) switch. When a monitor group switch is turned OFF, the counter elements related to that group are automatically reset to zero, and all of the data elements associated with the monitor group will contain either zero or blank values, depending upon their data types.

You can set default values for each snapshot monitor by using the appropriate DB2 Database Manager and database configuration file parameters. If a snapshot monitor group switch is turned on in the configuration file and an application takes a snapshot without updating or resetting that monitor group switch, the data returned will reflect the database activity since the DB2 Database Manager was started. Every application that connects to a database automatically inherits these default switch settings.

NOTE: *The snapshot monitor always collects some basic snapshot information, even if all monitor group switches are turned off. Obtaining detailed information from some monitor groups can significantly affect application performance. Take this into consideration whenever you turn a monitor group switch on.*

When Counting Starts

A snapshot contains, among other things, cumulative information that covers all database activity from the time database monitoring was started to the time the snapshot is taken. This cumulative information is collected by various activity counters. When counters are used to monitor activity, the counting begins at the following times:

- When an application connects to the database (at the application level, when the application establishes a connection; at the database level, when the first application establishes a connection; at the table level, when the table is first accessed; and at the table space level, when the table space is first accessed)

- When counters are reset

- When a monitor group switch is turned on

In many cases, you will want to collect counter information for a specific period of time. This means that you might need to reset counters while an application is running. (For example, if you are running iterative tests and obtaining snapshot information for each iteration, you might want to reset the counters between iterations.) You can reset counters for one or all databases controlled by the DB2 Database Manager by calling the RESET MONITOR function. When counters are reset, their current values are set to zero. If the counters for all active databases are reset, some DB2 Database Manager information will also be reset to maintain consistency.

You cannot selectively reset specific data items of a monitor group with the RESET MONITOR function. When this function is called, all resettable data items for the database specified or for all active databases are set to zero. You can, however, reset all the data items related to a specific monitor group by turning that monitor group switch off and then on again.

Retrieving Snapshot Monitor Data

Before an application program can collect snapshot monitor data, the program must first allocate a memory storage buffer that is large enough to hold the snapshot information retrieved. The amount of memory required for this buffer depends on the number of monitoring applications (snapshot and event) being run, the types of monitor information being collected, and the level of database activity.

NOTE: *Stopping certain applications allows you to focus on a single application or on a group of applications, which might make it easier for you to interpret the database system monitor output. Subsequently, as the number of applications running decreases, the amount of memory required to hold snapshot monitor data also decreases.*

An application can accurately estimate the amount of memory to allocate for this buffer by calling the ESTIMATE DATABASE SYSTEM MONITOR BUFFER SIZE function. After memory for the buffer has been allocated, you can collect a snapshot of the monitor data specified by calling the GET SNAPSHOT function. When this function is executed, snapshot data is collected and copied directly to the previously allocated memory storage buffer (provided a large enough buffer has been allocated). Portions of this buffer must then be typecast to specially defined data structures before the application can retrieve the snapshot data collected.

If all applications disconnect from a database, that database's snapshot monitor data will no longer be available. Alternatively, you can maintain one permanent connection to the database that will not be terminated until your final snapshot is taken. Keep in mind that if you are maintaining a permanent connection to a database, there is some amount of resource overhead associated with that connection.

Working with Multiple Databases

In its simplest form, a database application will only access and/or update data stored in a single database. However, it is often desirable for an application to access and/or update data that is distributed across two or more different databases. In either case, applications that interact with databases must ensure that data consistency is always maintained.

One of the best ways to maintain data consistency when working with two or more databases is to combine several read and/or write operations in a single transaction (known as a distributed unit of work). Applications that execute in a distributed unit of work environment (DUOW in DRDA terminology) can utilize a process known as two-phase commit to roll back or commit changes made by a transaction. This process is designed to maintain data consistency across multiple databases while transactions are executing.

How the Two-Phase Commit Process Works

The DB2 Database Manager contains a component known as the transaction coordinator that is designed to coordinate read/write operations that are made to several databases within a single transaction. The transaction coordinator uses a special database, known as the Transaction Manager database, to register each transaction (unit of work) and to track the completion status of that transaction across all databases that the transaction is involved with. The database that is to be used as a Transaction Manager database is determined by the value stored in the *tm_database* parameter of the DB2 Database Manager configuration file. The Transaction Manager database can be any database that an application can connect to; however, for operational and administrative reasons, the database must reside on a robust machine that is up and running most of the time. Additionally, all connections to the Transaction Manager database should be made by the transaction coordinator. An application program should never attempt to connect directly to the Transaction Manager database.

The following list describes the actual steps that are taken during the two-phase commit process:

1. When the application program starts a transaction, it will automatically connect to the Transaction Manager database.

2. Just before the first SQL statement in the transaction is executed, the transaction coordinator sends a *Transaction Register* (XREG) request to the Transaction Manager database in order to register the new transaction.

3. The Transaction Manager database responds to the application program by providing a unique global transaction ID for the new transaction (because the XREG request was sent without a predefined ID).

4. After receiving the transaction ID, the application program registers the new transaction (using the transaction ID) with the database containing the

required user data. A response is sent back to the application program when the transaction has been successfully registered.

5. SQL statements issued against the database containing the user data are handled in the normal manner, with the return code for each SQL statement processed being returned in the SQLCA data structure.

6. Steps 2 and 5 are repeated for each database that is accessed by the transaction. All other databases accessed in the transaction receive the global transaction ID just before the first SQL statement is executed against it. The SET CONNECTION SQL statement is used to switch between each database connection.

7. When the application program requests that the current transaction be committed, the transaction coordinator sends a "PREPARE" message to all databases that have been accessed by the transaction. Each database that receives this message writes a "PREPARED" record to their log files and sends a response back to the transaction coordinator.

8. When the transaction coordinator receives a positive response from all databases that the "PREPARE" message was sent to, it sends a message to the Transaction Manager database to inform it that the transaction has been prepared and is now ready to be committed. This completes the first phase of the two-phase commit process.

9. The Transaction Manager database writes a "PREPARED" record to its log file and sends a message back to the transaction coordinator, informing it that the second phase of the commit process can now be started. The transaction coordinator then forwards this message to the application program.

10. When the application program receives the message to begin the second phase of the commit process, it sends a "COMMIT" message to all databases that the "PREPARE" message was sent to (telling them to commit all changes made by the transaction). Each database that receives this message writes a "COMMITTED" record to its log file and releases all locks that were held by the transaction. When each database has completed committing its changes, it sends a reply back to the transaction coordinator.

11. When the transaction coordinator receives a positive response from all databases that the "COMMIT" message was sent to, it sends a message to the Transaction Manager database to inform it that the transaction has been completed. The Transaction Manager database then writes a "COMMITTED" record to its log file to indicate that the transaction is complete—and sends a message to the transaction coordinator to indicate that it has finished processing. The transaction coordinator then forwards this message to the application program. Figure 13–1 illustrates this sequence of events.

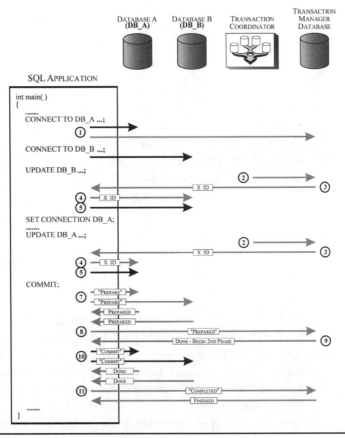

SQL APPLICATION

```
int main( )
{
    ........
    CONNECT TO DB_A ...;

    CONNECT TO DB_B ...;

    UPDATE DB_B ...;



    SET CONNECTION DB_A;
    ........
    UPDATE DB_A ...;



    COMMIT;



    ........
}
```

Figure 13–1   How the two-phase commit process works

Recovering from Errors Encountered While Using Two-Phase Commits

When databases are distributed over several remote servers, the potential for error situations resulting from network or communication failures is greatly increased. To ensure data integrity while using two-phase commits, the DB2 Database Manager handles two-phase commit errors as follows:

First Phase Errors

If a database responds that it failed to PREPARE a transaction, the transaction will be rolled back during the second phase of the commit process. In this case, a "PREPARE" message will not be sent to the Transaction Manager database. During the second phase of the commit, the application program sends a roll back message to all participating databases that successfully prepared the transaction during the first phase of the commit. Each database that receives this message writes an "ABORT" record to its log file and releases all locks that were held by the transaction.

Second Phase Errors

Error handling at the second stage of a commit is dependent upon whether the second phase is to commit or roll back the transaction. The second phase will only roll back the transaction if the first phase encountered an error.

If one of the participating databases fails to commit the transaction (possibly due to a communications failure), the transaction coordinator will continue (until successful) to try to commit the transaction to the database that failed. The value stored in the *resync_interval* parameter of the DB2 Database Manager configuration file is used to determine how long the transaction coordinator will wait between attempts to commit the transaction.

Transaction Manager Database Errors

If for some reason the Transaction Manager database fails, the transaction coordinator will resynchronize the transaction when the Transaction Manager database is restarted. This resynchronization process will attempt to complete all *indoubt transactions*; that is, all transactions that have completed the first phase, but not the second phase, of the two-phase commit process. The DB2 Database Manager instance where the Transaction Manager database resides will perform the resynchronization by:

1. Connecting to the databases that replied that they were "PREPARED" to commit during the first phase of the commit process.

2. Attempting to commit the indoubt transactions at that database. (If no indoubt transactions can be found, the DB2 Database Manager assumes that the database successfully committed the transaction during the second phase of the commit process.)

3. Committing the indoubt transactions in the Transaction Manager database after all indoubt transactions have been committed in the participating databases.

Other Database Errors

If one of the databases accessed in the transaction fails and is restarted, the DB2 Database Manager for that database will check the log files of the Transaction Manager database to determine whether the transaction should be rolled back or committed. If the transaction is not found in the Transaction Manager database log files, the DB2 Database Manager assumes the transaction was rolled back, and the indoubt transactions for this database will be rolled back. Otherwise, the database will wait for a commit request from the transaction coordinator.

Manually Resolving Indoubt Transactions

If, for some reason, you cannot wait for the transaction coordinator to automatically resolve indoubt transactions, you can manually resolve them by "making a heuristic decision" and applying that decision to all applicable records. In order to apply a heuristic decision to an indoubt transaction, its global transaction ID must first be acquired. The LIST INDOUBT TRANSACTIONS function can be used to obtain the global transaction ID for all indoubt transactions that exist for a specified database. Once an indoubt transaction's global transaction ID has been obtained, the COMMIT AN INDOUBT TRANSACTION function can be used to heuristically commit the transaction, and the ROLLBACK AN INDOUBT TRANSACTION function can be used to heuristically roll it back. After a transaction has been heuristically committed or rolled back, the FORGET TRANSACTION STATUS function can be used to tell the DB2 Database Manager to "forget it" by removing all log records that refer to it—and by releasing its log space.

NOTE: *If the* LIST INDOUBT TRANSACTIONS *command is executed with the* WITH PROPMTING *option, it can also be used to heuristically roll back, commit, or forget indoubt transactions.*

The indoubt transaction processing command and APIs should be used with extreme caution and only as a last resort. The best way to resolve indoubt transactions is to wait for the transaction coordinator to drive the resynchronization process. Otherwise, you could cause data integrity problems to occur (for example, if you manually commit or roll back a transaction in one database and perform the opposite action for another database). Recovering from data integrity problems requires that you understand the application logic and the data changed or rolled back—and to perform a point-in-time recovery of the database (or manually undo/redo the database changes made).

If the transaction coordinator will not be available for an extended period of time (to initiate the resynchronization process), and if an indoubt transaction is tying up resources that are urgently needed (i.e., locks on tables and indexes, log space, and storage taken up by the transaction), manually resolving the indoubt transaction may be necessary. There are no foolproof ways to manually recover indoubt transactions. However, the following steps can be used as a guideline:

1. Connect to the database for which you require all transactions to be complete.

2. Use the LIST INDOUBT TRANSACTIONS function to display the indoubt transactions. The transaction ID returned represents the global transaction ID and is identical in all other databases that were accessed by a transaction—including the Transaction Manager database.

3. For each indoubt transaction found, use your knowledge about the application and the *tm_database* parameter of the DB2 Database Manager configuration file to determine the names of the Transaction Manager database and the other databases that were accessed by the transaction.

4a. Connect to the Transaction Manager database. If you were able to connect to this database, use the LIST INDOUBT TRANSACTIONS function to display the indoubt transactions recorded in the Transaction Manager database. If there is an indoubt transaction with the same global transaction ID as that found in step 2 and with type "TM," you can connect to each database participating in the transaction and heuristically commit the transaction using the COMMIT AN INDOUBT TRANSACTION function or the LIST INDOUBT TRANSACTIONS WITH PROMPTING command.

If there is no indoubt transaction with the same global transaction ID (and with type "TM") as that found in step 2, you can connect to each database participating in the transaction and heuristically roll back the transaction using the ROLLBACK AN INDOUBT TRANSACTION function or the LIST INDOUBT TRANSACTIONS WITH PROMPTING command.

4b. If you are unable to connect to the Transaction Manager database, you will have to use the status of the transaction in the other participating databases to determine which action you should take:

■ If at least one of the other databases has committed the transaction, then you should heuristically commit the transaction in all the participating databases using the COMMIT AN INDOUBT TRANSACTION function or the LIST INDOUBT TRANSACTIONS WITH PROMPTING command.

■ If at least one of the other databases has rolled back the transaction, then you should heuristically roll back the transaction in all the participating databases using the ROLLBACK AN INDOUBT TRANSACTION function or the LIST INDOUBT TRANSACTIONS WITH PROMPTING command.

■ If the transaction is in "PREPARED" (indoubt) state in all of the participating databases, then you should heuristically roll back the transaction in all the participating databases using the ROLLBACK AN INDOUBT TRANSACTION function or the LIST INDOUBT TRANSACTIONS WITH PROMPTING command.

■ If you are unable to connect to one or more of the other participating databases, then you should heuristically roll back the transaction in all the participating databases using the ROLLBACK AN INDOUBT TRANSACTION function or the LIST INDOUBT TRANSACTIONS WITH PROMPTING command.

If you heuristically commit or roll back an indoubt transaction, you do not have to "forget it" immediately afterward. Instead, it is a good idea to wait until the Transaction Manager database is accessible so that your decisions can be verified. That way, if a transaction was committed or rolled back incorrectly, the Transaction Manager database can detect the error. When errors of this type are found, the Transaction Manager will write a message to the *db2diag.log* file indicating "heuristic damage" has occured to a particular database (this will occur when the Transaction Manager attempts to synchronize).

Two-Phase Commit Processing Using an XA-Compliant Transaction Manager

The XA interface is a widely used interface that was defined by the X/Open Company. This interface is used to exchange information between transaction managers (such as CICS) and resource managers (such as DB2 C/S) to ensure data consistency when working with multiple databases in a single transaction. If your application needs to perform read/write operations to resources that use the XA interface, the application will have to use an XA-compliant transaction manager in place of DB2's transaction coordinator. In this case, each database referenced in a transaction must be identified with an XA open string that has the following format:

```
"database_alias <,username,password>"
```

The *database_alias* specifies the alias name for the database and the *username* and *password* (optional) are used to provide authentication information to the database manager instance. After each database has been identified, the XA-compliant transaction manager treats it as a separate resource manager.

An XA-compliant transaction manager uses a two-phase commit process similar to that used by DB2 Universal Database. The primary difference between the two environments is that a Transaction Processing Monitor provides the function of logging and controlling a transaction, rather than a Transaction Manager database. Because the rest of the process is virtually the same, there is no difference in the way errors are handled.

The DB2 Database Monitor and Indoubt Transaction Processing Functions

Table 13–1 lists the DB2 API functions that are used to set/reset database monitor switches, collect database monitor data, and manually resolve indoubt transactions.

Each of these functions is described in detail in the remainder of this chapter.

Table 13–1   Database Monitor and Indoubt Transaction Processing APIs

Function Name	Description
GET/UPDATE MONITOR SWITCHES	Turns various database system monitor switches on or off and queries the DB2 database system monitor for a group monitoring switch's current state.
RESET MONITOR	Resets the internal data monitor switches of a specified database (or of all active databases) to zero.
ESTIMATE DATABASE SYSTEM MONITOR BUFFER SIZE	Estimates the size of the buffer needed to hold the information collected by the GET SNAPSHOT function.
GET SNAPSHOT	Retrieves specific DB2 Database System Monitor information and copies it to a user-allocated data storage buffer.
LIST DRDA INDOUBT TRANSACTIONS	Retrieves a list of all indoubt transactions that exist between partner logical units (LUs) that are connected by LU 6.2 protocol.
LIST INDOUBT TRANSACTIONS	Retrieves a list of all indoubt transactions for the current connected database.
COMMIT AN INDOUBT TRANSACTION	Heuristically commits an indoubt transaction.
ROLLBACK AN INDOUBT TRANSACTION	Heuristically rolls back an indoubt transaction.
FORGET TRANSACTION STATUS	Tells the Resource Manager to erase all knowledge of an indoubt transaction that was heuristically committed or rolled back.

GET/UPDATE MONITOR SWITCHES

Purpose   The GET/UPDATE MONITOR SWITCHES function is used to selectively turn various
database monitor switches (information groups to be monitored) on or off and to
query the database monitor for a group monitoring switch's current state.

Syntax
```
int SQL_API_FN sqlmon  (unsigned long        Version,
                        char                 *Reserved,
                        sqlm_recording_group GroupStates[ ],
                        struct sqlca         *SQLCA);
```

Parameters   *Version*   Specifies the version number of the database monitor data to collect.
This parameter must be set to one of the following values:

■ SQLM_DBMON_VERSION5
DB2 Version 5.0 (or later) database monitor data is to be
collected.

■ SQLM_DBMON_VERSION2
DB2 Version 2.1 database monitor data is to be collected.

■ SQLM_DBMON_VERSION1
DB2 Version 1.0 database monitor data is to be collected.

Reserved   A pointer that is currently reserved for later use. For now, this
parameter must always be set to NULL.

GroupStates   A pointer to a location in memory that contains the starting address
of an array of six *sqlm_recording_group* structures that contain
state information about each group monitor switch available.

SQLCA   A pointer to a location in memory where a SQL Communications
Area (SQLCA) data structure variable is stored. This variable returns
either status information (if the function executed successfully) or
error information (if the function failed) to the calling application.

Includes   #include <sqlmon.h>

Description The GET/UPDATE MONITOR SWITCHES function is used to selectively turn various
database monitor switches (associated with information groups that are to be
monitored) on or off and to query the database monitor for a group monitoring
switch's current state. This function uses an array of six *sqlm_recording_group*
structures to retrieve and update database monitor switch values. The
sqlm_recording_group structure is defined in *sqlmon.h* as follows:

```
struct sqlm_recording_group
{
unsigned long    input_state;  /* Indicates whether the specified    */
                               /* information group monitoring        */
```

```
                                     /* switch should be turned on       */
                                     /* (SQLM_ON), turned off            */
                                     /* (SQLM_OFF), or left in its        */
                                     /* current state (SQLM_HOLD).       */
      unsigned long   output_state;  /* The current state of the specified */
                                     /* group monitoring switch. Indicates */
                                     /* whether the specified information */
                                     /* group monitoring switch is       */
                                     /* currently turned on (SQLM_ON)    */
                                     /* or turned off (SQLM_OFF).        */
      sqlm_timestamp  start_time;    /* The date and time that the       */
                                     /* specified group monitoring switch */
                                     /* was turned on. If the specified   */
                                     /* group monitoring switch is turned */
                                     /* off, this field is set           */
                                     /* to 0.                            */
      };
```

This structure contains a reference to an additional structure, *sqlm_timestamp*, that stores timestamp information about when a group monitoring switch was turned on. The *sqlm_timestamp* structure is defined in *sqlmon.h* as follows:

```
typedef struct sqlm_timestamp
{
unsigned long   seconds;       /* The date and time, expressed as   */
                               /* the number of seconds since       */
                               /* January 1, 1970 (GMT).            */
unsigned long   microsec;      /* The number of elapsed            */
                               /* microseconds, ranging from 0 to   */
                               /* 999999, in the current second.    */
} sqlm_timestamp;
```

An array of six *sqlm_recording_group* structures must be defined or allocated before this function is called. If this function is used to set the value of one or more group monitor switches, each corresponding structure in the array must also be initialized before this function is invoked. After this function executes, this array will contain information about the current state of each group monitor switch available. You can obtain information about a specific group monitor switch by indexing the array with one of the following symbolic values:

▪ **SQLM_UOW_SW**
References unit of work (transaction) group monitor switch information.

▪ **SQLM_STATEMENT_SW**
References SQL statement group monitor switch information.

▪ **SQLM_TABLE_SW**
References table group monitor switch information.

■ SQLM_BUFFER_POOL_SW
References buffer pool group monitor switch information.

■ SQLM_LOCK_SW
References lock group monitor switch information.

■ SQLM_SORT_SW
References sort group monitor switch information.

Refer to the beginning of the chapter for more information about the database system monitor elements associated with each of these monitoring group switches.

Comments   ■ If database monitor data is to be collected for earlier versions of DB2 (i.e., if the *Version* parameter is set to SQLM_DBMON_VERSION1), this function cannot be executed remotely.

■ You can use this function to query the current state of different information group switches without modifying them by specifying SQLM_HOLD for the *input-state* element of each structure in the *Group States* array.

■ If this function attempts to obtain database monitor data for a version that is higher than the current server version, only information that is valid for the server's level will be returned.

■ For detailed information on using the database system monitor, refer to the *IBM DB2 Universal Database System Monitor Guide and Reference*.

Connection   This function can only be called if a connection to a DB2 Database Manager
Requirements instance exists. In order to obtain or set the database monitor switch settings for a remote instance (or for a different local instance), an application must first attach to that instance.

Authorization Only users with System Administrator (SYSADM), System Control (SYSCTRL), or System Maintenance (SYSMAINT) authority can execute this function call.

See Also   ESTIMATE DATABASE SYSTEM MONITOR BUFFER SIZE, GET SNAPSHOT, RESET MONITOR

Example   The following C++ program illustrates how to use the GET/UPDATE MONITOR SWITCHES function to retrieve and change the current values of the database monitor group switches:

```
/*─────────────────────────────────────────────────────────────── */
/* NAME:    CH13EX1.CPP                                             */
/* PURPOSE: Illustrate How To Use The Following DB2 API Function    */
/*          In A C++ Program:                                       */
/*                                                                  */
/*                 GET/UPDATE MONITOR SWITCHES                      */
/*                                                                  */
/*─────────────────────────────────────────────────────────────── */
```

```cpp
// Include The Appropriate Header Files
#include <windows.h>
#include <iostream.h>
#include <sqlmon.h>
#include <sqlca.h>

// Define The API_Class Class
class API_Class
{
    // Attributes
    public:
        struct sqlca   sqlca;

    // Operations
    public:
        long GetSetMonSwitches();
};

// Define The GetSetMonSwitches() Member Function
long API_Class::GetSetMonSwitches()
{
    // Declare The Local Memory Variables
    struct sqlm_recording_group   GroupStates[6];

    // Initialize The Database Monitor Group States Array
    // (Turn The Table Switch On, The Unit Of Work Switch Off,
    // And Query The Settings Of The Other Switches)
    GroupStates[SQLM_UOW_SW].input_state        = SQLM_OFF;
    GroupStates[SQLM_STATEMENT_SW].input_state  = SQLM_HOLD;
    GroupStates[SQLM_TABLE_SW].input_state      = SQLM_ON;
    GroupStates[SQLM_BUFFER_POOL_SW].input_state = SQLM_HOLD;
    GroupStates[SQLM_LOCK_SW].input_state       = SQLM_HOLD;
    GroupStates[SQLM_SORT_SW].input_state       = SQLM_HOLD;

    // Set/Query The Database Monitor Switches
    sqlmon(SQLM_DBMON_VERSION5, NULL, GroupStates, &sqlca);

    // If The Database Monitor Switches Were Set/Queried, Display
    // Their Current Values
    if (sqlca.sqlcode == SQL_RC_OK)
    {
        cout << "Current values of the Database Monitor Switches :";
        cout << endl << endl;

        cout << "Unit Of Work Switch   : ";
        if (GroupStates[SQLM_UOW_SW].input_state == SQLM_ON)
            cout << "ON" << endl;
        else
            cout << "OFF" << endl;

        cout << "SQL Statements Switch : ";
        if (GroupStates[SQLM_STATEMENT_SW].input_state == SQLM_ON)
            cout << "ON" << endl;
        else
```

```
                                cout << "OFF" << endl;

                   cout << "Table Switch           : ";
                   if (GroupStates[SQLM_TABLE_SW].input_state == SQLM_ON)
                        cout << "ON" << endl;
                   else
                        cout << "OFF" << endl;

                   cout << "Buffer Pool Switch     : ";
                   if (GroupStates[SQLM_BUFFER_POOL_SW].input_state == SQLM_ON)
                        cout << "ON" << endl;
                   else
                        cout << "OFF" << endl;

                   cout << "Lock Switch            : ";
                   if (GroupStates[SQLM_LOCK_SW].input_state == SQLM_ON)
                        cout << "ON" << endl;
                   else
                        cout << "OFF" << endl;

                   cout << "Sort Switch            : ";
                   if (GroupStates[SQLM_SORT_SW].input_state == SQLM_ON)
                        cout << "ON" << endl;
                   else
                        cout << "OFF" << endl;
              }

         // Return The SQLCA Return Code To The Calling Function
         return(sqlca.sqlcode);
    }


/*---------------------------------------------------------------------*/
/* The Main Function                                                   */
/*---------------------------------------------------------------------*/
int main()
{
         // Declare The Local Memory Variables
         long  rc = SQL_RC_OK;

         // Create An Instance Of The API_Class Class
         API_Class  Example;

         // Get/Update Monitor Switch Values
         rc = Example.GetSetMonSwitches();

         // Return To The Operating System
         return(rc);
    }
```

RESET MONITOR

Purpose   The RESET MONITOR function is used to reset the internal database system monitor data monitor switches of a specified database (or of all active databases) to zero.

Syntax
```
int SQL_API_FN sqlmrset (unsigned long    Version,
                         char             *Reserved,
                         unsigned long    ResetAllIndicator,
                         char             *DBAlias,
                         struct sqlca     *SQLCA);
```

Parameters *Version*

Specific version number of the database monitor data switches to reset. This parameter must be set to one of the following values:

- SQLM_DBMON_VERSION5
  DB2 Version 5.0 (or later) database monitor data switches are to be reset.

- SQLM_DBMON_VERSION2
  DB2 Version 2.1 database monitor data switches are to be reset.

- SQLM_DBMON_VERSION1
  DB2 Version 1.0 database monitor data switches are to be reset.

Reserved

A pointer that is currently reserved for later use. For now, this parameter must always be set to NULL.

ResetAllIndicator

Specifies whether to reset data monitor switches for a specific database or for all active databases. This parameter must be set to one of the following values:

- SQLM_OFF
  Reset the data monitor switches and areas for a specific database.

- SQLM_ON
  Reset the data monitor switches and areas for all active databases.

DBAlias

A pointer to a location in memory where the alias of the database whose data monitor switches are to be reset is stored.

SQLCA

A pointer to a location in memory where a SQL Communications Area (SQLCA) data structure variable is stored. This variable returns either status information (if the function executed successfully) or error information (if the function failed) to the calling application.

Includes	`#include <sqlmon.h>`
Description	The RESET MONITOR function is used to reset the internal database system monitor data monitor switches of a specified database (or of all active databases) to zero. When the data monitor switches of a database are set to zero, the database's internal system monitor data areas are automatically cleared. These data areas include the data areas that are used by each application connected to the database and by the database itself.

Each application attached to a database has its own private view of database system monitor data. If an application resets or turns off a database system monitor switch, other applications are not affected.

Comments	■ If database monitor data switches are to be reset for earlier versions of DB2 (i.e., if the *Version* parameter is set to SQLM_DBMON_VERSION1), this function cannot be executed remotely.

■ If this function is called with the *ResetAllIndicator* parameter set to SQLM_ON, the value in the *DBAlias* parameter is ignored, and the data monitor switches for all active databases are reset.

■ To make global changes to a database system monitor switch, modify the settings of the monitor switch configuration parameters in the DB2 Database Manager configuration file. Refer to the UPDATE DATABASE MANAGER CONFIGURATION function for more information.

■ If all database system monitor switches for all active databases are reset, some DB2 Database Manager information is also reset to maintain consistency with the data that is returned.

■ This function cannot be used to selectively reset specific data items or monitor groups. However, a specific monitor group can be reset by turning its switch off and then back on with the GET/UPDATE MONITOR SWITCHES function.

■ For detailed information about using the database system monitor, refer to the *IBM DB2 Universal Database System Monitor Guide and Reference*.

Connection Requirements	This function can only be called if a connection to a DB2 Database Manager instance exists. In order to obtain or set the database monitor switch settings for a remote instance (or for a different local instance), an application must first attach to that instance.
Authorization	Only users with System Administrator (SYSADM) authority, System Control (SYSCTRL) authority, or System Maintenance (SYSMAINT) authority can execute this function call.
See Also	GET/UPDATE MONITOR SWITCHES, ESTIMATE DATABASE SYSTEM MONITOR BUFFER SIZE, GET SNAPSHOT
Example	The following C++ program illustrates how to use the RESET MONITOR function to reset the database monitor group switches for the SAMPLE database:

```
/*————————————————————————————————————————————————*/
/* NAME:      CH13EX2.SQC                                    */
/* PURPOSE: Illustrate How To Use The Following DB2 API Function   */
/*          In A C++ Program:                                */
/*                                                           */
/*                 RESET MONITOR                             */
/*                                                           */
/*————————————————————————————————————————————————*/

// Include The Appropriate Header Files
#include <windows.h>
#include <iostream.h>
#include <sqlmon.h>
#include <sql.h>

// Define The API_Class Class
class API_Class
{
    // Attributes
    public:
        struct sqlca   sqlca;

    // Operations
    public:
        long ResetMonitor();
};

// Define The ResetMonitor() Member Function
long API_Class::ResetMonitor()
{
    // Reset The Database System Monitor Data Areas For The SAMPLE
    // Database
    sqlmrset(SQLM_DBMON_VERSION5, NULL, SQLM_OFF, "SAMPLE", &sqlca);

    // If The Database System Monitor Data Areas For The SAMPLE
    // Database Were Reset, Display A Success Message
    if (sqlca.sqlcode == SQL_RC_OK)
    {
        cout << "The Database System Monitor Data Areas for the ";
        cout << "SAMPLE database have" << endl;
        cout << "been reset." << endl;
    }

    // Return The SQLCA Return Code To The Calling Function
    return(sqlca.sqlcode);
}


/*————————————————————————————————————————————————*/
/* The Main Function                                         */
/*————————————————————————————————————————————————*/
int main()
```

```
{
    // Declare The Local Memory Variables
    long        rc = SQL_RC_OK;
    struct sqlca  sqlca;

    // Create An Instance Of The API_Class Class
    API_Class  Example;

    // Attempt To Connect To The SAMPLE Database
    EXEC SQL CONNECT TO SAMPLE USER userID USING password;

    // Reset The Monitors For The SAMPLE Database
    rc = Example.ResetMonitor();

    // Issue A Rollback To Free All Locks
    EXEC SQL ROLLBACK;

    // Disconnect From The SAMPLE Database
    EXEC SQL DISCONNECT CURRENT;

    // Return To The Operating System
    return(rc);
}
```

ESTIMATE DATABASE SYSTEM MONITOR BUFFER SIZE

Purpose   The ESTIMATE DATABASE SYSTEM MONITOR BUFFER SIZE function is used to estimate the size of the buffer needed by the GET SNAPSHOT function.

Syntax
```
int SQL_API_FN sqlmonsz (unsigned long   Version,
                         char            *Reserved,
                         sqlma           *SQLMA,
                         unsigned long   *BufferSize,
                         struct sqlca    *SQLCA);
```

Parameters   *Version*   Specifies the version number of the database monitor data to estimate the buffer size for. This parameter must be set to one of the following values:

■ SQLM_DBMON_VERSION5
  The buffer size for DB2 Version 5.0 (or later) database monitor data is to be estimated.

■ SQLM_DBMON_VERSION2
  The buffer size for DB2 Version 2.1 database monitor data is to be estimated.

■ SQLM_DBMON_VERSION1
  The buffer size for DB2 Version 1.0 database monitor data is to be estimated.

Reserved	A pointer that is currently reserved for later use. For now, this parameter must always be set to NULL.
SQLMA	A pointer to a *sqlma* data structure that contains a list of objects that database monitor data is to be collected for.
BufferSize	A pointer to a location in memory where this function is to store the estimated size of the buffer needed by the GET SNAPSHOT function.
SQLCA	A pointer to a location in memory where a SQL Communications Area (SQLCA) data structure variable is stored. This variable returns either status information (if the function executed successfully) or error information (if the function failed) to the calling application.

Includes   `#include <sqlmon.h>`

Description   The ESTIMATE DATABASE SYSTEM MONITOR BUFFER SIZE function is used to estimate the size of the buffer needed by the GET SNAPSHOT function. You can manually calculate the size of the buffer needed by adding the sizes of the structures returned for each object to be monitored, but you should use this function instead, because the GET SNAPSHOT function can return an unknown number of data structures (if, for example, a snapshot of all active databases is requested).

A special structure, *sqlma*, is used to pass information about the list of objects that are to be monitored to the DB2 Database System Monitor when this function is called. The *sqlma* structure is defined in *sqlmon.h* as follows:

```
typedef struct sqlma
{
unsigned long     obj_num;      /* The number of objects that are     */
                                /* to be monitored                    */
sqlm_obj_struct   obj_var[1];   /* An array of sqlm_obj_struct         */
                                /* structures that contains            */
                                /* descriptions about the objects      */
                                /* that are to be monitored            */
} sqlma;
```

This structure contains an array of one or more *sqlm_obj_struct* structures that are used to store characteristics about each object that is to be monitored. The *sqlm_obj_struct* structure is defined in *sqlmon.h* as follows:

```
typedef struct   sqlm_obj_struct
{
unsigned long     agent_id;     /* The ID of the agent that is to be   */
                                /* monitored                           */
unsigned long     obj_type;     /* The type of object that is to be    */
                                /* monitored                           */
char              object[36];   /* The name of the object that is to   */
                                /* be monitored                        */
} sqlm_obj_struct;
```

Comments
- The *obj_type* field of each *sqlm_obj_struct* structure used must contain one of the following values:

  - **SQLMA_DB2**
  DB2-related information is to be monitored.

  - **SQLMA_DBASE**
  Database-related information is to be monitored.

  - **SQLMA_APPL**
  Application information, organized by the application ID, is to be monitored.

  - **SQLMA_AGENT_ID**
  Application information, organized by the agent ID, is to be monitored.

  - **SQLMA_DBASE_TABLES**
  Table information for a database is to be monitored.

  - **SQLMA_DBASE_APPLS**
  Application information for a database is to be monitored.

  - **SQLMA_DBASE_APPLINFO**
  Summary application information for a database is to be monitored.

  - **SQLMA_DBASE_LOCKS**
  Locking information for a database is to be monitored.

  - **SQLMA_DBASE_ALL**
  Database related information for all active databases in the Database Manager instance is to be monitored.

  - **SQLMA_APPL_ALL**
  Application information for all active applications in the Database Manager instance is to be monitored.

  - **SQLMA_APPLINFO_ALL**
  Summary application information for all active applications in the Database Manager instance is to be monitored.

  - **SQLMA_DCS_APPLINFO_ALL**
  Summary DCS application information for all active applications in the Database Manager instance is to be monitored.

- If database monitor data is to be collected for earlier versions of DB2 (i.e., if the *Version* parameter is set to **SQLM_DBMON_VERSION1**), this function cannot be executed remotely.

- Because this function generates a significant amount of overhead, you may find it more desirable to allocate a buffer of a fixed size (than to call this function repeatedly) if the **GET SNAPSHOT** function is to be called several times.

- If no active databases or applications are found, this function may return a buffer size of zero. Therefore, applications should verify that the estimated buffer size returned by this function is greater than zero *before* allocating a buffer and calling the **GET SNAPSHOT** function. If the **GET SNAPSHOT** function returns an error because of insufficient buffer space, call this function again to determine the new buffer size requirements.

- ▓ For detailed information on using the database system monitor, refer to the *IBM DB2 Universal Database System Monitor Guide and Reference*.

Connection Requirements   This function can only be called if a connection to a DB2 Database Manager instance exists. In order to obtain buffer size information for a remote instance (or from a different local instance), an application must first attach to that instance.

Authorization   Only users with System Administrator (SYSADM) authority, System Control (SYSCTRL) authority, or System Maintenance (SYSMAINT) authority can execute this function call.

See Also   GET SNAPSHOT, GET/UPDATE MONITOR SWITCHES, RESET MONITOR

Example   See the example provided for the GET SNAPSHOT function on page 531.

▓▓ ▓▓ **GET SNAPSHOT**

Purpose   The GET SNAPSHOT function is used to retrieve specific DB2 database monitor information and copy it to a user-allocated data storage buffer.

Syntax
```
int SQL_API_FN sqlmonss  (unsigned long    Version,
                          char             *Reserved,
                          sqlma            *SQLMA,
                          unsigned long    BufferSize,
                          void             *Buffer,
                          sqlm_collected   *Collected,
                          struct sqlca     *SQLCA);
```

Parameters   *Version*   The version number of the database monitor data to collect. This parameter must be set to one of the following values:

- ▓ SQLM_DBMON_VERSION5
  DB2 Version 5.0 (or later) database monitor data is to be collected.

- ▓ SQLM_DBMON_VERSION2
  DB2 Version 2.1 database monitor data is to be collected.

- ▓ SQLM_DBMON_VERSION1
  DB2 Version 1.0 database monitor data is to be collected.

Reserved   A pointer that is currently reserved for later use. For now, this parameter must always be set to NULL.

SQLMA   A pointer to a *sqlma* data structure that contains a list of objects that a snapshot of database monitor data is to be collected for.

BufferSize   The size, in bytes, of the memory storage buffer where this function is to store the database monitor data retrieved.

Buffer	A pointer to a location in memory where this function is to store the database monitor data retrieved.
Collected	A pointer to the address of an *sqlm_collected* structure where this function is to store summary information about each type of database monitor data that is written to the memory storage area (*Buffer*).
SQLCA	A pointer to a location in memory where a SQL Communications Area (SQLCA) data structure variable is stored. This variable returns either status information (if the function executed successfully) or error information (if the function failed) to the calling application.

Includes

```
#include <sqlmon.h>
```

Description The GET SNAPSHOT function is used to retrieve specific DB2 database monitor information and copy it to a user-allocated data storage buffer. The database monitor information returned represents a snapshot of the DB2 Database Manager's operational status at the time this function was executed. Therefore, you can only update this information by reexecuting the GET SNAPSHOT function call.

A special structure (*sqlma*) is used to pass information about the list of objects that are to be monitored to the DB2 Database System Monitor when this function is called. Refer to the ESTIMATE DATABASE SYSTEM MONITOR BUFFER SIZE function for a detailed description of this structure. After this function is executed, summary statistics about the snapshot information that was collected is stored in a *sqlm_collected* structure which is defined in *sqlmon.h* as follows:

```
typedef struct sqlm_collected
{
unsigned long  size;              /* The size of the sqlm_collected    */
                                  /* structure                         */
unsigned long  db2;               /* Indicates whether DB2 Database    */
                                  /* Manager instance information       */
                                  /* was collected in the snapshot (1), */
                                  /* or not (0). This field is obsolete */
                                  /* in Version 5.0 and later.          */
unsigned long  databases;         /* The number of databases           */
                                  /* that snapshot information was      */
                                  /* collected for. This field is obsolete */
                                  /* in Version 5.0 and later.          */
unsigned long  table_databases;   /* The number of databases           */
                                  /* that table snapshot information was */
                                  /* collected for. This field is       */
                                  /* obsolete in Version 5.0 and later. */
unsigned long  lock_databases;    /* The number of databases           */
                                  /* that locking snapshot information was */
                                  /* collected for. This field is       */
                                  /* obsolete in Version 5.0 and later. */
unsigned long  applications;      /* The number of applications        */
                                  /* that snapshot information was      */
```

```
                                    /* collected for. This field is obsolete */
                                    /* in Version 5.0 and later.             */
    unsigned long  applinfos;       /* The number of applications            */
                                    /* that summary information was          */
                                    /* collected for. This field is obsolete */
                                    /* in Version 5.0 and later.             */
    unsigned long  dcs_applinfos;   /* The number of applications            */
                                    /* that DCS summary information was       */
                                    /* collected for. This field is obsolete */
                                    /* in Version 5.0 and later.             */
    unsigned long  server_db2_type; /* The DB2 Database Manager              */
                                    /* server type                           */
    sqlm_timestamp time_stamp;      /* The date and time the snapshot        */
                                    /* was taken                             */
    sqlm_recording_group
                   group_states[6];
                                    /* The current state of the information  */
                                    /* group monitoring switches             */
    char           server_prdid[20];         /* The product name and version
                                    */
                                    /* number of the DB2 Database Manager    */
                                    /* on the server workstation             */
    char           server_nname[20];          /* The workstation name stored in
                                    */
                                    /* the nname parameter of the DB2        */
                                    /* Database Manager configuration        */
                                    /* file on the server workstation        */
    char           server_instance_name[20];
                                    /* The instance name of the              */
                                    /* DB2 Database Manager                   */
    char           reserved[22];    /* Reserved for future use               */
    unsigned short node_number;     /* The number of the node that sent the  */
                                    /* snapshot information                  */
    long           time_zone_disp;  /* The difference, in seconds, between   */
                                    /* Greenwich Mean Time (GMT) and         */
                                    /* local time                            */
    unsigned long  num_top_level_structs;
                                    /* The total number of high-level        */
                                    /* structures returned in the snapshot   */
                                    /* output buffer. This counter replaces  */
                                    /* the individual counters (i.e., fields */
                                    /* 2 through 8 of this structure) which  */
                                    /* are obsolete in Version 5.0 and higher */
    unsigned long  tablespace_databases;
                                    /* The number of databases for which     */
                                    /* table space snapshot information      */
                                    /* was collected                        */
    unsigned long  server_version;  /* The version number of the server      */
                                    /* returning the snapshot data          */
} sqlm_collected;
```

This structure contains references to two additional structures (*sqlm_recording_ group* and *sqlm_timestamp*) that are used to store information about the current state of specific group monitoring switches and the exact date and time a group monitoring switch was turned on. Refer to the GET MONITOR SWITCHES function for a detailed description of each of these structures.

When snapshot information is collected, it is stored in a user-allocated buffer (whose address is stored in the *Buffer* parameter). Portions of this buffer must be typecast with special structures before the information collected can be extracted from it. For more information about these structures, refer to the *IBM DB2 Universal Database System Monitor Guide and Reference*.

Comments

■ The *obj_type* field of each *sqlm_obj_struct* structure used in the array of structures referenced by the *SQLMA* parameter must contain one of the following values:

■ `SQLMA_DB2`
DB2-related information is to be monitored.

■ `SQLMA_DBASE`
Database-related information is to be monitored.

■ `SQLMA_APPL`
Application information, organized by the application ID, is to be monitored.

■ `SQLMA_AGENT_ID`
Application information, organized by the agent ID, is to be monitored.

■ `SQLMA_DBASE_TABLES`
Table information for a database is to be monitored.

■ `SQLMA_DBASE_APPLS`
Application information for a database is to be monitored.

■ `SQLMA_DBASE_APPLINFO`
Summary application information for a database is to be monitored.

■ `SQLMA_DBASE_LOCKS`
Locking information for a database is to be monitored.

■ `SQLMA_DBASE_ALL`
Database-related information for all active databases in the Database Manager instance is to be monitored.

■ `SQLMA_APPL_ALL`
Application information for all active applications in the Database Manager instance is to be monitored.

■ `SQLMA_APPLINFO_ALL`
Summary application information for all active applications in the Database Manager instance is to be monitored.

■ `SQLMA_DCS_APPLINFO_ALL`
Summary DCS application information for all active applications in the Database Manager instance is to be monitored.

■ If database monitor data is to be collected for earlier versions of DB2 (i.e., if the *Version* parameter is set to `SQLM_DBMON_VERSION2` or `SQLM_DBMON_VERSION1`), this function cannot be executed remotely.

■ You can determine the amount of memory needed to store the snapshot information returned by this function by calling the ESTIMATE DATABASE SYSTEM MONITOR BUFFER SIZE function. If one specific object is being monitored, only the amount of memory needed to store the returned data structure for that object needs to be allocated. If the buffer storage area is not large enough to hold all the information returned by this function, a warning will be returned, and the information returned will be truncated to fit in the assigned storage buffer area. When this happens, you should resize the memory storage buffer and call this function again.

■ No snapshot data will be returned by a request for table information if any of the following conditions exist:

—The TABLE recording switch is turned off.

—No tables have been accessed since the TABLE recording switch was turned on.

—No tables have been accessed since the last time the RESET MONITOR function was called.

■ If this function attempts to obtain database monitor data for a version that is higher than the current server version, only information that is valid for the server's level will be returned.

■ For detailed information about using the database system monitor, refer to the *IBM DB2 Universal Database System Monitor Guide and Reference*.

Connection Requirements   This function can only be called if a connection to a DB2 Database Manager instance exists. In order to obtain a snapshot of database monitor data settings for a remote instance (or for a different local instance), an application must first attach to that instance.

Authorization   Only users with System Administrator (SYSADM) authority, System Control (SYSCTRL) authority, or System Maintenance (SYSMAINT) authority are allowed to execute this function call.

See Also   GET/UPDATE MONITOR SWITCHES, ESTIMATE DATABASE SYSTEM MONITOR BUFFER SIZE, RESET MONITOR

Example   The following C++ program illustrates how to use the GET SNAPSHOT function to collect snapshot information for the SAMPLE database and the DB2 Database Manager:

```
/*----------------------------------------------------------------------*/
/* NAME:     CH13EX3.CPP                                                */
/* PURPOSE:  Illustrate How To Use The Following DB2 API Functions      */
/*           In A C++ Program:                                          */
/*                                                                      */
/*                ESTIMATE DATABASE SYSTEM MONITOR BUFFER SIZE          */
/*                GET SNAPSHOT                                          */
/*                                                                      */
/*----------------------------------------------------------------------*/
```

```cpp
// Include The Appropriate Header Files
#include <windows.h>
#include <iostream.h>
#include <time.h>
#include <sqlmon.h>
#include <sqlca.h>

// Define The API_Class Class
class API_Class
{
    // Attributes
    public:
        struct sqlca   sqlca;

    // Operations
    public:
        long GetMonSnapshot();
    private:
        void Process_DB2_Info(struct sqlm_db2   *DB2Info);
        void Process_DBase_Info(struct sqlm_dbase *DBaseInfo);
};

// Define The GetMonSnapshot() Member Function
long API_Class::GetMonSnapshot()
{
    // Declare The Local Memory Variables
    char                    *Buffer;
    char                    *BufferIndex;
    unsigned long           BuffSize;
    unsigned int            NumStructs = 0;
    struct sqlma            *sqlma;
    struct sqlm_collected   Collected;
    struct sqlm_db2         *DB2Info;
    struct sqlm_dbase       *DBaseInfo;

    // Specify The Data Monitors To Collect Information For
    sqlma = (struct sqlma *) malloc(SQLMASIZE(2));
    sqlma->obj_num = 2;
    sqlma->obj_var[0].obj_type = SQLMA_DB2;
    strcpy(sqlma->obj_var[0].object, "SAMPLE");
    sqlma->obj_var[1].obj_type = SQLMA_DBASE;
    strcpy(sqlma->obj_var[1].object, "SAMPLE");

    // Estimate The Size Of The Database Monitor Buffer Needed
    sqlmonsz(SQLM_DBMON_VERSION5, NULL, sqlma, &BuffSize, &sqlca);

    // If The Database Monitor Buffer Size Was Estimated, Allocate
    // Memory For It
    if (sqlca.sqlcode == SQL_RC_OK)
        Buffer = (char *) malloc(BuffSize);
    else
        goto EXIT;

    // Collect Monitor Snapshot Information
```

```cpp
sqlmonss(SQLM_DBMON_VERSION5, NULL, sqlma, BuffSize, Buffer,
         &Collected, &sqlca);

// If The Snapshot Information Was Collected, Display It
if (sqlca.sqlcode == SQL_RC_OK)
{
    // Add Up All Structures Returned In The Buffer
    NumStructs =  Collected.db2 +
                  Collected.databases +
                  Collected.table_databases +
                  Collected.lock_databases +
                  Collected.applications +
                  Collected.applinfos +
                  Collected.dcs_applinfos +
                  Collected.tablespace_databases;

    // Loop Until All Data Structures Have Been Processed
    for (BufferIndex = Buffer; NumStructs > 0; NumStructs-)
    {

        // Determine The Structure Type
        switch ((unsigned char) *(BufferIndex + 4))
        {

        // Display Select DB2 Information Collected
        case SQLM_DB2_SS:
            DB2Info = (struct sqlm_db2 *) BufferIndex;
            Process_DB2_Info(DB2Info);
            BufferIndex += DB2Info->size;
            break;

        // Display Select Database Information Collected
        case SQLM_DBASE_SS:
            DBaseInfo = (struct sqlm_dbase *) BufferIndex;
            Process_DBase_Info(DBaseInfo);
            BufferIndex += DBaseInfo->size;
            break;

        // If Anything Else Was Collected, Display An Error
        default:
            cout << "ERROR : Unexpected data in buffer." << endl;
            goto EXIT;
            break;
        }
    }
}

EXIT:

// Free All Allocated Memory
if (sqlma != NULL)
    free(sqlma);

if (Buffer != NULL)
```

```cpp
        free(Buffer);

    // Return The SQLCA Return Code To The Calling Function
    return(sqlca.sqlcode);
}


// Define The Process_DB2_Info() Member Function
void API_Class::Process_DB2_Info(struct sqlm_db2  *DB2Info)
{
    // Declare The Local Memory Variables
    long  Time;

    // Display The DB2 Status Information
    cout << "DB2 DATABASE MANAGER STATUS INFORMATION" << endl;
    cout << "————————————————————————————————————————————————————————";
    cout << "——————————" << endl;
    cout << "DB2 Database Manager Status           : ";
    switch (DB2Info->db2_status)
    {
    case SQLM_DB2_ACTIVE:
        cout << "Active" << endl;
        break;
    case SQLM_DB2_QUIESCE_PEND:
        cout << "Quiesce Pending" << endl;
        break;
    case SQLM_DB2_QUIESCED:
        cout << "Quiesced" << endl;
        break;
    }

    // Display Time Started Information
    Time = DB2Info->db2start_time.seconds;
    cout << "Time DB2 Database Manager Was Started  : ";
    cout << ctime(&Time) << endl << endl;

    // Display Select DB2 Connection Information
    cout << "DB2 DATABASE MANAGER CONNECTION INFORMATION" << endl;
    cout << "————————————————————————————————————————————————————————";
    cout << "——————————" << endl;
    cout << "Remote Connections To The DB2 Instance : ";
    cout << DB2Info->rem_cons_in << endl;
    cout << "Local Connections To The DB2 Instance  : ";
    cout << DB2Info->local_cons << endl;
    cout << "Local Active Databases                 : ";
    cout << DB2Info->con_local_dbases << endl;

    // Return To The Calling Function
    return;
}


// Define The Process_DBase_Info() Member Function
void API_Class::Process_DBase_Info(struct sqlm_dbase *DBaseInfo)
{
    // Declare The Local Memory Variables
```

```
        char   TempStr[20];

        // Display The Database Identification Information
        cout << "DATABASE INFORMATION" << endl;
        cout << "—————————————————————————————————————————————";
        cout << "——————————" << endl;
        cout << "Database Alias                          : ";
        strncpy(TempStr, DBaseInfo->input_db_alias, 19);
        TempStr[19] = 0;
        cout << TempStr << endl;
        cout << "Database Name                           : ";
        strncpy(TempStr, DBaseInfo->db_name, 19);
        TempStr[19] = 0;
        cout << TempStr << endl;
        cout << "Database Path (Truncated)               : ";
        strncpy(TempStr, DBaseInfo->db_path, 19);
        TempStr[19] = 0;
        cout << TempStr << endl;

        // Display The DB2 Status Information
        cout << "Current Database Status                 : ";
        switch (DBaseInfo->db_status)
        {
        case SQLM_DB_ACTIVE:
            cout << "Active" << endl << endl << endl;
            break;
        case SQLM_DB_QUIESCE_PEND:
            cout << "Quiesce Pending" << endl << endl << endl;
            break;
        case SQLM_DB_QUIESCED:
            cout << "Quiesced" << endl << endl << endl;
            break;
        }

        // Return To The Calling Function
        return;
}


/*————————————————————————————————————————————————————————————————*/
/* The Main Function                                              */
/*————————————————————————————————————————————————————————————————*/
int main()
{
        // Declare The Local Memory Variables
        long   rc = SQL_RC_OK;

        // Create An Instance Of The API_Class Class
        API_Class  Example;

        // Collect Monitor Snapshot Information
        rc = Example.GetMonSnapshot();

        // Return To The Operating System
        return(rc);
}
```

LIST DRDA INDOUBT TRANSACTIONS

Purpose   The LIST DRDA INDOUBT TRANSACTIONS function is used to retrieve a list of all indoubt transactions that exist between partner logical units (LUs) that are connected by LU 6.2 protocol.

Syntax
```
int SQL_API_FN sqlcspqy (SQLCSPQY_INDOUBT    *TransactionData,
                         long                *NumTransactions,
                         struct sqlca        *SQLCA);
```

Parameters   *TransactionData*   A pointer to a location in memory where this function is to store the address of a *SQLCSPQY_INDOUBT* structure that contains a list of DRDA indoubt transactions.

NumTransactions   A pointer to a location in memory where this function is to store the number of DRDA indoubt transactions found.

SQLCA   A pointer to a location in memory where a SQL Communications Area (SQLCA) data structure variable is stored. This structure returns either status information (if the function executed successfully) or error information (if the function failed) to the calling application.

Includes   `#include <sqlxa.h>`

Description The LIST DRDA INDOUBT TRANSACTIONS function is used to retrieve a list of all indoubt transactions that exist between partner logical unites (LUs) that are connected by LU 6.2 protocol. DRDA indoubt transactions occur when communications between coordinators and participants in two-phase commit transactions is lost.

Information obtained about a DRDA indoubt transaction is stored in a *sqlcspqy_indoubt_t* structure (type defined as *SQLCSPQY_INDOUBT*), which is defined in *sqlxa.h* as follows:

```
typedef struct sqlcspqy_indoubt_t
{
struct sqlxa_xid_t  xid;              /* The XA identifier assigned by the    */
                                      /* Transaction Manager that uniquely    */
                                      /* identifies the global transaction    */
char            luwid[36];            /* The logical unit workstation ID      */
char            corrtok[33];          /* Coordinator token                    */
char            partner[18];          /* The partner ID                       */
char            dbname[9];            /* The name of the database where the   */
                                      /* indoubt transaction was found        */
char            dbalias[9];           /* The alias of the database where the  */
                                      /* indoubt transaction was found        */
char            role;                 /* The role                             */
char            uow_status;           /* Unit of work (transaction) status    */
char            partner_status;       /* Partner status                       */
} SQLSCPQY_INDOUBT;
```

This structure contains a reference to an additional structure, *sqlxa_xid_t*, which is used to store the unique XA identifier that is assigned to all transactions by the Transaction Manager. The *sqlxa_xid_t* structure is defined in *sqlxa.h* as follows:

```
struct sqlxa_xid_t
{
long            formatID;       /* XA format identifier             */
long            gtrid_length;   /* The length of the global         */
                                /* transaction identifier           */
long            bqual_length;   /* The length of the branch identifier */
char            data[128];      /* The global transaction identifier, */
                                /* followed by trailing blanks for a */
                                /* total of 128 characters (bytes)  */
};
```

When this function is executed, a memory storage area that is sufficient to hold the list of DRDA indoubt transactions found is allocated and a pointer to this area is returned in the *TransactionData* parameter.

Comments ■ Before this function can be executed, an application must be connected to the Sync Point Manager (SPM) instance. This connection can be established by using the value of the *spm_name* DB2 Database Manager configuration file parameter in place of a database name in a CONNECT SQL statement.

Connection Requirements This function can only be called if a connection to a DB2 Database Manager instance exists.

Authorization Only users with System Administrator (SYSADM) authority are allowed to execute this function call.

See Also LIST INDOUBT TRANSACTIONS, COMMIT AN INDOUBT TRANSACTION, ROLLBACK AN INDOUBT TRANSACTION, FORGET TRANSACTION STATUS

Example The following C++ program illustrates how to use the LIST DRDA INDOUBT TRANSACTIONS function to retrieve a list of all DRDA indoubt transactions that exist for the MYDB1 database:

```
/*---------------------------------------------------------------*/
/* NAME:    CH13EX4.SQC                                          */
/* PURPOSE: Illustrate How To Use The Following DB2 API Function */
/*          In A C++ Program:                                    */
/*                                                               */
/*               LIST DRDA INDOUBT TRANSACTIONS                  */
/*                                                               */
/*---------------------------------------------------------------*/

// Include The Appropriate Header Files
#include <windows.h>
#include <iostream.h>
#include <sqlenv.h>
```

```cpp
#include <sqlxa.h>
#include <sql.h>

// Define The API_Class Class
class API_Class
{
    // Attributes
    public:
        struct sqlca  sqlca;

    // Operations
    public:
        long ListTransactions();
};

// Define The ListTransactions() Member Function
long API_Class::ListTransactions()
{
    // Declare The Local Memory Variables
    SQLCSPQY_INDOUBT  *IndoubtTrans = NULL;
    long              NumIDTrans;

    // Restart The MYDB1 Database
    cout << "Restarting the database. Please wait." << endl << endl;
    sqlerstd("MYDB1", "userID", "password", &sqlca);

    // If Unable To Restart The Database, Display An Error Message
    // And Exit
    if (sqlca.sqlcode != SQL_RC_OK && sqlca.sqlcode != 1061)
    {
        cout << "ERROR : Unable to restart the MYDB1 database.";
        cout << endl;
        goto EXIT;
    }

    // Retrieve A List Of All DRDA Indoubt Transactions
    sqlcspqy(&IndoubtTrans, &NumIDTrans, &sqlca);

    // If A List Of DRDA Indoubt Transactions Was Obtained,
    // Display It
    if (sqlca.sqlcode == SQL_RC_OK)
    {
        // Display Information About All Indoubt Transactions Found
        for (; NumIDTrans > 0; NumIDTrans--)
        {
            cout << "Transaction ID" << endl;
            cout << "  Format ID         : ";
            cout << IndoubtTrans->xid.formatID << endl;
            cout << "  GTRID Length      : ";
            cout << IndoubtTrans->xid.gtrid_length << endl;
            cout << "  BQUAL Length      : ";
            cout << IndoubtTrans->xid.bqual_length << endl;
            cout << "  Data              : ";
            cout << IndoubtTrans->xid.data << endl << endl;
```

```
                    cout << "LUW ID               : ";
                    cout << IndoubtTrans->luwid << endl;
                    cout << "Coordinator Token    : ";
                    cout << IndoubtTrans->corrtok << endl;
                    cout << "Partner              : ";
                    cout << IndoubtTrans->partner << endl;
                    cout << "Databas              : ";
                    cout << IndoubtTrans->dbname << endl;
                    cout << "Alias                : ";
                    cout << IndoubtTrans->dbalias << endl;
                    cout << "Role                 : ";
                    cout << IndoubtTrans->role << endl;
                    cout << "Status               : ";
                    cout << IndoubtTrans->uow_status << endl;
                    cout << "Partner Status       : ";
                    cout << IndoubtTrans->partner_status << endl << endl;
                    IndoubtTrans++;
                }
        }

EXIT:

        // Return The SQLCA Return Code To The Calling Function
        return(sqlca.sqlcode);
    }


/*————————————————————————————————————————————————— */
/* The Main Function                                 */
/*————————————————————————————————————————————————— */
int main()
{
    // Declare The Local Memory Variables
    long          rc = SQL_RC_OK;
    struct sqlca  sqlca;

    // Create An Instance Of The API_Class Class
    API_Class  Example;

    // List All DRDA Indoubt Transactions Found
    rc = Example.ListTransactions();

    // Issue A Rollback To Free All Locks
    EXEC SQL ROLLBACK;

    // Disconnect From The MYDB1 Database
    EXEC SQL DISCONNECT CURRENT;

    // Return To The Operating System
    return(rc);
}
```

LIST INDOUBT TRANSACTIONS

Purpose The LIST INDOUBT TRANSACTIONS function is used to retrieve a list of all indoubt transactions that exist for the current connected database.

Syntax
```
int SQL_API_FN sqlxphqr  (int           RequestNode,
                          SQLXA_RECOVER **TransactionData,
                          long          *NumTransactions,
                          struct sqlca  *SQLCA);
```

Parameters   *RequestNode*   Specifies the node to list indoubt transactions for. This parameter must be set to one of the following values:

- SQLXA_EXE_THIS_NODE
  List indoubt transactions found on the node from which this function was called.

- SQLXA_EXE_ALL_NODES
  List indoubt transactions found in all nodes (in a multi-node datatbase environment).

TransactionData   A pointer to a location in memory where this function is to store the address of an *sqlxa_recover_t* structure that contains a list of indoubt transactions.

NumTransactions   A pointer to a location in memory where this function is to store the number of indoubt transactions found.

SQLCA   A pointer to a location in memory where a SQL Communications Area (SQLCA) data structure variable is stored. This variable returns either status information (if the function executed successfully) or error information (if the function failed) to the calling application.

Includes `#include <sqlxa.h>`

Description The LIST INDOUBT TRANSACTIONS function is used to retrieve a list of all indoubt transactions that exist for the currently connected database. Information obtained about an indoubt transaction is stored in an *sqlxa_recover_t* structure (type defined as *SQLXA_RECOVER*), which is defined in *sqlxa.h* as follows:

```
typedef struct sqlxa_recover_t
{
unsigned long    timestamp;     /* The date and time when the        */
                                /* transaction entered the indoubt   */
                                /* state                             */
struct sqlxa_xid_t xid;         /* The XA identifier assigned by the */
                                /* Transaction Manager that uniquely */
                                /* identifies the global transaction */
char             dbalias[8];    /* The alias of the database where   */
```

```
                                       /* the indoubt transaction was found    */
     char              applid[32];     /* The application identifier assigned  */
                                       /* to this transaction by the DB2       */
                                       /* Database Manager                      */
     char              sequence_no[4];                                         /* */
                                       /* The sequence number assigned as      */
                                       /* an extension to the application      */
                                       /* identifier by the DB2 Database       */
                                       /* Manager                              */
     char              auth_id[8];     /* The authorization ID of the user     */
                                       /* who initiated this transaction       */
     char              log_full;       /* Indicates whether the transaction    */
                                       /* caused a LOG FULL condition to occur  */
                                       /* (SQLXA_TRUE) or not (SQLXA_FALSE)     */
     char              connected;      /* Indicates whether the transaction is */
                                       /* undergoing normal syncpoint processing */
                                       /* and is waiting for the second phase of */
                                       /* a two-phase commit (SQLXA_TRUE) or the */
                                       /* transaction was left indoubt by an    */
                                       /* earlier failure and is awaiting a     */
                                       /* resync from the Transaction Manager   */
                                       /* (SQLXA_FALSE)                         */
     char              indoubt_status;                                         /* */
                                       /* Indicates whether the transaction    */
                                       /* has been prepared (SQLXA_TS_PREP),    */
                                       /* heuristically committed (SQLXA_TS_HCOM), */
                                       /* heuristically rolled back             */
                                       /* (SQLXA_TS_HROL), idle (SQLXA_TS_END),  */
                                       /* missing commit acknowledgement        */
                                       /* (SQLXA_TS_MACK), prepared and         */
                                       /* heuristically committed (SQLXA_TS_PHC), */
                                       /* prepared and (SQLXA_TS_PHR),          */
                                       /* heuristically rolled back heuristically */
                                       /* committed and heuristically rolled    */
                                       /* back (SQLXA_TS_HCHR), or prepared,    */
                                       /* heuristically committed, and          */
                                       /* heuristically rolled back (SQLXA_TS_PHCHR) */
     char              originator;     /* Indicates whether the transaction was */
                                       /* originated by XA (SQLXA_ORIG_XA) or   */
                                       /* by DB2 in a MPP                       */
                                       /* environment (SQLXA_ORIG_PE)           */
     char              reserved[9];    /* The first byte of this field          */
                                       /* indicates the indoubt transaction     */
                                       /* type; the rest of this field is set   */
                                       /* to zeros                              */
} SQLXA_RECOVER;
```

This structure contains a reference to an additional structure, *sqlxa_xid_t* (type defined as *sqlxa_tid*) which is used to store the unique XA identifier that is assigned to all transactions by the Transaction Manager. Refer to the LIST DRDA INDOUBT TRANSACTIONS function for a detailed description of the *sqlxa_xid_t* structure.

When this function is executed, a memory storage area that is sufficient to hold the list of indoubt transactions found is allocated by DB2 and a pointer to this area is returned in the *TransactionData* parameter.

Comments
- The memory that is allocated by this function is released automatically when the application that called this function terminates. Do not use the FREE MEMORY function to free this memory, because this function contains pointers to other dynamically allocated structures that will not be freed by the FREE MEMORY function.

- The maximum value that can be specified for both the *gtrid_length* and *bqual_length* fields of the *sqlxa_xid_t* structure is 64.

- For detailed information on using two-phase commits and indoubt transaction recovery, refer to the *IBM DB2 Universal Database Administration Guide*.

Connection Requirements   This function can only be called if a connection to a database exists.

Authorization   Only users with either System Administrator (SYSADM) authority or Database Administrator (DBADM) authority can execute this function call.

See Also   COMMIT AN INDOUBT TRANSACTION, ROLLBACK AN INDOUBT TRANSACTION, FORGET TRANSACTION STATUS

Example   The following C++ program illustrates how to use the LIST INDOUBT TRANSACTIONS function to retrieve a list of all indoubt transactions that exist for the MYDB1 database (this example was created and tested on the AIX operating system):

```
/*————————————————————————————————————*/
/* NAME:    CH13EX5.SQC                                    */
/* PURPOSE: Illustrate How To Use The Following DB2 API Function */
/*          In A C++ Program:                              */
/*                                                         */
/*              LIST INDOUBT TRANSACTIONS                  */
/*                                                         */
/*————————————————————————————————————*/

// Include The Appropriate Header Files
#include <iostream.h>
#include <sqlenv.h>
#include <sqlxa.h>
#include <sql.h>

// Define The API_Class Class
class API_Class
{
    // Attributes
    public:
        struct sqlca  sqlca;

    // Operations
    public:
        long ListTransactions();
};
```

```cpp
// Define The ListTransactions() Member Function
long API_Class::ListTransactions()
{
    // Declare The Local Memory Variables
    SQLXA_RECOVER   *IndoubtTrans = NULL;
    long            NumIDTrans;

    // Restart The MYDB1 Database
    cout << "Restarting the database. Please wait." << endl << endl;
    sqlerstd("MYDB1", "userID", "password", &sqlca);

    // If Unable To Restart The Database, Display An Error Message
    // And Exit
    if (sqlca.sqlcode != SQL_RC_OK && sqlca.sqlcode != 1061)
    {
        cout << "ERROR : Unable to restart the MYDB1 database.";
        cout << endl;
        goto EXIT;
    }

    // Retrieve A List Of All Indoubt Transactions
    sqlxphqr(SQLXA_EXE_THIS_NODE, &IndoubtTrans, &NumIDTrans,
        &sqlca);

    // If A List Of Indoubt Transactions Was Obtained, Display It
    if (sqlca.sqlcode == SQL_RC_OK)
    {
        // Display Information About All Indoubt Transactions Found
        for (; NumIDTrans > 0; NumIDTrans--)
        {
            cout << "Transaction ID" << endl;
            cout << "  Format ID      : ";
            cout << IndoubtTrans->xid.formatID << endl;
            cout << "  GTRID Length   : ";
            cout << IndoubtTrans->xid.gtrid_length << endl;
            cout << "  BQUAL Length   : ";
            cout << IndoubtTrans->xid.bqual_length << endl;
            cout << "  Data           : ";
            cout << IndoubtTrans->xid.data << endl << endl;
            cout << "Database         : ";
            cout << IndoubtTrans->dbalias << endl;
            cout << "Application ID   : ";
            cout << IndoubtTrans->applid << endl;
            cout << "Timestamp        : ";
            cout << IndoubtTrans->timestamp << endl;
            cout << "Sequence No.     : ";
            cout << IndoubtTrans->sequence_no << endl;
            cout << "Authorization ID : ";
            cout << IndoubtTrans->auth_id << endl;
            cout << "Log Full         : ";
            if (IndoubtTrans->log_full == SQLXA_TRUE)
                cout << "Yes" << endl;
            else
                cout << "No" << endl;
```

```
            cout << "Connected        : ";
            if (IndoubtTrans->connected == SQLXA_TRUE)
                cout << "Yes" << endl;
            else
                cout << "No" << endl;
            cout << "Originator       : ";
            if (IndoubtTrans->originator == SQLXA_ORIG_PE)
                cout << "DB2" << endl;
            else
                cout << "XA" << endl;
            cout << "Status           : ";
            cout << IndoubtTrans->indoubt_status << endl << endl;
            IndoubtTrans++;
        }
    }

EXIT:

    // Return The SQLCA Return Code To The Calling Function
    return(sqlca.sqlcode);
}

/*----------------------------------------------------------------*/
/* The Main Function                                              */
/*----------------------------------------------------------------*/
int main()
{
    // Declare The Local Memory Variables
    long        rc = SQL_RC_OK;
    struct sqlca  sqlca;

    // Create An Instance Of The API_Class Class
    API_Class  Example;

    // List All Indoubt Transactions Found
    rc = Example.ListTransactions();

    // Issue A Rollback To Free All Locks
    EXEC SQL ROLLBACK;

    // Disconnect From The MYDB1 Database
    EXEC SQL DISCONNECT CURRENT;

    // Return To The Operating System
    return(rc);
}
```

COMMIT AN INDOUBT TRANSACTION

Purpose   The COMMIT AN INDOUBT TRANSACTION function is used to heuristically commit an indoubt transaction.

| **Syntax** | ```
int SQL_API_FN sqlxphcm (int         RequestNode,
                         SQLXA_XID   *TransactionID,
                         struct sqlca *SQLCA);
``` |

Parameters   *RequestNode*   Specifies which node to heuristically commit indoubt transactions for. This parameter must be set to one of the following values:

> ■ `SQLXA_EXE_THIS_NODE`
> Heuristically commit indoubt transactions on the node from which this function was called.

> ■ `SQLXA_EXE_ALL_NODES`
> Heuristically commit indoubt transactions on all nodes (in a multi-node database environment).

TransactionID   A pointer to a location in memory where the XA identifier of the indoubt transaction to be heuristically committed is stored.

SQLCA   A pointer to a location in memory where a SQL Communications Area (SQLCA) data structure variable is stored. This variable returns either status information (if the function executed successfully) or error information (if the function failed) to the calling application.

Includes   `#include <sqlxa.h>`

Description   The COMMIT AN INDOUBT TRANSACTION function is used to heuristically commit an indoubt transaction. If this function is successfully executed, the specified transaction's state becomes *"Heuristically Committed."*

  When a transaction is initiated, the transaction is assigned a unique XA identifier by the Transaction Manager (which is then used to globally identify the transaction). This unique XA identifier is used to specify which indoubt transaction this function is to heuristically commit. Refer to the LIST DRDA INDOUBT TRANSACTIONS function for a detailed description of the XA identifier structure (*sqlxa_xid_t*).

Comments   ■ The maximum value that can be specified for both the *gtrid_length* and the *bqual_length fields* of the *sqlxa_xid_t* structure is 64.

                   ■ You can obtain *sqlxa_xid_t* structure information for a particular transaction by calling the LIST INDOUBT TRANSACTIONS function.

                   ■ Only transactions with a status of "Prepared" or "Idle" can be placed in the "Heuristically Committed" state.

                   ■ The Database Manager remembers the state of an indoubt transaction, even after the transaction has been heuristically committed, unless the FORGET TRANSACTION STATUS function is executed.

Connection Requirements   This function can only be called if a connection to a database exists.
```

Authorization   Only users with either System Administrator (SYSADM) or Database Administrator (DBADM) authority are allowed to execute this function call.

See Also   LIST INDOUBT TRANSACTIONS, ROLLBACK AN INDOUBT TRANSACTION, FORGET TRANSACTION STATUS

Example   The following C++ program illustrates how to use the COMMIT AN INDOUBT TRANSACTION function to heuristically commit an indoubt transaction (this example was created and tested on the AIX operating system):

```
/*————————————————————————————————————————————*/
/* NAME:    CH13EX6.SQC                                          */
/* PURPOSE: Illustrate How To Use The Following DB2 API Functions */
/*          In A C++ Program:                                    */
/*                                                               */
/*               COMMIT AN INDOUBT TRANSACTION                   */
/*               FORGET TRANSACTION STATUS                       */
/*                                                               */
/* OTHER DB2 APIs SHOWN:                                         */
/*          LIST INDOUBT TRANSACTIONS                            */
/*                                                               */
/*————————————————————————————————————————————*/

// Include The Appropriate Header Files
#include <iostream.h>
#include <sqlenv.h>
#include <sqlxa.h>
#include <sql.h>

// Define The API_Class Class
class API_Class
{
    // Attributes
    public:
        struct sqlca   sqlca;

    // Operations
    public:
        long CommitIDTransaction();
};

// Define The CommitIDTransaction() Member Function
long API_Class::CommitIDTransaction()
{
    // Declare The Local Memory Variables
    SQLXA_RECOVER   *IndoubtTrans = NULL;
    long            NumIDTrans;

    // Restart The MYDB1 Database
    cout << "Restarting the database. Please wait." << endl << endl;
    sqlerstd("MYDB1", "userID", "password", &sqlca);
```

```cpp
    // If Unable To Restart The Database, Display An Error Message
    // And Exit
    if (sqlca.sqlcode != SQL_RC_OK && sqlca.sqlcode != 1061)
    {
        cout << "ERROR : Unable to restart the MYDB1 database.";
        cout << endl;
        goto EXIT;
    }

    // Retrieve A List Of All Indoubt Transactions
    sqlxphqr(SQLXA_EXE_THIS_NODE, &IndoubtTrans, &NumIDTrans,
        &sqlca);

    // If A List Of Indoubt Transactions Was Obtained ...
    if (sqlca.sqlcode == SQL_RC_OK)
    {
        // Display Information About The First Indoubt Transaction
        // Found
        cout << "Transaction ID" << endl;
        cout << "  Format ID      : ";
        cout << IndoubtTrans->xid.formatID << endl;
        cout << "  GTRID Length   : ";
        cout << IndoubtTrans->xid.gtrid_length << endl;
        cout << "  BQUAL Length   : ";
        cout << IndoubtTrans->xid.bqual_length << endl;
        cout << "  Data           : ";
        cout << IndoubtTrans->xid.data << endl << endl;

        // Heurstically Commit The First Indoubt Transaction Found
        sqlxphcm(SQLXA_EXE_THIS_NODE, &IndoubtTrans->xid, &sqlca);

        // If The Indoubt Transaction Was Heurstically Committed,
        // Display A Success Message And Forget It
        if (sqlca.sqlcode == SQL_RC_OK)
        {
            cout << "Transaction has been heurstically committed.";
            cout << endl;

            // Forget The Heurstically Committed Indoubt Transaction
            sqlxhfrg(&IndoubtTrans->xid, &sqlca);

            // If The Indoubt Transaction Was Forgotten, Display A
            // Success Message
            if (sqlca.sqlcode == SQL_RC_OK)
                cout << "Transaction has been forgotten." << endl;
        }
    }

EXIT:

    // Return The SQLCA Return Code To The Calling Function
    return(sqlca.sqlcode);
}
```

```
/*------------------------------------------------------------------*/
/* The Main Function                                                */
/*------------------------------------------------------------------*/
int main()
{
    // Declare The Local Memory Variables
    long         rc = SQL_RC_OK;
    struct sqlca  sqlca;

    // Create An Instance Of The API_Class Class
    API_Class  Example;

    // Commit The First Indoubt Transaction Found
    rc = Example.CommitIDTransaction();

    // Issue A Rollback To Free All Locks
    EXEC SQL ROLLBACK;

    // Disconnect From The MYDB1 Database
    EXEC SQL DISCONNECT CURRENT;

    // Return To The Operating System
    return(rc);
}
```

ROLLBACK AN INDOUBT TRANSACTION

Purpose   The ROLLBACK AN INDOUBT TRANSACTION function is used to heuristically roll back an indoubt transaction.

Syntax
```
int SQL_API_FN sqlxphrl (int          RequestNode,
                         SQLXA_XID    *TransactionID,
                         struct sqlca *SQLCA);
```

Parameters   *RequestNode*   Specifies which node to heuristically roll back indoubt transactions for. This parameter must be set to one of the following values:

■ SQLXA_EXE_THIS_NODE
Heuristically roll back indoubt transactions on the node from which this function was called.

■ SQLXA_EXE_ALL_NODES
Heuristically roll back indoubt transactions on all nodes (in a multi-node database environment).

TransactionID   A pointer to a location in memory where the XA identifier of the indoubt transaction to be heuristically rolled back is stored.

SQLCA   A pointer to a location in memory where a SQL Communications Area (SQLCA) data structure variable is stored. This variable returns either status information (if the function executed successfully) or error information (if the function failed) to the calling application.

Includes   `#include <sqlxa.h>`

Description   The ROLLBACK AN INDOUBT TRANSACTION function is used to heuristically roll back an indoubt transaction. If this function is successfully executed, the specified transaction's state becomes *"Heuristically Rolled Back."*

When a transaction is initiated, the transaction is assigned a unique XA identifier by the Transaction Manager (which is then used to globally identify the transaction). This unique XA identifier is used to specify which indoubt transaction this function is to roll back. Refer to the LIST DRDA INDOUBT TRANSACTIONS function for a detailed description of the XA identifier structure (*sqlxa_xid_t*).

Comments
- The maximum value that can be specified for both the *gtrid_length* and the *bqual_length fields* of the *sqlxa_xid_t* structure is 64.

- You can obtain *sqlxa_xid_t* structure information for a particular transaction by calling the LIST INDOUBT TRANSACTIONS function.

- Only transactions with a status of "Prepared" or "Idle" can be placed in the "Heuristically Rolled Back" state.

- The Database Manager remembers the state of an indoubt transaction, even after the transaction has been heuristically rolled back, unless the FORGET TRANSACTION STATUS function is executed.

Connection Requirements   This function can only be called if a connection to a database exists.

Authorization   Only users with either System Administrator (SYSADM) authority or Database Administrator (DBADM) authority are allowed to execute this function call.

See Also   COMMIT AN INDOUBT TRANSACTION, LIST INDOUBT TRANSACTIONS, FORGET TRANSACTION STATUS

Example   The following C++ program illustrates how to use the ROLLBACK AN INDOUBT TRANSACTION function to heuristically roll back an indoubt transaction (this example was created and tested on the AIX operating system):

```
/*-------------------------------------------------------------*/
/* NAME:     CH13EX7.SQC                                       */
/* PURPOSE:  Illustrate How To Use The Following DB2 API Functions */
/*           In A C++ Program:                                 */
/*                                                             */
/*                ROLL BACK AN INDOUBT TRANSACTION             */
/*                FORGET TRANSACTION STATUS                    */
/*                                                             */
/* OTHER DB2 APIs SHOWN:                                       */
/*                LIST INDOUBT TRANSACTIONS                    */
/*                                                             */
/*-------------------------------------------------------------*/
```

```cpp
// Include The Appropriate Header Files
#include <iostream.h>
#include <sqlenv.h>
#include <sqlxa.h>
#include <sql.h>

// Define The API_Class Class
class API_Class
{
    // Attributes
    public:
        struct sqlca   sqlca;

    // Operations
    public:
        long RollbackIDTransaction();
};

// Define The RollbackIDTransaction() Member Function
long API_Class::RollbackIDTransaction()
{
    // Declare The Local Memory Variables
    SQLXA_RECOVER   *IndoubtTrans = NULL;
    long            NumIDTrans;

    // Restart The MYDB1 Database
    cout << "Restarting the database. Please wait." << endl << endl;
    sqlerstd("MYDB1", "userID", "password", &sqlca);

    // If Unable To Restart The Database, Display An Error Message
    // And Exit
    if (sqlca.sqlcode != SQL_RC_OK && sqlca.sqlcode != 1061)
    {
        cout << "ERROR : Unable to restart the MYDB1 database.";
        cout << endl;
        goto EXIT;
    }

    // Retrieve A List Of All Indoubt Transactions
    sqlxphqr(SQLXA_EXE_THIS_NODE, &IndoubtTrans, &NumIDTrans,
        &sqlca);

    // If A List Of Indoubt Transactions Was Obtained ...
    if (sqlca.sqlcode == SQL_RC_OK)
    {
        // Display Information About The First Indoubt Transaction
        // Found
        cout << "Transaction ID" << endl;
        cout << "  Format ID                : ";
        cout << IndoubtTrans->xid.formatID << endl;
        cout << "  GTRID Length             : ";
        cout << IndoubtTrans->xid.gtrid_length << endl;
        cout << "  BQUAL Length             : ";
        cout << IndoubtTrans->xid.bqual_length << endl;
```

```
        cout << "    Data                    : ";
        cout << IndoubtTrans->xid.data << endl << endl;

        // Heurstically Roll Back The First Indoubt Transaction Found
        sqlxphrl(SQLXA_EXE_THIS_NODE, &IndoubtTrans->xid, &sqlca);

        // If The Indoubt Transaction Was Heurstically Rolled Back,
        // Display A Success Message And Forget It
        if (sqlca.sqlcode == SQL_RC_OK)
        {
            cout << "Transaction has been heurstically rolled back.";
            cout << endl;

            // Forget The Heurstically Rolled Back Indoubt
            // Transaction
            sqlxhfrg(&IndoubtTrans->xid, &sqlca);

            // If The Indoubt Transaction Was Forgotten, Display A
            // Success Message
            if (sqlca.sqlcode == SQL_RC_OK)
                cout << "Transaction has been forgotten." << endl;
        }
    }

EXIT:

    // Return The SQLCA Return Code To The Calling Function
    return(sqlca.sqlcode);
}

/*------------------------------------------------------------------*/
/* The Main Function                                                */
/*------------------------------------------------------------------*/
int main()
{
    // Declare The Local Memory Variables
    long          rc = SQL_RC_OK;
    struct sqlca  sqlca;

    // Create An Instance Of The API_Class Class
    API_Class  Example;

    // Roll Back The First Indoubt Transaction Found
    rc = Example.RollbackIDTransaction();

    // Issue A Rollback To Free All Locks
    EXEC SQL ROLLBACK;

    // Disconnect From The MYDB1 Database
    EXEC SQL DISCONNECT CURRENT;

    // Return To The Operating System
    return(rc);
}
```

FORGET TRANSACTION STATUS

Purpose   The FORGET TRANSACTION STATUS function is used to tell the Transaction Manager (or Resource Manager) to erase knowledge of an indoubt transaction that has been heuristically committed with the COMMIT AN INDOUBT TRANSACTION function or heuristically rolled back with the ROLLBACK AN INDOUBT TRANSACTION function.

Syntax
```
int SQL_API_FN sqlxhfrg (sqlxa_xid_t    *TransactionID,
                         struct sqlca   *SQLCA);
```

Parameters   *TransactionID*   A pointer to a location in memory where the XA identifier of the indoubt transaction to be erased is stored.

               SQLCA   A pointer to a location in memory where a SQL Communications Area (SQLCA) data structure variable is stored. This variable returns either status information (if the function executed successfully) or error information (if the function failed) to the calling application.

Includes   `#include <sqlxa.h>`

Description   The FORGET TRANSACTION STATUS function is used to tell the Transaction Manager (or Resource Manager) to erase knowledge of an indoubt transaction that has been placed in either the "Heuristically Committed" or "Heuristically Rolled Back" state. Indoubt transactions can be placed in either of these states when the COMMIT AN INDOUBT TRANSACTION function or the ROLLBACK AN INDOUBT TRANSACTION function is executed.

When a transaction is initiated, the transaction is assigned a unique XA identifier by the Transaction Manager (which is then used to globally identify the transaction). This unique XA identifier is used to specify which indoubt transaction this function is to erase. Refer to the LIST DRDA INDOUBT TRANSACTIONS function for a detailed description of the XA identifier structure (*sqlxa_xid_t*).

Comments   ■ Only transactions with a status of "Heuristically Committed" or "Heuristically Rolled Back" can be processed by this function.

Connection   This function can only be called if a connection to a database exists.
Requirements

Authorization Only users with either System Administrator (SYSADM) authority or Database Administrator (DBADM) authority can execute this function call.

See Also   LIST INDOUBT TRANSACTIONS, COMMIT AN INDOUBT TRANSACTION, ROLLBACK AN INDOUBT TRANSACTION

Example   See the examples provided for the COMMIT AN INDOUBT TRANSACTION function on page 546 and ROLLBACK AN INDOUBT TRANSACTION function on page 549.

14

Thread Context Management Functions

By default, all DB2 database access acquired by threaded applications is serialized. That is, if one thread attempts to perform a database operation that is blocked for some reason (usually because a requested table has been locked for "exclusive" by another application), all other threads are blocked as well—even if those threads access other unlocked tables. Additionally, by default, all threads within a process share a common commit scope. Thus, two or more threads can only access a database concurrently if each thread runs under a different process—or if each thread runs under a different *context*. This chapter is designed to introduce you to the set of DB2 API functions that are used to allocate and manipulate separate contexts (environments) that enable two or more threads within an application to access a database concurrently. The first part of this chapter provides a general discussion about threads and contexts. Then, a detailed reference section covering each DB2 API function that can be used to allocate and/or manipulate a thread context is provided.

Contexts

As mentioned earlier, a *context* is simply an environment that enables two or more threads to run concurrently. Each context is a separate entity, and any connection or attachment made to a database or to a DB2 Database Manager instance within a context is isolated (and independent) from any connection or attachments made within other contexts. Once allocated, a context is virtually useless until the context has been associated with (attached to) a thread. Likewise a thread must be associated with a context before it can execute SQL statements or DB2 API function calls. By default, all threads within a process (the primary thread of the application) share the same context and the same commit scope. However, if the CREATE AND ATTACH TO AN APPLICATION CONTEXT function is called from within a thread, that thread will have its own context and its own commit scope.

Once created, contexts remain available for use until they are explicitly destroyed by the DETACH AND DESTROY APPLICATION CONTEXT function. In addition, contexts do not have to be associated with a given thread for the duration of a connection to a database or an attachment to a DB2 Database Manager instance. In fact, one thread can attach to a context, establish a connection or instance attachment, and then detach from the context. Another thread can then attach to the same context and begin doing work using the connection or instance attachment that was established by the first thread. In this manner, contexts can be passed around among threads within a given process (but not among threads in different processes).

NOTE: *Even when contexts are used, the following DB2 API functions will continue to run serialized:* PRECOMPILE PROGRAM, BIND, IMPORT, *and* EXPORT.

The DB2 Thread Context Management Functions

Table 14–1 lists the DB2 API functions that are used to allocate and manipulate separate contexts that enable threads within an application to access a database concurrently.

Each of these functions are described in detail in the remainder of this chapter.

Table 14–1 DB2 Thread Context Management Functions

Function Name	Description
`SET APPLICATION CONTEXT TYPE`	Identifies the type of context that a multi-threaded application will use to process threads.
`CREATE AND ATTACH TO AN APPLICATION CONTEXT`	Creates an application context, or creates and then attaches to an application context.
`DETACH AND DESTROY APPLICATION CONTEXT`	Makes the current thread stop using a specified context and frees all memory associated with that context.
`ATTACH TO CONTEXT`	Makes the current thread use a specified context.
`DETACH FROM CONTEXT`	Makes the current thread stop using a specified context.
`GET CURRENT CONTEXT`	Gets the context that the current thread is attached to.
`INTERRUPT CONTEXT`	Sends an interrupt to the specified context.

SET APPLICATION CONTEXT TYPE

Purpose The SET APPLICATION CONTEXT TYPE function is used to identify the type of context a multi-threaded application is to use to process threads.

Syntax
```
int sqleSetTypeCtx (long    ContextType);
```

Parameters *ContextType* Specifies the type of context that all threads in an application are to use. This parameter must be set to one of the following values:

- SQL_CTX_ORIGINAL
  All threads will use the same context, and concurrent database access will not be allowed. This is the default value used.

- SQL_CTX_MULTI_MANUAL
  All threads will use separate contexts, and it is up to the application to manage the context for each thread.

Includes
```
#include <sql.h>
```

Description The SET APPLICATION CONTEXT TYPE function is used to identify the type of context that a multi-threaded application will use to process threads. This function should be the first DB2 API function called in a multi-thread application.

Comments
- The following restrictions apply when this function is called with the *ContextType* parameter set to SQL_CTX_MULTI_MANUAL:
  - When termination is normal, automatic commit is disabled. Therefore, all commits must be done explicitly. At process termination, all outstanding transactions are rolled back.
  - The INTERRUPT function interrupts all contexts used. In order to interrupt a single context, the INTERRUPT CONTEXT function must be used instead.
- The scope of this function is limited to the current process.

- This function has no effect when it is executed on platforms that do not support application threading.

Connection Requirements This function can be called at any time.; a connection to a DB2 Database Manager instance or to a DB2 database does not have to be established first.

Authorization No authorization is required to execute this function call.

See Also CREATE AND ATTACH TO AN APPLICATION CONTEXT, ATTACH TO CONTEXT, DETACH AND DESTROY APPLICATION CONTEXT, DETACH FROM CONTEXT, INTERRUPT CONTEXT

Example The following C++ program illustrates how to use the SET APPLICATION CONTEXT TYPE function to identify the type of context a multi-threaded application will use to process threads:

```
/*------------------------------------------------------------*/
/* NAME:     CH14EX1.CPP                                      */
/* PURPOSE: Illustrate How To Use The Following DB2 API Function */
/*          In A C++ Program:                                 */
/*                                                            */
/*                 SET APPLICATION CONTEXT TYPE               */
/*                                                            */
/*------------------------------------------------------------*/

// Include The Appropriate Header Files
#include <windows.h>
#include <process.h>                    // _beginthread(), _endthread()
#include <stddef.h>
#include <stdlib.h>
#include <conio.h>
#include <iostream.h>
#include <sql.h>
#include <sqlenv.h>
#include <sqlca.h>

// Define The Thread Function Prototypes
void CheckKey(void *Dummy);
void GetInstance(void *Count);

// Declare The Global Memory Variables
BOOL   ContinueThread = TRUE;           // End Thread Flag
char   Instance[9];                     // Current Instance

/*------------------------------------------------------------*/
/* The Main Function                                          */
/*------------------------------------------------------------*/
int main()
{
    // Declare The Local Memory Variables
    long       rc = SQL_RC_OK;
    char       Counter = 0;

    // Set The Application Context Type To Normal (All Threads Will
    // Use The Same Context)
    sqleSetTypeCtx(SQL_CTX_ORIGINAL);

    // Launch The CheckKey() Thread To Check For A Terminating
    // Keystroke
    _beginthread(CheckKey, 0, NULL);

    // Loop Until CheckKey() Thread Terminates The Program
    while(ContinueThread == TRUE)
    {
        // Launch Up To Ten GetInstance() Threads
        if (Counter < 10)
            _beginthread(GetInstance, 0, (void *) (Counter++));

        // Wait One Second Between Loop Passes
        Sleep(1000L);
```

```
        // Display The Current Value Of The DB2INSTANCE Environment
        // Variable
        cout << "Current value of the DB2INSTANCE environment ";
        cout << "variable : " << Instance << endl;
    }

    // Return To The Operating System
    return(rc);
}

// Define The CheckKey() Thread Function
void CheckKey(void *Dummy)
{
    // Wait For A Keystroke
    _getch();

    // Set The ContinueThread Flag So The GetInstance() Threads Will
    // End
    ContinueThread = FALSE;

    // Terminate This Thread
    _endthread();
}

// Define The GetInstance() Thread Function
void GetInstance(void *Count)
{
    // Declare The Local Memory Variables
    struct sqlca  sqlca;

    // Loop Until CheckKey() Thread Terminates The Program
    while(ContinueThread == TRUE)
    {
        // Pause Between Loops
        Sleep(100L);

        // Obtain The Current Value Of The DB2INSTANCE Environment
        // Variable
        sqlegins(Instance, &sqlca);
        Instance[8] = 0;

        // If The Current Value Of The DB2INSTANCE Environment
        // Variable Was Not Obtained, Clear The Memory Storage Area
        if (sqlca.sqlcode != SQL_RC_OK)
            Instance[0] = 0;

        // Beep To Signal The Loop Is Still Running
        Beep(1000, 175);
    }

    // Terminate The Thread
    _endthread();
}
```

CREATE AND ATTACH TO AN APPLICATION CONTEXT

Purpose   The CREATE AND ATTACH TO AN APPLICATION CONTEXT function is used to either create an application context or to create and then attach to an application context.

Syntax
```
int  sqleBeginCtx  (void          **Context,
                    long          Action,
                    void          *Reserved,
                    struct sqlca  *SQLCA);
```

Parameters   *Context*   A pointer to a location in memory where this function is to store the starting address of a data storage area that is to be used to store context information.

Action   Specifies the action that this function is to perform. This parameter must be set to one of the following values:

- SQL_CTX_CREATE_ONLY
  Allocate context memory without attaching to the current thread.

- SQL_CTX_BEGIN_ALL
  Allocate context memory and attach to the current thread.

Reserved   A pointer that, at this time, is reserved for later use. For now, this parameter must always be set to NULL.

SQLCA   A pointer to a location in memory where a SQL Communications Area (SQLCA) data structure variable is stored. This structure returns either status information (if the function executed successfully) or error information (if the function failed) to the calling application.

Includes   `#include <sql.h>`

Description   The CREATE AND ATTACH TO AN APPLICATION CONTEXT function is used to either create an application context or to create and then attach to an application context. Once a thread attaches to an application context, all subsequent database operations performed on that thread are no longer serialized with other threads.

Comments
- More than one application context can be created. Each context has its own commit scope.
- Different threads can attach to different contexts.
- If this function is called with the *Action* parameter set to SQL_CTX_BEGIN_ALL, the *Context* parameter can contain a NULL pointer.
- If this function is called with the *Action* parameter set to SQL_CTX_BEGIN_ALL when the current thread is already attached to a context, an error will occur.

■ The scope of this function is limited to the current process.

■ This function has no effect when it is executed on platforms that do not support application threading.

Connection Requirements This function can be called at any time; connection to a DB2 Database Manager instance or to a DB2 database does not have to be established first.

Authorization No authorization is required to execute this function call.

See Also ATTACH TO CONTEXT, DETACH AND DESTROY APPLICATION CONTEXT

Example The following C++ program illustrates how to use the CREATE AND ATTACH TO AN APPLICATION CONTEXT function to create a new application context:

```
/*------------------------------------------------------------*/
/* NAME:    CH14EX2.CPP                                       */
/* PURPOSE: Illustrate How To Use The Following DB2 API Function */
/*          In A C++ Program:                                 */
/*                                                            */
/*              CREATE AND ATTACH TO AN APPLICATION CONTEXT   */
/*              ATTACH TO CONTEXT                             */
/*                                                            */
/*------------------------------------------------------------*/

// Include The Appropriate Header Files
#include <windows.h>
#include <process.h>                        // _beginthread(), _endthread()
#include <stddef.h>
#include <stdlib.h>
#include <conio.h>
#include <iostream.h>
#include <sql.h>
#include <sqlenv.h>
#include <sqlca.h>

// Define The Thread Function Prototypes
void CheckKey(void *Dummy);
void GetInstance(void *Count);

// Declare The Global Memory Variables
BOOL   ContinueThread = TRUE;              // End Thread Flag
char   Instance[9];                        // Current Instance
void   *ContextData = NULL;                // Context Data Storage Area

/*------------------------------------------------------------*/
/* The Main Function                                          */
/*------------------------------------------------------------*/
int main()
{
    // Declare The Local Memory Variables
    long      rc = SQL_RC_OK;
    char      Counter = 0;
```

```
    // Set The Application Thread Context Type To Manual
    sqleSetTypeCtx(SQL_CTX_MULTI_MANUAL);

    // Launch The CheckKey() Thread To Check For A Terminating
    // Keystroke
    _beginthread(CheckKey, 0, NULL);

    // Loop Until The CheckKey() Thread Terminates The Program
    while(ContinueThread == TRUE)
    {
        // Launch Up To Ten GetInstance() Threads
        if (Counter < 10)
            _beginthread(GetInstance, 0, (void *) (Counter++));

        // Wait One Second Between Loop Passes
        Sleep(1000L);

        // Display The Current Value Of The DB2INSTANCE Environment
        // Variable
        cout << "Current value of the DB2INSTANCE environment ";
        cout << "variable : " << Instance << endl;
    }

    // Return To The Operating System
    return(rc);
}

// Define The CheckKey() Thread Function
void CheckKey(void *Dummy)
{
    // Declare The Local Memory Variables
    struct sqlca   sqlca;

    // Create A New Application Context And Attach To It
    sqleBeginCtx(&ContextData, SQL_CTX_BEGIN_ALL, NULL, &sqlca);

    // If A New Context Was Created, Display A Success Message
    if (sqlca.sqlcode == SQL_RC_OK)
        cout << "A new context has been created." << endl;

    // Wait For A Keystroke
    _getch();

    // Set The ContinueThread Flag So The GetInstance() Threads Will
    // End
    ContinueThread = FALSE;

    // Terminate This Thread
    _endthread();
}

// Define The GetInstance() Thread Function
void GetInstance(void *Count)
{
```

```
// Declare The Local Memory Variables
struct sqlca  sqlca;

// Attach To The Context Created By The CheckKey() Thread
sqleAttachToCtx(ContextData, NULL, &sqlca);

// If Attached To The New Context, Display A Success Message
if (sqlca.sqlcode == SQL_RC_OK)
    cout << "Attached to the new context." << endl;

// Loop Until CheckKey() Thread Terminates The Program
while(ContinueThread == TRUE)
{
    // Pause Between Loops
    Sleep(100L);

    // Obtain The Current Value Of The DB2INSTANCE Environment
    // Variable
    sqlegins(Instance, &sqlca);
    Instance[8] = 0;

    // If The Current Value Of The DB2INSTANCE Environment
    // Variable Was Not Obtained, Clear The Memory Storage Area
    if (sqlca.sqlcode != SQL_RC_OK)
        Instance[0] = 0;

    // Beep To Signal The Loop Is Still Running
    Beep(1000, 175);
}

// Terminate The Thread
_endthread();
}
```

DETACH AND DESTROY APPLICATION CONTEXT

Purpose

The DETACH AND DESTROY APPLICATION CONTEXT function is used to make the current thread stop using a specified context and to free all memory associated with that context.

Syntax

```
int sqleEndCtx (void      **Context,
                long        Action,
                void       *Reserved,
                struct sqlca *SQLCA);
```

Parameters

Context   A pointer to a location in memory where the starting address of a data storage area that is used to store context information is stored.

Action   Specifies the action that this function is to perform. This parameter must be set to one of the following values:

■ SQL_CTX_FREE_ONLY
Only free context memory if no thread is currently attached to the context.

■ SQL_CTX_END_ALL
Free context memory after detaching the thread that is currently attached it.

Reserved   A pointer that, at this time, is reserved for later use. For now, this parameter must always be set to NULL.

SQLCA   A pointer to a location in memory where a SQL Communications Area (SQLCA) data structure variable is stored. This structure returns either status information (if the function executed successfully) or error information (if the function failed) to the calling application.

Includes   `#include <sql.h>`

Description   The DETACH AND DESTROY APPLICATION CONTEXT function is used to make the current thread stop using a specified context and to free all memory associated with that context.

Comments   ■ If this function is called with the *Action* parameter set to SQL_CTX_END_ALL, the *Context* parameter can contain a NULL pointer (in which case, the current context will be used). Otherwise, the *Context* parameter must reference a valid context information storage area that was allocated by the CREATE AND ATTACH TO AN APPLICATION CONTEXT function.

■ If this function is called while a database connection exists or while the context is attached to other threads, an error will occur.

■ If a context is used by a thread that executes an API that establishes an attachment to a DB2 Database Manager instance, the thread must detach from the Database Manager instance (by calling the DETACH function) before this function is called.

■ The scope of this function is limited to the current process.

■ This function has no effect when it is executed on platforms that do not support application threading.

Connection Requirements   This function can be called at any time; a connection to a DB2 Database Manager instance or to a DB2 database does not have to be established first.

Authorization   No authorization is required to execute this function call.

See Also   DETACH FROM CONTEXT, CREATE AND ATTACH TO AN APPLICATION CONTEXT

Example   The following C++ program illustrates how to use the DETACH AND DESTROY APPLICATION CONTEXT function to make the current thread stop using a specified context and to free all memory associated with that context:

```
/*------------------------------------------------------------*/
/* NAME:     CH14EX3.CPP                                       */
/* PURPOSE: Illustrate How To Use The Following DB2 API Function */
/*          In A C++ Program:                                  */
/*                                                             */
/*               DETACH FROM CONTEXT                           */
/*               DETACH AND DESTROY APPLICATION CONTEXT        */
/*                                                             */
/*------------------------------------------------------------*/

// Include The Appropriate Header Files
#include <windows.h>
#include <process.h>                      // _beginthread(), _endthread()
#include <stddef.h>
#include <stdlib.h>
#include <conio.h>
#include <iostream.h>
#include <sql.h>
#include <sqlenv.h>
#include <sqlca.h>

// Define The Thread Function Prototypes
void CheckKey(void *Dummy);
void GetInstance(void *Count);

// Declare The Global Memory Variables
BOOL  ContinueThread = TRUE;        // End Thread Flag
char  Instance[9];                  // Current Instance
void  *ContextData = NULL;          // Context Data Storage Area

/*------------------------------------------------------------*/
/* The Main Function                                          */
/*------------------------------------------------------------*/
int main()
{
    // Declare The Local Memory Variables
    long            rc = SQL_RC_OK;
    char            Counter = 0;
    struct sqlca    sqlca;

    // Set The Application Thread Context Type To Manual
    sqleSetTypeCtx(SQL_CTX_MULTI_MANUAL);

    // Launch The CheckKey() Thread To Check For A Terminating
    // Keystroke
    _beginthread(CheckKey, 0, NULL);

    // Loop Until The CheckKey() Thread Terminates The Program
    while(ContinueThread == TRUE)
    {
        // Launch Up To Ten GetInstance() Threads
        if (Counter < 10)
            _beginthread(GetInstance, 0, (void *) (Counter++));
```

```cpp
        // Wait One Second Between Loop Passes
        Sleep(1000L);

        // Display The Current Value Of The DB2INSTANCE Environment
        // Variable
        cout << "Current value of the DB2INSTANCE environment ";
        cout << "variable : " << Instance << endl;
    }

    // Destroy The Application Context That Was Created By The
    // CheckKey() Thread
    sqleEndCtx(&ContextData, SQL_CTX_FREE_ONLY, NULL, &sqlca);

    // If The Context Was Destroyed, Display A Success Message
    if (sqlca.sqlcode == SQL_RC_OK)
        cout << "Context has been destroyed." << endl;

    // Return To The Operating System
    return(rc);
}

// Define The CheckKey() Thread Function
void CheckKey(void *Dummy)
{
    // Declare The Local Memory Variables
    struct sqlca    sqlca;

    // Create A New Application Context And Attach To It
    sqleBeginCtx(&ContextData, SQL_CTX_BEGIN_ALL, NULL, &sqlca);

    // If A New Context Was Created, Display A Success Message
    if (sqlca.sqlcode == SQL_RC_OK)
        cout << "A new context has been created." << endl;

    // Wait For A Keystroke
    _getch();

    // Set The ContinueThread Flag So The GetInstance() Threads Will
    // End
    ContinueThread = FALSE;

    // Detach From The The New Context That Was Created At The Start
    // Of This Thread
    sqleDetachFromCtx(ContextData, NULL, &sqlca);

    // If Detached From The New Context, Display A Success Message
    if (sqlca.sqlcode == SQL_RC_OK)
        cout << "Detached from the new context." << endl;

    // Terminate This Thread
    _endthread();
}
```

```
// Define The GetInstance() Thread Function
void GetInstance(void *Count)
{
    // Declare The Local Memory Variables
    struct sqlca  sqlca;

    // Attach To The Context Created By The CheckKey() Thread
    sqleAttachToCtx(ContextData, NULL, &sqlca);

    // If Attached To The New Context, Display A Success Message
    if (sqlca.sqlcode == SQL_RC_OK)
        cout << "Attached to the new context." << endl;

    while(ContinueThread == TRUE)
    {
        // Pause Between Loops
        Sleep(100L);

        // Obtain The Current Value Of The DB2INSTANCE Environment
        // Variable
        sqlegins(Instance, &sqlca);
        Instance[8] = 0;

        // If The Current Value Of The DB2INSTANCE Environment
        // Variable Was Not Obtained, Clear The Memory Storage Area
        if (sqlca.sqlcode != SQL_RC_OK)
            Instance[0] = 0;

        // Beep To Signal The Loop Is Still Running
        Beep(1000, 175);
    }

    // Detach From The Context Created By The CheckKey() Thread
    sqleDetachFromCtx(ContextData, NULL, &sqlca);

    // If Detached From The New Context, Display A Success Message
    if (sqlca.sqlcode == SQL_RC_OK)
        cout << "Detached from the new context." << endl;

    // Terminate The Thread
    _endthread();
}
```

ATTACH TO CONTEXT

Purpose   The ATTACH TO CONTEXT function is used to make the current thread use a specified context.

Syntax
```
int sqleAttachToCtx (void          *Context,
                     void          *Reserved,
                     struct sqlca  *SQLCA);
```

Parameters	*Context*	A pointer to a location in memory where a valid context information storage area that was allocated by the CREATE AND ATTACH TO AN APPLICATION CONTEXT function is stored.
	Reserved	A pointer that, at this time, is reserved for later use. For now, this parameter must always be set to NULL.
	SQLCA	A pointer to a location in memory where a SQL Communications Area (SQLCA) data structure variable is stored. This structure returns either status information (if the function executed successfully) or error information (if the function failed) to the calling application.

Includes   `#include <sql.h>`

Description   The ATTACH TO CONTEXT function is used to make the current thread use a specified context. Once this function is called, all subsequent database operations performed by the calling thread will use the context specified.

Comments
- If more than one thread is attached to a given context, data access is serialized for each thread, and each thread shares a common commit scope.
- The scope of this function is limited to the current process.
- This function has no effect when it is executed on platforms that do not support application threading.

Connection Requirements   This function can be called at any time; a connection to a DB2 Database Manager instance or to a DB2 database does not have to be established first.

Authorization   No authorization is required to execute this function call.

See Also   CREATE AND ATTACH TO AN APPLICATION CONTEXT, DETACH FROM CONTEXT

Example   See example for CREATE AND ATTACH TO AN APPLICATION CONTEXT on page 560.

■ ■ DETACH FROM CONTEXT

Purpose   The DETACH FROM CONTEXT function is used to make the current thread stop using a specified context.

Syntax
```
int sqleDetachFromCtx (void       *Context,
                       void       *Reserved,
                       struct sqlca  *SQLCA);
```

Parameters   *Context*   A pointer to a location in memory where a valid context information storage area that was allocated by the CREATE AND ATTACH TO AN APPLICATION CONTEXT function is stored.

Reserved	A pointer that, at this time, is reserved for later use. For now, this parameter must always be set to NULL.
SQLCA	A pointer to a location in memory where a SQL Communications Area (SQLCA) data structure variable is stored. This structure returns either status information (if the function executed successfully) or error information (if the function failed) to the calling application.

Includes   `#include <sql.h>`

Description   The DETACH FROM CONTEXT function is used to make the current thread stop using a specified context.

Comments
- The current thread will not be detached from the context specified if it has never been attached to the context.
- The scope of this function is limited to the current process.
- This function has no effect when it is executed on platforms that do not support application threading.

Connection Requirements   This function can be called at any time; a connection to a DB2 Database Manager instance or to a DB2 database does not have to be established first.

Authorization   No authorization is required to execute this function call.

See Also   DETACH AND DESTROY APPLICATION CONTEXT, ATTACH TO CONTEXT

Example   See example for DETACH AND DESTROY APPLICATION CONTEXT on page 564.

■■ GET CURRENT CONTEXT

Purpose   The GET CURRENT CONTEXT function is used to get the context that the current thread is attached to.

Syntax
```
int sqleGetCurrentCtx  (void        **Context,
                        void        *Reserved,
                        struct sqlca *SQLCA);
```

Parameters
Context	A pointer to a location in memory where this function is to store the starting address of a data storage area that contains context information.
Reserved	A pointer that, at this time, is reserved for later use. For now, this parameter must always be set to NULL.
SQLCA	A pointer to a location in memory where a SQL Communications Area (SQLCA) data structure variable is stored. This structure

returns either status information (if the function executed successfully) or error information (if the function failed) to the calling application.

Includes   `#include <sql.h>`

Description   The GET CURRENT CONTEXT function is used to get the context that the current thread is attached to.

Comments   ■ The scope of this function is limited to the current process.

■ This function has no effect when it is executed on platforms that do not support application threading.

Connection   This function can be called at any time; a connection to a DB2 Database Manager
Requirements   instance or to a DB2 database does not have to be established first.

Authorization   No authorization is required to execute this function call.

See Also   ATTACH TO CONTEXT, DETACH FROM CONTEXT

Example   The following C++ program illustrates how to use the GET CURRENT CONTEXT function to get the context to which the current thread is attached:

```
/*———————————————————————————————————————————————————*/
/* NAME:     CH14EX4.CPP                              */
/* PURPOSE: Illustrate How To Use The Following DB2 API Function */
/*          In A C++ Program:                         */
/*                                                    */
/*              GET CURRENT CONTEXT                   */
/*                                                    */
/*———————————————————————————————————————————————————*/

// Include The Appropriate Header Files
#include <windows.h>
#include <process.h>                     // _beginthread(), _endthread()
#include <stddef.h>
#include <stdlib.h>
#include <conio.h>
#include <iostream.h>
#include <sql.h>
#include <sqlenv.h>
#include <sqlca.h>

// Define The Thread Function Prototypes
void CheckKey(void *Dummy);
void GetInstance(void *Count);

// Declare The Global Memory Variables
BOOL  ContinueThread = TRUE;            // End Thread Flag
char  Instance[9];                      // Current Instance
void  *ContextData = NULL;              // Context Data Storage Area
```

```cpp
/*-------------------------------------------------------------*/
/* The Main Function                                           */
/*-------------------------------------------------------------*/
int main()
{
    // Declare The Local Memory Variables
    long   rc = SQL_RC_OK;
    char   Counter = 0;

    // Set The Application Thread Context Type To Manual
    sqleSetTypeCtx(SQL_CTX_MULTI_MANUAL);

    // Launch The CheckKey() Thread To Check For A Terminating
    // Keystroke
    _beginthread(CheckKey, 0, NULL);

    // Loop Until CheckKey() Thread Terminates The Program
    while(ContinueThread == TRUE)
    {
        // Launch Up To Ten GetInstance() Threads
        if (Counter < 10)
            _beginthread(GetInstance, 0, (void *) (Counter++));

        // Wait One Second Between Loop Passes
        Sleep(1000L);

        // Display The Current Value Of The DB2INSTANCE Environment
        // Variable
        cout << "Current value of the DB2INSTANCE environment ";
        cout << "variable : " << Instance << endl;
    }

    // Return To The Operating System
    return(rc);
}

// Define The CheckKey() Thread Function
void CheckKey(void *Dummy)
{
    // Declare The Local Memory Variables
    struct sqlca   sqlca;

    // Create A New Application Context And Attach To It
    sqleBeginCtx(&ContextData, SQL_CTX_BEGIN_ALL, NULL, &sqlca);

    // If A New Context Was Created, Display A Success Message
    if (sqlca.sqlcode == SQL_RC_OK)
        cout << "A new context has been created." << endl;

    // Wait For A Keystroke
    _getch();

    // Set The ContinueThread Flag So The GetInstance() Threads Will
    // End
    ContinueThread = FALSE;
```

```
    // Terminate This Thread
    _endthread();
}

// Define The GetInstance() Thread Function
void GetInstance(void *Count)
{
    // Declare The Local Memory Variables
    struct sqlca  sqlca;

    // Attach To The Context Created By The CheckKey() Thread
    sqleAttachToCtx(ContextData, NULL, &sqlca);

    // If Attached To The New Context, Display A Success Message
    if (sqlca.sqlcode == SQL_RC_OK)
        cout << "Attached to the new context." << endl;

    // Get Information About The Current Context
    sqleGetCurrentCtx(&ContextData, NULL, &sqlca);

    // If The Information Has Been Collected, Display A Success
    // Message
    if (sqlca.sqlcode == SQL_RC_OK)
        cout << "Context information has been collected." << endl;

    // Loop Until CheckKey() Thread Terminates The Program
    while(ContinueThread == TRUE)
    {
        // Pause Between Loops
        Sleep(100L);

        // Obtain The Current Value Of The DB2INSTANCE Environment
        // Variable
        sqlegins(Instance, &sqlca);
        Instance[8] = 0;

        // If The Current Value Of The DB2INSTANCE Environment
        // Variable Was Not Obtained, Clear The Memory Storage Area
        if (sqlca.sqlcode != SQL_RC_OK)
            Instance[0] = 0;

        // Beep To Signal The Loop Is Still Running
        Beep(1000, 175);
    }

    // Terminate The Thread
    _endthread();
}
```

INTERRUPT CONTEXT

Purpose   The INTERRUPT CONTEXT function is used to send an interrupt to the specified context.

Syntax
```
int sqleInterruptCtx    (void          *Context,
                         void          *Reserved,
                         struct sqlca  *SQLCA);
```

Parameters   *Context*   A pointer to a location in memory where a valid context information storage area that was allocated by the CREATE AND ATTACH TO AN APPLICATION CONTEXT function is stored.

Reserved   A pointer that, at this time, is reserved for later use. For now, this parameter must always be set to NULL.

SQLCA   A pointer to a location in memory where a SQL Communications Area (SQLCA) data structure variable is stored. This structure returns either status information (if the function executed successfully) or error information (if the function failed) to the calling application.

Includes   `#include <sql.h>`

Description The INTERRUPT CONTEXT function is used to send an interrupt to the specified context. When invoked, this function:

1. Switches to the specified context
2. Sends an interrupt signal
3. Switches back to the original context
4. Returns control to the current thread

Comments   ■ The scope of this function is limited to the current process.

■ This function has no effect when it is executed on platforms that do not support application threading.

Connection Requirements This function can be called at any time, a connection to a DB2 Database Manager instance or to a DB2 database does not have to be established first. However, this function will not have any effect unless it is called when a connection to a DB2 database exists.

Authorization No authorization is required to execute this function call.

See Also   CREATE AND ATTACH TO AN APPLICATION CONTEXT

Example   The following C++ program illustrates how to use the INTERRUPT CONTEXT function to send an interrupt to the specified context:

```
/*————————————————————————————————————————————*/
/* NAME:    CH14EX5.CPP                                          */
/* PURPOSE: Illustrate How To Use The Following DB2 API Function */
/*          In A C++ Program:                                    */
/*                                                               */
/*                  INTERRUPT CONTEXT                            */
/*                                                               */
/*————————————————————————————————————————————*/

// Include The Appropriate Header Files
#include <windows.h>
#include <process.h>                     // _beginthread(), _endthread()
#include <stddef.h>
#include <stdlib.h>
#include <conio.h>
#include <iostream.h>
#include <sql.h>
#include <sqlenv.h>
#include <sqlca.h>

// Define The Thread Function Prototypes
void CheckKey(void *Dummy);
void GetInstance(void *Count);

// Declare The Global Memory Variables
BOOL  ContinueThread = TRUE;            // End Thread Flag
char  Instance[9];                      // Current Instance
void  *ContextData = NULL;              // Context Data Storage Area

/*————————————————————————————————————————————*/
/* The Main Function                                             */
/*————————————————————————————————————————————*/
int main()
{
    // Declare The Local Memory Variables
    long  rc = SQL_RC_OK;
    char  Counter = 0;

    // Set The Application Thread Context Type To Manual
    sqleSetTypeCtx(SQL_CTX_MULTI_MANUAL);

    // Launch The CheckKey() Thread To Check For A Terminating
    // Keystroke
    _beginthread(CheckKey, 0, NULL);

    // Loop Until CheckKey() Thread Terminates The Program
    while(ContinueThread == TRUE)
    {
        // Launch Up To Ten GetInstance() Threads
        if (Counter < 10)
            _beginthread(GetInstance, 0, (void *) (Counter++));

        // Wait One Second Between Loop Passes
        Sleep(1000L);
```

```cpp
            // Display The Current Value Of The DB2INSTANCE Environment
            // Variable
            cout << "Current value of the DB2INSTANCE environment ";
            cout << "variable : " << Instance << endl;
        }

    // Return To The Operating System
    return(rc);
}

// Define The CheckKey() Thread Function
void CheckKey(void *Dummy)
{
    // Declare The Local Memory Variables
    struct sqlca  sqlca;

    // Create A New Application Context And Attach To It
    sqleBeginCtx(&ContextData, SQL_CTX_BEGIN_ALL, NULL, &sqlca);

    // If A New Context Was Created, Display A Success Message
    if (sqlca.sqlcode == SQL_RC_OK)
       cout << "A new context has been created." << endl;

    // Wait For A Keystroke
    _getch();

    // Set The ContinueThread Flag So The GetInstance() Threads Will
    // End
    ContinueThread = FALSE;

    // Terminate This Thread
    _endthread();
}

// Define The GetInstance() Thread Function
void GetInstance(void *Count)
{
    // Declare The Local Memory Variables
    struct sqlca  sqlca;
    char          ThreadNum = (char) Count;

    // Attach To The Context Created By The CheckKey() Thread
    sqleAttachToCtx(ContextData, NULL, &sqlca);

    // If Attached To The New Context, Display A Success Message
    if (sqlca.sqlcode == SQL_RC_OK)
       cout << "Attached to the new context." << endl;

    // If This Thread Number Is Greater Than 5...
    if (ThreadNum >= 5)
    {
        // Interrupt The Context
        sqleInterruptCtx(ContextData, NULL, &sqlca);
```

```
        // If The Context Has Been Interrupted, Display A Success
        // Message And Terminate The Thread
        if (sqlca.sqlcode == SQL_RC_OK)
        {
            cout << "Context has been interrupted." << endl;
            _endthread();
            return;
        }
    }

    // Otherwise, Loop Until CheckKey() Thread Terminates The
    // Program
    while(ContinueThread == TRUE)
    {
        // Pause Between Loops
        Sleep(100L);

        // Obtain The Current Value Of The DB2INSTANCE Environment
        // Variable
        sqlegins(Instance, &sqlca);
        Instance[8] = 0;

        // If The Current Value Of The DB2INSTANCE Environment
        // Variable Was Not Obtained, Clear The Memory Storage Area
        if (sqlca.sqlcode != SQL_RC_OK)
            Instance[0] = 0;

        // Beep To Signal The Loop Is Still Running
        Beep(1000, 175);
    }

    // Terminate The Thread
    _endthread();
}
```

APPENDIX A

SQL Data Structures

The SQL Communications Area (SQLA) Structure

The SQL communications area (SQLCA) structure is a collection of variables that are updated at the end of the execution of every SQL statement and DB2 API function call. Application programs that contain embedded SQL statements (other than embedded **DECLARE**, **INCLUDE**, and **WHENEVER** statements) or API function calls must define at least one SQLCA data structure variable (you can also place one SQLCA data structure variable in each thread of a multithreaded application). You can use the **INCLUDE** SQL statement to provide the declaration of the SQLCA data structure in embedded SQL applications written in C and C++. The *sqlca* structure is defined in *sqlca.h* as follows:

```
struct sqlca
{
char   sqlcaid[8];      /* An "eye catcher" for storage dumps. This   */
                        /* field contains the value "SQLCA    ".      */
long   sqlcabc;         /* The size of the SQLCA structure (136 bytes) */
long   sqlcode;         /* The SQL return code value. A value of 0    */
                        /* means "successful execution," a positive   */
                        /* value means "successful execution with     */
                        /* warnings," and a negative value means      */
                        /* "error." Refer to the IBMDB2 Universal     */
                        /* Database Messages Reference for specific    */
                        /* meanings of SQL return code values.        */
short  sqlerrml;        /* The size, in bytes, of the data stored in  */
                        /* the sqlerrmc field of this structure. This */
                        /* value can be any number between 0 and 70. A */
                        /* value of 0 indicates that no data is stored */
                        /* in the sqlerrmc field.                     */
char   sqlerrmc[70];    /* One or more error message tokens, separated */
                        /* by 0xFF, that are substituted for variables */
                        /* in the descriptions of error conditions.   */
                        /* This field is also used when a successful  */
                        /* connection is established. Refer to the IBM */
                        /* DB2 Universal Database Messages Reference for */
                        /* specific meanings of SQL return code values. */
char   sqlerrp[8];      /* A diagnostic value that begins with a three- */
                        /* letter code identifying the product followed */
                        /* by five digits that identify the version,  */
                        /* release, and modification level of the     */
                        /* product. For example, "SQL05020" means DB2 */
                        /* Universal Database, version 5, release 2,  */
                        /* modification level 0. If the sqlcode field */
                        /* contains a negative value, this field      */
```

```
                              /* identifies the module that returned an error. */
        long    sqlerrd[6];   /* An array of six integer values that provide    */
                              /* additional diagnostic information              */
        char    sqlwarn[11];  /* An array of warning indicators, each           */
                              /* containing a blank or the letter 'W'. If       */
                              /* compound SQL was used, this field will         */
                              /* contain an accumulation of the warning         */
                              /* indicators set for all SQL sub-statements      */
        char    sqlstate[5];  /* The SQLSTATE value that indicates the outcome  */
                              /* of the most recently executed SQL statement    */
        };
```

Table A-1 describes the types of diagnostic information that can be returned in the *sqlerrd* array, and Table A-2 describes the types of warning information that can be returned in the *sqlwarn* array.

Table A-1 Elements of the *sqlca.sqlerrd* Array

Array Element	Diagnostic Information
sqlerrd[0]	If a CONNECT statement was successfully invoked, this element will contain the maximum expected difference in length of mixed character data (CHAR data types) when converted from the application code page to the database code page. A value of 0 or 1 indicates no expansion; a value greater than 1 indicates a possible expansion in length; a negative value indicates a possible contraction in length.
sqlerrd[1]	If the SQLCA data reflects a NOT ATOMIC compound SQL statement that encountered one or more errors, this element will contain a count of the number of SQL statements that failed.
sqlerrd[2]	If the SQLCA data reflects a PREPARE statement that was successfully invoked, this element will contain an estimate of the number of rows that will be returned.
	If the SQLCA data reflects an INSERT, UPDATE, or DELETE statement that was successfully invoked, this element will contain a count of the number of rows that were affected by the operation.
	If the SQLCA data reflects a compound SQL statement that was successfully invoked, this element will contain a count of the number of rows that were affected by all sub-statements.
	If the SQLCA data reflects a CONNECT statement that was successfully invoked, this element will contain 1 if the database can be updated; 2 if the database is read only.
sqlerrd[3]	If the SQLCA data reflects a PREPARE statement that was successfully invoked, this element will contain a relative cost estimate of the resources required to process the statement.
	If the SQLCA data reflects a compound SQL statement that was successfully invoked, this element will contain a count of the number of sub-statements that were successful.

Table A-1 Elements of the sqlca.sqlerrd Array (Continued)

Array Element	Diagnostic Information
	If the SQLCA data reflects a CONNECT statement that was successfully invoked, this element will contain 0 if a one-phase commit from a down-level client is being used; 1 if a one-phase commit is being used; 2 if a one-phase, read-only commit is being used; and 3 if a two-phase commit is being used.
sqlerrd[4]	This element contains the total number of rows that were inserted, updated, or deleted as a result of:
	■ The enforcement of constraints after a successful delete operation.
	■ The processing of triggered SQL statements from activated triggers.
	If the SQLCA data reflects a compound SQL statement was successfully invoked, this element will contain a count of all such rows for all SQL sub-statements processed.
	If the SQLCA data reflects a CONNECT statement that was successfully invoked, this element will contain 0 if server authentication is used; 1 if client authentication is used; 2 if authentication is handled by DB2 Connect; 3 if authentication is handled by DCE Security Services; 255 if authentication is not specified.
	In some cases, when an error is encountered this field contains a negative value that is used as an internal error pointer.
sqlerrd[5]	For a partitioned database, this element contains the partition number of the partition that encountered the error or warning. If no errors or warnings were encountered, this element contains the partition number of the coordinator node (the number stored in this element is the same as that specified for the partition in the *db2nodes.cfg* file).

Table A-2 Elements of the sqlca.sqlwarn Array

Array Element	Warning Information
SQLWARN0	This element is blank if all other indicators are blank; it contains a 'W' if at least one other indicator is not blank.
SQLWARN1	This element contains a 'W' if the value of a string column was truncated when assigned to a host variable. It contains a 'N' if the null terminator was truncated.
SQLWARN2	This element contains a 'W' if NULL values were eliminated from the argument of a function.
SQLWARN3	This element contains a 'W' if the number of columns is not equal to the number of host variables provided.
SQLWARN4	This element contains a 'W' if a prepared UPDATE or DELETE statement does not include a WHERE clause.
SQLWARN5	Reserved for future use.
SOLWARN6	This element contains a 'W' if the result of a date calculation was adjusted to avoid an invalid date.
SQLWARN7	Reserved for future use.

Table A-2   Elements of the *sqlca.sqlwarn* Array (Continued)

Array Element	Warning Information
SQLWARN8	This element contains a 'w' if a character that could not be converted was replaced with a substitution character.
SQLWARN9	This element contains a 'w' if arithmetic expressions containing errors were ignored during column function processing.
SQLWARNA	This element contains a 'w' if there was a conversion error while converting a character data value in one of the fields in the SQLCA data structure.

The SQLCHAR STRUCTURE

The SQLCHAR structure is a combination of a character string and a string length value. This structure works with VARCHAR data types. The *sqlchar* structure is defined in *sql.h* as follows:

```
struct sqlchar
{
short    length;        /* The length of the character string    */
                        /* stored in the data field of this      */
                        /* structure.                            */
char     data[1];       /* A character string.                   */
};
```

APPENDIX B

DB2 Log Records

This section describes the structure of the log records that are returned by the **ASYNCHRONOUS READ LOG** function. All log records begin with a "log manager header". This header contains generic information about the log record including the total log record size, the log record type, and transaction-specific information. The structure of the log manager header is shown in Table B–1.

Table B–1 Log Record Header Structure

Offset	Size (Bytes)	C Data Type	Description
0	4	integer	Length of the entire log record
4	2	short integer	Type of log record

The following log record types are valid:

"a" Datalink Manager	"o" Backup Start
"A" Normal Abort	"O" Backup End
"B" Backout Free	"p" Tablespace Roll Forward To Point-In-Time Start
"c" MPP Coordinator Commit	"P" Table Quiesce
"C" Compensation	"q" Tablespace Roll Forward To Point-In-Time End
"D" Tablespace Rolled Forward	"Q" Global Pending List
"E" Local Pending List	"R" Redo
"F" Forget Transaction	"s" MPP Subordinate Commit
"g" MPP Log Synchronization	"S" Compensation Required
"G" Load Pending List	"T" Partial Abort
"H" Table Load Delete Start	"U" Undo
"i" Propagate Only	"V" Migration Start
"I" Heuristic Abort	"W" Migration End
"J" Load Start	"X" TM Prepare
"K" Load Delete Start Compensation	"Y" Heuristic Commit
"L" Lock Description	"z" MPP Prepare
"M" Normal Commit	"Z" XA Prepare
"N" Normal	

Table B–1   Continued

Offset	Size (Bytes)	C Data Type	Description
			A Propogate Only ("i") log record is an informational log record that will be ignored by DB2 during roll forward, roll back, and crash recovery operations.
			Note: When a transaction performs writable work against a table that has DATA CATPURE CHANGES turned on, or when a transaction invokes a DB2 API that generates log records, that transaction is said to be *propagatable*.
6	2	short integer	Log record general flag
			The following log record general flags are valid:
			0x0001 Redo Always
			0x0002 Propagatable
			0x0080 Conditionally Recoverable
8	6	SQLU_LSN	Log Sequence Number of the previous log record written by this transaction. This value is used to chain log records by transaction. If the value is 0000 0000 0000, this is the first log record written by the transaction.
			The SQLU_LSN data type is defined as:

			union { char[6];
			      short[3];
			    };

14	6	SQLU_TID	Unique transaction identifier
			The SQLU_TID data type is defined as:

			union { char[6];
			      short[3];
			    };

20	6	SQLU_LSN	Log Sequence Number of the log record for this transaction prior to the log record being compensated.
			This value is only used for Compensation ("C") and Backout Free ("B") log records
26	6	SQLU_LSN	Log Sequence Number of the log record for this transaction being compensated.
			This value is only used for Propagatable compensation log records.

Total length of Log Manager Log Record Header :

     Non-Compensation: 20 bytes

     Compensation: 26 bytes

     Propagatable-Compensation: 32 bytes

Adapted from Table 90 on pages 529-531 of IBM DB2 Universal Database API Reference

Each log record is identified by a unique log sequence number (LSN). The log sequence number represents a relative byte address, within the database log file, for the first byte of the log record. In other words, the log sequence number marks the offset of the log record from the beginning of the database log file.

Log records that are written as a result of the execution of a single transaction can be identified by the value of the transaction identifier field in the log record header. These log records are assigned a unique transaction identifier, which is a six-byte field that is incremented by one each time a new transaction is started. All log records that are generated by the same transaction are assigned the same transaction identifier.

DB2 can generate up to forty different log records. The remaining pages in this appendix describe the structures of each log record that can be generated.

Data Manager Log Records

Data Manager log records are generated whenever Data Definition Language (DDL) SQL statements, Data Manipulation Language (DML) SQL statements, or some Utility APIs are executed. Two types of Data Manager log records exist: *Data Management System (DMS)* log records and *Data Object Manager (DOM)* log records.

Data Management System log records contain the header information shown in Table B–2, along with additional, record-specific information.

Table B–2 Data Management System (DMS) Log Record Header Structure

Offset	Size (Bytes)	C Data Type	Description
0	1	unsigned char	Component identifier (Always 1)
1	1	unsigned char	Function identifier
			The following function identifier values are valid:
			SQLD_MIN_DP (100) Minimum DBMS Log Function ID
			SQLD_MAX_DP (149) Maximum DBMS Log Function ID
			ADDCOLUMNS_DP (102), Add columns via **ALTER TABLE**
			CRNEWPG_DP (103) Create new page
			UNDOADDCOLUMNS_DP (104) Undo add columns
			ALTERPROP_DP (105) Alter property flag
			DELREC_DP (106) Delete record on page
			UNDOALTERPROP_DP (107) Undo alter property flag
			ALTERPENDING_DP (108) Alter check pending flag
			ALTERDEFAULTS_DP (109) Alter user defaults add flag

Table B–2 Continued

Offset	Size (Bytes)	C Data Type	Description		
			UNDOADD_DP	(110)	Undo add a record
			UNDODEL_DP	(111)	Undo delete a record
			UNDOUPDT_DP	(112)	Undo update a record
			CRSYSPGR_DP	(114)	Initialize system page DTR
			REORGPAGE_DP	(117)	Reorganize page
			INSREC_DP	(118)	Insert record on page
			UPDREC_DP	(120)	Update record on page
			UPDCHGONLY_DP	(121)	Log only updated
			CREATEPERM_DP	(128)	Initialize a DAT object
			UNDOALTERDEFAULTS_DP	(131)	Undo alter user default flag
			UNDOALTERPENDING_DP	(132)	Undo alter pending flag
2	2	unsigned short	Table identifier/Tablespace identifier		

Total length of DMS Log Record Header : 6 bytes

Adapted from Table 91 on page 532 of IBM DB2 Universal Database API Reference

Data Object Manager log records contain the header information shown in Table B–3, along with additional, record-specific information.

Table B–3 Data Object Manager (DOM) Log Record Header Structure

Offset	Size (Bytes)	C Data Type	Description		
0	1	unsigned char	Component identifier (Always 4)		
1	1	unsigned char	Function identifier		
			The following function identifier values are valid:		
			SQLD_MIN_DP	(100)	Minimum DBMS Log Function ID
			SQLD_MAX_DP	(149)	Maximum DBMS Log Function ID
			ADDCOLUMNS_DP	(102),	Add columns via **ALTER TABLE**
			CRNEWPG_DP	(103)	Create new page
			UNDOADDCOLUMNS_DP	(104)	Undo add columns
			ALTERPROP_DP	(105)	Alter property flag
			DELREC_DP	(106)	Delete record on page

Table B–3 Continued

Offset	Size (Bytes)	C Data Type	Description		
			UNDOALTERPROP_DP	(107)	Undo alter property flag
			ALTERPENDING_DP	(108)	Alter check pending flag
			ALTERDEFAULTS_DP	(109)	Alter user defaults add flag
			UNDOADD_DP	(110)	Undo add a record
			UNDODEL_DP	(111)	Undo delete a record
			UNDOUPDT_DP	(112)	Undo update a record
			CRSYSPGR_DP	(114)	Initialize system page DTR
			REORGPAGE_DP	(117)	Reorganize page
			INSREC_DP	(118)	Insert record on page
			UPDREC_DP	(120)	Update record on page
			UPDCHGONLY_DP	(121)	Log only updated
			CREATEPERM_DP	(128)	Initialize a DAT object
			UNDOALTERDEFAULTS_DP	(131)	Undo alter user default flag
			UNDOALTERPENDING_DP	(132)	Undo alter pending flag
2	2	unsigned short	Object identifier/Tablespace identifier		
6	2	unsigned short	Table identifier/Tablespace identifier		
10	1	unsigned char	Object type		
11	1	unsigned char	Flags		

Total length of DOM Log Record Header : 12 bytes

Adapted from Table 92 on pages 532-533 of IBM DB2 Universal Database API Reference

All Data Manager log records whose function identifier value begins with "UNDO" are written during the UNDO or ROLLBACK operation specified. A ROLLBACK operation can occur when:

- The ROLLBACK SQL statement is executed

- A deadlock situation causes a selected transaction to be rolled back

- Uncommitted transactions are rolled back during a crash recovery

- Uncommitted transactions are rolled back after a RESTORE DATABASE and ROLLFORWARD DATABASE operation has occurred.

Initialize Table Log Record

The initialize table log record is written whenever a new database table is created. The structure of the initialize table log record is shown in Table B–4.

Table B–4 Initialize Table Log Record Structure

Offset	Size (Bytes)	C Data Type	Description
0	6		DMS Log Record Header (See Table B–2)
6	6	SQLU_LSN	File create Log Sequence Number
			The SQLU_LSN data type is defined as:
			union { char[6];
			short[3];
			};
12	1	unsigned char	Table record type
13	1	char	Reserved
14	2	unsigned short	Index flag
16	4	unsigned long	Index root page
20	4	long	TDESC record ID
24	56	char	Reserved
80	4	unsigned long	Table directory flags
			The table directory flag 0x00000020 indicates that the table was created with the **NOT LOGGED INITIALLY** option specified and that no DML activity will be logged until the transaction that created the table is committed.
84	4	unsigned long	Table description length
88	1	unsigned char	Table description record type
89	1	char	Reserved
90	2	unsigned short	Number of columns
92	variable	long[]	An array of column and/or large object (LOB) descriptors (See Tables B–5 and B–6)

Total length of Initialize Table Log Record : 88 + *Table description record length* bytes

Adapted from Table 93 on pages 533-535 of IBM DB2 Universal Database API Reference

This is a Redo log record.

This table contains one or more column descriptor arrays and/or one or more large object (LOB) descriptor arrays. The structure of a column descriptor array is shown in Table B–5 and the structure of a LOB descriptor array is shown in Table B–6.

Table B–5   Column Descriptor Array Details

Offset	Size (Bytes)	C Data Type	Description
0	2	unsigned short	Field type
			The following field type values are valid:
			SMALLINT (0x0000)
			INTEGER (0x0001)
			DECIMAL (0x0002)
			DOUBLE (0x0003)
			REAL (0x0004)
			BIGINT (0x0005)
			CHAR (0x0100)
			VARCHAR (0x0101)
			LONG VARCHAR (0x0104)
			DATE (0x0105)
			TIME (0x0106)
			TIMESTAMP (0x0107)
			BLOB (0x0108)
			CLOB (0x0109)
			GRAPHIC (0x0200)
			VARGRAPH (0x0201)
			LONG VARG (0x0202)
			DBCLOB (0x0203)
2	2	short	Field length
			If field type is BLOB, CLOB, or DBCLOB, field length is not used.
			If field type is not DECIMAL, field length is the maximum length of the field.
			If field type is DECIMAL, field length is defined as follows: Byte 1 (unsigned char) contains the precision (total width) and Byte 2 (unsigned char) contains the scale (fraction digits).
4	2	unsigned short	Null flag
			The following null flag values are valid:
			ISNULL (0x01)
			NONULLS (0x02)
			TYPE_DEFAULT (0x04)
			USER_DEFAULT (0x08)

Table B–5 Continued

Offset	Size (Bytes)	C Data Type	Description
			Null flag values are mutually exclusive: a field can either allow nulls, or not allow nulls (valid options: no default, type default, or user default).
6	2	unsigned short	Field offset
			This is the offset from the start of the formatted record to where the field's fixed value can be found.

Total length of Column Descriptor Array : (number of columns) * 8 bytes

Adapted from Table 93 on pages 533-535 of IBM DB2 Universal Database API Reference

Table B–6 Large Object (LOB) Descriptor Array Details

Offset	Size (Bytes)	C Data Type	Description
0	4	unsigned long	Field length
4	4	unsigned long	Reserved
8	4	unsigned long	Log flag
			Indicates whether or not the column is to generate log records when data is loaded.

The first LOB, CLOB, or DBCLOB encountered in the column descriptor array uses the first element in the LOB descriptor array. The second LOB, CLOB, or DBCLOB encountered in the column descriptor array uses the second element in the LOB descriptor array, and so on.

Total length of LOB Descriptor Array : (number of LOB, CLOB, and DBCLOB fields) * 12 bytes

Adapted from Table 93 on pages 533-535 of IBM DB2 Universal Database API Reference

Import Replace (Truncate) Log Record

The import replace (truncate) log record is written whenever an IMPORT REPLACE operation is performed. The structure of the import replace log record is shown in Table B–7.

Table B–7 Import Replace (Truncate) Log Record Structure

Offset	Size (Bytes)	C Data Type	Description
0	12		DOM Log Record Header (See Table B–3)
12	variable	variable	Internal

Total length of Import Replace Log Record : 12 + size of *Internal* bytes

Adapted from Table 94 on page 536 of IBM DB2 Universal Database API Reference

The second set of pool and object IDs stored in the log record header identify the table being truncated. This is a Redo log record.

Rollback Insert Log Record

The rollback insert log record is written whenever an insert row operation is rolled back. The structure of the rollback insert log record is shown in Table B–8.

Table B–8   Rollback Insert Log Record Structure

Offset	Size (Bytes)	C Data Type	Description
0	6		DMS Log Record Header (See Table B–2)
6	2	char[2]	Padding
8	4	long	Record identifier
12	2	unsigned short	Record length
14	2	unsigned short	Free space

Total length of Rollback Insert Log Record : 16 bytes

Adapted from Table 95 on page 536 of IBM DB2 Universal Database API Reference

This is a Compensation log record.

Reorganize Table Log Record

The reorganize table log record is written whenever a reorganize table operation is performed. The structure of the reorganize table log record is shown in Table B–9.

Table B–9   Reorganize Table Log Record Structure

Offset	Size (Bytes)	C Data Type	Description
0	12		DOM Log Record Header (See Table B–3)
12	252	variable	Internal
264	2	unsigned short	Index token
			If the index token is not 0, it is the number that corresponds to the index that was used to cluster the reorganization (clustering index).
266	2	unsigned short	Temporary tablespace ID
			If the temporary tablespace ID is not 0, it is the number that corresponds to the tablespace that was used to build the reorganized table.

Total length of Reorganize Table Log Record : 268 bytes

Adapted from Table 96 on page 536 of IBM DB2 Universal Database API Reference

This is a Normal log record.

Create/Drop Index Log Record

The create/drop index log record is written whenever an index is created or destroyed (dropped). The structure of the create/drop index log record is shown in Table B–10.

Table B–10   Create/Drop Index Log Record Structure

Offset	Size (Bytes)	C Data Type	Description
0	12		DOM Log Record Header (See Table B–3)
12	2	char[2]	Padding
14	2	unsigned short	Index token
			This token is equilivant to the IID column in the SYSIBM.SYSINDEXES system table. If the index token is 0, the log record represents a create/drop action that was performed on an internal index (as opposed to a user index).
16	4	unsigned long	Index root page
			This is an internal index identifier.

Total length of Create/Drop Index Log Record : 20 bytes

Adapted from Table 97 on page 537 of IBM DB2 Universal Database API ReferenceThis is an Undo log record.

This is an Undo log record.

Create/Drop Table, Rollback Create/Drop Table Log Record

The create/drop table, rollback create/drop table log record is written whenever a table is created or destroyed (dropped) or whenever a create/drop table operation is rolled back. The structure of the create/drop table, rollback create/drop table log record is shown in Table B–11.

Table B–11   Create/Drop Table, Rollback Create/Drop Table Log Record Structure

Offset	Size (Bytes)	C Data Type	Description
0	12		DOM Log Record Header (See Table B–3)
12	56	variable	Internal

Total length of Create/Drop Table, Rollback Create/Drop Table Log Record : 68 bytes

Adapted from Table 98 on page 537 of IBM DB2 Universal Database API Reference

A create/drop table log record is a Normal log record. A rollback create/drop table log record is a Compensation log record.

Alter Propagation/Check Pending, Rollback Propagation/Check Pending Change Log Record

The alter propagation/check pending, rollback propagation/check pending change log record is written whenever the state of a table is changed as a result of adding or validating check constraints or whenever such a table change operation is rolled back. The structure of the alter propagation/check pending, rollback propagation/check pending change log record is shown in Table B–12.

Table B–12 Alter Propagation/Check Pending, Rollback Propagation/Check Pending Change Log Record Structure

Offset	Size (Bytes)	C Data Type	Description
0	6		DMS Log Record Header (See Table B–2)
6	2	char[2]	Padding
8	4	integer	Old flag value
			The following old flag values are valid:
			0 (FALSE) Propagation Off
			1 (TRUE) Propagation On
12	4	integer	New flag value
			The following new flag values are valid:
			0 (FALSE) Propagation Off
			1 (TRUE) Propagation On

Total length of Alter Propagation/Check Pending, Rollback Propagation/Check Pending Change Log Record : 16 bytes

Adapted from Table 99 on page 538 of IBM DB2 Universal Database API Reference

An alter propagation/check pending log record is a Normal log record. A rollback propagation/check pending change log record is a Compensation log record.

Alter Table Add Columns, Rollback Add Columns Log Record

The alter table add columns, rollback add columns log record is written whenever columns are added to an existing table with the **ALTER TABLE** SQL statement or whenever such a table change operation is rolled back. The structure of the alter table add columns, rollback add columns log record is shown in Table B–13.

Table B–13 Alter Table Add Columns, Rollback Add Columns Log Record Structure

Offset	Size (Bytes)	C Data Type	Description
0	6		DMS Log Record Header (See Table B–2)
6	2	char[2]	Padding
8	4	integer	Old column count
			The old number of columns in the table.
12	4	integer	New column count
			The new number of columns in the table. The number of new or added columns is determined by subtracting the old column count from the new column count.
16	4	integer	Old LOB count
			The old number of BLOB, CLOB, and DBCLOB columns in the table (used internally).
20	4	integer	New LOB count
			The new number of BLOB, CLOB, and DBCLOB columns in the table (used internally).
24	4	integer	Old LF count
28	4	integer	New LF count
32	4	integer	Old VAR flag value
			The old number of variable length columns in the table (used internally).
36	4	integer	New VAR flag value
			The new number of variable length columns in the table (used internally).
40	variable	Old column array	Information about the columns that were defined for the table before the **ALTER TABLE** SQL statement was executed.
			Each element in this array is 8 bytes long

Table B–13 Continued

Offset	Size (Bytes)	C Data Type	Description
variable	variable	New column array	Information about the columns that are defined for the table after the ALTER TABLE SQL statement is executed.
			Each element in this array is 12 bytes long

Total length of Alter Table Add Columns, Rollback Add Columns Log Record : 40 + (Number of old column arrays * 8) + (Number of new column arrays * 12) bytes

Adapted from Table 100 on pages 538–539 of IBM DB2 Universal Database API Reference

This table contains one or more column descriptor arrays and/or one or more large object (LOB) descriptor arrays in both the old column array and the new column array. The structure of a column descriptor array is shown in Table B–5 and the structure of a LOB descriptor array is shown in Table B–6. An alter table add columns log record is a Normal log record. A rollback add columns log record is a Compensation log record.

Insert/Delete Record, Rollback Update/Delete Record Log Record

The insert/delete record, rollback update/delete record log record is written whenever a row of data is added to (inserted) or removed from (deleted) a table or whenever a update/delete record operation is rolled back (both an insert record and a delete record log record is generated during an update operation if a row of data is altered). The structure of the insert/delete record, rollback update/delete record log record is shown in Table B–14.

Table B–14 Insert/Delete Record, Rollback Update/Delete Record Log Record Structure

Offset	Size (Bytes)	C Data Type	Description
0	6		DMS Log Record Header (See Table B–2)
6	2	char[2]	Padding
8	4	long	Record ID
12	2	unsigned short	Record length
14	2	unsigned short	Free space
16	2	unsigned short	Record offset
18	variable	variable	Record header and data

Total length of Insert/Delete Record, Rollback Update/Delete Record Log Record : 18 + *Record length* bytes

Adapted from Table 101 on pages 539-540 of IBM DB2 Universal Database API Reference

This table contains one or more data records. The structure of a data record header is shown in Table B–15 and the structure of a data record is shown in Table B–16.

Table B–15 *Data Record Header Details*

Offset	Size (Bytes)	C Data Type	Description
0	1	unsigned char	Record type
			Records are classified as follows:
			Updatable
			Special Control
			Each class has three record types:
			Normal
			Pointer
			Overflow
			Record data can only be viewed if the record type is updatable.
1	1	char	Reserved
2	2	unsigned short	Record length

Total length of Data Record Header : 4 bytes

Adapted from Table 101 on pages 539-540 of IBM DB2 Universal Database API Reference

Table B–16 *Data Record Details*

Offset	Size (Bytes)	C Data Type	Description
0	1	unsigned char	Record Type
			Records are classified as follows:
			Internal Control
			Formatted User Data
			A record type value of 1 indicates that the record is a formatted user data record.
1	1	char	Reserved
2	2	unsigned short	Fixed length
			Specifies the length of all fixed portions of the data. Note: If the record is an internal control record, this information cannot be viewed.
4	variable	unsigned short	Formatted record
			The formatted record can be a combination of fixed and variable length data. All fields contain a fixed length portion and, there are seven field types that have variable length parts. They are:
			VARCHAR
			LONG VARCHAR

Table B–16 Continued

Offset	Size (Bytes)	C Data Type	Description
			BLOB
			CLOB
			VARGRAPHIC
			LONG VARG
			DBCLOB
			The length of the fixed portion of the different field types can be determined as follows:
			DECIMAL
			The length is a standard packed decimal in the form: *nnnnnn ... s*. The length of the field is: (precision + 2)/2. The sign nibble (*s*) is xC for positive (+), and xD or xB for negative (-).
			SMALLINT
			INTEGER
			BIGINT
			DOUBLE
			REAL
			CHAR
			GRAPHIC
			The length is the fixed length size of the field.
			DATE
			The length is a 4-byte packed decimal in the form: *yyyymmdd* where *yyyy* is year, *mm* is month, and *dd* is day. For example, April 3, 1996 is represented as x'19960403'.
			TIME
			The length is a 3-byte packed decimal in the form: hhmmss where hh is hour, mm is minute, and ss is seconds. For example, 1:32PM is represented as x'133200'.
			TIMESTAMP
			This field is a 10-byte packed decimal in the form: *yyyymmddhhmmssuuuuuu* where *yyyy* is year, mm is month, *dd* is day, *hh* is hour, *mm* is minute, *ss* is seconds, and *uuuuuu* is microseconds.
			VARCHAR
			LONG VARCHAR
			BLOB
			CLOB
			VARGRAPHIC
			LONG VARG

Table B–16 Continued

Offset	Size (Bytes)	C Data Type	Description
			DBCLOB
			The length of the fixed portion of all variable length fields is 4.
			Note: If the record is an internal control record, this information cannot be viewed.

Total length of Data Record Details: 4 bytes

Adapted from Table 93 on pages 533-535 of IBM DB2 Universal Database API Reference

An insert/delete record log record is a Normal log record. A rollback update/delete record log record is a Compensation log record.

The table descriptor record describes the column format of the table. It contains an array of column structures, whose elements represent field type, field length, null flag, and field offset. The later is the offset, from the beginning of the formatted record, where the fixed length portion of the field is located. For columns that are nullable (as specified by the null flag), an additional byte follows the fixed length portion of the field. This byte contains one of the following values:

NOT NULL   (0x00): There is a valid value in the fixed length data portion of the record.

NULL   (0x01): The data field value is NULL.

The formatted user data record contains the table data that is visible to the user. It is formatted as a fixed length record, followed by a variable length section. All variable field types have a 4-byte fixed data portion in the fixed length section (plus a null flag, if the column is nullable). The first 2 bytes of the variable length section represent the offset from the beginning of the fixed length section, where the variable data is located. The next 2 bytes specify the length of the variable data referenced by the offset value.

Update Record Log Record

The update record log record is written whenever a row is updated and its storage location is not affected. The structure of the update record log record is shown in Table B–17.

Table B–17 Update Record Log Record Structure

Offset	Size (Bytes)	C Data Type	Description
0	6		DMS Log Record Header (See Table B–2)
6	2	char[2]	Padding
8	4	long	Record ID
12	2	unsigned short	New record length
14	2	unsigned short	Free space

Table B–17 Continued

Offset	Size (Bytes)	C Data Type	Description
16	2	unsigned short	Record offset
18	variable		Old record header and data
variable	6		DMS Log Record Header (See Table B–2)
variable	2	char[2]	Padding
variable	4	long	Record ID
variable	2	unsigned short	Old record length
variable	2	unsigned short	Free space
variable	2	unsigned short	Record offset
variable	variable		New record header and data

Total length of Update Record Log Record : 36 + *New record length* + *Old record length* bytes

Adapted from Table 104 on page 543 of IBM DB2 Universal Database API Reference

This is a Normal log record.

Long Field Manager Log Records

Long Field Manager log records are generated whenever long field data is inserted, updated, or deleted and only if a database's *logretain* and/or *userexits* configuration parameter has been turned on (enabled). To conserve log space, long field data inserted into tables is not logged if the database is configured for circular logging. In addition, when a long field value is updated, the "before" image is shadowed and not logged.

Long Field Manager log records contain the header information shown in Table B–18, along with additional, record-specific information.

Table B–18 Long Field Manager Log Record Header Structure

Offset	Size (Bytes)	C Data Type	Description
0	1	unsigned char	Originator code (Always 3)
1	1	unsigned char	Operation type
			The following operation type values are valid:
			110 Add long field record
			111 Delete long field record
			112 Non-update long field record
2	2	unsigned short	Pool identifier
4	2	unsigned short	Object identifier
6	2	unsigned short	Parent pool identifier (Pool ID of the data object)
8	2	unsigned short	Parent object identifier (Object ID of the data object)

Total length of Long Field Manager Log Record Header : 10 bytes

Adapted from Table 105 on page 544 of IBM DB2 Universal Database API Reference

Add/Delete/Non-Update Long Field Record Log Record

The add/delete/non-update long field record log record is written whenever long field data is inserted, updated, or deleted. The structure of the add/delete/non-update long field record log record is shown in Table B–19.

Table B–19　Add/Delete/Non-Update Long Field Record Log Record Structure

Offset	Size (Bytes)	C Data Type	Description
0	10		Long Field Manager Log Record Header (See Table B–18)
10	2	unsigned short	Long field length (in 512-byte sectors)
			The value for this field is always positive. The long field manager never writes log records for zero length long field data that is being inserted, updated, or deleted.
12	4	unsigned long	File offset (512-byte sector offset into long field object where data is located)
16	variable	char[]	Long field data

Total length of Add/Delete/Non-Update Long Field Record Log Record : 16 + *Long field length* bytes

Adapted from Table 106 on page 544 of IBM DB2 Universal Database API Reference

When a table has be altered to capture LONG VARCHAR or LONG VARGRAPHIC columns (by issuing the **ALTER TABLE** SQL statement with the **INCLUDE LONGVAR COLUMNS** option specified), the Long Field Manager will write the appropriate long field log record, as follows:

- If long field data is added, an add long field record log record will be written
- If long field data is removed, a delete long field record log record will be written
- If long field data is updated, an add long field record log record will be written for the new value(s) and a delete long field record log record will be written for the original value(s)
- If a table with a long field column is updated, but the long field columns themselves are not modified, a non-update long field record log record will be written

LOB Manager Log Records

LOB Manager log records are generated whenever large object (LOB) data inserted into a table – and only if a database's *logretain* and/or *userexits* configuration parameter has been turned on (enabled). When LOB data is updated, the update is treated as a delete of the old LOB value, followed by an insert of the new value. If the LOB Manager is able to determine that the new value is simply the old value with new data appended to it, the new data is appended to the old data and only the new data is logged.

A log record is always written for LOB columns if the database is forward recoverable, even if the LOB columns were created with the **NOT LOGGED** option. However, instead of logging the actual data, only the quantity of data and its position within the LOB object are logged. During forward recovery, zeros instead of user data, are written to the LOB object.

Multiple LOB log records may be written whenever any LOB value is added (inserted) to a table. That's because a single LOB log record cannot contain more than 32,768 bytes of data – thus, in order to handle large LOB data values, the data must be split into smaller pieces.

In order to conserve log space, LOB data itself is not logged if the database is configured for circular logging. In addition, when a LOB value is updated, the "before" image is shadowed instead of being logged.

LOB Manager log records contain the header information shown in Table B–20, along with additional, record-specific information.

Table B–20   *Large Object (LOB) Manager Log Record Header Structure*

Offset	Size (Bytes)	C Data Type	Description
0	1	unsigned char	Originator code (Always 5)
1	1	unsigned short	Operation identifier
2	2	unsigned short	Pool identifier
4	2	unsigned short	Object identifier
6	2	unsigned short	Parent pool identifier
8	2	unsigned short	Parent object identifier
10	1	unsigned char	Object type

Total length of Large Object (LOB) Manager Log Record Header : 11 bytes

Adapted from Table 107 on page 545 of IBM DB2 Universal Database API Reference

Insert LOB Data (Logging On) Log Record

The insert LOB data (logging on) log record is written whenever LOB data is inserted into a LOB column, or appended to existing data in a LOB column (and logging of the data has been specified). The structure of the insert LOB data (logging on) log record is shown in Table B–21.

Table B–21   *Insert LOB Data (Logging On) Log Record Structure*

Offset	Size (Bytes)	C Data Type	Description
0	11		LOB Manager Log Record Header (See Table B–20)
11	1	char	Padding

Table B–21   Continued

Offset	Size (Bytes)	C Data Type	Description
12	4	unsigned long	Data length
16	8	double	Byte address in object
24	variable	variable	LOB data

Total length of Insert LOB Data (Logging On) Log Record : 24 + *Data length* bytes

Adapted from Table 108 on page 546 of IBM DB2 Universal Database API Reference

Insert LOB Data (Logging Off) Log Record

The insert LOB data (logging off) log record is written whenever LOB data is inserted into a LOB column, or appended to existing data in a LOB column (and logging of the data has been turned off). The structure of the insert LOB data (logging off) log record is shown in Table B–22.

Table B–22   Insert LOB Data (Logging Off) Log Record Structure

Offset	Size (Bytes)	C Data Type	Description
0	11		LOB Manager Log Record Header (See Table B–20)
11	1	char	Padding
12	4	unsigned long	Data length
16	8	double	Byte address in object

Total length of Insert LOB Data (Logging Off) Log Record : 24 bytes

Adapted from Table 109 on page 546 of IBM DB2 Universal Database API Reference

Transaction Manager Log Records

The Transaction Manager generates log records that signify the completion of transaction events (i.e. commits and rollbacks). The timestamp values stored in these log records are in Coordinated Universal Time (CUT) format and mark the time, in seconds, since January 1, 1970.

Normal Commit Log Record

The normal commit log record is written whenever a COMMIT operation is performed. A COMMIT operation can occur when:

- The COMMIT SQL statement is executed
- An implicit COMMIT is performed during a CONNECT RESET operation.

  The structure of the normal commit log record is shown in Table B–23.

Table B–23 Normal Commit Log Record Structure

Offset	Size (Bytes)	C Data Type	Description
0	20		Log Record Header (See Table B–1)
20	4	unsigned long	Time transaction committed
24	9	char[9]	Authorization ID of the application (if the log record is marked as propagatable)

Total length of Normal Commit Log Record :

Propagatable:	33 bytes
Non-propagatable:	24 bytes

Adapted from Table 110 on pages 546 -547 of IBM DB2 Universal Database API Reference

This log record is written for XA transactions in a single-node environment, or on the coordinator node in a multi-node environment.

Heuristic Commit Log Record

The heuristic commit log record is written whenever an indoubt transaction is committed. The structure of the heuristic commit log record is shown in Table B–24.

Table B–24 Heuristic Commit Log Record Structure

Offset	Size (Bytes)	C Data Type	Description
0	20		Log Record Header (See Table B–1)
20	4	unsigned long	Time transaction committed
24	9	char[9]	Authorization ID of the application (if the log record is marked as propagatable)

Total length of Heuristic Commit Log Record :

Propagatable:	33 bytes
Non-propagatable:	24 bytes

Adapted from Table 111 on page 547 of IBM DB2 Universal Database API Reference

MPP Coordinator Commit Log Record

The MPP coordinator commit log record is written on a coordinator node (in a multi-node environment) whenever an application performs updates on one or more subordinator nodes. The structure of the MPP coordinator commit log record is shown in Table B–25.

Table B–25 *MPP Coordinator Commit Log Record Structure*

Offset	Size (Bytes)	C Data Type	Description
0	20		Log Record Header (See Table B–1)
20	20	SQLP_GXID	MPP Identifier of the transaction
40	2	unsigned short	Maximum node number
42	variable		TNL ((Maximum node number / 8) + 1)
variable	9	char[9]	Authorization ID of the application

Total length of MPP Coordinator Commit Log Record : 49 + (*Maximum node number* / 8) + 1 bytes

Adapted from Table 112 on page 547 of IBM DB2 Universal Database API Reference

MPP Subordinator Commit Log Record

The MPP subordinator commit log record is written on a subordinator node (in a multi-node environment) whenever an application performs updates. The structure of the MPP subordinator commit log record is shown in Table B–26.

Table B–26 *MPP Subordinator Commit Log Record Structure*

Offset	Size (Bytes)	C Data Type	Description
0	20		Log Record Header (See Table B–1)
20	20	SQLP_GXID	MPP Identifier of the transaction
40	9	char[9]	Authorization ID of the application

Total length of MPP Subordinator Commit Log Record : 49 bytes

Adapted from Table 113 on pages 547-548 of IBM DB2 Universal Database API Reference

Normal Abort Log Record

The normal abort log record is written whenever a transaction aborts after one of the following events occurs:

- The ROLLBACK SQL statement is executed
- A deadlock situation causes a selected transaction to be rolled back
- Uncommitted transactions are rolled back during a crash recovery
- Uncommitted transactions are rolled back after a RESTORE DATABASE and ROLLFORWARD DATABASE operation has occurred.

The structure of the normal abort log record is shown in Table B–27.

Table B–27   Normal Abort Log Record Structure

Offset	Size (Bytes)	C Data Type	Description
0	20		Log Record Header (See Table B–1)
20	9	char[9]	Authorization ID of the application (if the log record is marked as propagatable)

Total length of Normal Abort Log Record :

Propagatable:	29 bytes
Non-propagatable:	20 bytes

Adapted from Table 114 on page 548 of IBM DB2 Universal Database API Reference

Heuristic Abort Log Record

The heuristic abort log record is written whenever an indoubt transaction is aborted. The structure of the heuristic abort log record is shown in Table B–28.

Table B–28   Heuristic Abort Log Record Structure

Offset	Size (Bytes)	C Data Type	Description
0	20		Log Record Header (See Table B–1)
20	9	char[9]	Authorization ID of the application (if the log record is marked as propagatable)

Total length of Heuristic Abort Log Record :

Propagatable:	29 bytes
Non-propagatable:	20 bytes

Adapted from Table 115 on page 548 of IBM DB2 Universal Database API Reference

Local Pending List Log Record

The local pending list log record is written whenever a transaction is committed and a pending list exists. A pending list is a linked list of non-recoverable operations (for example, the deletion of a file) that can only be performed when the COMMIT SQL statement is executed. The structure of the local pending list log record is shown in Table B–29.

Table B–29   Local Pending List Record Structure

Offset	Size (Bytes)	C Data Type	Description
0	20		Log Record Header (See Table B–1)
20	4	unsigned long	Time transaction committed

Table B–29   Continued

Offset	Size (Bytes)	C Data Type	Description
24	9	char[9]	Authorization ID of the application (if the log record is marked as propagatable)
33	variable	variable	Pending list entries

Total length of Local Pending List Log Record :

Propagatable:	33 + size of *Pending list* bytes
Non-propagatable:	24 + size of *Pending list* bytes

Adapted from Table 116 on pages 548-549 of IBM DB2 Universal Database API Reference

Global Pending List Log Record

The global pending list log record is written whenever a transaction using two-phase commit is committed and a pending list exists. A pending list is a linked list of non-recoverable operations (for example, the deletion of a file) that can only be performed when the COMMIT_SQL statement is executed. The structure of the global pending list log record is shown in Table B–30.

Table B–30   Global Pending List Record Structure

Offset	Size (Bytes)	C Data Type	Description
0	20		Log Record Header (See Table B–1)
20	4	unsigned long	Time transaction committed
24	9	char[9]	Authorization ID of the application (if the log record is marked as propagatable)
33	variable	variable	Global pending list entries

Total length of Global Pending List Log Record :

Propagatable:	33 + size of *Global pending list* bytes
Non-propagatable:	24 + size of *Global Pending list* bytes

Adapted from Table 117 on page 549 of IBM DB2 Universal Database API Reference

XA Prepare Log Record

The XA prepare log record is written to mark the preparation of a transaction as part of a two-phase commit. The structure of the XA prepare log record is shown in Table B–31.

Table B–31 XA Prepare Log Record Structure

Offset	Size (Bytes)	C Data Type	Description
0	20		Log Record Header (See Table B–1)
20	4	unsigned long	Log space used by transaction
24	140	variable	XA identifier of the transaction
164	20	char[20]	Application name
184	32	char[32]	Application identifier
216	4	char[4]	Sequence number
220	8	char[8]	Authorization ID of the application
228	20	char[20]	Database alias used by client
248	4	unsigned long	Code page identifier
252	4	unsigned long	Time transaction prepared
256	variable	variable	Log synchronization information

Total length of XA Prepare Log Record : 256 + size of *Log synchronization information* bytes

Adapted from Table 118 on pages 548-549 of IBM DB2 Universal Database API Reference

This log record is written for XA transactions in a single-node environment, or on the coordinator node in a multi-node environment. This log record describes the application that started the transaction, and is used to recreate indoubt transactions.

MPP Subordinator Prepare Log Record

The MPP subordinator prepare log record is written on a coordinator node (in a multi-node environment) to mark the preparation of a transaction as part of a two-phase commit. The structure of the XA subordinator prepare log record is shown in Table B–32.

Table B–32 MPP Subordinator Prepare Log Record Structure

Offset	Size (Bytes)	C Data Type	Description
0	20		Log Record Header (See Table B–1)
20	4	unsigned long	Log space used by transaction
24	6	unsigned char[6]	Coordinator Log Sequence Number
30	20	SQLP_GXID	MPP Identifier of the transaction
50	20	char[20]	Application name
70	32	char[32]	Application identifier
102	4	char[4]	Sequence number
106	8	char[8]	Authorization ID of the application
114	20	char[20]	Database alias used by client

Table B-32 Continued

Offset	Size (Bytes)	C Data Type	Description
134	4	unsigned long	Code page identifier
138	4	unsigned long	Time transaction prepared

Total length of MPP Subordinator Prepare Log Record : 142 bytes

Adapted from Table 119 on page 550 of IBM DB2 Universal Database API Reference

This log record describes the application that started the transaction, and is used to recreate indoubt transactions.

Backout Free Log Record

The backout free log record is written to mark the end of a backout free interval. The backout free interval is a set of log records that are not to be compensated if a transaction is aborted. The structure of the backout free log record is shown in Table B-33.

Table B-33 Backout Free Log Record Structure

Offset	Size (Bytes)	C Data Type	Description
0	20		Log Record Header (See Table B-1)
20	6	unsigned char[9]	Compensate Log Sequence Number
			When this log record is read during a ROLLBACK operation the Compensate Log Sequence Number marks the next log record that is to be compensated.

Total length of Backout Free Log Record : 26 bytes

 **Utility Manager Log Records**

The Utility Manager generates log records that are associated with the following DB2 API functions:

- MIGRATE DATABASE
- LOAD
- BACKUP DATABASE
- ROLLFORWARD DATABASE

Utility manager log records mark the beginning and the end of the activities that each of these functions perform and all of these log records are propagatable, regardless of which tables are affected when the function is executed.

Migration Start Log Record

The migration start log record is written whenever a catalog migration operation is started. The structure of the migration start log record is shown in Table B–34.

Table B–34 Migration Start Log Record Structure

Offset	Size (Bytes)	C Data Type	Description
0	20		Log Record Header (See Table B–1)
20	10	char[10]	Migration start time
30	2	unsigned short	Migrate from release
32	2	unsigned short	Migrate to release

Total length of Migration Start Log Record : 34 bytes

Adapted from Table 120 on page 551 of IBM DB2 Universal Database API Reference

Migration End Log Record

The migration end log record is written upon the successful completion of a catalog migration operation. The structure of the migration end log record is shown in Table B–35.

Table B–35 Migration End Log Record Structure

Offset	Size (Bytes)	C Data Type	Description
0	20		Log Record Header (See Table B–1)
20	10	char[10]	Migration end time
30	2	unsigned short	Migrated to release

Total length of Migration End Log Record : 32 bytes

Adapted from Table 121 on page 551 of IBM DB2 Universal Database API Reference

Load Start Log Record

The load start log record is written whenever a load operation is started. The structure of the load start log record is shown in Table B–36.

Table B–36 Load Start Log Record Structure

Offset	Size (Bytes)	C Data Type	Description
0	20		Log Record Header (See Table B–1)
20	4	unsigned long	Log record identifier
24	2	unsigned short	Pool identifier

Table B–36 Continued

Offset	Size (Bytes)	C Data Type	Description
26	2	unsigned short	Object identifier
28	1	unsigned char	Flag
29	variable	variable	Object pool list

Total length of Load Start Log Record : 29 + size of *Object pool list* bytes

Adapted from Table 122 on page 552 of IBM DB2 Universal Database API Reference

Table Load Delete Start Log Record

The table load delete start log record is written whenever the delete phase of a load operation is started (the delete phase is only started if duplicate primary keys are found). The structure of the table load delete start log record is shown in Table B–37.

Table B–37 Table Load Delete Start Log Record Structure

Offset	Size (Bytes)	C Data Type	Description
0	20		Log Record Header (See Table B–1)

Total length of Table Load Delete Start Log Record : 20 bytes

Adapted from Table 123 on page 552 of IBM DB2 Universal Database API Reference

Load Delete Start Compensation Log Record

The load delete start compensation log record is written at the end of the delete phase of a load operation (the delete phase is only started if duplicate primary keys are found). The structure of the load delete start compensation log record is shown in Table B–38.

Table B–38 Load Delete Start Compensation Log Record Structure

Offset	Size (Bytes)	C Data Type	Description
0	20		Log Record Header (See Table B–1)

Total length of Load Delete Start Compensation Log Record : 20 bytes

Adapted from Table 124 on page 552 of IBM DB2 Universal Database API Reference

Load Pending List Log Record

The load pending list log record is written whenever a transaction associated with a load operation is committed and a pending list exists. A pending list is a linked list of non-recoverable operations (for example, the deletion of a file) that can only be performed when the transaction is committed. The structure of the load pending list log record is shown in Table B–39.

Table B–39   Load Pending List Record Structure

Offset	Size (Bytes)	C Data Type	Description
0	20		Log Record Header (See Table B–1)
20	4	unsigned long	Time transaction committed
24	9	char[9]	Authorization ID of the application (if the log record is marked as propagatable)
33	variable	variable	Pending list entries

Total length of Load Pending List Log Record :

Propagatable:	33 + size of *Pending list entries* bytes
Non-propagatable:	24 + size of *Pending list entries* bytes

Adapted from Table 125 on pages 552-553 of IBM DB2 Universal Database API Reference

A normal commit log record does not follow the load pending list log record.

Backup End Log Record

The backup end log record is written upon the successful completion of a database or table space backup operation. The structure of the backup end log record is shown in Table B–40.

Table B–40   Backup End Log Record Structure

Offset	Size (Bytes)	C Data Type	Description
0	20		Log Record Header (See Table B–1)
20	4	unsigned long	Backup end time

Total length of Backup End Log Record : 24 bytes

Adapted from Table 126 on page 553 of IBM DB2 Universal Database API Reference

Tablespace Rolled Forward Log Record

The tablespace rolled forward log record is written upon the successful completion of a table space rollforward recovery operation. The structure of the tablespace rolled forward log record is shown in Table B–41.

Table B–41 Tablespace Rolled Forward Log Record Structure

Offset	Size (Bytes)	C Data Type	Description
0	20		Log Record Header (See Table B–1)
20	2	unsigned short	Table space identifier

Total length of Tablespace Rolled Forward Log Record : 22 bytes

Adapted from Table 127 on page 553 of IBM DB2 Universal Database API Reference

Tablespace Roll Forward To Point-In-Time Start Log Record

The tablespace roll forward to point-in-time Start log record is written whenever a table space rollforward recovery to a specific point-in-time operation is started. The structure of the tablespace roll forward to point-in-time Start log record is shown in Table B–42.

Table B–42 Tablespace Roll Forward To Point-In-Time Start Log Record Structure

Offset	Size (Bytes)	C Data Type	Description
0	4	unsigned long	Timestamp for this log record
4	4	unsigned long	Timestamp to which table spaces are being rolled forward
8	2	unsigned short	Number of pools being rolled forward
10	variable	integer	*List of pool IDs that are being rolled forward

Total length of Tablespace Roll Forward To Point-In-Time Start Log Record : 10 + size of *Pool ID list* bytes

Adapted from Table 128 on pages 553-554 of IBM DB2 Universal Database API Reference

Tablespace Roll Forward To Point-In-Time End Log Record

The tablespace roll forward to point-in-time end log record is written upon the successful completion of a table space rollforward recovery to a specific point-in-time operation. The structure of the tablespace roll forward to point-in-time end log record is shown in Table B–43.

Table B–43 Tablespace Roll Forward To Point-In-Time End Log Record Structure

Offset	Size (Bytes)	C Data Type	Description
0	4	unsigned long	Timestamp for this log record
4	4	unsigned long	Timestamp to which table spaces were rolled forward
8	4	integer	A flag whose value is TRUE if the rollforward operation was successful and FALSE if the rollforward operation was canceled.

Total length of Tablespace Roll Forward To Point-In-Time End Log Record : 12 bytes

Adapted from Table 129 on page 554 of IBM DB2 Universal Database API Reference

Datalink Manager Log Records

Datalink Manager log records are generated whenever DDL and DML operations involving DATALINK columns with the file link control attributes set are performed. Datalink Manager log records contain the header information shown in Table B–44, along with additional, record-specific information.

Table B–44 Datalink Manager Log Record Header Structure

Offset	Size (Bytes)	C Data Type	Description
0	1	unsigned char	Component identifier (Always 8)
1	1	unsigned char	Function identifier
			The following function identifier values are valid:
			LINK_FILE (33) Link file
			UNLINK_FILE (33) Unlink file
			DELETE_GROUP (33) Delete group
			DELETE_PGROUP (33) Delete PGroup
			DLFM_PREPARE (33) DLFM Prepare
2	2	char[2]	Padding

Total length of Datalink Manager Log Record Header : 4 bytes

Adapted from Table 130 on pages 554-555 of IBM DB2 Universal Database API Reference

Link File Log Record

The link file log record is written whenever an insert or update operation on a DATALINK column creates a link to a file. The structure of the link file log record is shown in Table B–45.

Table B–45 Link File Record Structure

Offset	Size (Bytes)	C Data Type	Description
0	10		Datalink Manager Log Record Header (See Table B–44)
4	4	long	Server ID
8	4	integer	ReadOnly Flag
12	8	char[8]	Authorization ID
20	17	char[17]	Group ID
37	1	char[1]	Padding
38	2	unsigned short	Access Control

Table B–45 Continued

Offset	Size (Bytes)	C Data Type	Description
40	9	char[9]	Prefix ID
49	3	char[3]	Padding
52	7	char[7]	Recovery ID
59	1	char[1]	Padding
60	4	unsigned long	Stem name length
64	variable	variable	Stem name

Total length of Link File Log Record : 64 + *Stem name length* bytes

Adapted from Table 131 on page 555 of IBM DB2 Universal Database API Reference

One link file log record is written for each new link to a file. This is an Undo log record.

Unlink File Log Record

The unlink file log record is written whenever an update or delete operation on a DATALINK column destroys (drops) a link to a file. The structure of the unlink file log record is shown in Table B–46.

Table B–46 Unlink File Record Structure

Offset	Size (Bytes)	C Data Type	Description
0	10		Datalink Manager Log Record Header (See Table B–44)
4	4	long	Server ID
8	9	char[9]	Prefix ID
17	3	char[3]	Padding
20	7	char[7]	Recovery ID
27	1	char[1]	Padding
28	4	unsigned long	Stem name length
32	variable	variable	Stem name

Total length of Unlink File Log Record : 32 + *Stem name length* bytes

Adapted from Table 132 on page 556 of IBM DB2 Universal Database API Reference

One link file log record is written for each link that is dropped. This is an Undo log record.

Delete Group Log Record

The delete group log record is written whenever a table containing one or more DATALINK columns (that have the file link control attribute) is dropped. The structure of the delete group log record is shown in Table B–47.

Table B–47 Delete Group Record Structure

Offset	Size (Bytes)	C Data Type	Description
0	10		Datalink Manager Log Record Header (See Table B–44)
4	4	long	Server ID
8	7	char[7]	Recovery ID
15	1	char[1]	Padding
16	17	char[17]	Group ID
33	3	char[3]	Padding

Total length of Delete Group Log Record : 36 bytes

Adapted from Table 133 on page 556 of IBM DB2 Universal Database API Reference

One delete group log record is written for each DATALINK column for each DataLinks File Manager (DLFM) configured in the datalinks configuration file. A log record is only written for a given DLFM if that DLFM has the group defined on it when the table is dropped. This is an Undo log record.

Delete PGroup Log Record

The delete pgroup log record is written whenever a table space containing one or more DATALINK columns (that have the file link control attribute) is dropped. The structure of the delete pgroup log record is shown in Table B–48.

Table B–48 Delete PGroup Record Structure

Offset	Size (Bytes)	C Data Type	Description
0	10		Datalink Manager Log Record Header (See Table B–44)
4	4	long	Server ID
8	6	SQLU_LSN	Pool life log sequence number
			The SQLU_LSN data type is defined as:
			union { char[6];
			short[3];
			};
14	2	unsigned short	Pool ID

Table B–48 Continued

Offset	Size (Bytes)	C Data Type	Description
16	7	char[7]	Recovery ID
23	1	char[1]	Padding

Total length of Delete PGroup Log Record : 24 bytes

Adapted from Table 134 on pages 556-557 of IBM DB2 Universal Database API Reference

One delete pgroup log record is written for each DataLinks File Manager (DLFM) configured in the datalinks configuration file. A log record is only written for a given DLFM if that DLFM has the pgroup defined on it when the table space is dropped. This is an Undo log record.

DLFM Prepare Log Record

The DLFM prepare log record is written to mark the preparation of a transaction that interacts with one or more DataLink File Managers (DLFMs) as part of a two-phase commit. The structure of the DLFM prepare log record is shown in Table B–49.

Table B–49 DLFM Prepare Log Record Structure

Offset	Size (Bytes)	C Data Type	Description
0	10		Datalink Manager Log Record Header (See Table B–44)
4	4	unsigned short	Number of DataLink File Managers (DLFMs)
8	variable	variable	Server IDs

Total length of DLFM Prepare Log Record : 8 + (*Number of DLFMs* * 4) bytes

Adapted from Table 135 on page 557 of IBM DB2 Universal Database API Reference

This log record is used to recreate indoubt transactions that are associated with DLFMs.

APPENDIX C

How The Example Programs Were Developed

All of the example programs shown in this book were developed with Visual C++ 6.0 on the Windows NT 4.0 operating system, using the SAMPLE database provided with DB2 Universal Database.

Configuring The Client Workstation

To establish communications between a client workstation and a DB2 Universal Database server, perform the following steps (after installing the DB2 Universal Database *Client Application Enabler* (CAE) and the DB2 Universal Database *Software Development Kit* (SDK) software):

1. Invoke the Client Configuration Assistant by making the appropriate selection from the DB2 for Windows NT Programs menu. The panel shown in Figure C–1 will appear if no database connections have been defined.

Figure C–1 The DB2 Client Configuration Assistant Welcome Panel

2. When this panel appears, press the *Add Database* push button to start the *Add Database SmartGuide*. The panel shown in Figure C–2 should appear.

3. When the *Add Database SmartGuide* appears, select how you want to set up a connection by choosing the appropriate radio button on the *Source* page. In this example, we will search the network for the desired database (see Figure C–2).

4. When a selection has been made, press the *Next* push button to move to the *Target Database* page of the *Add Database SmartGuide* and select the desired (target) database by traversing the network tree (see Figure C–3).

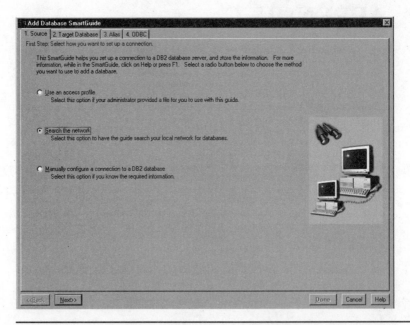

Figure C–2   The Source page of the DB2 Add Database SmartGuide

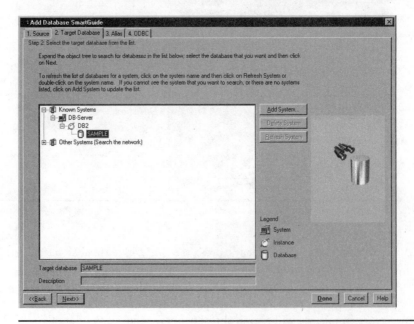

Figure C–3   The Target Database page of the DB2 Add Database SmartGuide

5. Once the database is selected, press the *Next* push button to move to the *Alias* page of the *Add Database SmartGuide* and enter a database alias and description (see Figure C–4).

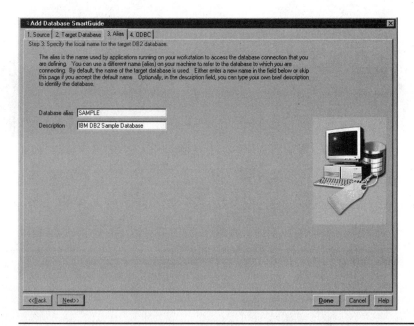

Figure C–4   The Alias page of the DB2 Add Database SmartGuide

6. When an alias and a description have been entered, press the *Next* push button to move to the *ODBC* page of the *Add Database SmartGuide* and specify how the database is to be registered with ODBC (see Figure C–5).

7. Finally, press the *Done* push button to complete the configuration setup. If everything has been entered correctly, the *Confirmation* dialog shown in Figure C–6 will be displayed you can test the connection to make sure it is working properly by pressing the *Test Connection* push button (see Figure C–6).

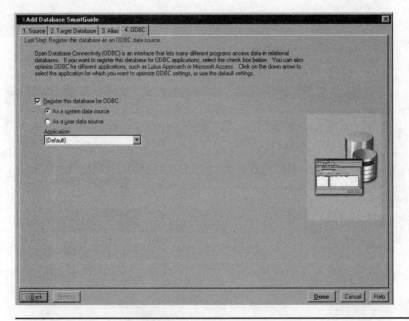

Figure C–5   The ODBC page of the DB2 Add Database SmartGuide

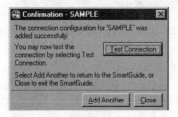

Figure C–6   The configuration confirmation dialog

Testing The Connection

8. After the *Test Connection* push button on the *Confirmation* dialog is pressed, the *Connect To DB2 Database* dialog shown in Figure C–7 will be displayed and you will be prompted for a user ID and password.

9. When this panel is displayed, provide a valid user ID and password and press the *OK* push button. A *DB2 Message* dialog like the one shown in Figure C–8 should appear.

10. After the connection has been configured and tested, the *Client Configuration Assistant* panel similar to the one shown in Figure C–9 should replace the *Add Database SmartGuide* and the newly configured database should be listed in the *Available DB2 Databases* list control.

Figure C–7   The DB2 connection information dialog

Figure C–8   The "connection test successful" message dialog.

Figure C–9   The Client Configuration Assistant main panel

How The Examples Are Stored On The Diskette

To aid in application development, each of the examples shown throughout the book are provided, in electronic format, on the CD that accompanies this book. This CD contains both a 90 day evaluation copy of DB2 Universal Database Personal Edition and a subdirectory that contains the example programs. This subdirectory (*examples*) is divided into the following nine subdirectories:

- Chapter_05
- Chapter_06
- Chapter_07
- Chapter_08
- Chapter_09
- Chapter_10
- Chapter_11
- Chapter_12
- Chapter_13
- Chapter_14

Each of these directories contains the examples that were presented in the corresponding chapters in the book.

How To Compile And Execute The Examples

The following steps can be performed to recompile and execute any example program stored on the diskette:

1. Create a directory on your hard drive and copy the example program into it.
2. Invoke the Visual C++ 6.0 Developer Studio.
3. Select *New* from the Visual C++ 6.0 Developer Studio *File* menu.
4. When the *New* panel is displayed, highlight *Win32 Console Application*, enter the appropriate location (hard drive and directory), and a project name that corresponds to the name of the directory that contains the example program (see Figure C–10).
5. When the *Win32 Console Application* wizard is displayed, select the *Empty Project* radio button and press the *Finish* button (see Figure C–11).
6. When the new project is created, select the *Project, Settings . . .* menu item, choose *All Configurations* in the *Settings For:* combo box, and enter the location (path) of the DB2 SDK header files in the *C/C++, Preprocessor, Additional include directories* entry field (see Figure C–12).

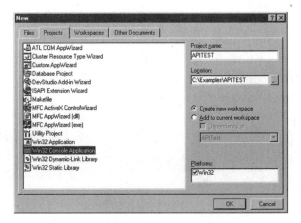

Figure C–10   The New Projects panel of the Visual C++ 6.0 Developer Studio

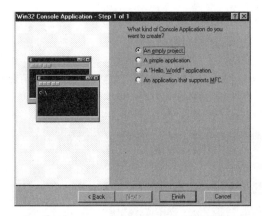

Figure C–11   The first panel of the Win32 Console Application wizard

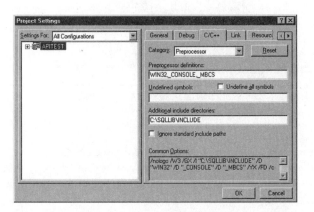

Figure C–12   The C/C++ Project Settings panel of the Visual C++ 6.0 Developer Studio.

7. Next, enter the location (path) of the DB2 SDK library files in the *Link, Input, Additional library path* entry field (see Figure C–13).

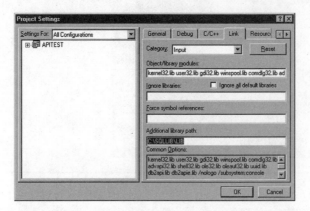

Figure C–13   The Link/Input Project Settings panel of the Visual C++ 6.0 Developer Studio.

8. Then, add the **DB2API.LIB** and **DB2APIE.LIB** libraries to the list of library files shown in the *Link, General, Object/library modules* entry field (see Figure C–14).

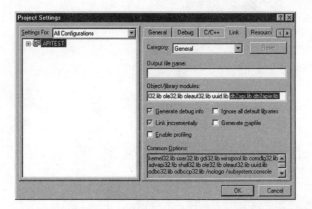

Figure C–14   The Link/General Project Settings panel of the Visual C++ 6.0 Developer Studio.

9. Once the new project settings have been saved, select the *File View* tab in the right-hand window, highlight the *Source Files* project files entry, press the right mouse button to display the pop-up menu, and select the *Add Files to Folder . . .* menu item (see Figure C–15).

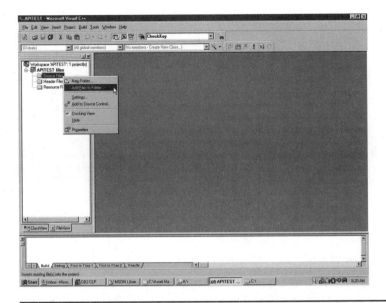

Figure C–15 The Add New Files to Folder **. . .** menu item

10. Highlight the example file name shown in the *Insert Files into Project* dialog and press the **OK** push button (see Figure C–16).

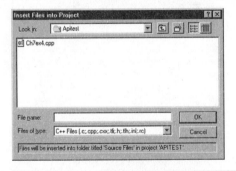

Figure C–16 The file selection window.

NOTE: *All files with .SQC extensions must be precompiled before they will appear in the file selection window (and before they can be added to a project). The following batch file (sqc_comp.bat) was used to precompile the .SQC examples:*

```
REM *** BUILD EMBEDDED SQL-API EXAMPLES COMMAND FILE ***
echo off

REM *** CONNECT TO THE SAMPLE DATABASE ***
db2 connect to sample user userid using password

REM *** PRECOMPILE THE .SQC SOURCE CODE FILE ***
db2 prep %1.sqc target cplusplus bindfile using %1.bnd

REM *** RENAME THE GENERATED FILE ***
copy %1.cxx %1.cpp
del  %1.cxx

REM *** BIND THE APPLICATION TO THE SAMPLE DATABASE ***
db2 bind %1.bnd

REM *** DISCONNECT FROM THE SAMPLE DATABASE ***
db2 connect reset
```

11. Compile and execute the program.

NOTE: *An appropriate User ID, and Password must be provided in the* SQLConnect()
function calls that are used to connect to the DB2 SAMPLE database. Also, if the user ID
specified is not the same as the user ID of the creator of the SAMPLE database, SQL
statements that interact with tables in the SAMPLE database may have to be qualified. If
this is the case, contact the System Administrator for information about the appropriate
qualifier to use.

BIBLIOGRAPHY

International Business Machines Corporation. 1997. *IBM DB2 Universal Database Administration: Getting Started, Version 5*. S10J–8154-00. IBM Corporation.

International Business Machines Corporation. 1998. *IBM DB2 Universal Database Administration Guide, Version 5.2*. S10J–8157–01. IBM Corporation.

International Business Machines Corporation. 1997. *IBM DB2 Universal Database API Reference, Version 5*. S10J–8167–01. IBM Corporation.

International Business Machines Corporation. 1998. *IBM DB2 Universal Database Command Reference, Version 5.2*. S10J–8166–01. IBM Corporation.

International Business Machines Corporation. 1997. *IBM DB2 Universal Database Embedded SQL Programming Guide, Version 5*. S10J–8158–00. IBM Corporation.

Index

Note: Boldface numbers indicate illustrations.

API INDEX

ABOUT THE AUTHOR

Roger Sanders is an Educational Multimedia Assets Specialist with SAS inSchool™, a division of SAS Institute, Inc. focusing on school technologies. He has been designing and programming software applications for the IBM Personal Computer for more than 15 years and specializes in system programming in C, C++, and 80 × 86 Assembly Language. He has written several computer magazine articles, and he is the author of *The Developer's Handbook to DB2 for Common Servers*, *ODBC 3.5 Developer's Guide*, and *DB2 Universal Database Application Programming Interface Developer's Guide*. His background in database application design and development is extensive. It includes experience with DB2 Universal Database, DB2 for Common Servers, DB2 for MVS, INGRES, dBASE, and Microsoft ACCESS.

SOFTWARE AND INFORMATION LICENSE

The software and information on this diskette (collectively referred to as the "Product") are the property of The McGraw-Hill Companies, Inc. ("McGraw-Hill") and are protected by both United States copyright law and international copyright treaty provision. You must treat this Product just like a book, except that you may copy it into a computer to be used and you may make archival copies of the Products for the sole purpose of backing up our software and protecting your investment from loss.

By saying "just like a book," McGraw-Hill means, for example, that the Product may be used by any number of people and may be freely moved from one computer location to another, so long as there is no possibility of the Product (or any part of the Product) being used at one location or on one computer while it is being used at another. Just as a book cannot be read by two different people in two different places at the same time, neither can the Product be used by two different people in two different places at the same time (unless, of course, McGraw-Hill's rights are being violated).

McGraw-Hill reserves the right to alter or modify the contents of the Product at any time.

This agreement is effective until terminated. The Agreement will terminate automatically without notice if you fail to comply with any provisions of this Agreement. In the event of termination by reason of your breach, you will destroy or erase all copies of the Product installed on any computer system or made for backup purposes and shall expunge the Product from your data storage facilities.

LIMITED WARRANTY

McGraw-Hill warrants the physical diskette(s) enclosed herein to be free of defects in materials and workmanship for a period of sixty days from the purchase date. If McGraw-Hill receives written notification within the warranty period of defects in materials or workmanship, and such notification is determined by McGraw-Hill to be correct, McGraw-Hill will replace the defective diskette(s). Send request to:

Customer Service
McGraw-Hill
Gahanna Industrial Park
860 Taylor Station Road
Blacklick, OH 43004-9615

The entire and exclusive liability and remedy for breach of this Limited Warranty shall be limited to replacement of defective diskette(s) and shall not include or extend any claim for or right to cover any other damages, including but not limited to, loss of profit, data, or use of the software, or special, incidental, or consequential damages or other similar claims, even if McGraw-Hill has been specifically advised as to the possibility of such damages. In no event will McGraw-Hill's liability for any damages to you or any other person ever exceed the lower of suggested list price or actual price paid for the license to use the Product, regardless of any form of the claim.

THE McGRAW-HILL COMPANIES, INC. SPECIFICALLY DISCLAIMS ALL OTHER WARRANTIES, EXPRESS OR IMPLIED, INCLUDING BUT NOT LIMITED TO, ANY IMPLIED WARRANTY OF MERCHANTABILITY OR FITNESS FOR A PARTICULAR PURPOSE. Specifically, McGraw-Hill makes no representation or warranty that the Product is fit for any particular purpose and any implied warranty of merchantability is limited to the sixty day duration of the Limited Warranty covering the physical diskette(s) only (and not the software or information) and is otherwise expressly and specifically disclaimed.

This Limited Warranty gives you specific legal rights; you may have others which may vary from state to state. Some states do not allow the exclusion of incidental or consequential damages, or the limitation on how long an implied warranty lasts, so some of the above may not apply to you.

This Agreement constitutes the entire agreement between the parties relating to use of the Product. The terms of any purchase order shall have no effect on the terms of this Agreement. Failure of McGraw-Hill to insist at any time on strict compliance with this Agreement shall not constitute a waiver of any rights under this Agreement. This Agreement shall be construed and governed in accordance with the laws of New York. If any provision of this Agreement is held to be contrary to law, that provision will be enforced to the maximum extent permissible and the remaining provisions will remain in force and effect.